FIFTY
SOUTHERN
WRITERS
AFTER
1900

FIFTY SOUTHERN WRITERS AFTER 1900

A BIO-BIBLIOGRAPHICAL SOURCEBOOK

EDITED BY
JOSEPH M. FLORA
AND
ROBERT BAIN

GREENWOOD PRESS
NEW YORK • WESTPORT, CONNECTICUT • LONDON

Library of Congress Cataloging-in-Publication Data

Fifty southern writers after 1900.

Bibliography: p.
Includes index.
1. American literature—Southern States—History and
criticism.   2. American literature—20th century—
History and criticism.   3. American literature—Southern
States—Bio-bibliography.   4. American literature—20th
century—Bio-bibliography.   5. Southern States in
literature.   6. Authors, American—Southern States—
Biography—Dictionaries.   7. Authors, American—20th
century—Biography—Dictionaries.   8. Southern States—
Biography—Dictionaries.   I. Flora, Joseph M.   II. Bain,
Robert (Robert A.).   III. Title.   IV. Title: 50 southern
writers after 1900.
PS261.F54   1987   810'.9'975   86-19460
ISBN 0-313-24519-3 (lib. bdg. : alk. paper)

Library of Congress Catalog Card Number: 86-19460
ISBN: 0-313-24519-3

First published in 1987

Greenwood Press, Inc.
88 Post Road West, Westport, Connecticut 06881

Printed in the United States of America

The paper used in this book complies with the
Permanent Paper Standard issued by the National
Information Standards Organization (Z39.48-1984).

10   9   8   7   6   5   4   3   2   1

Copyright Acknowledgments

The editors gratefully acknowledge permission to use portions of the following copyrighted material.

From *Let Us Now Praise Famous Men* by James Agee and Walker Evans. Copyright 1939 and 1940 by James Agee. Copyright 1941 by James Agee and Walker Evans. Copyright renewed 1969 by Mia Fritsch Agee. Reprinted by permission of Houghton Mifflin Company and Peter Owen, London.

From "90 North," "Seele in Raum," "Children Selecting Books," "The Death of the Ball Turret Gunner," "The Night Before Christmas," and "Nestus Gurley" from *The Complete Poems* by Randall Jarrell. Copyright © 1941, 1945, 1949, 1950, 1956, copyright renewed © 1968, 1969, 1972 by Mrs. Randall Jarrell. Reprinted by permissin of Farrar, Straus and Giroux, Inc.

From the *John Peale Bishop Papers*, box 8, folder 3. Published with permission of Princeton University Library.

From "The Case of Motorman 17: Commitment Proceedings," "The Tall Men," and "Lee in the Mountains" by Donald Davidson. Reprinted by permission of University of Minnesota Press.

The lines from *Essay on Poetics* and from *Hibernaculum* from *Selected Longer Poems* by A. R. Ammons are reprinted by permission of W. W. Norton & Company, Inc. Copyright © 1980, 1975, 1972 by A. R. Ammons.

The lines from "Corsons Inlet," "The Arc Inside and Out," "Hippie Hop," and "Small Song" from *Collected Poems, 1951-1971*, by A. R. Ammons are reprinted by permission of W. W. Norton and Company, Inc. Copyright © 1972 by A. R. Ammons.

From "Mr. Pope," "Ode to the Confederate Dead," "The Seasons of the Soul," "The Mediterranean," and "The New Provincialism," from *Collected Poems 1919-1976* by Allen Tate. Copyright © 1952, 1953, 1970, 1977 by Allen Tate. Copyright © 1931, 1932, 1937, 1948 by Charles Scribner's Sons. Copyright renewed © 1959, 1960, 1965 by Allen Tate. Reprinted by permission of Farrar, Straus and Giroux, Inc. and Faber and Faber Ltd.

From "The Hours," in *The Collected Poems of John Peale Bishop*, edited by Allen Tate, used with the permission of Charles Scribner's Sons. Copyright 1948 Charles Scribner's Sons; copyright renewed © 1976 Charles Scribner's Sons (Originally published in *The New Republic*, 3/3/41).

The lines from "Georgia Dusk" and "Song of the Son" from *Cane* by Jean Toomer. Copyright © 1923 by Boni & Liveright, renewed ® 1951 by Jean Toomer.

To
Frances Neumann
and
Wesley G. Neumann
with love and gratitude
and to the memory of
Raymond D. Flora
also with love and gratitude

—Joseph M. Flora

Contents

Introduction

"Far from slipping quietly into the American mainstream—whatever that may be—a new generation of Southern novelists and short-story writers seems to be staging what amounts to yet another literary uprising, a far better word than 'renaissance,' with its intimations of mugged-up classicism." So said Gene Lyons in "The South Rises Again," a lively essay in *Newsweek* of 30 September 1985. And so said Donald R. Noble in the final chapter of *The History of Southern Literature*, published by Louisiana State University Press in 1985. In the chapter entitled "The Future of Southern Writing," Noble wrote, "Yet, for every sign of homogenization there is equal evidence that Southern life retains traditions and values, attitudes and accents that will be a very long time in the erasing. For the foreseeable future, there is a South, therefore a Southern literature." *Fifty Southern Writers After 1900* is about these uprisings and continuities.

Though *Renascence* might sound to Lyons even more mugged up than *renaissance*, *Fifty Southern Writers After 1900*, a companion volume to *Fifty Southern Writers Before 1900*, uses that word to describe Southerners' remarkable literary achievements during William Faulkner's generation. These Renascence writers, publishing between 1919 or thereabouts and mid-century, include such diverse talents as Thomas Wolfe, Richard Wright, Ellen Glasgow, Jean Toomer, James Branch Cabell, Allen Tate, Zora Neale Hurston, John Crowe Ransom, and Eudora Welty.

Now a new generation of Southerners, publishing within the last three decades, has created an uprising full of wit, outrageousness, pity, violence, compassion, love, honor, courage, and human perversity. Like the Renascence writers before them, authors of this new generation tap Southern regional peculiarities and experience to create art that talks of the griefs that grieve upon universal bones. Besides recounting the lives and achievements of the Renascence authors, *Fifty*

Southern Writers After 1900 documents some rumblings from this new generation with essays about Harry Crews, Doris Betts, and others.

Fifty Southern Writers After 1900 offers students and teachers an overview of the writers' lives and work. Each essay, written by a knowledgeable scholar, contains five parts: a biographical sketch, a discussion of the author's major themes, an assessment of the scholarship, a chronological list of the author's works, and a bibliography of selected criticism. Readers working their way through this volume and its companion will have, we hope, a valuable complement to *The History of Southern Literature*, which emphasizes chronology and movements.

For several reasons, we have fixed the dividing line between our two volumes at 1900 rather than the Civil War. First, to give as much coverage as our format of 100 authors would permit, we decided to concentrate in our second volume on those twentieth-century writers important in the literary uprising known as the Renascence. Such a volume would have to include essays about Erskine Caldwell, Paul Green, Shelby Foote, Hamilton Basso, and Caroline Gordon, as well as those authors more often anthologized in collections of Southern and American writing. And because much Southern writing before the turn of the century is significant for cultural and historical reasons rather than artistic achievements, we chose 1900 as our dividing line in order to make our portrait of the period and its artists as comprehensive as we could.

Another reason for setting 1900 as the dividing line between the two volumes seems even more compelling. Though the Civil War and Reconstruction were the cataclysmic events in Southern history, it took a generation's distance before Southerners began to transmute this experience into enduring art. With the exceptions of Mark Twain, George Washington Cable, Charles W. Chesnutt, and a few others, most Southerners writing between 1865 and 1900 defended proudly and fiercely their father's choices and lamented the consequences of the Lost Cause. Though these Southerners produced little enduring art, they created a powerful mythology that still captures the imagination. In this myth, moonlight and magnolias surround dashing gentlemen and beautiful ladies attended by faithful slaves who treasure their servitude. Often set in the South before the war, these tales recount the tragic consequences of the Lost Cause. Thomas Nelson Page's "Marse Chan" (1884) draws the archetypal outlines of this Southern myth. Margaret Mitchell's *Gone with the Wind* (1936), probably the most popular American novel in the twentieth century, presents this myth powerfully and imaginatively, but Mitchell also transforms it by celebrating the bourgeois values of the antebellum South and by adopting Freudian insights to comment on the Southern social order.

Other Renascence writers questioned even more mercilessly than Mitchell their inherited Southern mythology. In their quest for truth rather than justification, they created new and more powerful mythologies that set aside the evasions and sentimentality of the old myth for a clear-eyed, humane look at the comedies, tragedies, and grotesqueries of their Southern heritage. Firing one of the uprising's first shots, H. L. Mencken in "The Sahara of the Bozart" (1917) castigated Virginia for being "senile" and Georgia for being "crass, gross, vulgar and obnoxious." In between, said Mencken, "lies a vast plain of mediocrity, stupidity, lethargy, almost of dead silence." But the iconoclastic Mencken was only partly right. In such novels as *The Deliverance* (1904) and *Virginia* (1913), Ellen Glasgow had already begun writing Virginia's social history; she had questioned Southern stereotypes about the social order and about the roles of men and women in that order. James Weldon Johnson's *The Autobiography of an Ex-Colored Man*, published privately in 1912 and reissued in 1927, had portrayed dramatically the plight of talented, sensitive blacks in a segregated society. In 1919, two years after Mencken's essay, James Branch Cabell published *Jurgen*. Banned as a lewd and lascivious book, *Jurgen* mingled mythmaking, adventure, philosophy, and sex in an assault on the genteel tradition—South and North. In addition to putting the genteel tradition on the defensive, *Jurgen* provided Southerners with a model of the avante-garde in art. The rebellion was under way.

In the fall of 1920, there gathered in Nashville, Tennessee, an extraordinary group of young men who spearheaded another arm of the rebellion by becoming first-rate critics, editors, poets, and fiction writers, and by changing radically the study of literature in the United States. John Crowe Ransom, already the author of *Poems About God* (1919), and Donald Davidson began meeting privately with Vanderbilt faculty, students, and Nashville citizens to talk of literature and culture. Joined shortly by Allen Tate and Robert Penn Warren, this group published the *Fugitive* (1922–25). Fleeing from the "high-caste Brahmins of the Old South," the *Fugitive* sounded new Southern poetic voices, particularly in the experimental verse of Ransom and Tate. The immediate impact of this shared concern for poetic excellence was the publication of several volumes: Ransom's *Chills and Fever* and *Grace After Meat*, both published in 1924; Tate's *Mr. Pope and Other Poems* (1928); Davidson's *The Outland Piper* (1924) and *The Tall Men* (1928); and later, Warren's first collection, *Thirty-six Poems* (1935). Equally important were the critical ideas emerging from conversations and correspondence—and appearing in periodical essays. Such works as Ransom's *The World's Body* (1938) and *The New Criticism* (1941) and Tate's *On the Limits of Poetry, Selected Essays, 1928–1948* (1948) defined central critical issues, not just for the South but for the country. Cleanth Brooks and Warren translated much of this theoretical criticism into a practical text, *Understanding Poetry* (1938), the most influential and imitated textbook in twentieth-century literary study.

By 1928, when *The Fugitives: An Anthology of Verse* appeared, the Fugitive era had ended. Tate had moved to New York and Warren was continuing his studies in California and Italy. More important, the Nashville group's interests had turned from a preoccupation with literature as such to a concern with Southern culture. Partly in response to Mencken's attacks on Southern fundamentalism during the Scopes Trial and partly in reaction to growing fears of business and industrialism, a new and larger group formed. Calling themselves Agrarians, this group published in 1930 a collection of twelve essays entitled *I'll Take My Stand: The South and the Agrarian Tradition*. The book's major theme—the superiority of Southern rural community life over Northern urban industrialism—explored the social, cultural, moral, and aesthetic values of these two different ways of living. The book's distinguished contributors included Ransom, Davidson, Tate, Warren, Frank Lawrence Owsley, John Gould Fletcher, Lyle H. Lanier, H. C. Nixon, Andrew Lytle, John Donald Wade, Henry Blue Kline, and Stark Young.

Assailed by both Southern and Northern critics as a trumped-up version of the moonlight and magnolia myth, *I'll Take My Stand* stirred controversy in its own day and continues to do so in ours. Published at the beginning of the Great Depression, the book enraged many New South writers concerned with the misery and poverty of a region not yet recovered from the Civil War and Reconstruction. To many, the book's racial views seemed uninformed or ill-formed. But as Louis D. Rubin, Jr., William C. Havard, and Thomas Daniel Young have noted, *I'll Take My Stand* belongs in the tradition of Ralph Waldo Emerson's and Henry David Thoreau's attacks on the dehumanizing effects of materialism and industrialism. As a "Southern Manifesto," *I'll Take My Stand* advocated the agrarian tradition because it offered individual and social values that gave life and art meaning. Never as cohesive a group as the Fugitives, the Agrarians soon turned their attention again to literature. The major figures in the group—Ransom, Davidson, Tate, Warren, Lytle, and Young—all achieved national reputations as poets, fiction writers, critics, and editors. The young rebels of Nashville left large marks.

In 1919 another young rebel named Thomas Wolfe watched the Carolina Playmakers of Chapel Hill produce two of his one-act plays—"The Return of Buck Gavin" and "The Third Night." Hoping to be a dramatist, he enrolled in George Pierce Baker's playwriting workshop at Harvard University, completed at least three more plays, but failed to find professional producers for his work. Turning to prose fiction, Wolfe earned immediate success with *Look Homeward, Angel* (1929). The novel both delighted and shocked Southerners with its unsentimental portraits of characters, of family and community life in Wolfe's Altamont (Asheville). A Raleigh newspaper accused Wolfe of betraying his region, of spitting upon his native state and the South. But Wolfe believed otherwise. He wrote to his mother in April 1930:

I belong to a different generation from that of certain older people who were perhaps shocked by some things in my book, but I really do not think my own generation is worse than theirs; I think in many respects it is much more honest. Every writer who is honest, I think, feels the tragedy of destiny and much of living, but I hope that I shall never be bitter, in what I write, against people. I think some people made that mistake about my first book—they thought the author was bitter about people, but he was not: he may have been bitter about the toil, waste, and tragedy of living.

Eugene Gant, the novel's portagonist and a thinly veiled portrait of Wolfe himself, calls the South "the dark, ruined Helen of his blood." Wolfe's South is filled with moonlight and ghosts, but the magnolias of the aristocratic plantation were missing. His Altamont was not Eden; it was a place where people's warts showed and men got drunk and cursed the world. But it was also the stage for Wolfe's human comedies and tragedies.

Always a prolific writer who had trouble shaping his novels, Wolfe completed three more books before his death in 1938: *Of Time and the River* (1935), a collection of stories, *From Death to Morning* (1935), and *The Story of a Novel* (1936). From a mountain of manuscript material Wolfe had written before his death, Edward Aswell of Harper and Brothers edited and patched together, without comment, three books that were published posthumously—*The Web and the Rock* (1939), *You Can't Go Home Again* (1940), and *The Hills Beyond* (1941), stories of Wolfe's family set in the North Carolina mountains. Though Wolfe's work after *Look Homeward, Angel* included "lyric paeans to the American scene," his novels and stories about Eugene Gant and George Webber were always rooted in the "dark, ruined Helen of his blood."

Also in 1919, another young rebel from Oxford, Mississippi—mustered out after a brief tour of duty with the Royal Air Force of Canada—published his first fiction, a story entitled "Landing in Luck" in the 26 November number of *The Mississippian*, and a poem entitled "L'Apres-Midi d'un Faune" in the *New Republic*. At home in Oxford, William Faulkner contributed verse to local papers, wrote a verse drama (*The Marionettes*) in 1920, and with the help of Phil Stone, published his first book, *The Marble Faun*, a volume of poems, in 1924. The year 1925, according to Cleanth Brooks, was "a most important one in the process of Faulkner's maturation" because he discovered A. E. Housman's poetry and Cabell's *Jurgen*. The following year, with the help of Sherwood Anderson, he published his first novel, *Soldiers' Pay*. Then, in a burst of creative energy, he invented or discovered Yoknapatawpha County, his own little postage stamp, and between 1927 and 1936, wrote thirteen books, among them his greatest: *Sartoris* (1929), his first Yoknapatawpha volume; *The Sound and the Fury* (1929), which he called his most successful failure; *As I Lay Dying* (1930); *Sanctuary* (1931), a book even more sensational than *Jurgen*; *Light in August* (1932); and his greatest work, *Absalom, Absalom!* (1936). Before his death in 1962, he would publish fourteen more volumes, among them the Snopes trilogy and *Go Down, Moses* (1942).

Faulkner's experimental fictions about Yoknapatawpha County and the Deep South—especially in *Absalom, Absalom!*—cast aside the moonlight and magnolia myth, which he associated with "hoop skirts and plug hats," for a new mythology that got closer to the truth of what it meant to tell about the South. To tell his stories of Yoknapatawpha County and of the truths of the human heart, Faulkner combined in original ways fictional techniques old and new to create a voice so distinctive that it would damn imitators to oblivion. Multiple narrators, stream of consciousness, repetitions with variations, tales filled with allusions, stories with a strong sense of the oral tradition, a combining of old literary genres in new ways (including detective and mystery stories), and a convoluted prose style—these became Faulkner's stock-in-trade. Perhaps more important, he generally refused to tell his stories chronologically, a fact that confused and frustrated many early readers (and still does). Instead, he made his readers work, made them sort and arrange and judge. In doing so, Faulkner abjured chronology (the written tale's traditional mode) to create in his readers a consciousness of the complicated process of discovering truth. Faulkner also created such a list of memorable characters that he mapped the territory of the Deep South more completely than any other writer. Southern letters would never be the same after Faulkner.

But Faulkner's recognition came slowly. Although he early had a small, enthusiastic following, he was always pressed for money and could not support his family on the proceeds from his writing. He wrote short stories furiously, hoping for quick sales, and in May 1931 made the first of his forays to Hollywood as a screenwriter, again hoping for big money. *Sanctuary*, published early in 1931, brought him notoriety, and *Time* magazine featured Faulkner on its 23 January 1939 cover. Money problems, however, plagued Faulkner throughout the early 1940s. *The Portable Faulkner* (1946), with Malcolm Cowley's influential introduction, enhanced Faulkner's reputation by making his work readily available, and when Metro-Goldwyn-Mayer paid $50,000 for movie rights to *Intruder in the Dust* (1948), Faulkner's finances improved considerably. When he won the Nobel Prize for Literature in 1950, both his finances and his literary reputation were secure. As Thomas E. Dasher notes in this volume, Faulkner "ranks among the greatest writers of his nation and century."

If Faulkner's recognition came slowly, black Southerners fought even harder battles against the region's hard segregation laws designed to deny them their humanity and to crush their creativity. Like Richard Wright, who dramatizes his struggles for survival in *Black Boy* (1945), many Southern blacks fled North to look for more congenial climates. During New York City's Harlem Renaissance of the 1920s, Southern blacks especially found encouragement for their creative efforts. James Weldon Johnson, one of the earlier Southern artists to head North, published privately in 1912 *The Autobiography of an Ex-Colored Man*, a novel about the vicissitudes of its light-skinned protagonist who in desperation decides to pass for white. Reissued in 1927 with an introduction by Carl Van Vechten, *The Autobiography* encouraged other blacks—South and North—to cast their experience in fiction and poetry. More important than Johnson's *Autobiography* is his *God's Trombones* (1927), a collection of seven free verse Negro sermons that capture "the essence of the old-time rural black ministers who, through their magnificent and moving sermons, served as eloquent instruments of God, God's trombones." For years associated with the National Association for the Advancement of Colored People, Johnson never forgot his Southern heritage and advanced the cause of black artists from both South and North.

The careers of Jean Toomer and Zora Neale Hurston, both strongly rooted in the South and both associated with the Harlem Renaissance, illustrate two strikingly different paths. After writing *Cane* (1923), a boldly experimental novel with sections set in rural Georgia, Toomer published little during the remainder of his life. Though he continued to write, he turned his interest to philosophical reform, but *Cane* influenced many black writers, among them Langston Hughes. Though Hurston published stories in the mid–1920s, she did not complete her first book, *Jonah's Gourd Vine*, until 1934. Between 1934 and 1948, Hurston wrote seven books, the most famous of which is *Their Eyes Were Watching God* (1937), the story of Janie Crawford's search for love and selfhood. At her death in 1960, Hurston had received recognition as a folklorist, but scholars and critics rediscovered her fiction in the early 1970s, and her stock has risen to that of a major writer.

The major Southern black voice, however, belonged to Richard Wright, born in 1908 on a cotton plantation east of Natchez, Mississippi. Wright published his first story in 1924 in the *Southern Register*, a black weekly newspaper, but he found his native South oppressive and headed for Chicago in 1927. By the mid–1930s, his stories, essays, and poems were appearing in Northern magazines, and in 1937 he moved to New York City, where he became Harlem editor of the *Daily Worker*, a Communist publication. His first book, *Uncle Tom's Children*, appeared in 1938; then in 1940 *Native Son* won critical accolades and sold 200,000 copies in three weeks. Three more books—among them *Black Boy* (1945)—and a play appeared before Wright moved to France in 1947. *The Outsider* (1953), his first novel after *Native Son*, reflected Wright's disenchantment with and abandonment of his Communist associations in 1944. By the time *The Long Dream* appeared in 1958, Wright had fallen from favor with American critics, but he had firmly established himself as the major black writer of the South and the nation.

Among the galaxy of women writers during the Renascence, Ellen Glasgow stands first. *The Descendant* (1897), her first novel, and much of her early fiction, including *The Battle Ground* (1902), were marked by sentimentality, but even in these early works, she created strong women characters who often challenged received opinions and attitudes. By the time she wrote *Virginia* (1913), Glasgow had discovered her fictional milieu (her "social history of Virginia") and was sharpening her craft as a writer. In such books as *Barren Ground* (1925), *The Sheltered Life* (1932), and *Vein of Iron* (1935), Glasgow produced her best work. Her psychological realism, her satiric portraits of romantic men, and her tough-minded view of her region's social history have assured Glasgow a secure place in Southern letters. Recent feminist criticism indicates that her stature grows.

Fifty Southern Writers After 1900 takes obvious risks—even in representing the Renascence. In identifying our fifty authors, we have included some whose reputations have declined and excluded others whose achievements warrant inclusion. Though the reputations of Elizabeth Madox Roberts, Jesse Stuart, and John Gould Fletcher have waned, these writers deserve continued study as significant figures of the Renascence. We hope this volume will help readers to rediscover their appeal. To include some writers of the new uprising, we omitted such authors as Evelyn Scott, Anne Spencer, and Julia Peterkin, all still worth reading. Our format demanded some exclusions.

Though we believe we have covered the Renascence well within the limits of our format, we stand in quicksand in representing the new writers—mainly because there are so many of them writing so well. The writers we have included—Harry Crews, Doris Betts, Ernest Gaines, Reynolds Price, and Anne Tyler—were born mostly in the 1930s and have already published a sizable body of work. Texan Larry McMurtry, sometimes identified with the South, appears in *Fifty Western Writers*, a just placement in our view. But the list of Southerners achieving regional and national reputations is long.

Fifty Southern Writers After 1900 and its companion volume, *Fifty Southern Writers Before 1900*, owe their existence to many people. Foremost, we are indebted to the many scholars who have contributed to the making of these books. Their willingness to share their love and knowledge of Southern letters constitutes an act of faith. To Fred Erisman and Richard W. Eutlain, editors of *Fifty Western Writers* (1982), we owe the format of our volumes. We thank especially Louis D. Rubin, Jr., who has given us wise counsel about our work. We are grateful to Cynthia Harris and her associates at Greenwood Press for their patience and help in a complex job of editing. We also wish to thank our colleagues at Chapel Hill and the Department of English for their support and advice. Suzanne Booker Canfield proved an able sleuth at uncovering many of our errors. Cheryl Baxley, Toni Carter, Diana Dwyer, Jo Gibson, Kim Lassiter, Angela Miller, Tobi P.B. Schwartzman and Sandi Monroe helped us with typing and clerical duties. Nancy West aided us in compiling the index. Ramona Cook, Christine Flora, Maggie Boone Ford, and Charlotte McFall assisted us with numerous details. Frustrations there were, but these good people helped us to keep our sense of humor and our confidence in a good cause.

———————— RICHARD R. SCHRAMM ————————

James Agee
(1909–1955)

When James Agee died in 1955, he had published only three works of any length: *Permit Me Voyage, Let Us Now Praise Famous Men*, and *The Morning Watch*. The volume of poetry was largely forgotten; the documentary had been proclaimed a failure; the novel had received mixed reviews. A version of the genius-destroyed-by-the-system legend had grown up around Agee, based primarily upon his monumentally self-destructive personality and his long association with the Luce empire, but he seemed destined for the ranks of America's forgotten writers. Publication of *A Death in the Family* in 1957 and its award of the Pulitzer Prize for literature increased interest in Agee and his work and led to the reissue of *Let Us Now Praise Famous Men* in 1960. Reconsidered, *Famous Men* appeared to be one of the most important books of the 1930s. This judgment, along with the success of *A Death in the Family*, seems to have won for Agee a permanent place in American literary history.

BIOGRAPHY

James Rufus Agee was born 27 November 1909 in Knoxville, Tennessee, the son of Hugh James Agee ("Jay"), an employee of the Postal Services, and Laura Whitman Tyler, a graduate of the University of Tennessee and a devout Anglo-Catholic. A bright, verbal, precocious, and solitary child, Agee grew up in a household that was loving but strict. His emotional life was shaped on one hand by his mother's coolness and piety and on the other by his father's warmth and vitality. One of his biographers, Laurence Bergreen, notes that Agee "yearned to ally himself with both parents, but the impossibility of reconciling their divergent temperaments left him in a continual state of unease and hyper-sensitivity to every undercurrent of tension in the household."

On 18 May 1916 Agee's life was disrupted by the death of his father in an automobile accident. This event came to occupy a central place in his imagination. By the time he was sixteen, Agee wanted to write about his father's death and its effect upon him and his family. Eventually he did so in the novel *A Death in the Family*.

The Agees remained in Knoxville for three years after Jay Agee's death. In 1919 Mrs. Agee, James, and his sister Emma moved to a house adjacent to the campus of St. Andrew's School, an Episcopal school for boys near Sewanee, Tennessee. Because of the school's religious atmosphere and because it afforded her son the opportunity to be taught by men, Mrs. Agee enrolled Rufus, as he was then called, in St. Andrew's. There he developed a friendship with Father James Harold Flye, a history teacher who became his confidant for the rest of his life. Agee addressed a remarkable series of letters to Father Flye from 1929 to 1955. Through the influence of St. Andrew's and his mother's pious example, religion played an important role in Agee's life. Years later in *The Morning Watch* he examined this period of his life, reacting against the damage he felt was done him by the oppressive piety of his youth.

Early in 1924 the Agees returned to Knoxville so that Mrs. Agee could nurse her ailing father. In spring 1924 she married Father Erskine Wright, an Episcopal priest she had met at St. Andrew's. Agee felt that his mother was somehow abandoning him and betraying his father. Some months later he accompanied Father Flye on a trip to Europe.

Back in the United States, Agee entered Phillips Exeter Academy in New Hampshire in autumn 1925. His mother and her new husband joined him in New England, settling in Rockland, Maine, in 1926. Agee's entry into Exeter marks his removal from the South.

Scruffy, clumsy, unrefined—sometimes deliberately so—Agee felt out of place at Exeter. A lackluster student, he nevertheless read widely and wrote for the *Phillips Exeter Monthly*, the school's literary magazine. Both the quality and quantity of his writing impressed his teachers, who repeatedly awarded him prizes in literary contests. In his senior year, his skill led him to the editorship of the *Monthly*. Agee also received encouraging criticism from Edna St. Vincent Millay, Ezra Pound, and Hilda Doolittle, to whom he sent copies of a verse play he had written. By the time of his graduation from Exeter in 1928, he had resolved to become a writer.

This resolve remained firm throughout his four years at Harvard. Although he felt as out of place there as he had at Exeter and although he suffered from attacks of melancholy and depression, he continued to write. Many of his short stories and poems appeared in the *Harvard Advocate*, a campus literary magazine. After serving as secretary of the *Advocate*, he became its president and editor in March 1930. The high point of his tenure came two years later when the *Advocate* published an elaborate parody of *Time* magazine. It so impressed Henry Luce, editor of *Time*, that he offered Agee a position on the staff of *Fortune*, another of his publications. Although journalism was not the kind of writing he hoped to do, Agee accepted Luce's offer and headed for New York immediately after graduation.

In New York Agee found no refuge from the melancholy that had gripped him in Cambridge. He quickly became frustrated with his work at *Fortune*, feeling that his imagination and talent were atrophying. With the help of Archibald MacLeish, then also on the staff of *Fortune*, Agee became reconciled to his lot as a salaried writer, but he never accepted the opinions of the magazine. Although he was not the most docile writer at *Fortune*, he proved to be one of the most promising. At the end of his probationary period, he was offered a permanent position. Also at this time, after much internal debate, he married Olivia (Via) Saunders, whom he had met during his Harvard years, on 28 January 1933.

His married life proved unhappy. Via's affection could not dispel Agee's melancholy, which increased as the decade proceeded and eventually led him to attempt suicide. In August of 1937 Via left him, but by that time he had become involved with Alma Mailman, a woman he had met at the home of Via's parents. In fall 1937 he decided to divorce Via. The divorce was completed the following year, and on 6 December 1938 he and Alma were married.

Although his job at *Fortune* demanded most of Agee's time, he was able to do some of his own work. In 1934 MacLeish convinced him to submit some of his poems to the Yale Press. Under the title *Permit Me Voyage*, the poems were published as the 1934 installment in the Yale Series of Younger Poets. By the end of the 1930s Agee had published poems in such journals as *Partisan Review*, *New Masses, Common Sense*, and *transition*.

Publication of *Permit Me Voyage* only intensified Agee's frustration with the routine at *Fortune*. By 1935 his work load had expanded so that time for his own writing became increasingly scarce. While Agee was on a leave of absence from November 1935 to May 1936, he and Via retired to Anna Maria, Florida. Agee began some projects there, but his own inertia defeated his ambitious plans.

Ironically, it was on *Fortune*'s time that Agee began his major work of the 1930s. In 1936 the magazine sent him and photographer Walker Evans to Alabama to prepare a story on cotton sharecropping. Returning to his native South so moved Agee that the work he produced proved inappropriate for *Fortune*. What began as a routine magazine assignment turned into a five-year struggle with a body of recalcitrant material and a bevy of unsympathetic editors. The struggle ended in 1941 with the publication of *Let Us Now Praise Famous Men*.

Early in 1938 he and Alma moved to a farm near Frenchtown, New Jersey. He made occasional forays into New York but generally remained on the farm, where he worked on the Alabama book. Financial problems soon forced him to return to New York, but a few months later he abandoned the city once again and established himself at Monk's Farm in Stockton, New Jersey. In 1939 he resigned from *Fortune*.

His separation from the Luce publishing empire was brief. In September 1939 he became a book critic for *Time*. After two years of reviewing books exclusively, Agee began to review films as well. Because of the anonymity of the work and because of the extensive editing to which his essays were subjected, he found film reviewing at *Time* unsatisfying. His criticism was of such consistently high quality, however, that in 1942 the editor of the *Nation* invited him to write a regular film column. For three years he served double duty as a reviewer for both *Time* and the *Nation*. His signed reviews won him a devoted following, and today Agee is recognized as one of America's finest film critics. He gave up his reviewing chores at *Time* in 1945 but continued his column in the *Nation*. For two years thereafter he was not attached to any particular department at *Time* and wrote on a variety of subjects.

Although his new position at *Time* provided more freedom than he had had as a reviewer, the change offered little comfort, for his second marriage was also troubled. In 1941 Alma left him, taking with her their son born the preceding year. Agee's second divorce soon followed. That same year saw *Famous Men* fail both critically and commercially. This accumulation of woe brought Agee to the emotional nadir of his life. As he approached his thirty-sixth year in 1945, he began to experience premonitions of death. His father died at the age of thirty-six, and Agee did not expect to live beyond that age.

Throughout this dark time, Agee was encouraged by Mia Fritsch, a woman with whom he had worked at *Fortune*. She and Agee were married in 1944—a few months after the death of their son, born in July, over two months premature. Two years later, on 7 November 1946, Mia gave birth to Agee's third child, Julia Teresa. But a new family did not alleviate Agee's sense of doom. The belief that his life was ending intensified his conviction that he had wasted his talent and caused him to feel more acutely the pressure of his own neglected writing. In 1948 he gave up his column in the *Nation* and resigned his position at *Time*. He planned to support himself by writing film scripts and perhaps an occasional article. This arrangement, he hoped, would enable him to concentrate on the work he most fervently wanted to do.

In 1947 he had returned in earnest to a project he had begun in 1935, an autobiographical novel about his childhood. A trip to St. Andrew's in 1949 to visit his dying stepfather reawakened memories of the years he had spent there and prompted him to transform those memories into fiction. Thus by the end of the decade he had begun *A Death in the Family* and *The Morning Watch*, his major novels. Agee saw *The Morning Watch* (1950) to completion. That same year he began his collaboration on *The African Queen* with film director John Huston. In the fall of 1950 Agee traveled to California to watch the shooting of the film and to seek more screenwriting assignments. His wife remained in New York, where she was recuperating from the birth of their third child, Andrea.

In Los Angeles Agee spent a good deal of time with Huston, whose way of life was congenial to his own. The two men spent their days working, playing tennis, talking, smoking, drinking, and occasionally sleeping. The pace proved too much for Agee. In January 1951 he suffered a serious heart attack. During his convalescence he wrote "A Mother's Tale," a symbolic story that dramatizes the principle by which he lived, warning us, as Laurence Bergreen writes, that "Nothing matters but the survival of the individual; to follow the norms of society is to die." After his recuperation he continued his film work, but another heart attack in October sent him back to the hospital.

In 1952 he returned to New York to work on a television screenplay about the life of Abraham Lincoln. This project claimed his attention for the entire year. His heart trouble continued, but he refused to relax his pace. Brief retreats to a farm he and Mia had purchased in Hillsdale, New York, afforded him some rest, but not enough to improve his condition. In 1953 he wrote *Noa Noa*, a script based on the life of Paul Gauguin. The need to support his family—which in 1954 came to include a son, John Alexander—forced him to carry a work load that further taxed his health.

In March 1955 Agee suffered a series of heart attacks. Even though he was severely debilitated, he planned to finish current projects and return to Hollywood to solicit new ones. He never realized those plans. On 16 May 1955, while riding in a taxicab on his way to his doctor's office in New York City, he died of a heart attack.

Interest in Agee's work did not die with him. In 1957 *A Death in the Family* was published and won the Pulitzer Prize for fiction. Under the title *All the Way Home* it was later adapted for the stage, for television, and finally for the screen. His film reviews were collected and published in 1958 under the title *Agee on Film*. A companion volume, *Agee on Film, Volume II*, containing five of his movie scripts, appeared in 1960. That year also saw the reissue of *Let Us Now Praise Famous Men* to a more sympathetic critical reception than the one that greeted it in 1941. Agee's letters to Father Flye were gathered and published in 1962. Four years later *The Morning Watch* appeared in paperback. In 1968 Agee's poems and short stories were gathered and published in separate collections. Since then an additional story, "1928 Story," has been published.

MAJOR THEMES

> How were we caught?
>
> What, what is it has happened? What is it has been happening that we are living the way we are?
>
> The children are not the way it seemed they might be:
>
> She is no longer beautiful:
>
> He no longer cares for me, he just takes me when he wants me:
>
> There's so much work it seems like you never see the end of it:
>
> I'm so hot when I get through cooking a meal it's more than I can do to sit down to it and eat it:
>
> How was it we were caught?

In its imagery and point of view, this passage from *Famous Men* provides a summary of James Agee's major themes. The imagery is domestic:

children, married love, and housework. The narrators, Alabama sharecroppers, are looking back, surveying their pasts, trying to figure out how they came to live as they do. These two concerns, the family and the impact of the past upon the present, are the central themes in Agee's most important work. In *Let Us Now Praise Famous Men*, as well as in his poetry and fiction, he repeatedly sought to discover how the past gave rise to the present. This concern naturally led him to reflect upon family, for the past reaches us most intimately through the family. Much of his poetry, most of *Famous Men*, and all of his major fiction grew out of his preoccupation with one question: How did I become the man I am?

When Agee sought to answer that question, he did not restrict his inquiry to the span of years represented on his family tree. He saw the individual set within an expanse of time that stretches back to mythic and geologic beginnings. For Agee an individual's situation in life is not simply the result of recent developments but rather the product of forces and events that reach well beyond remembering. Agee's view of man is thus essentially tragic because he sees us trapped within time, doomed from the very outset.

His cosmic perception of time and his tragic view of man inform a sequence of 25 sonnets he included in *Permit Me Voyage* (1934). "In them," Bergreen writes, "he tried to uncover a link between his present discontent and troubled family history." In the first sonnet he takes his family history back about as far as it can go to Adam's fall. In the next two sonnets Agee elaborates on man's inescapable plight in time. "Our doom is in our being," he writes in the second sonnet. Throughout life we are "Ravened with hunger death alone may spell." Thus the family seems little more than a means to perpetuate suffering: the "generations" merely "advance" our "many hungerings." In the fourth sonnet, however, the family makes of time something more than the mere extension of tragedy through the ages: it links one human to another and imbues time with purpose. Agee follows a "chain of flesh" from Adam to himself and defines his life in terms of the generations that preceded him. Like his ancestors', his fate will be tragic: his strivings, too, will come to "naught." But he draws courage from their example and purpose. It is his "trust" "to touch with deathlessness their clay," his responsibility to overcome the tragedy time has in store for all by erecting an edifice of memory. He sought to achieve that purpose through his art.

Although Agee sees himself as part of a "chain of flesh," his place in it is ambiguous. He is at once bound to a "trust" but wears wings his ancestors "never wore" and knows hope they "never knew." He is with them but not of them and in the end will both "join" and "betray" them. This sense of being part of yet alienated from a particular heritage also informs his major fiction and lies at the heart of *Let Us Now Praise Famous Men*.

A combination of photographs and prose, *Famous Men* resembles a number of documentaries published in the 1930s that sought to expose the depredations of tenant farming in the South. It does not, however, fit comfortably into that genre. While it records the exploitation of the rural poor, it advocates neither the reforms of the New Deal nor those of the Communist Party. In fact, Agee contends that the solution to the tenants' problems is not to be found on this earth. His skepticism about political and economic reform stems directly from his view of time. Tracing the historical roots of the tenants' plight through the life of a single anonymous sharecropper, Agee does not begin with the stock market crash or even the Civil War. He moves all the way back to "the substance and bowels of the stars and of all space." Eventually, his farmer becomes "a crucifixion of cell and whip-lashed sperm" and gets born "weaponless" and "defenseless" into a world that is nothing more than a prison "of habituation, of acceptance [and] of resignation." Finally, Agee "specializes" this life, locating it within "the depths of the working class; of southern alabamian tenant farmers." In Agee's view the tenants' troubles have little to do with the Great Depression, landlords, or the price of cotton and everything to do with what he calls "certain normal predicaments of human divinity." There is nothing unusual about the tenants' plight; only its form is distinctive. He tells us that "born otherwise" his farmer would have broken "his shell on other forms of madness" and been as abused as the people we meet in *Famous Men*. Thus Agee's great documentary is suffused with the same tragic sense that permeates his sonnets, and as in the sonnets, the family is the means through which the tragedy of time reaches us. In spite of its tragic viewpoint, *Famous Men* is still a highly effective political statement because it conveys the full weight of the tenants' misery. Agee presents them not as "social integers in a criminal economy" but rather as suffering human beings.

When Agee arrived in the South, he found that he was painfully out of place. The three vignettes that appear early in *Famous Men*—"Late Sunday Morning," "At the Forks," and "Near a Church"—make this clear. Each shows a man whose best efforts and good intentions only alienate him from the people he wants to know. At one point in his sojourn in Alabama the bug-infested beds and indigestible food become so intolerable that he and Walker Evans flee the countryside for such urban pleasures as provincial Birmingham can provide. Yet Agee gradually accepts rural Southern society and recognizes that it is his real home, albeit one that he will never be able to reclaim.

The culmination of this gradual acceptance forms the climax of *Famous Men*. It occurs when Agee visits the Gudgers, one of the tenant families he and Evans have decided to write about and photograph. A rainstorm turns the roads to mud so that when he leaves, his car slides into a deep ditch. He returns to the Gudgers' home, wakes them, and asks for a place to sleep. Over his protests they fix him a meal. Seated between George Gudger and his wife, eating heavy, simple food, Agee is enveloped in a memory that comes not so much from his own experience as from the collective memory of his family, and he realizes that his roots lie with these people in this region.

The epiphany in the Gudgers' kitchen prompted Agee to reflect upon far more than his own family and heritage. It led him to contemplate families in general and the family's function in time. He emphasized these themes in the title he planned to give to the overall project, of which *Famous Men* was to be the first volume: *Three Tenant Families*. The work records the way families live, and one of its most poignant sections illustrates how families, like living cells, grow and extend themselves in time by splitting apart. In the section entitled "A Country Letter" Agee describes the Gudgers' anguish when Emma, Annie Mae Gudger's sister, departs for Mississippi. Agee presents the episode for its intrinsic dramatic merit, but he places it in a context that shows he clearly saw a larger meaning in it. As in the sonnet sequence, he assumes a cosmic view of time. Through the family, he tells us, "Each is intimately connected with the bottom and extremest reach of time."

Agee maintains that in addition to providing continuity to human experience, families also provide comfort in the face of time's vast indifference. They make our plight in time bearable by imposing upon it a human structure that gives us a home in its endless, indifferent expanse.

Agee did not see the family solely as a source of continuity and comfort. He was painfully acquainted with its baneful influences. "In what dry agony of despair," he writes, "a mother may fasten her talons and her vampire mouth upon the soul of her struggling son and drain him empty, light as a locust shell." The image of the locust shell stayed with Agee: nearly a decade later he used it as a symbol of growth and change in *The Morning Watch* (1950), a novel that illustrates how a family can stifle the life of its members.

Agee wrote *The Morning Watch* while working on the manuscript that eventually became *A Death in the Family*. Thinking about his childhood, he certainly could not avoid probing his relationship with his mother. *The Morning Watch* is the result of this probing. It is Agee's judgment of his life as it was shaped by his mother in the absence of his father.

The most salient feature of Agee's life after the death of his father was the extreme piety inculcated in him by his mother. In *The Morning Watch* he looked back upon his four years at St. Andrew's School and judged the way that piety affected him. The novel is another part of the answer to his question: How did I become the man I am? Hence its meaning must not be sought in the perspective of Richard, Agee's twelve-year-old autobiographical protagonist, but in that of Agee himself, the novel's narrator. From his perspective he understands the meaning of the events that take place at St. Andrew's on Holy Thursday and Good Friday, 1923; Richard does not.

Richard is extremely pious, aspiring to sainthood. His piety has led him to practice one form of self-debasement after another. He sees this behavior as atonement for his sins, as self-abnegation for the greater honor and glory of God. But Richard's self-inflicted pain and humiliation derive not from a desire to glorify God but from a deep sense of guilt and self-loathing that in turn stems from an impossible burden of religiosity. The narrator's judgment of conventional religion in *The Morning Watch* is severe. For him it is life-denying, and as long as Richard is in its grip, he is moving toward death, which he almost accomplishes when he attempts to drown himself in an abandoned quarry near the school. The climax of *The Morning Watch* occurs when Richard discovers the source of his desire to torment himself. His actions after he realizes his mother's stifling piety indicate that his desire to be a saint is fading. After their watch he and his companions retreat to an abandoned quarry to enjoy a forbidden early morning swim. There one of the boys wounds a snake, which Richard then beats to death. The snake carries with it all the connotations of evil usually associated with snakes, but Agee makes it a richer symbol of moral complexity, the inextricable weave of good and evil that Richard must learn to accept within himself if he is to overcome his destructive guilt. The slime of the snake clings to him. He refuses to wash it off and wears it back to school, Agee tells us, as he might wear ashes on Ash Wednesday. The slime, like the ashes, testifies to man's fallen nature. Richard's refusal to wash it off suggests that he is abandoning his pursuit of sainthood and moving towards an acceptance of his flawed humanity.

It is a direction quite different from that which we see at the end of *A Death in the Family*. In a sense, however, *A Death in the Family*, like *The Morning Watch*, completes itself only in the life of its author, for only there do we find the meaning of the events it narrates. As in *The Morning Watch*, Agee's aesthetic process is that of recapturing moments in time. Once again he looks back upon his past and asks, How did I become the man that I am? Here he works out his answer by creating another autobiographical protagonist, the six-year-old Rufus, and placing him in a family shaped by two distinctive heritages: that of the mother's family, the Lynches, and that of the father's, the Follets.

The Lynch heritage is relatively sophisticated, urban, and religious. The family reads the *New Republic* and the *Nation*. Andrew Lynch, Rufus's uncle, is an artist. His grandfather, Joel Lynch, quotes Shakespeare and Hardy. His mother Mary is proper, pious, and prudish. A devout Catholic, she insists upon bringing her children up in her faith. Mary's piety is obsessive to the point of hysteria. She uses her faith to escape reality, and it isolates her from her family.

In contrast to the Lynches stand the Follets. They come from the Tennessee mountains. Grandpa Follet is a lazy but likable hill-country man, his wife a strong, silent, enduring woman. Their son Jay, Rufus's father, is vital, earthy, and, one suspects, sometimes bawdy. He is no stranger to barrooms, and has little regard for the pieties of religion. To his son "he smelled like dry grass, leather and tobacco" and radiated a "great energy and a fierce kind of fun."

Agee casts young Rufus clearly in the mold of Jay Follet. The boy shares his father's love of Charlie Chaplin. When Jay laughs at Mary's prudishness, Rufus laughs, too, and feels "enclosed . . . with his father." The same taste that led Jay to buy ornately patterned linoleum leads Rufus to choose a "thunderous" jade green, canary yellow, black, and white cap over a more conservative dark serge. Jay's instinct for the unvarnished truth is evident in his son. We also see traces of Jay's attitude toward religion in his son. When his aunt explains that his father died because "God wanted him with Him," Rufus asserts that a concussion killed his father, "*not* God."

With Jay's death, Rufus loses the Follet heritage. Agee suggests the implications of this loss in the novel's final scene. *A Death in the Family* begins with
Rufus's walking home with his father. It concludes with his walking home with
his Uncle Andrew, a member of the Lynch family and an artist. The Lynch
family will become the dominant influence in his life and will transform him
into the saintly, self-destructive Richard of *The Morning Watch*.

SURVEY OF CRITICISM

As more of Agee's works were published through the 1960s, critical interest
in him quickened. In 1966 Peter Ohlin published *Agee*, a study of his poetry,
prose, film scripts, and film criticism. Ohlin offers useful critical insights and
intelligently discusses Agee's theories of writing. Kenneth Seib published an
introductory study entitled *James Agee: Promise and Fulfillment* (1968). His
treatment of Agee's poetry is sound, but his discussion of *Famous Men* is
superficial, and his reading of the fiction is characterized by interpretations
unsupported by the texts. Erling Larsen's pamphlet *James Agee* (1971) provides
a good brief summary of Agee's career and contains much on Agee's film writing.
Its discussion of *The Morning Watch* is weak, but the analysis of *A Death in
the Family* contains useful comments about the tension between its narrative and
subnarrative. Larsen also places *Famous Men* into the context of *Fortune* journalism of the 1930s. Alfred T. Barson's *A Way of Seeing* (1972) attempts to
"identify the sources of Agee's art in his life and at times to trace its development
and decline." Barson claims that the years from 1947 to 1950 were Agee's best.
He spends a good deal of time discussing Agee's aesthetic theory and practice
and traces the influence of James Joyce in his work. He offers particularly detailed
analyses of Agee's poetry and film scripts. The best general study of Agee's
work is Victor A. Kramer's *James Agee* (1975). Thorough, detailed, and intelligent, Kramer's readings provide an excellent introduction to Agee's writing.

Agee is remembered chiefly for *Let Us Now Praise Famous Men* and *A Death
in the Family*. The best study of *Famous Men* appears in William Stott's *Documentary Expression and Thirties America* (1973). Stott argues that *Famous
Men* is the best of the period's documentaries. He carefully and sensitively
discusses the photographs and the prose. The best study of *A Death in the Family*
is Robert Cole's discursive, comprehensive, and sympathetic essay in *Irony in
the Mind's Life* (1974).

All of the general studies of Agee's work contain a biographical chapter, but
they are of necessity sketchy. In 1974 David Madden provided some much-
needed detail when he edited *Remembering James Agee*, a collection of memoirs
that includes pieces by Father Flye, Walker Evans, John Huston, and Agee's
colleague at *Time* Whittaker Chambers. In 1977 Genevieve Moreau published
a full-length biography, *The Restless Journey of James Agee*. It is a disappointing
performance that adds little to our knowledge of Agee's life. Moreau's criticism
never rises above summarizing and theme labeling. Perhaps her most egregious

failing is her confusion of Agee's fiction with his life. At times in her discussion of *A Death in the Family* it is impossible to tell if she is referring to Rufus Follet, the novel's protagonist, or James Rufus Agee, the author. She accepts the fiction as a literal transcription of biographical fact but does not offer any nonfictional justification for doing so. Mark A. Doty in *Tell Me Who I Am: James Agee's Search for Selfhood* (1981) does not make that mistake. When Doty mines Agee's novels for biographical facts, he corroborates the fictional material with testimony from people who knew Agee. Doty's study often relies on psychoanalytical theories to explain Agee's life and argues that religion was "the all-important element in his quest for selfhood." It also provides a useful critical survey of the question of Agee's wasted talent. The need for a comprehensive, first-rate biography was met with the publication of Laurence Bergreen's *James Agee: A Life* in 1984. Like Moreau, Bergreen confuses Agee's life with his art: he passes off whole passages of *A Death in the Family* and *The Morning Watch* as detailed, exact transcriptions of what actually happened when Jay Agee died or when James Agee attended St. Andrew's. He uses the short stories in the same way. Neither Bergreen nor Moreau seems to realize that Agee's novels and stories are fiction—autobiographical fiction, to be sure, but fiction nonetheless. Agee worked out an interpretation of his life through his art. In his novels and stories he ordered and shaped his experience for interpretive and aesthetic reasons. Thus his fictional portrayal of his life may not be historically accurate in every detail. To claim that his novels and stories tell us exactly how it was, in the absence of nonfictional corroboration, is therefore risky and misleading. Yet the quality of Bergreen's biography more than makes up for this flaw. He provides a complete picture of Agee that reveals his insatiable sexual appetite as well as the appalling severity of his alcoholism. Bergreen does justice to a complex and contradictory writer whose life and work have fascinated us and will continue to do so for many years to come.

BIBLIOGRAPHY

Works by James Agee

Permit Me Voyage. New Haven: Yale University Press, 1934.
Let Us Now Praise Famous Men. Boston: Houghton Mifflin, 1941.
The Morning Watch. Boston: Houghton Mifflin, 1951.
A Death in the Family. New York: McDowell, Obolensky, 1957.
Agee on Film: Reviews and Comments, vol. 1. New York: McDowell, Obolensky, 1958.
Agee on Film, Volume II: Five Film Scripts. New York: McDowell, Obolensky, 1960.
Four Early Stories by James Agee. Collected by Elena Harap. West Branch, Iowa: Cummington Press, 1964.
The Collected Poems of James Agee. Ed. Robert Fitzgerald. Boston: Houghton Mifflin, 1968.
The Collected Short Prose of James Agee. Ed. Robert Fitzgerald. Boston: Houghton Mifflin, 1968.

The Letters of James Agee to Father Flye. New York: George Braziller, 1962; 2d ed.
    Boston: Houghton Mifflin, 1971.

Studies of James Agee

Barson, Alfred T. *A Way of Seeing: A Critical Study of James Agee*. Amherst: University
    of Massachusetts Press, 1972.
Bergreen, Laurence. *James Agee: A Life*. New York: E. P. Dutton, 1984.
Coles, Robert. *Irony in the Mind's Life: Essays on Novels by James Agee, Elizabeth
    Bowen, and George Eliot*. Charlottesville: University Press of Virginia, 1974.
Doty, Mark A. *Tell Me Who I Am: James Agee's Search for Selfhood*. Baton Rouge:
    Louisiana State University Press, 1981.
Kramer, Victor A. *James Agee*. New York: Twayne, 1975.
Larsen, Erling. *James Agee*. Minneapolis: University of Minnesota Press, 1971.
Madden, David, ed. *Remembering James Agee*. Baton Rouge: Louisiana State University
    Press, 1974.
Moreau, Genevieve. *The Restless Journey of James Agee*. New York: William Morrow,
    1977.
Ohlin, Peter. *Agee*. New York: Ivan Obolensky, 1966.
Seib, Kenneth. *James Agee: Promise and Fulfillment*. Pittsburgh: University of Pittsburgh
    Press, 1968.
Stott, William. *Documentary Expression and Thirties America*. London: Oxford Uni-
    versity Press, 1973.

A. R. Ammons
(1926–   )

Of all the American poets born in the South, only Robert Penn Warren can compare with A. R. Ammons in importance, and since Warren's reputation has to do as much with fiction and criticism as with poetry, it is probable that, among poets, Ammons is the best and the most influential.

BIOGRAPHY

Archie Randolph Ammons was born in Columbus County, North Carolina, on 18 February 1926. Columbus County, of which the county seat is the small town of Whiteville, is within a few miles of the ocean. After graduation from Whiteville High School in 1943, Ammons worked in a shipyard in nearby Wilmington and then in 1944, at the age of eighteen, began a two-year term of service with the U.S. Navy. On his discharge in 1946 he entered Wake Forest College, then in Wake Forest, North Carolina (this school is now Wake Forest University and has moved a hundred miles westward to Winston-Salem). He was awarded a B.S. in general science in 1949 and, soon afterwards, married Phyllis Plumbo; their son John was born in 1956.

Between 1949 and 1964 Ammons served as principal of an elementary school in Hatteras, North Carolina (on the Outher Banks, not far from Columbus County); spent one year at the University of California at Berkeley; and lived for a dozen years in the southern part of New Jersey, where he worked at a number of jobs, including an executive position with a firm manufacturing biological glassware. In 1964 he joined the faculty of Cornell University as an instructor, rose through the ranks in seven years to become a professor, and now holds the prestigious Goldwin Smith Professorship.

Among Ammons's many honors are a Traveling Fellowship from the American Academy of Arts and Letters, a Guggenheim Fellowship, a National Book

Award, the Bollingen Prize, a National Book Critics Circle Award, the Levinson Award, an award from the National Institute of Arts and Letters, and a MacArthur Prize Fellow Award. He has been given honorary Doctor of Letters degrees by Wake Forest University and the University of North Carolina at Chapel Hill.

After a seemingly slow start, Ammons has become one of the most productive and versatile of American poets. With the exception of a few short pieces of critical prose, his entire literary output consists of poetry, but that poetry comprises a full range of forms, from short, intense lyrics to long, relaxed verse essays. He teaches literature and creative writing, and since about 1975 he has become known as a painter as well as a poet.

MAJOR THEMES

Ammons's publishing career began rather inauspiciously in 1955, when he was twenty-nine years old, with the appearance of his first book, *Ommateum*, which was printed in a small edition by the subsidy firm of Dorrance in Philadelphia. His next book, *Expressions of Sea Level*, did not come out until nine years later, but this time the publisher was a respected university press (Ohio State), and since then—since, that is, the age of thirty-eight—Ammons has published abundantly in some of the best magazines and anthologies and with the most distinguished of commercial publishers. As of this writing (1985), he is fifty-nine, the holder of an honored chair at one of the finest American universities, and the recipient of many awards and much recognition.

Ammons's epochal *Collected Poems 1951–1971* comprises, without significant change or omission, almost all of the contents of six volumes: *Ommateum*, *Expressions of Sea Level* (1964), *Corsons Inlet* (1965), *Northfield Poems* (1966), *Uplands* (1970), and *Briefings* (1971). All of Ammons's trade volumes since *Collected Poems 1951–1971* have been published by Norton: *Sphere: The Form of a Motion* (1974), *Diversifications* (1975), *The Snow Poems* (1977), *A Coast of Trees* (1981), *Worldly Hopes* (1982), and *Lake Effect Country* (1983). There have been, as well, some limited editions of short works and three "selected" volumes: *Selected Poems* (1968), *The Selected Poems 1951–1977* (1977), and *Selected Longer Poems* (1980). The important book-length *Tape for the Turn of the Year* (1965) has not been included in *Collected Poems 1951–1971* or in any of the "selected" volumes.

With all such abundance, celebrity, and distinction, it remains possible to think of Ammons as a thoroughly American poet whose work cannot be readily exported because it cannot be readily understood apart from its native environment. For all its scope and variety, the work as a whole can be called original, inventive, organic, homely, anti-institutional, nonestablishment, unacademic, eccentric, unpredictable, idiosyncratic, iconoclastic in some senses but earnestly patriotic in others. Not one American in a hundred thousand is a devoted reader of poetry, but *People* magazine at one time saw fit to give Ammons a modest spread. The Ammons canon includes some of the shortest (one line) and some of the longest (hundreds of pages) poems in modern literature; some of the easiest and some of the obscurest; some sublimely transcendent mystical visions and flights of philosophy but also some moments of vulgarity, obscenity, and scatology (though no blasphemy or pornography). It is a total canon.

Ammons has glossed his own poems with internal commentary and explication. The reader can find overt references to Emerson, Williams, and Eliot, along with covert allusions to Pound, Stevens, Frost, and several other poets, and critics, ancient and modern. Ammons's capacious idiom can, at the drop of a hat, embrace Homer, Aristophanes, Xenophon, or Dostoevsky, and one whole long poem is called *Essay on Poetics*, but one never gets the feeling that learning or affectation has gotten the upper hand and choked the spontaneous life out of the poems. Each poem is a cross section, small or large, axial or angular, of a lyric moment wholly faithful to the momentum of the immediate present—gross, hankering, mystical, nude; also fine, easy, secular, and dapper. The poems are executed in pure obedience to a common impulse to meet the world pretty much as it is and not to leave anything important out. The poems also seem experimental and novel, but only as an expression of fresh authenticity of vision and voice, with no atmosphere of avant-garde formaldehyde or chloroform. Ammons is an artist of the Luminist school, not a taxidermist.

In the historical setting of these past 30 years, and in the environment of poems by his contemporaries (particularly W. D. Snodgrass, James Merrill, Robert Creeley, Frank O'Hara, and John Ashbery, all born in 1926 or 1927), Ammons's poetry reads like irony's obituary. And high time, too. When *Ommateum* was being composed during the end of Truman's presidency and the early years of Eisenhower's, American poets faced a hideous dilemma: if you were not T. S. Eliot (or some clone like W. H. Auden), then you had to be Joyce Kilmer. There seemed to be no viable means of coping with *The Waste Land*, despite the numerous robust counterattacks by Frost, Williams, Hart Crane, Rexroth, John Berryman, J. D. Salinger, Karl Shapiro, and several others, in poetry and prose. Allen Ginsberg (also born in 1926) promised some relief with *Howl* (1956), which had at least the momentary virtues of novelty and energy. There is something to be said in favor of the shock and humor echoing from "hydrogen jukebox" to "boxcars boxcars boxcars racketing through snow toward lonesome farms in grandfather night" and all that, but it is finally impossible to believe that a uniformly silly and affected crowd of opium-eaters are really, deep down, the best minds of anybody's generation.

Probably neither minds nor generations make much difference, so that to found one's idiom on bureaucratic language like "the best minds of my generation" is to enter a vapid claim that cannot readily be validated except by cheap irony or tenuous melodrama. The diction of Columbia University (where Eisenhower had lately been), no matter how much parody and irony one can employ to mock and distort it, remains the diction of Columbia University. In the wordstorm of controversy and publicity, in the protracted spat between the Beats on one side and James Dickey on the other, *Ommateum* had to go almost completely ignored.

In the match between Liberal Irony and Conservative Irony, there may seem to be little for those without Irony to do except to look for a way to hide their membership in the 4-H Club. Robert Bly (b. 1926) shifted allegiance and style somewhat but maintained a stubborn fidelity to a populist-humanist ideal. W. S. Merwin (b. 1927) and James Wright (1927–80) gave up the lineaments of their earlier symmetrical poesy and concomitantly enlarged the scope of their poetry, Merwin in the direction of unearthly surrealism, Wright mostly in the direction of loving populist lyrics and kindhearted satires. As the dust settles and the water clears, it begins to seem that Ammons's most congenial and semblable contemporaries are Bly, Merwin, and Wright. Even in that company, Ammons stands head and shoulders over the nearest competitors. After a lengthy contest with the all-but-inescapable poetics of discrepancy and discontinuity—a robust poetics that thrives on negation, denial, irony, and satire—Ammons has emerged as a brilliantly versatile champion of positive affirmation and celebration. That victory is not a matter of blind faith, indifference, or Pollyanna-ism, but rather of clarity and toughness.

Practically from the beginning, in *Ommateum*, Ammons has exercised his talents in three chief modes: the short poem, the sustained sequence, and between those extremes of minimum and maximum, a middle-length poem of perception, recollection, nostalgia, and meditation. The last mode may be one that the poet is abandoning, since there seem to be very few such poems in his recent books, and some of the finest of these poems, which are among the finest that Ammons has ever written, are not included in *The Selected Poems 1951–1977*.

These mid-length poems being those with which the general reader may be most familiar, they can be discussed first. The earliest one-sixth of Ammons's *Collected Poems 1951–1971* is devoted to tentative experimental poems in various modes and keys, so to speak—some virtually prehistoric, some virtually posthumous. The speaker, often calling himself "Ezra," can talk, in language with a strangely flat trajectory, about Sumer and Babylon, about Antioch in 1098 and Strasbourg in 1349, about one's own death and transfiguration. These early poems, written mostly before 1960, can be read as an entity complete in itself, comprising a unified immemorial world rendered through the multiplying planes and lenses of an insect's compound eye (*ommateum* in a now-obsolete zoological lexicon). The personae seem to be provisional tangents drawn at various angles to describe a number of concentric peripheries, all variable as to time, place, and orientation. The same group of poems can be read also as a grand overture preliminary to later poems in which the sometimes extravagant peripheries are contracted to something like a central self more or less coextensive with the poet himself. (It has often happened that a poet cannot deal with his immediate self directly but must, since language and literature are both radically discontinuous, take some ostensibly roundabout course to arrive at a personal origin. Pound, for example, shuffled a whole deck of personae before coming up with a truly personal poem with an uncluttered idiom, and it turns out that his clearest expression is technically assigned to someone nearly Pound's opposite: an adolescent Chinese girl married to a middle-class river merchant, on the other side of the world a thousand years ago.) With Ammons, once the "Ezra" overture had established the range of themes and styles, the poet was finally free to write about himself as he now is and has been earlier, growing up in rural North Carolina during the Depression. Still Ammons's most accessible poems, these are "Silver" and "Mule Song" (about a mule), "Hardweed Path Going" (a bird and a hog), "Coon Song," "Nucleus," "Nelly Myers," the two "Carolina Said-Songs," and a few others. In these poems of honesty, decency, candor, and tenderness, the poet records, in an unadorned but sometimes playful idiom, memories of a childhood and youth marked by poverty, uncertainty, and even tragedy but all somehow assuaged by the lucidity of the poetry itself.

"Corsons Inlet" (1965) marks an epoch of sorts: with this poem Ammons takes leave of the preoccupations and styles of his earlier poems and begins to concentrate on what was to become his typical engagement with respect to theme and technique. The poem, which takes its name from Corson's Inlet on the New Jersey shore, is a beach poem in several important senses. We recall that Ammons's upbringing and early occupations have to do with sand, shore, and glass. A sea-beach is an ideal poetical threshold, the special sort of place that we charge with personal and ritual significance. (The anthropologist Victor Turner has given currency to the useful term "liminality," which amounts to a way of assigning social meaning to thresholds that symbolize our passage from state to state. With Turner's help, we can recognize the literary importance of thresholds, windows, bridges, tunnels, waterfalls, twilight, equinoxes, turnings of the tide, and suchlike.) "Corsons Inlet" is like "Dover Beach," "The Love Song of J. Alfred Prufrock," "Neither Out Far Nor In Deep," and "The Idea of Order at Key West"—a poem that is at once personal and philosophical, poised between physical elements and using that in-between vantage point as a fulcrum for the examination of order and disorder, including the verbal and musical orders in the poem itself. "Corsons Inlet" represents a liminal walk between land and water, north and south, summer and autumn, with low tide made maximally low by a full moon (just as in "Dover Beach"). The poem ends in an unironic assertion of equation, identity, and novelty: "that I have perceived nothing completely, / that tomorrow a new walk is a new walk."

Now, the defining discrepancy of irony, whereby nothing is quite itself, eventually generates odd statements like Eliot's characteristic "April is the cruellest month" or "In my end is my beginning" or "midwinter spring" (a strange season in which the fire and the rose are one). These are calamitous dislocations that seem to cry out for correction and restoration. Against, say, the prevailing irony and satire of eighteenth-century literature, Burns opposes a new harmonic equation: "A man's a man for a' that." Ammons, who resembles Burns in more than one way, often traffics in equations like "tomorrow a new walk is a new walk." One of his long poems, *Essay on Poetics*, opens with a diapason of identifications:

> Take in a lyric information
> totally processed, interpenetrated into
> wholeness where

a bit is a bit, a string a string, a
cluster a cluster. . . .

The last words of *Collected Poems 1951–1971* come at the end of "The Arc
Inside and Out" in a breathtaking series of absolutes and ellipses:

. . . the apple an apple with its own hue
or streak, the drink of water, the drink,

the falling into sleep, restfully ever the
falling into sleep, dream, dream, and
every morning the sun comes, the sun.

This account of Ammons's writing is not an allegorical mural depicting the
triumphant overthrow of Misanthropic-Pessimistic Irony by the dimpled cupids
and cherubim of Philanthropic-Optimistic-Patriotic-Monogamous Harmony—not
quite. The combat is neither so simple nor so one-sided, nor is Ammons himself
reducible to a caricature compounded of features from James Whitcomb Riley,
Rudyard Kipling, the sunny side of Frost, or the new conglomerate formed when
Walt Disney Enterprises acquired the Gibson Greeting Card Company. Sooner
or later, however, the pose of bitterness and the glamour of apocalypse turn out
to be as romantically phony as G. F. Babbitt's Rotarian zeal, and particularly
after the turmoil that reigned from 1963 to 1974 in this country, it is refreshing
in the extreme to know that we have among us a great poet who can write a
piece like "Hippie Hop":

I have no program for
saving this world or scuttling
the next: I know no political,
sexual, racial cures: I make
analogies, my bucketful of
flowers: I give flowers to people
of all policies, sexes, and races
including the vicious, the
uncertain, and the white.

This is a poet who can, in the bicentennial year of 1976, which happens to mark
his own fiftieth birthday, inscribe *The Snow Poems* with a dedicatory "for my
country."

To place Ammons in literary history, we need to see that the prevailing mode
of modern literature has been irony, marked usually by a negation or denial or
discrepancy on or near the surface of a powerful work. In simple terms, we can
say that *Ulysses* is not about Ulysses, *The Autobiography of Alice B. Toklas* is
not the autobiography of Alice B. Toklas, "The Love Song of J. Alfred Prufrock" is not a love song. Irony is realized as the kind of distorted utterance
typical of the *eiron*, who is a character who does not and perhaps cannot speak

directly and so must speak indirectly, sometimes to the extent of manifestly saying the opposite of what we know he latently means. Prufrock's mildly anguished exclamation—"It is impossible to say just what I mean!"—says, ironically, just what he means, and that self-consuming property of irony permits the luxuriance of queer vocabulary, syntax, verbal form, and prosody.

In time, the great generation of ironists—Stevens, Joyce, Pound, Eliot—so exploited the vein of irony that an entire generation of critics had to come along with an arsenal of concepts like ambiguity, paradox, antithesis, and irony itself. With this body of literature so firmly in the saddle and with an academically established criticism acting as a loyal corps of equerries, a book like *Ommateum* scarcely stood a chance of succeeding in 1955.

Ammons's first great theme is continuity and harmony. His early technique delivers that theme in an answerable style by embodying and dramatizing certain lyric conformations, multifaceted like the eye of an invertebrate but yielding finally a single image. The theme involves oneness and sameness, often registered as resemblance, and the technique involves repetition and analogy. Unavoidably, the technique leads Ammons into a good deal of fairly serious wordplay. At its most modest level, this play simply recognizes the capacity of language for ranges of meaning, particularly in the idiomatic clustering of atomically simple terms in normal discourse: the rather weird tune of "how do you do," for instance, or the enigmatic richness of such varied combinations as "in all," "all in," and "all in all." Ammons's "Small Song" provides prismatic exemplification of such play:

> The reeds give
> way to the
>
> wind and give
> the wind away

—a poem wherein the absence of punctuation suggests the uncultivated condition of simple elements. The space after the "the" in the second line seems an analogue of the airy wind, and the play of the reeds in the wind is analogous to the play in language between the idiomatic "give way" (meaning to yield) and "give away" (meaning both to get rid of and to disclose). There is positive, rich ambiguity here but no paradox or irony. In the manifold of acoustic analogs, all of the consonants are voiced (with the single possible exception of the beginning of "to"), and the voicing itself is analogous to the small sound of wind and reeds.

Not long after he had so mastered the poetics of analogy—by which the concept, diction, acoustics, and graphic layout of the poem all combine to present a concentric image so puissantly focused that it takes on a large scope of philosophical and theological significance—Ammons added another kind of mastery. In current jargon, analogy is opposed to "digital" readouts, a notion that involves the design of instruments for measuring something quantitative. A standard clock is an analog device that tells time by the movement of hands in a circle that is analogous to the sun's movement around the earth. The mechanism is relatively simple, but it takes a long time for a child to master the literacy required to interpret what the clock means. A digital clock is a device with a much less simple mechanism but a much easier vocabulary and syntax, and the computation by this instrument is not a matter of overt analogy but of digital movement. It may take months for a child to learn that the short hand between II and III and the long hand on V mean that it is 25 minutes past two, but he can figure out what "2:25" means as soon as he can read numerals.

We are accustomed to think of poetry as a matter of analogs and analogies. Similes and metaphors are common figures, and the operation of analogy can be expanded to the scale of allegory with many levels. The ordonnance of foot, line, stanza, and so forth is itself a kind of ambitious analogy uniting what the eye sees, what the ear hears, and what the mind imagines. The graphic line reinforcingly records an acoustic line, which is an analog of a sentence or other sort of grammatical line, all of which is analogous to a line of thought. Where the graphic line stops in space, the acoustic line stops in time, and the visible pause mirrors the audible pause. Each poem becomes an elaborate analogy. "Small Song" is analogous to such an extent that we can say that even the suspension of the end of the second line creates "whitespace" that represents space, air, and wind in the world. Ammons has explored this potential for analogy to the extent of writing "th'elision fields" (*Hibernaculum*), a complex analogical pun involving the near-identical sounds of "elision" and "Elysian" and the immediate application of the concept of elision in "th'elision," which is an elision. This process is almost a mockery of analogy—one of those metalinguistic models of self-realization or self-contradiction (as in the pair: "It is incorrect ever to split an infinitive" and "It is incorrect to ever split an infinitive") leading quickly to eschatological headaches.

Much commoner in Ammons's persistent wordplay is a strain that exploits the digital or arbitrary properties of language, as in such anagrams as "cold clod clam calm" or "scared sacred" or in the description of earthworms as "wads of worthy long fellows." The arbitrary or accidental element here has to do with the usual operation of language whereby a man named Longfellow need not be a long fellow. By an ironic critique of language, "Wadsworth Longfellow" is decomposed into quasi-significant elements (wads, worth, long, fellow) and then precariously recombined into a phrase, "wads of worthy long fellows," which has nothing essential to do with the great nineteenth-century American poet. To Ammons, who can describe himself as "not a whit manic," the latter sort of digital wordplay seems much more negotiable than the analog wordplay exemplified by "th'elision." More than anyone else writing today, Ammons has taken advantage of the unlimited possibilities offered by what might be called digital poetry, in which the letters, words, feet, lines, and stanzas all have their own peculiar order *internally* but no analogous, reinforcing concentering of orders. (This is a poet who can find his own first name embedded in the name of a particular model of Pontiac, the "Starchief.")

Many years ago, John Crowe Ransom spoke of the local texture of a poem as "irrelevant" to its logical structure, but no poet before Ammons has so thoroughly gone into the exploitation of a verse line that begins and ends in obedience to a predetermined format without having anything to do with the musical or grammatical structure of what the lines say. *Hibernaculum*, for example, consists of 112 uniform stanzas of three tercets each, with Arabic numeration. But the lines and stanzas can end at some arbitrarily set margin, like that of standard typewritten prose. Typically, his poems avoid periods, even at the end, relying instead on commas and colons, which are the punctuation of continuity and identity without pat finality. Here is a passage from *Hibernaculum*, beginning with the last line of stanza 27:

> I really do not want to convince anyone of anything except
>
> 28
>
> that conviction is cut loose, adrift and aswim, upon the
> cool (sometimes sweltering) tides of roiling energy:
> that's not to despise conviction, definition, or other
>
> structure but to put them in their place: I hope
> you are in the middle income bracket (at least): I
> desire to be in the very high upper outgo bracket:
>
> to furnish forth energy out of nothing, except reflection,
> a few hard years, several procedures of terror and
> astonishment, New Hope Elementary School, assorted
>
> 29
>
> mothers and fathers (with the one and the one), fifty
> acres of ground, half swamp, half hill, Whiteville High
> School, the Pacific Ocean, a small sweep through the arc
>
> of the galaxy, one arm of the spiral in particular,
> etc.: . . .

And so on: seemingly random, relaxed, and almost pointless. One of the usual functions of verse form—and of rhyme and meter especially—is to provide an extra dimension of necessity in the array of verbal matter. A poem that ends with a rhyme and an iambic foot seems to say, as a prosodic subtext, that the final word has to be what it is, for it is the word that completes the grammatical pattern and also the sound that satisfies the pattern of stress and rhyme. In Ammons's digital prosody, this adventitious necessity is replaced by the physical limit of the typewriter's margin; in *Tape for the Turn of the Year*, the gross physical limitation is even more pronounced, because the poem was originally typed on a whole roll of adding machine tape. In *The Snow Poems*, the wordplay becomes more extravagant, descending even to typewriter games that no one has associated with any experience later than high school:

(o(o   a look-see

(oo)   slightly more direct

(-(-   shut-eye

($($ American dream

(*(*   34″ bust

This seems to be the fooling around suitable in a poem called "It's April 1," but it is also a serious demonstration of Ammons's nostalgic devotion to novelty and to maneuvers of redemption for all creatures great and small—the smaller the better. *The Snow Poems* also presents multiple poems, with one in a parallel column glossing another, and all of the 120 poems are uniformly titled with their first lines, even when this means calling a poem by a queerly curtailed digital name like "The Hen Pheasants Streak Out of the," "Snow of the," and "My Father Used to Tell of an." When there seems to be nothing new under the sun except perhaps new ways to imitate poems that are themselves derivative and parasitic, it is uncommonly refreshing to recognize that America has a poet who is still capable of genuine novelty, originality, and purity of vision. And there seems to be no slacking off in the offing.

SURVEY OF CRITICISM

Although the thirtieth anniversary of the publication of *Ommateum* is coming up soon, there has been little criticism of Ammons's poetry. The only whole book devoted to his work is the Twayne United States Authors Series volume: Alan Holder, *A. R. Ammons* (1978). In the Twayne tradition—and the Ammons volume is the 303d in the series—this book is solid, reliable, serviceable, and dutiful. It cannot be called an inspired study, and it is not always quite accurate, but it is useful.

Two critics of Ammons's own generation have done the most conspicuous work on his poetry. Richard Howard, whose criticism amounts mostly to appreciation and delectation, has recently gathered most of his reviews into a single essay called "A. R. Ammons: 'The Spent Seer Consigns Order to the Vehicle of Change,' " printed now as the first chapter of the enlarged edition of *Alone with America*. Howard is both sympathetic and brilliant, and he seems to try to take Ammons's poetry on its own terms as much as possible.

For most readers, if not for all, Harold Bloom may present something of a problem. He has written a good deal about Ammons's poetry, and he is generally encomiastic and scrupulous. Bloom's writings on Ammons, for the present distributed in essays in *The Ringers in the Tower* and *Figures of Capable Imagination* and in odd passages in other books, make up about a book's worth of material, some of which can be illuminating. Bloom's stock-in-trade has become an idiosyncratically revisionist approach to literary history and an even more idiosyncratic approach to reading, which he persists in calling "misreading." He classifies Ammons as a "strong" poet, and in many of Ammons's "strong" poems he finds a sixfold bill of tropes associated with rhetorical figuration, Freudian defense mechanisms, and the lofty quasi-familial struggles among poets. Bloom can also sweeten the pot with terms and concepts drawn from his vast accumulation of data: the Kabbala, English literature from Milton on, American Romanticism, Continental philosophy and criticism, and daily life. One may not accept or even understand what Bloom says, but it has to be recognized that he has paid profound attention to Ammons's works. The two of them have been colleagues, and each has dedicated a work to the other. None of that guarantees that Ammons endorses everything Bloom may say, but it certainly does not suggest that Ammons considers Bloom all wet. Readers will have to judge for themselves whether they need Bloom's criticism, either to help them enjoy Ammons's poetry or just for the pleasure of reading Bloom's prose poems for their own sake.

A special issue of *Diacritics* (No. 3, Winter 1973) contains an interview with Ammons and some interesting critical studies, and there have been valuable isolated essays, articles, and chapters on his work, but except for good studies by Robert Morgan and Hyatt H. Waggoner, none seems to call out for special mention.

BIBLIOGRAPHY

Works by A. R. Ammons

Ommateum, with Doxology. Philadelphia: Dorrance, 1955.
Expressions of Sea Level. Columbus: Ohio State University Press, 1964.
Corsons Inlet: A Book of Poems. Ithaca: Cornell University Press, 1965.
Tape for the Turn of the Year. Ithaca: Cornell University Press, 1965.
Northfield Poems. Ithaca: Cornell University Press, 1966.
Selected Poems. Ithaca: Cornell University Press, 1968.
Uplands: New Poems. New York: Norton, 1970.
Briefings: Poems Small and Easy. New York: Norton, 1971.
Collected Poems 1951–1971. New York: Norton, 1972.
Sphere: The Form of a Motion. New York: Norton, 1974.
Diversifications: Poems. New York: Norton, 1975.
For Doyle Fosso. Winston-Salem, N.C.: Press for Privacy, 1977.
Highgate Road. Ithaca: Inkling X Press, 1977.
The Selected Poems 1951–1977. New York: Norton, 1977.
The Snow Poems. New York: Norton, 1977.

Breaking Out. Winston-Salem, N.C.: Palaemon, 1978.
Six-Piece Suite. Winston-Salem, N.C.: Palaemon, 1978.
Selected Longer Poems. New York: Norton, 1980.
Changing Things. Winston-Salem, N.C.: Palaemon, 1981.
A Coast of Trees: Poems. New York: Norton, 1981.
Worldly Hopes: Poems. New York: Norton, 1982.
Lake Effect Country: Poems. New York: Norton, 1983.

Studies of A. R. Ammons

Bloom, Harold, "A. R. Ammons: 'When You Consider the Radiance.' " Ch. 18 of *The Ringers in the Tower: Studies in Romantic Tradition.* Chicago: University of Chicago Press, 1971.
———. "Dark and Radiant Peripheries: Mark Strand and A. R. Ammons"; "The New Transcendentalism: The Visionary Strain in Merwin, Ashbery, and Ammons"; "A. R. Ammons: The Breaking of the Vessels." Chs. 7, 8, and 10 of *Figures of Capable Imagination.* New York: Seabury-Continuum, 1976.
Diacritics, no. 3 (Winter 1973). Contains an interview with Ammons and articles by Josephine Jacobsen, David Kalstone, Jerome Mazzaro, Josephine Miles, Linda Orr, and Patricia A. Parker.
Harmon, William. " 'How Does One Come Home': A. R. Ammons's *Tape for the Turn of the Year.*" *Southern Literary Journal* 7, no. 2 (Spring 1975): 3–32.
Holder, Alan. *A. R. Ammons.* Boston: Twayne, 1978.
Howard, Richard. "A. R. Ammons: 'The Spent Seer Consigns Order to the Vehicle of Change.' " Ch. 1 of *Alone with America: Essays on the Art of Poetry in the United States Since 1950.* enl. ed. New York: Atheneum, 1980.
Morgan, Robert. "The Compound Vision of A. R. Ammons' Early Poems." *Epoch* 22, no. 3 (Spring 1973): 343–63.
Waggoner, Hyatt H. "A. R. Ammons: Ezra 'Perishing for Deity.' " Ch. 6 of *American Visionary Poetry.* Baton Rouge: Louisiana State University Press, 1982.

John Barth
(1930–   )

Sometimes identified as a novelist of ideas, sometimes as a creator of metafictions, John Barth has gained followers through his deft presentation of ideas and through his experimentation with fictional forms. He is one of the most important novelists to emerge since World War II.

BIOGRAPHY

Mason and Dixon's line runs east and west along Maryland's upper border, then north and south down the state's Eastern Shore. Born 27 May 1930, in the town of Cambridge on Maryland's Eastern Shore, John Barth is a Southerner because he was born *east* of the Mason-Dixon line, an appropriate paradox for our most paradoxical of writers. Other than a verse column entitled "Ashcan Pete" that Barth wrote for his high school newspaper, little in his youth predicted his later success as a novelist. His chief passion was music, particularly jazz and the drums. Indeed, he was to play with jazz groups for 25 years—for money during high school, college, and the early years of his first marriage, for pleasure thereafter.

After high school graduation, Barth spent summer 1947 in New York City, studying harmony and orchestration at the Juilliard School of Music. He made A's in both his courses, but tuition and the cost of city living were high, and his musical talent, he came quickly to realize, was limited, so he returned to Cambridge only to discover that Johns Hopkins University had awarded him a scholarship he had forgotten applying for. Barth enrolled that fall, tentatively declaring himself a journalism major in the newly instituted Department of Writing, Speech, and Drama. In his junior year, a number of events helped determine his future as a teacher and writer. Several professors including the Spanish poet Pedro Salinas, the first writer Barth had ever known, provided the young Barth with "splendid models" of the literary life. He also met fellow students whose passionate interest in writing inspired his own desire to write. Most important, he began to read—over three thousand short stories in his junior year alone. Barth's determination to catch up on his reading was abetted by his job as book-filer in the library stacks of the Classics Department and William Foxwell Albright's Oriental Seminary. The job helped Barth support his new wife, Harriet Anne Strickland, whom he married 11 January 1950. But it also introduced him to the great Oriental Tale cycles that have been an enduring influence on his imagination and work—Petronius's *Satyricon*, the *Panchatantra*, the eleventh-century Sanskrit *Ocean of Story*, and Burton's annotated *Book of the Thousand Nights and a Night*, whose Scheherazade remains for Barth the perfect image of the storyteller.

By Barth's senior year two of his stories had appeared in the student literary magazine; a third, "Lilith and the Lion," was published in the *Hopkins Review*, Barth's first in a professionally edited magazine. He graduated in spring 1951 with the highest grade point average in the College of Arts and Sciences. That summer, on 31 July 1951, his first child, Christine, was born. In the fall he entered the graduate writing program at Hopkins. His M.A. thesis, a realistic novel entitled *Shirt of Nessus*, was too mediocre, Barth insists, to qualify him for the graduate creative writing workshop he now teaches. Receiving his M.A. in 1952, he enrolled that summer in the Hopkins Ph.D. program, studying literary aesthetics through summer 1953. By then the Barths' second child, John, had been born (on 14 October 1952); their third child was due (Daniel, Barth's last child, was born 21 January 1954); and money was short. So Barth decided to accept a position at Pennsylvania State University teaching remedial English and, like his character Jake Horner, prescriptive grammar.

That fall he began "Dorchester Tales," a projected tale cycle of 100 stories modeled upon those Oriental Tale cycles he had discovered in the classics library at Hopkins. Barth had completed about half of the stories, most of which he later destroyed, when in 1954 he happened upon an old photograph of a showboat that had toured the Chesapeake Bay when he was a boy and decided to write a novel involving a similar showboat. He began *The Floating Opera* in January 1955, completing it in three months. But the grim conclusion of his "nihilistic comedy" discouraged publishers from accepting it. Appleton-Century-Crofts, the sixth house to review the novel, offered to publish it if Barth would soften the climax. Eager to break into print, Barth agreed, revising the ending so that Todd Andrews attempts suicide by asphyxiation rather than by blowing up himself and 699 fellow townspeople as they watch a minstrel show on board a showboat. Published on 24 August 1956, *The Floating Opera* was runner-up for that year's National Book Award. But Barth regretted having changed the novel's conclusion, and when Doubleday reissued the book in 1967, he restored the original ending.

Barth wrote his next novel, a "nihilistic tragedy," during the last three months of 1955. Because it resembled *The Floating Opera*, which had not sold well,

Appleton-Century-Crofts was reluctant to publish it right away, so Barth sought another publisher. After Knopf refused the novel, Doubleday accepted it but asked that Barth change its original title, "What To Do Until the Doctor Comes," to *The End of the Road*. Published in August 1958 to enthusiastic reviews, the novel almost doubled the sales of *The Floating Opera* (3,000 copies compared to 1,682) but was still a commercial failure.

Barth's first two novels had brought him fame but little fortune. When he began *The Sot-Weed Factor* in early 1956, his salary at Penn State was low, and his family's financial condition, in Barth's words, "pretty desperate." His 1958 application for a Guggenheim Fellowship was unsuccessful, but Penn State provided a small raise and a $250 grant that allowed him to do research in Maryland for *The Sot-Weed Factor*. Published by Doubleday on 19 August 1960, it, too, was critically acclaimed but commercially unsuccessful. In April 1959, *The Sot-Weed Factor* finally finished, Barth immediately began a new project, a novel to be entitled *The Seeker* or *The Amateur*. But he abandoned it in June for another book, *Giles Goat-Boy*, whose theme and structure were greatly influenced by his recent readings in myth, particularly Joseph Campbell's *The Hero With a Thousand Faces* and Lord Raglan's *The Hero*. After applying, again unsuccessfully, for a Guggenheim Fellowship in 1961, Barth received a sabbatical leave from Penn State, spending the first six months of 1963 in Europe, where the Barths lived for a while in rainy Spain (a biographical detail Barth bestows upon the Turners in *Sabbatical*).

In 1965 the State University of New York (SUNY) at Buffalo offered Barth a full professorship, a reduced teaching load, and an attractive salary. Somewhat reluctantly, Barth moved his family from their home in the Allegheny mountain village of Pine Grove Mills, Pennsylvania, to Buffalo, where he became Edward S. Butler Professor of Literature at SUNY. The year before, Grosset and Dunlap had reissued *The Sot-Weed Factor* in paperback. The enormous "underground" success of the book, particularly on college campuses, prepared the way for *Giles Goat-Boy*, Barth's first best-seller, published by Doubleday on 31 May 1966. The commercial success of *Giles*, coupled with Barth's improved financial status at Buffalo, ended the money problems the Barths had suffered for the first dozen years of his career as a writer.

Barth remained at Buffalo from 1965 to 1973, a period he calls the "American High Sixties." Rebellion was in the air, not only the political rebellion of Vietnam protesters but artistic rebellion as well: "Pop Art popping at the Albright-Knox Museum; strange new music from Lukas Foss, Lejaren Hiller, and their electronic colleagues; . . . and, also the Peace Bridge . . . from which Professor [Marshall] McLuhan expounded on the limitations, indeed the obsolescence, of the printed word in our electronic culture" (*Friday Book*, p. 63). Barth had also discovered the short fiction of the Argentine Jorges Luis Borges and was beginning to research the oral traditions of narrative. Out of this milieu came Barth's influential essay "The Literature of Exhaustion," published in the *Atlantic* in August 1967, and his "series" of short fictions, *Lost in the Funhouse*, which he began writing in early 1966, finished in February 1968 and saw published by Doubleday on 27 September 1968. Nominated for the 1968 National Book Award, *Funhouse* is Barth's most experimental work, containing fictions intended not only for print but for live voice and for tape. Doubleday had actually agreed to include in the book itself cassette recordings of some of the stories, but Barth, deciding to rebel along more traditional lines, backed off.

As soon as *Funhouse* was completed, Barth, as is his habit, launched a new project, a long novel he called *LETTERS*. In fall 1969 he and his wife of almost twenty years separated, and Barth moved into their summer cottage on Lake Chautauqua in western New York, commuting up the New York State Thruway to teach his classes at Buffalo. Enjoying the solitude of his new surroundings, he continued to work on his novel in progress and, in his spare time, learned to sail—a pastime that figures prominently in everything he has written since. Among Barth's plans for *LETTERS* were two "core texts" that were to appear six-sevenths of the way through the novel and that were to be narrated by two mythological figures, Perseus and Bellerophon. But after completing "The Perseid," Barth decided to write two more novellas that, when combined with the first, would form a separate volume called *Chimera*.

Barth began "Bellerophoniad" in fall 1969. Before its completion in 1971, a number of key events in his life transpired: he was divorced, married to Shelly Rosenberg, a former student, on 27 December 1970, and suffered his first serious case of writer's block. The writer's block disappeared in late summer 1970 when he realized that the difficulties he was having in composing "The Bellerophoniad" actually duplicated the difficulties his protagonist was having getting Pegasus to fly. His creative juices flowing once more, Barth wrote "Dunyazadiad" during the summer of 1971. *Chimera* was published by Random House in September 1972, gaining Barth his third National Book Award nomination. But this time he won.

Barth spent the 1972–73 academic year on leave from SUNY, teaching at Boston University. Late that year, Johns Hopkins offered him a position teaching in the University Writing Seminar. So in the fall of 1973 the Barths moved to Baltimore, Shelly to teach at the St. Timothy's School, Barth to become the Alumni Centennial Professor of English and Creative Writing in the same program from which he had graduated two decades before. Perseus-like, Barth's life had come full circle. Although not fallen from Olympus, he, like Bellerophon, had again landed in the Maryland marshes.

The Hopkins years have been productive. In 1979 *LETTERS: a Novel* was completed at last and published by Putnam's. An encyclopedic reorchestration of characters and themes from his first six books, it is Barth's most demanding and most brilliant literary performance to date. That same year, Barth wrote "The Literature of Replenishment," which appeared in the January 1980 *Atlantic*. In 1982 Putnam's published *Sabbatical: A Romance*, Barth's most straightforward narrative since his first two novels. *The Friday Book: Essays and Other Nonfiction*, a collection of essays and lectures Barth wrote on Fridays, the other four days of the workweek having been reserved for fiction, was published by Putnam's in October 1984. *Tidewater Tales: A Novel*, the working title of his current project, concerns a married couple who tell stories to one another as they sail the Chesapeake.

MAJOR THEMES

If by *theme* we mean the idea or set of ideas embodied and expanded upon in a work of art, then Barth's themes are difficult to pinpoint. Ideas abound in his novels, to the extent that he has frequently been called a novelist of ideas. But Barth, an opposite-sex twin whose novels also tend to come in pairs, almost always contradicts in the second novel of the pair whatever philosophical position he seems to have arrived at in the first. For example, *The Floating Opera* apparently makes a case for ethical subjectivism. After concluding that in a world without absolutes suicide is no more rationally defensible than choosing to live, Todd Andrews further considers whether "in the real absence of absolutes, values less than absolute mightn't be regarded as in no way inferior and even be lived by" (p. 114). In *The End of the Road*, on the other hand, Barth first attributes Todd's conclusion to Joe Morgan, then has Jake Horner "undo that position . . . and carry all *non-mystical* value-thinking to the end of the road" (quoted in Harris, p. 46). Values, Barth seems to say in this novel, lie outside the province of rational discourse. Similarly, *The Sot-Weed Factor*, the first of Barth's pair of "gigantistic" novels, apparently rejects the possibility of attaining transcendental unity represented by Eben's quixotic quest for ideal Beauty and Henry's desire for coalescence. But in *Giles Goat-Boy*, which completes Barth's pair of "meganovels," George does transcend categories, perceiving at once, in no time, universal unity.

Barth's books are novels of ideas only insofar as they "dramatize alternatives to philosophical positions" (Prince, p. 57). His philosophical skepticism is rooted in the belief that "reality" is nothing more than our ideas about "reality" hypostatized. As a brief glance at intellectual history indicates, such hypostatizations last briefly, as one age, one *Weltanschauung*, one coordinating myth inevitably gives way to its successor. By refuting in one book a position he seems to have upheld in a prior book, Barth creates a metaphor for this ineluctable process. Taken collectively, his books achieve the effect of a constant grasping for meaning, on the one hand, balanced by the realization that all meaning is projected—invented rather than discovered and therefore relevant and contingent—on the other. Yet Barth's desire to imagine alternatives to "reality" affirms the value of such imaginings. Their value remains constant from age to age, although the "realities" imagined are themselves ephemeral. In Barth's fictions, the passionate desire to construct meaning, not meaning itself, assumes the status of a universal value. If anything is sacred, it is not a particular form of human "reality" but that which is *formative* of human "reality": imagination and its medium, language.

The world we perceive, and in the act of perception help to create, is therefore no more ontologically secure than the "world" contained in works of fiction. To reinforce this idea, Barth's work draws attention to its own artificiality in a variety of ways. In *Lost in the Funhouse*, self-reflexive fictions such as "Title," "Autobiography," and "Life-Story" are primarily about their own processes. In works such as *LETTERS*, *The Floating Opera*, "Bellerophoniad," and *Sabbatical*, however, self-reflexiveness is almost completely absorbed into the work's narrative flow. Each of these works is narrated by a protagonist or protagonists acutely aware of the problems they are having composing the work we are reading. Since the writing process forms a central element in the novel's plot, references to that process, which in another context would constitute foregrounding, become wholly appropriate to the work's "realistic" base. Although virtually free of narrative self-consciousness, *Giles Goat-Boy* also affirms its artificiality when, in a famous scene, George meets someone who is reading the book in which she and he are characters, *Giles Goat-Boy* itself. Resonating in both ontological directions, such devices suggest the similarly fictive nature of the "real" world.

Not only do Barth's fictions comment upon their own processes, but as metafictions they comment upon the history and nature of the genre they exemplify. In its imitation of the conventions of the eighteenth-century novel, for example, *The Sot-Weed Factor* allows Barth to draw analogies between the age that produced the first novels and our own milieu, also a time of transition, out of which postmodernist texts such as *The Sot-Weed Factor* have risen. Among the metafictional elements of *LETTERS* is the relationship between two characters: Lady Amherst, who represents the Great Tradition of Western Literature, and Ambrose Mensch, whose career as a writer replicates the novel's historical progress from realism through Modernism to the sterile archformalism of High Modernism. Ambrose wishes to get Lady Amherst "one final time with child" (767); but she is menopausal, he the victim of an exhausted silence. To transcend his aesthetic dilemma, Ambrose must find a form that neither repudiates the past nor slavishly emulates it. Whereas premodernism overemphasizes the world of objective reality, thereby blinding itself to that subjectivism that participates in the construction of "reality," and whereas modernism overemphasizes the essentially subjective ordering properties of the human mind, thereby blinding itself to the ontological "thereness" of the world of physical fact, Ambrose must strive for a middle ground between these apparent oppositions, thereby achieving a postmodernist synthesis of both. Such is the postmodernist "program" Barth outlines in "The Literature of Replenishment" and embodies in *LETTERS*, which among other things is a history of the novel from its origins through postmodernism.

Despite such formal considerations, Barth's books are not just virtuoso performances. Form for Barth is always a metaphor for other concerns, never an end in itself. "My feeling about technique in art," he has said, "is that it has about the same value as technique in love-making. That is to say, on the one hand, heartfelt ineptitude has its appeal and, on the other hand, so does heartless skill; but what you want is *passionate virtuosity*'' (quoted in Harris, p. 3). Barth has often referred to the Jungian notion that writers are to a large extent transcribers of preexisting archetypes. But archetypes are merely formative, possessing no form of their own. Thus the forms they inspire, the aesthetic constructs, must be unique. To use Barth's favorite metaphor from Borges, the archetypal fire remains constant and unchanging from generation to generation; the algebra—the artifact itself—varies, not only between generations but from artist to artist. To allow the artist's ''algebra,'' his form and technique, to harden into stale, exhausted formulae is to risk extinguishing the ''fire.'' Thus Barth's constant drive for unique and original expression. Yet this drive also involves risk: the writer may become so concerned with formal means that calculation totally replaces inspiration—a danger that Barth's characters J. Bray, Bellerophon, and Ambrose Mensch fail to avoid. Passionate virtuosity: algebra and fire—poetic power requires a dynamic unity of each.

Within Barth's fiction, love functions as the chief emblem of this unity. Mystical illumination in his books almost always coincides with sexual embrace, as in the cases of George and Anastasia, Ambrose and Lady Amherst, Fenwick and Susan. Indeed, it is this search for unity that links all of Barth's work, which otherwise shifts in mode and manner from book to book. Barth's vision may therefore be described as mythopoeic, since unity, as Joseph Campbell and others have demonstrated, is the central idea of the mythic. Barth's first two protagonists, terrified by the unity they seek, retreat behind a shield of words. In *The Sot-Weed Factor*, on the other hand, Henry Burlingame deliberately seeks cosmic harmony, and in *Giles Goat-Boy* George, transcending categories, achieves it. But each of Barth's protagonists, like Barth himself, is a writer in the world, not a mystic. The problem of the mythopoeic writer is how to translate mythic intimations, which are finally ineffable, into words capable of evoking that which may not be articulated. Barth's next two books, *Lost in the Funhouse* and *Chimera*, address this difficulty, the former focusing primarily on the relationship between sex, language, and myth; the latter, by far the most socially conscious of Barth's first six books, showing how myth may inform life as well as art. *LETTERS*, Barth's seventh book, and *Sabbatical*, his eighth and most ''realistic,'' complete this return to the world while affirming that it is a *worded* world after all. Language, properly employed, is the mythic if not mystic ligature connecting man, time, and world in a dynamic unity. Barth's recent books, then, illuminate that which is hidden, incipient, in his first two novels and which emerges gradually through the next four books: the true source and nature of the unity he has sought from the beginning. This unity is not located beyond the categories of subject and object, in the mystic realm to which George ascends or in the mythic past of *Funhouse* and *Chimera*, but in the reciprocal, dialogic interchange between self and other. The poetic act of saying delivers the world to man and man to the world. The world, Barth has come to understand over the course of his career thus far, does not exist *in* so much as *through* the word. This notion informs as it explains the passionate virtuosity of John Barth.

SURVEY OF CRITICISM

The major critical statements about Barth fall into three rather obvious categories: articles in professional journals, chapters in books, and book-length studies. A representative sampling of articles has been collected by Joseph J. Waldmeir (1980). Included in this collection are two important essays: Earl Rovit's "The Novel as Parody: John Barth," one of four essays on Barth's fiction that *Critique* published in its winter 1963 issue, the first extended commentary Barth's work received; and Campbell Tatham's "John Barth and the Aesthetics of Artifice" (1971), still one of the best statements of the Barthian aesthetic. Curiously omitted from Waldmeir's collection is Thomas LeClair's important essay "John Barth's *The Floating Opera*: Death and the Craft of Fiction" (1973), the first article to argue that, despite its realistic surface, Barth's novel displays many of the "aesthetic qualities" of his later, more innovative fiction.

The earliest book to devote a full chapter to Barth's fiction was Robert Scholes's *The Fabulators* (1967). British and American writers such as Barth, Scholes maintains, take an especial delight in formal design for its own sake, an observation that almost singlehandedly redirected critical attention away from theme toward Barth's formal inventiveness. Three more general studies of recent American fiction containing chapters on Barth's novels appeared in 1971: Tony Tanner's *City of Words*, which focuses on Barth's verbal play; Richard Boyd Hauck's *A Cheerful Nihilism*, which places Barth in the tradition of the absurd that Hauck believes began with the Puritans; and Charles B. Harris's *Contemporary American Novelists of the Absurd*, also a study of absurdist tendencies in Barth's fiction.

Other books in the second category that deserve mention include the following: Raymond M. Olderman's *Beyond the Waste Land* (1972), which devotes its single chapter on Barth exclusively to *Giles*; Max F. Schulz's *Black Humor Fiction of the Sixties* (1973), which adroitly examines the thematic and formal implications of multiplicity in Barth's work; and Charles Caramello's *Silverless Mirrors* (1983), the first application of poststructuralist critical methods to *Funhouse*. Lengthy interviews with Barth are contained in collections edited by Joe David Bellamy (1974), Frank Gado (1973), L. S. Dembo and Cyrena N. Pondrom (1972), and Thomas LeClair and Larry McCaffery (1982). Finally, John Gardner (1978), Gerald Graff (1979), and Jerome Klinkowitz (1975) have each attacked Barth's fiction, the first two because they find Barth willfully difficult and excessively experimental, the last because he finds Barth insufficiently innovative.

The third category of Barth criticism remains the slightest. Only four book-length studies plus Joseph Weixlmann's bibliography (1976) have been published, and two of these are introductions, thus necessarily quite general. In 1970 Gerhard Joseph's Minnesota pamphlet appeared, remaining the standard introduction to Barth's life and works until David Morrell's book superseded it in 1976. Despite the excessive generality of Morrell's interpretations, which often consist of plot summaries, his book provides a compendium of pertinent facts about Barth's life and works and is an indispensable biographical source. Unlike these introductions, Jac Tharpe's terse study (1974) should be turned to by the nonspecialist only after a close acquaintance with Barth's fiction and some of the more accessible commentaries have been consulted. Tharpe's thesis is that, together, Barth's novels form a history of philosophy. Yet, Tharpe argues, Barth is primarily an aesthetician for whom form is content. The first book-length study of Barth's fiction, Tharpe's book is eminently worthy of its subject and a book no serious critic of Barth can responsibly omit from account. The most recent book on Barth is Charles B. Harris's *Passionate Virtuosity: The Fiction of John Barth* (1983), which argues that Barth's vision is essentially mythopoeic and that his considerable virtuosity as an artist is balanced by a passionate commitment to life and love.

BIBLIOGRAPHY

Works by John Barth

The Floating Opera. New York: Appleton-Century-Crofts, 1956; rev. ed., Garden City, N.Y.: Doubleday, 1967.
The End of the Road. Garden City, N.Y.: Doubleday, 1958; rev. ed., 1967.
The Sot-Weed Factor. Garden City, N.Y.: Doubleday, 1960; rev. ed., 1967.
Giles Goat-Boy or, The Revised New Syllabus. Garden City, N.Y.: Doubleday, 1966.
Lost in the Funhouse. Garden City, N.Y.: Doubleday, 1968.
Chimera. New York: Random House, 1972.
LETTERS: A Novel. New York: Putnam's, 1979.
Sabbatical: A Romance. New York: Putnam's, 1982.
The Friday Book: Essays and Other Nonfiction. New York: Putnam's, 1984.

Studies of John Barth

Bellamy, Joe David, ed. *The New Fiction: Interviews with Innovative American Writers*. Urbana: University of Illinois Press, 1974.
Caramello, Charles. *Silverless Mirrors: Book, Self, and Postmodern American Fiction*. Tallahassee: Florida State University Press, 1983.
Dembo, L. S. and Cyrena N. Pondrom, ed. *The Contemporary Writer: Interviews with Sixteen Novelists and Poets*. Madison: University of Wisconsin Press, 1972.
Gado, Frank, ed. *First Person: Conversations on Writers and Writing*. Schenectady, N.Y.: Union College Press, 1973.
Gardner, John. *On Moral Fiction*. New York: Basic Books, 1978.

Graff, Gerald. *Literature Against Itself: Literary Ideas in Modern Society*. Chicago: University of Chicago Press, 1979.

Harris, Charles B. *Contemporary American Novelists of the Absurd*. New Haven: College and University Press, 1971.

————. *Passionate Virtuosity: The Fiction of John Barth*. Urbana: University of Illinois Press, 1983.

Hauck, Richard Boyd. *A Cheerful Nihilism: Confidence and The Absurd in American Humorous Fiction*. Bloomington: Indiana University Press, 1971.

Joseph, Gerhard. *John Barth*. Minnesota Pamphlets on American Writers, No. 91. Minneapolis: University of Minnesota Press, 1970.

Klinkowitz, Jerome. *Literary Disruptions: The Making of a Post-Contemporary American Fiction*. Urbana: University of Illinois Press, 1975.

LeClair, Thomas. "John Barth's *The Floating Opera*: Death and the Craft of Fiction." *University of Texas Studies in Language and Literature* 14 (Winter 1973): 711–30.

LeClair, Thomas and Larry McCaffery, ed. *Interviews with Contemporary American Novelists*. Urbana: University of Illinois Press, 1982.

Morrell, David. *John Barth: An Introduction*. University Park: Pennsylvania State University Press, 1976.

Olderman, Raymond M. *Beyond the Waste Land: A Study of the American Novel in the Nineteen-Sixties*. Madison: University of Wisconsin Press, 1972.

Prince, Alan. "An Interview with John Barth." *Prism* (Sir George Williams University, Spring 1968): 42–62.

Scholes, Robert. *The Fabulators*. New York: Oxford University Press, 1967.

Schulz, Max F. *Black Humor Fiction of the Sixties: A Pluralistic Definition of Man and His World*. Athens: Ohio University Press, 1973.

Tanner, Tony. *City of Words: American Fiction, 1950–1970*. New York: Harper and Row, 1971.

Tatham, Campbell. "John Barth and the Aesthetics of Artifice." *Contemporary Literature* 12, no. 1 (1971): 60–73.

Tharpe, Jac. *John Barth: The Comic Sublimity of Paradox*. Carbondale: Southern Illinois University Press, 1974.

Waldmeir, Joseph, ed. *Critical Essays on John Barth*. Boston: G. K. Hall, 1980.

Weixlmann, Joseph. *John Barth: A Bibliography*. New York: Garland, 1976.

JOSEPH R. MILLICHAP

Hamilton Basso
(1904–1964)

Hamilton Basso was a prolific and popular writer. Although neglected in recent years, his work remains important for its liberal realism, its connections to the work of other Southern writers, and its own literary merits. Basso is a minor but interesting figure in the mosaic of the Southern Renascence.

BIOGRAPHY

Joseph Hamilton Basso was born on 5 September 1904 in New Orleans. His family background and place of birth anticipated the development of both his personal life and his literary career. Most of his life was spent in New Orleans and in New York City. His literary subject was the Southern myth; his attitude toward it was detached and cosmopolitan.

Basso was named for his grandfather, an Italian immigrant who established a small shoe factory that supported the family comfortably. As a boy, Basso lived upstairs over the business in the old French Quarter, a colorful neighborhood he later described in a series of sketches published in the *New Yorker* in the 1950s. When Basso was ten, his family moved to the "American" section beyond Canal Street, where he progressed through the local schools to Tulane University.

Basso entered Tulane in 1922, the year that marked the maturation of literary modernism with the publication of Eliot's *The Waste Land* and Joyce's *Ulysses*. Modernism had reached New Orleans a year earlier, when a group of Tulane professors and sojourning writers founded the *Double Dealer*, a literary periodical second only to Nashville's *Fugitive* in its importance to Southern letters. Basso studied law at Tulane, but his lifelong interests in history and literature led him to the *Double Dealer* group, which in those years included Sherwood Anderson, Edmund Wilson, Oliver La Farge, and the youthful William Faulkner. After Faulkner's death, Basso wrote about their playing drunken, dangerous tag across the roofs of the French Quarter. More important, Faulkner and the other writers influenced Basso's decision to leave law school for journalism and literature, his lifelong profession and vocation respectively.

At various times Basso worked for all three of the city's major papers. During the late 1920s he lived for a time in New York City, trying his hand at advertising, which he detested. Finally, he devoted himself entirely to his own writing, finishing an autobiographical novel, *Relics and Angels*, in 1929. This rather imitative first effort about a young man who cannot return home to New Orleans met an indifferent critical and popular response in the months following the stock market crash, and Basso later rejected the work himself.

In 1930 Basso married Etolia Moore Simmons, a local woman he met at Tulane, and he went back to newspaper work to support them. Over the next two years, he completed a biography of the Confederate general, P.G.T. Beauregard, published by Scribner's in 1933. *Beauregard: The Great Creole* was Basso's first important book, and its modest success provided the money to write a second novel in Asheville, North Carolina, where Basso had gone to visit a new friend, novelist Thomas Wolfe. Wolfe recommended Basso's new novel to editor Maxwell Perkins, and Scribner's published it in 1934. *Cinnamon Seed* was a much better novel than Basso's first, and it set the tone of his fiction during the 1930s, realistic pictures of the Depression South formed by the confluence of its geography and history.

In 1935 Basso went back to journalism as an associate editor of the liberal *New Republic*. His home base became New York City, but his writing assignments brought him back to the South to cover such events as the Scottsboro trial, the Huey Long assassination, and the Gastonia strike. A textile strike forms the background for Basso's third novel, *In Their Own Image* (1935), though the novel stays mostly in the foreground that depicts with Jamesian irony the horsey set of Aiken, South Carolina. The book is also notable as his only novel without a protagonist who is identifiable with Basso.

The autobiographical figure reappears as David Barondess, the novelist-hero of *Courthouse Square* (1936), Basso's best novel to date. David tries to return to Macedon, South Carolina, and discovers he cannot accept the injustice of Southern society. More important, he matures as he discovers his own complicity in the tangled web of Southern history. The book was well reviewed by the critics, well received by the public, and optioned by Hollywood.

The commercial success of *Courthouse Square* allowed Basso a sabbatical from his editorial duties, and he returned to Asheville, where he renewed his intellectual energies through wide reading and study. Out of this period came his next set of books, novels that could be called more philosophical than social. The best of them is *Days Before Lent* (1939), which traces the maturation of its protagonist against the background of Mardi Gras in New Orleans. Dr. Jason Kent is more concerned with global issues than are Basso's earlier protagonists, though he too must come to terms with his Southern heritage before he can marry, the conventional ending Basso usually favored. The book proved both a critical and commercial success, winning the Southern Authors Award over formidable competition and later being made into a movie under the title *Holiday for Sinners*. *Wine of the Country* (1940) is centered on a young anthropologist who tries to study his home county in lowland South Carolina but discovers he must understand his patrimony through his heart as well as his head. *Sun in Capricorn* (1942) is notable for the antagonism between its Basso-like hero and Gilgo Slade, an obvious fictional incarnation of Huey Long. Although this novel was a popular success, Slade is too much the stock villain.

Sun in Capricorn was Basso's last novel until after World War II. He was excused from military service because of weak health but worked for the Office of Strategic Services as a home front journalist. In 1944 he joined the staff of the *New Yorker*, a periodical that published his best short fiction and nonfiction. Basso's only child, Keith, was born in 1940, and the family settled permanently in Weston, Connecticut, a pleasant suburb of New York. During the war, Basso produced one book, *Mainstream* (1943), a series of biographies of representative Americans notable for its patriotic conclusions about the American Dream.

Basso's next book did not appear until 1949; *The Greenroom* is his only novel set outside the United States, though his characters are expatriated Americans. In this instance the Basso-like protagonist matures through his relationship with an aged American novelist, probably modeled on Edith Wharton. Indeed, the novel is reminiscent of Wharton's books, or those of her mentor Henry James. Because of its more complex feminine personalities, it proves perhaps his best novel.

Basso returned to Southern settings for his most popular novel, *The View from Pompey's Head* (1954). The book topped the *New York Times* best-seller list for several weeks and was made into a highly successful film under the same title. This success guaranteed good sales for the second volume of a projected trilogy about the fictional port city of Pompey's Head, South Carolina. *The Light Infantry Ball* (1959) is a realistic Civil War novel, called an "adult Southern" by one critic. Basso never completed a projected third novel (which was to have been set during the Reconstruction) in the Pompey's Head trilogy. Instead he finished his weakest novel, *A Touch of the Dragon* (1964).

Basso died of cancer at age fifty-nine, on 13 May 1964. His funeral was crowded with his literary friends, and his former editor Malcolm Cowley wrote an affectionate reminiscence in the *Saturday Review*. Undoubtedly, Basso's illness explains the weakness of his final novel; had he lived he might well have produced other works meriting both popular and critical acclaim.

MAJOR THEMES

A lifelong friend of William Faulkner and a confidant of Thomas Wolfe, Basso stood near the center of the Southern Renascence in both a historical and a geographical sense. He was a member of the *Double Dealer* group in New Orleans after World War I and an exile in the North after World War II. His fiction as much as his life proves central to the Southern Renascence. Like Faulkner, he probed the symbolism of plantation house culture; like Wolfe, he pictured the exiled Southerner; like Warren, he portrayed a Southern demagogue.

At the same time, Basso's fiction represents a strain different in many ways from that of these major male figures, or of the best women writers of the Renascence: Eudora Welty, Carson McCullers, or Flannery O'Connor. Although Basso began his fiction in the imitation of Faulkner, Wolfe, and Warren, his journalistic bent brought him to a more realistic, liberal, and popular fiction. In his best work, Basso considers the tragic results of the South's preoccupation with its own "myth" of Southern history. In these novels, he strikes that fitful balance between individual and society that obtains in the best realistic fiction.

Although he always worked in a realistic mode, Basso's vision sometimes faltered in his effort to be both liberal and popular. His fiction sometimes oversimplifies the complexities of Southern historical relations in an attempt to further liberal politics. His fictional portrait of Huey Long in *Sun in Capricorn* provides a good example; betraying the cause of populism, Gilgo Slade becomes the consummate villain of stock romance, joining many of Basso's heroines and minor characters. Basso had a weakness for popular turns of plot. Often he allowed his realistic vision to be weakened by such action sequences as the hunt in *Wine of the Country*, such mystery plots as Cameron's disappearance in *The Light Infantry Ball*, or such happy ending romances as the marriage in *Days Before Lent*. *A Touch of the Dragon* suffers greatly from melodramatic twists and stock characters.

Yet Basso's finest works avoid or overcome these problems to repay the thoughtful reader even today. Although he cannot be counted in the first rank of Southern writers, the popular Basso may have done as much as any single writer in shaping American attitudes toward the South in the period from the Depression to the Supreme Court decision on desegregation. In many ways his best novels are also his most popular—*Courthouse Square, Days Before Lent*, and *The View From Pompey's Head*.

Courthouse Square was both the culmination of earlier, less competent fiction and the prototype of later, more professional work. The line of development in the author's earlier novels is easily traced. *Relics and Angels*, his first novel, establishes the Basso protagonist, a sensitive young Southerner who cannot go home again. Whereas his first novel is more personal in its hero's search for maturity, his second novel, *Cinnamon Seed*, is more social in its concerns for the South. The protagonist disappears entirely in favor of social analysis in Basso's third novel, *In Their Own Image. Courthouse Square* combines the best elements of the three earlier novels, creating one of Basso's best works.

In *Courthouse Square* Basso returned to the autobiographical protagonist found most often at the center of his books. David Barondess, his central character, is a young Southerner who has published two novels critical of the South, but who returns to his home in Macedon, South Carolina, at a crisis in his literary and personal life. David is psychologically blocked in the creation of his new novel, and his frustration vents itself in rejection of his wife, a Northern girl he married in New York. His return home gives him the chance to reconsider both his vocation a novelist and his personal commitment to Letitia.

Macedon, a typical county seat and market town, sits in the hill country, like its namesake populated by a race of hearty, barbarous warriors. David Barondess must find his place in this world before he can understand his place in the larger world represented by New York. Like Faulkner's Ike McCaslin or Wolfe's Monk Webber, he is a young man defining himself in relation to the history of his family, his town, and his region. David discovers in the diary of his grandfather Edward Barondess, a Southern abolitionist, not only his next book but an index to his personal identity. He learns that the Barondess family has always complemented the romanticism of the Legendres and the pragmatism of the Lamars, the two other notable families of Macedon, with a liberal, moral sense. The Legendres have disappeared over the years, like Faulkner's Sutpens, leaving only the ruin of the family mansion to haunt the town. The Lamars, like Faulkner's Snopses, have emerged as courthouse crooks who control the local culture. When David returns to Macedon, he excites the envy of the local newspaper editor, Pick Eustis, and the jealousy of Dan Lamar, the scion of the local boss. Julie Lamar, Dan's wife, is an old girlfriend of David's, and their romance threatens to heat up once again over the long, hot summer.

The spark igniting this dangerous situation is provided by a local pharmacist, a black man named Fauget. Although he seems to be an Uncle Tom, respected in both the white and black communities, Fauget shocks the town by offering to buy the Legendre mansion and renovate it into a hospital for blacks. Later his motivation becomes clearer when he is revealed as the illegitimate son of Cincinnatus Legendre, a Confederate general, and a quadroon woman. While the newspaper's editorials fulminate against the plan, Dan Lamar organizes a lynch mob against Fauget. David Barondess manages to rescue the old black man, but not before he is badly hurt himself in the destruction of the Legendre mansion.

Basso's narrative is exciting, and its symbolism effective. The myth of the Old South proves inoperative in modern Macedon; the Legendre house and the values it represents are useless to the contemporary citizens of Macedon, both white and black. Basso also underlines these themes with the historical contrast between David's crusade and that of his abolitionist grandfather Edward.

If the Southern sections of the book are successful, the New York sections are less so. Almost a third of the book concerns David's years in New York, his marriage, and his literary career. Unfortunately, the literati of Basso's novel are not always convincing. The major difficulty is the insubstantial characterization of David's wife Letitia. Although David has in essence deserted her, indirectly causing the loss of their unborn baby, she runs to his bedside at the news of his injury. She not only forgives David but recognizes what an admirable character he is and pledges herself to his support. This character development smacks of the movies, particularly the "woman's picture" of that decade, wherein wives nobly sacrificed themselves for noble husbands.

These problems of characterization and plotting do not cancel out the strengths of the book, though they do weaken them. *Courthouse Square* presents the tragedy of history working itself out in the modern South through the person of a sensitive Southern writer. Basso's next novel would take a similar central character and use him to view the tragedy of a world on the brink of war.

Like *Courthouse Square, Days Before Lent* (1939) combines successful elements of earlier novels. Dr. Jason Kent, the protagonist, is a complex and engaging variation of the Basso type. The New Orleans setting provides a good deal of symbolic meaning, while the plot skillfully unfolds events both romantic and violent against the backdrop of Mardi Gras. These elements were blended with a good deal of stylistic achievement, thematic integrity, and realistic intelligence. Only a romantic and redundant happy ending weakens the total success of the novel.

Basso's multiple epigraphs all point toward his theme: the unity of human experience within the physical life of the universe. Jason Kent's maturation comes about in his recognition of this unity, and in his evolution of successful life from it. Young Dr. Kent's name, Jason, symbolizes his search for the treasure of personal integrity. As the novel opens he has just turned thirty, finally completing his medical studies after a number of side trips into the realms of religion, science, and the humanities.

Like Basso's other protagonists, Jason must choose a father figure. His own father, now dead for a decade, was a romantic—a doctor who devoted himself to the derelicts of the French Quarter, an amateur anthropologist, and a skilled boxing coach. Jason knows he must be more realistic in the difficult days preceding World War II. Should he use medicine for social purposes, as he is advised by his old friend Father Carducci? Or should he devote himself to pure medical research under the tutelage of his former professor Dr. Hunt? Or should he take the medical directorship offered by a large corporation, as suggested by another mentor, Dr. Muller?

His choice is complicated by the people dependent on him. Like most of Basso's heroes, Jason has found his heroine, the beautiful Susanna Fuller. They plan to marry, and he must fit her interests into his vocational plans. He also has inherited from his father the care of Joe Piavi, a broken-down pug. Another unstable character is Tyrell Surtees, his father's cousin, who resembles a Tennessee Williams version of a Southern playwright. The two men represent dark sides of Jason, as well as of his father, the temptations of physical and intellectual irresponsibility.

The novel opens on the Thursday before Mardi Gras. Jason is trying to finish his monograph on *Kala-azar*, a tropical disease he had encountered in the bayous along the Gulf coast three years earlier. A long and interesting flashback recalls his fight against a local outbreak of the deadly disease. The affair made him something of a medical hero and led to the career offers he now contemplates.

Unable to work, Jason wanders the streets of the Quarter, encountering all of the major characters and another old friend of his father, Dr. Gomez. A Central American medical doctor, Gomez has been exiled by a military dictatorship in his native land. His career parallels the decline of modern civilization into the throes of totalitarianism of both the left and the right. The old doctor tells Jason that only a truly scientific education will lead humankind to true freedom. Dr. Gomez is returning to his homeland to make one last attempt at revolution, and he offers Jason his New Orleans practice. Jason now has another alternative: he can follow more closely in his father's footsteps into the French Quarter.

The novel then jumps to Sunday and the arrival of Susanna from New England. Here the rather clichéd romance plot develops, but on Monday Jason sets romance aside when he discovers that Joe Piavi has killed a local racketeer. Jason resolves to save his old friend from the gangster's gunmen, enlisting the help of a young newspaper reporter. He sets off on a nightmarish search through the mean streets mobbed by masked revelers.

Mardi Gras, Fat Tuesday, itself resolves all the plot developments. Danny O'Neill, the reporter, finds Piavi first and tries to hide him out for an exclusive interview. The local mob has access to the newspaper, however, and their thugs gun both men down in the midst of the mad celebration. Meanwhile, Tyrell Surtees chooses Mardi Gras to commit suicide, haunted by the specter of his wife, who killed herself after his repeated infidelities. He flies his private airplane above the sordid violence of the streets, out over the Gulf into oblivion.

Stunned by the dark world around him, Jason finds his own human balance. Rejecting the solutions of his various surrogate fathers, he decides to buy his father's practice, finish his medical monograph, and marry Susanna. This resolution proves a sensible human compromise in the holistic vision posited earlier in the novel. Unfortunately, it also smacks slightly of the commercial happy ending of the movies of the decade. Yet the novel's careful structuring of this solution makes it acceptable in human terms as a dramatization of the maturation process found at the heart of Basso's best books. Combined with the intellectual complexity of the novel, this maturation makes *Days Before Lent* one of Basso's finest novels, one which merited the Southern Authors Award over such formidable competition as Thomas Wolfe's last novel and Robert Penn Warren's first.

Basso's most popular novel was undoubtedly *The View from Pompey's Head*. It was selected by the Literary Guild, listed by the *New York Times* as a best-seller for 42 weeks, and sold to the movies for a large sum. The book's blockbuster sales were spurred by the almost entirely enthusiastic reviewing in the major periodicals. Colman Rosenberger, writing in the New York *Herald-Tribune*, realized the source of the book's success when he characterized it in terms of three separate "novels" within its structure: the novel of character, the novel of suspense, and the novel of ideas.

The "novel of character" concerns Anson Page, a forty-year-old version of the Basso protagonist. A successful lawyer with a large New York firm, Anson is another Southerner in Northern exile, wondering if he can return to his home in Pompey's Head, South Carolina. The town's striking name is taken from the shape of a jutting bluff at the estuary of the Cassava River; in the classical spirit of the times, the town's colonial governor named it for the noble Roman. An amalgam of Charleston and Savannah, Pompey's Head paralleled their history from the glory days of the cotton trade, to the Civil War blockade and destruction, to twentieth-century somnolence.

Anson Page is trapped in a middle-aged stasis as the novel opens. His life is circumscribed by his office and his apartment, both nice enough places. Yet he still preserves enough of his youthful, romantic view of life to wonder if he should have left the slower, softer, more sensual life of South Carolina. For him, Pompey's Head becomes a symbol of Edenic innocence and youthful exuberance.

His mid-life crisis is precipitated by a return to Pompey's Head after an absence of fifteen years. The occasion of his trip provides "the novel of suspense" within the book. One of his corporate clients, a large publishing company, has been accused of embezzling over $20,000 from the royalties of its most famous writer, the eccentric Southern novelist, Garvin Wales. The reclusive author resides on a small island near Pompey's Head, and Anson's errand is to clear up the mystery of the missing money. This proves to be a delicate and complicated mission, as the money was taken by Wales's editor, the now deceased Phillip Greene. This part of the novel is something of a *roman à clef*, as Wales seems compounded from Faulkner, Hemingway, and Wolfe, while Greene is clearly based on Maxwell Perkins.

The implications of Anson's trip in both a personal and a professional sense develop the "novel of ideas." The protagonist discovers in the revival of old friendships and romances how much he has grown. "Sonny" Page has left behind his best friend, the ambitionless scion of the founding family, as well as his old sweetheart, the wife of a newly rich social climber. Anson's fling with the dissatisfied, middle-aged club woman finally convinces him of how shallow his past has been. Clearly his future is in New York with his career and family.

Meanwhile, his investigation into the missing royalty money introduces him to another Southern gentlewoman, Lucy Wales, the aging author's redoubtable wife. Lucy is the one who has brought the charges against her husband's dead editor. Anson knows the money has been paid to a woman named Anna Jones, a shadowy figure from Wales's past. Later he discovers that the mulatto woman was Wales's mother, and that he has kept the knowledge from Lucy in his fear that a daughter of the Devereaux family will leave him at the revelation of his parentage. Finally, Anson forces Wales to face up to the reality of his past, just as he faces up to his own.

Both developments confirm Anson's and Basso's view of the Southern tradition. The weight of the past warping the present is a theme in all of Basso's novels; here it is identified as an ancestor worship that distorts both the ancestors and the worshippers. Even a Southerner as creative as Garvin Wales bows to the slavery of tradition in the South. If a great writer can be choked by the dead hand of the past, Anson concludes that he also would be throttled if he returned to Pompey's Head. Thus the "novel of ideas" emerges naturally from character development and the suspense narrative, creating one of Basso's best books from a critical viewpoint and certainly his most successful from a popular viewpoint.

SURVEY OF CRITICISM

Criticism of Basso's work is not extensive. Only two full-length studies about him exist at present; only two articles are at all important. A number of recent survey books and articles mention Basso or his individual novels, but many of the contemporary essays or reviews of his work prove more insightful.

The most important single work on Basso is Joseph Millichap's volume in the Twayne United States Authors Series. *Hamilton Basso* (1979) is the only study to consider all the author's canon and to make use of his unpublished papers. The biographical portrait was also based on extensive interviews with the novelist's widow, Mrs. Etolia Moore Basso. The book discusses Basso as a realistic novelist of the Renascence and analyzes all of his novels, short stories, and nonfiction in these terms. It also features a selected but extensive bibliography of primary and secondary sources.

The other full-length work on Basso, an unpublished doctoral dissertation at the University of North Carolina at Chapel Hill, is Clarence F. Ikerd's "Hamilton Basso: A Critical Portrait" (1974), which provides a thorough and intelligent assessment of Basso's life and works.

The best article on Basso is James Rocks's "The World View from Pompey's Head." It provides a sensible overview of Basso's work, though Rocks finally judges Basso as a popular novelist and journalist. His assessment of individual works, *Wine of the Country*, for example, is also interesting. Another important article is Malcolm Cowley's reminiscence piece, which appeared in the *Saturday Review* after Basso's death in 1964.

Several survey volumes mention Basso or his books in connection with their own particular interests. Perhaps the most favorable analysis of Basso appears in John Bradbury's *Renaissance in the South* (1963). Bradbury views Basso as an important social novelist. By contrast, in *The Art of Southern Fiction* (1963) Frederick J. Hoffman dismisses Basso as a popular novelist. Another interesting perspective is provided by Rose Basile Green in *The Italian-American Novel* (1973). Several of Basso's novels, in particular *Sun in Capricorn*, are frequently mentioned in surveys of Southern, political, or liberal fiction.

Much of the best criticism of Basso and his works remains in the contemporary articles and reviews. In this regard, Basso's own reviews and articles on the state of Southern or American letters are informative. The most important are "Letters in the South" (*New Republic*, 1935); "The Future of the South" (*New Republic*, 1939); and "William Faulkner: Man and Writer" (*Saturday Review*, 1962).

BIBLIOGRAPHY

Works by Hamilton Basso

Relics and Angels. New York: Macauley, 1929.
Beauregard: The Great Creole (biography). New York: Scribner, 1933.
Cinnamon Seed. New York: Scribner, 1934.
In Their Own Image. New York: Scribner, 1935.
Courthouse Square. New York: Scribner, 1936.
Days Before Lent. New York: Scribner, 1939.
Wine of the Country. New York: Scribner, 1941.
Sun in Capricorn. New York: Scribner, 1942.
Mainstream (biographical essays). New York: Reynal & Hitchcock, 1943.
The Greenroom. Garden City, N.Y.: Doubleday, 1949.
Exploration of the Valley of the Amazon (1854), by William Lewis Herndon. Ed. Hamilton
    Basso. New York: McGraw-Hill, 1952.
The View from Pompey's Head. Garden City, N.Y.: Doubleday, 1954.
The Light Infantry Ball. Garden City, N.Y.: Doubleday, 1959.
A Quota of Seaweed (travel essays). Garden City, N.Y.: Doubleday, 1960.
A Touch of the Dragon. New York: Viking, 1964.

Studies of Hamilton Basso

Aaron, Daniel. *Writers on the Left.* New York: Columbia University Press, 1961.
Bradbury, John. *Renaissance in the South.* Chapel Hill: University of North Carolina
    Press, 1963.
Carolan, Pamela Jean. "An Examination of Structure in Hamilton Basso's *The Green-
    room.*" M.A. thesis, University of North Carolina, 1971.
Cowley, Malcolm. "The Writer as Craftsman: The Literary Heroism of Hamilton Basso."
    Saturday Review 47 (June 27, 1964): 17–18.
Green, Rose Basile. *The Italian-American Novel.* Rutherford, N.J.: Fairleigh Dickinson
    University Press, 1973.
Hoffman, Frederick J. *The Art of Southern Fiction.* Carbondale: Southern Illinois Uni-
    versity Press, 1963.
Ikerd, Clarence F. "Hamilton Basso: A Critical Portrait." Ph.D. diss., University of
    North Carolina, 1974.
Millichap, Joseph R. *Hamilton Basso.* Boston: G. K. Hall, 1979.
Rocks, James. "The World View from Pompey's Head." *South Atlantic Quarterly* 71
    (1972): 326–41.
Rubin, Louis D., Jr. "All the King's Meanings." *Georgia Review* 8 (1954): 422–34.
Snyder, Robert E. "The Concept of Demagoguery: Huey Long and His Critics." *Lou-
    isiana Studies* 15 (1976): 61–84.

Doris Betts
(1932–   )

In 1954 when she was twenty-two, Doris Betts published her first book, a collection of twelve short stories. Entitled *The Gentle Insurrection*, this volume won a $2,000 prize given by Putnam Publishers and the University of North Carolina. Reviewers praised the book, commenting upon the high quality of her work, the youth of the author, and the great promise of her career. Since that time Betts has published two more volumes of short fiction and four novels, as well as articles and stories in a variety of periodicals.

Her reputation as a writer has grown slowly and incrementally. She mastered the short-story form early and is often put in the company of Flannery O'Connor, Peter Taylor, and Katherine Anne Porter, but her development as a novelist has been gradual. She describes herself as a natural short-story writer, but an "artificial and contrived and forced novelist." Her short stories are included in many anthologies, and her poetry, fiction, and articles are published in scholarly journals and popular periodicals; a film entitled "Violet," adapted from her short story "The Ugliest Pilgrim," won an Academy Award in 1982. Each novel has been different; each has shown growth. Her 1981 novel *Heading West* was a Book-of-the-Month Club selection. For many years she has been highly regarded by critics, teachers of literature, and specialists in Southern letters, but her reputation is growing steadily with the general public. After over 30 years on the national literary scene, Doris Betts is an artist whose work continues to surprise, inform, and delight the reader.

BIOGRAPHY

Doris June Waugh was born on 4 June 1932 in Statesville, North Carolina, the only child of William Elmore and Mary Ellen Freeze Waugh. Her father worked in a cotton mill, and she grew up in this small Southern town during the Depression and World War II years. Because everyone she knew was poor, she had no sense of material deprivation. Surrounded by an extended and loving family of grandparents, cousins, aunts, and uncles, she was an imaginative child who found her vocation early. She seems to have known always that she would be a writer.

This small rural town of Statesville, the community of neighbors and family members, and the Associate Reformed Presbyterian Church all exerted strong influences in forming Betts the artist. Probably the most important early influence was her mother, a woman neither intellectual nor bookish. Her mother's values resided in home and hearth and church, but she supported Doris's literary precocity. Doris Waugh began composing poems before she learned to write, and her mother nurtured this literary gift by writing down the poems and carefully saving them for her daughter. And although her mother instinctively found the written word in books threatening and dangerous, she allowed her daughter to read widely. Mrs. Waugh once asked her what she did when she got to bad words in a novel; Doris solemnly assured her mother that she skipped them.

The public library provided books for the young girl who read eagerly and indiscriminately. If she was not wandering in the neighborhood or playing with other children, she was reading. Her passion for the printed word has stayed with her, and she remains an adventurous reader of poetry, fiction, philosophy, and nonfiction.

No doubt the book that has had the most impact on Betts is the King James Bible. Her family were devout churchgoers, members of the Associate Reformed Presbyterian Church. Betts's mother described the ARPs as "All Right People," and the Waugh family attended church frequently—morning and evening services on Sunday, choir practice, prayer meetings, and revivals. Biblical stories touched her, as did the rhythms of the Bible. She found the stories in the Bible "very physical, very specific and concrete. . . . And you come out of them with a great sense of the flesh, and the blood, and the same material which I did see about me, and about which I have written extensively." Her fundamental Protestant background profoundly influenced her writing—convincing her early of the power of the word. She has explained that in the first book of the Bible, "the universe appears to be created not by action or event but by an imperative sentence. . . ." And religion informs Betts's life as well as her work. A person of deep religious faith, she has described herself as a member of the "tribe of Apostle Thomas—a natural doubter" whose faith has been hard-won. Her next novel will be a long family chronicle set in Iredell County, North Carolina, with a Presbyterian minister as the main character. She says the novel will trace the decline of religion as an influence in American life.

Home and community, church and library—these were the boundaries of the physical world of Doris Waugh, who wrote poems and fiction throughout her childhood. Her first novels were written in composition books, illustrated with pictures cut out of magazines, and shared with her classmates. She left this world at eighteen to attend Woman's College of the University of North Carolina at

Greensboro (now UNC-Greensboro). There her freshman English teacher introduced to her the idea of quality in literature and the disturbing notion that some writing was better than others. He gave her Dos Passos and Dostoevsky and other writers to read, and he judged her own writing, encouraging her in fiction but dismissing her poetry.

Doris Waugh continued to write, and after her second year of college, she married Lowry Betts on 5 July 1952 and moved to Chapel Hill, where her young husband attended law school. She enrolled at the University of North Carolina in 1954, when their second child was also born, but did not complete her degree. Her professional career was launched that year with the publication of *The Gentle Insurrection* (1954), which included some short stories written in her teens. Thus, 1954 was a signal year for Betts, marking her auspicious debut as a writer and the beginning of what would eventually become a long relationship with the University of North Carolina at Chapel Hill.

Betts has never had a room of her own nor an income that freed her for writing. She now writes in an easy chair centered in her house, surrounded by stacks of books and piles of paper—close to the kitchen, convenient to the front door. When her children were young, she wrote wherever she could—the kitchen table, an office where she worked, or the laundromat. And she wrote in brief periods, an hour here and an hour there.

Beginning as a teenager, she has worked all her life at such jobs as clerk, typist, and salesperson. She wrote for newspapers and served as editor for the Sanford (N.C.) *News Leader* in 1960. Starting in 1966 as a part-time teacher at UNC, she has moved up the ranks, serving as director of freshman composition from 1972 to 1978 and as assistant dean of the honors program from 1978 to 1981. Since 1980 she has been Alumni Distinguished Professor of English. During 1982–85 she served as (the first woman) chair of the faculty at the university. Her academic career as an award-winning teacher and outstanding administrator has been distinguished.

For many years she resided with her family in Sanford, North Carolina, where her husband practiced law. The Betts family includes three children—Doris LewEllyn, born in 1953; David Lowry, 1954; and Erskine Moore II, 1960. In addition to home, family, writing, and other employment, Betts has always been involved in public service activities. Two examples of her community service are her membership from 1960 to 1965 on the Lee County (N.C.) library board of trustees and her two terms, 1965–72, as an elected member of the Sanford (N.C.) city school board. Betts is an elder in the Presbyterian Church.

Now that the children are grown and away from home, she and her husband live on an 80-acre farm called Araby in Pittsboro, North Carolina, some twenty miles from Chapel Hill. She has always separated her private life and her academic life, commuting to her teaching position at the University of North Carolina.

Betts is an attractive, charismatic woman with chestnut brown hair and dark brown eyes. Articulate and comfortable with an audience, she is at home in public whether she is presenting a scholarly paper on the work of Anne Tyler, reading from her own work, speaking about style in literature to a conference of writers, talking to undergraduate members of Chi Omega sorority on being presented a service award, delivering a commencement address to the graduating class at Chapel Hill, conducting a course in writing or literature, or conversing with an interviewer. She has been particularly generous and open with interviewers, and her opinions on a broad spectrum of subjects are in print. Her voice is deep, and she speaks in the accents of her native North Carolina. Her manner—warm, curious, intelligent, earthy, witty, disarming—is effective with children, undergraduate students, men, women, dogs, horses, and interviewers.

MAJOR THEMES

Most of Betts's fiction is set in North Carolina among ordinary people. She is a regionalist in the sense that she draws on the weather, language, culture, and habits of a particular region. But, as she has explained, "The kind of fiction that comes out of a region and lasts, lasts not because of the region nor the latitude in which it is cast, but because of whatever is in the story that is human, that is sustained over more than a geographic area." Although she draws on her native North Carolina roots for setting, the landscape of her fiction is psychological and not geographical.

People of the lower and lower-middle class fascinate her, she says, "because the mortality is much closer to the edge of the veil there." She has described the "tribe" she knows best: "Mostly Scotch-Irish with a featherweight of Cherokee. Farmers, beauticians, policemen, millworkers, squirrel hunters, army privates. Earthy, joking people without college degrees, often without high school diplomas, living hard in piedmont North Carolina—red clay, red rivers. Use-it-up, wear-it-out, make-it-do people. Thrifty, stubborn, honest, hot-tempered. Their occasional fist fights were over money or sex but rarely ideas."

Although her characters do not come exclusively from this tribe, her fiction often depicts these people of the lower and lower-middle class, and she has written consistently of love and death, of growing up and growing old. She says her themes are "time and mortality," but there's hardly a subject close to the human heart that she has not treated, portraying families and their relationships, isolated people, the relationships of blacks and whites, the submerged and passionate life of her ordinary characters.

Her fiction most often presents conflict within the characters, and many of the tales involve the main character's quest or journey toward realizing some truth. But in form, both short stories and novels show great variety. Short stories include farcical tales, dark comedies, other worldly happenings, and lyrical pieces, as well as more traditional stories. Betts sketches the experience of all life in her fiction, but she returns to certain subject matter—the treatment of children and old people (frequently facing death), the depiction of love in all its various manifestations, and the pathetic failure of human beings to communicate with one another. Many characters live suppressed lives, and while they function conventionally on the surface, they suffer an emotional tumult below that plane.

Of the twelve stories in her first book, *The Gentle Insurrection*, more than half deal with death; others deal with love. In "A Sense of Humor" two children climb up to peer in a casket and find the body of their Uncle John unrecognizable to them. At the end of the story, they collapse in laughter when the young girl realizes that Uncle John, a practical joker, was himself the victim of an immense practical joke—locked in a box deep in the ground. The child at the center of "Child So Fair" is afflicted with a cleft palate, but in the clouded eyes of his almost-blind grandmother, he is a fair child. This starkly told story depicts the transcending beauty and simplicity of love.

Two of the stories show a failure of love and feature suppressed spinsters. In "Miss Parker Possessed" the forty-year-old librarian, overcome by a "wild springtime of thinking," falls in lust with a banker. Miss Parker suppresses those strong feelings and keeps her job by putting an end to her own passion. Miss Ward in "The Sympathetic Visitor" makes a condolence call on a young black woman employee. As the proper Miss Ward speaks the platitudes of conventional sympathy, she undergoes a tumultuous and exhausting journey that leaves her weeping—not for the dead or the bereaved, but for herself.

In each of these stories a character mounts a gentle insurrection, and in the title story, a young woman who lives with her mother and brother attempts to escape a mean life of poverty and hard work. She plans to run away with her lover, but her attempt fails, and like Miss Ward, she weeps for herself. Like Miss Parker, she will suppress her desires because she tells herself she is weeping for the last time.

In this volume of a dozen stories are the seeds of the work—both short and long fiction—that would follow. All of the characters might be neighbors in some rural community in North Carolina. Their world is not an easy one that grants happy endings, but rather a world of hard work and pain and desire and frustration, to which the healing power of laughter sometimes brings pleasure. The transcending joy of love is as rare as the ability of characters to communicate. Beneath provincial and conventional surfaces, these characters suffer the torment of bottled-up passion and desire and need. And life, as Betts has explained, is lived close to the veil—to birth and violence and death and love. Her fictional world is a palpable, concrete place, rich in the sights, smells, and sounds of a particular time and setting. In this place she treats that passion of the human heart—as William Faulkner has explained—that grieves on universal bones.

Betts's second volume of short fiction, *The Astronomer and Other Stories* (1966), contains seven short stories and a novella. Although these stories resemble her earlier work in theme, setting, and subject, there are new elements. Two stories, "Spies in the Herb House" and "All That Glisters Is Not Gold," are autobiographical and are told in the first person. Two are comic tales, one the humorous story of an inept bootlegger whom the sheriff catches with 56 bottles of "white mule" hidden in the carcass of a mule, the other a farce that recounts the antics of a small-town lawyer at an egg festival in Parsonville, the egg center of the state.

The most important piece in this collection, however, is the novella that gives the book its title. A small masterpiece, "The Astronomer" is the story of a lonely, uncommunicative man whose wife and two sons are dead. After he retires from the knitting mill where he has been a weaver, a chance reading of a Walt Whitman poem leads him on an unexpected journey of discovery that begins when he takes up the subject of astronomy.

Betts's third volume of short fiction, *Beasts of the Southern Wild* (1973), includes seven stories that feature women characters at the center of the action, among them the title story. In this tale a schoolteacher lives a boring and conventional life with her insensitive husband and two children, but she also enjoys a rich and erotic fantasy life with its own sustained story line. The volume also contains Betts's most chilling story of childhood, "The Spider Gardens of Madagascar," and an otherworldly after-death journey, "Benson Watts Is Dead and in Virginia."

The first story in this collection, "The Ugliest Pilgrim," is frequently anthologized. The naive narrator is Violet Karl, a young woman who has embarked on a pilgrimage across the country to Tulsa with the purpose of beseeching a television evangelist to heal her disfiguring facial scar. Violet keeps a journal as she travels on a Greyhound bus where she meets a black soldier and a handsome blonde paratrooper. She plays poker with the two men and spends the night with them in a hotel where she and the paratrooper make love. A religious young woman, Violet has amassed Scripture verses to argue her case with the preacher for a miracle of healing, but she is terribly disappointed in the evangelist, whose program is beamed on tape and who is not even in Tulsa. Redemption comes to her in a most unexpected way as she finds love with the paratrooper. A touching and ironic love story—the heroine is smart and good but terribly disfigured, the hero a paratrooper interested in motorcycles—"The Ugliest Pilgrim" is a most moving contemporary story about the mystery of God's grace.

These three collections of short fiction have secured Doris Betts's position as a contemporary master of the short story. Reviewers have consistently praised her work, commenting upon her powers of observation and imagination, her feeling for time, place, character, form, and structure. In the *New York Times* review of her third volume of short stories, Michael Mewshaw called Betts's stories "deceptively simple and entertaining on the surface," but, he continued, "They resist interpretation the way Wallace Stevens said poems should—almost completely." He went on to remark that the "writing escapes categorization and remains very much an index of one woman's intriguing mind, and the finest fruit of her imagination falls to the reader in a shower of startling images, metaphors, and similes."

To date, Betts has published four novels: *Tall Houses in Winter* (1957), *The Scarlet Thread* (1964), *The River to Pickle Beach* (1972), and *Heading West* (1981). Although these works are similar to the short fiction in subject, theme, setting, and character, the longer form has enabled Betts to depict characters in complex relationships and to follow these characters over time. Her novels are particularly excellent in characterization, and even minor characters are often fully drawn and memorable. Her rich, allusive style works well with the larger canvas provided by long fiction, and the action of the novels—as in the short stories—frequently reverberates with larger meanings. *The Scarlet Thread*, for example, follows a family over time, but it also tells the story of the community where that family lives. The community's development from rural to industrial suggests the same pattern enacted in many communities during the early years of the twentieth century. Similarly, *The River to Pickle Beach* focuses on a childless couple and their personal experience with violence during the same time that the larger community of the United States is coping with the unreasonable violence that killed political figures. *Heading West* suggests meanings on a number of levels, as the text echoes with allusions to the American past, to the Bible, and to literature. Betts's novels return to the old verities of morality and time, love and the absence of love, pain and joy, and the problem of evil, but each novel is quite different in form, structure, and meaning.

Tall Houses in Winter, an apprentice novel, is an introspective work, autumnal in tone. After a decade's absence, an English professor comes homes to North Carolina with a death sentence hanging over him. He has cancer of the larynx and has decided not to seek treatment. The book is a lengthy remembrance of things past for Ryan Godwin, who must come to terms not only with the living members of his family but also with the dead ones—mother, father, brother, and the sister-in-law who was the great love of his life. Eventually he chooses life over death and decides to seek treatment, primarily because of the love and responsibility he feels for ten-year-old Fen, ostensibly his nephew but probably his own son. The most lively part of this novel is the retrospective account of Godwin's doomed love affair with his brother's wife. But reviewers compared this work unfavorably with Betts's short stories. In choosing to make a middle-aged academic the center of consciousness in this work, she seems to be on less certain ground than she was in her earlier short fiction. And characters who fail in communicating with each other also fail to engage the sympathy of the reader.

Betts's second novel, *The Scarlet Thread*, differs from the first in telling a story over a longer period of time and featuring a larger cast of characters. A historical novel set at the turn of the century, it chronicles a quarter of a century in the lives of the Allen family. It also tells the story of a rural community as it develops into a mill town. This novel succeeds remarkably in depicting character, in showing complex relationships within a family, and in re-creating time and place. It focuses on each of the three Allen children in turn and presents a sensitive, moving, and authentic portrayal of growing up in a family. The characterization of Esther Allen, an imaginative and unconventional young woman, is especially fine. But Betts seemed to have trouble with structure in this work—chapters seems almost detachable, unified elements—and she was criticized for sensational gothic elements in the text.

For the setting of *The River to Pickle Beach*, Betts moved her characters from rural North Carolina to the beach and her time from the past to the present, 1968. At the center of this novel is a married couple in their forties, Bebe and Jack Sellers. Their relationship is warm and loving, comfortably sensual. Into their lives intrudes an old army buddy of Jack's, Mickey McCane, who is strongly attracted to Bebe. He is sexually frustrated, racially prejudiced, and mightily interested in guns and hunting. In a senseless, apparently unmotivated act of violence, McCane shoots and kills a retarded mother and her son. His destructive act mirrors violence on a national scale in the year of the King and Kennedy murders. This book was well received, with critics noting the timeliness of themes such a sex, violence, the generation gap, racial unease, family ties, the place of religion, and the viability of friendship. In the *New York Times* Jonathan Yardley called Betts a "tough, wise, and compassionate writer," one who "has never quite got her due."

With her fourth novel, *Heading West*, Betts moved the action out of North Carolina and across the highways of the country to the Grand Canyon. For the first time in her long fiction a woman is the protagonist. Nancy Finch is a librarian, and she is perhaps Betts's definitive treatment of the repressed spinster. With this smart, strong, witty character, Betts seems to find her voice in a novel that both attempts and achieves much.

On one level the novel is a psychological thriller that follows the kidnapping of a woman by a psychopathic, small-time criminal. But it is also the story of a woman's growth into independence and maturity as she breaks the yoke that ties her neurotically to her family and actively makes a choice about her life. At the same time the book marks Betts's fullest treatment of time and mortality, depicted graphically in Nancy's descent into a dark night of the soul as she descends through layers of time into the canyon. *Heading West* is a rich, many-layered, allusive book—Betts's finest work of long fiction.

With a collection of short stories ready for the press and a novel close to publication, Doris Betts has a career still very much in progress. It is too early to offer any grand assessment of her work. She will no doubt continue to produce fiction, short and long, with the themes and subject matter that have remained fairly constant throughout her career. No doubt she will also continue to surprise, inform, and touch the reader with her art.

SURVEY OF CRITICISM

Critical material on Doris Betts is not abundant, but there are some sources of information. Among these are several critical articles, entries in reference books, interviews given by Betts, and reviews of her books. Her manuscripts and correspondence are in the Doris Betts Collection, Boston University Libraries in Massachusetts.

In "Doris Betts's Nancy Finch" (1983), Dorothy Scura surveys the four novels with particular emphasis on *Heading West*. David Marion Holman's "Faith and the Unanswerable Questions" (1982) examines the dilemma of Betts's characters who "are trying to solve mysteries of faith, trying to make sense out of their lives and their world." In "Negro Characters in the Fiction of Doris Betts" (1975), Elizabeth Evans finds Betts "extremely competent in presenting a great variety of Negro characters distinguished by personality and individualized by special traits." In two brief articles Evans shows similarities in Amy Lowell's "Patterns" and Betts's "The Mandarin" (1976) and analyzes humor in "The Dead Mule" (1981). Ruth Moose's brief "Superstition in Doris Betts's New Novel" (1973) points out the use of folk wisdom in *The River to Pickle Beach*.

Three articles in *Survey of Contemporary Literature* provide detailed readings of three of Betts's books: John C. Coleman on *The Scarlet Thread* (1977), David Madden on *The Astronomer and Other Stories* (1977), and A. Wesley Jones on *Beasts of the Southern Wild* (1982).

Increasingly, Betts is listed in various reference books. Entries in *Southern Writers: A Biographical Dictionary* (1979) and *Contemporary Authors* (1975) are primarily biographical. Two others that include critical commentary are Jean W. Ross's (1983) survey of Betts's fiction (includes an interview with Betts focusing on *Heading West*) and Mary Anne Ferguson's (1979) brief overview of the fiction.

The best sources of information on Betts's life and art are published interviews. Particularly noteworthy are the ones by Rod Cockshutt (1981), George Wolfe (1972), and William E. Ray (1972).

Each of Doris Betts's books has been reviewed by major newspapers and periodicals since 1954. These reviews provide interesting materials for assessing her critical reputation.

BIBLIOGRAPHY

Works by Doris Betts

The Gentle Insurrection and Other Stories. New York: G. P. Putnam's, 1954; London: Gollancz, 1955.

Tall Houses in Winter. New York: G. P. Putnam's, 1957; London: Gollancz, 1958; Milan: Rizolli, 1959; New York: Curtis, 1973.

The Scarlet Thread. New York: Harper & Row, 1964; New York: Curtis, 1973.

The Astronomer and Other Stories. New York: Harper & Row, 1966.

The River to Pickle Beach. New York: Harper & Row, 1972; New York: Curtis, 1973.

Beasts of the Southern Wild and Other Stories. New York: Harper & Row, 1973; Atlanta: Peachtree Publishers, 1985.

Heading West. New York: Knopf, 1981; New York: Signet American Library, 1982.

Studies of Doris Betts

Bain, Robert. "Doris Betts." *Southern Writers: A Biographical Dictionary*. Ed. R. Bain, J. M. Flora, and L. D. Rubin, Jr. Baton Rouge: Louisiana State University Press, 1979, pp. 25–26.

Cockshutt, Rod. "Q & A with Doris Betts." *Tar Heel: A Magazine of North Carolina* 9 (December 1981): 44–49.

Coleman, John C. "The Scarlet Thread." *Survey of Contemporary Literature*. Ed. Frank Magill. Rev. and enl. ed. Englewood Cliffs, N.J.: Salem, 1977, pp. 6647–49.

Eaton, Evelyn. "A Fine Debut." Rev. of *The Gentle Insurrection*, by Doris Betts. *Saturday Review* 37 (10 July 1954): 14.

Evans, Elizabeth. "Another Mule in the Yard: Doris Betts's Durable Humor." *Notes on Contemporary Literature* 11 (March 1981): 5–6.

———. "The Mandarin and the Lady: Doris Betts's Debt to Amy Lowell." *Notes on Contemporary Literature* 6 (1976): 2–5.

———. "Negro Characters in the Fiction of Doris Betts." *Critique: Studies in Modern Fiction* 17 (1975): 59–76.

Ferguson, Mary Anne. "Doris Betts." *American Women Writers*. Ed. Lina Maniero. New York: Ungar, 1979, pp. 151–52.

Holman, David Marion. "Faith and the Unanswerable Questions: The Fiction of Doris Betts." *Southern Literary Journal* 15 (Fall 1982): 15–22.

Jones, A. Wesley. *"Beasts of the Southern Wild and Other Stories."* *Survey of Contempoary Literature*. Ed. Frank N. Magill. Rev. and enl. ed. Englewood Cliffs, N.J.: Salem, 1977, pp. 579–83.

Kinsman, Clarke D., ed. "Betts, Doris (Waugh)." *Contemporary Authors*. Detroit: Gale, 1975, pp. 75–76.

Leonard, John. "Books of the Times." Rev. of *Heading West*, by Doris Betts. *New York Times* 17 Dec. 1981, sec. c: 23.

Madden, David. *"The Astronomer and Other Stories."* *Survey of Contemporary Literature*. Ed. Frank N. Magill. Rev. and enl. ed. Englewood Cliffs, N.J.: Salem, 1977, pp. 418–23.

Mewshaw, Michael. "Surrealism and Fantasy." Rev. of *Beasts of the Southern Wild and Other Stories*, by Doris Betts. *New York Times Book Review* 28 October 1973: 40–41.

Moose, Ruth. "Superstitution in Doris Betts's New Novel." *North Carolina Folklore Journal* 21 (1973): 61–62.

"Notes on Current Books." Rev. of *The Astronomer and Other Stories*, by Doris Betts. *Virginia Quarterly Review* 42 (Spring 1966): xlviii.

Ray, William E. "Doris Betts on the Art and Teaching of Writing." *Man in 7 Modes*. Ed. William E. Ray. Winston-Salem, N.C.: Southern Humanities Conference, 1972, pp. 40–50.

Rogoff, Leonard. "Culture & Its Rightful Heirs: Doris Betts on Higher Education." *Spectator Magazine* (Raleigh, North Carolina) 5 June 1985: 5–8.

Ross, Jean W. "Doris Betts." *Dictionary of Literary Biography Yearbook: 1982*. Ed. Richard Ziegfield. Detroit: Gale, 1983, pp. 219–27.

Scura, Dorothy. "Doris Betts's Nancy Finch: A Heroine for the 1980s." *Southern Quarterly* 22 (Fall 1983): 3–12. Repr. in *Women Writers of the Contemporary South*. Ed. Peggy W. Prenshaw. Jackson: University Press of Mississippi, 1984, pp. 135–45.

Wolfe, George. "The Unique Voice: Doris Betts." *Kite Flying and Other Irrational Acts*. Ed. Jonn Carr. Baton Rouge: Louisiana State University Press, 1972, pp. 149–73.

Yardley, Jonathan. "The Librarian and the Highwayman." Rev. of *Heading West*, by Doris Betts. *Washington Post* 29 November 1981: 3–4.

————. Rev. of *The River to Pickle Beach*, by Doris Betts. *New York Times Book Review*, 21 May 1972: 12.

John Peale Bishop
(1892–1944)

In the introduction to their 1981 edition of the correspondence of Allen Tate and John Peale Bishop, Thomas D. Young and John J. Hindle argue that Tate's friendship and encouragement were instrumental in rekindling in the middle-aged Bishop the literary ambitions of his youth, that "Except for Tate's well intended and genuinely felt praise, the world of letters would not have two dozen or so highly original and structurally superior poems, a book of excellent short stories, an undeservedly neglected novel, and nearly a dozen perceptive and illuminating critical essays" (*Republic of Letters*, p. 9). Young and Hindle's thesis is neither provable nor unprovable. Tate of course made no claim to being the prime begetter of Bishop's mature art; in reply to a letter from Bishop thanking him for his "aid and encouragement," Tate said: "I've done nothing to deserve gratitude; I saw some fine work, said it was fine, and thereby only did my simple duty by the republic of letters" (*Republic of Letters*, pp. 91, 94). Young and Hindle's estimate of the worth of Bishop's work however, is not likely to be gainsaid by any reader who knows that work.

BIOGRAPHY

Bishop was born 21 May 1892 in the northeastern neck of West Virginia, in Charles Town, close to Harper's Ferry. (John Brown's trial and execution for treason took place in Charles Town, which had been laid out in 1786 by George Washington's brother, Charles.) Bishop's heritage on his mother's side was pioneer Virginian—an amalgam of English, Scots, and German settlers of the seventeenth and eighteenth centuries. His father's family, however, had moved to Charles Town from Connecticut after the Civil War. Bishop always thought of himself as a Southerner, but he was deeply attached to his father, Jonathan, who died when John was just nine years old. According to Tate, Bishop's dual heritage compounded the "deep conflict of loyalties felt by many people in the border South from 1865 to 1914"; Tate also felt that Bishop, in the last decade of his life, "more and more took imaginatively the part of his father, of the outsider, of the *déraciné*," and that this "split in loyalty" was "the condition of his special sensibility, liberating his powers of observation" (*Collected Poems*, p. xii).

A protracted childhood illness that delayed Bishop's matriculation at Princeton was probably also a factor in his widespread childhood reading and his early interest in poetry. He attended day school in Hagerstown, Maryland, and was later a student at the Mercersburg Academy, in Pennsylvania. He had published a poem in *Harper's Weekly* while a student at Mercersburg, and his verses appeared almost immediately in the *Nassau Literary Magazine* after his arrival at Princeton in 1913. At Princeton, among a talented group of classmates, Bishop stood out—personally, academically, and literarily. (F. Scott Fitzgerald portrayed him as Tom D'Invilliers in *This Side of Paradise*.) By the time of his graduation in 1917, followed soon after by his acceptance of a commission in the U.S. Army, Bishop had accumulated enough poems, based on Romantic and fin de siècle models, for a slim volume of verse bearing the ironically modest title *Green Fruit*. Military service overseas did not have the same impact on Bishop as it did on writers such as Cummings and Hemingway, but it did provide him with his first experience of France, where he was afterwards to live for several years and which was to become for him a model of a civilized nation. Upon his return to America, Bishop was caught up in the bustle of postwar New York City. From 1920 to 1922 he was one of the editors of *Vanity Fair*; in 1922 he and Edmund Wilson, his friend from the Princeton years, jointly published *The Undertaker's Garland*, a collection of prose and poetry. Also in 1922 he married and departed with his bride, Margaret Hutchins, for a three-year sojourn in Europe, where he became friends with such writers as Cummings, Hemingway, Ezra Pound, Ford Madox Ford, and Archibald MacLeish. Back in New York once more, he renewed his contributions to *Vanity Fair* and found employment in the east coast office of Paramount Pictures. He also worked hard to complete a novel, *The Huntsmen Are Up in America*, which Scribner's encouraged but finally declined to publish. Disappointed in their hopes for the novel and unhappy with life in the United States, in 1926 Bishop and his wife returned to Europe, this time for an even more extended stay. In Orgeval, northeast of Paris, they purchased the Chateau de Tressancourt, an old house reputed to have been one of Henry of Navarre's hunting lodges, where they settled down to a life of studied domesticity, and to the raising of three sons born in the next five years.

Bishop continued with his reading and with various literary projects, but his productivity during the first years of his residence in Orgeval was minimal. Tate, who had first met Bishop in a New York speakeasy in 1925 but who only got to know him in France after 1928, was of the opinion that "he had not been happy in that charming isolation. . . . he seemed in that period remote and without concentration, except in intervals when he produced, in a burst of energy, a group of poems or an occasional story.'' As the 1920s drew to a close, Bishop's output increased and the quality of his work heightened apace. In 1930 he won the *Scribner's Magazine* prize for short fiction, with the winning story providing the title for a collection of stories, *Many Thousands Gone*, published the following year. In 1933 Scribner's also published *Now with His Love*, a collection of recent as well as earlier poems. In that same year, soon after the book of poems appeared, and partly as a consequence of the decline in the value of the Depression dollar, the Bishops returned to the United States permanently.

For a while the Bishops lived in Connecticut, and afterwards for a longer spell in New Orleans. Then, in 1935, they moved to Cape Cod, where they eventually built a new house, christened Sea Change, in South Chatham. Bishop continued to produce work of high quality. His poetry and reviews appeared frequently in important literary journals, and he published a number of significant critical essays. In 1935 Bishop's only published novel, *Act of Darkness*, appeared, as did another verse collection, *Minute Particulars*. In 1940 he lectured at major American universities and became chief poetry reviewer for the *Nation*; the next year his *Selected Poems* was published, and he again became a temporary resident of New York, where he served as director of the publications program in the office of the Coordinator of Inter-American Affairs. For some years Bishop had suffered from high blood pressure; in mid–1942 he was forced to give up his New York job and return to Cape Cod. In 1943 his old friend Archibald MacLeish persuaded him to accept a post at the Library of Congress, but Bishop suffered a heart attack after only two weeks in Washington. Back once more in his beloved Sea Change, he continued to work at his poetry, but his health steadily worsened. He died on 4 April 1944 at the Cape Cod Hospital in Hyannis, Massachusetts.

Among the Bishop Papers on deposit at the Dulles Memorial Library at Princeton is an epitaph, in his wife's hand, which Bishop dictated shortly before his death:

> Here far from the lovely land that bore me,
> By the cold sea I lie.
> Let none who have known love deplore me,
> The rest may pass me by.

Bishop traveled far from the South, but he never forgot it, and the love that he and his art celebrated was to a very large extent bound up with his sense of, his consciousness of, the South of his boyhood.

MAJOR THEMES

''The ceremony must be found / That will wed Desdemona to the huge Moor'' are the opening lines of Bishop's 1925 poem ''Speaking of Poetry.'' But the burden of the poem—that poetry results from the wedding of disparate impulses

and materials, that it is both enactment and outcome of a "ceremony" simultaneously "traditional" and "strange, with never before heard music"—ad-
umbrates thematic patterns central to all of Bishop's mature work. That work is
quintessentially concerned with ambiguities, polarities, opposed tensions, conflicting loyalties. In 1931 Bishop wrote Tate, "In a healthy society there are
various tensions opposed. There is a continual effort necessary to maintain
equilibrium which must be (this the Americans will not admit) an unstable
equilibrium. They want it stable. They want everything finally settled. Whereas
nothing should ever be settled" (*Republic of Letters*, p. 47). For Bishop, art
was a chief means for achieving such a perilous balance, and in his eyes the
artist was potentially a heroic figure within a fragmented culture. The mature
Bishop, however, always insisted upon the ambiguities of the artistic enterprise.
As he put the case in two of the many aphorisms Edmund Wilson printed in his
edition of Bishop's *Collected Essays*: "The poet is a product of a border country,
of the mixed race and the misalliance," and "The instinct toward art is profoundly, essentially conservative; the technique of art is profoundly revolutionary" (pp. 375, 376).

   Bishop's critical essays constitute, in Wilson's words, "not a series of literary
critiques—though there are some admirable studies of literary subjects—but a
set of discourses on various aspects of contemporary civilization: literature,
painting, moving pictures, architecture, manners, religion" (*Collected Essays*,
p. vii). Bishop's attitude toward many aspects of contemporary civilization was
questioningly critical, but he was not a programmatic, polemical critic such as
Tate and John Crowe Ransom. His essays, rather, indirectly reflect the quality
of his thinking and are suggestive of the range of his temperament.

   Like most American artists during the 1920s and 1930s, Bishop was unhappy
with American culture and society. He was dismayed by the ugliness and brutality
of industrial capitalism, depressed by the canting hypocrisies of American morality, and upset by American philistinism with regard to art. In his criticism he
attempted to point up those forces he considered responsible for American cultural
disorder, and to point out admirable features of other cultures, cultures which
in various fashions provided models for right living and thinking. He felt, for
example, that New England Puritanism, while of great influence in shaping
American thought, "had never provided the new country with a particularly
satisfactory morality." Carried across the Appalachians by the pioneers, the
ideals of New England "began to go bad" (*Collected Essays*, pp. 70–71), the
result being an American culture stripped of a sense of community and bereft
of moral standards. Unhappy with twentieth-century America, Bishop found
much to admire in the culture of the eighteenth century, particularly as it had
taken shape in France and in the colonial South. He also thought the legacy of
the eighteenth century could still be discerned in modern France and in the
contemporary South.

   In Bishop's view, France had emerged as "arbiter of the arts and of all the
attributes of civilization" because she had so successfully mediated between the

Latin and Germanic cultures of Europe, being "able to consider both, to control both, to bring both into a single and harmonious whole" (*Collected Essays*, p. 173). Bishop thought that both France and the American South had developed and still maintained societies in which tradition was of great importance. In one of his most important essays, "The South and Tradititon," which argues that modern man can learn much from Southern respect for traditional codes of conduct, he observes, "The use of tradition is, as the French abundantly prove, to provide a technique of living and offer a discipline and a pride" (*Collected Essays*, p. 9). Bishop, a veteran of the Great War, found much to admire in the soldiers of the Confederate army, who were, he thought, bound together by a sense of tradition: "They, at all events, had a tradition. . . . Their attitude toward life was alike, and when they faced death it was in the same way. This makes for integrity, as it certainly also makes for a sounder emotional life" (*Collected Essays*, p. 5).

Bishop's art is ultimately concerned with the opposing forces of life and death, with the body and its dissolution; in his criticism this concern is most significantly manifest in his explorations of the meaning of myth and his discussions of the nature of art. In praising the culture of France, which insisted upon classical "balance and grace," Bishop noted how "the French never forgot that these qualities . . . are those of a living body at its perfection, the body which we derive from a remoter past than that of Greece" (*Collected Essays*, p. 174). Believing man to be essentially animal and the bases of life to be sensual and instinctual, Bishop insisted that "we must live from the instincts, for the mind unsupported not only cannot tell us how to behave, it cannot give us any very satisfactory reasons for living at all" (*Collected Essays*, p. 9). Patterns for living might be supplied by vital traditions; reasons for living might ultimately be gained from the lessons of myth, "true creations" (p. 124) of the primitive mind not yet dissociated from the body; and tropes for living might be supplied by the discipline of art. Bishop's thinking about the function of myth is best illustrated in two essays: one on Frazer's *The Golden Bough* (1936) and "The Myth and Modern Literature" (1939); his concern for the discipline of art is evident in most of his criticism, but especially so in "Homage to Hemingway" (1936) and "The Discipline of Poetry" (1936).

In praising Hemingway, Bishop noted, "It is the privilege of literature to propose its own formal solutions for problems which in life have none." Hemingway's "vision of life is one of perpetual annihilation," but that vision is both sustained and made bearable by Hemingway's command of his craft: "He has mastered his *métier* as has no American among his contemporaries. That is his pride and his distinction" (*Collected Essays*, pp. 45–46). In "The Discipline of Poetry" Bishop argues it is the goal of all the arts "to present the conflict of man with time. This is as true for those arts, like architecture, which we ordinarily call spatial, as it is for those arts which, like music, are strictly temporal. And the famous release which the arts afford is essentially a release from time" (*Collected Essays*, p. 104). In a 1941 radio program, after observing that the "very essence of being a *man* is to own a poignant and inescapable conviction of being a creature of time," Bishop argued that "the essential task of *poetry* is to display a man in relation to time" (Bishop Papers, Princeton). In his essay on the craft of poetry, Bishop held that it is not in man's power to control time, but that the artist can control "the consciousness of it." In Bishop's view, "The means which the poet uses to that end is verse." For Bishop, consequently, "there is no such thing as free verse. The one freedom which is allowed the poet is the possibility of expanding or contracting these limits. To do away with them entirely is to lose, not only the chief advantage his craft allows him, but his fecundity. In art, as in love, nothing is more sterile than limitless desire" (*Collected Essays*, p. 104).

As S. C. Moore has remarked, Bishop's criticism provides "a prose mirror of the values implicit in his poetry. . . . Both criticism and poetry had the same function: resolving what he considered the chaos of his time" (p. 69). To effect such a resolution, Bishop brought to bear upon his poetry, and made alive in his poetry, those aesthetic impulses he deemed central to the artistic culture of France, where, in Bishop's view, "the artist was allowed the utmost possible freedom in the choice of his material; he was praised in the end in proportion to his ability to unite force and form" (*Collected Essays*, p. 174). Or, as the poet-critic Louis Coxe has observed of Bishop's poetic goals and accomplishments: "Ceremony, ritual, virtue, power. All these must exist in concert and alliance with sensibility, delicacy, grace" (p. 156).

Although there is a thematic coherence to the poetry Bishop produced over a period of 30 years, it should be noted that during much of his poetic career Bishop tended to be greatly influenced by the poetic styles of his predecessors as well as his contemporaries; not until late in his life did he achieve an identifiably personal idiom and manner. In his juvenilia, in his youthful contributions to the Princeton student literary magazine, there are successively echoes of Shelley and Poe and Swinburne; then the influence of Yeats, which was long to continue, makes itself evident, as does that of such French poets as Baudelaire, Gautier, and Verlaine. French accents continue to sound in many of the poems in *Green Fruit* (1917); there are also hints of Pound and Eliot. The influence of Eliot is even more apparent in some of Bishop's contributions to *The Undertaker's Garland* (1922), particularly in the long meditation upon mortality, "The Death of a Dandy." The poem is indebted to "Gerontion," but it is nevertheless a success in its own right—welding language, structure, and form into a coherent whole.

Similar successes are abundant in the pages of *Now with His Love* (1933), even if the poems in this volume, the fruit of more than a decade of work, are also frequently imitative in mode and idiom. The particularities of Bishop's sensibility and intelligence, however, are concretely evident in the thematic emphases of the volume: reflection upon the nature and function of art, commentary on the mutability of individual lives and human societies, and celebration of the release provided by sensuality in a world of seeming chaos. In addition to "Speaking of Poetry," the most accomplished poems in the 1933 volume are "Perspectives Are Precipices," "Beyond Connecticut, Beyond the Sea," "The Return," and "And When the Net was Unwound Venus Was Found Ravelled with Mars." In *Minute Particulars* (1935), new thematic groupings are discernible, reflective of Bishop's heightened concern with the lineaments of American culture and his increasing sense of the contrasting values of ancient myth and modern rationalism. Most impressive among the poems in this book are the two verse sequences, "New England" and "Experience in the West," along with "Your Chase Had a Beast in View," "The Mothers," "The Tree," and "Divine Nativity." Bishop's *Selected Poems* (1941) do not, as Joseph Frank has observed, "reveal any significant development in Bishop's work; only his accustomed mastery of familiar themes and styles" (Frank, the "Achievement," of JPB, p. 339), but by now Bishop's "mastery" is so complete that the various idioms and personae he essays are completely his own; he no longer echoes other poets. And any poet might take pride in such a celebration of sexual love as "Invitation at Dawn," in such a meditation upon history as "The Parallel." Finally, there are a number of superbly achieved poems from Bishop's last years not in the *Selected Poems* but included among *The Collected Poems* of 1948. "Resurrection" is the culmination of Bishop's persistent exploration of mythological themes; "A Subject of Sea Change" (the Phi Beta Kappa poem of 1942) is perhaps the finest of his meditations upon man's mortality and the impermanence of history; and "The Hours," prompted by F. Scott Fitzgerald's death in 1941, is one of the most moving elegies in English. It is a poem of grief, and perhaps of despair, but Bishop's trust in the redemptive power of love and art breathes through the entire poem, particularly in its last stanza:

> I cannot animate with breath
> Syllables in the open mouth of death.
> Dark, dark. The shore here has a habit of light.
> O dark! I leave you to oblivious night!

In his poetry, Bishop only infrequently dealt with the South and with Southern history. In his fiction, however, the South and its history are of central concern. In the fiction, even more so than in his essays, he imaginatively took possession of the ambiguous legacy of his West Virginia birth.

Death, both physical and symbolic, is a basic thematic concern of practically all of Bishop's fiction. Death is admitted, and perhaps kept at bay, in a compelling story in *The Undertaker's Garland*, "Resurrection," about a young American officer's reactions to the disinterment of the corpse of an American soldier hastily buried during the fighting in the Argonne. The uncollected (until 1948) story "Toadstools Are Poison," which rivals Faulkner's "That Evening Sun" in its command of a child's point of view, deals with the confusions and terror of a three-year-old taken by his nurse to witness the public hanging of a black man.

And death, along with responses to death, is a central preoccupation of the short-story sequence, *Many Thousands Gone*, and the novel, *Act of Darkness*.

In *Many Thousands Gone*, set in the fictional upper Shenandoah Valley town of Mordington (the town's name is significant), the first of the five stories takes place prior to the Civil War, the next three during the war years, and the last at the turn of the century. The first story, "The Corpse in the House," deals with a young lawyer's realization that he no longer loves the girl to whom he has been engaged for several years. That girl, now aging, lacks the vitality of the old woman, born in the eighteenth century, who is the corpse of the story's title. The next three stories narrate episodes of death and defiance of death during the fighting that raged up and down the Valley. In all three, the fact of death spurs a heightened awareness of life. In the last story, "If Only," a brilliantly successful fusion of romance and realism, a black servant named "Bones" is the prop and mainstay of two elderly maiden sisters, providing them with the illusion, and the substance, of a life lived according to antebellum ideals. Bones, the past as embodied in an ambiguously smiling black man, *is* Death, but he also brings vitality and a certain fulfillment to the lives of the maiden sisters; he is, as the last sentence of the story observes, "a dear obsession"—costly to be sure, but worthy of love. Together, the stories reveal not only Bishop's fascination with the Southern past but also his double-edged judgment of that past, which he saw as both heroic and tragically flawed, with the nineteenth century exhibiting both a pattern of pathetic decline and signs of organic wholeness.

Act of Darkness, also set in the fictional Mordington, picks up the threads of Southern history just after the turn of the century and interweaves them with the coming-of-age of the novel's observer-narrator (that the novel is to some extent autobiographical is suggested by the narrator's name, John). At one very important level, the novel is about John's coming to grips with the fact of death, his father's death most of all, and with the troublesome nature of his own sexuality. The novel is also about the distortions of Southern values and ideals in the twentieth century, particularly as those distortions are reflected in the persons and personalities of the two primary actors in the novel's central "act of darkness": John's uncle, Charlie Marston, and Virginia Crannock, the woman he is accused of raping. Charlie and Virginia are in no wise embodiments of Shakespeare's Othello and Desdemona; instead, they represent the decline of Southern tradition, the collapse of the Southern code as a guide to conduct. More important, Charlie represents a turning away from the agrarian foundations of Southern society. Bishop wrote Tate in 1931 that "the great service of the South was to provide a proper tension in two directions. First it gave a pull toward agriculture, the land as against the machine; secondly, one toward the past, traditional living as opposed to progress. And this was good" (*Republic of Letters*, p. 47). In *Act of Darkness* the tensions between past and present, between agrarian order and industrial progress, are becoming unbalanced. And John's doubts about himself and his future are exacerbated by the social and cultural disorder of the world in which he grows up. The novel's end, however, signals a hopeful note; the John of the novel, at least, comes to think: "No further defeat or disillusion was possible to me; none could overcome me, I felt within myself too great strength to oppose them" (*Act of Darkness*, p. 367).

SURVEY OF CRITICISM

In 1966, concluding what is still the single extended study of Bishop's work, Robert White declared Bishop to be a very good writer, one who "should be known for all his work—and by more than a handful of contemporary readers" (White, *John Peale Bishop*, p. 161). White's high opinion of Bishop's work reiterated assessments arrived at by earlier critics and seconded by later commetators. A decade after Allen Tate's "Note" of the 1930s, the publication of the *Collected Essays* and *Collected Poems* in 1948 prompted praise from such distinguished critics as Joseph Frank, William Arrowsmith, Stanley Edgar Hyman, Babette Deutsch, and Robert W. Stallman. Subsequently, Leslie Fiedler and Louis Coxe published essays emphasizing Bishop's accomplishments. More recently, Andrew Lytle has sounded a similar note. The critical instruments agree: Bishop was a writer of distinction; however, he is still not much attended to. All his books but *The Undertaker's Garland* are out of print, and critical articles about him are infrequent. Yet two provocative articles about *Act of Darkness* appeared in the early 1980s, and maybe the Young-Hindle edition of the Bishop-Tate correspondence will spark a new interest in the writer from West Virginia who died on Cape Cod.

BIBLIOGRAPHY

Works by John Peale Bishop

Green Fruit. Boston: Sherman, French, 1917.
The Undertaker's Garland (in collaboration with Edmund Wilson). New York: Alfred A. Knopf, 1922.
Many Thousands Gone. New York: Charles Scribner's Sons, 1931.
Now with His Love. New York: Charles Scribner's Sons, 1933.
Act of Darkness. New York: Charles Scribner's Sons, 1935.
Minute Particulars. New York: Alcestis Press, 1935.
Selected Poems. New York: Charles Scribner's Sons, 1941.
The Collected Essays of John Peale Bishop. Ed. With introduction by Edmund Wilson. New York: Charles Scribner's Sons, 1948.
The Collected Poems of John Peale Bishop. Ed. with introduction by Allen Tate. New York: Charles Scribner's Sons, 1948.
The Republic of Letters in America: The Correspondence of John Peale Bishop & Allen Tate. Ed. with introduction by Thomas D. Young and John J. Hindle. Lexington: University Press of Kentucky, 1981.

Studies of John Peale Bishop

Arrowsmith, William. "An Artist's Estate." *Hudson Review* 2 (Spring 1949): 118–27.
Bier, Jesse. "A Critical Biography of John Peale Bishop." Ph.D. dissertation, Princeton University, 1956.
———. "John Peale Bishop: The Memory Lingers On." *Western Humanities Review* 9 (Summer 1955): 243–48.
Coxe, Louis. "Romance of the Rose: John Peale Bishop and Phelps Putnam." *Michigan Quarterly Review* 14 (Spring 1975): 150–58.
Deutsch, Babette. *Poetry in Our Time*. New York: Henry Holt, 1952, pp. 189–95.
Eby, Cecil D., Jr. "The Fiction of John Peale Bishop." *Twentieth Century Literature* 7 (April 1961): 3–9.
Fiedler, Leslie. "John Peale Bishop & the Other Thirties." *Commentary* 43 (April 1967): 74–82. Reprinted in *The Collected Essays*, vol. 2. New York: Stein and Day, 1971, pp. 256–70.
Frank, Joseph. "The Achievement of John Peale Bishop." *Minnesota Review* 2 (Spring 1962): 325–44. Reprinted in *The Widening Gyre*. New Brunswick: Rutgers University Press, 1963, pp. 203–28.
———. "Force and Form: A Study of John Peale Bishop." *Sewanee Review* 55 (January-March 1947): 71–107.
Haun, Eugene. "John Peale Bishop: A Celebration." *Reality and Myth*. Ed. William Walker and Robert Welker. Nashville: Vanderbilt University Press, 1964, pp. 80–97.
Hayhoe, George F. "John Peale Bishop's Theory of Poetry." *Markham Review* 4 (February 1974): 34–38.
Hindle, Thomas F. "The Poet as Novelist: *Act of Darkness* and *The Fathers*." *Mississippi Quarterly* 35 (Fall 1982): 375–85.
Hyman, Stanley Edgar. "Notes on the Organic Unity of John Peale Bishop." *Accent* 9 (Autumn 1948): 102–13. Reprinted in *The Promised End*. Cleveland: World, 1968, pp. 49–62.
Lytle, Andrew. "Allen Tate and John Peale Bishop." *Grand Street* 2 (Autumn 1982): 148–56.
Moore, S. C. "The Criticism of John Peale Bishop." *Twentieth Century Literature* 12 (July 1966): 66–77.
Stallman, Robert W. "The Poetry of John Peale Bishop." *Southern Renascence*. Ed. Louis D. Rubin, Jr. and Robert Jacobs. Baltimore: Johns Hopkins University Press, 1953, pp. 369–91.
Tate, Allen. "A Note on Bishop's Poetry." *Southern Review* 1 (Autumn 1935): 357–64. Reprinted in *Essays of Four Decades*. Chicago: Swallow Press, 1968, pp. 348–57.
Vauthier, Simone. "The Meaning of Structure: Toward a New Reading of John Peale Bishop's *Act of Darkness*." *Southern Literary Journal* 7 (Spring 1975): 50–76.
———. "Perspectives Are Precipices: Points of View in John Peale Bishop's *Act of Darkness*." *Recherches Anglaises et Américaines* 15 (1982): 195–211.
White, Robert L. *John Peale Bishop*. New York: Twayne, 1966.

——————— JOSEPH M. FLORA ———————

James Branch Cabell
(1879–1958)

When John S. Sumner, executive secretary of the New York Society for the Suppression of Vice, ordered the plates and all copies of James Branch Cabell's *Jurgen* (1919) seized for alleged obscenities, he insured for Cabell, at least for a time, the dominant literary reputation of the 1920s, the decade some critics called the James Branch Cabell Period. Middle-aged as the decade began, Cabell was senior to such writers as F. Scott Fitzgerald and Ernest Hemingway, now more popularly identified with the 1920s. Furthermore, several of Cabell's books had been published prior to *Jurgen*. Although Cabell wrote many fine books during and after the Great Depression, critics increasingly judged him irrelevant, finding his work lacking in substance and his manner offensive. When Cabell died in 1958, few sang his praises.

But there remained the few. Shortly before Cabell's death, Edmund Wilson wrote a provocative essay for the *New Yorker* "reopening" the Cabell case. Wilson's praise failed to restore Cabell to his earlier position, and the Cabell revival that followed has been modest. Nevertheless, in the 1960s, there existed the Cabell Society and the James Branch Cabell Society, and both societies sponsored journals. Cabell would probably have been wryly amused by the phenomenon, but he would have understood the politics of academicians. In time, only the Cabell Society remained, and it still issues *Kalki*, though there have been noticeable interruptions. Although the Society has influenced the reprinting of several of Cabell's books, his work seldom appears in anthologies of American literature. Cabell will not challenge the younger writers of the 1920s who replaced him, but he will continue to attract readers who delight in keen irony, wry satire, and manipulation of myth and language. Students of Southern literature will continue to explore the special ways in which his work expresses the Southern experience.

BIOGRAPHY

Cabell's pedigree is spectacularly Southern and aristocratic, even by the exacting standards of Virginia. James Branch Cabell's great-grandfather Cabell had been governor of the state, and one grandfather, Robert Gamble Cabell I, had been next-door neighbor as well as personal physician to General Robert E. Lee. James's mother, Anne Branch, came from one of Richmond's most prominent families. Through the marriages of his mother's sisters, James was related to several other prominent families. By publishing under the bulky name of James Branch Cabell, he paid homage to both lineages. The name fits the distinctiveness of his style and method. Most writers were opting for the simpler: Ernest M. Hemingway (under which an early poem by Hemingway was published in the *Double Dealer*) quickly became Ernest Hemingway. Unlike his grandfather William Clark Falkner, Faulkner wanted a simple William Faulkner. The difference is instructive for clarification of the numerous ties between Cabell and Faulkner. Faulkner's Deep South Mississippi presents a different face of the complex entity known as the South. Cabell epitomizes the Tidewater aristocracy of Virginia, and his choice of publication name reflects the difference.

Cabell was born on 14 April 1879 in Richmond, in the family home that stood where the Richmond Public Library is presently located. Much of the care of James and his brothers Robert and John was entrusted to a "mammy" (who was part Indian and part Caucasian as well as black). Part of the family for a quarter of a century, Mrs. Louisa Nelson helped instill in the children an aristocratic egoism. In Cabell's Richmond, memories of the Confederacy, the Civil War, and Reconstruction were fresh and often narrated—and, of course, fact was often embellished. A shy and sensitive child, Cabell was a good listener, and tales of the Lost Cause influenced him early. He noticed that many of the stories about the Confederate heroes that his elders told on private occasions carried innuendoes not found in the high rhetoric that characterized public occasions. In his childhood reading, Cabell took an immediate and abiding interest in Greek and Roman myths and especially in the Arthurian legends. His reading and the atmosphere of late-nineteenth-century Richmond converged to set him on a course that made him one of the greatest students of myth among American writers. The "mythical method" fell naturally to him. In time Cabell would be reckoned a revolutionary force in twentieth-century literature, but it should not be forgotten that he lived his formative years in the nineteenth century, and in important ways was a product of it. Even while he used classical myths to comment on modernity as Joyce and Eliot were doing, he also commented on the mythmaking of the Old South.

A precocious lad, Cabell was only fifteen years old when he matriculated at the College of William and Mary. Williamsburg contrasted sharply with industrial and expanding Richmond, but its association with heroes of the Colonial past must have found responsive chords in Cabell, and he deepened his sense of the ironies of time while he pondered Virginia's history. He participated actively in campus life, joining Alpha Sigma Alpha fraternity. By the time he was an upperclassman, he had been hired to teach French and Greek to undergraduates. He became one of the editors of the *William and Mary Quarterly*, to which he contributed regularly. Ever the economist, he later revised these essays for inclusion in *Beyond Life* (1919), the statement of his aesthetic and philosophic principles that forms a delightful prelude to all of his work and the book that Cabell later designated as the "preface" to the eighteen volumes of *The Works of James Branch Cabell*. The fictional setting for the dialogues in *Beyond Life* is Fairhaven, which was modeled on Williamsburg. Cabell's years there were important for the writer who was to be.

In Williamsburg Cabell also experienced affairs of the heart that profoundly affected his thinking and colored his fictions. The young woman who was behind Cabell's numerous witch-women was Gabriella Brooke Moncure, whom Cabell had known briefly in his childhood and whom he rediscovered in Williamsburg, where the Moncures then lived. Although she was four years his senior, she and Cabell developed a deep friendship, and they probably would have married sometime had not scandal marred Cabell's last semester in college. Cabell had also been a close friend to Charles W. Coleman, the librarian. Rumors of homosexual liaisons involving Coleman and several of the more intellectual students, including Cabell, led to a college investigation. Cabell withdrew from school in protest, and his mother arrived on campus with a lawyer. The charges were discredited, and Cabell, after requesting reinstatement, received his degree on 23 June 1898. But he had been stung by the incident, and his relationship with Gabriella Moncure was decisively altered.

After graduation Cabell served an apprenticeship in a series of newspaper jobs, first with the Richmond *Times*, then from 1899 to 1901 with the New York *Herald*, then again with the Richmond *Times*. In New York he began a correspondence with his cousin, Miss Norvell Harrison, who lived in Brooklyn, but the affair lacked the depth of emotion Cabell had had with Gabriella and was perhaps essentially literary.

Soon after his return to Richmond, Cabell was involved in an even more dramatic scandal. He was thought to be the murderer of his cousin, John W. Scott, whose brutally assaulted body was found near the Cabell residence. The supposed motive was protection of the family honor, for Scott was rumored to be the lover of Cabell's mother. When the police could not solve the crime, many believed family influence had had its way. Years later, the evidence pointed to the brothers of a country girl whom Scott had seduced. Cabell, meanwhile, recoiled again from the community's willingness to condemn on the basis of gossip and hearsay.

For the next ten years Cabell worked as a professional genealogist, an activity that took him to France, Ireland, and England. His work as genealogist also colored his vision of human experience and dictated some of his writing methods. The divorce of Cabell's parents in 1907 added a further complication to his heightened sense of family as destiny. The divorce coincided with publication of *Brachiana*, one of Cabell's two genealogical records of the Branch family. After publication of *Branch of Abingdon* in 1911, Cabell worked in West Virginia for two years in the office of a Branch uncle who owned and operated coal mines.

By then Cabell was in his thirties, and he had come to enjoy a libertine's reputation, seeing it, and the adventures behind it, in the tradition of the court of Charles II as well as appropriate to his status in Southern society, and he doubtless wished to allay lingering rumors from the Coleman episode in Williamsburg. Rockbridge Alum was a Viriginian resort for those like Cabell who wished to practice their gallantry. There in the summer of 1912 he met a well-to-do widow who caused him to depart from his bachelor ways. She was Mrs. Emmett A. Shepherd, formerly Rebecca Priscilla Bradley, of Charles City County, Virginia. Mrs. Shepherd was four-and-a-half years older than Cabell, but he was drawn to her affability and social charm and her courage (her firstborn child was a virtually helpless polio victim). Mrs. Shepherd was also a good manager, and a part of Cabell wanted that. A persistent wooer, Cabell prevailed, and he and "Percie" were married on 8 November 1913.

Since Cabell inherited numerous children by taking a wife, the challenge of the marriage was considerable, but Cabell and Percie complemented each other effectively. Although Percie never pretended to understand—or even read—Cabell's work, she knew that writing was his calling, and in her careful way she gave priority to his creative work, insuring his privacy and assisting him as the gracious hostess of a well-managed household. She also presented him with his own son on 25 August 1915. Born when his mother was forty, Ballard did not have normal intelligence and his body remained "dwarfish"; although he never lived as an independent adult, he had charming ways and brought pleasure to his family. Not surprisingly, marriage became a major subject of Cabell's fiction. The numerous wives in Cabell's fiction were often based on women from myth and legend, but assuredly on Percie as well.

Coincident with Cabell's marriage, he found his true voice as a writer. He had earlier written numerous stories (published in such magazines as *Argosy, Smart Set, Lippincott's,* and *Harper's Monthly*), work that found its way into several books, the first of which was *The Eagle's Shadow* (1904). But by Cabell's reckoning as well as that of most of his admirers, the apprenticeship ended with *The Cream of the Jest* (1917). Revisiting his work for *The Works of James Branch Cabell* (1927–30), Cabell underscored the point in a preface: "only in *The Cream of the Jest* and its temporal successors had I any sense of dealing with my own work." *The Cream of the Jest* was succeeded by the most highly prized volumes in the Cabell canon: *Jurgen* (1919), *Figures of Earth* (1921), *The Silver Stallion* (1926), and *Something about Eve* (1927).

The most famous was *Jurgen*; its notoriety in the Jazz Age earned Cabell the reputation as a writer whose work embodied the avant-garde. In his earliest work, Cabell had taken sexual comedy as a province. Usually he made the necessary adjustments to accepted decorum, although his departures were enough to cause the artist Howard Pyle to let the editors of *Harper's Monthly* know he was unwilling to provide illustrations for Cabell's stories. The element of sexual play in *Jurgen* far exceeded that of anything Cabell had previously attempted, to the horror of genteel readers and critics and to the delight of a new generation that welcomed forthright treatment of sexuality in human affairs and recognition of its importance for the imagination. The ensuing conflict was important in the history of censorship in the United States.

With the suppression of *Jurgen*, Cabell became the object of national as well as local censure, but he also sensed opportunity. Before the court found for McBride, Cabell's publisher, on 19 October 1922, an impressive army of influential writers and critics had voiced their outrage at the censorship, and readers everywhere clamored for copies of the suppressed book. The drama insured exceptional sales for the book once it was exonerated and, for a time, good sales for all of Cabell's forthcoming books. Cabell had played a major part in the imbroglio; McBride published his *Taboo*, a satire on John Sumner and his supporters, in 1921. Realizing that in the long run his admirers would be a select company, Cabell let *Jurgen* do all for him that it could. He cultivated lionhood.

Richmond became a literary center, and various of Cabell's champions journeyed there to talk of books and life and to enjoy Cabell's hospitality. When four of Richmond's young literati started the *Reviewer*, one of the most important little magazines of the Southern Renascence, they naturally sought Cabell's advice. During the period of the suppression of *Jurgen*, Cabell was guest editor of three issues—making them, by design, collectors' items. For the *Reviewer*, Cabell's effort was to parallel Poe's contributions to Richmond's earlier literary magazine, the *Southern Literary Messenger*. Cabell foresaw that much of the attention would end; although only in his forties, he sensed that the boom of the 1920s was the time for the publication of *The Works of James Branch Cabell*, and by 1930 the eighteen volumes were in print. When the University of Virginia hosted a conference for Southern writers in October 1931, Cabell was among the participants, but so was William Faulkner. By then the most shocking book on the scene was *Sanctuary*, not *Jurgen*. Increasingly, Faulkner was the Southern writer who was viewed with awe; increasingly, in the decade of the Depression, Cabell seemed a symbol of the decadent, frivolous 1920s.

By the time Cabell had seen *The Works of James Branch Cabell* to completion, he was fifty-one years old. Writing was his chief passion, but he knew there would have to be new directions in his writing. He marked this change by publishing his new work as Branch Cabell, a further sign of affectation to those who did not approve of him. He eventually returned to his full name, although to little fanfare.

More than the sharp decline in his popularity gave a darker hue to his late work. The Depression and the grim struggles of a world at war disturbed him, too. And by the mid–1930s health problems increasingly reminded him of his own mortality. Victim of repeated attacks of pneumonia, he discovered the value of spending winters in St. Augustine, Florida. The warmer winters also helped Priscilla, who had developed acute arthritis. Cabell was devastated when she died in St. Augustine on 29 March 1949 after a heart attack.

There were some new compensations in the later years. Wintering in Florida not only gave Cabell new material for his writing; it also provided him with some new friendships that replaced the dazzling nexus of champions he knew in the 1920s. Chief among the new company were Stephen Vincent Benét, A. J. Hanna of Rollins College (with whom Cabell collaborated for a book on the St. John's River), and Marjorie Kinnan Rawlings. And there were some new champions to insist on his merits—most important, Edmund Wilson.

Cabell's last days were also brightened by marriage on 15 June 1950 to Margaret Waller Freeman, with whom he had worked in the exciting time of the *Reviewer*. Margaret was a splendid stepmother for Ballard and a loyal caretaker of Cabell's interests after his death. Cabell died in Richmond from cerebral hemorrhage on 5 May 1958 at age seventy-nine. Margaret first buried him next to Priscilla in Brook Hill, Virginia, but later moved him and Priscilla to Richmond's Hollywood Cemetery. She is now also buried next to Cabell. The library of Virginia Commonwealth University bears his name. The Cabell Room in the library is in the style of Cabell's birthplace and houses his personal library.

MAJOR THEMES

Aristocrat that he was, Cabell was understandably attracted to the novel of manners. Not for him was the impulse of the *Bildungsroman* or the confessional novel, at least in their more obvious forms. He was drawn to the intellectual, the detached, the ironic—and his first five novels had contemporary settings that mirrored Richmond and Williamsburg. His characters were, for the most part, of his own class. The most obviously autobiographical of the novels was the second, *The Cords of Vanity*, whose protagonist has love affairs that recall those of Cabell's young manhood. The early novel that touched readers most deeply was *The Rivet in Grandfather's Neck*. It was also the novel that seemed to have a depiction of Virginia mores as a primary intent. (Zelda Fitzgerald wept over the novel, and William Faulkner in his apprenticeship read it carefully.) Common to all of the "contemporary novels" was the air of the aesthete, the world of Lord Henry Wooten of Oscar Wilde's *The Picture of Dorian Gray*. Finally, what interested Cabell most in these novels was the artist, his place and his meaning, not the manners of Virginia. Through these novels, Cabell discovered his real subject—himself.

Thus it was that Cabell would identify *The Cream of the Jest* as the first of his books recognizably his own. Felix Kennaston, the book's protagonist, was also the protagonist of *The Eagle's Shadow*. This later Felix is important not for what he says, but for what he dreams. Dream life is the primary reality, for—as Felix reflects—the only certainty is the prison of the individual consciousness. Although *The Cream* is set in Lichfield (Cabell's name for Richmond

translates "field of corpses"), much of the novel portrays Felix's rich dream
life that brings him into contact with key figures of history, especially with the
lovely Ettarre, a princess in the mythical kingdom of Poictesme. Cabell acknowledges the poignant pull of the loves of the "real" world, but for the most
part we are such stuff as dreams are made of. Thus, the drama of Poictesme
and Cabell's mythical people portrays the essence of Cabell's inner life, and the
title of the chief work of his life takes on a double meaning—*The Biography of
the Life of Manuel: The Works of James Branch Cabell*. Although the work
purports to relate the biography of Dom Manuel of Poictesme, it also relates the
biography of Cabell; Manuel the swineherd set out to make a figure for himself
and followed his own thinking, except when Dame Naifer, his wife, asserted
her claims. The basic tension of Cabell's work is between the dream and the
real; counterpointing this tension is the drama between the male and the female.

Cabell revised his early work slightly to make it "fit" the grand design of
the biography of Manuel that he had developed about the time of *The Cream*.
He made clear the major philosophical concepts, or attitudes, of his work in
Beyond Life. There are three major attitudes in the biography: the Chivalric, the
Gallant, and the Poetic. Individual works often emphasize a single one of these,
but usually presentation of one attitude causes reflection on another. A character
may progress from attitude to attitude, and *Beyond Life* presents, in part, a
history of these attitudes in the Western world.

According to the code of Chivalry, man's chief struggle is religious, and man
is on earth briefly to prove his worthiness for another existence. Since the Maker
is necessarily distant, man finds a focus in the worship of a good, true, and
beautiful woman. For the medieval mind, the Virgin Mary was her most important
embodiment, but various women of medieval ritual and legend also gave powerful
embodiment to the theme. Because Cabell believed man to be a worshipping
creature, the medieval and chivalrous attracted him. Even while Cabell was
writing his Virginia novels, he was also writing short stories set in medieval
times. He was always aware that man might practice his Chivalry complexly,
but that man needed faith Cabell knew. Domnei, or "woman worship," played
an important role in Southern culture. In his various tales on the theme, Cabell
was addressing a Southern concern, but with much more subtlety and complexity
than most of his countrymen had managed.

The burden domnei places on women is, of course, staggering. The role of
the veiled, virginal doll was often not one that women wanted. In *Jurgen* and
subsequent works Cabell insisted that women's sexual drives could be as strong
as those of men. Discovering this reality, a particular male might abandon his
domnei (as Europe abandoned Chivalry) and adopt the attitude of Gallantry. In
English literature this attitude reached its highest perfection in the drama of the
Restoration period. Faith in a caring Creator having been shaken, man concluded
that he had his body for a short time, and it was capable of giving him keen
pleasure. In place of the one woman of the code of Chivalry, there would usually
be many women, but a woman must always be pursued with ritual and grace.

Wit and detachment made the game worth playing for its own sake. Cabell insists on the comic aspects of human sexuality, but he also portrays it as an affront to death. Man could use the force creatively to counter what reason declared was essential void. For the Gallant, the surface was everything.

But Gallantry has its drawbacks, for the body's vigor becomes less. The Gallant may conclude that the game is not worth playing. The fortunate may find refuge in the attitude of Poetry. Poetry can transcend bodily limitations, can recapture something of the lovely spirit of Chivalry. It allows its practitioner to bystep the pain of Naturalistic reductionism. Thus it is that John Charteris of *Beyond Life* opts for the dynamic illusion, what Ibsen called the life-saving lie.

Passage through these attitudes is one of Cabell's structural devices for his masterpiece *Jurgen*. There are other devices as well, particularly the device of mythic structure. The myth of Faustus provides the initial counterpart for the forty-year-old Jurgen's progress from the realm of Glathion to the realm of Cocaigne to the land of Leukê and finally to the hell of his father and the heaven of his grandmother. Like Faustus, Jurgen does not fear to make compacts with the devil; like Faustus he is desirous of "tasting any drink once." Because he put in a kind word for the devil, Jurgen is granted the body of a twenty-year-old, but he retains the perspective of middle age. This duality provides the intellectual comedy of his adventures, which become a return to his own past. Reliving his youthful passion for Dorothy la Désirée, once again no better than she should be, Jurgen loses her a second time, but he soon finds interesting companions in three queens of mythology. With Queen Guenevere he enacts the code of Chivalry. With Queen Anaïtis (her name is an anagram for Insatia) he enacts the code of Gallantry. Finally, like Faustus, he gets to see Queen Helen, but he wisely refrains from sexual intercourse with her. He knows that he should keep the realm of Poetry intact. The three queens represent, respectively, Faith, Desire, and Vision. Jurgen visits both hell and heaven after his journey in Leukê, after which he gets to view the three queens once again, choosing finally to return to his wife, Dame Lisa (who represents aspects of each of these queens even if she is a shrew with a tongue as sharp as that of Dame Van Winkle). Not only is Jurgen like Faustus; he is like Odysseus, and his adventures finally take him to his own Penelope. In part a portrayal of the adventures of Everyman, *Jurgen* is also a profoundly personal odyssey—rich in layers of meaning—and a convincing celebration of marriage, much as its predecessor *The Cream of the Jest* had been. As Joe Lee Davis observed, Cabell's vision is much like that of Frost in "Birches." There is a splendid coming and going for the Swinger of Birches, but Earth is the right place for love.

The love that Cabell portrays most consistently and effectively is not young love, but the love of mature years. His world is that of *The Tempest* rather than *Romeo and Juliet*. Indeed, Prospero is the Shakespearean character most attractive to Cabell, the one whose spirit is closest to his own. There is an impressive population of magicians in Cabell's fiction, but he was most sympathetic to Prospero, who had not been overly impressed with the realities of this world.

Cabell was the poet of middle age and old age, and he often captured the poignancy of their most profound moments as a character looks across his own isolation to the beloved wife or child. He was obsessed by Time that often seemed to render human activities pointless and pathetic, but even at the end of his long life, he could find the drama amusing. At the least, art could provide a pleasant means to occupy oneself before Grandfather Death appeared. In that regard, Cabell counted himself most fortunate. He had been able to do with his life what he wished to do, be a writer. Although readers often considered Cabell spokesman of a sophisticated nihilism, his work also expresses a powerful drive towards faith and purpose. Paradoxically, uncannily, he also celebrates the heroic in man. Jurgen put matters thus after Pan had shown him "all": "Yes, you can kill me if you choose, but it is beyond your power to make me believe that there is no justice anywhere, and that I am unimportant. For I would have you know I am a monstrous clever fellow. As for you, you are either a delusion or a god or a degraded Realist. But whatever you are, you have lied to me, and I know that you have lied, and I will not believe in the insignificance of Jurgen." (Storiesende ed., p. 135).

SURVEY OF CRITICISM

Cabell always had his eye on the future. Like Milton, he wanted to write books with a life beyond life. Taking note of posterity, he revised his printed books carefully for the Storiesende edition, writing prefaces to describe the genesis and reception of each work, and the importance of the book to the "Biography" or to him. Thereafter, he regularly wrote some preface or introductory statement for his books. When he died, he had his work essentially in the form he wanted it, and he died knowing that there was academic readiness for scholarship and research on his work. Among American writers, he had credentials that marked him as enduring. He had, in fact, written the foreword for Frances Joan Brewer's *James Branch Cabell: A Bibliography of His Writings, Biography and Criticism* (1957). Brewer's work contains extensive descriptions of Cabell's books as well as listings of items about him. This recognition of Cabell's achievement—and invitation to scholars—was reinforced with the companion volume by Matthew J. Bruccoli, *James Branch Cabell: A Bibliography, Part II: Notes on the Cabell Collections at the University of Virginia*, also published in 1957. James N. Hall's *James Branch Cabell: A Complete Bibliography* (1974) was not "complete," and publication by Revisionist Press meant that the book would not have the audience of its predecessors. The photoprocessed book was expensive, and few copies were printed. Maurice Duke's *James Branch Cabell: A Reference Guide* (1979) is also not as elegant as the bibliographies of Brewer and Bruccoli, but it is an important research tool offering strong evidence that Cabell's reputation has survived the neglect of the 1930s. And although the listings on Cabell in any particular year may not be many, there is a sizable body of criticism on him, and Duke's work provides valuable assistance in identifying it.

During the 1920s Cabell could scarcely have been more fortunate in his defenders. H. L. Mencken's brief *James Branch Cabell* (1927) is still invigorating. Like Carl Van Doren's *James Branch Cabell* (1932), it captures the special appeal of Cabell's work for many readers of the 1920s. Joseph Hergesheimer's praise for Cabell in the *American Mercury* of January 1928 was also part of the tune Mencken played.

The reaction against Cabell is most vehemently stated in Oscar Cargill's *Intellectual America: Ideas on the March* (1941). Cargill declared Cabell to be "beyond all shadow of a doubt, the most tedious person who has achieved high repute as a *literatus* in America." In *On Native Grounds* (1942) Alfred Kazin labeled Cabell "an exquisite," and he emphasized his assessment of Cabell's importance to the mainstream of American writing by deleting him from the abridged paper version of his book.

Cargill and Kazin did not persuade everyone, and Edmund Wilson's 1956 essay, "The James Branch Cabell Case Reopened," signaled shift of opinion in Cabell's favor and a prelude to more careful scrutiny of Cabell's work. Louis D. Rubin's *No Place on Earth* (1959) emphasized the importance of the South to Cabell's imagination by pairing his career with that of Ellen Glasgow. Rubin's book was the forerunner of other attention in the academy. Joe Lee Davis's *James Branch Cabell* (1962) surveys the whole of Cabell's career. It emphasizes the variety and the complexity of Cabell's work. In *Jesting Moses: A Study of Cabellian Comedy* (1962) Arvin R. Wells seeks to define the essence of Cabellian comedy, finding it more Rabelaisian than Meredithian, a means of confronting Naturalistic despair. He illustrates his thesis almost exclusively through reference to the major romances of *The Biography of Manuel*. In 1967 a book by an Englishman, Desmond Tarrant's *James Branch Cabell: The Dream and the Reality*, gave further encouraging impetus to the Cabell revival. Tarrant emphasizes Cabell's powers of myth and the religious dimensions of his work. Unlike Wells, he treats the later fictions as well as the later romances of the "Biography." The best overview of Cabell's work remains Davis's study.

Although the Revisionist Press brought out four collections of essays by Cabell scholars, these books did little to promote Cabell's reputation in the academies. But *James Branch Cabell: Centennial Essays* (1983), edited by M. Thomas Inge and Edgar E. MacDonald, should have an impact in those places. Its essays, written especially for the Cabell centennial, pay tribute to his achievements without making unwarranted prophecies of the growth of Cabell studies. Louis D. Rubin's "A Virginian in Poictesme" sets the tone for the collection. The essays that follow suggest the scope of Cabell's impressive achievement and a good deal about his life. Edgar MacDonald's fine essay "Cabell in Love," as well as his impressive photographic essay, reminds us of the need for a full-scale biography. Dorothy M. Scura discusses Cabell's literary relationship with Guy Holt, his editor at McBride. Joseph M. Flora discusses the fictions Cabell published under the name Branch Cabell, finding them strong commentary on the grim political realities of the late 1930s and early 1940s. W. L. Godshalk compares *Figures of Earth* with Shakespeare's *Troilus and Cressida*. Mark Allen writes on "Enchantment and Delusion: Fantasy in the Biography of Manuel," and Leslie A. Fiedler recalls the rebellion inherent in his youthful reading of Cabell, but wonders, "How is it possible today to respond without guilt to Cabell's travesties of male/female relations, when women everywhere around us are protesting such stereotypes of them and us?" (p. 140). The book concludes with a solid review of Cabell scholarship by Ritchie D. Watson, Jr.

BIBLIOGRAPHY

Works by James Branch Cabell

The Eagle's Shadow. New York: Doubleday, Page, 1904.

Gallantry. New York & London: Harper, 1907.

The Line of Love. New York & London: Harper, 1907.

Chivalry. New York & London: Harper, 1909.

The Cords of Vanity. New York: Doubleday, Page, 1909.

The Soul of Melicent. New York: Stokes, 1913. Rev. as *Domnei*. New York: McBride, 1920.

The Rivet in Grandfather's Neck. New York: McBride, 1915.

The Certain Hour. New York: McBride, 1916.

From the Hidden Way. New York: McBride, 1916.

The Cream of the Jest. New York: McBride, 1917.

Beyond Life. New York: McBride, 1919.

Jurgen. New York: McBride, 1919.

Figures of Earth. New York: McBride, 1921.

The Jewel Merchants. New York: McBride, 1921.

The High Place. New York: McBride, 1923.

Straws and Prayer-Books. New York: McBride, 1924.

The Music from Behind the Moon. New York: Day, 1926. Revised and republished as *The Witch-Woman*. New York: Farrar, Straus, 1948.

The Silver Stallion. New York: McBride, 1926.

Something about Eve. New York: McBride, 1927.

Ballades from the Hidden Way. New York: Crosby Gaige, 1929.

Sonnets from Antan. New York: Fountain Press, 1929.

The Way of Ecben. New York: McBride, 1929. Revised and republished in *The Witch-Woman* (1948).

The White Robe. New York: McBride, 1929. Revised and republished in *The Witch-Woman* (1948).

Some of Us. New York: McBride, 1930.

Storiesende Edition of The Works of James Branch Cabell in Eighteen Volumes. New York: McBride, 1927–1930.

These Restless Heads. New York: McBride, 1930.

Special Delivery. New York: McBride, 1933.

Ladies and Gentlemen. New York: McBride, 1934.

Smirt. New York: McBride, 1934.
Smith. New York: McBride, 1935.
Preface to the Past. New York: McBride, 1936.
Smire. Garden City, N.Y.: Doubleday, Doran, 1937.
Hamlet Had an Uncle. New York & Toronto: Farrar and Rinehart, 1940.
The First Gentleman of America. New York & Toronto: Farrar & Rinehart, 1942.
The St. Johns, with A. J. Hanna. New York: Farrar & Rinehart, 1943.
There Were Two Pirates. New York: Farrar, Straus, 1946.
Let Me Lie. New York: Farrar, Straus, 1947.
The Witch-Woman. New York: Farrar, Straus, 1948.
The Devil's Own Dear Son. New York: Farrar, Straus, 1949.
Quiet, Please. Gainesville: University of Florida Press, 1952.
As I Remember It. New York: McBride, 1955.

Studies of James Branch Cabell

Blish, James. "The Long Night of a Virginia Author." *Journal of Modern Literature* 2 (1972): 393–405.

Brewer, Frances Joan. *James Branch Cabell: A Bibliography of His Writings, Biography and Criticism*. Charlottesville: University Press of Virginia, 1957.

Bruccoli, Matthew J. *James Branch Cabell: A Bibliography, Part II: Notes on the Cabell Collections at the University of Virginia*. Charlottesville: University Press of Virginia, 1957.

Cargill, Oscar. "The Intelligentsia." *Intellectual America: Ideas on the March*. New York: Macmillan, 1941, pp. 495–503.

Davis, Joe Lee. *James Branch Cabell*. New York: Twayne, 1962.

Duke, Maurice. *James Branch Cabell: A Reference Guide*. Boston: G. K. Hall, 1979.

Flora, Joseph M. "From Virginia to Poictesme: The Early Novels of James Branch Cabell." *Mississippi Quarterly* 32 (Spring 1979): 219–39.

Godshalk, William L. "Cabell and Barth: Our Comic Athletes." *The Comic Imagination in America*. Ed. Louis D. Rubin, Jr. New Brunswick: Rutgers University Press, 1973, pp. 275–83.

Hergesheimer, Joseph. "James Branch Cabell." *American Mercury* 13 (January 1928): 38–47.

Hinz, Evelyn J. and John J. Teunissen. "Life Beyond Life: Cabell's Theory and Practice of Romance." *Genre* 10 (1977): 299–327.

Howard, Leon. "Figures of Allegory." *Sewanee Review* 62 (January-March 1934): 54–66.

Inge, M. Thomas and Edgar E. MacDonald, eds. *James Branch Cabell: Centennial Essays*. Baton Rouge: Louisiana State University Press, 1983.

Kazin, Alfred. "The Exquisites." *On Native Grounds: An Interpretation of American Prose Literature*. New York: Reynal & Hitchcock, 1942, pp. 227–46.

Mencken, H. L. *James Branch Cabell*. New York: McBride, 1927.

Parks, Edd Winfield. "James Branch Cabell." *Southern Renascence: The Literature of the Modern South*. Ed. Louis D. Rubin, Jr., and Robert D. Jacobs. Baltimore: Johns Hopkins University Press, 1953, pp. 251–61.

Parrington, Vernon Louis. "The Incomparable Mr. Cabell." *Main Currents in American Thought*, Vol. 3. New York: Harcourt, Brace, 1930, pp. 335–45.

Rubin, Louis D., Jr. "A Southerner in Poictesme." *No Place on Earth: Ellen Glasgow, James Branch Cabell and Richmond-in-Virginia*. Austin: University of Texas Press, 1959.

————. "Two in Richmond: Ellen Glasgow and James Branch Cabell." *Southern Renascence*. Ed. Louis D. Rubin, Jr. and Robert D. Jacobs. Baltimore: Johns Hopkins University Press, 1953, pp. 115–41.

Schlegel, Dorothy B. "Cabell and His Critics," *The Dilemma of the Southern Writer*. Ed. Richard K. Meeber. Farmville, Va.: Longwood College, 1961, pp. 119–40.

Tarrant, Desmond. *James Branch Cabell: The Dream and the Reality*. Norman: University of Oklahoma Press, 1967.

Van Doren, Carl. *James Branch Cabell*. New York: Literary Guild, 1932.

Wagenknecht, Edward. "James Branch Cabell: The Anatomy of Romanticism." *Cavalcade of the American Novel*. New York: Henry Holt, 1952, pp. 339–53.

Wells, Arvin R. *Jesting Moses: A Study in Cabellian Comedy*. Gainesville: University of Florida Press, 1962.

Wilson, Edmund. "The James Branch Cabell Case Reopened." *The Bit Between My Teeth*. New York: Farrar, Straus and Giroux, 1965.

—————————— RONALD WESLEY HOAG ——————————

Erskine Caldwell
(1903–   )

Erskine Caldwell is among the most prolific and controversial of Southern writers. Both his popular and critical reception have fluctuated dramatically over a half-century career. Recent interest in his work has focused on its regional and historical importance as well as on its stylistic and thematic development.

BIOGRAPHY

Erskine Preston Caldwell was born in Moreland, Coweta County, Georgia, on what he believes to be 17 December 1903; there is no accurate record of his birth. The only child of the Reverend Ira Sylvester Caldwell and Caroline Preston Bell, Caldwell spent his boyhood and early teenage years moving with his parents throughout the Southeast. Ira's position with the Associate Reformed Presbyterian (ARP) Church necessitated this peripatetic life, an experience that contributed to at least four characteristics that have marked Erskine Caldwell as a man and writer: a restless pursuit of new places, people, and events; a sensitivity to the problems of the underprivileged and the underdog; a lingering preoccupation with the South-as-place and with the forms of Southern life; and a search for new perspectives from which to regard past experience.

Although Caldwell received little formal schooling in his youth, he was regularly tutored at home by his parents. Caroline, a former teacher, and Ira, who had compiled a brilliant college record, were equal to the task of educating their son. Supplementing this parental instruction was a brief term at the Wrens Institute in Wrens, Georgia, where the family settled in 1918 when Ira was recalled to the state by the ARP. In this period, Caldwell also gained his first writing experience working for the local weekly paper and, as a stringer, for several major Georgia dailies. Valuable, too, were his excursions into the tobacco country with his father, with one of the local doctors, or with the county tax assessor. These trips constituted Caldwell's first conscious exposure to the hard life in the east Georgia sand hills.

In fall 1920 Caldwell entered his father's alma mater, Erskine College in South Carolina, where for two years he established a reputation as a poor student and a distinguished traveler, the latter by dint of boxcar-hopping weekend visits to cities on the line. During his second year this yen for travel and adventure led to an abortive quest for a deckhand's job on a gulf freighter and to a brief incarceration in the Bogalusa, Louisiana, jail as a vagrant and suspected "wobbly" agitator. From 1923 to 1925 Caldwell was an in-and-out student at the University of Virginia, where his desire to write, his restlessness, and his preference for experience to schooling all intensified. He used his frequent absences from Charlottesville to enrich his experiences by working as a milkman in Washington, D.C., and as a store clerk and professional football player in Pennsylvania. Before returning to Virginia, he briefly studied economics at the University of Pennsylvania.

Abandoning college to work full-time for the Atlanta *Journal* in 1925, Caldwell returned to Georgia with a new bride, the daughter of a University of Virginia faculty member. His thirteen-year marriage to Helen Lannigan produced three children. During his year at the *Journal*, Caldwell's interest in writing became an obsession that governed the rest of his life. His acquaintance with Margaret Mitchell, then a feature writer for the paper, along with his own labors as a book reviewer, prompted him to try writing fiction. Although his short-story submissions netted only an album filled with rejection slips, he resolved to spend the next ten years making himself a proficient professional writer.

To further that goal, Caldwell took his family and small savings to an isolated farmhouse in Mount Vernon, Maine. In that outpost he hoed potatoes, chopped wood, wrote book reviews to slow the drain on his finances, and—most of all— wrote his stories. No slave to inspiration, he used his journalist's discipline to generate several stories a week. Occasional wanderlust took him to such faraway places as a one-room cabin in the piney woods of South Carolina, but always his typewriter went along and always he used it to swell his supply of stories.

After three years of writing during Maine hibernations and intermittent escapes, Caldwell in 1929 placed stories with several "little" magazines, including the Paris-based *transition*. That October his first book, a seamy novelette called *The Bastard*, was published in a small-press limited edition and was promptly banned in nearby Portland, Maine. Caldwell's long feud with censors had begun. A second novelette, *Poor Fool*, appeared the next year in a similar format and to similar response.

The most important advance for Caldwell in 1930 was the budding of a relationship with Maxwell Perkins, Scribner's famous editor in chief, who had written to request stories and then for months had rejected all submissions. Early in the year, however, Perkins accepted not just one but two stories, both of which were printed in the June issue of *Scribner's Magazine*. (Thinking he had been offered a mere $2.50 instead of $250 for the stories, Caldwell brazenly rejected Perkins' first proposal and so, in his confusion, earned a robust $350 for his first major magazine publication.) Perkins was so impressed by Caldwell's work that he soon contracted to publish a collection of his stories. *American Earth*, a mix of new and previously published pieces, appeared in 1931 under the Scribner imprint; it was Caldwell's first significant book.

While visiting his parents in Georgia at the end of 1930, Caldwell explored again the back roads of Burke, Jefferson, and Richmond counties, sharpening impressions from former journeys and finding the subject of his first major novel. Written in a New York hotel room and polished at the homestead in Maine, *Tobacco Road* was accepted by Perkins for Scribner's in the summer of 1931, just two weeks after its submission. Unfortunately, the initial reception of the novel by its reviewers in early 1932 was considerably cooler than that of its editor.

When another new novel, written partly at a hotel managed by his friend Nathanael "Pep" West, failed to find a home at Scribner's, Caldwell reluctantly switched allegiance to Viking Press, where his rendering of life in rural Maine was again turned down. (Twenty years later it was published as *A Lamp for Nightfall*.) Retreating to Mount Vernon, Caldwell wrote in a single draft during summer 1932 the manuscript of his next Southern novel, *God's Little Acre*. Published by Viking in 1933, the book in its first year sold twice as well— approximately 10,000 copies—as *Tobacco Road* and attracted greater, if still mixed, notice.

For Caldwell, 1933 was a year of both honor and disapprobation. His story "Country Full of Swedes" won the *Yale Review* award for fiction, a windfall that enabled him to buy the Maine house in which his family had long resided. Public attention of a different sort resulted when the New York Society for the Suppression of Vice took exception to the antics of Ty Ty Walden and company in *God's Little Acre*. Defended by a parade of intellectuals, the book was exonerated in a famous judicial decision. (Later controversies over other works brought Caldwell notoriety and contributed to his vast sales, especially in the growing paperback market.) To improve his finances, Caldwell spent three months working as a scriptwriter for MGM, a lucrative interlude but one he condemned in later life as hackwork and a waste of time. More to his liking were two other events of 1933, the publication of a second collection of stories, *We Are the Living*, and the opening on Broadway of Jack Kirkland's adaptation of *Tobacco Road*. After a slow start, the play established a then-record run of seven years, ultimately earning Caldwell a substantial fortune and making "Tobacco Road" part of the American literary landscape.

During 1935 and 1936 Caldwell published in rapid succession four of his best books. In 1935 he brought out two works of fiction: *Kneel to the Rising Sun*, a story collection graced by the title piece about a lynching, and *Journeyman*, a humorously trenchant account of a visit by a con man–preacher to the town of Rocky Comfort. The social consciousness reflected in these books finds alternate expression in *Some American People* (1935), a volume of travel essays mellowed by their sympathetic portraits of men and women in a sometimes quixotic struggle to outlast hard times. Not to be overlooked from this period is the stylistically eccentric and experimental *The Sacrilege of Alan Kent*, published in 1936. A prose poem later judged by its author to be too self-conscious, the book is a loosely narrative progression of images, many of which haunt the memory.

The latter half of the 1930s was dominated by Caldwell's productive professional association with the renowned *Life* photographer Margaret Bourke-White, the woman he made his second wife in 1939. Their automobile tour of the South in the summer of 1936 generated the 1937 photo-essay volume *You Have Seen Their Faces*, which graphically portrays the problems caused by sharecropping and peonage. Of the other three books they brought out together before their divorce in 1942, *North of the Danube* (1939), a study of Czechoslovakia and the fruit of Caldwell's first European travel, has earned more praise than *Say, Is This the U.S.A.* (1941) and *Russia at War* (1942).

While critics generally have consigned to lesser status or dismissed entirely Caldwell's work after the 1930s, the next decade in fact saw the publication of three important new novels: *Trouble in July* (1940), a story about the personal and political circumstances surrounding a lynching; *Georgia Boy* (1943), a masterful story cycle that whimsically evokes the youth of imagination; and *Tragic Ground* (1944), a study of displaced persons whose actions are both humorously and disquietingly grotesque. During this decade Caldwell also began his editorship of the *American Folkways* series, a multivolume celebration of different regions of the country. He was also a reporter-broadcaster from Moscow in the early days of World War II and subsequently worked in Hollywood on the propaganda film *Mission to Moscow*. In 1942 he married his third wife, June Johnson, who became the mother of his fourth and last child.

Since 1950 Caldwell's most significant writing has been in nonfiction. He abandoned the short story—which he still terms his favorite genre—in the 1950s and, after a flurry of novel writing in the 1960s, turned exclusively to reminiscences and travel books such as his latest all new publication, *Afternoons in Mid-America* (1976). Among the notable books of this period are *Call It Experience* (1951), a chronicle of his rise to fame that holds its peace on personal matters; *In Search of Bisco* (1965), his exploration of racial attitudes in the context of a quest for a lost friend; *Writing in America* (1967), an interesting hodgepodge of literary opinions; and *Deep South* (1968), a tribute to his father and an examination of Southern religion.

Ever the traveler, Caldwell shifted his residence in the 1970s from Florida to Scottsdale, Arizona, where he lives with his wife and occasional illustrator of his work, Virginia Moffet Fletcher, whom he married in 1957. He still travels extensively throughout a world that knows him as the author of some 60 books that have been translated into 40 languages and have sold, collectively, more than 80 million copies. Despite his cosmopolitan awareness, Erskine Caldwell remains a most proper subject for the present volume. When told of this project, he responded in a letter to the author: "I'm glad they still consider me a Southern writer. I do too."

MAJOR THEMES

Not a critical theorist, Caldwell has nonetheless expressed over the years many opinions about writing. From these statements emerges an essentially romantic aesthetic that asserts the primacy of imagination in the creative process. Caldwell's art emphasizes spontaneous linear storytelling rather than either plotting or revising. He views himself as a recorder, not a manipulator, of his characters' words and deeds. "I don't manufacture tapestries," he says. "I let the people say or do what's going to happen next" (Broadwell and Hoag, *Paris Review* 131). Admitting to no influence over his characters, he refuses to censor their behavior because such restraint would invalidate his laissez-faire method.

Curiously wedded to Caldwell's belief in unfettered imagination is his insistence on experience as the true school for a writer. Deliberately rejecting both influence and instruction, he says he was shaped to no significant degree either by books or by the study of books. (Although he has read more than he sometimes pretends, it is probably a fact that he has not read very much.) Rather, he uses an experientially acquired knowledge of psychology, economics, and sociology as the foundation on which his imagination builds. His is a fiction of more-or-less real gardens inhabited by more-or-less imaginary toads. Following the dreamlike flights of his imagination, Caldwell's people stumble over problems observable in the real world. Thus, his hybrid art often vacillates between surrealism and realism.

Consistent with Caldwell's spontaneous approach to storytelling is his preference for "content" over "style," since by style he means something akin to conscious manipulation. For example, he maintains that he is neither a deliberate humorist nor an intentional distorter of reality. Of humor he says: "What can be humorous one moment can be very sad the next. It all depends upon the circumstances, and I don't think humor should be forced" (Broadwell and Hoag, *Mississippi Quarterly* 581). About distortions of reality, he attributes any disparities between his world and the real world to the unforced workings of his artistic imagination and says that he has not "distorted anything beyond recognition" (Broadwell and Hoag, *Georgia Review* 91).

In *Call It Experience* Caldwell defines fiction as "an imaginary tale with a meaning"; elsewhere he declares himself to be a man who means no meanings. His explanation for this superficial contradiction is that he is as perplexed as the reader by the doings of his people who are "their own creations," but like the reader he believes that the stories do have some meaning. Disclaiming intentions of philosophy, evangelism, or reform—although he concedes a degree of the last in some of his nonfiction books—he says that the purpose of his fiction is "to provide a mirror into which people may look" (*Call It Experience* 235).

What is Fiddler in "The Growing Season"? Are Jeeter Lester in *Tobacco Road* and Spence Douthit in *Tragic Ground* victims of circumstance or of themselves? In Caldwell's open-ended, reflexive fiction the stories and their readers interpret each other.

Although readers must judge for themselves the degree to which Caldwell's precepts, as summarized, inform his literary example, some of his other opinions are less subject to debate. Although he considers the short story to be "the essence of writing," he does not distinguish hierarchically between fiction and nonfiction: "In the end it's how well you do it that's going to count" (Broadwell and Hoag, *Paris Review* 148:137). Neither does he admit a qualitative difference between popular and serious fiction; in fact, he regards large sales as something of an imprimatur. He must please himself first, he says; however, his next most valued appreciator is not the reviewer or critic but "the ordinary man in the street, the golden mean" (Broadwell and Hoag, *Paris Review* 152). Finally, while he resents being thought of as "some sort of regional character" (Broadwell and Hoag, *Georgia Review* 84), he prefers regional writing because of his interest in the varying local interplay among economics, sociology, and psychology.

A frequent experimenter with home-brewed literary modes, Caldwell varies his prevailing approach, often identified as naturalistic realism or symbolic naturalism, with a smorgasbord of other tactics. *The Bastard* and *Poor Fool*, apprentice works, share with parts of *God's Little Acre* an expressionistic technique. On the other hand, his prose poem *The Sacrilege of Alan Kent* is a series of epiphanies impressionistically rendered. When his stories seem, as Kenneth Burke says, "subtly guided by the logic of dreams," they are surrealistic (in MacDonald, *Critical Essays* 172); and when his often grotesque characters behave in perversely humorous ways, there is black humor afoot. "Caldwell," declares James Devlin, "paints with a palette knife, smearing flamboyant daubs of humor and gross characterization" to create "vivid" and "pulsating" works (121). Says Caldwell himself: "I do not have a velvet touch. . . . I like to hammer-hammer-hammer and make all the noise I can" (*Writing in America* 10). Despite the emotional impact of outrageous characters and bizarre events, Caldwell almost never breaks his narrative stance of distanced objectivity. Indeed, among the many ironies in his work—and irony is Caldwell's principal stock-in-trade—none is greater than this gap between the flat, detached narrative voice and the circus of extremes it describes.

Contrasting with this proliferation of techniques are the structural simplicity of his stories and the primitive quality of his narration and dialogue. Held together by controlling themes and recurrent images rather than elaborate architectonics, his fictions move linearly, chronologically, and episodically to their swift climaxes. A disciple of oral storytelling, Caldwell makes effective use of anecdotal narration and conversational prose. In "Candy-Man Beechum" and other tales that feature a black protagonist, he eschews the phonetic representation of dialect in favor of a rhyming, syncopated prose meant to capture the movement and tone of black speech. Although Caldwell makes little use of metaphor and

figurative language in general, he does employ—in keeping with the oral tradition—repetition for a variety of purposes, including characterization and choric
commentary.

Ideologically, Caldwell's fiction is about needs, obsessions, frustrations, and
sublimations. In *Tobacco Road* Jeeter Lester needs to farm cotton, his wife needs
a dress, his mother needs food, one daughter needs an operation, and another
needs freedom from her husband. But because of a hard-to-determine meld of
social, economic, and personal handicaps, they cannot have what they need.
Instead, these people get by on anodynes ranging from snuff to sex, from mindless
daydreaming to pointless excursions in an automobile whose rapid demise un-
derscores the decline of the South, the fall of the family, and the yielding of the
human spirit to the spirit of animal survival. In *God's Little Acre* Will Thompson
is obsessed with turning on the power at the mill just as Ty Ty Walden is
obsessed with finding gold on his Georgia farm. In these vain pursuits, the
former loses his life, the latter his sons. Similarly, in *Journeyman*, *Tragic
Ground*, and other stories, people want what they do not know how to get and
are forced to live without. Essentially unthoughtful and unperceptive, Caldwell's
characters learn little from their suffering; they endure or die, but almost never
do they change. The feeling that builds for the reader is of an itch that sometimes
tickles and sometimes torments, but is seldom satisfactorily scratched. In Caldwell's best work a romantic belief in emotion and a primitive faith in the agrarian
worker exist side by side with a naturalistic sense of futility in the face of
environmental and biological determinism. Difficult to unravel, this knot at the
core of things gives his books their power.

Several notable shifts characterize Caldwell's writing over the past half century. Perhaps the most obvious is in prevailing genres. From a concentration on
short stories in the 1920s and early 1930s, he moved to an emphasis on novels,
his dominant form of the 1940s and 1950s. Then, in the mid–1960s he turned
largely to nonfiction, exclusively his province in recent years. Other movements
have been, in fiction, away from the prickly humor that spiked his best work
until the end of the 1940s and, in nonfiction, away from observations of troubled
men and women to travel books and reminiscences. What social wrongs do find
their way into the later books usually involve race, as in *In Search of Bisco*, his
nonfiction contribution to the literature of the civil rights period, and many of
the novels.

The best of Erskine Caldwell's fiction appeared in the 1930s and early 1940s,
any list of which must include the novels *Tobacco Road* (1932), *God's Little
Acre* (1933), *Journeyman* (1935), *Trouble in July* (1940), and *Tragic Ground*
(1944). Together with the less-distinguished novels—*A House in the Uplands*
(1946), *The Sure Hand of God* (1947), *This Very Earth* (1948), *Place Called
Estherville* (1949), and *Episode in Palmetto* (1950)—these comprise what Caldwell refers to as a "cyclorama" of "representative vistas, or visions, of the
South" (Broadwell and Hoag, *Georgia Review* 93). Also among his best works
are the long prose poem *The Sacrilege of Alan Kent* (1936) and the story cycle

Georgia Boy (1943), the latter of which is arguably his masterpiece. Although all of his story collections contain interesting pieces, nowhere does he surpass the achievement of *American Earth* (1931), *We Are the Living* (1933), *Kneel to the Rising Sun* (1935), and *Southways* (1938). The more extensive offerings in *Jackpot* (1940) and *The Complete Stories of Erskine Caldwell* (1953) make them, also, important titles in his canon. Many commentators have suggested that Caldwell's forte is the short story; and the large measure of truth in this assertion is demonstrated by such sparkling creations as "Midsummer Passion," "Saturday Afternoon," "Country Full of Swedes," "Maud Island," "Candy-Man Beechum," "The Growing Season," "Kneel to the Rising Sun," "The Fly in the Coffin," and perhaps twenty others that, collected, would constitute a classic of the genre. In nonfiction his best works are *Some American People* (1935), *Call It Experience* (1951), *In Search of Bisco* (1965), *Deep South* (1968), and— with Margaret Bourke-White—*You Have Seen Their Faces* (1937) and *North of the Danube* (1939).

SURVEY OF CRITICISM

In view of the quantity of his production, the variety of his literary forms, the high quality of his best work, and the paucity of critical response to date, Erskine Caldwell studies are now only a shadow of what they will become. For the critic and teacher, one of the rewards of Caldwell scholarship is the chance to help refurbish the reputation of a neglected and worthy writer, ultimately restoring his best works to circulation and enlightened consideration. The superior novels belong on bookstore shelves just as the superior stories deserve to be included in the anthologies that introduce students to important writers. What Malcolm Cowley's *The Portable Faulkner* once did to revive flagging interest in William Faulkner, a similar volume could do to hasten the long-delayed reconsideration of Erskine Caldwell. The American Academy of Arts and Letters has recently embraced his company; it remains for the American academy of students, teachers, and scholars to do the same.

The history of Caldwell criticism from its beginning in the 1930s through the 1960s is one of acclaim and anticipation followed by disregard, disdain, and dismissal. The more he wrote, the more his reputation sagged, leaving behind what was perceived as the unfulfilled promise of the early books and stories. By the 1950s Caldwell-baiting had become a sport for reviewers who used him as a target for their often mindless showmanship. Since the late 1960s, however, his stock has gradually risen until now a full-scale revival seems imminent.

Many early commentators, among them Randall Jarrell and Carl Van Doren, praised Caldwell for his humor, while others such as Norman MacLeod, writing in *New Masses*, were attracted to his social consciousness. In 1935 Kenneth Burke argued that Caldwell was not primarily a social realist, humorous or otherwise, but rather a dreamer of the fantastic and surreal. In that same decade Southern advocates such as John Donald Wade and Donald Davidson accused him of grossly distorting and selling out his homeland. Joseph Warren Beach, in 1941, saw Caldwell's fiction as a laudable hybrid in which social consciousness served art without losing its own import and impact. Three years later Malcolm Cowley cited unresolved difficulties in his own attempt to reconcile Caldwell's social criticism with the seemingly willful disreputableness of his largely unsympathetic fictional characters. In the 1950s Robert Cantwell, in his introduction to *The Humorous Side of Erskine Caldwell*, defended his subject as a great humorist and, in a separate article, discussed the complex relationship between Caldwell's characters and the land that holds them in its sway. Despite kind words from C. Hugh Holman, George Snell, and Walter Allen, generally negative assessments by John M. Bradbury, Louise Y. Gossett, and others comprise the majority of what little serious consideration Caldwell received during most of the 1960s.

The first comprehensive study of Caldwell's work is James Korges's pamphlet *Erskine Caldwell* (1969), which, despite its excesses, offers useful insights into the novels and focuses deserved attention on the nonfiction. In a 1971 article, James J. Thompson, Jr., examines Caldwell's portrayal of Southern religion. The only English-language book on Caldwell to appear during the 1970s is William A. Sutton's *Black Like It Is/Was* (1974), an ambitious if uneven attempt to describe Caldwell's treatment of race. In 1975 R. J. Gray discussed Caldwell's comedy of frustration in light of the tradition of old Southwest humor. The following year saw two important statements: Sylvia Jenkins Cook's comparison of Caldwell and Faulkner in *From Tobacco Road to Route 66* and Malcolm Cowley's support for a Caldwell revival (subsequently published as part of *And I Worked at the Writer's Trade*). Scott MacDonald's examination of repetition as technique in the stories (1977) and Guy Owen's articles on the unpublished poetry (1978) and *The Sacrilege of Alan Kent* (1979) are also worthwhile. Of considerable interest, despite its stylistic and structural flaws, is the 1979 issue of *Pembroke Magazine*, which devotes 184 pages to a potpourri of Caldwelliana.

The 1980s have thus far generated several articles and, more significantly, the two most important books to date on Caldwell's work. Notable articles include Guy Owen's consideration of *The Bastard* and *Poor Fool*, published in *A Fair Day in the Affections* (1980); John Seelye's study of Caldwell and Harry Crews (1980); and Robert D. Jacobs's discussion of *Tobacco Road* and the low-life comic tradition in Southern humor (1980). The two highlights of 50 years of Caldwell criticism are *Critical Essays on Erskine Caldwell* (1981), edited by Scott MacDonald, and James E. Devlin's *Erskine Caldwell* (1984). In an excellent introductory essay MacDonald both surveys at length the history of Caldwell scholarship and offers a new approach to his subject based on Caldwell's own aesthetic of spontaneous storytelling. This book reprints many of the most important reviews of and essays on Caldwell's work, introduces Sylvia Jenkins Cook's new essay on the nonfiction, and reprints twenty essays by Caldwell himself. Although MacDonald labels Caldwell "a great writer," Devlin assesses him more modestly as "an important minor figure in the broad tradition of

American naturalism.'' Both agree, however, that Caldwell has been the victim of unwarranted neglect. *Erskine Caldwell* is flawed by a somewhat disjointedly amorphous structure and the unevenness of its interpretations. For example, although Devlin's analysis of *God's Little Acre* in terms of its Dionysian orientation is a real contribution, his estimation of *Journeyman* reductively wrings darkness and gloom out of this lively, often funny, book. On balance, Devlin's is the most comprehensive treatment of Caldwell's canon and career. Even its deficiencies should stimulate profitable discussion among potential correctors.

Students of Caldwell eventually must account for the disparity between his reputation in America, which sagged for decades, and his more stable reputation abroad, especially in Europe, the Soviet Union, and Japan. As early as 1961 Stewart Benedict posited cultural and psychological differences as reasons for the greater esteem in which Caldwell was held by the French critical establishment. More recently, Hartmut Heuermann's excellent *Erskine Caldwell's Short Stories* (1974), in German, surveys Caldwell's European reputation. Despite these beginnings, the bulk of work on Caldwell from a culturally comparative perspective remains to be done.

Although there is no full biography of Caldwell, the bibliographical compilation of his work has been given a good start by Scott MacDonald and William White. The former's contribution to *First Printings of American Authors* and his evaluative checklist of Caldwell's short fiction, both of which appeared in 1978, are substantially complete. The latter's checklist of reviews and criticism through 1980 is a boon to all Caldwell scholars. Good sources of information on both Caldwell's life and writings are the many interviews with Caldwell published over the years. The most comprehensive of these is that conducted by Elizabeth Broadwell and Ronald Hoag in 1980 and published serially by three journals in 1982–83. Substantive earlier interviews include those with Richard Sale and Jac Tharpe.

Erskine Caldwell's contribution to American literature can no longer be ignored. To evaluate that contribution is a significant opportunity and challenge.

BIBLIOGRAPHY

Works by Erskine Caldwell

The Bastard. New York: Heron Press, 1929.
Poor Fool. New York: Rariora Press, 1930.
American Earth. New York: Scribner's Sons, 1931.
Tobacco Road. New York: Scribner's Sons, 1932.
God's Little Acre. New York: Viking, 1933.
We Are the Living. New York: Viking, 1933.
Journeyman. New York: Viking, 1935.
Kneel to the Rising Sun. New York: Viking, 1935.
Some American People. New York: R. M. McBride, 1935.
The Sacrilege of Alan Kent. Portland, Maine: Falmouth Book House, 1936.

You Have Seen Their Faces, with Margaret Bourke-White. New York: Viking, 1937.

Southways. New York: Viking, 1938.

North of the Danube, with Margaret Bourke-White. New York: Viking, 1939.

Jackpot. New York: Duell, Sloan and Pearce, 1940.

Trouble in July. New York: Duell, Sloan and Pearce, 1940.

Say, Is This the U.S.A., with Margaret Bourke-White. New York: Duell, Sloan and
    Pearce, 1941.

All-Out on the Road to Smolensk. New York: Duell, Sloan and Pearce, 1942.

Russia at War, with Margaret Bourke-White. London and New York: Hutchinson, 1942.

Georgia Boy. New York: Duell, Sloan and Pearce, 1943.

Tragic Ground. New York: Duell, Sloan and Pearce, 1944.

A House in the Uplands. New York: Duell, Sloan and Pearce, 1946.

The Sure Hand of God. New York: Duell, Sloan and Pearce, 1947.

This Very Earth. New York: Duell, Sloan and Pearce, 1948.

Place Called Estherville. New York: Duell, Sloan and Pearce, 1949.

Episode in Palmetto. New York: Duell, Sloan and Pearce, 1950.

Call It Experience. New York: Duell, Sloan and Pearce, 1951.

A Lamp for Nightfall. New York: Duell, Sloan and Pearce, 1952.

The Complete Stories of Erskine Caldwell. Boston: Little, Brown, 1953.

Close to Home. New York: Farrar, Straus and Cudahy, 1962.

In Search of Bisco. New York: Farrar, Straus and Giroux, 1965.

Miss Mamma Aimee. New York: New American Library, 1967.

Writing in America. New York: Phaedra, 1967.

Deep South. New York: Weybright and Talley, 1968.

The Weather Shelter. New York: World, 1969.

Afternoons in Mid-America. New York: Dodd, Mead, 1976.

"Interview with Erskine Caldwell," ed. Jac Tharpe. *Southern Quarterly* 20, no. 1 (1981):
    64–74.

"The Art of Fiction LXII: Erskine Caldwell," ed. Elizabeth Pell Broadwell and Ronald
    Wesley Hoag. *Paris Review* 24, no. 4 (1982): 126–57.

" 'A Writer First': An Interview with Erskine Caldwell," ed. Elizabeth Pell Broadwell
    and Ronald Wesley Hoag. *Georgia Review* 36 (1982): 82–101.

"Erskine Caldwell on Southern Realism," ed. Elizabeth Pell Broadwell and Ronald
    Wesley Hoag. *Mississippi Quarterly* 36 (1983): 579–84.

Studies of Erskine Caldwell

Those studies mentioned in the survey of criticism that do not receive a separate citation
here are included in *Critical Essays on Erskine Caldwell*, edited by Scott MacDonald.

Cantwell, Robert. "Caldwell's Characters: Why Don't They Leave?" *Georgia Review*
    11 (1957): 252–64.

———. Introduction. *The Humorous Side of Erskine Caldwell*. New York: Duell, Sloan
    and Pearce, 1951, pp. ix-xxxi.

Cook, Sylvia Jenkins. *From Tobacco Road to Route 66: The Southern Poor White in
    Fiction*. Chapel Hill: University of North Carolina Press, 1976, pp. 64–84.

Devlin, James E. *Erskine Caldwell*. Boston: Twayne, 1984.

"Erskine Caldwell: America's Great 20th Century Writer." *Pembroke Magazine* 11 (1979): 2–185.

Gossett, Louise Y. *Violence in Recent Southern Fiction*. Durham, N.C.: Duke University Press, 1965, pp. 3–47.

Heuermann, Hartmut. *Erskine Caldwell's Short Stories*. Frankfurt/Main, Germany: Peter Lang, 1974.

Holman, C. Hugh. "The View from the Regency-Hyatt: Southern Social Issues and the Outer World." *Southern Fiction Today: Renascence and Beyond*. Ed. George Core. Athens: University of Georgia Press, 1969, pp. 16–32.

Jacobs, Robert D. "*Tobacco Road*: Lowlife and the Comic Tradition." *The American South: Portrait of a Culture*. Ed. Louis D. Rubin, Jr. Baton Rouge and London: Louisiana State University Press, 1980, pp. 206–26.

Korges, James. *Erskine Caldwell*. Minneapolis: University of Minnesota Press, 1969.

MacDonald, Scott, ed. *Critical Essays on Erskine Caldwell*. Boston: G. K. Hall, 1981.

———. "Erskine Caldwell 1903–   ." *First Printings of American Authors: Contributions Toward Descriptive Checklists*. Ed. Matthew J. Bruccoli and others. Detroit: Gale Research, 1978. 2: 85–97.

Owen, Guy. "The Apprenticeship of Erskine Caldwell: An Examination of *The Bastard* and *Poor Fool*." *A Fair Day in the Affections: Literary Essays in Honor of Robert B. White, Jr*. Ed. Jack D. Durant and M. Thomas Hester. Raleigh, N.C.: Winston Press, 1980, pp. 197–204.

———. "Erskine Caldwell's Unpublished Poems." *South Atlantic Bulletin* 43, no. 2 (1978): 53–57.

———. "*The Sacrilege of Alan Kent* and the Apprenticeship of Erskine Caldwell." *Southern Literary Journal* 12, no. 2 (1979): 36–46.

Sale, Richard B. "An Interview in Florida with Erskine Caldwell." See MacDonald, *Critical Essays*.

Seelye, John. "Georgia Boys: The Redclay Satyrs of Erskine Caldwell and Harry Crews." *Virginia Quarterly Review* 56 (1980): 612–26.

Snell, George. *The Shapers of American Fiction 1798–1947*. New York: Cooper Square, 1961, pp. 263–88.

Sutton, William A. *Black Like It Is/Was: Erskine Caldwell's Treatment of Racial Themes*. Metuchen, N.J.: Scarecrow Press, 1974.

Wade, John Donald. "Sweet Are the Uses of Degeneracy." *Southern Review* 1 (1936): 449–66.

White, William. "About Erskine Caldwell: A Checklist, 1933–1980." *Bulletin of Bibliography* 39 (1982): 9–16.

———. "About Erskine Caldwell: Addenda." *Bulletin of Bibliography* 39 (1982): 224–26.

HELEN S. GARSON

Truman Capote
(1924–1984)

Truman Capote was an extremely visible writer, thrusting himself constantly before the public. Throughout his life he gave carefully choreographed, sometimes flamboyant, interviews; but almost always, Capote stressed his seriousness as an artist. Another side of Capote appeared in front of television cameras where he seemed to enjoy the role of jester and clown. Even the most private facts of his personal life became part of the entertainment.

Most television viewers and even some readers of his books took Capote's self-mockery both as the measure of the man and the writer. His short stature, his high-pitched voice, and his speech mannerisms led much of the public to focus on him rather than his writing. Some forgot and some never discovered the diversity and complexity of the work.

BIOGRAPHY

Although Truman Capote rejected the designation "Southern writer" (he was a resident of New York for almost 50 years), readers and critics continue to see him as a Southerner. Named Truman Persons at his birth, 30 September 1924, in New Orleans, he lived in Louisiana until he was four. During the next six years he was cared for by his mother's relatives in rural Alabama. His parents had been divorced, and his mother had moved to New York, where she married Joseph Capote. After several years she sent for her son, who was then adopted by her second husband. Truman Persons became Truman Capote.

Capote's schooling was fragmentary and brief; he attended both public and private schools, including a military academy. He did not finish high school, dropping out at the age of seventeen. Educationally, Capote was the "intellectual hitchhiker" he calls one of his fictional doubles, P. B. Jones of the "Answered Prayers" stories.

After leaving school, Capote held a number of jobs, several of them at the *New Yorker* magazine, where he worked for two years. He had begun writing during the time he was still in school, and he continued to write while working full-time. He was still in his teens when several of his short stories were published, among them "Miriam," for which he won the O. Henry Prize. Characteristically, Capote gave several different reasons for the brevity of his stint at the *New Yorker*. In retrospect, the important fact is that his leaving enabled him to give all his time to writing his first novel.

Although Capote had begun a work called *Summer Crossing*, he soon abandoned it for the book that made him famous at the age of twenty-four: *Other Voices, Other Rooms*. Controversial though it was, harshly criticized by some and hailed by others as part of a new movement in literature, the novel was a commercial success. Nobody had been able to determine how important Capote's self-publicizing ability was in creating an audience, but few critics have spoken of that first novel without mentioning his use of public relations and provocative photographs.

Playwright, essayist, short-story writer, film scenarist, and novelist, Capote tried many modes, though not with equal success. Different works show different sides, like the man himself: sad and funny, melancholy and happy; some have a joyful sense of life, whereas others are filled with overtones of death.

He told stories of children growing up in the country, learning about the seasons, learning about tenderness; he depicted another world of children who are preyed upon by adults; he created young girls who long for those irreconcilable opposites, fame and security; he wrote of stars and of cleaning ladies; he drew—and empathized with—murderers; and he showed victims of many kinds—young, middle-aged, and old.

The contrary sides of Capote's work have been described as daylight and darkness, terms that seem applicable to the writer's own personality. Capote never escaped from the sorrows and bitterness of his childhood, although some of the happier moments are also woven into his writing. Nevertheless, to the end of his life Capote saw himself as an abandoned child, unwanted and unloved by either parent. Many of his stories contain orphan figures, a type he identified with—lost, solitary, vulnerable children who belong nowhere. Even one of his very late stories, "Dazzle," written in 1980, gnaws on the old, unresolved issues.

Autobiographical elements are inherent in Capote's characters. Not only do the fictional children portray something of the author himself, but also several versions of various relatives appear in the stories: for example, Miss Sook Faulk, a cousin with whom Capote lived for a while during his childhood, is his "friend" in "A Christmas Memory," Dolly in "The Grass Harp," and herself in "The Thanksgiving Visitor." In the short stories, young and middle-aged men who are destructive, cruel, and sometimes decadent often may be identified with Capote himself. Indeed, the writer almost insists on such a reading in the stories written in the 1970s. In the nonfiction work, the essays, *The Muses Are Heard*, and the "nonfiction novel," *In Cold Blood*, Capote appears both as observer and occasional participant.

A list of Capote's books might suggest that he was a prolific writer; however, that was not the case. He had most of his work published as short pieces in magazines and later collected them, occasionally publishing parts of these collections under different titles. As a result, *The Selected Writings of Truman Capote* (1963) contains stories from *A Tree of Night and Other Stories* (all of which had appeared originally in magazines), parts of *Breakfast at Tiffany's: A Novel and Three Stories*, and selections from *Local Color*. *The Dogs Bark* (1973) also has parts of *Local Color*, as well as selections from *Observations* and *The Muses Are Heard*. Capote's last book, *Music for Chameleons* (1980), was publicized and reviewed as "new writings," but it consisted of pieces that had appeared in several magazines, predominantly Andy Warhol's *Interview*.

A widely traveled man, Capote occasionally lived abroad, often writing about the places he visited or settled in. His longtime friend and companion, Jack Dunphy, was generally with him. Dunphy occupied Capote's house in Switzerland but recently has been living in another Capote home in Long Island, where Capote spent much of his time before his death in Los Angeles, 24 August 1984. He died at the home of Joanne Carson, a former wife of the famed talk show host, Johnny Carson.

There were many ironies associated with Capote's death; not the least was the fact that it took place in a city he claimed to despise. Several of his essays about Hollywood, in particular, and California, in general, stress the deathlike quality of what he saw as an artificial world. Yet the artificial world was the one Capote deliberately chose for himself in the last two decades of his life.

With the success of *In Cold Blood* (1966), Capote was at the high point of his career. Not only was he famous, he was rich; and he was in demand everywhere. To commemorate his achievement he gave a ball, which several people called "the party of the decade." Reporters reviewed the party as if it were one of Capote's plays, and it was written up in newspapers and magazines for weeks. What is important about the party is that it punctuates the end of Capote's significant writing as well as his charmed social life. Never again was he able to write a sustained work of any value. The stories of the 1970s were failures. Not only were they badly written, they were cruel, gossipy tales about the jet set that had accepted him as one of their own.

Attacks and counterattacks were common for a time. Doors were closed to Capote, who declared himself friendless but still an artist. There were frequent accounts of the writer's bouts of drinking and drug taking. There were arrests for drunk driving. Capote and those sympathetic to him blamed his condition on the trauma left by his relationship with the murderers depicted in *In Cold Blood*. Although he wrote and socialized less in the last decade of his life, newspapers continued to treat him as a celebrity, reporting his illnesses, hospital stays, and nights on the town.

After the failure of the stories intended as the nucleus of *Answered Prayers*,

Capote kept announcing that he was rewriting the book. Although he published another collection, *Music for Chameleons* (1980), there continued to be statements about the rewriting of the novel. Obituaries and eulogies following his death noted that Capote had just completed the final chapter of *Answered Prayers* while visiting in California. Whether that is fact or a final example of Capote's personal inventiveness remains to be seen. Planning to have yet another splashy party in celebration of the book's completion, Capote died a month before his sixtieth birthday.

MAJOR THEMES

Capote's first novel, *Other Voices, Other Rooms* (1948), belongs to what Irving Malin has called "New American Gothic." It also represents, along with the work of other young writers of Capote's era, a different type of fiction, a change from the predominantly sociological and realistic mode popular in Capote's youth. The only link *Other Voices, Other Rooms* has to the realistic mode is that it contains a taboo subject, homosexuality.

Other Voices, Other Rooms is a novel unlike others that use elements of Southern gothic to symbolize a dying civilization or a corrupted world. Capote's novel is concerned with a small cast of characters and a limited landscape. There is no examination of the Southern past, its history, its failures, its guilt. Written in a highly stylized form, the novel tells of a boy's search for love and of his entrapment in a narcissistic existence from which there is no escape. The novel reveals qualities that became characteristic of Capote's writing: poetic language, with strong use of symbols and images; the lost child motif; and the themes of betrayal and loss of innocence.

The collection *A Tree of Night and Other Stories* (1949), published a year after *Other Voices, Other Rooms*, has some of the same dark and gothic elements of the novel, although not all of the stories are set in the South. Five of the stories—"Master Misery," "Miriam," "The Headless Hawk," "Shut a Final Door," and "A Tree of Night"—contain aspects of fantasy, fear, and horror. Each is about loneliness and disintegration. The young women in "Master Misery" and "A Tree of Night" are victimized in part because of their own fears. The elderly woman in "Miriam" slides into a schizophrenic world because of her isolation from the real one. The young men in "The Headless Hawk" and "Shut a Final Door" betray everyone who loves them and ultimately come to a point of paralysis and collapse. "Children on Their Birthdays," one of the three "sunny" stories in the collection, is in numerous ways a forerunner of Capote's novel *Breakfast at Tiffany's* (1958). The aspiring young female character, the devoted swains, and the poetic use of nostalgia appear in both.

The light and humorous side of Capote permeates "Children on Their Birthdays," with its sparkling dialogue, succession of funny episodes, and eccentric characters. The central figure, Miss Lily Jane Bobbit, is obviously a fantasy child, a compendium of the wishes, desires, dreams and hopes of children, and, perhaps at some level, of adults. Her longing to be a star, to be somebody, to be extraordinary, mirrors the longings of everyone, including Capote himself as a boy. Miss Bobbit is a creature who lives in the sky, an idea that Capote uses in other stories and develops more completely in *Breakfast at Tiffany's*. Those who live in the sky are not like the rest of us: they are wild things; they cannot be captured; and even if they long for peace and security and fame they cannot attain them. They vanish like our dreams of childhood.

Nostalgia, or a type of pleasurable melancholy, is a hallmark of much of Capote's writing; the sweet, brief moments of joy that disappear like flower petals or autumn leaves are inherent to his narrative devices. The teller of the tale, sometimes Capote or his persona, looks back to a time or episode of happiness. In "Children on Their Birthdays" the narrator tells of a single year when a young girl came to his town. To create the aura of reality within a dream, the author uses both structure and symbol, something like movement within a paperweight. At the beginning we are told the ending. In the novel *The Grass Harp* (1951), which appeared two years after *A Tree of Night and Other Stories*, the narrator tells about the "lovely years," for him the years between the ages of eleven and sixteen. Like many of Capote's other characters, Collin Fenwick, the narrator, is an orphan—shy, delicate, and sensitive—like the boys in *Other Voices, Other Rooms*, "A Christmas Memory," and "The Thanksgiving Visitor." Raised by two maiden sisters, Collin enters an idyllic world and from his cousin Dolly he learns about love and happiness. But Collin also learns about death and memory, sadness and sweetness that are blended together.

The air of nostalgia and remembrance in the story is close to that of *Breakfast at Tiffany's*, as is the circular structure. The gentle, elderly cousin who teaches the boy about nature and about love is a forerunner of the old, eccentric cousin in "A Christmas Memory," and there are certain resemblances in the conclusions to the two stories. The tonal qualities of the endings are, however, very different. Although *The Grass Harp* ends with an air of melancholy, it is a melancholy that also contains a kind of joy, the joy of memory, the wholeness of existence. In the later story the melancholy is not tempered by joy of any kind, and the reader is left with a sense of loss and pain.

Holly Golightly, of *Breakfast at Tiffany's*, is another one of Capote's lost children—sweet, touching and vulnerable. But, like Miss Lily Jane Bobbit, and unlike the lost boys of Capote's stories, Holly is also tough. A survivor, she is also one of the "wild things," one of the creatures who live in the sky. She wants what all the young people of Capote's stories want—a secure world, a place "where nothing very bad could happen."

To the narrator, Holly is a part of his own beginnings: a time when he was starting out, a time of hopefulness and disappointments, a time of finding out who one is, a time of youth. The story is not a true one, and Capote never suggests it is anything but an invention; nevertheless, Capote puts himself into it, just as he does in "Children on Their Birthdays." Because he takes no fictional guise, wears no masks, and because he is who he says he is and attaches real facts about himself (his own birthday, for example), the story seems closer than fiction. Once again, it is a story filled with dualities: humor and sadness, happiness and pain, with madcap episodes and moments of tenderness. But it is the tone painting of the story that strikes the reader with greatest force, the colors and scenes that sometimes have the qualities of stained-glass paintings.

"A Christmas Memory" shares many of the characteristics of other Capote stories. The nostalgia and sadness are greater in it than in the earlier stories, perhaps because the loss that occurs is one with which the reader may easily identify. It is not so much the specific loss of a beloved person, although that does occur, but rather all that is suggested in the passing of a world that can never be recaptured, the lost Edenic world. In memory that strips away what it chooses, the childhood world comes to us as idyllic; the reader mourns its loss at the end of the story.

While he was writing his short stories, novels, and plays, Capote also produced nonfiction of various kinds. In 1950 he published, under the title *Local Color*, a collection of sketches written over a period of years. The eight sketches are accompanied by photographs that lend another dimension to the writing. Although Capote was not a photographer, his sensitivity to the medium was recognized by Richard Avedon, who asked him to write the narrative for his book *Observations* (1959). The essays in *Local Color* describe New Orleans, Manhattan, Brooklyn, Hollywood, Haiti, Paris, Ischia, Tangiers. Unlike his next nonfiction book, the articles in *Local Color* have no relationship to each other, except in the persona of Capote.

The Muses Are Heard (1956), originally a series of travel articles in the *New Yorker*, connects each segment to the central story, a cultural exchange between the United States and the USSR. In this story about the theatrical troupe that put on the opera *Porgy and Bess*, the people who accompanied the performers, and the Russians involved in the venture, Capote is at his wittiest; he also captures the gloom and fear in the Russia of the late 1950s.

The Dogs Bark (1973), a collection of Capote's essays, includes one of his most famous, "The Duke in His Domain," a portrait of Marlon Brando at the height of his career. Capote's skill as an interviewer and his ability to stand back from the subject, as well as his unobtrusiveness, are evident in this article, qualities that are even more important in *In Cold Blood*. Capote is, however, often more personal in some of the other pieces in *The Dogs Bark*. "Louis Armstrong," which had accompanied Avedon's portrait in *Observations*, describes Capote's long-standing appreciation of Armstrong's kindness.

Another memorable piece from *Observations*, and reprinted in *The Dogs Bark*, is about Marilyn Monroe. The commentary, written a few years before the actress's death, captures much about Monroe's personality that led to her suicide. Capote's interest in the childlike, insecure Monroe later prompted another essay that became part of *Music for Chameleons* (1980).

With *In Cold Blood* (1966), Capote brought together all the skills he had learned throughout his career of writing both fiction and nonfiction. In this work he is both reporter and creative artist, displaying what he considered a new art form, the "nonfiction novel." Both the term and Capote's claim to be the originator of the type have been the source of much controversy. There is no question, however, that the technique has been extremely influential since the appearance of the novel. Further, the book was one of the century's greatest commercial successes. It sold in great numbers not only in the United States but also in translation in 25 foreign countries.

Capote's interest in what Robert Langbaum called "motiveless malignancy" came about from reading a news account of a murder that took place in Kansas in 1959. When he decided that he wanted to write a book about the events, he arranged to publish in the *New Yorker* a series of articles that he would later rework for a book. To prepare himself for this new project, he researched material about criminals, meeting a number of them, including the two accused of murdering the Clutter family in Kansas.

Capote's techniques in relating the story suggest a mixture of reporter, painter, photographer, and novelist. Even though the outcome was known to every reader, the four-part book is a masterful study in suspense. Only the final section lacks the drama of the three preceding segments. The sometimes overwhelming number of details about the last five years of the murderers' lives spent in effort to avoid the death penalty necessarily detracts from the taut drama of the story. There is also a certain lopsidedness in Capote's interest in one of the criminals, Perry Smith. His attraction to Smith is easy to understand: Smith had been a lonely boy, a deserted child, someone who never found a place for himself in society. In many ways, Capote identified with Smith, who felt himself unloved and unwanted, who, as boy and man, always expected to be betrayed.

After publication of *In Cold Blood*, Capote was to publish only one more book before his death, *Music for Chameleons*, another collection of unrelated pieces: short stories, a novella, and "Conversational Portraits." Although a number of reviewers praised the work, the part they focused on was the novella, *Handcarved Coffins*, which Capote called "A Nonfiction Account of an American Crime." Because of its subject and Capote's participation in the story, the work invited comparison with *In Cold Blood*, but readers generally found it less forceful, less interesting, and too derivative.

Three of the "Conversational Portraits" received passing praise from reviewers: the essay on Marilyn Monroe, entitled "Beautiful Child"; a piece called "A Day's Work," in which Capote tells about his cleaning woman; and the very personal "Nocturnal Turnings," where the writer talks about his fears and beliefs and many of his experiences from childhood through adulthood. He also makes a statement that was picked up by numerous commentators: "I'm an alcoholic . . . a drug addict . . . [a] homosexual." Once more the familiar note is sounded at the end, the conviction that he has nobody but himself, that he is completely alone.

Several of the stories in *Music for Chameleons* are reworkings of those published in the 1970s in *Esquire*. Although each story had an individual title, it was to be part of the book-length *Answered Prayers*. Each story is about the sexual behavior of famous people, known nationally and internationally. Readers familiar with Capote's circle have identified the characters, but in many instances the guessing game is unnecessary because the names of numerous celebrities are undisguised. In the stories Capote gossips about socialites, artists, writers, photographers, movie and television stars, presidents and their wives. The stories are cruel, often crude, and rambling. For the reader, aside from the dubious pleasure of learning about the secrets of the rich and famous, the one value of the stories is that they provide more information about Capote himself. Three of the four stories of *Answered Prayers* have a narrator named P. B. Jones, with whom Capote chose to identify himself. Much autobiographical information is given through Jones, a writer who is drawn to be Capote's stand-in. The reader wonders about Capote's intentions in creating a monstrous and corrupt figure in Jones, for Jones is not only given Capote's own background but is also made the author of Capote's stories.

Jones makes an important statement in "Unspoiled Monsters": that his one "obligation was to his talent." That is exactly the point that Capote made frequently in the last years of his life. When interviewers questioned him about the kind of material he wrote, Capote answered that the artist uses what he has, what is available to him. He and those he wrote about are merely mortal, but art is everlasting, "durable and perfect."

SURVEY OF CRITICISM

When *Other Voices, Other Rooms* was published in 1948, it was praised by Mary McGrory, but disliked by Elizabeth Hardwick and Diana Trilling, whereas Leslie Fiedler, John Aldridge, and Orville Prescott gave it mixed evaluation. Such splitting is characteristic of the critical reaction to all Capote's work. Of the 25 reviews of *A Tree of Night and Other Stories* (1949), four were unfavorable, nine were mixed, and twelve were favorable. Even the nonfiction book *Local Color* (1950) got mixed reviews. John Aldridge, writing about Capote in *After the Lost Generation: A Critical Study of the Writers of Two Wars* (1951), saw him as unable to create works of any social significance. Malcolm Cowley, however, in "American Novels Since the War" (*New Republic*, 28 December 1953), called Capote a significant new writer. Although Capote lacks interest in social realism, Cowley noted, he is concerned with significant personal questions.

In an early interview with Rochelle Girson, (*Saturday Review of Literature*, 12 February 1949), Capote disclaimed being a Southern writer or a Freudian. Although Capote gave many interviews over the years, some of the subject matter remained constant. When *The Grass Harp* both as book and play received the usual mixed reception, Capote defended himself in a number of interviews. Harvey Breit, in "Talk with Truman Capote," in the *New York Times Book Review*, recounts Capote's criticism of the critics as well as his statement that he sought to write things "psychologically and emotionally true." In interviews with Henry Hewes and with Norton Elliot, who wrote "Fable Drawn From Life: Capote's 'Grass Harp' Deals with Character He Knew As a Child" for the *New York Times*, Capote discussed not only his childhood relationship to the story of *The Grass Harp* but also the role Robert Frost played in his leaving the *New Yorker*.

Like the reviews of the play *The Grass Harp*, those of the play *The House of Flowers* were generally unfavorable; however, Capote's next endeavor, his nonfiction book *The Muses Are Heard*, was praised by most critics, as was his next novel, *Breakfast at Tiffany's* (1958). Also, beginning in 1958, numerous articles about Capote's style and subjects began to appear. Paul Levine, in "Truman Capote: The Revelation of the Broken Image," finds two kinds of stories, dark and light, and discusses a search for identity as a theme of the early stories. In "The Grotesque in Modern American Fiction," William Van O'Connor comments on Capote's use of abnormal characters and situations (1959). Considering Capote to be a writer of romances, Ihab Hassan, in "The Daydream and Nightmare of Narcissus" (1960), discusses Capote's themes and his two styles—dark and light. In another essay, "The Character of Post-war Fiction in America" (*The English Journal*, 51, 1962), Hassan counts Capote one of ten major American writers.

Avedon's *Observations* (1959), with commentary by Capote, also received mixed reviews. In 1961 Walter Sullivan, writing for *South: Modern Southern Literature in the Fifties*, criticizes Capote's grotesquerie, but Irving Malin's *New American Gothic* (1962) expresses a completely different opinion of gothicism and grotesquerie and the ways Capote used them. A chapter entitled "Truman Capote and the Twisted Self" in Chester Eisinger's *Fiction in the Forties* (1963) also examines Capote's use of the gothic tradition. Louise Gossett, in *Violence in Recent Southern Fiction* (1965), finds that though Capote's abnormal characters are unable to love, they still search for love. She also points out that the characters lack moral dimensions.

In 1965 Kenneth Tynan accused Capote of moral irresponsibility in relationship to the criminals he wrote about in *In Cold Blood*; Tynan echoed the most frequent criticism of Capote from the beginning to the end of his career—that he lacked moral involvement. (The other was that his characters lacked substance.) In 1966 there were more interviews on as well as an outpouring of reviews of *In Cold Blood* and articles about the author and his work. Many critics saw the book as a brilliant work of art, whereas others saw it as hollow, immoral, voyeuristic, and self-promoting. In an interview with George Plimpton for the *New York Times Book Review* ("The Story Behind a Nonfiction Novel," 16 January 1966, pp. 2–3), Capote discussed his choice of subject, his invention of the nonfiction novel, and the two Kansas murderers.

At that time Capote declared he would write no more plays but would work only in forms that were more congenial to him; however, in 1966 he saw "A Christmas Memory" made into a television play. A year later, the short story "Among the Paths of Eden" appeared on television and received excellent reviews. But a revised version of *House of Flowers* was shown on Broadway, and, like its predecessor, failed.

In the late 1960s, Capote began to talk in interviews about his new project, *Answered Prayers*. He discussed it in a lengthy interview with Eric Norden for *Playboy* magazine (1968), with Alden Whitman for the *New York Times* in 1971, and with Gerald Clarke for *Esquire* in 1972. In the *Rolling Stone* interview with Jann Wenner, Capote stated he had begun writing *Answered Prayers* as early as 1956. In the *Village Voice* Arthur Bell's article on "La Côte Basque, 1965" (one of the stories of *Answered Prayers*) is entitled, "A Suicide Follows Capote's Latest Tale" (1975). Capote defended himself then, as he had in 1968 in an interview for *Mademoiselle*, when he talked about differences between artists and craftsmen, a point he was to make frequently over the following years. In interview after interview for the remainder of his life, he continued to stress the importance of writing over relationships. *Esquire* printed numerous letters praising the stories, but the majority of critics see them as mischievous, vengeful, and debauched. One of the best interviews with Capote is Ann Taylor Fleming's in the *New York Times Magazine* (1978): part 1, "The Descent from the Heights," and part 2, "The Private World of Truman Capote." Here Capote surveys his own life, talking of his childhood, his loneliness, and his homosexuality.

There are several bibliographies and checklists of Capote's work. The most important of them is Robert Stanton's *Truman Capote: A Primary and Secondary Bibliography* (1980). It lists everything written about Capote through 1979, as well as his works and the places of publication.

Although there are few book-length studies of Capote's work and fewer about the man, there are some lengthy treatises. Craig Goad's 50-page pamphlet, entitled *Daylight and Darkness, Dream and Delusion: The Works of Truman Capote* (1967), treats the psychological aspects of Capote's characters. One of the most revealing portraits of Capote himself appears in John Malcolm Brinnin's "The Picture of Little T. C. in a Prospect," in *Sextet: T. S. Eliot and Truman Capote and Others* (1981). Brinnin describes meeting Capote at Yaddo when Capote was writing his first novel; he describes the period of rising success, taking the story up to the writing of *In Cold Blood*. Brinnin shows Capote changing from naive charmer to cynical social climber for whom everything and everyone were material to put between the covers of a book. William Nance wrote the first book-length study; his *The Worlds of Truman Capote* (1970) traces the developement of the writer from the first stories through *In Cold Blood*. Nance's prophecy that Capote would go on to produce even more significant literature proved inaccurate. Helen S. Garson's *Truman Capote* (1980), the second and most recent book on Capote, presents biographical information and critical appraisal of Capote's work.

To date there is no full-scale biography of Capote, although Stanton calls Gerald Clarke Capote's biographer and says in his introduction to his bibliography that Clarke's book "is scheduled to be published . . . in late 1979." Clarke himself announced in television interviews after Capote's death that he was working on the biography. Undoubtedly, a large audience awaits the publication of a Capote biography, whoever writes it.

BIBLIOGRAPHY

Works by Truman Capote

Other Voices, Other Rooms. New York: Random House, 1948.

A Tree of Night and Other Stories. New York: Random House, 1949.

Local Color. New York: Random House, 1950.

The Grass Harp. New York: Random House, 1951.

The Grass Harp [Play]. New York: Random House, 1952.

The Muses Are Heard. New York: Random House, 1956.

Breakfast at Tiffany's: A Short Novel and Three Stories. New York: Random House, 1958.

Observations. Photographs by Richard Avedon, commentary by Truman Capote. New York: Simon and Schuster, 1959.

The Selected Writings of Truman Capote. New York: Random House, 1963.

A Christmas Memory. New York: Random House, 1966.

In Cold Blood. New York: Random House, 1966.

The Thanksgiving Visitor. New York: Random House, 1967.

House of Flowers [A Play]. New York: Random House, 1968.

Trilogy: An Experiment in Multimedia, with Eleanor Perry and Frank Perry. New York: Macmillan, 1969.

The Dogs Bark: Public People and Private Places. New York: Random House, 1973.

Music for Chameleons. New York: Random House, 1980.

Studies of Truman Capote

Aldridge, John. *After the Lost Generation: A Critical Study of the Writers of Two Wars*. New York: Noonday Press, 1958.

Bradbury, John. *Renaissance in the South: A Critical History of the Literature, 1920–1960*. Chapel Hill: University of North Carolina Press, 1963.

Breit, Harvey. *The Writer Observed*. Cleveland: World, 1956.

Brinnin, John Malcolm. *Sextet: T. S. Eliot and Truman Capote and Others*. New York: Delacorte Press, 1981.

Bryer, Jackson R. "Truman Capote: A Bibliography." *In Cold Blood: A Critical Handbook*. Ed. Irving Malin. Belmont, Cal.: Wadsworth, 1968.

Cowley, Malcolm. *The Literary Situation*. New York: Viking Press, 1954.

Eisinger, Chester. *Fiction of the Forties*. Chicago: University of Chicago Press, 1963.

Garson, Helen S. *Truman Capote*. New York: Frederick Ungar, 1980.

Gordon, Caroline and Allen Tate. *The House of Fiction*. New York: Charles Scribner's, 1960.

Gossett, Louise. *Violence in Recent Southern Fiction*. Durham, N.C.: Duke University Press, 1965.

Hassan, Ihab. *Radical Innocence: The Contemporary American Novel*. Princeton, N.J.: Princeton University Press, 1961.

Hill, Patti. "Truman Capote." *Writers at Work: The "Paris Review" Interviews*. Ed. Malcolm Cowley. New York: Viking Press, 1959.

Kazin, Alfred. *Bright Book of Life*. Boston: Little, Brown, 1971; New York: Delta, 1974.

———. *Contemporaries*. Boston: Little, Brown, 1962.

———. *The Open Form: Essays for Our Time*. New York: Harcourt, Brace, and World, 1961.

Klein, Marcus. *After Alienation: American Novels in Mid-Century*. Cleveland: World, 1962.

Levine, Paul. "Truman Capote: *The Revelation of the Broken Image*." *Virginia Quarterly Review* 34 (1958): 600–17.

Malin, Irving. *New American Gothic*. Carbondale: Southern Illinois University Press, 1962.

Nance, William. *The Worlds of Truman Capote*. New York: Stein and Day, 1970.

Newquist, Roy. *Counterpoint*. Chicago: Rand McNally, 1964.

O'Connor, William Van. "The Grotesque in Modern American Fiction." *College English* 20 (April 1959): 342–47.

Schorer, Mark. "McCullers and Capote: Basic Patterns." *The Creative Present: Notes on Contemporary American Fiction*. Ed. Nona Balakian and Charles Simmons. Garden City, N.Y.: Doubleday, 1963.

Stanton, Robert J. *Truman Capote: A Primary and Secondary Bibliography*. Boston: G. K. Hall, 1980.

Starosciak, Kenneth. *Truman Capote: A Checklist*. New Brighton, Minn.: Starosciak, 1974.

Sullivan, Walter. "The Continuing Renascence: Southern Fiction in the Fifties." *South: Modern Southern Literature in Its Cultural Setting*. Ed. Louis Rubin, Jr., and Robert Jacobs. New York: Doubleday, 1961.

Waldmeir, Joseph, ed. *Recent American Fiction: Some Critical Views*. Boston: Houghton Mifflin, 1963.

Wall, Richard and Carl Craycraft. "A Checklist of Works about Truman Capote." *Bulletin of the New York Public Library* 71 (March 1967): 165–72.

West, Ray B. *The Short Story in America*. Chicago: Henry Regnery, 1952.

Harry Crews
(1935–   )

Although without great critical reputation at the time of this writing, Harry Crews is an important contemporary Southern novelist. Straddling the traditional rural South and the modern urban South, Crews has written novels demonstrating how a contemporary Southern writer can adapt traditional Southern concerns to a contemporary setting.

BIOGRAPHY

Harry Crews is unique among modern white Southern writers: when he writes about poor whites, he gives an insider's perspective. He grew up a member of the poorest class, so he does not observe poor whites with the detachment of many white Southern writers. He was born on 7 June 1935 near Alma in Bacon County, Georgia. Since his parents were tenant farmers, Crews's early life involved a great deal of moving around in search of better land and better living conditions. The life Crews's family lived was hard and violent, and in his fiction he presents man's struggle in the stark, simple terms he encountered as a child. His father died when Crews was two years old; in fact, Crews himself discovered his father's body. His mother remarried, to a violent, hard-drinking man. After his mother left his stepfather, the Crews family periodically spent time in Jacksonville, Florida, where his mother worked in a cigar factory. During his childhood, at least one event of direct relevance to his fiction occurred. At age five, he was afflicted with infantile paralysis, the treatment of which involved his lying in bed for a year or so. Often friends and neighbors would visit to examine his physical condition. Partly as a result of this experience, Crews developed his sympathy for freaks, who appear frequently in his fiction.

The society in which Crews grew up was essentially illiterate—Crews was the first of his family to graduate from high school—so to these people the oral tradition was very important. Feeling akin to his neighbors who liked to sit on the porch and tell stories, Crews considers himself a traditional storyteller.

Upon graduation from high school at age seventeen, Crews joined the Marines because, he has said, he did not know how to do anything and there were too many mouths to feed at home already. Although he has not written or said a great deal about his time in the Marines, he has indicated that parts of it were hard, but the experience did make him a man. He spent four years in the Marine Corps and then entered the University of Florida under the GI Bill. Growing restless after two years at the university, Crews left for eighteen months, spending that time traveling around the United States on a motorcycle. He then returned to the university to complete his degree. At the University of Florida he met Andrew Lytle, who was teaching creative writing there and who became a father figure to him. Crews retains great respect and admiration for Lytle, who taught him the discipline of writing. But he also feels that a barrier exists between him and Lytle because Lytle's background is aristocratic and agrarian while Crews's is poor white.

After graduating from the university, Crews put in a stint teaching junior high school English, returned to the university to earn an M.A. and then taught English at Broward Community College in Fort Lauderdale, Florida. In 1968, the year *The Gospel Singer*, his first novel, was published, he returned to his alma mater to teach English and creative writing and has remained there ever since. Unlike some writers who regard teaching as at best a necessary evil, Crews enjoys the association with aspiring young writers and feels that the job of teaching gives his life a necessary order.

Although Crews was something of a late bloomer as a writer (he was thirty-three when his first novel was published), he had served a long apprenticeship, writing even when he was a child. He has repeatedly acknowledged his debt to Graham Greene, whose novels he studied obsessively in order to learn the techniques of fiction writing. After *The Gospel Singer* was published, other novels followed quickly: *Naked in Garden Hills* (1969), *This Thing Don't Lead to Heaven* (1970), *Karate Is a Thing of the Spirit* (1971), *Car* (1972), *The Hawk Is Dying* (1973), *The Gypsy's Curse* (1974), and *A Feast of Snakes* (1976). Most of these novels were respectfully reviewed, though his works have elicited some negative comment. Since 1976 Crews has written mostly nonfiction. From 1975 to 1977 he wrote a regular monthly column for *Esquire* called "Grits," in which he dealt with personal or regional subjects. In 1978 he published his autobiography, *A Childhood: the biography of a place*, to almost universal acclaim. Then in 1979 *Blood and Grits*, a collection of magazine journalism previously published in *Esquire*, *Playboy*, and elsewhere, was released. *Florida Frenzy*, a collection of previously published fiction and nonfiction plus a new story, "The Enthusiast," appeared in 1982.

Crews is a remarkably direct and honest person. He has given numerous interviews, which along with his nonfiction are important sources for understanding his works and his personality. He is very open about his drinking problem and about his obsessions, anxieties, and uncertainties. Although he seems reasonably content and comfortable in Gainesville, Florida, he wrote his autobiography out of the feeling that he needed to discover who he is. He still feels more a part of the Bacon County of his childhood, with all the hardships and deprivation he and his family suffered, than of the comfortable university town where he now lives. In fact, *A Childhood* ends with Crews not really feeling a part of anywhere. It is this very sense of alienation and displacement, a result especially of his uncertain early life, out of which and about which he writes his fiction.

MAJOR THEMES

The novels of Harry Crews are short, intense, violent, and often very funny. As with most Southern writers, place is very important to him. He sets his novels either in primitive rural Georgia or in urban Florida. Yet the novels reveal the interconnection of rural and urban, for most of the important characters in the urban novels are of rural backgrounds, having moved, as did Crews himself and many other residents of South Georgia, from rural Georgia to urban North Florida. Much of the tension in the novels arises from the contrast between rural and urban, since even his rural settings are invaded by the modern world: television cameras and tourists are often seen invading formerly insular rural communities. Crews is sensitive to the impact of modernism on the South, yet he remains conscious of traditional ways of life. Ultimately, his novels are of the contemporary world, registering the shocks and changes of modern life.

Crews's novels reveal the human consequences of the disruption of tradition. His characters are filled with anxiety about the absence of meaning in their lives. And while they, like Crews himself, cannot find a place within any viable community, they do manifest an awareness of and desire for tradition and continuity. Ultimately, Crews is a religious writer, though he can find no creed in which to believe. His characters search for faith, belief, a sense of perfection. Yet they are finally forced to admit their human limitation.

In this connection Crews's use of freaks is revealing. He includes midgets in his first three novels, *The Gospel Singer*, *Naked in Garden Hills*, and *This Thing Don't Lead to Heaven*. In *Naked in Garden Hills* there appears a grotesquely fat man, and the protagonist of *The Gypsy's Curse* is a deaf mute with withered legs. Other characters, while not physically freakish, commit grotesque actions. Writing about grotesque characters, Crews follows an honorable Southern tradition, suggesting by grotesqueness man's incompleteness and alienation and the absurdity of human existence. Yet the significance of the grotesque in his world differs from that of Flannery O'Connor, Carson McCullers, or Erskine Caldwell, writers with whom he has often been compared. For those writers, grotesque characters are deviations from some at least implicit norm, religious in O'Connor's case, social in Caldwell's, and human in McCullers's. Crews is much less sure than are these other writers of the existence of any standards by which to measure the grotesque's deviation. To Crews, grotesques are individuals who cannot hide their aberrations, while the rest of us, who have our own abnormalities, can conceal them with impunity. In such a view normality becomes a meaningless term, a concept clung to in order to avoid the truth that all people are grotesques. Above all, in both fiction and life Crews demands honesty, so he removes the disguises by which humans attempt to conceal the truth about themselves and human existence.

His characters search for meaning through ritual activities they hope will gain them membership in communities or contact with some kind of continuity. For example, the protagonist of *The Hawk Is Dying* attempts to train a hawk in a time-honored way; the main character of *Karate Is a Thing of the Spirit* wants to become a member of a karate *dojo* by learning the proper method of practicing karate; the protagonist of *The Gypsy's Curse* resides in a kind of male commune centered upon a gymnasium—he disciplines both body and spirit through body building and hand balancing. These rituals, and others in other novels, however, are finally contaminated by the appearance of vulgar and raucous crowds and the particularly contemporary rituals of television and show business. Thus most of his characters finally fail to sustain meaningful membership in a community and are left at the end stripped of all but their individual resources.

Crews portrays man as, paradoxically, very primitive, acting on instinct and obsession, yet at least attempting to nourish the spiritual as well, for the aim of his protagonists is always to unite the self through ritual with some higher order of being, association with which will redeem their inherent incompleteness. Such actions are often violent, for Crews sees man as by nature violent. His characters, and Crews himself, are strongly attracted to physical confrontations with the world, and while he is aware of the potential social harm or destructiveness violence may bring, he sees violence as an attempt on the part of the individual to establish some kind of personal meaning. In a bankrupt social order inimical to the individual, man seeks to become a part of some larger order, not through denying his violent impulses but through disciplining them ritualistically. The rioting crowds that often appear at the ends of the novels express violence out of control. But his protagonists attempt to discipline those forces in themselves so that they and others will not be swept away by them.

A clear development in Crews's treatment of the theme of man's search for meaning can be seen in the course of his eight novels. The first three, *The Gospel Singer*, *Naked in Garden Hills*, and *This Thing Don't Lead to Heaven*, as the titles suggest, directly treat religion as a possible source of meaning. Since religion is found to be inadequate, the next four novels—*Karate Is a Thing of the Spirit*, *Car*, *The Hawk Is Dying*, and *The Gypsy's Curse*—consider various alternative kinds of physical rituals as avenues to meaning. Further, they deal with love and human companionship as possible solutions to man's dilemma. Finally, his latest novel, *A Feast of Snakes*, suggests that all solutions are inadequate and that violence of the most horrible kind is the only available response to man's condition. Thus, Crews's vision has grown progressively darker over his career.

The Gospel Singer treats man's religious hungers directly, yet religion seems finally an illusion. Not only is religion commercially exploited, the Gospel Singer himself, to whom the frustrated and yearning characters in the novel look for spiritual comfort, is a fake. Unable to believe in what he sings, he can only hold to the truth by seducing and corrupting his childhood sweetheart, MaryBell. Like a Graham Greene character, he is haunted by at least the possibility of the existence of God. The Gospel Singer is alienated and alone, constantly drawn back to the rural town of his childhood but able to find no more meaning there than in the cities where he performs in large arenas and on television. In his first novel Crews directly presents one of his main themes: the disjunction of body and soul. Although the Gospel Singer would like to help those who so desperately look to him for meaning, he cannot forget his own corruption. The most he can do is confess his sinfulness and endure being lynched by the irate crowd. Yet it becomes clear that they do not really hear his confession—they continue to believe in him and the hope he offered, hope, the novel makes clear, which is entirely illusory.

Naked in Garden Hills treats religion in an almost allegorical way, with the industrialist Jack O'Boylan functioning as the absent God figure. The novel illustrates how human beings exploit one another in a modern, industrialized, Godless landscape. Implicitly, the novel criticizes modern industrialism, but it most essentially deals with the human hunger for love. Fat Man (weighing 600 pounds) and Jester (three feet tall) are trapped in grotesque bodies and seek meaning through exploiting one another. The triumphant figure in the novel is Dolly Furgeson, who learned in New York that her beauty is a commodity to be traded upon. She bends everyone in Garden Hills to her will, offering the only hope in the blasted landscape. Her plan for Garden Hills involves a go-go establishment in which many of the characters are performers who end up exploited. Dolly is the only person in the novel equipped to live in the modern world, but her way of living is through materialism and exploitation and through the denial of human love and interconnection. Such, Crews suggests, is the nature of success in a world from which God has absented Himself.

This Thing Don't Lead to Heaven effectively disposes of institutional religion as a subject for Crews, for the title implicitly refers to earthly life itself. Set in a home for the elderly, the novel treats the sometimes absurd and grotesque things people attempt to do to cope with or evade death. Although the novel suffers from a diffuse focus, all the characters seek some kind of meaning for their lives. Unlike *Naked in Garden Hills*, this novel suggests that some hope can be found in human love: it concludes with Junior Bledsoe, a grave plot salesman who has had so little faith in life that he only finds meaning in selling grave plots, and Pearl Lee Gates, who was born and raised in the old folks home and hence has lived surrounded by old age and death, united in the hope that love will redeem their heretofore sterile lives.

Karate Is a Thing of the Spirit is the first Crews novel to be set in urban Florida, and its subject is karate, a secular ritual and a secular avenue to meaning. Through karate the devotees seek purity, self-control, order and meaning, and if they qualify they earn membership in a community of karateka headed by Belt, a black belt. Although karate is a physical activity and hence of this world and the body, in its purest form it is also a thing of the spirit. The novel focuses on John Kaimon, a wanderer and seeker of wide experience who joins the *dojo* for a while, and Gaye Nell, a brown belt and beauty queen who is one of the leaders of the commune. Although they are both attracted to the purity of karate and Gaye Nell at least is very adept at it, by the end of the novel they leave the *dojo*, for they ultimately are unable to transcend the flesh through devotion to the spirit. John and Gaye Nell are in love and she is pregnant with his child: the hope of the novel lies in the interpersonal relationship of the two young people. Crews respects what karate attempts to accomplish, but in the novel he portrays its goal as unrealistic, and at this point in his career he places whatever hope he sees for human beings in human love.

Car, set in a Jacksonville dominated by streets, superhighways, and automobiles, continues Crews's treatment, begun in *Naked in Garden Hills*, of the impact of modern technology on the individual. An idealist who has been raised in an automobile junkyard, Herman Mack can find only one way to express his aspirations to something higher: eating an automobile. As grotesque as this activity seems, in essence it is his attempt to forge a union with his god through the ritual of communion. Around Herman are arrayed various characters who pervert his desire by seeking material gain from it through commercialization and show business. Yet Herman must finally abandon his attempt. Crews suggests that the spiritual cannot be found through the material, indeed that the spiritual cannot be found at all. The conclusion of this novel replicates the end of *Karate Is a Thing of the Spirit*, for Herman leaves Jacksonville with Margo, the hotel prostitute who loved and encouraged him during his ordeal. The novel's ending again implies the possibility of human love as a source of meaning.

The Hawk Is Dying carries man's search one step further, and the level of desperation is much greater. George Gattling, like Crews born and raised in rural Bacon County, Georgia, regards life in urban Gainesville, Florida, as empty and false. Although he is a material success, he finds life lived entirely on the material level witahout meaning. For him, love provides no answer; only training hawks puts him in contact with something he feels is real, something primitive and elemental. So while funeral preparations for his nephew Fred progress, he affronts civilized sensibilities by attempting to train a hawk. It is important to him that he do it properly by following the ritual ways of the thirteenth century. Furthermore, his training of the hawk involves self-discipline. It is the only way George can conceive of getting in touch with tradition and gaining a sense of continuity. Even though the end of the novel reflects some ambiguity, the reader does feel that George is successful. His success, however, involves a rejection of the modern world and all it stands for.

The Gypsy's Curse continues Crews's treatment of the role of love as opposed to discipline and training. Here Marvin Molar, a deaf-mute with withered legs who does a hand-balancing act for a living, attempts to create meaning for himself through the disciplining of his body in workouts in a gymnasium. Marvin regards himself as a conscientious artist, an artist of the body who finds meaning through the physical. He lives in the gym with other defectives in a peaceable male commune. It is love, however, that upsets his equilibrium. Because of his love for Hester and out of fear that he will lose her, he allows her to move into the gym. Subsequently, she sets out to destroy the peaceful lives of the men. A sensitive, thoughtful man, Marvin feels forced to kill her, thus purifying his world of evil. He is left at the end of the novel to continue his workouts in the prison gym. Thus the avenue through which meaning can be found is much reduced in this novel.

In Crews's latest novel, *A Feast of Snakes*, such avenues are virtually non-existent. Crews returns to rural Georgia for his setting, and frustration, madness, and violence are omnipresent. Joe Lon Mackey, the protagonist, is a former high school all-American football player denied the opportunity to attend college because he is functionally illiterate. Deprived of the ritual outlet of football for his violent tendencies and burdened with a wife and two small babies, Joe Lon is full of rage, despair, and sadness. Unlike all Crews's previous novels, no outlets seem available in *A Feast of Snakes*. Love is nonexistent, having been replaced by brutal and brutalizing sex; drinking and random violence occur constantly. The best that Joe Lon can do is recognize the truth of his dead-end life and act accordingly. He can feel in control of his life only through killing four people, after which he is thrown into a pit of snakes by an enraged mob. Thus, the possibility of control has been reduced in Crews's latest novel. No ritual, no equilibrium, no balance seem possible. Hope is nonexistent; the only redemption lies in accepting the truth.

Since the appearance of *A Feast of Snakes*, Crews has published only one other work of fiction, a short story called "The Enthusiast." It is intended as the first chapter of another novel, but whether that novel appears or not, Crews has published a substantial corpus of works. His novels are powerful portraits of modern man *in extremis*, cut off from traditional sources of meaning. Sensitive to the forces of modern life and of those within the individual which are inimical to the achievement of full humanity, Crews has written books full of sadness and frustration. They explore various solutions to man's dilemma: religion, ritual, love. Finally, all such potential solutions are revealed to be inadequate, and man is left alone in the void. Perhaps the best man can do is survive, yet even that is a tenuous proposition in the later novels. Though now without the critical reputation his novels merit, Harry Crews is one of the most important writers of his generation practicing fiction in the South.

SURVEY OF CRITICISM

Harry Crews has been the subject of numerous interviews over the years, but only recently has substantial criticism been devoted to his fiction, in part perhaps stimulated by the publication of his autobiography in 1978. For anyone interested in critical study of Crews's novels, the place to begin is his nonfiction. A beautifully written and powerful book, *A Childhood*, purporting to be the story of only one year in his life when he was five, provides a great deal of material to aid the reader in understanding Crews's art and personality. One learns, for example, that for him storytelling is a way of imposing order and meaning on what was and continues to be an extremely chaotic existence.

His nonfiction collected in *Blood and Grits* and *Florida Frenzy* is also an essential source for background information on the fiction. Crews is by no means a practicing literary critic; however, his journalism, personal in nature and employing many of the techniques appearing in his fiction, sheds illuminating light on his interests and obsessions. Some of the articles are particularly relevant to his fiction: "Television's Junkyard Dog," an essay on the television star Robert Blake, treats Crews's own early life in interesting asides; "Carny" describes Crews's experiences with freaks; "The Car" can be directly related to *Car*; "The Hawk Is Flying" can be read with interest in conjunction with *The Hawk Is Dying*. And "Climbing the Tower," his meditation on Charles Whitman, the disturbed young man who killed twelve people from the tower on the University of Texas campus, contains important connections with *A Feast of Snakes*. Both his fiction and his nonfiction are expressions of and attempts to gain some control over his obsessions; so reading the two types of works together is unusually rewarding.

A surprisingly large number of interviews in which Crews's open, honest, and forthright personality comes through have also appeared. Although they unavoidably repeat one another, each interview has its own strengths. Anne Foata elicits important comments from Crews on his background, his opinions of other Southern writers, and his general beliefs. V. Sterling Watson's interview focuses directly on Crews's recent novel at the time, *The Hawk Is Dying*, whereas Joe David Bellamy concentrates his questions on the fictional process and Crews's techniques. David K. Jeffrey and Donald R. Noble deal retrospectively with all the novels and with Crews's attitude toward his audience and reviewers. A recent interview, conducted by Kay Bonetti, concentrates on *A Childhood* and Crews's life as a writer.

Important critical analyses of Crews's works have begun to appear. Allen Shepherd provides a general treatment and evaluation of the novels, focusing directly on the novels he thinks are best, *Car*, *The Hawk Is Dying*, and *A Feast of Snakes*. Frank W. Shelton provides an overview of the development of Crews's career. John Seelye makes the case for Crews's importance as a writer by asserting that his world is one of chrome and steel, not the traditional agrarian South. Seelye's wide-ranging essay includes suggestive remarks on such other writers as Caldwell, Faulkner, Percy, and Nathanael West. Patricia V. Beatty concentrates on the failure of language in *The Gypsy's Curse*; Larry W. DeBord and Gary L. Long, two sociologists, treat the theme of social mobility in the novels.

An important source of materials for the Crews scholar is the collection of essays *A Grit's Triumph*, edited by David K. Jeffrey. Besides the previously published essay by Shelton and the interview by Jeffrey and Noble, it includes original essays on such subjects as Crews and the Southern fictional tradition, the role of the land and ethnics, Crews's freaks, Crews and the church, Crews and sports, and Crews's women characters. In addition, two essays on *Car* are included. The essays are uneven and to some degree repetitive, but the book as a whole provides the fullest treatment to date of Crews's fiction and career.

Although his critical reputation at present is not secure and although his works (and perhaps his personality) occasionally elicit strongly negative reactions, this recent critical activity provides some hope that eventually Harry Crews will be seen as one of the significant writers of his generation.

BIBLIOGRAPHY

Works by Harry Crews

The Gospel Singer. New York: William Morrow, 1968.

Naked in Garden Hills. New York: William Morrow, 1969.

This Thing Don't Lead to Heaven. New York: William Morrow, 1970.

Karate Is a Thing of the Spirit. New York: William Morrow, 1971.

Car. New York: William Morrow, 1972.

"Interview with Harry Crews," ed. Anne Foata. *Recherches Anglaises et Américaines* 5 (1972): 207–25.

The Hawk Is Dying. New York: Knopf, 1973.

"Arguments Over an Open Wound: An Interview with Harry Crews," ed. V. Sterling Watson. *Prairie Schooner* 48 (Spring 1974): 60–74.

The Gypsy's Curse. New York: Knopf, 1974.

A Feast of Snakes. New York: Atheneum, 1976.

"Harry Crews: An Interview," ed. Joe David Bellamy. *Fiction International* 6/7 (1976): 83–93.

A Childhood: the biography of a place. New York: Harper and Row, 1978.

Blood and Grits. New York: Harper and Row, 1979.

"Harry Crews: An Interview," ed. David K. Jeffrey and Donald R. Noble. *Southern Quarterly* 19 (Winter 1981): 65–79.

Florida Frenzy. Gainesville, Florida: University Presses of Florida, 1982.

"Harry Crews on the American Dream," ed. Larry W. DeBord and Gary L. Long. *Southern Quarterly* 20 (Spring 1982): 35–53.

"An Interview with Harry Crews," ed. Kay Bonetti. *Missouri Review* 6 (Winter 1983): 145–64.

Studies of Harry Crews

Beatty, Patricia V. "Body Language in Harry Crews's *The Gypsy's Curse*." *Critique* 23 (Winter 1981–82): 61–66.

Gann, Daniel H. "Harry Crews: A Bibliography." *Bulletin of Bibliography* 39 (September 1982): 139–45.

Jeffrey, David K., ed. *A Grit's Triumph: Essays on the Works of Harry Crews*. Port Washington, N.Y.: Associated Faculty Press, 1983.

Seelye, John. "Georgia Boys: The Redclay Satyrs of Erskine Caldwell and Harry Crews." *Virginia Quarterly Review* 56 (Autumn 1980): 612–26.

Shelton, Frank W. "Harry Crews: Man's Search for Perfection." *Southern Literary Journal* 12 (Spring 1980): 97–113.

Shepherd, Allen. "Matters of Life and Death: The Novels of Harry Crews." *Critique* 20 (1978): 53–62.

Donald Grady Davidson
(1893–1968)

Despite the scandal (for some) of his fierce and unyielding conservatism, his public and unwavering devotion to the social, cultural, and political traditions of his region, it is difficult to overestimate the influence of Donald Davidson on the development of the profession of letters in the contemporary South. Although critics often argue that Davidson's traditionalism mitigated against (or even prevented) a general recognition of his stature as a poet, critic, and social commentator, the truth is the other way around. What most distinguished Davidson in all of his lifetime as a poet, professor, historian, literary critic, and diagnostician of cultural change was the purity and disinterestedness of his character, his indifference to considerations of personal advantage and intellectual fashion. In almost 50 years of consistency in the disciplines he mastered, Davidson identified himself as a member of the Party of Memory. What began for him in simple ancestral piety and an instinct for making—for poetry as a social act and for the history that defines such activity—deepened over the years into self-consciously traditionalist politics and poetics, a general view of how best to embody and preserve a civilization and of how we might forfeit such a patrimony.

BIOGRAPHY

Donald Grady Davidson was born 18 August 1893 in Campbellsville, Tennessee, the eldest son of William Eluford Davidson, a rural schoolmaster, and Elma Wells Davidson, from whom he derived much of his abiding love for music. His father gave him an early awareness of his heritage as a Southerner—and the discipline of the classical languages. In 1905 Donald Davidson went up from a series of small schools and from the "deep country" of Middle Tennessee to complete his preparatory training at Branham and Hughes School at Spring Hill. After four years of thorough instruction there, he entered Vanderbilt University in fall 1909 "on a loan of $100 and a little odd cash." These resources dwindled, and from 1910 to 1914 Davidson taught school back in the country and saved his money for a return to Nashville. During his second undergraduate period (1914–16) he continued to teach in a private school, to read widely, and to enlarge a circle of friends who were to be an important part of his life. In these years he wrote occasionally for student magazines and absorbed the rich intellectual atmosphere of what was the most ambitious of Southern universities. In fall 1916 Davidson took another post at a country school; but as the United States moved toward war, he was admitted to Officers Training School (OTS). In May 1917 he reported to Fort Oglethorpe, Georgia, and was subsequently commissioned second lieutenant in the 324th Infantry, 81st Division.

While in the army, Davidson received his B.A. in absentia from Vanderbilt. After being assigned to Camp Sevier, Greenville, South Carolina, he married Theresa Sherrer, an Ohio woman whom he had met in 1916 while they were teaching at neighboring schools in Pulaski, Tennessee.

In late July 1918 the 81st Division shipped out to France. In September the division was sent into the line toward the Vosges Mountains. During the next six weeks, the 81st took part in the great offensive in the Meuse-Argonne that brought about the armistice of 11 November. Davidson (now a first lieutenant) experienced bombing near Bruyères, fought in a pitched battle in the Manheuelle Woods near Moranville, and was shelled by a retreating German force. In these engagements his regiment suffered more than 200 casualties. In spring 1919 he toured various parts of France and learned of the birth of his daughter, Mary Theresa. The 81st Division embarked for America in June 1919. They landed in Charleston and were released on terminal leave a few days later.

Davidson had difficulty in recovering his sense of vocation after discharge from the army. There was no instructorship available to him at Vanderbilt and no other way of resuming his education. For a time he sought work in Ohio, where his wife and child had awaited his return from Europe. Instead, he found a post at Kentucky Wesleyan College, teaching there during the 1919–20 school year. In late spring 1920 Davidson was finally offered an instructorship at Vanderbilt, where he was to continue a member of the faculty for the next 44 years. In 1922 he finished his M.A., with a thesis on Joseph Conrad—work that he later published in the *Sewanee Review*. He resumed meeting regularly with literary friends, but with a new emphasis on the form of literature and the art of the poet. Davidson had already been influenced and inspired by the example of his teacher and comrade-in-arms, John Crowe Ransom; while he was still overseas he wrote some experimental poetry of his own—a part of his achievement preserved only in "The Roman Road," which appears in *The Long Street*. He had read Ransom's first book of verse in manuscript in Georgia while they were together at OTS in 1917. In 1919 he returned to Vanderbilt and to the special conversations with his colleagues and friends at the home of James M. Frank. With the rest of their discussion group (and especially with Allen Tate, a brilliant undergraduate who had joined it in 1921), Davidson and Ransom in 1922 founded the *Fugitive*, a magazine of verse unlike any other published in the South (or United States).

Davidson handled much of the practical work involved in publishing the *Fugitive*. Forty-eight of his early poems first appeared in its pages and only fifteen from the same period in other outlets such as the *Double Dealer*. Twenty-four of the 34 poems gathered in his first collection, *The Outland Piper* (1924), are from the *Fugitive*. The magazine, containing so much of his early poetry, may be properly described as the setting of Davidson's literary apprenticeship. Numerous passages in this early work anticipate his mature style, the tropology and the mythic substructure that inform his finest productions. Understandably he chose to preserve a few of these poems from the record of his beginnings. But much of this work is diminished by poeticism and aureate diction, an Edwardian or fin de siècle confusion of the nature of poetry with conscious manipulation of sound and imagery, an effort to make it, as he later wrote Tate, "exceedingly beautiful." This youthful poetry is filled with images of contrived transcendence and, although it treats of no large political or philosophical questions, sometimes sounds a fashionable but unconvincing note of cynicism or despair.

In 1926 Davidson began to work seriously on *The Tall Men*, a many-faceted composition of almost two thousand lines that heralded a new direction in his development. *The Tall Men* (1927) is a suite of nine parts, a structured set, not a collection, a poem of magnitude, scale, and scope. It echoes a wide range of English poetry—models and prototypes from the Anglo-Saxons to the Courtly Makers, from Spenser to the modern dramatic monologues—as it considers the life of the speaker in relation to that of his forebears, the frontiersmen who crossed over the mountains to "locate the blood" and their ancestors, reaching all the way back to the beginnings of civilized life in Northern Europe. This persona is at once like Davidson *and* a corporate symbol. In this formula, considerations of identity lead to the question of present duty and the question is answered, out of the tradition, either directly or by implication, in blank verse that is eloquent, concrete, forceful, and dignified. Promoted to assistant professor in 1924, Davidson was made associate professor in 1929, partly on the strength of *The Tall Men*. There is a direct line that runs from *The Tall Men* to the essay he contributed to *I'll Take My Stand*, "A Mirror for Artists." Although as Tate later acknowledged, there would have been no reconstitution and redirection of the Nashville circle and no Agrarian manifesto without "the devotion and determination" of Davidson, his contribution to the 1930 symposium in defense of things Southern was less directly concerned with the conflict between the sections in American history than with the general question of the proper role of the artist. Part of the reason, he argues, for preferring "societies which were for the most part stable, religious and agrarian" to the ostensibly efficient malaise of industrialism is the useful and honorable function reserved to the poet under the former dispensation. But if Davidson speaks in broad, more than Southern terms of the trivial status of literature in an industrial regime when he writes as one of the twelve who rejected the gospel of "progress," he had already been explicitly and particularly Southern on more than one occasion in publishing poetic defenses of the embattled fundamentalists of his region who were caught in the aftermath of the Scopes trial in Dayton, Tennessee.

From 1925 in such places as *Forum* and the *Saturday Review of Literature* Davidson, like Ransom, wrote "unorthodox defenses of orthodoxy." In them he maintained that the fundamentalist and the poet have two things in common: "a fierce clinging to poetic supernaturalism," and also a common mortal enemy in the rationalist mind that has made (and continues to operate) modern industrial society. Davidson took this position in 1926 and never retreated from it. Agrarianism, a preference for a customary, landowning society over the frenetic anonymity of the modern city, was not a phase in his life. It was its central fact, its organizing core.

The Nashville Agrarians functioned as a school or circle from 1930 through 1937, debating alternative versions of the South's future with Southern progressives, writing social commentary on a variety of public questions, developing an inclusive doctrine on most of these issues and in general resisting what Frank Owsley warned against as "the conquest of the Southern mind." They wrote countless essays and reviews in the *Virginia Quarterly Review*, the *Sewanee Review*, *Hound and Horn*, the *Southern Review*, and the *American Review*—their favorite outlet from 1933 to 1937. Davidson himself wrote more than 40 essays in support of the Agrarian enterprise, and also some new, very Southern poetry, this time concerned directly with the Confederate component of his heritage.

As he later wrote, "I set out to compose a series of poems—largely narrative in character—in which I would attempt to present some of the major figures in Southern history, at decisive or tragic moments in their careers." The resulting poems did not follow this plan precisely, but they did dramatize the difficulty of being a Southerner in the modern world by tracing the present concern of Southern traditionalists back to the political impotence of the region following its military defeat: to that cause, and to the disappearance of the heroic will to independence that had been a natural feature of the disposition of most Southerners. One of these poems, perhaps Davidson's most famous composition, gave a title to the new collection, *Lee in the Mountains and Other Poems* (1938). This verse, even at its lyric and dramatic best, fits Davidson's theory of the social utility of literature. It is not private poetry, which he believed his contemporaries had overproduced. The design of this poetry is calculated to bring the regional past to life. But what is also noteworthy about such poems as "Sanctuary," "The Running of Streight," "On a Replica of the Parthenon," "Randall, My Son," "Twilight on Union Street," and "Lee in the Mountains" is that they were written at a time of great political engagement, while Davidson was simultaneously putting together the contents of his most important contribution to Agrarian social theory, *The Attack on Leviathan: Regionalism and Nationalism in the United States* (1938).

Without any official moment of dispersal, the Agrarians began to stand aside from their campaign to preserve the cultural integrity of their homeland. Or rather, all of them save Davidson, who was not attenuated in his primary loyalties by a transregional understanding of what was at stake in the struggle or by distractions unrelated to them. For he was in the process of learning new reasons for doing what loyalty would have required of him even without access to the "larger picture": even if he had not come to believe, as he summarized the matter in his Lamar Lectures, "Behind the vituperative particulars . . . of anti-Southern attacks of the nineteen-twenties . . . [was] a more general pattern of condemnation in which the South was but an incidental, if important, object of criticism." By the time he had finished with his restatement of traditional Southern anti-federalism, he had become a systematic political conservative and a mortal enemy of Franklin D. Roosevelt's New Deal.

Hobbes's monster suggests a civil power with absolute authority to create peace and prevent the war of each against all, "the idea of a Great Society, organized under a single, complex, but strong and highly centralized national government, motivated ultimately by men's desire for economic welfare of a specific kind rather than a desire for personal liberty." Yet even in 1936–38 Davidson perceived the pressures on his own people as part of a larger action, threatening Western civilization with "the subtlest and most dangerous foe of humanity—the tyranny that wears the mask of humanitarianism and benevolence." That such a foe was the same in Tennessee or Vermont he was quick to acknowledge. The true targets of the spirit of modernity, whatever language it spoke, were self-government and sound education, "the entire Western tradition in the arts" and, especially, the "American political and governmental system in general . . . the basic American principle of free enterprise in labor, agriculture and industry."

By the time he was promoted to professor in 1937, Davidson had developed a set of courses that occupied his attention for the remainder of his tenure at Vanderbilt and also at Middlebury College in Vermont, where he taught in the Bread Loaf School of English almost every summer from 1931 through 1964. Working on the English and Scottish popular ballads caused him to think about traditionalist societies per se—and thus to write about Thomas Hardy and Yeats and the cultural theories of Arnold Toynbee. It made him focus on folklore, manners, and other properties of nomocratic cultures not "poured in from the top": to produce marvelous essays on the "Sacred Harp" hymnody of the South and the unsentimental "irreverence" of American folk songs. He was a conservative in the largest and most reflective sense. The intensification of this mood is reflected in the powerful two-volume study *The Tennessee*, which he prepared for the Rinehart and Company Rivers of America Series, a work in which he re-creates dramatically—as an action *and* an experience—the origins of his world and then its declension under the ideological influence of the Tennessee Valley Authority. The image he constructs of the interaction of people and place is both a positive and then a negative instance of the political theory advanced in *The Attack on Leviathan*. It is an exemplum in both directions, and it results in some of his most carefully crafted artistic production, better suited than mere analysis to its rhetorical purpose in rendering what is usually discursive in the earlier book.

The Tennessee: The Old River, Frontier to Secession (1946) and *The Tennessee: The New River, Civil War to TVA* (1948) are works of history in the old humanistic tradition—inquiries into the meaning of the American experience as lived out in the valley of a great river. Together they illustrate and interpret the story of a free and proud society put at risk by "benevolence." The premise undergirding Davidson's account is a doctrine that might now be called "ecological," but it was for him part of an inherited religious truth. His point is not that he objects to all forms of flood control or hydroelectric power. To the contrary, he is careful to recognize every success of the TVA. But he is uneasy about the feckless spirit of domination that attempts against nature whatever the fancy of man may desire and his ingenuity accomplish, and distrustful of other "planning" for a teleocratic remaking of the Valley in ways that have nothing to do with high water or electricity. Davidson's *The Tennessee* is also filled with a rich and respectful sense of the physical presence of the river. He speaks of terrain he has covered in person and of travel on the river in earlier times and in his own. The Agrarians had written in *I'll Take My Stand* that "religion is our submission to the general intention of a nature that is fairly inscrutable" and "the sense of our role as creatures within it." Working from such a presumption, one could not approve of the TVA.

As Davidson became more and more the political man and conscious conservative, as his career diverged dramatically from those of his fellow Fugitives, he began to write his best criticism and some of his finest poetry. The reading of his life that maintains that he was prevented from fulfilling the promise of his youth by being "too ferocious" and "too Southern" is a tendentious distortion of the record, resting on doubtful political and aesthetic assumptions. In 1952 Davidson and his friend Charles Faulkner Bryan finished their folk opera, *Singin' Billy*, and saw it through to production. Bryan composed the music and Davidson the libretto, which illustrated some of his theories concerning traditional poetry as practical song and the socially cohesive function of art.

In May 1956 Davidson took part in a reunion of the Fugitives held at Vanderbilt, where he defended his view of the oral origins of poetry. In 1957 the Louisiana State University Press brought out *Still Rebels, Still Yankees*, a distinguished collection of Davidson's literary and cultural criticism. Also in 1957 Davidson delivered the first series of the Eugenia Dorothy Blount Lamar Memorial Lectures at Mercer University in Georgia. These addresses, treatments and interpretations of the Fugitive and the Agrarian past, were published as *Southern Writers in the Modern World* (1958).

Scattered throughout these later years are splendid essays still uncollected. But what is most noteworthy about the last eighteen years of Davidson's career is that they included an onset of new poetic activity, culminating in the 1961 publication of *The Long Street*. Louis D. Rubin, Jr., speaks of this verse as "less ideological . . . [and] gentler in tone . . . than much of [Davidson's] earlier work" and then refers to it as a "surprising late flowering of talent." This late poetry, though as conservative in its implications and as free of any suggestion of the modernist aesthetic as any he composed, demonstrates the poet's mastery of modernist techniques and a refinement of irony, of indirection, not apparent in his earlier work.

Davidson retired from teaching in 1964; but he did not withdraw from the causes he had served throughout his adult life or from fostering and advising the host of friends and former students to whom he was always generous with counsel and sponsorship. Neither did he at any time cease to work. In 1966 the University of Minnesota Press published his *Poems: 1922–1961*. In spring 1968 he was prevented by failing health from attending a reunion of the Agrarians at the University of Dallas.

Davidson died in Nashville on 25 April 1968. For many conservatives and men and women of letters he continues to be, as Russell Kirk suggested some years ago, the figure of reference for his kind, "the most Southern of Southerners," a measure after whose example they at their best aspire.

MAJOR THEMES

Davidson wrote several poems about the role of the poet, his function as *vates* or keeper of the communal memory, and the magic and peril of his estate. Another group has an apocalyptic theme, a note of warning, "judgment" or trouble to come. But David A. Hallman is on the mark in observing that "Davidson chose as the dominant metaphor for his verse the image of 'the long street.' " This metaphor allowed him to treat of the human costs of modernity, to join in the almost universal outcry of the poets of his age against "the total negation of existence resulting from the . . . quest, undertaken in fulfillment of the scientific world view, for a totally rational society." Many of Davidson's poems, however, have nothing to do with the desiccating costs of rationalism or the harm done in the name of improving the world, none of which touch on the besetting emphasis earlier identified as standing at the heart of his achievement, the difference between modern and traditional societies. But that distinction is rarely far from Davidson's artistic nexus, even when, as in "The Ninth Part of Speech," "Gradual of the Northern Summer," or the Joe Clisby songs, his motif is celebration, what lifts the heart and calls for praise.

"Old Harp" and "The Demon Brother" are early poems recalling the function of the scop or bard of heroic times, little understood by modern men "who never knew the glee" and "read, as read they must, what once was sung," and then warning against the curse of isolation that comes to another kind of singer, the outland piper, who with the beauty of his song beguiles those who hear him to wander the earth in search of "unknown kin." The former image of the poet he affirms throughout his entire career; concerning the latter, of the artist as magician, he is at first equivocal and then (except in a very narrow sense) almost negative. The mature Davidson writes most memorably about the artist in the birthday poem, "Lines Written for Allen Tate on His Sixtieth Anniversary," in "Meditation on Literary Fame," and in "Woodlands, 1956–1960." Or, in a context also apocalyptic, in "The Case of Motorman 17: Commitment Proceedings," in which a poet testifies on behalf of poor Orestes Brown, who knows better than what lawyers, psychiatrists, and liberal clergymen tell him concerning "the old family trouble." In this dramatic poem the poet is ignored; and Motorman 17, who fears "the hounds of hell" that come to punish his blasphemous cousin, a progressive minister, is put away. Those who are involved in Brown's commitment have, like the Reverend Dr. Brown in his wicked sermon on the unreality of evil, denied what the Eumenides teach in Aeschylus's play:

> Did we not know of old that fear keeps watch
> Over the soul of man; and reason alone
> Cannot give courts of law a sacred place?
> What force would else restrain the breakers of oaths,
> Or stand guard at our doors against the foe?

Where reductionist psychiatry and secularized, meliorist theology hold sway, Brown's story of the three old women following his impious kinsman cannot be believed. Yet "poetry and justice [will] come again," and will arrive together— "unless the world be dead." For when the redemption contained in suffering is recognized, the poet who makes the connection will be an acknowledged authority and justice an axiom rendered by his singing. The "elder law" may, however, first "rage through the world again"—according to the prediction of that most religious of Greek poets, when he makes the benign transformation of the Furies conditional. The linking of poetry and "the old harsh way" is Davidson in his most sober vein. The imitation of Aeschylus reminds us that the forms for making never go out of date, are no more in danger of obsolescence than the promises of Apollo or the dark predictions of the prophet that

> *His fury goes out like fire*
> *And burns that none can quench it.*

In "Lines Written for Allen Tate on His Sixtieth Anniversary," Davidson delivers his personal note of tribute. The dramatic recollection of Agrarian festivities when they all were young and the reference to his own "shortened breath" frame the use he makes of Tate's achievement to specify what service it is that the Muses reward, what art that can expect an audience among a people who live beyond history. Poetry, as produced by Allen Tate, gives back to rootless moderns their sense of identity, of purpose, of the continuity of civil life and the fearful struggle that will be required to preserve it. "Woodlands, 1956–1960" concludes on the same note.

Davidson's two-part poem written on the occasion of a sequence of visits to the home of South Carolina's most famous novelist is at once a tribute to William Gilmore Simms, to his art as it relates to his society, and a "great house" poem in the tradition of Ben Jonson's "To Penshurst," Marvell's "Upon Appleton House," and Yeats's "Coole Park, 1929." The motif of Simms's novels of the American Revolution is traditionalist persistence such as survives in the way of life at Woodlands. An "established order" protected in war is again protected in the act of poet as guardian, as he recalls its behavior in defending itself. Simms had done what Davidson does, making sure that we are one "with Marion's men," using heroic art to arm us against "the Great Dragoon," whose malevolence goes far beyond "chains to fetter, fire to burn." The Simms poems are among Davidson's most fully realized, defining his own artistic motives almost as much as they do those of his "unseen host." As in so many of his best works, imitation becomes re-creation; poetry, living tradition.

Davidson honors Simms as the "saga man" of the early South who perpetuated a living heritage, a "fable" among people to whom it belongs by rightful inheritance. And a living heritage is at least potentially a present force to call upon when at "hour zero" it is time to "ring alarm." For warning, the poem implies, is as much a part of the business of the poet as *vates*, as are panegyric, satire, and celebration. Said another way, sometimes the poet's duty is to anticipate the worst. Davidson does this with great force in the concluding section of *The Tall Men*, "Fire on Belmont Street," heroic satire as the Renaissance humanists defined such verse. Here the poet cries out,

> "Citizens, awake! Fire is upon you, fire
> That will not rest, invisible fire that feeds
> On your quick brains, your beds, your homes, your steeples
> Fire in your sons' veins and in your daughters',
> Fire like a dream of Hell in all your world. . . ."

Yet a vision of the normative is not missing from this poem of warning, or from any of the other poems like it in the Davidson canon. He counsels, "Fly . . . to the hills . . . / Where water is and the slow peace of time"—an alternative to what the urban scene has come to mean in his symbolic system: ontological acceptance of the human condition in all of its contingent frailty, which is a predicate for any form of grace. Davidson does this foreboding more artfully in the late poem "A Touch of Snow," where reading weather becomes a carefully managed trope for another kind of sensitivity to signs of change; and does it also in his two poems concerning the ironic status of public monuments in Nashville, "Twilight on Union Street" and "On a Replica of the Parthenon." In these brief, bitter lyrics he speaks from the authority of anger. Tennesseans of his own time have an inverted relation to Andrew Jackson and the Athenians. They raise as "bribes against their fate" misleading tributes to "wisdom and virtue." But the gestures can only make "uncertainty more sure" as "the traffic leads," while the hero turns his horse's rump to us, "saluting James K. Polk."

The apocalyptic "sense of ending" is, in certain Davidson poems, as severe as anything to be found in the poetry of his era. Yet he writes as well in joy and affirmation as he does in doleful anticipation—in "The Ninth Part of Speech" and "Gradual of the Northern Summer," concerning the right formula for education without rationalism and the sacramental sense of nature as the locus of a "mountain church." These poems are masterful and evocative employment of the Vermont scene, as are "Joe Clisby's Song" and "On Culleoka Road" of rural Middle Tennessee. There Davidson's countryman persona speaks to our time in tribute to love, as spokesman for a generation who knew the difference between heart's "truth" and distortions of it. Joe's voice is one of those heard while traveling "the long street." Others, more urgent, speak to Davidson out of the Southern past.

"Lee in the Mountains" and "Sanctuary" represent at his best the Davidson of "ancestral voices," the rendering of consciousness by dramatic means—a characteristic device of the modernist mode in both fiction and poetry.

In "Lee in the Mountains" we confront Robert Lee, erstwhile soldier and, in his old age, caught and surrounded by his enemies. He now presides over Southern boys who study at Washington College. Lee walks toward the college chapel, and we share his thoughts, going back to the early Republic of his father and forward to the devotional he will offer once that morning's services begin. He is in the last years of his life, both an "outlaw" and the acknowledged patriarchal chieftain of all the people he defended in war; both a "voice commanding in a dream" and the man who with a "word" might "this torn earth . . . quicken into shouting / Beneath the feet of ragged bands." Davidson preserves, however, not just Lee the patriarch and Lee the soldier, but primarily Lee the man of faith, who looks to the mountains not for military refuge but for another kind of deliverance—a variety he recommends to his charges in the passage toward which the entire poem builds:

> It is not the bugle now, or the long roll beating.
> The simple stroke of a chapel bell forbids
> The hurtling dream, recalls the lonely mind.

Instead of further testing in the field, Lee recommends trust in God's grace,

> To bring this lost forsaken valor
> And the fierce faith undying
> And the love quenchless
> To flower among the hills to which we cleave,
> To fruit upon the mountains whither we flee,
> Never forsaking, never denying

His children and His children's children forever
Unto all generations of the faithful heart.

In "Sanctuary" the voice speaking is not that of a famous figure but of an anonymous Tennessean who warns his son to prepare himself for the return of the ancient enemy: to seek refuge in the mountains once he sees "*his* great dust rising in the valley." But even though there is talk of "harrying" the foe, the conclusion of this monologue is once again religious—not the orthodox Anglicanism of General Lee but an older religiousness inspired by high and sacred places, yet not unrelated to the more conventional variety reserved for the house of God.

Davidson wrote all kinds of poems, knowing what purpose each of them was to serve. His "long street" begins as far back as the "song which Moses made" and the narrative of Troy. It runs beyond him toward an unpromising future which must, even so, be confronted. Traveling on it is the poet's way of having something to tell us. To find his direction in the continuum, Davidson took along the forms that had marked the path others had made while on their journey. Employing these structures was a merging with the larger prescription, with a way of seeing, as useful as any discursive argument or manifesto might be—as in "Old Sailor's Choice," in which Odysseus reports on a contemporary version of his voyage, one whose dangers are more insidious than those known to Homer's sailor king. Davidson's art was a method of discovery, though as much of old things as of new.

SURVEY OF CRITICISM

Serious critical discussion of Davaidson's work has been impeded by preoccupation with (and hostility toward) his cultural analysis and his political commitments. Nonetheless, since his death some progress has been made toward the development of an overview and inclusive theory of his poetry, his poetics, his reading of modern history and historical change. In *Donald Davidson* (1972), Thomas Daniel Young and M. Thomas Inge laid a firm foundation for further study of specific works and of Davidson's career. Their listing of Davidson's work and of commentary upon it in *Donald Davidson: An Essay and a Bibliography* (1965) is also an invaluable tool for any research on the writer. Louise Cowan's "Donald Davidson: The 'Long Street' " (1964) is the best critical essay on Davidson's poetry to be published thus far. It emphasizes Davidson's concept of tradition. Her book *The Fugitive Group: A Literary History* (1959) contains a substantial account of the beginnings of Davidson's career as a poet. David A. Hallman's "Donald Davidson's 'Long Street': An Agrarian's Conservative Testament" (1984) is an excellent interpretation of Davidson's conservatism as a positive influence on his art.

Lewis Simpson's 1972 foreword to the Louisiana State University Press reissue of *Still Rebels, Still Yankees* is the best discussion thus far of Davidson's poetics.

M. E. Bradford's "A Durable Fire: Donald Davidson and the Profession of Letters" (1967) explains the relation of component parts of Davidson's complex, many-sided performance. Louis D. Rubin, Jr.'s discussion of Davidson in *The Wary Fugitives: Four Poets and the South* (1978) is also an important piece. Essays on Davidson as social thinker by Michael O'Brien in his *The Idea of the American South, 1920–1941* (1977) and Fred Hobson in his *Tell About the South: The Southern Rage to Explain* (1983) are useful but, when politically myopic, sometimes unsatisfactory. Comment on Davidson in the works of John M. Bradbury, John Lincoln Stewart, and Richard Gray serves chiefly as a negative example, of how not to write criticism. Marion Montgomery's "Bells for John Stewart's Burden" (1966) is an appropriate response to the worst of this academic derogation.

Most needed in the study of Davidson is the explication of single poems or groups of poems, as in Lawrence E. Bowling's "An Analysis of Davidson's 'Lee in the Mountains' " (1952), M. E. Bradford's "Meaning and Metaphor in Donald Davidson's 'A Touch of Snow' " (1966), and Martha E. Cook's "Dryads and Flappers: Donald Davidson's Early Poetry" (1979); or serious treatments of his political thought, as in Edward S. Shapiro's "Donald Davidson and the Tennessee Valley Authority: The Response of a Southern Conservative" (1974). Davidson's work in relation to the conservative revival of the 1950s, his influence on younger conservatives, is a subject that would repay careful study.

BIBLIOGRAPHY

Works by Donald Davidson

An Outland Piper. Boston and New York: Houghton Mifflin, 1924.
"Joseph Conrad's Directed Indirections." *Sewanee Review* 33 (April 1925): 163–77.
"Artist as Southerner." *Saturday Review of Literature* 2 (May 15, 1926): 781–83.
The Tall Men. Boston and New York: Houghton Mifflin, 1927.
"First Fruits of Dayton, The Intellectual Evolution of Dixie." *Forum* 79 (June 1928): 896–907.
"A Mirror for Artists." *I'll Take My Stand*. By Twelve Southerners. New York: Harper and Brothers, 1930, pp. 28–60.
"The Trend of Literature, A Partisan View." *Culture in the South*. Ed. W. T. Couch. Chapel Hill: University of North Carolina Press, 1935, pp. 183–210.
"White Spirituals: The Choral Music of the South." *American Scholar* 4 (Autumn 1935): 460–73.
"The Political Economy of Regionalism." *American Review* 6 (February 1936): 410–34.
"That This Nation May Endure, The Need for Political Regionalism." *Who Owns America? A New Declaration of Independence*. Ed. Herbert Agar and Allen Tate. Boston: Houghton Mifflin, 1936, pp. 113–34.
The Attack on Leviathan: Regionalism and Nationalism in the United States. Chapel Hill: University of North Carolina Press, 1938.

Lee in the Mountains and Other Poems. Boston and New York: Houghton Mifflin, 1938.
  Reissued New York: Charles Scribner's Sons, 1949.
"Agrarianism and Politics." *Review of Politics* 1 (April 1939): 114–25.
American Composition and Rhetoric. New York: Charles Scribner's Sons, 1939. Reissued
  1943, 1947, 1953, 1959, 1964, 1968.
"The Preface to Decision." *Sewanee Review* 53 (Summer 1945): 394–412.
The Tennessee. 2 vols. The Rivers of America Series. New York and Toronto: Rinehart,
  1946 and 1948. Vol. 1, *The Tennessee: The Old River: From Frontier to Secession*,
  reprinted with introduction by Thomas Daniel Young. Knoxville: University of
  Tennessee Press, 1978.
Introduction. *The Letters of William Gilmore Simms*, 5 vols. Ed. Mary C. Simms Oliphant,
  Alfred Taylor Odell, and T. C. Duncan Eaves. Columbia: University of South
  Carolina Press, 1952. 1: xxxi–lviii.
"The Talking Oaks of the South." *Shenandoah* 5 (Winter 1953): 3–8.
Still Rebels, Still Yankees. Baton Rouge: Louisiana State University Press, 1957. Reissued
  with foreword by Lewis Simpson in 1972.
Southern Writers in the Modern World. Lamar Memorial Lectures. Athens: University
  of Georgia Press, 1958.
"The New South and the Conservative Tradition." *National Review* 9 (September 10,
  1960): 141–46.
The Long Street: Poems. Nashville: Vanderbilt University Press, 1961.
The Spyglass: Views and Reviews, 1922–1961. Selected and edited by John Tyree Fain.
  Nashville: Vanderbilt University Press, 1963.
"Decorum in the Novel." *Modern Age* 9 (Winter 1964–65): 34–48.
"The Gardens of John Donald Wade." *Georgia Review* 19 (Winter 1965): 385–403.
  Repr. in *Selected Essays and Other Writings of John Donald Wade*. Ed. Donald
  Davidson. Athens: University of Georgia Press, 1966, pp. 1–20.
"The Meaning of War: A Note on Allen Tate's 'To the Lacedemonians.' " *Southern
  Review* 1 (July 1965): 720–30.
"Odyssey of a Litterateur." *Intercollegiate Review* 2 (May-June 1966): 363–370.
Poems: 1922–1961. Minneapolis: University of Minnesota Press, 1966.
"The Vision of Richard Weaver: A Foreword." *The Southern Tradition at Bay*. By
  Richard M. Weaver. Ed. George Core and M. E. Bradford. New Rochelle, N.Y.:
  Arlington House, 1968, pp. 13–25.
The Literary Correspondence of Donald Davidson and Allen Tate. Ed. John Tyree Fain
  and Thomas Daniel Young. Athens: University of Georgia Press, 1974.
"The Center That Holds: Southern Literature & The Oldtime Religion." *Southern Par-
  tisan* 4 (Fall 1984): 17–22.
Singin' Billy: An Opera in Two Acts. Text by Donald Davidson; music by Charles Faulkner
  Bryan. Glendale, S.C.: Foundation for American Education, 1985.

Studies of Donald Davidson

Allen, Ward. "Donald Davidson." *Sewanee Review* 78 (Spring 1970): 390–404.
Bowling, Lawrence E. "An Analysis of Davidson's 'Lee in the Mountains.' " *Georgia
  Review* 6 (Spring 1952): 69–85.
Bradbury, John M. *The Fugitives: A Critical Account*. Chapel Hill: University of North
  Carolina Press, 1958.

Bradford, M. E. "A Durable Fire: Donald Davidson and the Profession of Letters." *Southern Review* 3 (Summer 1967): 721–41.

———. "Meaning and Metaphor of Donald Davidson's 'A Touch of Snow.' " *Southern Review* 2 (Summer 1966): 516–23.

Buffington, Robert. "Mr. Davidson in the Formal Garden." *Georgia Review* 24 (Summer 1970): 121–31.

Cook, Martha E. "Dryads and Flappers: Donald Davidson's Early Poetry." *Southern Literary Journal* 12 (Fall 1979): 18–26.

Cowan, Louise. "Donald Davidson: The 'Long Street.' " *Reality and Myth: Essays in American Literature in Memory of Richmond Croom Beatty.* Ed. William E. Walker and Robert L. Welker. Nashville: Vanderbilt University Press, 1964, pp. 98–110.

———. *The Fugitive Group: A Literary History.* Baton Rouge: Louisiana State University Press, 1959.

———. "The *Pietas* of Southern Poetry." *South: Modern Southern Literature in Its Cultural Setting.* Ed. Louis D. Rubin, Jr., and Robert D. Jacobs. Garden City, N.Y.: Doubleday, 1961, pp. 95–114.

Dessommes, Lawrence. "The Epistemological Implications in 'The Ninth Part of Speech.' " *Mississippi Quarterly* 23 (Winter 1973–74): 21–32.

Doyle, John Robert, Jr. "Pacing the Long Street with Donald Davidson." *Sewanee Review* 74 (Autumn 1966): 946–50.

Eaton, Charles Edward. "Donald Davidson and the Dynamics of Nostalgia." *Georgia Review* 20 (Fall 1966): 261–69.

Gray, Richard. *The Literature of Memory: Modern Writers of the American South.* Baltimore: Johns Hopkins University Press, 1977, pp. 94–105.

Hallman, David A. "Donald Davidson's 'Long Street': An Agrarian Conservative Testament." *Southern Literary Journal* 16 (Spring 1984): 63–80.

Hobson, Fred. *Tell About the South: The Southern Rage to Explain.* Baton Rouge: Louisiana State University Press, 1983.

Kirk, Russell. "The Poet as Guardian: Donald Davidson," *Confessions of a Bohemian Tory: Episodes and Reflections of a Vagrant Career.* New York: Fleet, 1963, pp. 152–54.

Landess, Thomas. "The Art of Intimacy." *University Bookman* 16 (Autumn 1975): 10–13.

Lasseter, Rollin A., III. "The Southern Myth in Donald Davidson's Poetry." *Kentucky Review* 1 ((Fall 1967): 31–43.

Montgomery, Marion. "Bells for John Stewart's Burden." *Georgia Review* 20 (Summer 1966): 145–81.

O'Brien, Michael. *The Idea of the American South, 1920–1941.* Baltimore: Johns Hopkins University Press, 1977, pp. 185–227.

Purdy, Rob Roy, ed. *The Fugitives' Reunion: Conversations at Vanderbilt, May 3–5, 1956.* Nashville: Vanderbilt University Press, 1959.

Ransom, John Crowe. "The Most Southern Poet." *Sewanee Review* 70 (Spring 1962): 202–07.

Rubin, Louis D., Jr. *The Wary Fugitives: Four Poets and the South.* Baton Rouge: Louisiana State University Press, 1978, pp. 136–86; 256–66.

Shapiro, Edward S. "Donald Davidson and the Tennessee Valley Authority: The Response of a Southern Conservative." *Tennessee Historical Quarterly* 33 (Winter 1974): 436–51.

Simpson, Lewis. Foreword. *The Literary Correspondence of Donald Davidson and Allen Tate*. Ed. John Tyree Fain and Thomas Daniel Young. Athens: University of Georgia Press, 1973, pp. vii-xix.

————. "Introduction: Donald Davidson and the Southern Defense of Poetry." *Still Rebels, Still Yankees and Other Essays*. Baton Rouge: Louisiana State University Press, 1972, pp. v-xvi.

Stewart, John Lincoln. *The Burden of Time: The Fugitives and Agrarians*. Princeton, N.J.: Princeton University Press, 1965.

Stewart, Randall. "Donald Davidson." *South: Modern Southern Literature in Its Cultural Setting*. Ed. Louis D. Rubin, Jr., and Robert D. Jacobs. Garden City, N.Y.: Doubleday, 1961, pp. 248–59.

Tate, Allen. "The Gaze Past, The Glance Present," *Memoirs and Opinions, 1926–1974*. Chicago: Swallow, 1975, pp. 35–38.

Thorp, Willard. *American Writing in the Twentieth Century*. Cambridge: Harvard University Press, 1960, pp. 243–44.

Wade, John Donald. "Oasis." *Sewanee Review* 70 (Spring 1962): 208–12.

Young, Thomas Daniel and M. Thomas Inge. *Donald Davidson*. New York: Twayne, 1972.

————. *Donald Davidson: An Essay and a Bibliography*. Nashville: Vanderbilt University Press, 1965.

RICHARD J. CALHOUN

James Dickey
(1923–   )

Praised more for his force than for his grace, James Dickey often portrays the strange and monstrous. He has been called a gothic poet, much as Flannery O'Connor is often described as a gothic story writer. He gained great fame for his novel *Deliverance* (1970), particularly when it was made into a successful motion picture. But Dickey is first of all a poet, and he had made a substantial name as such before the novel was published. Generally, critics regard Dickey's work that preceded *Deliverance* as superior to that which followed it. Especially since Dickey is still writing, there is no clear consensus about his ultimate place in modern letters.

BIOGRAPHY

Although he became a student of the rural South, James Dickey was a product of the urban South. He was born on 2 February 1923 in a suburb of Atlanta, Georgia. His father was a successful lawyer who encouraged his son to read law, not literature. His mother had minor literary interests, a fondness for Long-fellow and Tennyson, but little beyond that. Dickey's one literary passion was Lord Byron, an interest solely occasioned by his reading of John Drinkwater's popular biography *The Pilgrim of Eternity*. What was read in the Dickey family was not literature but case histories of trials, as Dickey liked to say, "from Jesus to Fatty Arbuckle." His idea of a hero was Clarence Darrow. The good life for Dickey as a youth was working with his hands and, above all, playing football. Football at North Fulton High in Atlanta determined his selection of Clemson College, now Clemson University, where he played freshman football during fall 1942 until he was promoted with other promising freshmen during that war-depleted season to the varsity for the final game against archrival South Carolina.

Rather than waiting to be drafted, Dickey enlisted in the Army Air Corps soon after the football season.

Dickey's serious reading began with off-duty boredom at Army Air Corps bases as a by-product of a romantic interest in a post librarian. But the Air Corps was not all boredom. He flew more than a hundred combat missions in the Philippines, Okinawa, and firebombing raids over Tokyo. He learned for the second time the importance of being a survivor; the first had been his knowledge of the death of his older brother Eugene, for whom Dickey was a replacement child. As a part of his literary education at post libraries, he developed a special interest in "failed poets," writers such as Melville and James Agee, who turned from attempts to write poetry to crafting prose carefully in narrative fiction. Poetic prose became something he wanted to emulate because these writers were attempting to use prose for "higher things."

After the war Dickey transferred from Clemson to Vanderbilt and turned from football to track, eventually becoming Tennessee state champion in the 120-yard high hurdles. His interest in literature grew as he studied at a university with a strong literary reputation from such predecessors as John Crowe Ransom, Robert Penn Warren, Allen Tate, and Donald Davidson; historian Frank Owsley made him aware for the first time what it was to be Southern. Among the Vanderbilt writers Dickey especially admired were Warren, for his vividness in depicting violence, and Randall Jarrell, for his gentleness and compassion. Monroe K. Spears was the teacher from whom Dickey learned the most, especially the notion that the imagination escaped from the literal fact in order to create good literature. Belief in "the creative possibilities of the lie" continues to fascinate Dickey. At Vanderbilt the study of anthropology was also important to him. The differences between the primitive mind and the civilized modern mind later became a thematic preoccupation of his work.

In November 1948, before his graduation the next June, Dickey married Maxine Syerson, then a graduate student in nursing. He graduated magna cum laude and was rewarded with a graduate fellowship in English at Vanderbilt. His debut as a poet came when he published in the student literary magazine. This publication was closely followed by another in the *Sewanee Review*, for which he later served as the chief poetry reviewer.

Next to writing, Dickey's true career is teaching. He accepted an instructorship at Rice Institute, but the Korean War occasioned his recall as a pilot by the Air Force. When he returned to Rice in 1952, over thirty and without a Ph.D., he hoped to publish enough poetry to enable him to have a career teaching creative writing. The Vanderbilt connection paid off. At the urging of Monroe Spears, Dickey applied for a *Sewanee Review* fellowship, and with Allen Tate and Andrew Lytle judging, won the award. He spent the year writing poetry in Europe, predominantly in Italy. At the conclusion of his fellowship, with new credentials, he accepted Andrew Lytle's invitation to join him at the University of Florida, where, disappointingly, his assignment was freshman composition rather than creative writing. There were complaints when at a public reading, mostly for faculty and faculty wives, Dickey read a poem, "The Father's Body," about a child discovering his own sexual identity by comparing his body to his father's. Rather than apologize, Dickey resigned.

At age thirty-three Dickey began a career as a copywriter with an advertising firm, McCann-Erickson—his primary responsibility, the Coca-Cola account. He wrote copy by day and poetry by night. As writing poetry became more and more important, he changed jobs, returning to Atlanta from New York, to continue with the Coca-Cola account, then moving to a smaller company, with responsibility for the Lay's Potato Chip account. Finally, he became advertising director and vice president for the Atlanta agency Burke Dowling Adams, which handled the Delta Air Lines account. The publication of his first two books, *Into the Stone* (1960) and *Drowning with Others* (1962), helped him win a Guggenheim Fellowship, leading to his final break with the business world and his surrender of a well-paying job for only the promise of success as a poet.

After his fellowship Dickey began a brief itinerant career serving as poet-in-residence at several colleges (Reed College, San Fernando Valley, and the University of Wisconsin at Madison) and undertaking lecture tours, reading his poems on a mission for what he described in an essay as "Barnstorming for Poetry." *Buckdancer's Choice* (1965) won him his first major award, the National Book Award for poetry in 1966. That year he was named consultant in poetry for the Library of Congress. The next year, with the publication of his first collected poems, *Poems 1957–1967*, he was recognized as a major force in American poetry, perhaps even as important as Robert Lowell. What was miraculous was that he accomplished this at age forty-five with only slightly more than a decade of full-time writing. In 1969 he accepted the position he still holds, Carolina Professor of English and Writer-in-Residence at the University of South Carolina at Columbia.

In the 1970s Dickey's greatest success was with his prose rather than with his poetry, especially with his first novel, *Deliverance* (1970), and to a lesser degree with two works of very personal literary criticism, *Self-Interviews* (1970) and *Sorties* (1971). Even his poetry seemed more like prose, signaling perhaps a move toward the poetic prose he had always admired, especially in *The Eye-Beaters, Blood, Victory, Madness, Buckhead and Mercy* (1970), *The Zodiac* (1976), and *The Strength of Fields* (1979). In his work in the 1970s he also sought a wider and larger audience. Two books were financial, if not exactly artistic, successes: *Jericho: The South Beheld* (1974), prose poem descriptions of Southern landscape to accompany drawings and paintings by Hubert Shuptrine; and *God's Images* (1977), prose emulations of Blake or Milton to accompany biblical passages. Some critics thought they detected a serious decline in poetic quality. Richard Howard and Robert Penn Warren, however, praised the wild power of the unlyrical poetry in *The Zodiac*, Dickey's imitation of a 1941 poem by the Dutch poet Henrik Marsman. Perhaps indicative of a turning back to lyric grace are the poems published in *Puella* (1982), dedicated to the "male imagined'' girlhood of his second wife, Deborah, whom he married in 1977. His first wife had died of cancer the preceding year.

MAJOR THEMES

To date, Dickey has written his best poetry during the remarkable decade of creativity from 1957 to 1967. His earliest poems were largely affirmative, written from the grateful perspective of a survivor, first through birth, since only his brother Eugene's death permitted his own life, and then from the death and destruction of World War II. As a survivor with the guilt of one so fortunate, Dickey seeks to relate imaginatively to nonsurvivors. In his early poem "The String," he uses a family pastime of performing tricks with string as the narrative base, developing the fiction that his dead brother Eugene also performed these family tricks. This shared experience is suggested as a bond between the dead and the living, between his dead brother and Dickey's own son, Chris, who continues the family tradition of string tricks. In a second early poem, "The Performance," Dickey structures the poem around another nonsurvivor, Donald Armstrong, who crash-landed in the Philippines, was captured, and beheaded the next day. Pondering Armstrong's death, Dickey imagines him transcending his execution by achieving at last, to the amazement of his captors, what he had failed to do back at the base—a perfect handstand. What this poem illustrates is Dickey's use of the imagination to provide what factual knowledge cannot; through a creative lie, he takes a different view "from the official version that God made or the world made." With Whitmanesque empathy, he enters the experience of another and is able to imagine transcendence of the ordinary.

Even though Dickey's poems seek transcendence of the ordinary and the literal, he should not be regarded too simply as a romantic advocate of something called "the more life school." As a reviewer in the 1950s for the *Sewanee Review*, he always deplored ordinariness and literalness in contemporary poetry; he condemned them as "the suspect in poetry," those academic or garden variety styles of poetry into which modernism had deplorably degenerated. Intentionally, as critic and as poet, Dickey has contributed to that neo-romantic revolution in poetry that has been called, for the lack of a better name, postmodernism, but he never approved of some of its early manifestations, such as "Beat Poetry" or "Confessional Poetry." To Dickey, transcendence of some sort is necessary for poetry to possess life, but technique and language matter much more than some of the first postmodernists seemed to realize. Most important to Dickey is transcending the limitations of the ordinary self, achieving a vision of Byzantium while avoiding Babel by maintaining formal control over the poem. He has consistently sought to escape the literal by using devices such as "empathetic exchange of identity," establishing a narrative setting, with often a touch of surrealism; using "big forms" or archetypes; and, at his best, employing a distinctive voice or persona that would seem to restore to the poet control of the poem. His model, if Dickey can be said to have one, was Theodore Roethke, another practitioner of postmodernist romanticism and lyric grace.

In *Drowning with Others* (1962) Dickey employs his most famous device, his empathetic "way of exchange." In the most often quoted example, "A Dog Sleeping on My Feet," the narrator watches his dog asleep, feet moving, as he presumably dreams of a fox hunt, and through imaginative identification, experiences, though human, the long-forgotten animal excitement of the chase. What is gained is not just "more life" but forgotten life, an entrance into Jungian racial memory. In a similar poem, "Listening to the Foxhounds," the persona is a hunter without a dog, who, unlike the other hunters, identifies with the hunted fox, participating in the primitive excitement of the escape as the fox finds the safety of his den. He continues to employ this kind of "exchange" in his next book, *Helmets* (1964). In "Drinking from a Helmet" a soldier drinks from the helmet of a dead soldier and, on donning it, sees, so Dickey imagines, uncommonly through the eyes of the dead man. Dickey's idea of "exchange" is based on a premise that civilized man has lost the natural forces that were once essential for his survival. Through imaginative exchange a sense of what is lost—primitive powers such as instinct, intuition, participation in rituals, especially in the hunt, where the kill is the natural and expected thing—can be temporarily regained. As the title of his first collection, *Into the Stone* (1960), suggests, there is often some attempt to reidentify with nonhuman nature. In "The Vegetable King" an ordinary householder sleeps outside in early spring, and in a dream he is transformed into the sacrifical vegetable king whose Orphic dismemberment is necessary for the creation of spring. His persona sees everything from a perspective that becomes characteristic of Dickey's poetry—from beyond the ordinary human world, poetically expressed in "The Sheep Child" as "the grassy world seen from both sides." On waking he cannot distinguish between dream and reality. "Sleeping Out at Easter" is another early example of a persona losing human consciousness and gaining the feel of being nonhuman, through sleeping out in nature. But in Dickey the exchange is only a temporary event. The moment of exhilaration and terror soon passes. After a brief withdrawal there is a return to the human, but with a permanent change.

Dickey has been concerned with war, but not often enough to be a war poet on the scale of Jarrell or Shapiro. There are five war poems in *Into the Stone* (1960) and a few more in subsequent volumes. The best of these are one of the earliest, "The Performance," and one of his last, "The Firebombing," in *Buckdancer's Choice* (1965). In the later poem he can no longer feel the guilt of being a survivor, or even of being a killer who participated in the firebombing raids over Tokyo. He can briefly imagine a visit from one of the nonsurvivors below, the image of a fire-burned Japanese, an image that crumbles at his doorstep, on the threshold of entrance. There is now just too much distance in time, as there was even then too much distance in space, in his cockpit far above.

Love is also an early theme, and the mythical figure invoked most successfully in the early poems is Orpheus, who entered the underworld to redeem his beloved Eurydice. Love of man for woman approaches the power of the mystical love he feels for nature, but what is gained from this experience is much less clear than in his later poems. The climactic poem of *Into the Stone*, "The Landfall," begins promisingly as a narrative of two lovers who pull their boat to landfall, but it ends without a clear resolution. Not surprisingly, it was left out of *Poems 1957–1967*. In later poems Dickey is more successful and more meaningful in his treatment of love, even in a comic version, "Cherrylog Road" (*Buckdancer's Choice*). The persona's youthful desire (amid the wrecks of a junkyard) for Doris Holbrook expresses a desire for unrestrained access to all natural things in order to enhance life, but here there is a restraining element of fear of the father, Mr. Holbrook, and of his shotgun.

The concern with family has always remained strong in Dickey, but the concerns changed as Dickey grew older. In *Drowning with Others* the subject is not only his guilt over the chance for life that his brother's death gave him but also father and son relationships. Two of the best differ strikingly and show the range of Dickey's poetry. "The Owl King" is unrealistic and mythical, a fable of a father seeking his blind son lost in the woods, the province of the owl king. Each main character—father, owl, and son—has his section of the poem. Without sight the child transcends his father's knowledge and learns from the owl to see by means of imagination. "The Hospital Window" is a realistic tribute to the passing of generations; it utilizes an account of Dickey's departure from a visit with his father in the hospital. As he descends to earth in the elevator, he imagines that he feels his father ascending to heaven. As he faces the murderous traffic below, he has a vision in the window, ablaze from the light of the setting sun, of a wave from his father at the hospital window, conveying the message that his father above is unafraid, both of his own impending death and of his son's possible death below.

Transcendence of the ordinary is a major concern with Dickey, but it is never more than a brief escape that can give life renewed meaning. It is not even always possible for Dickey's personae, because they must occasionally remain prisoners of their natural states and limitations. In "The Lifeguard," one of his finest poems, Dickey compares the lifeguard to Christ, but any transcendence for the lifeguard is only a fantasy of his imagination; he cannot make the dead arise. Dickey portrays a human situation in which man is inescapably imprisoned by his own limitations. In "The Falling" (1967) the fantasies of rescue on the part of an airline hostess falling to her death are just that, only fantasies; all she can do in the brief moment of life left her is to plan how to prepare herself to enter earth and to make her death meaningful for the Kansas farm boys who will find her below. The climactic poem in Dickey's imaginative exchanges is a vision of a pastoral heaven, appropriate for animals, "The Heaven of Animals" (*Drowning with Others*). He draws on the Platonic idea of heaven as a continuation of the finer moments on earth. This is not the biblical heaven but a more primitive one where the animals are not deprived of the pleasures of the hunt, yet guilt and death do not exist, only pleasure without fatalities.

In such poems as "The Firebombing," "Falling," "The Sheep Child," and "May Day Sermon to the Women of Gilmer County, Georgia, by a Woman Preacher Leaving the Baptist Church," Dickey explored new themes, experimented with new forms (including his "split line"), and continued to use strong narrative. There were deeper and darker explorations of the psyche than before: in "May Day Sermon" he focuses on the eroticism that underlies the woman preacher's religious fundamentalism. This poem sets a standard by which Dickey has indicated he is willing to be judged. With his next book, *The Eye-Beaters, Blood, Victory, Madness, Buckhead and Mercy* (1970), he seemed to lose the balance between neo-romantic theme and careful formal control, and between an affirmative overview and pessimism in the face of destructive forces.

Dickey dropped his insistence on a narrative base, whether realistic or surrealistic, for his lyric perceptions and substituted a loose associational structure. What had been dramatic now seemed to some critics to have become merely rhetorical. Such poems as "Power and Light" and "The Eye-Beaters" had a certain terrible power, but the transcendent act, such as Donald Armstrong's death gesture or Dickey's father's wave, was no longer a climax. In "The Eyebeaters" the self-imposed bruises of the blind represent a horror that reason will not let imagination lie about; a creative lie will no longer suffice. In his imitation, *The Zodiac*, even the effective and reliable narrator has disappeared. Still there have been good short poems, such as "Pine" and "Madness" in *The Eye-Beaters* and a few of the lyrics in *Puella* (1982).

Few poets have left a clearer impression of their creative intention, or as detailed description of why and how individual poems were written than Dickey has in his many interviews or in his volumes of literary criticism, *Babel to Byzantium* (1968) and *Self-Interviews* (1971). He has consistently insisted that his poetry is for him "the center of the creative wheel" and that anything else he has written—including a screenplay, a television adaptation, his books of literary criticism, his two books of poetic prose, *Jericho* and *God's Images*—is simply a spin-off from his poetry. Dickey is right: his poetry is central, and his prose is simply further development of his thematic concerns in his poetry. His major effort so far in prose is *Deliverance*, and the deliverance from boredom sought there by Ed Gentry and Lewis Medlock is not very different from what Dickey's poetic personae seek. What Ed Gentry gains from his experience on the river is the ability to kill with skill and indifference. This ability must be only temporary, however, and Gentry must be delivered from this also on his return to the city and to his family.

What Dickey has promoted in his poetry is clearly not a return to primitivism as something better than civilized life, but an individual's "emotional primitivism" that permits him to join the primordial life in the collective unconscious in order to regain joy and to survive. Dickey has made clear his goal as a poet:

"he would point the way back to the first man himself, who stood on the shores and opened his arms to the world." This is a romanticism different from that of the nineteenth century. Although Dickey has expressed admiration for D. H. Lawrence, he knows he is not Lawrence seeking to regain the cosmos; he simply tries to show us how, if only briefly, we can find within ourselves something other than the ordinary. The poet too should be capable of finding other selves than the literal one for his poetic personae, as well as with protean creativity, other shapes for his verse. To achieve these goals, Dickey has taken risks. Neither his successes nor his failures are on a small scale, nor do they go unnoticed by his critics.

SURVEY OF CRITICISM

The first critical attention given to Dickey was as critic, specifically as an often notoriously harsh reviewer of current poetry for the *Sewanee Review*. He seemed consciously to write in the Southern tradition of judicial criticism, viable from Poe to Randall Jarrell, as a "hatchet man." He denied this intention and contended that what he admired in Jarrell was not the harshness of the early criticism but the compassion of the later. Dickey was simply trying to warn against a new, unexciting academic gentility in poetry, identified in his first slender volume of criticism as "the suspect in poetry." Today Dickey advocates a greater freedom in thematics in poetry, without neglecting language and form.

There were a few early appreciative reviews of his poetry, most notably by Howard Nemerov (*Sewanee Review* 1963) and Robert Duncan (*Poetry* 1964). Without being aware that a major talent was emerging, both poets praised many things in Dickey's poetry. Dickey's recognition as an important voice in poetry came two or three years later in articles more concerned with his techniques than with his themes. Foremost among these was H. L. Weatherby's *Sewanee Review* article (1966) that called attention to his "way of exchange," a Dickey variation on romantic empathetic imagination. Weatherby's concern was with isolating the quality that marked Dickey's best poems in *Drowning with Others*, *Helmets*, and especially in what Weatherby recognized as his best book, *Buckdancer's Choice*. His exemplar was "A Dog Sleeping on My Feet," illustrating an exchange between man and some form of bestiality, with the intention of evoking some inspirational light so that Dickey could show the world as he knew it to be. What provided this light, in Weatherby's opinion, was the exchange. Weatherby was not, however, a true believer in Dickey's poetry, arguing that there were both religious and aesthetic dangers in this kind of poetry. Richard Howard (*Partisan Review* 1966, reprinted in Calhoun, *James Dickey: The Expansive Imagination*) was the first critic to examine themes, symbols, and images in Dickey's poetry and to recommend his work as the product of an important new voice in contemporary poetry; he called him a poet of "processes." Howard has remained a champion of Dickey's poetry, even coming to the defense of the much-abused *The Zodiac*. In a third major article on Dickey, Peter Davison

(*Atlantic Monthly* 1967) focused on Dickey's treatment of war and reincarnation as the basis of his claim that Dickey and Robert Lowell were the two contemporary poets most nearly deserving of the designation major poet. In his contrast between Lowell as a poet already recognized and Dickey as a late arrival, Davison identifies the qualities that he believes mark Dickey's poetry for distinction— archetypal concerns and an overwhelming sense of urgency. He praises Dickey for both his range and style—and for his ambition. A fourth important early recognition of Dickey's importance was Laurence Lieberman's introduction to his selection of Dickey's poems, *The Achievement of James Dickey* (1968). Not only did Lieberman make available a comprehensive selection of the poetry, but he also explored Dickey's themes and subjects even more thoroughly than had Richard Howard, stressing implicitly a relationship to Theodore Roethke by singling out "joy/celebration" as a central quality in the poetic visions of both.

Soon after Lieberman's book the first collection of Dickey's poetry in a single volume, *Poems 1957–1967*, appeared, and what Weatherby, Howard, Davison, and Lieberman had found was now open to public inspection and critical acclaim. Edmund Fuller in the *Wall Street Journal* (24 May 1967) proclaimed the author of these poems "the most fertile, powerful American poet currently practicing." Lieberman added two essays, in the *Hudson Review* (August 1967) and in the *Yale Review* (Winter 1968). Other poets—Jean Garrigue (*New Leader*, 22 May 1967), Louis Simpson (*Harper's*, August 1967), Ann Stanford (Los Angeles *Times*, April 1967), Louis Untermeyer (*Saturday Review*, May 1967)—and a discriminating drama critic, John Simon (*Commonweal*, 1 December 1967), joined in the praise. Harsh appraisal of Dickey came from his former friend and publisher of *The Suspect in Poetry*, Robert Bly, who in a review (*Sixties*, Spring 1967) accused Dickey of a lack of social and political consciousness because he did not criticize the Vietnam War in his poetry. This view of Dickey as a socially and politically irresponsible Southern writer also prompted attacks on *Deliverance* as glorifying violence at a time when there was a violent war in Vietnam. *Deliverance* was a popular success and an immediate best-seller but was not at first highly praised by critics. Benjamin Demott pronounced Dickey simply another prominent member of "the more life school," an aspect of postmodern neo-romanticism that grasped for absolutes while dismissing conventional modes of living (*Saturday*, 28 March 1970). Others regarded *Deliverance* as merely an effective adventure story. Typical was Nelson Algren's view (*Critic*, May-June 1970) that Dickey was a good poet, but unable to sustain a novel. There were exceptions: Ed Yoder in *Harper's* found the novel both horrible and believable. Nevertheless, the view that *Deliverance* was too much horror with too little meaning was to change quickly; within a few years, *Deliverance* was praised for its complexity and its relationship to the themes of Dickey's poetry.

The praise for *Poems 1957–1967* was replaced by puzzlement and occasional harsh criticism in the 1970s. Some reviewers found the poems in *The Eye-Beaters* (1970) to be obsessed by disease, pain, and death. Other reviewers regretted the change in Dickey's style from direct statements and regular forms to experiments with a subdivided long-line free verse. Dickey's venture into imitation, *The Zodiac* (1976), was generally regarded as further evidence of decline from dramatic power and lyric grace into empty rhetoric, although it had its powerful advocates (see, for example, Robert Penn Warren, *New York Times Book Review*, 14 November 1976). Dickey's later books fared somewhat better. *The Strength of Fields* (1979) was recognized by Dave Smith as a continuation of Dickey's best work (*Poetry*, March 1981). *Puella* (1982) drew some praise and brief comments on his further experiments with language.

Two books on Dickey have appeared in the 1980s: Richard J. Calhoun and Robert W. Hill's Twayne volume, *James Dickey* (1983), and a new edition of mostly old essays, Bruce Weigl and T. R. Hummer's *The Imagination as Glory* (1984). A new volume of poetry is expected, and his long-awaited novel *Alnilan* is reported scheduled for publication.

BIBLIOGRAPHY

Works by James Dickey

Into the Stone and Other Poems. In *Poets of Today VII*. Ed. John Hall Wheelock. New York: Scribner's, 1960.
Drowning with Others. Middletown, Conn.: Wesleyan University Press, 1962.
Helmets. Middletown, Conn.: Wesleyan University Press, 1964.
The Suspect in Poetry. Madison, Minn.: Sixties Press, 1964.
Two Poems of the Air. Portland, Ore.: Centicore Press, 1964.
Buckdancer's Choice. Middletown, Conn.: Wesleyan University Press, 1965.
A Private Brinksmanship. Claremont, Calif.: Pilzer College, 1965.
Poems 1957–1967. Middletown, Conn.: Wesleyan University Press, 1967.
Spinning the Crystal Ball. Washington, D.C.: Library of Congress, 1967.
Babel to Byzantium: Poets & Poetry Now. New York: Farrar, Straus & Giroux, 1968.
Metaphor as Pure Adventure. Washington, D.C.: Library of Congress, 1968.
Deliverance. Boston: Houghton Mifflin, 1970.
The Eye-Beaters, Blood, Victory, Madness, Buckhead and Mercy. Garden City, N.Y.: Doubleday, 1970.
Exchanges. Bloomfield Hills, Mich.: Bruccoli Clark, 1971.
Self-Interviews. Ed. Barbara and James Reiss. Garden City, N.Y.: Doubleday, 1971.
Sorties: Journal and New Essays. Garden City, N.Y.: Doubleday, 1971.
Jericho: The South Beheld. Birmingham, Ala.: Oxmoor House, 1974.
The Zodiac. Garden City, N.Y.: Doubleday, 1976.
God's Images: The Bible, A New Vision. Birmingham, Ala.: Oxmoor House, 1977.
The Strength of Fields. Garden City, N.Y.: Doubleday, 1979.
Tucky the Hunter. New York: Crown, 1979.
The Water-Bug's Mittens. Bloomfield Hills, Mich.: Bruccoli Clark, 1979.
Puella. Garden City, N.Y.: Doubleday, 1982.

Studies of James Dickey

Ashley, Franklin. *James Dickey: A Checklist*. Intro. by James Dickey. Detroit: Gale Research, 1972.

Bruccoli, Matthew J. *James Dickey: Conversations with Writers*. Ed. Matthew J. Bruccoli et al. Detroit: Gale Research, 1977, 1: 25–45.

Calhoun, Richard J. and Robert W. Hill. *James Dickey*. Boston: Twayne, 1983.

Calhoun, Richard J., ed. *James Dickey: The Expansive Imagination; A Collection of Critical Essays*. Deland, Florida: Everett-Edwards, 1973.

Davison, Peter. "The Difficulties of Being Major." *Atlantic Monthly*, October 1967, pp. 116–21. Reprinted in Calhoun, *James Dickey: The Expansive Imagination*.

Elledge, Jim. *James Dickey: A Bibliography, 1947–1974*. Metuchen, N.J.: Scarecrow Press, 1979.

Glancey, Eileen. *James Dickey, the Critic as Poet: An Annotated Bibliography with an Introductory Essay*. Troy, N.Y.: Whitson, 1971.

Howard, Richard. *Alone with America: Essays on the Art of Poetry in the United States Since 1950*. New York: Atheneum, 1969, pp. 75–98.

Lieberman, Laurence. *The Achievement of James Dickey: A Comprehensive Selection of His Poems with a Critical Introduction*, Glenview, Ill.: Scott, Foresman, 1968.

Oates, Joyce Carol. *New Heaven, New Earth: The Visionary Experience*. New York: Vanguard Press, 1974, pp. 205–63.

Weatherly, H. L. "The Way of Exchange in James Dickey's Poetry." *Sewanee Review* 74 (1966): 669–80.

Weigl, Bruce and T. R. Hummer, ed. *The Imagination as Glory: The Poetry of James Dickey*. Urbana and Chicago: University of Illinois Press, 1984.

———————————— J. LEE GREENE ————————————

Ralph Ellison
(1914–   )

It is rare for an American novelist who publishes only one novel to receive the sustained critical acclaim that Ralph Ellison has received for *Invisible Man*. In less than two decades following its publication in 1952, *Invisible Man* was widely considered an American classic.

BIOGRAPHY

Oklahoma had been a state only seven years when on 1 March 1914 the second of three sons was born to young pioneer migrants Lewis and Ida Ellison. Lewis Alfred Ellison, an avid reader, named the infant Ralph Waldo Ellison, an expression of his desire that the child grow up to be a poet and a philosopher. During his childhood Ralph frequently was teased about being named after Ralph Waldo Emerson. Uncomfortable with his name, he later shortened the Waldo to W. But, like his namesake, he became a distinguished writer and thinker. Fifty-two years after Ralph Waldo Ellison was born in Oklahoma City, his native state held a special ceremony to honor his contributions to the creative arts.

Ralph was walking by the time he was six months old and was frequently his father's companion. Lewis Ellison died when Ralph was only three, and because such a strong bond had developed between the two, it was difficult for Ralph to accept the reality of his father's death. But Ida Millsap Ellison kept the vividness of Lewis Ellison alive for her two sons (the firstborn had died) by telling them of their father's life. Lewis Ellison was a native of Abbeville, South Carolina, where he ran away from home at a young age. Later he became what his son Ralph has characterized as a ''professional soldier,'' traveling eventually to Cuba, the Philippines, and China. Before migrating to Oklahoma from Chattanooga, Tennessee, Lewis tried several business ventures. He had a creative

imagination and a strong interest in the construction trades. In Oklahoma City
he worked as a construction foreman.

Ralph seemingly inherited his father's creative temperament, particularly the
desire to build and to create. As a child he attempted to build crystal set radios
from cast-off parts and to experiment with a chemistry set. Most of his creative
energies as a child, however, were devoted to music. Even before he was trained
in music he attempted to write marches, songs, and exercises in symphonic form.

Throughout Ralph's childhood and adolescence, Ida Ellison provided him with
an environment that stimulated his affinities for the creative arts. A lover of the
performing arts, she often played opera recordings in her home, frequently
attended plays in the city, and occasionally interacted with actors and other artists
who came through Oklahoma City. When Ralph was still a young child, his
mother bought him a secondhand cornet after their next-door neighbor had taught
him the fundamentals of playing an alto horn. Subsequently, he developed considerable skill as a trumpeter.

She also encouraged his interest in reading. From her work as a domestic she
brought home *Vanity Fair*, *Literary Digest*, cast-off copies of novels, and other
reading materials that Ralph absorbed. Attracted to fairy tales as a child, he
gradually moved to reading juvenile fiction, Westerns, detective novels, and the
classics, although he was about thirteen years old before he scaled down his
reading of fairy tales.

Ida Ellison was equally instrumental in helping shape her son's social consciousness. The year he was born she was canvassing for the socialists in Oklahoma City. In the 1920s, with the backing of the NAACP, she sustained a protest
against the city's segregated housing laws by living in a neighborhood reserved
for whites. That she was arrested several times did not deter her. Only after the
threat of violence affected her younger son, Herbert, did she relinquish this
campaign.

Although they moved frequently, the Ellisons lived primarily in the black
communities of Oklahoma City's East Side, where Ralph was exposed to different
types of music. It was here during his childhood and adolescence that he developed a strong interest in blues and jazz. Even at a young age he attended
dances and became acquainted with some of the prominent local blues and jazz
musicians, several of whom later became nationally famous. Music also was an
integral part of the curricula in the primary and secondary schools he attended
in Oklahoma City. Blues and jazz, however, were excluded. He took courses
in music appreciation, studied classical music, participated in the band, and,
from the ninth through the twelfth grades, took courses in music harmony.

Ellison also enjoyed activities and pursued interests typical of children and
adolescents of his time, place, and circumstance. In high school he was both
academician and athlete. From a relatively young age he worked at a variety of
jobs, including shining shoes, running errands, selling newspapers, and working
in a drugstore. While he was in high school, one of his jobs was cutting grass
for Dr. Ludwig Hebestreit in exchange for trumpet lessons. A German immigrant

who formed what became the Oklahoma Symphony, Hebestreit also taught Ellison the importance of musical technqiue and increased his understanding of classical composers such as Beethoven, Wagner, and Schumann.

In 1931 Ellison graduated from Douglass High School in Oklahoma City. Financially unable to enroll in college that fall, he found work in the city and saved toward his college education. At the end of two years his savings were meager, and even with a music scholarship to Tuskegee Institute, he still faced difficulty paying the expenses for his freshman year. Yet he was determined to take advantage of this opportunity to study classical music at Tuskegee under the black conductor-composer William L. Dawson. His goal was to write a symphony and have it performed by the time he was twenty-six. So in the late summer of 1933 he left Oklahoma City to enroll at Tuskegee. He could not spare from his savings the price of a train ticket. Riding the trains as a hobo and hitchhiking, he reached Tuskegee, Alabama, in a week.

At Tuskegee Institute he maintained his interest in blues and jazz, but his teachers there did not encourage this interest. He also continued to expand his reading, much of it independent of what he was taught in class. Melville and other writers of the American Renaissance, Marx, Freud, Pound, Hemingway, and Gertrude Stein particularly interested him. In 1935 he by chance read T. S. Eliot's *The Waste Land*, and this marked the beginning of his desire to become a writer instead of a musician.

Off to New York in the summer of 1936 with the intent of earning and saving enough money by the end of the summer to complete his education at Tuskegee, Ellison remained in New York because he did not achieve his aim. He enrolled in art classes to study sculpture and continued his formal study of music; however, two illnesses—his and his mother's—permanently halted his formal studies.

In 1937 Ida Ellison was living in Dayton, Ohio, and was seriously ill as the result of a fall and her physician's inaccurate diagnosis. Her sons moved to Dayton to care for her. Ralph and Herbert made their living that winter hunting and selling game. During the winter nights Ralph studied the craftsmanship of authors such as Joyce, Stein, Dostoevsky, and Hemingway, and seriously began to work on his own craft as a writer.

After his mother died in 1937, he returned to New York, was introduced to Richard Wright by a mutual friend, and formed a close friendship with Wright. With Wright's encouragement and guidance, Ellison wrote a book review and a short story, and continued to study the fictional technique of other writers. Within a few years his friendship with Wright began to dissipate. According to Ellison, as early as 1940 Wright had come to view him as a potential literary rival.

Although he first arrived in New York about five years after the wane of the Harlem Renaissance, he was aware of its literary, artistic, and cultural activities. He had studied Afro-American history in grade school and had been introduced to the works of Langston Hughes, Claude McKay, James Weldon Johnson, and other writers of the Harlem Renaissance before he graduated from high school.

In New York he met several of the Harlem Renaissance thinkers and artists, and some of them, such as Hughes, encouraged and helped guide his ambition to become a writer. Wright helped him get a job with the Work Projects Administration, and Ellison worked as a researcher with the New York Federal Writers' Project from 1938 to 1942.

By the early 1940s he had published a few short stories and several book reviews and had gained minor notice from the literati. In 1942 he became editor of *Negro Quarterly*, joined the merchant marine in 1943 (working as a baker and a cook), and received a Rosenwald Fellowship in winter 1944 to work on a novel. He worked for several months but made only minimal progress on this novel about the wartime experiences of a black soldier. He put the manuscript aside and began to plan the outline for a different novel. On sick leave from the merchant marine in the summer of 1945, he moved temporarily to a farm in Vermont in order to rest and to work on this second novel. While there, he wrote the opening paragraph of what became *Invisible Man*. During the next seven years he worked methodically and laboriously on the novel's form and meaning, interrupting his work on *Invisible Man* for about a year in an unsuccessful attempt to complete the short war novel he had begun in 1944.

In July 1946 he married his second wife, Fanny McConnell. His wife's interests and aspirations in the creative arts and her stalwart moral and financial support helped sustain their marriage and his efforts to complete *Invisible Man*. Ellison wrote a few short stories and articles and did some work as a free-lance photographer during this period, but he devoted most of his time to writing his novel.

For thirteen weeks following its publication in April 1952, *Invisible Man* was a best-seller. Ellison's stature as a first-rate American novelist was established immediately. The following year, 1953, the novel won for him the National Book Award and the National Newspaper Publishers Russwurm Award. Since then, he has led an active life as teacher, lecturer, and writer. From the 1960s through the 1970s he taught at Rutgers University, Bard College, the University of Chicago, and New York University. He was a favored speaker on the lecture circuit, even during the mid–1960s when his novel received its most scathing criticism.

Shadow and Act (1964) and *Going to the Territory* (1986), collections of essays, are his only other book-length publications. Yet he has continued to be a frequent contributor of essays and articles to journals and magazines. He also has published several short stories during the last 25 years, most of which are excerpts from a projected novel and are collectively referred to as the Hickman stories. While a fellow at the American Academy of Arts and Letters in Rome (1955–57), he began work on this projected novel. In the late 1960s a fire in his summer home destroyed several hundred pages of the manuscript. Although he is said to have reconstructed most of the manuscript pages that were destroyed, and to have written several hundred (even several thousand) additional pages, it remains unpublished, a fact that has generated much literary discussion about Ellison as an artist.

The recipient of several honorary degrees during the last two decades, he also has been awarded America's Medal of Freedom and the Chevalier de l'Ordre des Artes et Lettres, one of the most prestigious honors France accords a foreign artist. From 1970 until his retirement in 1980, Ellison was Albert Schweitzer Professor of Humanities at New York University. Since his retirement there have been renewed hopes and promises that the long-awaited Hickman novel, rumored to be in three volumes, will be published.

MAJOR THEMES

Ellison's *Invisible Man* is a quintessential example of how thoroughly the problem of identity pervades the form and meaning of a twentieth-century American novel. The novel's complex thematic structure is predicated on two interrelated questions: Who am I? How did I come to be? The posing and answering of these questions undergird the novel's point of view, its several structural layers, its major characterizations, its richness of language, its allusions, and its imagistic patterns. Ellison draws from various components of American life to chronicle the experiences of the novel's protagonist, a black Everyman who searches for an authentic identity through self-definition.

Integral aspects of the novel's form and meaning are based on a careful mixture of what can be called classicisms, Americanisms (both Afro- and Anglo-), and Africanisms. Its artistry derives from a harmonious blending of different traditions, of which the dominant influences are literature, folklore, history, and music, many of the same ingredients dominating Ellison's life and pervading his essays and short fiction.

In the novel (rather than in a musical composition) Ellison fulfilled an ambition he had as an adolescent to blend the traditions of blues and jazz with those of classical music. Like the author, the novel's protagonist is both writer and musician. Near the end of the prologue the protagonist intones the narrative perspective of his memoir: "And so I play the invisible music of my isolation." Thematically and structurally, the protagonist's dilemma is the blues, which Ellison defines in his essay "Richard Wright's Blues" as "an autobiographical chronicle of personal catastrophe expressed lyrically." At the same time, the novel's form coincides with the structure of a jazz composition. While a central theme runs throughout and hovers in the background, each of the novel's episodes is like a virtuoso performance, a variation on the central theme. Its tripartite structure of prologue, body, and epilogue also parallels the A-B-A structure of a classical composition.

This blending of different traditions as a characteristic of Ellison's fictional artistry in *Invisible Man* is not confined to his use of music. Both oral and written literary traditions figure prominently in the novel's form and meaning. European folklore and its Anglo-American remnants are as meaningfully woven into the fabric of the novel's fictive vision as the Afro-American folktales of Brer Rabbit and his African antecedent. Ellison's use of folklore in *Invisible Man* is only one example of his contention, expressed in many of his essays, that cross-cultural influences are essential in defining an American. To be sure, folklore such as that recorded by the Grimm brothers is as much a part of Afro-American culture as Brer Rabbit is a part of Anglo-American culture. The folk idioms Ellison absorbed as a child from barbershops, dance halls, street corners, and other places in the black community find a place in the novel along with the literary idioms of some of the Western world's most prominent authors, its recorders of folktales, and writers of fairy tales.

From the written literary traditions of classical cultures, Ellison's uses of Homer, Dante, Virgil, and others are obvious. From European literary traditions one hears in the novel echoes of Dostoevsky and Joyce. Aspects of the works of such writers as Emerson, Whitman, and Mark Twain blend with those of James Weldon Johnson, Langston Hughes, and Richard Wright. The philosophical, social, economic, and political ideas of Nikolai Lenin and Abraham Lincoln, of Thomas Jefferson and Jack Johnson, of Marcus Garvey and George Washington, of Andrews Norton and Booker T. Washington, of Henry Moton and John D. Rockefeller, among many others, find a functional place in the novel's artistry. The various comparisons and contrasts, ambiguities and ambivalences, affirmations and negations, and other ways of blending traditions in the novel help define the protagonist's identity as well as support one of the novel's basic themes that America—and thus, the individual American—is woven of many strands.

What Ellison demonstrates in *Invisible Man*, various essays, and some of his short stories (especially the Hickman stories) is that for any American to know who he is, he must understand how he came to be. In his works he concentrates on the dilemma of black Americans, but it is a dilemma other Americans, especially whites, share. It is the problem of an individual's, a race's, and a nation's relationship to the past, a past that is ever present.

In the novel black characters such as Bledsoe, Ras, and Rinehart, and white characters such as Norton, Jack, and Sybil all suffer from various degrees of an identity crisis, a crisis precipitated by tensions between their present circumstances and their personal and racial pasts. To be sure, as the last line of the novel states, the protagonist speaks for everyone. The theme of coming to terms with the past, presented through characterization, allusions, incidents, and scenes, is inextricably bound to the theme of history, especially American history. Thus, as the protagonist points out in the epilogue, what he says about individuals also applies to societies.

The problems of being an American and the problems of America are central concerns in Ellison's works. Often his works deal with problems of a character who rejects his ethnic past. Expanding the literary use of the black folk sermon in his story "Juneteenth" (itself a folk version of Afro-American history), Ellison explores this idea as it applies to black Americans in general. In the story, the power of music, language, and ritual, essential ingredients of the African past, aids the black American in attaining an authentic identity. His story "Night

Talk,'' part of the Hickman series, provides another perspective on how one's identity is integrally connected to the past. "Night Talk," as Ellison's headnote to its first publication indicates, is a strange dialogue between the two chief characters of the Hickman series, a dialogue that attempts "to arrive at the true shape and substance of a sundered past and its meaning."

The problems of the individual reflect the problems of the society in which he lives. In his essay "The Art of Fiction," Ellison states that "one function of serious literature is to deal with the moral core of a given society." For him, the black American "symbolizes among other things the human and social possibility of equality," a theme that resounds throughout his novel, his short fiction, and his essays. It is, overall, the inability or unwillingness of America to live out the principles of its democracy. The willful distortion of those principles, especially but not only as that distortion affects blacks, makes American democracy a joke, what elsewhere Ellison speaks of as a Jokeocracy.

Invisible Man and other of Ellison's characters eventually recognize and reject the illusion of the American Dream. In this context theirs is a journey from illusion to reality. In some instances, these characters change the joke and slip the yoke. In his story "Cadillac Flambé," for instance, the central character burns his Cadillac on the lawn of a racist white senator. The Cadillac is a symbol of American prosperity and of blacks' exclusion from that prosperity. In this story, as in Invisible Man, the themes of politics and technology merge. The result is a vision of America as a technocracy whose scientific approach to history, to life, has eroded the humanitarian spirit supposedly embedded in the idea and the ideal of America. In "Cadillac Flambé," a tragicomedy predicated on the use of myth and ritual, the character's ritualistic burning of his Cadillac signals his knowledge of the difference between the illusion and reality of American democratic principles.

One of the principles on which America was founded was the separation of church and state. In his Hickman stories and elsewhere in his writings, Ellison explores variations on the integration of religion and politics. Indeed, one of the chief characters in this series of short fictions is Bliss/Sunraider, a Southern black child evangelist (Bliss) who becomes a Northern white (apparently) racist politician (Sunraider). He is the essence of the contradiction that is America—politically, racially, culturally, morally, and ethically.

Ellison sees America as a glowing contradiction, and through a series of reversals he explores basic manifestations of this contradiction through characterization, language, theme, and allusion. In his essays he is an acute observer of literature and literary artists, of music and musicians, of politics and politicians, of history and historical figures, and of society in general. In his creative writings these are the sources upon which he frequently draws to shape his fictive world. It is the manner in which he incorporates these sources that provides a gloss on his major themes. He may parody or he may paraphrase both the form and the content of his source materials (such as in his use of Emerson, Whitman, or Booker T. Washington). At other times he may merge ideologically with his sources (as in the case of Melville). Seldom, however, is he a mere imitator of his literary predecessors or contemporaries. To be sure, he uses literary artists and their works as an integral part of the thematic fabric of his novel and stories, as another cultural component that provides a fictional perspective on American democracy.

SURVEY OF CRITICISM

During the year following the publication of *Invisible Man* in April 1952, there were numerous reviews and essay reviews of the novel published in some of the nation's leading newspapers, magazines, and journals. Most of the white critics who praised the novel added the qualification that for a black writer the novel was exemplary. A few critics thought the novel was at best second- or third-rate. In general, black critics gave the novel moderate praise. For the next 25 years, the most informative critical comments about the novel dealt with its style, its use of black American folk materials, its affinities with the works of Anglo-American and European writers, and its overall fictive vision of the place and plight of blacks in America.

In 1964 Ellison published his collection of essays, *Shadow and Act*. In 1965 *Book Week*'s poll of 200 prominent authors, editors, and critics declared that *Invisible Man* was the most distinguished work of fiction published since 1945. About the same time America's black awareness movement gained full stride. These three events marked a significant shift in focus in critical assessments of Ellison, of *Invisible Man*, and of his other writings. In effect, there developed a polarization of critical opinions (though not exclusively along racial lines) that lasted until the early 1970s. In the main, white critics continued to praise the novel but somewhat tempered the racial condescension evident in previous years. They concentrated on affinities between *Invisible Man* and works in the Anglo-American literary tradition. Many of them strained to make the definition of "universal" synonymous with "white," and overall they avoided thematic discussions that might have overt racial implications. One result was that more articles about the novel's craft began to appear.

On the other hand, many black (and a few white) critics during the period complained that Ellison's vision in *Invisible Man* strayed too far from the principles, motives, and aesthetics of black art and black artists as determined by the social and political orientation of the times. In 1963 Irving Howe had set much of the tone for this perspective and had drawn Ellison himself squarely into the debate over art and protest—the now-famous Howe-Ellison critical exchange. Ten years later the general debate itself was the subject of an informative article by William Walling.

The publication of *Shadow and Act* established Ellison as an astute critic of literature, music, and American culture. Since then, his collected and uncollected essays in large measure have determined the direction of critical responses to *Invisible Man* and to his other works. In his introduction to *Shadow and Act*

Ellison points out that the essays are autobiographical. His essays and his numerous interviews are the sources for published information about his life, thoughts, and experiences. He also contends in the collection that *Invisible Man* is not an autobiographical novel. Apparently, critics and scholars have taken this statement at face value, for comparatively few studies have focused on the parallels between Ellison's life and incidents, characters, and ideas in *Invisible Man*. This is true even of the most inclusive study of Ellison's life and writings yet to appear, Robert G. O'Meally's *The Craft of Ralph Ellison* (1980). There are conflicting details in the information Ellison and others have published about his life, and a full-length biography remains to be done.

In his essays and interviews Ellison frequently speaks of the literary influences on his life and art. He gives particular attention to writers in the Anglo-American and European literary mainstreams, whom he calls his "literary ancestors." Since 1964 several critics, many of them following what can be called the validation-by-association school of literary criticism, have concentrated on the direct parallels between *Invisible Man* and the works of Ellison's "literary ancestors."

The trend has been to deal with those writers whose inclusion in the form and meaning of the novel is obvious. In part, this trend accounts for the fact that far fewer critics have noted affinities between *Invisible Man* and the works of Ellison's Afro-American literary predecessors, whom he calls his "literary relatives." Critical discussions of similarities between *Invisible Man* and works by W.E.B. Du Bois, James Weldon Johnson, and, of course, Richard Wright, and literary discussions of the Wright-Ellison-Baldwin triad constitute the bulk of critical articles about Ellison and his "literary relatives." Except for very general and chronological studies of black American literature, critics (Houston Baker is one exception) basically have ignored Ellison's alignment with the Afro-American literary tradition.

Throughout his critical writings Ellison has focused on the significance of literary technique, a topic that itself has generated both positive and negative comments about his role and accomplishments as a literary artist. Shelby Steele, Ronald Walcott, Gene Bluestein, and several other critics have produced significant commentary about the influence of blues and jazz on the novel. The influence of classical music, gospel music, and spiritual music on the form and meaning of *Invisible Man* needs to be critically assessed. Susan Blake and Floyd Horowitz are among several critics who have written perceptively about Ellison's use of black American folklore in *Invisible Man*. Satire and comedy in the novel have been the topics of critical articles written from quite different critical perspectives. Numerous critics have dealt with various aspects of the novel's concern with identity, and existential themes in the novel have been the focus for several critical studies.

Although numerous articles since the 1960s have studied particular aspects of the artistry in *Invisible Man*—its structure, characterization, language, allusions, and patterns of imagery, among other techniques—there is need for a comprehensive and sophisticated study of the novel's craft and of Ellison as a literary artist. O'Meally's *The Craft of Ralph Ellison* was a major first step in this direction. O'Meally provides one of the fullest discussions of Ellison's short fiction yet to appear.

The decade of the 1970s indeed was a high mark in critical attention to Ellison. Between 1970 and 1975 alone he was the exclusive or a principal subject of more than twenty doctoral dissertations completed at American universities. He received widespread attention from literary critics in Italy, Germany, France, Great Britain, and other European countries. He was a favored subject of American literary critics and literary historians during the 1970s. The different articles, book chapters, and dissertations about Ellison that have appeared since 1952 now number in the hundreds. Bibliographical studies of him are appearing more frequently. His short fiction also is receiving more attention. Yet the critical focus remains on *Invisible Man*. Recent trends are toward a more in-depth exploration of the novel's language, its mythic, folkloric, and ritualistic ramifications and implications, and its various musical, political, religious, and literary sources. The novel's richness and complexity promise to generate critical studies for many years to come.

BIBLIOGRAPHY

Works by Ralph Ellison

Invisible Man. New York: Random House, 1952.
Shadow and Act. New York: Random House, 1964.
Going to the Territory. New York: Random House, 1986.

Short Fiction

"Slick Gonna Learn." *Direction* 2 (September 1939): 10–11, 14, 16.
"Afternoon." *American Writing*. Ed. Hans Otto Storm et al. Prairie City, Ill.: J. A. Decker, 1940, pp. 28–37.
"The Birthmark." *New Masses* 36 (July 1940): 16–17.
"Mister Toussan." *New Masses* 41 (November 1941): 19–20.
"That I Had the Wings." *Common Ground* 3 (Summer 1943): 30–37.
"Flying Home." *Cross Section*. Ed. Edwin Seaver. New York: L. B. Fischer, 1944, pp. 469–85.
"In a Strange Country." *Tomorrow* 3 (July 1944): 41–44.
"King of the Bingo Game." *Tomorrow* 4 (November 1944): 29–33.
"Invisible Man." *Horizon* 16 (October 1947): 104–18.
"Invisible Man: Prologue to a Novel." *Partisan Review* 19 (January 1952): 31–40.
"Did You Ever Dream Lucky?" *New World Writing* 5 (April 1954): 134–45.
"February." *Saturday Review* 1 (January 1955): 25.
"A Coupla Scalped Indians." *New World Writing* 9 (1956): 225–36.
"The Roof, the Steeple and the People." *Quarterly Review of Literature* 10 (September 1959): 115–28.
"And Hickman Arrives." *Noble Savage* 1 (1960): 5–49.

"It Always Breaks Out." *Partisan Review* 30 (Spring 1963): 13–28.

"Out of the Hospital and Under the Bar." *Soon, One Morning*. Ed. Herbert Hill. New York: Alfred A. Knopf, 1963, pp. 242–90.

"Juneteenth." *Quarterly Review of Literature* 13 (1965): 262–76.

"Night-Talk." *Quarterly Review of Literature* 16 (1969): 317–29.

"A Song of Innocence." *Iowa Review* 1 (Spring 1970): 30–40.

"Cadillac Flambé." *American Review* 16 (1973): 249–69.

"Backwacking: A Plea to the Senator." *Massachusetts Review* 18 (Autumn 1977): 411–16.

Studies of Ralph Ellison

Baker, Houston A. "Forgotten Prototype." *Virginia Quarterly Review* 49 (Summer 1973): 433–49.

Blake, Susan L. "Ritual and Rationalization: Black Folklore in the Works of Ralph Ellison." *PMLA* 94 (January 1979): 121–36.

Bluestein, Gene. "The Blues as a Literary Theme." *Massachusetts Review* 8 (Autumn 1967): 593–617.

Covo, Jacqueline. *The Blinking Eye: Ralph Waldo Ellison and His American, French, German, and Italian Critics, 1952–1971*. Metuchen, N.J.: Scarecrow Press, 1974.

Doyle, Mary Ellen. "In Need of Folk: The Alienated Protagonists of Ralph Ellison's Short Fiction." *CLA Journal* 19 (December 1975): 165–72.

Gayle, Addison. *The Way of the New World: The Black Novel in America*. Garden City, N.Y.: Doubleday, 1975.

Gibson, Donald B., ed. *Five Black Writers: Essays on Wright, Ellison, Baldwin, Hughes, and Le Roi Jones*. New York: New York University Press, 1970.

Giza, Joanne. "Ralph Ellison." *Black American Writers: Bibliographical Essays*, vol. 2. Ed. M. Thomas Inge, Maurice Duke, and Jackson R. Bryer. New York: St. Martin's Press, 1978.

Hersey, John R., ed. *Ralph Ellison: A Collection of Critical Essays*. Englewood Cliffs, N.J.: Prentice-Hall, 1974.

Horowitz, Floyd R. "Ralph Ellison's Modern Version of Brer Bear and Brer Rabbit in *Invisible Man*." *Midcontinental American Studies Journal* 4 (Fall 1963): 21–27.

O'Daniel, Thurman B. "Image of Man as Portrayed by Ralph Ellison." *CLA Journal* 10 (June 1967): 277–84.

O'Meally, Robert G. *The Craft of Ralph Ellison*. Cambridge, Mass.: Harvard University Press, 1980.

Steele, Shelby. "Ralph Ellison's Blues." *Journal of Black Studies* 7 (December 1976): 151–68.

Walcott, Ronald. "Some Notes on the Blues, Style and Space: Ellison, Gordone and Tolson." *Black World* 22 (December 1972): 4–29.

Walling, William. " 'Art' and 'Protest': Ralph Ellison's *Invisible Man* Twenty Years After." *Phylon* 34 (June 1973): 120–34.

THOMAS E. DASHER

William Faulkner
(1897–1962)

William Faulkner has achieved a greater influence on Southern writers than has any other. But his appeal is finally international, and he ranks among the greatest writers of his nation and century, as the continuous outpouring of criticism on his art testifies.

BIOGRAPHY

William Cuthbert Falkner (he would later add the *u* dropped by his great-grandfather) was born in New Albany, Mississippi, on 25 September 1897. The son of Murry Cuthbert and Maud Butler Falkner, he soon moved with his family to Ripley, Mississippi, but after the births of two more sons—Murry and Johncy—the family moved to Oxford, Mississippi, in September 1902. These moves were tied to family, for the Falkners had been prominent in north Mississippi for several decades. William Clark Falkner (1825–85), the "Old Colonel," had been a Confederate officer, a novelist (*The White Rose of Memphis*), and a cofounder of the Ripley Railroad Company. After the war, he practiced law and later was shot and killed by an irate former partner; an impressive eighteen-foot statue dominates the monument at his grave near Ripley. His son John Wesley Thompson Falkner, the "Young Colonel" (1848–1922), attended the University of Mississippi, practiced law, moved to Oxford in 1885, and briefly entered politics. His elder son Murry, however, never found the success his grandfather or father knew. Attracted to the railroad, William Faulkner's father moved his family to Oxford where he ran a livery stable; he loved to hunt and to drink.

Maud Butler, whose mother Lelia Butler, called Damuddy, lived with the Murry Falkners when they moved to Oxford, was a small, reserved, determined woman whose relationship with her husband was often strained. She loved to paint and to read, recommending Shakespeare, Balzac, Conrad, and contemporary fiction writers to her sons. She and her husband disagreed almost from the first about their oldest son, whose own relationship with his mother had an especially strong impact upon his life. Until her death in 1960, William Faulkner visited with her every day he was in Oxford, and while she often failed to understand his actions and his writing, she remained one of his staunchest defenders.

Initially, Faulkner was a good student, but by the eighth grade he was bored with school and far more involved in his own reading and writing, as well as the activities of the community and his father's livery stable. He already felt alienated from many of his peers who found him different and difficult. By the eleventh grade, the final year in high school, he had dropped out of school, briefly returning to play football but leaving for good in the fall of 1915. He was not, however, totally alone in a hostile environment, for he always enjoyed hunting with other boys and men, and he had become involved in two relationships that altered his life and career.

One was with Estelle Oldham. Twenty months older than Faulkner and a popular coquette in Oxford, she had known the Falkner boys since childhood, the oldest having always been her favorite. He shared books and poems with her and tried to please her with his clothes and constant attention. And she responded, for if he placed her and her world upon a pedestal, she, in turn, took his world and interests seriously and tried to share in them. By the time she entered college, they both acknowledged their mutual love even though she gladly received the attention of other men.

The other relationship was with Phil Stone, the scion of an established Oxford family, who was four years older than Faulkner and educated at Ole Miss and Yale. In June 1914 he and Faulkner met through a friend who recognized the younger man's talent and the older's learning. Thus began a lifelong friendship that changed and nearly crumbled, but that Faulkner still acknowledged with the dedication of his Snopes trilogy. At first, Stone served as mentor and resource. A man who loved to talk and teach, he found a willing, insatiable student. They spent much time together discussing classic and contemporary literature, philosophy, and history. Stone further opened a world into which Faulkner had begun to wander by encouraging the younger man to write his own poetry. Although Faulkner would have doubtlessly developed into a writer without Stone's influence, he benefited in a number of ways from their friendship in the early years of his career.

One benefit to Faulkner from Stone's friendship occurred in spring 1918 when Estelle gave in to family pressure and agreed to marry Cornell Franklin. To help Faulkner through this difficult period and to head off a possible elopement, Stone invited Faulkner to join him at Yale, where he was in law school. Working as a ledger clerk in New Haven, Faulkner experienced briefly the atmosphere and stimulation of a great university, but in mid-June, two months after Estelle's marriage, he joined the Royal Air Force in New York and later reported to

Toronto for active service. Although he desperately wanted to see action in World War I, he never left Canada and was discharged in early December. This experience, however, profoundly affected his fiction, and for many years, he cultivated the myth that he had been severely wounded during the war. He even wore his uniform and limped around Oxford. Only much later did he attempt to clarify his role during the war. Meanwhile, he used this experience repeatedly, even in his first published fiction, which appeared in the *Mississippian* a year later, "Landing in Luck."

Faulkner's sojourn in New Haven and Canada and his return to Oxford were only the first in a series of extended journeys that would take him in the next decade away from and back to Oxford. In 1919 he wandered around Mississippi, taking trips to Memphis and New Orleans. His poem "L'Apres-Midi d'un Faune" appeared in the *New Republic* in August, and he began to publish poems in the *Mississippian* and Oxford *Eagle*, having enrolled in the University of Mississippi as a special student. In the following year he joined the Marionettes, a university drama club for which he wrote a verse play, *The Marionettes*, even though he withdrew from Ole Miss in November 1920.

During the fall of 1921, after presenting Estelle Franklin with a gift volume of his poems, *Vision in Spring*, he went to New York, where he stayed with Stark Young and worked at a bookstore run by Elizabeth Prall. Reading such writers as Melville, Flaubert, Dostoevsky, and Cervantes, he continued his own writing and drawing. He briefly rented a room in Greenwich Village and revisited New Haven but returned to Oxford in December 1921 to become postmaster at the university post office, a position Phil Stone had helped to secure for him. As postmaster, Faulkner was a complete failure; he preferred to read and write— continuing to publish in the *Mississippian* and having one poem appear in the *Double Dealer* in June 1922. Stone helped to arrange the publication of his first volume of poems, *The Marble Faun*, with the Four Seas Company; Faulkner agreed to pay the $400 production costs. By the end of 1924, having lost his postmaster's job, Faulkner decided to visit New Orleans, where his New York employer Elizabeth Prall now lived with her husband, Sherwood Anderson.

New Orleans was a center for artists and writers, whose work often appeared in the *Double Dealer*. At the center of this group was Anderson, the author of *Winesburg, Ohio* and *Horses and Men*; he and Faulkner got along well together when they first met in late 1924. After *The Marble Faun* was published in December, Faulkner returned to New Orleans in early 1925 on his way to Europe. Since he would not sail until July, he frequently visited with the Andersons; and he began to contribute a series of sketches to the New Orleans *Times-Picayune*, met many people—including Helen Baird, with whom he fell in love—and wrote his first novel, *Soldiers' Pay*, which Anderson sent to his own publisher with his recommendation.

When Faulkner sailed with William Spratling to Europe after a brief trip to Oxford, he had no definite plans. He traveled in Italy and Switzerland and settled in Paris in mid-August. Enthralled with the city and its art, he began his second novel, *Elmer*, which he never published but from which he repeatedly used material in later published work. After a brief visit to England, he returned to Paris and then sailed in December for New York, where he checked on the progress of *Soldiers' Pay*.

When his first novel was published on 25 February 1926, he was back in New Orleans with Spratling. Most of the first printing of *Soldiers' Pay* sold quickly, and the good reviews encouraged Faulkner to begin his third novel, *Mosquitoes*, which drew heavily on his New Orleans experiences with Anderson and his circle of friends and on Helen Baird, to whom he dedicated the novel, completed in September 1926. Two other works composed during these New Orleans periods were written expressly for Helen: *Mayday* and *Helen: A Courtship*. Unlike Estelle, who was beginning to have marital problems, Baird rejected Faulkner's love. With his novel, however, he was more successful. Liveright accepted *Mosquitoes*, which was published on 30 April 1927.

During this period Faulkner had begun work on Snopes material called *Father Abraham*, but he put it aside to write *Flags in the Dust*, his first completed novel to deal with the Sartorises and Yoknapatawpha. He also returned briefly to New Orleans and collaborated with Spratling on *Sherwood Anderson & Other Famous Creoles*. When he returned to Oxford, he found Estelle, with her two children, who had decided to divorce Cornell Franklin; the divorce, however, would not be final for two years.

After revising *Flags* extensively, Faulkner sent it to Liveright in October 1927, confident that he had written a great novel. When his publisher rejected the manuscript and advised Faulkner not to try to publish it, the author was devastated. He was also having little success in trying to publish his short stories. Putting *Flags* temporarily aside, he plunged into his next novel with a fervor that remained unique in his career. He wrote *The Sound and the Fury*, convinced that no one would publish his work and that he was thus freed from outside considerations. He knew that this time he had truly written a great novel. Meanwhile, Harcourt, Brace accepted *Flags* on the condition that he cut it. He agreed and went to New York, taking the manuscript of his new novel with him. Ben Wasson, now his agent, actually did the cutting, and *Flags in the Dust* became *Sartoris*, Faulkner's third published novel; it appeared on 31 January 1929. By the time *The Sound and the Fury* was accepted by Cape and Smith in early 1929, Faulkner, determined also to write a novel that would sell, completed a draft of *Sanctuary*.

On 20 June 1929 he and Estelle married, two months after her divorce was final, and he corrected the proofs of *The Sound and the Fury* on his honeymoon. He had accomplished two great personal goals: he had written his first truly great novel and had married the woman whom he had always loved. His marriage, however, never matched the success of his career, and although he wrote many great novels, he and Estelle were seldom happy together. Neither could adjust to the other, and both used alcohol as an escape and a means of release. Although their marriage lasted and produced two daughters, one to die in infancy and the other to become her father's delight, their lives remained separate and often at war.

By the time *The Sound and the Fury* was published on 7 October 1929, Faulkner had a wife and little money; his short stories did not begin to sell until the following year. He found a job in the Ole Miss power plant where, during the night, he wrote *As I Lay Dying*. By the time it was published in October 1930, his stories had begun to sell, and he bought a home, Rowan Oak. When the galley proofs of *Sanctuary* arrived, he viewed them with dismay and insisted on extensive revision. *Sanctuary* was published in early 1931, assuring Faulkner the notoriety that he had known the novel would produce. *These 13*, a collection of his stories, soon followed, and in October he attended the Southern Writers' Conference in Charlottesville before a seven-week stay in New York, where he drank heavily, met many writers—including Dashiell Hammett, Lillian Hellman, and Nathanael West—and was treated as a famous and respected writer.

Back in Oxford, he continued to work on *Light in August* and to face severe financial problems. Thus in May 1932 he made his first trip to Hollywood, where he earned $500 a week writing for movies. In Hollywood he met the director Howard Hawks, for whom he worked on scripts for over two decades. In August Murry Falkner died, and on 9 October 1932 *Light in August* was published to considerable acclaim as a major novel by an internationally known author. Once again in Oxford, he continued to work on short stories and took flying lessons. *A Green Bough*, his second volume of verse, was published in April 1933, and his second volume of stories, *Doctor Martino and Other Stories*, appeared in April 1934. During this period he continued to fly and to work periodically on film scripts as well as his own work, a novel about the Snopes family and one he entitled *Requiem for a Nun*. By the end of 1933, he put both novels aside to begin the novel that would become *Absalom, Absalom!* He also earned his pilot's license and later attended the dedication of the Shushan Airport in New Orleans.

In mid–1934 he worked on a series of stories about Bayard Sartoris for the *Saturday Evening Post* and returned to Hollywood to make $1,000 per week. When he arrived back in Oxford in September 1934, he put *Absalom* aside and began work on *Pylon*, which drew heavily from his experiences with flying and with the people whom he had met at air shows and airports. He wrote quickly, finishing the manuscript in late November, and the novel was published on 25 March 1935. He continued to work on stories and returned to *Absalom* as his financial situation worsened once again. Then in November his beloved youngest brother Dean, whom he had encouraged to fly, was killed in a plane crash; he felt totally responsible. But he was not able to grieve in Oxford; he returned to Hollywood, this time not only for money, but although he did not yet know it, also for love. He was drawn to Meta Carpenter, Hawks's secretary, and an intimate relationship that lasted intermittently over much of the rest of his life developed. In Hollywood he also finally finished *Absalom*, which was published on 26 October 1936.

During the first half of 1937, still in Hollywood after several brief visits home, he revised his Bayard Sartoris stories and wrote a long, final story for the novel *The Unvanquished*, which was published in early 1938. By this time he had begun *The Wild Palms* and severely burned his back during a visit to New York. After the sale of *The Unvanquished* to Hollywood, he bought a farm not far from Oxford where Faulkner the novelist, who had never wanted to be seen as the literary man, could also be Faulkner the farmer. He finished *The Wild Palms* in June 1938. He had also returned to the Snopes material, which he already knew would become a trilogy; the first volume of the trilogy was later entitled *The Hamlet*.

Meanwhile, Faulkner was named to the National Institute of Arts and Letters, and his picture appeared on the cover of *Time* magazine. Between grief and nothing, he would choose grief, as he told several people in his life, including Meta Carpenter, but he would not be able to grieve away from the public eye. An intensely private man, he was now a public person whose reputation grew increasingly during the next decade and culminated in the Nobel Prize. It was a difficult decade: he continued to struggle financially and, at times, artistically. *The Hamlet*, however, progressed smoothly, and it was published in April 1940. During this period, Conrad Aiken published an essay favorably comparing him to Balzac, and Faulkner, who claimed to have little interest in politics, contributed the manuscript of *Absalom, Absalom!* to a relief fund for Spanish loyalists.

Faulkner's own funds, however, were depleted. The sole provider for much of his family, he asked for advances from his publisher, wrote more stories, worried about the impending war, and did civil defense work. He also began to revise stories for the novel *Go Down, Moses*, which was published in May 1942. During this period he tried for a screenwriting job and also a commission in the military. Always, he turned out stories, hoping to cover the constant bills.

Finally, in July 1942 he returned to Hollywood for only $300 per week as part of a long-term contract that sent him back and forth between Oxford and Hollywood for several years. He renewed his affair with Meta Carpenter, but the burden of his financial problems and his misery in Hollywood combined with his heavy drinking to create perhaps the lowest point in his life. As a result of a conversation in Hollywood he began the story that slowly evolved into *A Fable*, but he was able to produce little of his own work except for a few stories. He spent much of 1943, 1944, and 1945 working on scripts and trying to progress with his fable about Christ. In mid–1945 Malcolm Cowley began work on *The Portable Faulkner* for Viking Press. The book had a great impact upon Faulkner's reputation and the availability of his work. Published in April 1946, this volume included both a long introduction by Cowley and a new piece on the Compsons by Faulkner. Also in early 1946, Warner Brothers agreed to let Faulkner finish his fable, allowing him to stay in Oxford and to begin to extricate himself from his Hollywood bondage. The novel progressed slowly as Faulkner continued his life in Oxford—riding horses, hunting, participating in family activities, and meeting with English classes at Ole Miss in April 1947. Finally, in early 1948 he put aside the incredibly complex manuscript of his fable and began *Intruder in the Dust*, which he finished in April after careful but rapid revision. Not only did the novel receive enthusiastic reviews and sell well, but MGM bought the film rights for $50,000. Once again, he was the highly touted author, widely entertained when he arrived in New York in October. Almost immediately, back in Oxford, he began to plan two collections of short fiction—one to contain his collected stories and the other to focus on Gavin Stevens as detective. Clearly, much of the artist's agony of the past few years was behind him.

In early 1949 Faulkner helped the film crew who came to Oxford to film *Intruder*, and in November *Knight's Gambit* was published. Earlier, in August, he had met a young woman, Joan Williams, with whom he became involved first as confidant and mentor, and later as suitor and rejected older lover. He proposed that they coauthor a play that he would outline and she develop. She did little work on the play, which became *Requiem for a Nun*, the story he had conceived as early as 1933. Before he could finish it, however, he received the American Academy's Howells Medal for Fiction in May 1950, saw his *Collected Stories* published in August, and in November learned that he had been awarded the 1949 Nobel Prize for Literature. At first refusing to go to Stockholm, he did take his daughter Jill with him to the award ceremonies in December 1950 and delivered his famous acceptance speech, although no one in the audience could hear it. When the speech was published, it seemed to mark another turning point in his life. Many people saw it as an affirmation of man's ability to prevail over the agony, defeat, and suffering that some felt dominated his fiction; but as others recognized, Faulkner's work had always affirmed the verities of the human heart, and the short Stockholm speech said nothing new.

For the new Nobel Prize novelist, 1951 was a busy year. Agreeing to help Howard Hawks on a script, he went to Hollywood for two months at $2,000 a week and, once again, saw Carpenter. In March he received the National Book Award for Fiction for *Collected Stories*; in April he traveled to England and France. He also worked on the stage version of *Requiem*, which had been published as a novel in September. In October he received the French Legion of Honor in New Orleans and returned to his fable as the new year began. In early 1952 he stayed in Oxford, speaking in May to an enthusiastic audience at the Delta Council, where he attacked federal welfare programs. He then left for Paris where severe back pain—probably caused by a fall from a horse—proved almost crippling. He traveled to Norway, then back to New York and Oxford. He continued to see Williams and tried to help her with her writing. In late 1952, despite the back pain and heavy drinking, he worked on *A Fable* in Princeton and New York. In early 1953 he left Oxford again, this time planning to stay nearly six months, seeking for a way to finish his novel, to escape the physical pain, and to ease the emotional suffering.

In New York, although Faulkner remained physically ill from heavy drinking for several months, he managed to work steadily; his work included television scripts and a long piece on Mississippi for *Holiday* magazine. He returned home in April to work through the summer on *A Fable*, which he was convinced would be his best novel. Back in New York, Saxe Commins, his editor at Random House, helped him wrestle with the huge manuscript as he tried to continue the troubling relationship with Williams. Finally, with the novel finished, he left for Europe in November to work with Hawks on another movie.

In Europe, he traveled in France, Switzerland, England, and Italy; he became involved with yet another young woman, Jean Stein. In early 1954 he traveled to Egypt to meet Hawks; there he completed his script and learned of Williams's marriage to a younger man and the approaching marriage of his daughter. Back in Oxford in April, he continued to worry about *A Fable*, finally published on 2 August 1954 to mixed reviews nearly ten years after he had begun to write it. Before Jill's marriage on 21 August, he attended an international writers' conference in Brazil at the request of the government. After the wedding he divided his time between Oxford and New York writing stories and teleplays, continued his relationship with Stein, and received the National Book Award for *A Fable* in January 1955 and the Pulitzer Prize in May.

In 1955 he became embroiled in the heated dispute over desegregation; he was vehemently attacked for his opposition to the segregationists. Then in July he made a triumphant visit to Japan, again at the request of the State Department. On his way home he made stops in Manila, Europe, and Iceland, arriving in Oxford in October, not long after the publication of *Big Woods*, a carefully crafted collection of his hunting stories. Thus, he was assuming a more public voice even though he continued to cherish his privacy. His patriotism and his conscience combined to make him a spokesman for America, for writers, and for white Southerners struggling to deal with the growing civil rights movement.

By late 1955, when he began his second Snopes volume, royalties and movie sales of his novels had increasingly relieved his financial worries. Through 1956, he visited Charlottesville, Virginia, where Jill lived, as he traveled between New York and Oxford. In June he agreed to head a section of President Eisenhower's "people-to-people" program to establish better contacts between American and foreign writers, and in late September he finished *The Town*, published in May 1957. Meanwhile, he had agreed to serve as writer-in-residence at the University of Virginia for the second semester. Together, he and Estelle, who had lived separate lives for years, moved to Charlottesville. He also visited Greece in February for a production of *Requiem* and a medal from the Athens Academy. When he returned to Oxford from Virginia, he began the third Snopes volume, which he continued when he was again writer-in-residence at the University of Virginia in 1958. He divided his time between Oxford and Charlottesville, where he increasingly felt at home and especially enjoyed the fox hunting and horseback riding. *The Mansion* was published on 13 November 1959 after he had bought a home in Charlottesville; he had found a certain peace in his second home near his daughter and grandsons.

In early 1960 Faulkner was in Oxford but soon returned to Charlottesville, where he was appointed Balch Lecturer in American Literature; he continued to visit classes and give one public reading a year. In October his mother died, severing one of his major ties to Oxford, and he further cemented his ties to the University of Virginia when he decided to leave his manuscripts to the William Faulkner Foundation in Charlottesville. In April 1961 he paid a successful visit to South America as a guest of the North American Association of Venezuela and, soon after, began his next novel, *The Reivers*, published in June 1962. Throughout the last of 1961, he remained in Virginia, where he had another serious riding accident and complicated health problems. Returning to Rowan Oak in January 1962, he visited with friends and family.

When he and Estelle moved back to Virginia, they planned to make the move permanent. He visited West Point in April, and in May accepted the Gold Medal for Fiction of the National Institute of Arts and Letters in New York. He returned to Oxford in early June, and while he was there he had another riding accident. Making plans to buy an estate not far from Charlottesville, he relaxed at Rowan Oak. On 5 July he entered the hospital after a drinking bout and died there of a heart attack on 6 July, the old Colonel's birthday. He was buried in St. Peter's cemetery in Oxford on 7 July 1962.

MAJOR THEMES

In "Race at Morning," one of Faulkner's late stories written in 1954 and sold to the *Saturday Evening Post*, Mister Ernest tells the disbelieving narrator, a young boy, that the boy must go to school. The boy wants to stay with Mister Ernest, farming and hunting and leading the kind of life he observes the older man living. " 'That ain't enough any more [Mister Ernest tells him]. Time was when all a man had to do was just farm eleven and a half months, and hunt the other half. But not now. Now just to belong to the farming business and the hunting business ain't enough. You got to belong to the business of mankind.' " The boy must go to school to learn how to teach others not only what is right and wrong but, more important, *why* it is right and *why* the boy, later a man, acts the way he does. Thus, the boy must understand why *maybe* is " 'the best word in our language, the best of all. That's what mankind keeps going on: Maybe.' "

Mister Ernest realizes that man's most difficult challenge is to face choosing and then accepting the responsibility of living with the consequences of that choice. With a knowledge of Mister Ernest's world—the land, the hunt, the relationship of man with nature, man with his fellowman—the boy must go further to help others live in a complex world where the choices are perhaps no more difficult than those faced by previous generations, but which now demand response from individuals whose very consciousness of the complexity makes knowing *why* essential before they can make the choice. In other words, the boy's initiation into good and evil has only just begun, and he will spend a lifetime facing moral questions to which farming and hunting alone cannot provide the answers. He must develop the critical awareness of the educated individual, the ability to ask the difficult questions and then accept acting even though one knows that only after the action will he be able to judge whether or not he acted rightly. He also knows that even then he will never know whether or not choosing another response might have produced better or more just or more compassionate results. Yet belonging to the "business of mankind" forces the boy out of childhood, out of the world of the past, the world of Mister Ernest, into the future—all contained in the present moment of decision.

Critics continue to debate the merits of Faulkner's late fiction; all agree that the greatest work began with *The Sound and the Fury* and continued through *Go Down, Moses*. Most concur that Faulkner wrote at least five or six truly great novels during that period. About the work written after 1942, however, they still vehemently disagree. Some claim that although Faulkner continued to write great parts of novels, the great novels were behind him. Others maintain that he lost the drive, the spark, as he moved from the dark world of the earlier period to the brighter vision of the later period. Still others believe that he felt compelled to affirm man's ability to prevail over the human condition while he earlier denied that possibility. In all of Faulkner's work—both early and late— there emerges, however, a consistency of themes and commitment. His Nobel Prize Acceptance Speech does anticipate *A Fable*, "Race at Morning," and *The Reivers*, but it also incorporates *As I Lay Dying*, *Absalom, Absalom!*, and *The Wild Palms*. Faulkner's major themes do not divide neatly into dark and light, despair and hope, tragic and comic. They do, in many ways, merge into *Maybe*.

For Faulkner, an individual who must live in the modern world faces the traps that other twentieth-century writers have explored: alienation, isolation, fragmentation. Certainly in the post–World War I world, modern man is constantly in danger of following Prufrock's model or Yeats's "passionate intensity." Sadness at a world bereft of values, moral certainty, or belief in anything shaped the young Faulkner's poetry and prose. The early work is filled with epicene, faunlike creatures who exist only half-formed in world-weary despair or ennui and are replaced by young men seeking meaning in what they perceive to be a meaningless world. Their vision is turned inward, toward self, recoiling in horror from full involvement in the world around them; Little Sister Death lurks in the doorway, and they often turn to welcome her embrace. For Quentin Compson, this embrace results in his actual suicide; Horace Benbow, on the other hand, returns to Belle Mitchell and a death-in-life situation. Young Bayard Sartoris feels driven away from his family and the community as he pursues his own inevitable death in a plane crash, whereas Darl Bundren withdraws into insanity, unable to cope with his family's odyssey and his own ineffectual efforts to derive meaning from the lives around him. None of these men knows how to come to terms with time, history, the community, and Original Sin. Eating the apple only assured the knowledge of good and evil, not of what is good and what is evil. Thus, these great forces and influences overwhelm many Faulkner characters when they are unable to incorporate them into a whole rather than disparate fragments. For Faulkner, who chose to write mainly of Yoknapatawpha residents, Southerners were particularly appropriate examples of the universal condition of man. Yet he never saw the dilemmas or problems of his characters as unique to the South. On the contrary, he found in his native region the strengths and weaknesses, the supports and threats that assail all people.

Among those strengths is always community. As Cleanth Brooks states, community "is the circumambient atmosphere, the essential ether of Faulkner's fiction." From Joe Christmas to Lucius Priest, the community exerts a powerful influence over the lives of the individuals within it. At times it can be destructive, as when it is stirred by hatred, bigotry, and mindless respectability; however, in Faulkner it always provides the context, the framework in which people live their lives. It cannot save anyone, but it can help someone save himself. Joe Christmas in *Light in August* cannot fit, for he fails to learn who he is. His is the tragedy of a man who becomes subsumed by a passion to discover his identity fixed forever in being white or black. Like Ahab pursuing Moby Dick, he refuses to compromise and propels himself toward destruction. Gail Hightower also cuts himself off from the community by pursuing his own obsessions to the destruction of his home and life. In contrast to them, Lena Grove and Byron Bunch elicit the strengths of the community as they grope toward a family unit and a stable existence. This community does not depend upon some aristocracy at the top of a social hierarchy, but very often upon the yeoman farmer whose integrity and ties to the land make him able to reach out and embrace Lena and Byron. Similarly, in *Intruder in the Dust* the various elements of the community combine forces to save Lucas Beauchamp. Gavin Stevens, Aleck Sander, Chick Mallison, and Miss Habersham finally involve even the Gowries in proving Lucas's innocence. In the Snopes trilogy, Flem gains a wife, the presidency of the bank, and the mansion, but again through Gavin Stevens and Chick Mallison and especially V. K. Ratliff the community presides over Flem's self-ordained doom. The values of the community, chosen by Sarty Snopes in "Barn Barning" over his father's values, assure that Flem, who, unlike Sarty, chooses his own ruthless ambition over family, will face Mink's bullet without an attempt to save himself. In Faulkner's fiction those people who cut themselves off from the community deny themselves a vital strength and important foundation.

History also figures in much of Faulkner's work. Certainly history haunts Gail Hightower, whose obsession with his grandfather's exploits in the Civil War prevents him from living in the present. In *Go Down, Moses* Ike McCaslin's reaction to his discovery of his family's history dooms him to an ineffectual repudiation of the land and a hollow existence as every hunter's uncle and no child's father. Both Quentin Compson and Shreve McCannon in *Absalom, Absalom!* imaginatively reconstruct the past in order to understand the Sutpens' destruction. Quentin, however, cannot assimilate the past—his own in *The Sound and the Fury* or Sutpen's—and shivers in the cold, knowing he cannot move into the future. Shreve, his Canadian roommate, sees the search for the truth about the Sutpens as a challenging game and seems no wiser for his discoveries at the end of the novel. For these characters and others, time is a linear element that they hope to slice off as seconds on a clock. For Faulkner, time past and time future are contained in time present. One cannot escape history, as Temple Drake discovers in *Requiem for a Nun*, nor can one live successfully without history, as the Reporter sees in *Pylon*. Like Bayard Sartoris in *The Unvanquished*, man must learn from the past to live in a viable present, to adapt to change so that change will not control his existence.

That ability to live fully—to maintain standards of conduct and to strive to inculcate the verities of the human heart in oneself as well as others—is always balanced by the knowledge that man will not inhabit Eden again. There is no millenarianism in Faulkner. Some of his harshest criticism is leveled not at the villains Jason Compson, Flem Snopes, and Popeye but at ineffectual idealists: Gavin Stevens, Horace Benbow, and Ike McCaslin. Certainly Jason Compson is a thoroughly despicable character who lacks any compassion or pity or love. Faulkner condemns those incapable of love and those who exploit the love of others. Yet such characters are as "easy" to condemn in fiction as they are in life. Love, of course, can also be destructive, as Harry Wilbourne discovers in *The Wild Palms*. But idealism and softheadedness can be equally as destructive and perhaps more harmful. Stevens, Benbow, and McCaslin are indeed sympathetic characters, but they finally fail to do more good than harm. In *Go Down, Moses* and *Light in August*, Stevens obviously misinterprets the events he witnesses; and in *Requiem for a Nun*, *The Town*, and *The Mansion*, he does little more than maintain a watch. His self-righteousness and moral rigidity are no match for the forces at work in Linda Kohl, Temple Drake, or Flem Snopes. Benbow fares even worse, for in the face of evil he is powerless and collapses. Ike McCaslin is surely one of Faulkner's most appealing youths, but as a man he signs away his inheritance and, like Pilate, believes that he can escape responsibility for the failures of his family as well as for man's basic nature. Unable to be Christ, Ike crucifies the opportunities he has to use the past and his own ability in a meaningful, constructive way.

Faulkner believed in man's ability to prevail over the tragedies of the human condition. As Cleanth Brooks writes, "Faulkner's work speaks ultimately of the possibilities and capacities of the human spirit for finding and embodying meaning." Readers will not find central heroes who achieve mindless happiness. Yet throughout Faulkner's fiction his characters emerge triumphant in their denial of the meaninglessness of life. Judith Sutpen not only loves Bon, who in turn clearly loves her, but also commits her life to his child and the world that remains after 1865. Dilsey cannot save the Compsons, but she refuses to let their tortured lives overwhelm the compassion and pity and courage she insists upon within herself. Henry Armstid madly digs at the Old Frenchman's Place; but Ratliff, with his wisdom and integrity, always counterbalances Gavin Stevens's idealism and foolishness and finally surveys Flem's ruin in all its aspects. But avarice, selfishness, cruelty, and bigotry are never defeated in Faulkner. "Prevailing" does not mean the elimination of man's vices. In fact, one of man's greatest strengths is his capacity to recognize those very weaknesses that struggle internally with every virtue.

Harry Wilbourne in *The Wild Palms* spends much of his life in prison. He
and Charlotte try to escape time and responsibility, to make of love an absolute
into which they can entwine their lives. Attempting to make life all honeymoon,
they destroy the romance. Seeking a perfect union, they find separation. Yet
Harry refuses to escape, to commit suicide when the possibility is offered. He
wants to know why he should act in such a way and, more important, why he
and Charlotte failed so miserably in their attempt to prevail over the limitations
of life and human relationships. Although they have been foolish and have hurt
others, he and Charlotte are not wicked people who scorn all the verities of the
human heart. In fact, they try to redefine them all in terms of themselves, their
own personal lives. Throughout Faulkner's work, such attempts are doomed.
Yet Harry lives through the attempt, chooses to live with the wisdom he has
finally gained and the memory of the love that he and Charlotte shared. He
chooses grief over nothing. Faulkner believed in man's capacity to learn, to gain
a certain wisdom, to choose life, to discover meaning. In the word *maybe* lie
the possibilities of such capabilities; in man himself lies the potential to make
of the moment a continuum with the past and an assurance of the future.

SURVEY OF CRITICISM

Beginning in the 1950s and accelerating through the 1960s and 1970s, critical
and biographical studies of Faulkner have proliferated to the point that probably
no other American author has been so studied. Unfortunately, many of these
works are flawed by careless scholarship and needless repetition of prior critical
analyses.

Nevertheless, as O. B. Emerson's *Faulkner's Early Literary Reputation in
America* (1984) shows, Faulkner never lacked for astute critics. Although it has
been popular to decry his critical reception before the mid–1940s, his work has
been read carefully and with insight. Much of this work, however, was done by
foreign critics, especially the French, and the sale of his books was adversely
affected by unperceptive reviews in the popular press and, of course, the demands
that the novels themselves placed upon the reader. Yet by the mid–1930s Faulkner
was already seen as a major American writer, and when he won the Nobel Prize
in 1950, the sale of his books began to match the reputation he had already
established.

Perhaps the major lack in Faulkner scholarship today is a complete and up-
to-date bibliography of his work. Until it appears, James B. Meriwether's bibliographical work in *The Literary Career of William Faulkner* (1961), "The
Short Fiction of William Faulkner: A Bibliography" in *Proof 1* (1971), and
"The Books of William Faulkner: A Revised Guide for Students and Scholars"
in the *Mississippi Quarterly* (Summer 1982) must suffice.

There are, however, several fine bibliographies of work about Faulkner:
Thomas L. McHaney's *William Faulkner: A Reference Guide* (1976) and John

Earl Bassett's two works, *William Faulkner: An Annotated Checklist of Criticism* (1972) and *Faulkner: An Annotated Checklist of Recent Criticism* (1983). McHaney lists works chronologically through 1973 and includes an index to authors and titles, and a great number of subject entries. Bassett's first volume ends in 1971 and is organized under topical headings with some works listed alphabetically and others chronologically under the headings; the second volume covers from about 1971 through 1982 and is set up much like the 1971 checklist. The annual "Checklist of Scholarship on Southern Literature" published in the *Mississippi Quarterly* is also quite helpful. For critical assessments of work on Faulkner, one should begin with Meriwether's chapter on Faulkner in *Sixteen Modern American Authors* (1974) and consult the Faulkner chapter in the annual *American Literary Scholarship* and the "Survey of Research and Criticism" published annually in the Faulkner issue of the *Mississippi Quarterly* since 1978. Among the many guides, handbooks, and character indices to Faulkner, the most comprehensive index is Thomas E. Dasher's *Faulkner's Characters: An Index to the Published and Unpublished Fiction* (1981); Calvin S. Brown's *A Glossary of Faulkner's South* (1976) can also be useful.

Although Faulkner vehemently opposed intrusions into his private life such as Robert Coughlan's *The Private World of William Faulkner* (1954), based upon two unreliable articles in *Life*, scholars have repeatedly explored his life. Until 1974 the best biographical study was Michael Millgate's first chapter in *The Achievement of William Faulkner* (1966); it was superseded by Joseph Blotner's massive two-volume *Faulkner: A Biography* (1974), the authorized study. An overwhelming compilation of details and information, Blotner's work assiduously avoided critical analyses, and its omissions were pointed out by numerous reviewers. Still, it stands as probably the major biographical study of Faulkner; Carvel Collins's long-awaited biography has never appeared. Since Blotner's work appeared, Collins has published several intriguing introductions to Faulkner volumes, notably *Mayday* (1977) and *Helen: A Courtship* (1981). Of significance is Meta Carpenter Wilde's *A Loving Gentleman: The Love Story of William Faulkner and Meta Carpenter* (1976); Carpenter's long-term involvement was omitted from Blotner. Also of interest are Malcolm Franklin's *Bitterweeds: Life with William Faulkner at Rowan Oak* (1977) and Ben Wasson's *Count No 'Count* (1983). Blotner's edition of Faulkner's *Selected Letters* appeared in 1977. Judith B. Wittenberg's *Faulkner: The Transfiguration of Biography* (1979), a biographical study that overuses psychoanalytic methods, and David Minter's *William Faulkner: His Life and Work* (1980), a critical biography that does not totally successfully explore the relationship between Faulkner's life and his fiction, herald the probable deluge of biographical studies based upon Blotner's work. Certainly a study such as the one Minter purports to do would be a valuable addition to the field, but perhaps the most valuable addition since Blotner's 1974 biography is Blotner's 1984 one-volume biography. A condensed, revised, and updated version of his earlier work, *Faulkner: A Bi-*

ography is, in many ways, more reliable and usable than the 1974 volumes. Blotner has incorporated others' work published since 1974 and has greatly profited from the corrections that reviewers and scholars sent him.

Since Harry M. Campbell and Ruel E. Foster's *William Faulkner: A Critical Appraisal* (1951), over 150 critical books and several thousand articles have been published. As critical theories develop and go in and out of fashion, new studies proliferate. Many of these are thesis-ridden and reveal far more about a particular theory than about Faulkner. Several book-length studies are, however of unquestioned importance. Cleanth Brooks's *William Faulkner: The Yoknapatawpha Country* (1963) and *William Faulkner: Toward Yoknapatawpha and Beyond* (1978) head the list. Devoting a chapter to each of the novels, Brooks also considers Faulkner's treatment of nature, the common people, and time and history. Other critics have gone into greater depth on individual novels or developed more complex theories, but no one has surpassed the insight, balance, and usefulness of these works. Indeed, almost all of Brooks's many Faulkner essays have similar strengths and yield similar pleasure. Brooks remains the premier critic of Faulkner's work. Also very valuable, although more limited in its treatment of the individual novels, is Michael Millgate's *The Achievement of William Faulkner* (1966). Together with Brooks's, Millgate's work on Faulkner continues to be the starting point for any study of Faulkner.

Other useful studies that range over Faulkner's entire canon or focus on several novels include Olga Vickery's *The Novels of William Faulkner: A Critical Interpretation* (1959: rev. 1964) and Warren Beck's *Man in Motion: Faulkner's Trilogy* (1961), a complex and rewarding study of the Snopes novels. Most of the other critical books on Faulkner prior to 1970, such as Irving Howe's *William Faulkner: A Critical Study* (1952, 1962), were superseded by Brooks and Millgate.

Since 1970, reviewers have continued to debate the merits of the book-length studies that explore, often in great detail, particular aspects of Faulkner's work. Among these studies are Panthea Reid Broughton's *William Faulkner: The Abstract and the Actual* (1974), which stresses the relationship between experience and abstractions in Faulkner, and John T. Irwin's *Doubling and Incest/Repetition and Revenge: A Speculative Reading of Faulkner* (1975), a psychoanalytic study showing the influence of structuralism, Lacan, and Nietzsche. David Williams's *Faulkner's Women: The Myth and the Muse* (1977) is a provocative study discussing female characters through the use of Jungian archetypes and symbols. Arthur F. Kinney's *Faulkner's Narrative Poetics: Style as Vision* (1978) explores Faulkner's use of the narrative techniques in the modernist tradition; Hugh M. Ruppersburg focuses on narrative structure and technique in four of the novels in *Voice and Eye in Faulkner's Fiction* (1983). Heavily indebted to Derrida, John T. Matthews's *The Play of Faulkner's Language* (1982) is a stimulating addition to Faulkner criticism, as is Thadious M. Davis's *Faulkner's "Negro": Art and the Southern Context* (1983), perhaps the best of the several books focusing on Faulkner's treatment of Negroes in his fiction. Judith Sensibar's *The*

Origins of Faulkner's Art (1984) is a useful study of Faulkner's early work in poetry and prose. Several intriguing studies of individual novels are Thomas L. McHaney's *William Faulkner's "The Wild Palms": A Study* (1975), André Bleikasten's *The Most Splendid Failure: Faulkner's "The Sound and the Fury"* (1976), and Noel Polk's *Faulkner's "Requiem for a Nun": A Critical Study* (1981).

Also of interest are the volumes that have emanated from the annual Faulkner conference held at the University of Mississippi since 1974. Although greatly uneven in their quality and usefulness, these essays often offer interesting insights into the better-known Faulkner critics and scholars as well as Faulkner himself. Finally, it is important to stress that much of the best work on Faulkner continues to appear in journal articles. There is no indication that the Faulkner industry will taper off; thus, the student of Faulkner faces an awesome task of dealing with the outpouring of work on Faulkner and slowly sifting out the worthwhile from the worthless. Unfortunately, the latter often threatens to overwhelm the former.

BIBLIOGRAPHY

Works by William Faulkner

The Marble Faun. Boston: Four Seas, 1924.
Soldiers' Pay. New York: Boni & Liveright, 1926.
Mosquitoes. New York: Boni & Liveright, 1927.
Sartoris. New York: Harcourt, Brace, 1929.
The Sound and the Fury. New York: Jonathan Cape & Harrison Smith, 1929.
As I Lay Dying. New York: Jonathan Cape & Harrison Smith, 1930.
Idyll in the Desert. New York: Random House, 1931.
Sanctuary. New York: Jonathan Cape & Harrison Smith, 1931.
These 13. New York: Jonathan Cape & Harrison Smith, 1931.
Light in August. New York: Harrison Smith & Robert Haas, 1932.
Miss Zilphia Grant. [Dallas]: Book Club of Texas, 1932.
A Green Bough. New York: Harrison Smith & Robert Haas, 1933.
Doctor Martino and Other Stories. New York: Harrison Smith & Robert Haas, 1934.
Pylon. New York: Harrison Smith & Robert Haas, 1935.
Absalom, Absalom! New York: Random House, 1936.
The Unvanquished. New York: Random House, 1938.
The Wild Palms. New York: Random House, 1939.
The Hamlet. New York: Random House, 1940.
Go Down, Moses. New York: Random House, 1942.
Intruder in the Dust. New York: Random House, 1948.
Knight's Gambit. New York: Random House, 1949.
Collected Stories. New York: Random House, 1950.
Notes on a Horsethief. Greenville, Miss.: Levee Press, 1951.
Requiem for a Nun. New York: Random House, 1951.
A Fable. New York: Random House, 1954.

Big Woods. New York: Random House, 1955.

The Town. New York: Random House, 1957.

Faulkner in the University: Class Conferences at the University of Virginia, 1957–1958, ed. Frederick Gwyn and Joseph L. Blotner. New York: Vintage, 1959.

The Mansion. New York: Random House, 1959.

Early Prose and Poetry. Ed. Carvel Collins. Boston: Little, Brown, 1962.

The Reivers. New York: Random House, 1962.

The Wishing Tree. New York: Random House, 1967.

New Orleans Sketches. Ed. Carvel Collins. New York: Random House, 1968.

Lion in the Garden: Interviews with William Faulkner, 1926–1962, ed. James B. Meriwether and Michael Milgate. New York: Random House, 1968.

Flags in the Dust. Ed. Douglas Day. New York: Random House, 1973.

The Marionettes: A Play in One Act. Charlottesville: University Press of Virginia for the Bibliographical Society of the University of Virginia, 1975, 1978.

Mayday. [South Bend, Ind.]: University of Notre Dame Press, 1977, 1980.

Selected Letters of William Faulkner. Ed. Joseph Blotner. New York: Random House, 1977.

Mississippi Poems. [Oxford, Miss.]: Yoknapatawpha Press, 1979.

Uncollected Stories of William Faulkner. Ed. Joseph Blotner. New York: Random House, 1979.

Helen: A Courtship. New Orleans: Tulane University and Oxford, Miss.: Yoknapatawpha Press, 1981.

Sanctuary: The Original Text. Ed. Noel Polk. New York: Random House, 1981.

Elmer. Ed. Dianne L. Cox. Northport, Ala.: Seajay Press for the *Mississippi Quarterly*, 1983.

Father Abraham. Ed. James B. Meriwether. New York: Random House, 1984.

Vision in Spring. Austin: University of Texas Press, 1984.

Studies of William Faulkner

Adams, Richard P. *Faulkner: Myth and Motion*. Princeton, N.J.: Princeton University Press, 1968.

Bassett, John Earl. *Faulkner: An Annotated Checklist of Recent Criticism*. Kent, Ohio: Kent State University Press, 1983.

———. *William Faulkner: An Annotated Checklist of Criticism*. New York: David Lewis, 1972.

Beck, Warren. *Man in Motion: Faulkner's Trilogy*. Madison: University of Wisconsin Press, 1961.

Bleikasten, André. *Faulkner's "As I Lay Dying."* Bloomington: Indiana University Press, 1973.

———. *The Most Splendid Failure: Faulkner's "The Sound and the Fury."* Bloomington: Indiana University Press, 1976.

———. *William Faulkner's "The Sound and the Fury": A Critical Casebook*. New York: Garland, 1982.

Blotner, Joseph. *Faulkner: A Biography*. 2 vols. New York: Random House, 1974.

———. *Faulkner: A Biography*. 1 vol. New York: Random House, 1984.

Brooks, Cleanth. *William Faulkner: Toward Yoknapatawpha and Beyond*. New Haven: Yale University Press, 1978.

————. *William Faulkner: The Yoknapatawpha Country*. New Haven: Yale University Press, 1963.

Broughton, Panthea Reid. *William Faulkner: The Abstract and the Actual*. Baton Rouge: Louisiana State University Press, 1974.

Brown, Calvin S. *A Glossary of Faulkner's South*. New Haven: Yale University Press, 1976.

Butterworth, Keen. *A Critical and Textual Study of Faulkner's "A Fable."* Ann Arbor: UMI Research, 1983.

Cox, Dianne L. *William Faulkner's "As I Lay Dying": A Critical Casebook*. New York: Garland, 1984.

Dasher, Thomas E. *William Faulkner's Characters: An Index to the Published and Unpublished Fiction*. New York: Garland, 1981.

Davis, Thadious M. *Faulkner's "Negro": Art and the Southern Context*. Baton Rouge: Louisiana State University Press, 1983.

Emerson, O. B. *Faulkner's Early Literary Reputation in America*. Ann Arbor: UMI Research, 1984.

Franklin, Malcolm. *Life with William Faulkner at Rowan Oak*. Irving, Texas: The Society for the Study of Traditional Culture, 1977.

Hayashi, Tetsumaro. *William Faulkner: Research Opportunities and Dissertation Abstracts*. Jefferson, N.C.: McFarland, 1982.

Irwin, John T. *Doubling and Incest/Repetition and Revenge: A Speculative Reading of Faulkner*. Baltimore: Johns Hopkins University Press, 1975.

Kawin, Bruce F. *Faulkner and Film*. New York: Ungar, 1977.

————. *Faulkner's MGM Screenplays*. Knoxville: University of Tennessee Press, 1982.

Kinney, Arthur F. *Faulkner's Narrative Poetics: Style as Vision*. Amherst: University of Massachusetts Press, 1978.

Longley, John. *The Tragic Mask: A Study of Faulkner's Heroes*. Chapel Hill: University of North Carolina Press, 1963.

McHaney, Thomas L. *William Faulkner: A Reference Guide*. Boston: G. K. Hall, 1976.

————. *William Faulkner's "The Wild Palms": A Study*. Jackson: University Press of Mississippi, 1975.

Matthews, John T. *The Play of Faulkner's Language*. Ithaca, N.Y.: Cornell University Press, 1982.

Meriwether, James B., ed. *The Literary Career of William Faulkner: A Bibliographical Study*. Princeton, N.J.: Princeton University Library, 1961.

————. "William Faulkner," *Sixteen Modern American Authors*. Ed. Jackson R. Bryer. Durham, N.C.: Duke University Press, 1974. Pp. 223–75.

Millgate, Michael. *The Achievement of William Faulkner*. New York: Random House, 1966.

Minter, David. *William Faulkner: His Life and Work*. Baltimore: Johns Hopkins University Press, 1980.

Muhlenfeld, Elisabeth. *William Faulkner's "Absalom, Absalom!": A Critical Casebook*. New York: Garland, 1984.

Pitavy, François. *Faulkner's "Light in August."* Bloomington: Indiana University Press, 1973.

————. *William Faulkner's "Light in August": A Critical Casebook*. New York: Garland, 1982.

Polk, Noel. *Faulkner's "Requiem for a Nun": A Critical Study*. Bloomington: Indiana University Press, 1981.

Ruppersburg, Hugh M. *Voice and Eye in Faulkner's Fiction*. Athens: University of Georgia Press, 1983.

Sensibar, Judith. *The Origins of Faulkner's Art*. Austin: University of Texas Press, 1984.

Skei, Hans H. *William Faulkner: The Short Story Career*. Oslo: Universitetsforlaget, 1982.

Vickery, Olga. *The Novels of William Faulkner: A Critical Interpretation*. Baton Rouge: Louisiana State University, 1964.

Wagner, Linda W., ed. *William Faulkner: Four Decades of Criticism*. East Lansing: Michigan State University Press, 1973.

Wasson, Ben. *Count No 'Count: Flashbacks to Faulkner*. Jackson: University Press of Mississippi, 1983.

Wilde, Meta Carpenter and Orin Borsten. *A Loving Gentleman: The Love Story of William Faulkner and Meta Carpenter*. New York: Simon & Schuster, 1976.

Williams, David. *Faulkner's Women: The Myth and the Muse*. Montreal and London: McGill-Queen's University Press, 1977.

Wittenberg, Judith B. *Faulkner: The Transfiguration of Biography*. Lincoln: University of Nebraska Press, 1979.

————————— WILLIAM PRATT —————————

John Gould Fletcher
(1886–1950)

John Gould Fletcher began and ended his life in Little Rock, Arkansas, but lived much of the time away from his native home, achieving his first fame as a member of the Imagist group of poets in London in 1915, later fame as a member of the Fugitive group of poets in Nashville in 1922, and still later fame as one of the Southern Agrarian essayists who issued *I'll Take My Stand* in 1930. His career reached its zenith with the publication of his autobiography, *Life Is My Song*, in 1937, and his *Selected Poems*, in 1938, for which he was awarded a Pulitzer Prize in 1939. Because he was a Southerner as well as an expatriate, an Imagist as well as a Fugitive and an Agrarian, Fletcher held a unique place in modern American literature, despite the fact that he wrote neither a major literary work nor a classic anthology piece. It was chiefly as the one figure linking the two main American literary schools of the twentieth century, the international, or experimental, movement and the Southern, or traditional, movement, that Fletcher earned his measure of permanent significance as writer.

BIOGRAPHY

John Gould Fletcher was born on 3 January 1886 in Little Rock, Arkansas, the son of John G. and Adolphine Krause Fletcher. His paternal grandfather had migrated from Tennessee to Arkansas before the Civil War, and his father had been born on a farm in rural Arkansas. Gould was his great-great-grandmother's maiden name. In spite of his later years as an expatriate in Europe, Fletcher always identified himself as both American and Southern, attributing his love of travel to his father's Scottish pioneer stock, and his love of books and art to his mother's German ancestry. His father had become a prosperous cotton-broker and banker in Little Rock by the time Fletcher was born, and Fletcher was educated primarily at home by his mother, who passed on to him her German musical and literary culture. He grew up as the favored only son of a successful elder businessman (Fletcher's father was fifty-five at the time Fletcher was born) and a cultivated younger woman, in a mansion enriched with "the flavor of the Old South" and a legendary ghost. With the help of private tutors, he learned Latin and German as a boy, and developed an abiding love of art and literature in his own home, well before graduating from public high school at age sixteen.

His father wanted him to become a lawyer, and perhaps enter politics, but in 1902 his father was defeated in a campaign for governor of Arkansas against a rural demagogue named Jeff Davis, and Fletcher later wrote, "I began to loathe the sham and corruption that went on in America in the name of democracy fully seven years before I quit America for good and went abroad." To satisfy his mother's ambitions, he applied for admission to Harvard in 1902. Unable to pass Harvard's full battery of entrance examinations, he studied for a year at Phillips Academy in Andover, Massachusetts, where he found himself suddenly thrust as "an unprotected and hypersensitive southerner, into the midst of a school full of New Englanders, all contemptuously ignorant of the South and secure in their ignorance." Nominally a Christian when he left home, he entered Harvard in 1903 and soon turned from religion to art and philosophy, being much influenced in his college years by a fellow student who was an ardent disciple of Nietzsche. He also began writing poetry, under the stimulus of studying French and reading Arthur Symons's book *The Symbolist Tradition in Literature*. He was becoming serious about writing when his father's death in 1906 liberated him from the obligation of further study; as he later said, "My father's death had left the field open. I could go abroad." Over his mother's objections, he dropped out of Harvard without a degree in 1907, joining a summer archeological expedition that took him to New Mexico, Arizona, and Colorado; he returned to Boston for a time, and then, the next summer, left for Europe.

Fletcher arrived in Venice in summer 1908, and went on to Rome, where he became absorbed in Italian culture, but decided that it was largely of the European past, whereas English culture dominated the European present. Therefore in May 1909 he moved to London, staying there for most of the next quarter of a century. He had come to believe that the conservative Roman Catholicism of southern Europe was no match for the liberal Protestantism of northern Europe, and to recognize that medieval feudal society, for which he had much sympathy, had been effectively replaced by an industrial democracy with a creed of material progress that was sweeping civilization before it. Thus, Fletcher showed his special faculty for being a critic of cultural change while becoming caught up in the excitement of it, and he had the good fortune to arrive in London just at the moment when a new literary consciousness was being formed, chiefly in the pages of Ford Madox Hueffer's *English Review* and A. R. Orage's *New Age*, at Harold Monro's Poetry Bookshop, and in the activities of the first group of Imagist poets that T. E. Hulme had collected around him. He later said that he got his "second education" in London from 1909 to 1913, when he "took the first steps which were to transform me from a dilettante into a professional writer.''

Fletcher did not immediately become a part of the literary scene in London, but continued to study and imitate French poetry until, on a visit to Paris in spring 1913, he met Ezra Pound at the Closerie des Lilas cafe on the Left Bank. Impressed with Fletcher's extensive French library and his first five books of poetry (all published in London in 1913 at his own expense), Pound became Fletcher's friend and champion, arranging for the publication of some of his most recent and original poems, the ''Irradiations,'' in *Poetry* magazine in Chicago, writing a complimentary review of Fletcher's poetry to go with the poems, and then inducing Fletcher to become the financial patron of a new literary magazine, the *Egoist*, which would be the chief organ for the new school of Imagists in London. Grateful for Pound's help, Fletcher nonetheless declined Pound's invitation to be in the first Imagist anthology, *Des Imagistes*, in 1914. He asserted, ''I never considered myself in any way Pound's disciple,'' and when Amy Lowell came to London, he struck up a friendship with her that resulted in the publication, in Boston in 1915, of his first Imagist collection, *Irradiations, Sand and Spray*, and his appearance in the annual anthology, *Some Imagist Poets*, in 1915, 1916, and 1917. Fletcher thus became one of the six poets most closely identified with Imagism, along with two Americans—Amy Lowell and H. D.—and three Englishmen—Richard Aldington, F. S. Flint, and D. H. Lawrence. He now ''fully considered [himself] to be an Imagist,'' and was dismayed when Pound left the group to found the Vorticist school, intended to expand Imagism into all the arts. In Fletcher's opinion, Pound would have been better advised to ''rest his achievement on the more solid ground of the original Imagism, which was already being discussed and imitated in America.'' Fletcher himself built on this ground in his next book, *Goblins and Pagodas* (1916), which included a sequence called ''Ghosts of an Old House,'' inspired by a return visit to Little Rock in 1915 and signaling a new departure for him: ''I may claim for them that they are the only imagistic poems which are also southern poems.''

Although his return to the United States had renewed his American roots, Fletcher continued living in London until 1933, partly because in 1916 he married an Englishwoman, ''Daisy'' (Florence Emily Arbuthnot, wife of an English painter, who left her husband to marry Fletcher), and partly because he had begun to think of himself as a European as well as an American. He was publishing poetry and criticism in the leading little magazines, *Poetry* and the *Little Review* in America, and the *Egoist* in London and, like Amy Lowell, had begun to experiment with what he called ''polyphonic prose,'' a blend of prose and poetry that enjoyed a brief popularity. He extended his range of poetic subjects in *Japanese Prints* (1918), with its Oriental images; *Breakers and Granite* (1921), with its American landscapes; and *Preludes and Symphonies* (1922), with its ''color symphonies,'' which were compounded of French music, poetry, and painting. His critical taste expanded to include a biography of the French painter *Paul Gauguin, His Life and Art* (1921), a biography of the Elizabethan adventurer *John Smith—Also Pocahontas* (1928), and his most ambitious prose work, *The Two Frontiers: A Study in Historical Psychology* (1930), which drew prophetic parallels between the United States and Russia as modern civilizations that had evolved from contrary European political ideas, and which he saw— already in 1930—as threatening to dominate the whole world.

But while Fletcher seemed to be developing a more and more international viewpoint in his writing, he was being drawn increasingly toward his native region, to which he returned in 1933 to spend the remainder of his life. He had become associated with T. S. Eliot, another American expatriate, first in Pound's the *Egoist* and later in Eliot's own magazine, the *Criterion*, founded in London in 1922, to which he contributed several essays and reviews. He came to share Eliot's view that Western civilization was declining because of increasing materialism and decreasing religious faith, and he was attracted even more strongly to the view of the Southern Fugitive poets that the older agrarian society was more civilized than the newer industrial society. He learned of the Fugitives when lecturing on American poetry at Oxford University in 1922, because one of them, William Y. Elliott, who had come to England as a Rhodes scholar, happened to be in the audience and expressed surprise that Fletcher had not mentioned the poets of Nashville. Fletcher soon bridged the gap: his poems "The Last Frontier" and "Cro-Magnon" were published in 1923 in the *Fugitive*, and in 1927 he made a trip to Nashville for a lecture, meeting John Crowe Ransom and Donald Davidson there, and later meeting Allen Tate in New York. In 1927 he published the essay "Two Elements in Poetry" in which he contrasted the Imagists with the Fugitives, saying that the Imagists had concentrated on poetic form, thus creating a new style and movement in English poetry, whereas the Fugitives had concentrated on ideas, and so along with Eliot had created a new "school of intellectual poetry in America." He credited both the Imagists and the Fugitives with being "explorers of new experience" and said that "every age that produces poetry that will live, has to forge a new instrument for itself." As a result of his interest in Southern themes, Fletcher was invited to contribute to *I'll Take My Stand* in 1930, and for it he wrote an essay about the decline of Southern education, from the time when it was dominated by the classical humanism of the private academies to the time when it had changed to public schooling in the practical skills needed for a technological society. Thus he willingly joined the effort to produce "a critique of northern industrial civilization, and a defense of the culture of the old South," in the hope that "some part of America might in some way be delivered from the incubus of the machine."

Strongly drawn back to his native region by these new intellectual currents, which had convinced him that a revival of Southern culture was underway, Fletcher was impelled to leave his wife in England in 1933 (she had tried living in America, but found it impossible) and to divorce her in 1935. Then in 1936, having returned to Little Rock, he married again, to Charlie May Simon, another artist's wife attracted by his writing. But she was a writer herself, a native of Memphis who shared his desire to "maintain the rich variety, the color, and the charm of American life" by holding fast to "the genuine rural America of the beloved community." On a bluff near Little Rock he built a home that he called Johnswood, and he was content to live there, except for some summers spent in writing at the MacDowell Colony in New Hampshire, until his death in 1950. His principal later writings were his autobiography, *Life Is My Song*, possibly his most substantial and enduring work, and the *Selected Poems*, for which he won the somewhat belated tribute of a Pulitzer Prize—essentially for the poetry of his early Imagist period. Although he turned his pen to regional subjects in an effort to enrich Arkansas culture, his last books of poems, *South Star* (1941) and *The Burning Mountain* (1946), and his last prose work, a history of Arkansas (1947), showed neither the originality nor the liveliness of Fletcher's earlier works. Fletcher was known to suffer from periodic bouts of depression, and on 10 May 1950 he wandered from home alone; he was reported missing, and his body was found in a nearby pond. The coroner ruled that he had committed suicide by drowning. An obituary published the following day in the *New York Times* acknowledged that "John Gould Fletcher rose slowly, uncertainly, and with pain to a position of respect and even of eminence in this country."

MAJOR THEMES

Fletcher's poetic talent was highly adaptable, taking him from the French Symbolists to the Imagists to the Fugitives in his search for a suitable style, but there is no doubt that his best poems were written under the Imagist influence. In fact, his most creative period could be narrowed to the years 1913–14, the time of his closest association with Pound. It was then that he produced, in rapid succession, the series of short Impressionistic sketches he called "Irradiations"; the first of his "color symphonies," which he called the "Blue Symphony"; and two extended Imagist sequences titled "London Excursion" and "Ghosts of an Old House." About the "Irradiations," the best of which began with arresting lines like "Flickering of incessant rain" and "Trees like great jade elephants," Fletcher wrote that he had attempted "a presentation of daily life in terms of highly-orchestrated and coloured words." In his "Blue Symphony," he said he was trying "to describe certain predominant moods in terms of things happening. Thus one gets expectancy described as a traveler looking at blue mountains in the distance." The "London Excursion" was a more ambitious work, whose intention was "to leave the poet's mind entirely blank, like the *tabula rasa* which, as Locke has said, we all are endowed with at birth; and to make the resultant poem entirely naive in the simultaneous presentation to the consciousness of as many contrasting images as possible, derived openly from, say, one's association with them as one walked through the crowded streets of the city." And in "Ghosts of an Old House" he attempted "to evoke, out of the furniture and surroundings of a certain old house, definite emotions which I have had concerning them. I have tried to relate my childish terror concerning this house—a terror not uncommon among children, as I can testify—to the aspects that called it forth." These were the poems in which Fletcher most clearly achieved his aim of expressing personal feelings through objective descriptions, according to his own definition of Imagism, which was that "the chief object of a poem was to produce a certain aesthetic effect; that effect was implicit in an image or series of images, and the business of the poet was to present his images as clearly and concisely as possible."

Fletcher's later poems, and his "polyphonic prose," became more diffuse and verbose, since as Pound correctly judged in 1915, "He has a lawless and uncontrolled ability to catch certain effects, mostly of color, but no finishing sense." As Fletcher himself admitted of his experiments, "I may have pushed metrical variation too far towards anarchy." He had a prolific gift for the conception of poetry, but was less gifted in its execution, and thus his poems were often more interesting as ideas than as completed works. But Fletcher had a critical gift as well, with insight into both his own limitations and those of his age. In an illuminating passage in his autobiography, he explained that "in my own poetry, and in its development and achievement, I have been free to develop the forms in which I choose to write. But I have not been free to choose any or every subject. My subjects, as well as the interest I have taken in them, have been dictated to me by the given circumstances of my life. Thus in every case I have been governed not by free will, nor by necessity, but by a sort of necessitous free will, a free will always acting within the confines of some given set of conditions." Imagism provided Fletcher with a technique that enabled him to shape the raw material of his experience, as American expatriate and as Southerner, into poetic form, through brief verbal images of his adult urban life in London or of his earlier childhood home in Arkansas. But these poems did not coalesce into a unified whole; no single volume of Fletcher's poetry, including the *Selected Poems*, is completely satisfying in itself, although everything he wrote is infused with a highly intelligent and sensitive personality.

Because it was the personality that counted most in Fletcher's writing, his autobiography, *Life Is My Song*, is in many ways his most solid accomplishment. The story he tells of himself is truthful and revealing, and the portraits he gives of the writers with whom he collaborated in London and in the South, are well-drawn and memorable. One learns almost as much about the Imagists—Pound, Amy Lowell, H. D.—and the Fugitives—Ransom, Davidson, Tate—as about Fletcher himself, and in the process acquires some understanding of the ideas at work in each of these primary twentieth-century American poetic schools. Fletcher assumed the role of critic and historian of his age judiciously and realized how fortunate he had been to be born in a generation when "poets of high merit appeared on the American scene," although he doubted whether his own work would count significantly among them. He had joined the Imagists before World War I, when it was possible to make a religion of art, to feel that there was value in expressing the artist's private consciousness, and to believe in the permanence of Western culture. But his "aesthetic phase" ended with the war, and afterwards he sought a new "humanist phase," guided by Eliot's search for the lost religious faith underlying Western culture, and by the Fugitives' search for the lost agrarian community of the South. Fletcher came to the view that European culture was inevitably declining through material progress and spiritual decay and that the only hope for the survival of American culture lay in its retaining whatever remained of regional identity and the older agrarian way of life; otherwise, "It was a question of whether man could or would master the machines, or whether the machines would end by mastering him." In 1921 Fletcher had praised the French painter Paul Gauguin as an artist who "foresaw that material progress would end in annihilating humanity," and who had asserted against it "the duty of the artist," which in his view is "to affirm the dignity of life, the value of humanity." He saw the Fugitives as enlisting in the same effort, and as late as 1944 he defended them as "neither reactionaries nor sentimental liberals. They are merely people confronted with the conflict between the uniform meaninglessness of an industrial age resting upon the modern gadgets of science, and the purposefulness of humanity dependent on deep loyalty, on poetry and myth, on a strong-rooted folk tradition."

Other than his autobiography and the best of his Imagist poems, Fletcher's reputation rests on his critical essays—which, unfortunately, were never collected into a book—and on his broad historical-critical study of *The Two Frontiers* (1930), where he showed prophetic vision in pitting America against Russia as the dominant nations of the future, and demonstrated his wide reading by extended comparisons of the major American and Russian writers of the nineteenth century: Pushkin and Irving, Gogol and Hawthorne, Tolstoy and Whitman, Dostoevsky and Melville. Although he took an impartial attitude toward the relative merits of capitalism and communism as economic systems, he recognized that the increasing material success of both systems could result eventually in a conflict that might be catastrophic, and his book is therefore both prophetic and pessimistic in its conclusion: "The end of such a conflict might well be such a state of famine, disorder, and exhaustion as to leave no hope to mankind for the future." Fletcher held out little hope for a peaceful reconciliation of differences between the two nations, although he spoke eloquently of the need for some kind of "humanism that is at once scientific and aesthetic" through which the world might achieve "an ideal and supra-physical unity of spirit."

If Fletcher's sweeping view of world politics was more pessimistic than optimistic—a view that seems fully justified by historical events since 1930—he took a somewhat more hopeful view of poetry. His two most important summarizing essays are "The Impulse of Poetry," published in *American Caravan IV* in 1931, and "Herald of Imagism" in the *Southern Review* in 1936. In the first of these, Fletcher argued for the central role of poetry among the arts, contending that poetry alone makes use of the spatial and temporal media of all the arts and includes underlying philosophical themes as well, embodying the ethical values essential to human culture. He held that art evolves as nature does: "The evolution of new art-forms is always the same: a new way of looking at life creates a new form of art, and this form is elaborated up to the point where it becomes artificial, when it has to give way to a fresh outburst of creative genius, or perhaps I had better say, creative sensibility." In the early twentieth century, Imagism had represented the "return to nature": "It aimed at creating a new form by a stark stripping off of all detail in order to pursue the essential." Since then, he said, poets had been seeking some kind of unifying belief to undergird the new poetic form, but as Eliot's *The Waste Land* had demonstrated: "The chief difficulty about the creation or understanding of reasonably good poetry in our time, is the lack of a good dogmatic ground on which to base our poetic perceptions. We have to formulate a scheme of poetic values without relation to prevailing theological belief, and such a scheme is very difficult, if not altogether impossible."

In "Herald of Imagism" Fletcher wrote in appreciation of Amy Lowell's achievement, but saw her as a representative of New England culture, "the peculiar and paradoxical mixture of individual independence and Puritan conformity, of world-wide curiosity and rigid intolerance, of reformist zeal and of naive self-satisfaction," which was implicitly expressed in her poetry. He contrasted her culture with that of the Southern writers who succeeded the Imagists and made a revival of Southern culture possible—though, in Fletcher's eyes, it seemed most unlikely at the time he left the South for Europe. He testified to the fact that during his lifetime Southern literature had experienced a renascence, causing the "intellectual school" of American poets, the Fugitives, to be a dominant influence in the second quarter of the century, as the experimental school of the Imagists had been dominant in the first quarter of the century. He felt that in the South lay the best hope for the future of American culture.

SURVEY OF CRITICISM

The soundest criticism of Fletcher in his lifetime came from the writers he knew best, those of the Imagist and Fugitive schools. It was Pound who first gave him credit, in sending his poems to Harriet Monroe at *Poetry* magazine in Chicago in 1913, for his ability to "make a *book*, as opposed to the common or garden faculty of making a 'Poem.' " It was also Pound who saw his limitations, writing in 1915 of Fletcher's "Impressionist temperament, made intense at half-seconds." Amy Lowell became his second champion, devoting a section of her influential *Tendencies in Modern American Poetry* (1917) to his poetry, calling him a "virtuoso of words," who often found it "hard to curb his exuberance," with the result that "some of his symphonies, some of the poems in 'Irradiations,' are heaped too full of words."

René Taupin, in his study of the Imagist period, *The Influence of French Symbolism on Modern American Poetry* (first published in 1929), characterized both Fletcher and Amy Lowell as "American Symbolists," whose work was "a continuation of French Symbolism." Although he did not find Fletcher original enough to surpass the models he imitated, Taupin maintained that in the best poems of the "Irradiations" and "Symphonies" Fletcher achieved "a delicately descriptive symbolism, a musical and perfectly appropriate *vers libre*." R. P. Blackmur added to this estimate in a review in the March 1936 *Poetry* magazine, saying that in reading Fletcher one feels "the element of poetry presided over by a genuinely poetic figure," and that while no single poem stays in the mind, "Mr. Fletcher is a personal poet in that it is the prevalent sense of his personality that animates his poems and alone gives them form."

As for the Southern side of Fletcher, Allen Tate included two of his poems in the Southern Number of *Poetry* in May 1932, and Robert Penn Warren wrote for the same issue a review summing up Fletcher's achievement: "The ideal of his early poetry was clear—a sort of absolute poetic communication, a pure art." Warren went on to say that Fletcher's later interest in the social environment of poetry had brought him into touch with the Fugitives and the Agrarians, but while he became more concerned with regional values in his later writing, "he has not, apparently, clarified the principles from which he is working." Donald Davidson, however, viewed Fletcher's accomplishment more generously in his essay "In Memory of John Gould Fletcher" in the December 1950 *Poetry*, where he pictured him as rooted in his native Arkansas, "on a steep, pine-covered ridge near Little Rock," and standing firm—"no art-for-art's sake aesthete, but a man of broadest intellectual capacity and intense moral purpose." Davidson believed that Fletcher had become "more of a traditionalist than he intended to be," and saw in some of his later poetry the aim Fletcher had come to hold highest: "man's search for God as the theme of all great poetry." He praised "the rich and various intelligence that is revealed in Fletcher's remarkable, but poorly titled, autobiography, *Life Is My Song*," as well as "the combination of aristocratic and backwoodsy tendencies that social historians find it difficult to understand in persons of southern antecedents." Davidson felt that, after a rebellious early period as an expatriate, Fletcher had realized that his true subject and true audience were in America. Davidson credited him with a "prophetic study of Russia and America, *The Two Frontiers*," and concluded, "Not many writers, in any age, can attain his degree of lonely courage"—a courage he thought fit to compare with the heroic gallantry of Faulkner's fictional Colonel Sartoris, champion of the lost cause of the Old South.

Since his death, Fletcher has been accorded scant critical attention, and a full reassessment of his scope and stature seems long overdue. There is a need for a biographical and critical study that would take account of the early originality of his poetry and the later originality of his critical and historical essays, as well as his autobiography. The only full-length treatment of Fletcher to date is the volume by Edna Buell Stephens in the Twayne United States Authors Series in 1967, which provides the standard useful survey of his life and writings, but which attempts unsuccessfully to overcome the customarily applied labels of Imagist, Fugitive, and Agrarian by treating him as a "mystic." Somewhat juster treatment of the poetry is found in Edmund S. de Chasca's *John Gould Fletcher and Imagism* (1978), which concludes that Fletcher's most mature verse was written during the Imagist period from 1913 to 1916, after which he began "a long, downward spiral" that led him to "become a Southern poet, closing out his career with three regional volumes." No complete and balanced study of Fletcher as poet, critic, and historian of the modern period has yet appeared, although the basis of such a full treatment can certainly be found in the well-annotated and helpful *John Gould Fletcher: A Bibliography*, compiled by Bruce Morton in 1979, which notes in its introduction that "beyond recognition as a poet, [Fletcher] has received relatively little attention as a critic, or as an aesthetic and a social theoretician."

If Fletcher is to be appreciated for the full range of his achievement, there will have to be further studies of his work as a whole, of the critic as well as the poet, the traditionalist as well as the experimentalist, the Southerner as well as the expatriate. Perhaps the greatest need at present is for his best critical essays to be collected into a single volume, enabling readers to encounter Fletcher's mind anew, in its impressive breadth and depth, which is reflected in his critical writings as well as in his finest short poems and his autobiography.

BIBLIOGRAPHY

Works by John Gould Fletcher

The Book of Nature. London: Constable, 1913.
The Dominant City. London: Max Goschen, 1913.
Fire and Wine. London: Grant Richards, 1913.
Fool's Gold. London: Max Goschen, 1913.
Visions of the Evening. London: Erskine Macdonald, 1913.
Irradiations, Sand and Spray. Boston: Houghton Mifflin, 1915.
Goblins and Pagodas. Boston: Houghton Mifflin, 1916.
Japanese Prints. Boston: Four Seas, 1918.
The Tree of Life. London: Chatto & Windus, 1918.
La Poésie d'André Fontainas. Paris: Monde Nouveau, 1919.
Breakers and Granite. New York: Macmillan, 1921.
Paul Gauguin, His Life and Art. New York: Nicholas L. Brown, 1921.
Preludes and Symphonies. Boston: Houghton Mifflin, 1922.
Parables. London: Kegan Paul, 1925.
Branches of Adam. London: Faber & Gwyer, 1926.
The Black Rock. New York: Macmillan, 1928.
John Smith—Also Pocahontas. New York: Brentano's, 1928.
The Crisis of the Film. Seattle: University of Washington Bookstore, 1929.
The Two Frontiers: A Study in Historical Psychology. New York: Coward-McCann, 1930.
XXIV Elegies. Santa Fe: Writer's Editions, 1935.
Life Is My Song: The Autobiography of John Gould Fletcher. New York: Farrar & Rinehart, 1937.

Selected Poems. New York: Farrar & Rinehart, 1938.
South Star. New York: Macmillan, 1941.
The Burning Mountain. New York: E. P. Dutton, 1946.
Arkansas. Chapel Hill: University of North Carolina Press, 1947.

Studies of John Gould Fletcher

Aiken, Conrad. *Scepticisms: Notes on Contemporary Poetry*. New York: Knopf, 1919, pp. 105–14, 187–92.
Behrens, R. "John Gould Fletcher and Rimbaud's *Alchimie du Verbe*." *Comparative Literature* 8 (1956): 46–62.
Blackmur, R. P. "Versions of Fletcher." *Poetry* 76 (1936): 344–47.
Coffman, Stanley. *Imagism: A Chapter for the History of Modern Poetry*. Norman: University of Oklahoma Press, 1951, pp. 175–80.
Davidson, Donald. "In Memory of John Gould Fletcher." *Poetry* 77 (1950): 154–61.
De Chasca, Edmund S. *John Gould Fletcher and Imagism*. Columbia: University of Missouri Press, 1978.
Hughes, Glenn. *Imagism and the Imagists: A Study in Modern Poetry*. Stanford: Stanford University Press, 1931, pp. 125–52.
Kimpel, Ben. "John Gould Fletcher in Retrospect." *Poetry* 84 (1954): 284–96.
Lowell, Amy. *Tendencies in Modern American Poetry*. New York: Macmillan, 1917, pp. 233–343.
Lund, Mary Graham. "John Gould Fletcher, Geographer of the Uncharted Province of Beauty." *Sewanee Review* 76 (Winter 1968): 76–89.
Monroe, Harriet. "John Gould Fletcher." *Poetry* 27 (1926): 206–10.
Morton, Bruce. *John Gould Fletcher: A Bibliography*. Kent, Ohio: Kent State University Press, 1979.
Pound, Ezra. "Peals of Iron." *Poetry* 3 (1913): 111–13.
Quinn, Kerker. "Story of an Arkansas Poet." *Poetry* 58 (1941): 334–36.
Simon, Charlie May. *Johnswood*. New York: E. P. Dutton, 1953.
Stephens, Edna Buell. *John Gould Fletcher*. New York: Twayne, 1967.
Taupin, René. "John Gould Fletcher: American Symbolist." *The Influence of French Symbolism on Modern American Poetry*. Trans. William Pratt and Anne Pratt. New York: AMS Press, 1985, pp. 168–81.
Van Doren, Mark. "Poetic Space and Time." *Nation* 112 (13 April 1921): 252.
Warren, Robert Penn. "A Note on Three Southern Poets." *Poetry* 40 (1932): 103–13.
Webster, Harvey Curtis. "Music vs. Eloquence." *Poetry* 33 (1947): 353–56.
Zabel, Morton D. "Dust Discrowned." *Poetry* 33 (1929): 222–24.

ROBERT L. PHILLIPS

Shelby Foote
(1916–   )

A distinguished historian, Shelby Foote is also a skilled novelist. After the publication of his three-volume *The Civil War*, an accomplished narrative of the decisive drama in the South's history, he also began to receive a more just recognition for his achievements as a novelist.

BIOGRAPHY

Soon after Shelby Dade Foote, Jr., was born on 17 November 1916 in Greenville, Mississippi, his father, an executive with Armour and Company, began a migration, as his fortunes with the meat-packing firm rose, that took the family to Jackson, Vicksburg, Pensacola, and finally to Mobile, where he died suddenly in 1922. Following his father's death, Shelby and his mother, Lillian Rosenstock Foote, returned to Greenville, where they lived until 1924, when Mrs. Foote became a secretary for Armour and Company in Pensacola. Three years later, in summer 1927, mother and son had moved back to Greenville where Shelby lived for the next 26 years with interruptions for college and for World War II.

Greenville, the county seat of Washington County and a busy Mississippi River port, lies in one of the finest agricultural regions of the world, the Yazoo-Mississippi Delta. The region, together with the histories of the Foote and Rosenstock families, provided Foote with some of the raw ingredients his imagination later developed into fiction. Foote's paternal grandfather, Huger Lee Foote, came to the rapidly developing Delta in 1877 to manage three plantations in which his father, Hezekiah, a successful planter and lawyer in east Mississippi, had invested. His maternal grandfather, Morris Rosenstock, migrated from Vienna to Greenville a few years later. Both men accumulated substantial holdings, and both lost their fortunes. Hugh Foote sold his plantations, and, soon after the turn of the century, lost the proceeds at the poker table. Rosenstock saw his fortune disappear in the market failure of 1921.

Shelby Foote's closest friend during high school was Walker Percy who, along with his two brothers, had been adopted by William Alexander Percy, a poet who in 1941 published a highly admired autobiography, *Lanterns on the Levee*. Foote spent much time in the Percy household, where he saw many of the famous writers and artists who were often guests there. There, too, he heard William Alexander Percy's fine collection of classical music played on one of the first automatic record players imported into the Delta. Walker Percy and Foote began their literary apprenticeships as contributors to and editors of the Greenville High School newspaper, the *Pica*, by writing essays, poems, and reviews.

Foote's apprenticeship continued in Chapel Hill at the University of North Carolina, where he contributed to the *Carolina Quarterly* for the two years he was enrolled. Back in Greenville in 1937, he began writing the book that would later become *Tournament*, but World War II interrupted his work. The Army National Guard unit Foote had joined in 1939 was mobilized, and before he was dismissed by court-martial for insubordination in 1944 in Ireland, he had been promoted to captain. During the winter of 1944–45 he worked in New York briefly as a reporter for the Associated Press. Feeling that he needed to make a more direct contribution to the war effort, he enlisted in the Marine Corps, where he served in combat intelligence until the war ended.

In Greenville, after the war, he worked for a radio station and for the newspaper, the *Delta Democrat Times*, until 1947, when he decided to work full-time as a writer. His short story "Flood Burial" appeared in the *Saturday Evening Post* in 1946; his first separate publication appeared in 1947, *The Merchant of Bristol*, a pamphlet issued by the Levee Press in Greenville. In 1949 *Tournament*, the book he had begun before he left Greenville for the war, appeared and was followed in rapid succession by three other novels, *Follow Me Down* (1950), *Love in a Dry Season* (1951), and *Shiloh* (1952), and by a collection of inter-related stories, *Jordan County: A Landscape in Narrative* (1954). In these books Foote developed his history of Jordan County and Bristol, which closely resemble Washington County and Greenville, and he populated his county with characters who resemble members of his own family and other Washington County folk such as the Blantons, who founded Greenville.

In 1954 the success of *Shiloh* prompted the editors at Random House to ask Foote to write a brief history of the Civil War that could be released in connection with the centennial celebration. In Foote's hands one volume grew to three and into a project that, aided by three Guggenheim fellowships, occupied him for the better part of twenty years. Volume 1 of the history, *Fort Sumter to Perryville*, appeared in 1958; volume 2, *Fredericksburg to Meridian*, in 1963; and the final volume, *Red River to Appomattox*, in 1974. During these years Foote lived in Memphis except for a period in 1963–64 when he was a Ford Foundation Fellow and writer-in-residence at the Arena Stage in Washington. From there Foote moved to Mobile before returning to Memphis, and in 1968 he was in Virginia as writer-in-residence at Hollins College.

Foote has been married three times. It was his paying courtship to Tess Lavery in Belfast that led to his dismissal from the army. They were married before Foote left Ireland and divorced in 1946. From 1948 to 1953 he was married to Marguerite Dessommes; one daughter, Margaret Shelby Foote, was born to them. In 1956 he married his present wife, Gwyn Rainer; their son, Huger Lee Foote II, was born in 1961.

Following the completion of the *Civil War* Foote published *September, September* (1978), a novel set in Memphis but featuring characters who have relations with Bristol and Jordan County. Shelby and Gwyn Foote continue to live in Memphis, where Foote is working on another novel set in Jordan County.

MAJOR THEMES

Parker Nowell, a lawyer in Foote's 1950 novel, *Follow Me Down*, explains that in this century "Love has failed us," with the result that we are "irrevocably alone." "Anything that seems to combat that loneliness is a trap," Nowell feels. "We left our better destiny in '65, defeated though we fought with a fury that seems to indicate foreknowledge of what would follow if we lost. Probably it happened even earlier: maybe in Jackson's time. Anyhow—whenever—we left the wellsprings, and ever since then we have been moving toward this ultimate failure of nerve" (233). Nowell's view seems to be close to Foote's own, for major themes in his fiction have to do with the failure of love and the failure of characters to understand and adhere to their "wellsprings." The failures of individual characters must be seen as a part of a larger failure of the civilization to come to terms with its own traditions and history and to understand itself in the light shed by knowledge of the dynamics of history and tradition. Nowell is also interested, as is his creator, in music, particularly since music, like successful fiction, employs form. If there is an escape from loneliness at all, it is to be found in art or in the quiet but heroic assertion of a will to love.

A character needs to be able to define himself either intellectually, as Nowell is capable of doing, or intuitively with respect to history and tradition. The force of history is very strong in Foote's fiction, and characters who try to counter that flow are doomed to failure, just as engineers who try to divert the Mississippi River from its course in *Tournament* fail to prevent destruction. The "wellsprings" lie deep in characters molded over the centuries by Western civilization. Isaac Jameson in "Pillar of Fire," one of the seven stories that comprise *Jordan County: A Landscape in Narrative*, was one of the first settlers along the banks of Lake Jordan. Isaac, traveling with trappers through the western delta, dreamed that he saw the wilderness tamed under his hand. Following his dream, he created one of the region's largest, most productive plantations, which he named Solitaire to honor his bachelorhood. Isaac lost his bachelorhood and fathered one of the South's Civil War heroes, but the name stuck to the farm and came increasingly to represent the isolation Hugh Bart, the second successful owner of Solitaire, came to experience. Bart, the hero of *Tournament*, Foote's first completed novel, succeeded as long as he stuck to his intuitive sense of what best suited himself and his land. But gradually Bart moved away from his dream, lured by the image he saw of himself in lesser men's eyes and by false promises of finance capitalism.

Major Dubose, in an incident Foote took from his manuscript of *Tournament* and published as "Flood Burial" in the *Saturday Evening Post*, represents the separation from wellsprings of the history of the region. The major, a distinguished Civil War veteran, has spent years writing a history of the war, but he dies during a flood and is buried in a trunk containing the water-ruined manuscript that no one other than the major himself had read.

Characters who abandon and are abandoned by history exist in an isolation encompassed by their economic, social, even biological failures. Hugh Bart cannot pass on to his children, particularly his oldest son, the "spark" that made him the man he was. The son cannot farm Solitaire, and Hugh sells it only to lose the proceeds in poker and bank failure. Hector Sturgis in the long central story in *Jordan County*, "Child by Fever," is so revolted by his wife's labor in childbirth that he never resumes sexual relations with her. Characters in Foote's twentieth-century Bristol usually act out a loveless passion in a world of jazz, technological progress, and alcohol. *Love in a Dry Season*, Foote's novel of twentieth-century Bristol, depicts a wasteland of observers who watch other observers and who wait. No one emphatically and decisively *does*.

History cannot be moribund, the hollow observance of forms adapted from the past. It must be vital, dynamic. If the South were acting out its failure in the Civil War, then the causes may lie in what Metcalf, a Confederate staff officer in Foote's *Shiloh*, identifies as a love of the past, an "incurable romanticism," or "misplaced chivalry."

Although tradition and history assume powerful force in Foote's fictive world, history gives way to even deeper "wellsprings" so that "this ultimate failure of nerve" can be judged in a religious and mythical as well as a historical framework. On the surfaces of Foote's texts, reverberations of a more timeless human dimension sound. Hector Sturgis's name recalls Greek heroism and his furies Greek tragedy; against both Foote invites us to judge Hector's modern failure. Pauly Green, the principal figure in "Rain Down Home," has a name that invokes both Christianity and more primitive fertility rites. Against a background of a fecund earth, the delta's loamy soil, and a nature that annually renews itself, Foote's modern characters act out their failures. Oblivious to symbolic renewal, they grow cotton to sell. Some are sadly misled into the throes of revivalism, as is Luther Dade Eustis, whom Parker Nowell defends at his murder trial in *Follow Me Down*. Luther was sure that his killing the prostitute he had taken to an island in the Mississippi was in accordance with God's command.

Finally, however, the failure of love is not a necessary trap for modern man. Eben and Martha Kinship, a wealthy black couple in Foote's most recent novel,

September, September (1977), experience a kind of renewal from concern over their son who was kidnapped for ransom by three whites seeking to take advantage of civil rights unrest. But the most certain escape from loneliness for modern man, if there is to be an escape and reunion with the historical and mythical "wellsprings" that should give shape and direction to the modern world, occurs in the achievement of form in art. "Ride Out," a story in *Jordan County*, features a jazz trumpet player, Duff Conway. Emotion fills Duff's art, but as Duff's composer friend Van comes to understand, Duff's jazz lacks finally the achievement of form that would make it permanent. If Duff had not failed in love, and had not been condemned to death for the murder that resulted from the failure, then his trumpet, from which he had contracted tuberculosis, would have been the instrument of his death.

The achievement of form is one of the many accomplishments of Foote's *The Civil War: A Narrative*. Unlike Major Dubose in *Tournament*, Foote is not a failed historian; rather he has taken the most important event in the history of the American South and imposed upon the four years a form that makes that event in history observable from a consistent narrative point of view. Foote has considered himself a novelist first and a historian second and by doing so has created a fine work of art as well as a history. Again, as in the novels, the surface of the text is rich in allusions to the past, particularly the *Iliad*. Thus, in the eyes of the narrator the actions of the Civil War are observed and measured on a scale not limited to the events beginning in 1861 and concluding in 1865, but rather on one recalling the very beginnings of Western civilization.

SURVEY OF CRITICISM

In his entry for the *Bibliographical Guide to the Study of Southern Literature* (1969), James E. Kibler, Jr., complained that critical essays about Foote's work were "virtually nonexistent." He also noted that the reviews of his novels in periodicals with national circulation generally offered little in the way of critical evaluation, most of them amounting simply to brief notices. There were by 1969 critical reviews of the first two volumes of *The Civil War* commenting briefly on the artistic value of the books, but the professional historians generally complained that Foote's failure to document his history sufficiently ruined whatever other value it might have.

Since 1969 Foote has received increasing critical attention: a number of articles have appeared, two journals have published special issues about his work, and Helen White and Redding Sugg have published their excellent book-length study in the Twayne series. Reviews of the final volume of *The Civil War* and of *September, September* have been generally thoughtful.

In 1971 the *Mississippi Quarterly* published the first of the special issues, containing Thomas H. Landess's pioneering investigation of the themes in Foote's novels, two interviews with Foote, a critical study of form in *Love in a Dry Season* by Simone Vauthier, and James E. Kibler, Jr.'s excellent bibliography of primary and secondary material. Kibler's bibliography also contains excerpts from his correspondence with Foote.

The French critics have been much quicker than the Americans to appreciate the high quality of art in Foote's novels. The special issue of *Delta* (No. 4, May 1977) contains nine articles that investigate with some precision the questions of form in *Jordan County: A Landscape in Narrative*. *Delta* is published by the Centre d'Étude et de Recherches sur les Écrivains du Sud aux États-Unis at the Université Paul Valéry à Montpellier.

For many years compared to Faulkner, Foote willingly agrees that Faulkner has been a major influence, but Foote's Jordan County is markedly different from Faulkner's Yoknapatawpha, and reading Foote as a member of the tribe of Faulkner will cause one to miss a great deal. This argument has been forcefully advanced by Helen White and Redding Sugg in *Shelby Foote*; they point out Foote's indebtedness to Browning and Proust among others. The most thoroughgoing study to date of *The Civil War* also appears in their book.

Two general, brief surveys of Foote's career are Kibler's entry in the *Dictionary of Literary Biography* (1978) and Robert L. Phillips, Jr.'s booklet *Shelby Foote* (1977), published by the Mississippi Library Commission. In addition, articles about specific matters are beginning to appear in a number of academic journals, as is noted in the bibliography below. Particularly significant are those by Louis D. Rubin, Jr., George Garrett, and Wirt Williams, which explore Foote's accomplishments in *The Civil War*.

Foote has never liked to give speeches; however, he is a fascinating conversationalist and has allowed a number of interviews. In the interviews with Evans Harrington, John G. Jones, John Carr, Helen White and Redding Sugg, Foote discusses his literary interests extensively.

Much remains to be done. Of course, Foote's literary career is still in the making, but he is beginning to receive the attention that the strength and maturity of his art have earned.

BIBLIOGRAPHY

Works by Shelby Foote

The Merchant of Bristol. Greenville: Levee Press, 1947.

Tournament. New York: Dial Press, 1949.

Follow Me Down. New York: Dial Press, 1950.

Love in a Dry Season. New York: Dial Press, 1951.

Shiloh. New York: Dial Press, 1952.

"Talks With Shelby Foote," ed. Harvey Breit. *New York Times Book Review*, 27 April 1952, p. 16.

Jordan County: A Landscape in Narrative. New York: Dial Press, 1954.

The Night before Chancellorsville. Ed. Shelby Foote. New York: New American Library, 1957.

The Civil War: A Narrative, vol. 1, *Fort Sumter to Perryville*. New York: Random House, 1958.
The Civil War: A Narrative, vol. 2, *Fredericksburg to Meridian*. New York: Random House, 1963.
"The Novelist's View of History." *Mississippi Quarterly* 17 (Fall 1964): 219–25.
Three Novels: Follow Me Down, Jordan County, Love in a Dry Season. New York: Dial Press, 1964.
"Talking with Shelby Foote: June 1970," ed. John Graham. *Mississippi Quarterly* 24 (Fall 1971): 405–27.
"Interview with Shelby Foote," ed. Evans Harrington. *Mississippi Quarterly* 24 (Fall 1971): 349–77.
"It's Worth a Grown Man's Time." *Kite-Flying and Other Irrational Acts: Conversations with Twelve Southerners*, ed. John Carr. Baton Rouge: Louisiana State University Press, 1972, pp. 3–33.
The Civil War, vol. 3, *Red River to Appomattox*. New York: Random House, 1974.
September, September. New York: Random House, 1977.
"Growing Up in the Deep South: A Conversation with Eudora Welty, Shelby Foote, and Louis D. Rubin, Jr." *The American South: Portrait of Culture*. Baton Rouge: Louisiana State University Press, 1980, pp. 59–85.
"A Colloquium with Shelby Foote," ed. Helen White and Redding Sugg. *Southern Humanities Review* 15 (Fall 1981): 281–99.
"Shelby Foote." *Talking with Mississippi Writers*, ed. John G. Jones. Jackson: University Press of Mississippi, 1982, pp. 37–92.

Studies of Shelby Foote

Bruccoli, Matthew J. and C. E. Frazer Clark, Jr., ed. *First Printing of American Authors, Contributing Toward Descriptive Checklists*, vol. 2. Detroit: Gale Research, 1978, pp. 165–66.
Gale, Robert. "Shelby Foote Repeats Himself, a Review Article." *Journal of Mississippi History* 17 (January 1955): 56–60.
Garrett, George. "Foote's *The Civil War: The Version for Posterity?*" *Mississippi Quarterly* 28 (Winter 1974–75): 83–92.
Howell, Elmo. "The Greenville Writers and the Mississippi Country People." *Louisiana Studies* 86 (Winter 1969): 348–60.
Kibler, James E., Jr. "Shelby Foote." *Dictionary of Literary Biography*. Detroit: Gale Research, 1978. 2: 148–54.
———. "Shelby Foote: A Bibliography." *Mississippi Quarterly* 24 (Fall 1971): 437–65.
Landess, Thomas H. "Southern History and Manhood: Major Themes in the Works of Shelby Foote." *Mississippi Quarterly* 24 (Fall 1971): 321–47.
Phillips, Robert L., Jr. *Shelby Foote*. Jackson: Mississippi Library Commission, 1977.
———. "Shelby Foote's Bristol in 'Child by Fever.'" *Southern Quarterly* 19 (Fall 1980): 172–83.
Rubin, Louis D., Jr. "Shelby Foote's Civil War." *Prospects* 1 (1974): 313–33.
Shepherd, Allen. "Technique and Theme in Shelby Foote's *Shiloh*." *Notes on Mississippi Writers* 5 (Spring 1972): 3–10.

Skei, Hans. "History as Novel: Shelby Foote's *The Civil War: A Narrative.*" *Notes on Mississippi Writers* 13 (1981): 45–63.

Vauthier, Simone. "Fiction and Fictions in Shelby Foote's 'Rain Down Home.' " *Notes on Mississippi Writers* 8 (Fall 1975): 35–50.

———. " 'Pillar of Fire': The Civil War of Narratives." *Delta* 4 (May 1977): 71–81.

———. "The Symmetrical Design: The Structural Patterns of *Love in a Dry Season.*" *Mississippi Quarterly* 24 (Fall 1971): 379–403.

White, Helen and Redding Sugg. *Shelby Foote.* Boston: Twayne, 1982.

Williams, Wirt. "Shelby Foote's *Civil War*: The Novelist as Humanistic Historian." *Mississippi Quarterly* 24 (Fall 1971): 429–36.

—————— FRANK W. SHELTON ——————

Ernest J. Gaines
(1933–   )

Of the many contemporary Southern black writers who now look to their Southern roots for material, Ernest Gaines was one of the first to follow the footsteps of such writers as Jean Toomer and Zora Neale Hurston, and with the publication of *The Autobiography of Miss Jane Pittman* in 1971 he achieved both popular and critical recognition.

BIOGRAPHY

Ernest Gaines was born on a plantation near New Roads, Louisiana, northwest of Baton Rouge, on 15 February, 1933. The oldest of eight brothers and three sisters, he remembers beginning to work in the fields at age nine. Because his mother and father were separated when he was a child, he was raised by his aunt, Miss Augusteen Jefferson, a woman who had never walked a day of her life; Gaines indicated her importance to him by dedicating *The Autobiography of Miss Jane Pittman* to her. This aunt is the model not only of Miss Jane but of all the courageous, dignified old people who appear in his fiction. At his aunt's house, Gaines did many of the things he describes Jimmy Aaron doing in *The Autobiography*—he read to people, wrote letters for them, and above all listened to the stories they told. Although Gaines lived in Louisiana for only his first fifteen years, that period was extremely important to his development as a writer, providing him the fund of memories on which he has drawn throughout his career.

In 1948 Gaines and his mother moved to Vallejo, California, to live with his stepfather, who was in the merchant marine, and to enable Gaines to get the good education unavailable to him in rural Louisiana. It was after moving to California that he discovered books. When he became involved with a rough group of young people, his stepfather advised him to get off the streets, and

Gaines gravitated to the public library. He especially responded to novels that depicted the peasantry, and he reports that he was quickly drawn to Steinbeck and Cather. His favorite writers are still the nineteenth-century Russians: Chekhov, Tolstoy, and especially Turgenev, whose *Sportsman's Sketches* and *Fathers and Sons* had great impact on him. In addition, Gaines admires Hemingway and finds the theme of grace under pressure particularly applicable to blacks. Of Southern writers, he was of course influenced by Faulkner, especially by his style and use of dialect, but Gaines has said that although Southern writers compellingly describe the earth and sun, they do not do so well with black characters. Gaines developed early the desire to write about the Southern black peasantry he knew so well but could not find in the books he read.

Although he began writing in 1949, only after attending high school and junior college and then serving in the army did he begin serious study of the craft of fiction. He earned a B.A. at San Francisco State College, where some of his stories won him in 1958 the Wallace Stegner Creative Writing Fellowship for graduate study at Stanford University.

In 1962 Gaines had planned to go to Mexico to try to finish the novel he had been working on for years, but inspired by the courage of James Meredith at the University of Mississippi, he instead decided to return to Louisiana, a decision of great significance to his career. He lived there for six months in 1963, during which time he talked with people and absorbed the Louisiana environment, enabling him to write as he had never done before. His first publications—the stories "Just Like a Tree" and "The Sky Is Gray"—date from 1963, and his first novel, *Catherine Carmier*, appeared in 1964. Although it received the Joseph Henry Jackson Literary Prize, it did not receive much public attention and in light of Gaines's later career is more important for what it promises than for its own merits. Gaines spent years on it, finding the third-person point of view troublesome, for he is much more comfortable telling a story in the first person. In *Of Love and Dust* (1967) Gaines found a voice with which he was at ease, and with this novel he began to receive the generally positive, respectful reviews that have continued to the present time. *Bloodline*, a collection of previously published stories, appeared in 1968. The publication of *The Autobiography of Miss Jane Pittman* (1971) and the later well-regarded and popular television movie made from it, mark the high point of Gaines's career. Certainly his best thus far, this novel is a major contribution to American literature. He has published two novels since then. *In My Father's House* (1978) suggests that he had difficulty adapting to his prominence as a literary figure. His most recent novel, *A Gathering of Old Men* (1983), adapts the Faulknerian technique he earlier used in "Just Like a Tree"—telling the story in short sections from different characters' perspectives.

Ernest Gaines is a very private man. He does not make tours to promote his works and does not take public positions on political or racial matters (for example, he avoided the Black Arts Movement of the late 1960s). Certainly his novels reveal a great interest in political and social issues as they affect black people, but he believes he can best serve the cause of art and humanity by devoting himself to the craft of fiction.

Gaines divides his time between San Francisco and Louisiana, where he occasionally teaches at the University of Southwestern Louisiana. He lives in California in order to gain a perspective on his Southern material but returns to Louisiana every year to absorb and experience the region that provides his subject matter. He has written several novels set in California but finds they are not worth publishing. For most of his readers, it is hard to conceive of an Ernest Gaines novel not set in Louisiana.

MAJOR THEMES

Before it became fashionable among Southern black writers, Gaines wrote about his native area. Like William Faulkner with his Yoknapatawpha County, he has concentrated on a single limited area and has created works that interrelate both geographically and thematically. Dealing with the rural area around his fictional Bayonne, Louisiana, his works cover the time span from the Civil War to the present. He is particularly interested in the theme of historical, social, and personal change as it has occurred in the rural South. In general, his depiction of the changes in the South follows a Faulknerian line, at least as modified by a black perspective. The traditional plantation owners, weakened both personally and economically, lease more and more of their land to the Cajuns. Snopes-like, money-oriented vermin bring tractors to the land and ruin it. Since there are no jobs for blacks, most of the young leave; the old remain to watch the destruction of their land, their traditions, and their way of life. Gaines sees the Cajuns as particularly modern; their growing power reveals a weakening of values and a loss of determination to live in harmony with the land. Gaines depicts major historical events in his works but emphasizes the "folk" and daily life: historical change is filtered through the perspective of his average characters. Perhaps his strongest qualities are his humanity and compassion. He seems incapable of reducing character to stereotype, and even his most unsympathetic characters are presented with understanding.

Several themes consistently appear in Gaines's work. The most general is the role of history and the relationship between past and present. He explores, with particular regard to race relations, whether change is possible, both socially and individually. The issue of determinism and free will is central, for the pressures of oppression often threaten to deprive his black characters of the ability to transform their lives. Connected to this concern is his interest in the relationship between old and young, for the old are often resistant to change while the young want to fight for it. Yet Gaines and often his young characters revere the old, who embody the strength of black people—both as individuals and as a community. For it is often the community in which he finds a locus of values. A tension between men and women appears in the works. Slavery, Gaines feels, has denied black men their manhood. In order to attain or assert it, black men must take extreme, often violent, action that threatens to upset the stability of the community. Women, on the other hand, are often conservators and survivors and are strongly identified with the community. Gaines has clearly built his books around several dichotomies. Looking at the novels sequentially reveals how they all treat these issues and how *The Autobiography of Miss Jane Pittman*, Gaines's supreme artistic triumph, unites those opposites.

His first novel, *Catherine Carmier*, is filled with bleak determinism. Although the book is set in the present, to the characters in it the civil rights movement is only a vague rumor. Its protagonist is Jackson Bradley, a young black man born and reared in rural Louisiana but educated in California. He is a rootless modern man who does not know where he belongs, finding life in the North and West empty; but he is unable to live in the South either. He returns to visit his Aunt Charlotte, who raised him, and her disappointment that he will not live and teach in Louisiana indicates the barrier in this novel between old and young. Jackson's only hope lies in his love for Catherine, daughter of Raoul Carmier. In many ways Raoul is the most interesting character in the novel. A man of heroic pride who loves the land, he is virtually the only person to resist the encroachment of the Cajuns by working the land independently. But as a Creole he is trapped between the races; the whites don't treat him as an equal because of his black heritage, and because of his white blood he considers blacks beneath him. He loves only Catherine, who is caught between the two men in her life, loving and admiring her father but also sensing the dead end her life has become and seeing Jackson as a way to freedom and a new life. Although the novel ends ambiguously, with at least a hint that Catherine and Jackson may ultimately be able to have a life together, its thrust runs counter to that hope. Gaines suggests that history, caste, and race are prisons; no change is possible because the characters cannot break out of the cages their lives have become. Love and hope are victims; Catherine will continue to live a restricted life while Jackson will continue searching for something to fill the void within.

Set in the late 1940s, *Of Love and Dust* involves a movement into the past that culminates in *The Autobiography of Miss Jane Pittman* and also suggests a movement forward in terms of artistry and optimism. The novel is told by Jim Kelly, the straw boss on the plantation, an accepted member of the black community but also a man trusted by the whites. His perspective on the events of the novel thus conveys, both through his own voice and his relating of events other blacks observe, the perspective of the community. The protagonist of the novel, Marcus Payne, is the archetypal "bad nigger," selfish, rebellious, disrespectful, determined to do only what he wants. Initially, Jim and all the other blacks dislike and resent him as a troublemaker. Although the older members of the community are treated with sympathy in the novel, they are committed to the old ways of submission and accommodation and never move beyond that attitude, but Jim does change. He comes to realize that Marcus, by resisting what the white man wants, is asserting his pride and manhood. Although Marcus is killed in the end, he dies with dignity, and Gaines suggests that his rebellion is the precursor of events to come. Because of his example, Jim Kelly leaves the plantation, no longer simply accepting his fate but believing he can act to shape his life. The novel thus suggests that change can occur, although slowly and painfully. But love is again, as in *Catherine Carmier*, defeated by the system. Two instances of interracial love are included in the novel. Both relationships begin as purely sexual but eventually become genuinely loving; in both cases, however, racial considerations block the open, healthy expression of that love. In this novel, then, barriers still exist between men and women and between old and young; however, through the examples of Marcus and Jim, Gaines suggests that black men can reject the burdens of slavery and assert their manhood.

Bloodline is a collection of five previously published stories, intricately linked by locale and theme. Gaines carefully organizes the stories so their concerns progress from youth to maturity and finally to old age. All the stories indicate a potential for individual growth and change, and one development in the volume is their widening scope. The first two stories, "A Long Day in November" and "The Sky is Gray," focus primarily on individuals, but with "Three Men," and especially "Bloodline" and "Just Like a Tree," the concern, while remaining personal, also widens to include the public realm. The first three stories explore what manhood is for the black male: in the first story it is defined as assuming responsibility for family; in the second it involves enduring pain and hardship without complaint; in the third it means submitting to punishment from whites instead of taking an easy escape. The fourth story, "Bloodline," continues to deal with manhood but also attends to such issues as the clashes of the races and the generations, with the potential for violent revolution strongly present. Gaines's treatment is complex: he certainly admires his characters' search for manhood and struggle for change, but a hardening of character and loss of humanity may also occur, as is especially evident in someone like Copper Laurent. The final story of the book, "Just Like a Tree," combines all Gaines's usual concerns in a story of reconciliation. The change occurring in rural Louisiana results in the uprooting of old Aunt Fe, a pillar of the black community. The community gathers to bid her farewell, honoring what she represents and asserting their own solidarity. Aunt Fe accepts the young man who brings the disruption inevitable with change, and his love and respect for her reveal his reverence for what she represents. Thus a collection filled with conflict ends on a note of unity and acceptance.

With *The Autobiography of Miss Jane Pittman* Gaines completes the excursion into the past begun in *Of Love and Dust*. Building on the character of Aunt Fe, he creates a "folk autobiography" that relates the story of people who are not in history books, from the Civil War to the civil rights movement of the 1960s. Although the book centers on Miss Jane, she is an observer much of the time; what she sees is the chronicle of black Americans from slavery to the present. From the beginning of the novel, when Jane is determined to keep the name given to her by a Union soldier instead of her slave name, to the end, when she accompanies her people to Bayonne for a civil rights demonstration, she is in the best sense enduring and sustaining. Many of the dichotomies that run through Gaines's works are united in her character and story. The differing roles of men and women function as significant elements in the novel. Women preserve and sustain the community—as Miss Jane's longevity symbolizes. Men, on the other hand, must court danger by actively asserting their manhood, as the lives of the three men especially important to her reveal. Ned, in effect her "son," is a rebel like Marcus Payne, but Marcus's rebellion was purely personal whereas Ned returns to Louisiana in the early 1900s to teach and help his people. Although he is murdered by whites, Miss Jane and others perpetuate his legacy. In the 1960s Jimmy Aaron assumes Ned's role and urges his people to action. Again the older people hold back, fearful of change, but after Jimmy is killed, Jane unites old and young and past and present when she goes to Bayonne to complete Jimmy's mission. Marcus's purely personal rebellion has become political action. In Joe Pittman, Jane's husband, we also find the man's need to prove himself, in his case through horsebreaking. He too is killed—by a wild horse—but in her love and understanding of Joe, as well as Ned and Jimmy, Jane bridges the gap between men and women as well as between the generations. Her strength is rooted in the past but directed toward the future. When Jimmy returns, he tells the people that without their support he is helpless. Not simply a matter of numbers, their strength is their character as it has been forged by all they have endured through history. Although the people appear weak and fearful, the example of Miss Jane reveals their potential. They can shake off the shackles of bondage and determinism, assert their free spirit through direct action, and cause change. While the change has only begun at the end of *The Autobiography of Miss Jane Pittman*, the pride and dignity of Miss Jane and all those she represents imply that finally they will prevail.

The voice of Miss Jane provides much of the vitality of her novel, but in his next book, *In My Father's House*, Gaines returns to the third person for the first time since *Catherine Carmier* and produces a subdued, even bleak, novel. Both setting and protagonist are unusual for Gaines, the former a small town instead of a rural area and the latter Philip Martin, a minister, leader in the black community, and potential politician. Set in the period of disillusionment following the assassination of Martin Luther King, Jr., the novel suggests that the progress implicit in the conclusion of *The Autobiography of Miss Jane Pittman* was temporary or even illusory. Barriers between old and young remain, for the young, far from leading the fight for constructive change (as in earlier novels), are mostly cynical, apathetic, and hopeless, or devoted to anarchic violence. On the personal level, a conflict exists between fathers and sons and past and present, illustrated by Robert X, Martin's illegitimate son, who appears ghostlike to accuse Martin of ruining Robert's life and the lives of his mother and siblings. Robert is evidence that, by abandoning them years ago, Martin in effect destroyed them. Formerly an irresponsible gambler and drinker, Martin tries to explain to his son that his earlier weakness was a legacy of slavery. Although he seems through religion to have transcended his past and pridefully considers himself a man, that past rises up to haunt him and force him to face the consequences of his weakness. Martin wants to effect a reconciliation with his son and thus with his past, but Robert's suicide precludes that. So the book ends on a hopeless note, with Martin brought low. The novel suggests that the past is alive and inescapable, though not necessarily comforting. Martin himself, in his earlier self-satisfaction, is at least partly to blame for his fate. He had felt that his acceptance of religion and his devotion to his people would completely absolve him from his past, and he apparently gave no thought to the people he had earlier abandoned. Thus, Martin must pay the price for never assuming full responsibility for his actions.

A Gathering of Old Men marks something of a return of hope to the Gaines canon. Even though the time of the novel remains the present, Gaines returns to a familiar rural setting, a place where the young have left and only the old remain. By adapting the narrative method of "Just Like a Tree" to the novel form—telling the story in alternating sections from as many as fifteen different points of view—Gaines suggests that the perspective of the book is finally that of the black community. The novel is essentially a celebration of old age, as was at least the last section of *The Autobiography of Miss Jane Pittman*. In their willingness to assume responsibility for the murder of a Cajun in order to protect the black man they think killed him, the fifteen or twenty old men, all in their seventies or eighties, acquire heroic proportions. Certainly the past, during which they had simply allowed themselves to be humiliated by whites, weighs heavily on them. Although their memory of past cowardice and submission may seem a burden they must discard, it is the very thing that inspires their heroism; for they are determined to act courageously before it is too late. The most moving section of the novel appears at its center, when several of the old men step forward to voice their grievances, explaining their final courageous stance. A dominant presence in the book, the nearby graveyard embodies the collective past of the black people, a past that informs, strengthens, and endures in the present. This novel, unlike *In My Father's House*, posits a fruitful connection between past and present and is more hopeful about change, both personal and social. For rural Louisiana has been slowly changing. The Boutan family, Cajuns who have always believed in vigilante justice, allow the law to operate here. Mapes, the sheriff who has previously treated blacks with contempt and brutality, develops respect for the old men who defy him. Mathu, the one black man who has been strong and dignified all his life and therefore has looked with disdain on other blacks, also learns to respect the old men who have stood with him. In the union of a group of old black men for concerted action, Gaines creates an image of the potential dignity and courage of all blacks.

In his fiction Gaines returns again and again to the same ground, not only geographically but also thematically. Yet his works do not give the impression of repetition but rather of growing depth of perspective. In his small area of Louisiana, he attempts to capture all humanity in its beauty and ugliness, its strength and weakness. Gaines reveals a concern for people, a reverence for the everyday, and a love of the land, powerfully evoking the strength, pride, and dignity people can develop by living close to the soil.

SURVEY OF CRITICISM

As might be expected, little criticism of Gaines's work appeared prior to the publication of *The Autobiography of Miss Jane Pittman*, but since that time he has begun to receive a deserved critical recognition.

Although Gaines has published very little nonfiction, perhaps the best account of his early life and literary development through *The Autobiography of Miss Jane Pittman* is his essay "Miss Jane and I," which appears in *Callaloo* along with an interesting collection of photographs he has taken of his native Louisiana. Gaines has consented to numerous interviews as well, for he is quite willing to discuss literary influences and his intentions in his fiction. The most revealing interviews are those given to Charles Rowell, Ruth Laney, and John O'Brien.

The most comprehensive critical treatment of Gaines's work to date can be found in a chapter of a book on contemporary American fiction by Jack Hicks. Dealing with all the fiction through *In My Father's House*, Hicks traces the movement in Gaines's work from history as bondage to history as a part of the natural cycle and shows how his modes of expression change from the white existential novel to folk forms, including sermons and folktales. Gaines is the subject of a special issue of *Callaloo*, which includes the aforementioned essay by Gaines and his interview with Rowell. In addition, it contains essays on each of his works of fiction: a discussion by Alvin Aubert of the Creole absence in *Catherine Carmier*, an appreciation of *Of Love and Dust* by the novelist John Wideman, an essay by Todd Duncan applying Erik Erikson's conception of the life cycle of *Bloodline*, a treatment by Barry Beckham of the oral techniques used in *The Autobiography of Miss Jane Pittman*, a general consideration of Gaines's fictional world by Michael Fabre, and a checklist of material about Gaines's work compiled by Charles Rowell. This volume, providing the greatest amount of material on him in a single place, is an important resource for Gaines scholars.

Other criticism includes two general essays by Jerry H. Bryant that analyze *The Autobiography of Miss Jane Pittman* as Gaines's supreme accomplishment because of its generosity of spirit, its depth and humanity. Illuminating considerations of that work are also found in essays by William L. Andrews and Albert Wertheim, the former tracing the dialectic in the novel between progress and regress and the latter dealing with the epic form of the novel. Essays by John Callahan and Vilma Raskin Potter consider the relationship between the novel and the television film based on it. Although the film is generally highly regarded and Gaines himself likes it, both critics are concerned to point out its limitations. Sherley Anne Williams has written an interesting piece concerning *Of Love and Dust*, demonstrating how, in the character of Marcus Payne, Gaines has adapted the urban streetman figure to his rural setting. *Bloodline* has received more critical attention than any other Gaines work except *The Autobiography of Miss Jane Pittman*. Articles by William Burke, Walter R. McDonald, and Frank W. Shelton all treat, from different perspectives, the issue of manhood in the stories. Craig Hansen Werner deals with the volume's relationship to James Joyce's *Dubliners* and provides an unusual non-Southern perspective on the collection. The only extended consideration to date of Gaines's later work is Frank Shelton's essay on *In My Father's House*; this article traces the falling off of hope in that novel from the earlier ones.

Gaines's critical reputation seems secure. Particularly because of *The Autobiography of Miss Jane Pittman*, he is regarded as one of the finest contemporary Southern black writers. Work remains to be done, however, especially on his later novels, which have yet to receive their due. Although Gaines may never surpass *The Autobiography of Miss Jane Pittman*, he continues to produce interesting and important fiction.

BIBLIOGRAPHY

Works by Ernest J. Gaines

Catherine Carmier. New York: Atheneum, 1964.
Of Love and Dust. New York: Dial Press, 1967.
Bloodline. New York: Dial Press, 1968.
The Autobiography of Miss Jane Pittman. New York: Dial Press, 1971.
"Ernest J. Gaines," *Interviews with Black Writers*, ed. John O'Brien. New York: Liveright, 1973.
"A Conversation with Ernest Gaines," ed. Ruth Laney. *Southern Review* 10 (January 1974): 1–14.
"Home: A Photo-Essay." *Callaloo* 1 (May 1978): 52–67.
In My Father's House. New York: Alfred A. Knopf, 1978.
"Miss Jane and I." *Callaloo* 1 (May 1978): 23–38.
" 'This Louisiana Thing That Drives Me': An Interview with Ernest J. Gaines," ed. Charles H. Rowell. *Callaloo* 1 (May 1978): 39–51.
A Gathering of Old Men. New York: Alfred A. Knopf, 1983.

Studies of Ernest J. Gaines

Andrews, William L. " 'We Ain't Going Back There': The Idea of Progress in *The Autobiography of Miss Jane Pittman*." *Black American Literature Forum* 11 (Winter 1977): 146–49.
Aubert, Alvin. "Ernest J. Gaines's Truly Tragic Mulatto." *Callaloo* 1 (May 1978): 68–75.
Beckham, Barry. "Jane Pittman and Oral Tradition." *Callaloo* 1 (May 1978): 102–09.
Bryant, Jerry H. "Ernest J. Gaines: Change, Growth, and History." *Southern Review* 10 (October 1974): 851–64.
———. "From Death to Life: The Fiction of Ernest J. Gaines." *Iowa Review* 3 (Winter 1972): 106–20.

Burke, William. *"Bloodline*: A Black Man's South." *CLA Journal* 19 (June 1976): 545–58.

Callahan, John. "Image-Making: Tradition and the Two Versions of *The Autobiography of Miss Jane Pittman.*" *Chicago Review* 29 (Autumn 1977): 45–62.

Duncan, Todd. "Scene and Life Cycle in Ernest Gaines' *Bloodline.*" *Callaloo* 1 (May 1978): 85–101.

Fabre, Michel. "Bayonne or the Yoknapatawpha of Ernest Gaines." *Callaloo* 1 (May 1978): 110–24.

Hicks, Jack. *In the Singer's Temple*. Chapel Hill, N.C.: University of North Carolina Press, 1981.

McDonald, Walter R. " 'You Not a Bum, You a Man': Ernest J. Gaines's *Bloodline.*" *Negro American Literature Forum* 9 (Summer 1975): 47–49.

Potter, Vilma Raskin. *"The Autobiography of Miss Jane Pittman*: How to Make a White Film from a Black Novel." *Literature/Film Quarterly* 3 (Fall 1975): 371–75.

Rowell, Charles H. "Ernest J. Gaines: A Checklist, 1964–1978." *Callaloo* 1 (May 1978): 125–31.

Shelton, Frank W. "Ambiguous Manhood in Ernest J. Gaines's *Bloodline.*" *CLA Journal* 19 (December 1975): 200–9.

———. *"In My Father's House*: Ernest Gaines after Jane Pittman." *Southern Review* 17 (April 1981): 340–45.

Werner, Craig Hansen. *Paradoxical Resolutions: American Fiction Since James Joyce*. Urbana: University of Illinois Press, 1982.

Wertheim, Albert. "Journey to Freedom: Ernest Gaines's *The Autobiography of Miss Jane Pittman.*" *The Afro-American Novel Since 1960*. Ed. Peter Bruck and Wolfgang Karrer. Amsterdam: B. R. Gruner, 1982.

Wideman, John. *"Of Love and Dust*: A Reconsideration." *Callaloo* 1 (May 1978): 76–84.

Williams, Sherley Anne. *Give Birth to Brightness: A Thematic Study of Neo-Black Literature*. New York: Dial Press, 1972.

LINDA WAGNER-MARTIN

Ellen Glasgow
(1873–1945)

Ellen Glasgow was known not only as a Southern writer through most of her career: she was known as a Virginia writer. Many of her nineteen novels and her short stories are set in Virginia, or a location that might be Virginia. Even though she loved to travel and tried living in New York City, she found she could not write there. She returned to Virginia to finish the book she was then working on (titled, appropriately, *Virginia*) and soon thereafter came back to her home at One West Main in Richmond, where she remained until her death.

BIOGRAPHY

Ellen Glasgow was born 22 April 1873 or 1874 (there is no official record), the eighth child of Francis T. Glasgow, manager of the Tredegar Iron Works—a stern Presbyterian and Scotsman—and Anne Jane Gholson, who was descended from Virginia Tidewater aristocracy. An Episcopalian, Ellen's mother was worn with both the worry of depressed times and continuous dissension with her husband. Ellen's childhood was darkened by the uncertain economy, her mother's failing health, and her own fragility. "Born without a skin," her "mammy" said to describe her susceptibility to illness, Glasgow seldom attended school because of health problems.

Glasgow was, consequently, largely self-educated, but by the time she was eighteen, she was reading Darwin, Spencer, and Mill. Except for her brother-in-law Walter McCormack, also her tutor, and her sister Cary, Glasgow's family had little sympathy with her ambition to write. In 1897 she published *The Descendant* anonymously and was thrilled when critics attributed it to Harold Frederic. With the publication in 1898 of *Phases of an Inferior Planet*, under her own name, Glasgow's career was well launched, although her family never approved of her life as an independent woman.

The heavy infusion of philosophy and scientific argument in her first two novels indicates Glasgow's search for belief. (When her mother had a breakdown in 1890 after discovering her husband's black mistress, Ellen left the church as a gesture of protest against her father.) Her sympathy with a liberal and agnostic hero is evident in both these novels, where the spirited women characters— Rachel Gavin and Mariana Musin—are secondary to the male protagonists, Michael Akershem and Anthony Algarcife. Even early in her career, for Glasgow the "proper" subject of literature was mankind.

With her 1900 novel, *The Voice of the People*, Glasgow began to treat the theme of the "outsider." Nicholas Burr is poor, uneducated, and noble. Once again Glasgow portrays a strong woman, Eugenia Battle, but her focus falls more steadily on Burr as he develops into the governor of Virginia. This is Glasgow's first novel to use a Southern setting and history for plot and characterization. The book became a best-seller. Her ability to draw historical events in her fiction was unmistakable. She was clearly interested in her state, the South, and the conflicts inherent among established social classes—but that is not to say that she was primarily a social historian. Glasgow was, first, a novelist, albeit a novelist who made use of her Southern knowledge and heritage.

In 1902 she published one of her best early books, *The Battle-Ground*. A story of the Civil War, the novel gave American readers Betty Ambler, a determined, indomitable heroine whose persistence won for her the love of the book's hero. Glasgow's first happy ending reflected her own anticipation of personal happiness. The love she discovered for a man who was unfortunately already married never came to fruition (his identity has never been established definitely); so the tenor of her fiction later in this decade was remarkably chastened. But in both *The Deliverance* (1904)—the novel of the strong, unconventional heroine, Maria Fletcher, who waits for her love while he serves a prison term—and *The Wheel of Life* (1906)—where the beautiful poet Laura Wilde finally breaks her engagement and finds happiness in her own self-sufficiency— Glasgow tests the assumptions about romance that dominated most fiction by women. What she arrives at, even this early, is a kind of renunciation of "romance." For Glasgow, "love" comes to mean devotion transcendent of sexual passion. *The Ancient Law* (1908), her novel of Daniel Ordway Smith and Emily Brooks, is further illustration of love as renunciation.

The characters of Glasgow's next novels, *The Romance of a Plain Man* (1909) and *The Miller of Old Church* (1911), reflect her need to escape from reality. Several of her siblings had died; her beloved sister Cary was suffering from cancer; and Glasgow had just broken her engagement to the Reverend Frank Paradise. She turned to old friends, largely women friends, and to an interest in Eastern philosophy ("Peace dwells in impersonality alone," she wrote later in life, "—beyond the personal"). These novels feature both strong women characters and atypical social situations. Glasgow seems to be actively investigating the conventions of most interest to women at the turn of the century. *The Romance of a Plain Man* includes an abused wife, a wife who insists on attention from her busy businessman husband, and the portrayal of possible infidelity as a choice for women. *The Miller of Old Church* criticizes traditional notions of women's discreet silences by portraying the strong bond between Molly Merryweather and Blossom Revercomb. Despite its title, the novel is partly about friendships among women, as Glasgow says in the text, " . . . the relation of woman to woman. Deeper than the dependence of sex, simpler, more natural, closer to the earth, as if it still drew its strength from the soil . . . the need of woman for woman was not written in the songs and the histories of men, but in the neglected and frustrated lives which the songs and the histories of men had ignored."

Much of Glasgow's later fiction was an effort to illuminate those neglected and frustrated lives. *Virginia* (1913), the story of a woman who gives up any identity she once had for the roles of traditional wife and mother, is Glasgow's first mature novel. The long and moving rendition of Virginia's marriage to playwright Oliver Treadwell depicts her as a "good" woman, faithfully putting her husband first in all considerations, losing her beauty and her chance for mature development in this willful self-abnegation. Glasgow writes of Virginia, however, with great sympathy, and places the blame for much of her attitude on her mother (who has told her that love is all that matters and that a wife is always subordinate to her husband) and on all aspects of the Southern social code, including the church. This novel includes some of Glasgow's strongest criticism of the religious milieu (at one point she describes Virginia as "the logical result of an inordinate sense of duty, the crowning achievement of the code of beautiful behaviour and the Episcopal Church"). Susan Treadwell, Virginia's self-reliant friend in this novel, is re-created in *Life and Gabriella* (1916), a less successful book than *Virginia*. Gabriella as divorced "new" woman makes her living in New York and raises her children, alone. Eventually, however, she marries again—a conclusion that keeps her housed within traditional boundaries for a fictional heroine.

Life and Gabriella was the novel Glasgow tried to write in New York, but she had come to recognize the claims of Virginia on her imagination, and in 1916 returned to her family home in Richmond. She met and became engaged to a successful Richmond lawyer, Henry Anderson. They never married, but the anticipation of marriage—and then disappointment when it did not occur—kept Glasgow in suspension for the next decade. She was forty-three when she met Anderson, and she had to reconsider all the decisions about life-style and belief she had already made. The process was tumultuous, but from it came several of her most interesting books.

She drew a fond portrait of Anderson as David Blackburn in *The Builders* (1919). *One Man in His Time* (1922) is a kind of sequel to it. In this latter book Corinna Page, an independent woman in her late forties, finally decides to give up her lover because another woman—weaker, more desperate—needs his love. In this novel, Glasgow as Corinna Page advises an ingenue, Patty Vetch, about loving wholeheartedly: "Just so much and no more. . . . Give with the mind and the heart; but keep always one inviolable sanctity of the spirit—of the buried self beneath the self.'' Corinna is the character truest to the author's own self-image during these years, and were it not for her creation, Glasgow would probably not have been able to write her masterpiece, *Barren Ground* (1925).

In *Barren Ground*, Dorinda Oakley, the pregnant and unmarried girl who runs away from home and then returns to vanquish the poor farmland and build a comparative empire for her family, breaks all stereotypes—particularly for a Southern heroine. Dorinda properly deserves to be called a *hero*. She is passionate and fearless. She loves Jason Greylock and goes nearly mad when she realizes that he has married someone else. She even attempts to kill him. But she also knows that saving her own life means leaving her family and home. In New York, she learns about scientific farming—and also about financing. Returning to Virginia, she changes her allegiance from her mother to her father, works incredibly hard, is best friends with her black maid, and eventually settles her score with Greylock as she buys out his property and then cares for him in his dying days. Revenge has prompted a decade of her life, and Dorinda can be read as embittered as well as strong; but there is success and life at the end of her story. We may not like her in her marriage or her role as stepmother, but she has made something of the limited options for women—especially unmarried and pregnant women—without economic support of any kind.

Glasgow considered *Barren Ground* her best book, and the psychological realism and passion that inform the novel make it one of the period's best. But as if free of the intensity that prompted the book, Glasgow then turned to her trilogy of satiric novels about women's sanity in the face of men's romantic foibles—*The Romantic Comedians* (1926), *They Stooped to Folly* (1929), and the somewhat more biting *The Sheltered Life* (1932).

The first two of these satires are genteel treatments of older men who look for eternal romance through love for younger women. In *The Romantic Comedians* Judge Honeywell makes the mistake of marrying fortune-hunter Annabel Upchurch. In *They Stooped to Folly* Virginius Littlepage lives a fantasy life with the town's loose woman while his own wife dies, almost unnoticed, before his eyes. The innocence of the wandering male has drastic consequences in *The Sheltered Life*, however; there Glasgow portrays a philandering man's corruption of an adolescent girl who reveres both him and his beautiful wife, Eva Birdsong. In the tragedy of Jenny Blair Archbald and Eva's husband, George, Glasgow has written her devastating commentary on a society that condones a double standard of behavior. Some critics argue that *The Sheltered Life* may be Glasgow's best novel. It is certainly among her best.

When she was past sixty, Glasgow wrote *Vein of Iron*—a novel she thought worthy to be compared with *Barren Ground*. In some ways it is a sequel to that masterpiece. The characteristic ''vein'' of strength that made Dorinda Oakley persevere in her chosen life is also evident in Ada Fincastle and her gentle father, John. Through the 30 years of the story, Glasgow traces the Scots-Presbyterian family (John is a former minister turned agnostic and philosopher) through a chronology of misfortunes. Ada becomes pregnant and bears a child long before the child's father, Ralph McBride, is free to marry her. Once married, Ralph persists in liaisons that keep the already poor family destitute and lead to serious accidents for him. Yet the center of the novel is not Ada so much as it is her father, who sacrifices his final days—and his life—traveling back to their early home so that when he dies there, the family will be saved burial expenses. Ada and John together image the "vein of iron": Ada represents loving with "a single heart"; John has moved past the personal to fulfillment in a spiritual sense.

Between 1935, when *Vein of Iron* appeared (and sold over 100,000 copies in a single year), and 1945, when Glasgow died in her sleep after a heart attack, she wrote two more novels (*In This Our Life*, 1941, which was filmed, and *Beyond Defeat*, not published until 1966); her autobiography (*The Woman Within*, 1954, at her direction, not published until after her death); and the prefaces to those of her novels which were republished during the late 1930s as the Virginia Edition. The prefaces appeared as *A Certain Measure* in 1943. Together, these books show her persistence in the face of increasing ill health (during some of these years, her doctors would allow her to work only fifteen minutes a day). And they also reveal her increasing recognition that her place in American letters was secure, that she had written well about important subjects, and that her fellow writers and critics (Carl Van Doren, Stark Young, Marjorie Kinnan Rawlings, James Branch Cabell, Allen Tate, Howard Mumford Jones, and others) were willing to help her maintain her position as a best-selling author and—for her, more important—a respected author.

In 1942 Glasgow won the Pulitzer Prize for *In This Our Life*. In earlier years she had been elected to the American Academy of Arts and Letters and had received the Howells Medal for Fiction and a special award from the *Saturday Review of Literature*; she had also received several honorary doctorates from prestigious universities. Her books were nearly always on the best-seller lists, and *The Romantic Comedians* and *They Stooped to Folly* were book club selections. Despite a serious hearing impairment, which had plagued her from her twenties, she was able to travel, maintain friendships with writers and critics she admired, and live a strikingly independent and even unconventional life. As she wrote in an unpublished essay, "More than thirty years ago, I began my literary work as a rebel against conventions. I am still a rebel, but the conventions are different." She died on 21 November 1945.

MAJOR THEMES

Glasgow was the chronicler of the lives of Southern women as well as of social convention and individual manners in a large sense. Each of her novels tried to fit single characters into the matrix of either nineteenth-century society or modern society, or the difficult transitional period as the first gave way to the second. Although Glasgow was seldom dramatic, she did believe that fiction should instruct and that the conscience of the writer should inform the work.

In her earliest novels Glasgow drew women's lives as unhappy. Their search for success as artists, singers, or writers often ended in defeat—at least partly because they had at some point given up their career for marriage of a highly traditional kind. In Glasgow's mid-career novels the women tended to question accepted social patterns. Gabriella in *Life and Gabriella* chose to divorce her husband and to support herself and her children, just as Corinna Page broke her engagement rather than give up her freedom. Dorinda Oakley managed a large farm, doing much of the work herself, and became a productive member of the larger community.

By the time of her trilogy of manners—*The Romantic Comedians, They Stooped to Folly*, and *The Sheltered Life*—Glasgow had learned to criticize the male characters whom she once made heroic, but her criticism is for the most part gentle and good-humored. Throughout her work, the *mis*educated woman was a constant character; but in her later writing, women were less afraid to make changes in their lives, even if those changes meant a loss of public approval. Woman against society is a continual Glasgow theme.

Another pervasive theme is the power and beauty of nature. Glasgow's characters, male and female, fared best if they were in touch with the eternal pantheistic forces. Natural wisdom, the worship of the natural, is frequently set against formal religion, often to the detriment of the latter. Late in her career Glasgow reinforced the stances she had taken earlier in the portrayal of her women characters by choosing male characters who also defied convention. In *Vein of Iron* John Fincastle leaves the ministry to become a philosopher and an agnostic; in *In This Our Life* Ira Timberlake considers adultery. The personal choice, free from social coercion, was always the right choice.

Another consistent theme in Glasgow's fiction is the abhorrence of cruelty. Characters who are purposely mean, self-centered, or hurtful to others are evil. Jason Greylock's infidelity is no worse than Mrs. Timberlake's selfishness, and Judge Archbald's misunderstanding is every bit as evil—for all its innocence—as Oliver Treadwell's divorcing Virginia. Sternly moral, Glasgow holds her characters to their responsibilities, demanding that they live as they know how best to do—never accepting the excuse of human weakness or social convention.

The "world" that Glasgow creates is as complete and functioning as that of Faulkner or Balzac. Although she kept the settings of most of her novels within the South, and mostly within Virginia, she was less concerned with geographical reality than with the reality of her psychological portrayals. (This is not to say that she was careless about physical details; she often visited her "sites" so that description would be accurate.) She makes use of the common traits of her locations to build a base of social custom that her characters play against. For readers to understand the conventions that bind Virginia Pendleton Treadwell, they must understand some of Dinwiddie's traditions. For, finally, the heart of

Glasgow's fiction is character, not locale, and as she said in *Vein of Iron*, "It is only in the heart that anything really happens."

SURVEY OF CRITICISM

Much early criticism of Glasgow's work was heavily influenced by a theme in her prefaces, that of her fiction as a "social history of Virginia." Seeking to become more important to the world of letters, Glasgow took a lead from her friend and colleague James Branch Cabell, another Virginia writer, who saw her work as important social history. When Glasgow was writing these prefaces during the mid and late 1930s, she stressed that common perspective.

It seems natural that many of the Southern critics of Glasgow's work would follow her emphasis. Louis D. Rubin, Jr., C. Hugh Holman, Stark Young, Allen Tate, and Julius Rowan Raper all identify Glasgow as a Southern writer, and they see the novels as segments of a comprehensive history. Frederick P. W. McDowell did an important service to Glasgow criticism in 1963, when he discussed her style (*Ellen Glasgow and the Ironic Art of Fiction*), and Monique Parent Frazee, in *Ellen Glasgow: Romancière* (1962), gave the author broad coverage—from the perspective of social history as well as of craft, with some attention to Glasgow's interest in women's themes and characters. Blair Rouse edited Glasgow's letters in 1958; his study of her appeared in 1962 in the Twayne United States Authors Series. William W. Kelly's bibliography of Glasgow's work in 1964 provided scholars with a helpful tool, as did Carrington C. Tutwiler, Jr., with the book on Glasgow's library (1969).

With the publication in 1972 of E. Stanly Godbold, Jr.'s biography *Ellen Glasgow and the Woman Within* and the 1976 *Centennial Essays*, a strong collection of essays edited by M. Thomas Inge, Glasgow criticism came into its own. Those books were bracketed by two central studies by Julius Rowan Raper, *Without Shelter: The Early Career of Ellen Glasgow* (1971) and *From the Sunken Garden: The Fiction of Ellen Glasgow, 1916–1945* (1980). Since 1974 Edgar E. MacDonald has provided a valuable service by editing the *Ellen Glasgow Newsletter*. Also appearing recently, with attention to Glasgow as a woman writer, are Anne Goodwyn Jones's study of seven Southern women writers (*Tomorrow Is Another Day*, 1982); Barbro Ekman's *The End of a Legend: Ellen Glasgow's History of Southern Women* (1979); Linda Welshimer Wagner's *Ellen Glasgow: Beyond Convention* (1982); and Marcelle Thiébaux's *Ellen Glasgow* (1982). Such feminist critics as Annis Pratt, Elaine Showalter, and Elizabeth Ammons are also helping to prove the multidimensionality of Glasgow's fiction.

BIBLIOGRAPHY

Works by Ellen Glasgow

The Descendant. New York: Harper, 1897.
Phases of an Inferior Planet. New York: Harper & Brothers, 1898.

The Voice of the People. New York: Doubleday, Page, 1900.
The Battle-Ground. New York: Doubleday, Page, 1902.
The Deliverance. New York: Doubleday, Page, 1904.
The Wheel of Life. New York: Doubleday, Page, 1906.
The Ancient Law. New York: Doubleday, Page, 1908.
The Romance of a Plain Man. New York: Macmillan, 1909.
The Miller of Old Church. Garden City, N.Y.: Doubleday, Page, 1911.
Virginia. Garden City, N.Y.: Doubleday, Page, 1913.
Life and Gabriella. Garden City, N.Y.: Doubleday, Page, 1916.
The Builders. Garden City, N.Y.: Doubleday, Page, 1919.
One Man in His Time. Garden City, N.Y.: Doubleday, Page, 1922.
The Shadowy Third and Other Stories. Garden City, N.Y.: Doubleday, Page, 1923.
Barren Ground. Garden City, N.Y.: Doubleday, Page, 1925.
The Romantic Comedians. Garden City, N.Y.: Doubleday, Page, 1926.
They Stooped to Folly. Garden City, N.Y.: Doubleday, Doran, 1929.
The Sheltered Life. Garden City, N.Y.: Doubleday, Doran, 1932.
Vein of Iron. New York: Harcourt, Brace, 1935.
In This Our Life. New York: Harcourt, Brace, 1941.
A Certain Measure. New York: Harcourt, Brace, 1943.
The Woman Within. New York: Harcourt, Brace, 1954.
The Letters of Ellen Glasgow. Ed. Blair Rouse. New York: Harcourt, Brace, 1958.
The Collected Stories of Ellen Glasgow. Ed. Richard K. Meeker. Baton Rouge: Louisiana
      State University Press, 1963.
Beyond Defeat: An Epilogue to an Era. Ed. Luther Y. Gore. Charlottesville: University
      Press of Virginia, 1966.

Studies of Ellen Glasgow

Auchincloss, Louis. *Ellen Glasgow*. Minneapolis: University of Minnesota Press, 1964.
Cabell, James Branch. *As I Remember It*. New York: McBride, 1955.
Ekman, Barbro. *The End of a Legend: Ellen Glasgow's History of Southern Women*.
      Acta Universitatis Upsalensia, No. 37. Upsala, Sweden: Almgvist & Wiksell
      International, 1979.
Godbold, E. Stanly, Jr. *Ellen Glasgow and the Woman Within*. Baton Rouge: Louisiana
      State University Press, 1972.
Holman, C. Hugh. *Three Modes of Southern Fiction*. Athens: University of Georgia
      Press, 1966.
Inge, M. Thomas, ed. *Ellen Glasgow: Centennial Essays*. Charlottesville: University
      Press of Virginia, 1976.
Jones, Anne Goodwyn. *Tomorrow Is Another Day: The Woman Writer in the South,
      1859–1936.*. Baton Rouge: Louisiana State University Press, 1982.
Kelly, William W. *Ellen Glasgow: A Bibliography*. Charlottesville: University Press of
      Virginia, 1964.
McDowell, Frederick P. W. *Ellen Glasgow and the Ironic Art of Fiction*. Madison:
      University of Wisconsin Press, 1963.
Parent Frazee, Monique. *Ellen Glasgow: Romancière*. Paris: A. B. Nizet, 1962.
Raper, Julius Rowan. *From the Sunken Garden: The Fiction of Ellen Glasgow, 1916–
      1945*. Baton Rouge: Louisiana State University Press, 1980.

————. *Without Shelter: The Early Career of Ellen Glasgow*. Baton Rouge: Louisiana State University Press, 1971.

Richards, Marion K. *Ellen Glasgow's Development as a Novelist*. The Hague: Mouton, 1971.

Rouse, Blair. *Ellen Glasgow*. New York: Twayne, 1962.

Rubin, Louis D., Jr. *No Place on Earth: Ellen Glasgow, James Branch Cabell, and Richmond-in-Virginia*. Austin: University of Texas Press, 1959.

Thiébaux, Marcelle. *Ellen Glasgow*. New York: Frederick Ungar, 1982.

Tutwiler, Carrington C., Jr. *A Catalogue of the Library of Ellen Glasgow*. Charlottesville: Bibliographic Society of the University of Virginia, 1969.

Wagner, Linda Welshimer. *Ellen Glasgow: Beyond Convention*. Austin: University of Texas Press, 1982.

Caroline Gordon
(1895–1981)

Although Caroline Gordon has not been studied as much as some of her Southern contemporaries—Faulkner and Katherine Anne Porter, for instance—she has been a presence on the literary scene of the South since 1931, when her first novel, *Penhally*, was published. Her associations with a later generation, including Walker Percy and Flannery O'Connor, are extensive, and eventually she will have a secure place in the literary history of her period.

BIOGRAPHY

Caroline Gordon was born 6 October 1895 on a farm in Todd County, Kentucky, almost on the Tennessee border. Her mother, Nancy Meriwether, belonged to a family who had lived in this part of southwest Kentucky for several generations. Her father, James Morris Gordon, a Virginian, went to Kentucky as a tutor to the Meriwether children when he was a young man, and later married his student Nancy. After his marriage he ran a boys' academy in nearby Clarksville, Tennessee; his daughter Caroline received her early education in the classics there. She was awarded a B.A. from Bethany College in West Virginia in 1916. After teaching a few years in Clarksville, she started a career in journalism and worked for the Chattanooga *News*. An early admirer of the Nashville Fugitives, she was among the first to write favorable notices of their work. In the summer of 1924 she met Allen Tate through their friend Robert Penn Warren, who had roomed with Tate at Vanderbilt. Warren, ten years younger than Gordon, also came from Todd County, and his family and the Meriwethers were acquainted. By the end of 1924 Gordon and Tate were married and living in New York City. Thus began a literary partnership that lasted 35 years.

In the New York and Paris of the 1920s, the Tates were near the center of a brilliant new literary generation. Their friends included Hart Crane, Malcolm

Cowley, Katherine Anne Porter, John Peale Bishop, and especially Ford Madox Ford. Gordon served as a secretary to Ford during his visits to New York (he had become a transatlantic figure who divided his time between France and the United States). He became her mentor in the art of fiction, now a central concern in her life. She was directly associated with a man who had known James, Turgenev, and Flaubert: this was the tradition of the novel that Ford represented, and in time Gordon became an heiress to this tradition and tried to perpetuate it among her own students.

By comparison with most of her friends in the 1920s, she was a late starter. Her first story, "Summer Dust," came out in 1929 in the *Gyroscope*, a little magazine edited by Yvor Winters in California; her first novel, *Penhally*, was published in 1931 when she was thirty-six. But it was an altogether accomplished novel; she had mastered the problems of technique that some writers take several books to solve. She wrote much of this novel in Paris, where she and Tate lived from the autumn of 1928 to the end of 1929. They had gone there partly through the auspices of Ford, who had recommended Tate for the Guggenheim Fellowship that was their main source of income while they were abroad; once in Paris, they lived for some time in Ford's apartment on the left Bank. Through Ford they met other Americans, including Ernest Hemingway and Gertrude Stein. The Tates, however, were not typical members of the expatriate colony in Paris. They were already deeply involved in the history of the South as a literary subject, and it was many years before Gordon used France as a setting for her fiction.

The Tates returned from France with their young daughter Nancy in January 1930. After a brief residence in New York, they settled in an old house, which they called Benfolly (bought for them by Allen Tate's brother Ben), perched above the Cumberland River near Clarksville, Tennessee. This was to be the main setting for their life during the next eight years. Their original literary friends—John Crowe Ransom, Warren, Donald Davidson, Andrew Lytle, and others in the old Fugitive group at Vanderbilt—lived in the vicinity, mostly in Nashville, and for a few years they had a literary community of their own. It was the so-called Agrarian period in their lives, a period of furious creativity for them, as it was for their Southern contemporaries. None of them was more energetic than Gordon, who published four novels and several stories between 1931 and 1937. The Tates were often poor, but they lived with a certain style at Benfolly, which soon became a stopping point for many of their friends from the old days in New York and Paris. Many years later Gordon wrote a novel, *The Strange Children* (1951), about their life at Benfolly during the 1930s.

Gordon's first novel, *Penhally* (1931), was a critical success, and during the early 1930s she published stories in such magazines as *Scribner's, Hound and Horn*, and T. S. Eliot's *Criterion*. Then it was her turn to be awarded a Guggenheim Fellowship, and in 1932 the Tates returned to France for part of a year. By this time she was writing her second novel, *Aleck Maury, Sportsman*, based on the early life of her father. It was published in 1934; her most popular novel, it has been frequently reprinted. One reason for the novel's popularity may be that it is the central work of a cycle of fiction about Aleck Maury; several of the related stories, especially "Old Red" and "The Last Day in the Field," have often appeared in anthologies. In 1937 Gordon published two novels, *None Shall Look Back* and *The Garden of Adonis*. The first is set in Kentucky and Tennessee during the Civil War; the second, her "Agrarian" novel, is set in the same locale during the economic depression of the 1930s. Both of them deal with the same family at different stages of its history.

In 1938 Gordon, now rather well known, was appointed as the first writer-in-residence at the Woman's College of the University of North Carolina (now the University of North Carolina at Greensboro). She and Tate stayed there only a year because Tate accepted a teaching post at Princeton in 1939, and they lived in that university town for the next three years. She had already begun work on one of her most ambitious novels, *Green Centuries*, set on the North Carolina frontier at the time of the Revolution; it was published in 1941. The Tates spent the year 1942–43 in Tennessee, this time in a house at Monteagle in the Cumberlands, which they shared with a young couple, the poet Robert Lowell and his first wife, the novelist Jean Stafford. There much of Gordon's next novel, *The Women on the Porch*, was written. It was published in 1944. During 1943–44 the Tates lived in Washington, where he held the post of consultant on poetry at the Library of Congress. But in 1944 they returned to Tennessee so that he could edit the *Sewanee Review*.

The Women on the Porch, which deals with the restoration of a failed marriage, in retrospect seems to have anticipated the next phase of the Tates' life. Their own marriage fell apart during 1945, while they were living in Sewanee; Gordon left her husband to live in New York, and in January 1946 they were divorced. But a few months later Tate resigned his editorship and followed her to New York; they were remarried in April 1946. Meanwhile, she had published a collection of short stories called *The Forest of the South* (1945), in a sense a farewell to the South, where she never lived again. During the late 1940s the Tates were in Greenwich Village, the scene of their early years of marriage, but they were attracted by the life in Princeton, where they had many friends, including Jacques Maritain and Francis Fergusson. This was to be Gordon's home until 1973. During much of the remainder of her long life she was an ardent teacher, either at Columbia University and the New School for Social Research in New York, or at one of a number of universities where she had temporary appointments: the University of Washington, the University of Kansas, the University of California at Davis, Purdue, and Emory. But she always returned to Princeton to be near her daughter Nancy and her family.

No doubt the immense amount of time that Gordon devoted to teaching, lecturing, and critical writing for so many years diverted her attention from writing fiction. Still, she published *The Strange Children* in 1951, *The Malefactors* in 1956, *Old Red and Other Stories* in 1963, and *The Glory of Hera* in 1972. The two important private events in her life during this long period were her conversion to the Roman Catholic Church in the late 1940s and the end of her marriage to Allen Tate in 1959. These events, especially her conversion, certainly affected her fiction. She began to look at experience, and most of all her own early life, from a "Catholic" point of view. She spent many years doing extensive research on her most ambitious work, what was intended to be a two-part novel in which her own life and the life of her ancestors would be set against the career of the Greek hero Heracles, a prefiguration of Christ. Her research even took her to Greece for several months during 1967. *The Glory of Hera* was published in 1972. Although this book could stand alone, it was intended as only the first part of the longer work, which was never finished.

In 1973 Gordon left Princeton at age seventy-eight and moved to the University of Dallas, where the then-president, Donald Cowan, and his wife Louise, the critic, had established a program in creative writing. The University of Dallas, a small Catholic institution, provided her with a setting to her liking for the next five years. She continued to teach, but the Cowans tried to set aside as much time as possible for her writing. She worked on the second part of her novel, and at one time or another she published about 100 pages of it in various quarterlies. But her health declined, and she resigned from the university in 1978.

Her last move was to San Cristobal de las Casas in the state of Chiapas, Mexico. Her daughter and son-in-law had already moved there from Princeton, and in her last years she was probably closer to her family than she had ever been. She enjoyed being a matriarch and loved to be surrounded by young people. She died there on 11 April 1981 in her eighty-sixth year and was buried with Catholic Indian rites in the local cemetery. It was the end to a lifelong journey that had taken her back and forth across North America and much of Western Europe.

MAJOR THEMES

Caroline Gordon's earlier novels focus on the history of her region. *Penhally* (1931) is the story of a house and the decline of a family on the Kentucky-Tennessee border, the setting of most of her novels and stories. The novel turns on the dissension within the family created when the first master of Penhally, Nicholas Llewellyn, quarrels with his brother Ralph over the division of the property. Nicholas feels that the individuals composing the family should subordinate their happiness to it at any price. He succeeds in keeping the property intact, but his descendants, through weakness or historical defeat, cannot duplicate his role. The end comes during the 1920s with another pair of brothers: one of them, Chance, murders the other, the new Nicholas who inherited the property but betrayed it. The final act of violence is an index to the state of affairs now prevalent; private violence is melodramatic and lacks any social sanction. Chance can only express his personal outrage at the loss of Penhally, to him a loss of his manhood in a society of shifting values and nervous energies.

There is no tragedy in his act. Although fewer than 300 pages, the novel spans four generations in the life of the Llewellyns. To have presented so much history in a flat chronological sequence would have been ineffective. Gordon solved the problem by arranging the book in three parts, each with its center of action. Part 1, after a prologue, is compressed into several panels of action dated 1861–63. Part 2 is set in one afternoon in 1900. Part 3 runs through a few months during one year in the 1920s. Each phase of the action is extended through memory, and the continuity of a century is established by the "time shift." Past and present merge in images that are firmly realized, broken up, brought into new arrangements.

Penhally is a completely "rendered" novel, as Ford would have said. Its method—the shifting post of observation in the line of succession among the Llewellyns—allows a remarkable degree of control for such a large subject. Its author has seldom written better. But she was not content with the perfection of a method, and her subsequent books have realized her subject by a variety of means. Her second novel, *Aleck Maury, Sportsman* (1934), for instance, is based on the convention of the old-fashioned memoir. Aleck Maury is the only one of her major characters whom Gordon has permitted to tell his own story. Since she based the character closely on her own father, whom she "interviewed" when she was writing the novel and related stories, the fiction has an unusual degree of authority.

Aleck Maury, hunter and fisherman, is the sportsman par excellence, and his book can be enjoyed simply as something pleasurable, like Izaak Walton's *The Complete Angler*. But Gordon has deftly complicated things by introducing the image of Aeneas, fleeing the ruins of Troy with his decrepit father on his back. Aleck Maury himself is a Virginian, the son of a Latinist who undertakes the boy's education by teaching him to read the *Aeneid*. The image is occasionally alluded to later in the book, but never insisted on. It tells us something about Aleck's father, the inheritor of the classical and rhetorical tradition of the Old South who declaims poetry in the *ore rotundo* manner and who still retains the feeling for epic style even in near poverty. It also suggests that Aleck himself is an Aeneas, who will leave the ruins of his father's house, but not under the aegis of any Venus who will guide him to another Troy. He has only the memory of a civilization to perpetuate. Dispossessed almost from the start, he is thrown back upon his sportsman's instincts for survival. Gordon—like Tate in "The Mediterranean" (1933) and "Aeneas in Washington" (1933), composed while she was writing *Aleck Maury*—tends to identify the lost cause of the Old South with the cause of Troy, and thus the Southern attitude is placed within a larger perspective.

The pair of novels that she published in 1937, *None Shall Look Back* and *The Garden of Adonis*, extend her historical theme, and they complement each other in various ways. Both deal with the break up of a family estate, and apparently the same family, at different periods. *None Shall Look Back* has for its model nothing less than *War and Peace*, and like Tolstoy she has written a novel that has seemed to some readers to fall into its component parts. She has, to start with, taken a Kentucky family, the Allards, with their various connections, through the vicissitudes of the Civil War. Under the impact of the war their fortunes undergo a decline; they are almost ruined, but in the end we know that they will somehow survive. Yet the novel is also about the war in its western theater. We follow the highest officers of the Confederate and Federal forces as they direct the operations of the war, which is the enveloping action. The problem is how to relate the two levels of action, public and private. At the climax of the novel Gordon does this by having the young Confederate soldier Rives Allard, who is now in love with his adversary Death, shot from his horse. The author quickly takes the point of view from Rives to General Bedford Forrest, a procedure that would ordinarily violate the structure of a scene. But when Forrest sees the body, he recognizes it; then, as though there were a continuum of consciousness between the dead man and his commander, the focus moves entirely to Forrest, for the only time in the novel. Rives's tragedy is caught up in the larger action of which Forrest is the representative. But this is the only one of Gordon's novels in which the tragic movement is complete.

The Garden of Adonis deals with four families, including the Allards, during the Depression of the 1930s. Here there is no true center of action as there is in *None Shall Look Back*. The patriarch Mister Ben Allard is still the master of his property, but he is at the mercy of bankers, store keepers, a falling tobacco market, and other forces almost beyond control. The tenant families on the place are obvious victims, and even a rich manufacturing family that has moved into the locality is dependent on a remote banking system. There is no hero anywhere in sight, but Ote Mortimer, a young man from one of the tenant families, seems for a time to approach this role, and Mister Ben regards him as a son. Unfortunately, they never understand each other, and in the final scene misunderstanding leads to violence as Ote kills his master.

In *Green Centuries* (1941) Gordon deals with a subject far in the past—the migration westward through the mountains to Kentucky at the time of the Revolution. The assumption of the pioneers is not only that nature is to be subdued, it is to be shattered. (This assumption runs counter to the reverent attitude held by the Cherokees.) The very size of the American continent gives the sense of infinite expanses to be exploited. The central figure of the novel is Rion Outlaw, the successful and irresponsible conqueror of space. At the end he gazes into the sky and at last understands the meaning of his name: "Orion fixed upon his burning wheel, always pursuing the bull but never making the kill. . . . Like the mighty hunter he had lost himself in the turning. Before him lay the empty west, behind him the loved things of which he was made." A related work by Gordon is a long story called "The Captive" (1932), a masterpiece of sustained style about a pioneer woman captured by Indians on the same frontier.

The five novels that culminate in *Green Centuries* are conceived in a kind of grand design against the enveloping action of history. With these books behind her, Gordon had the choice of "filling out" her subject, perhaps using some of the characters she had already invented, or else of extending it by moving to another post of observation. Her second group of novels—*The Women on the Porch* (1944), *The Strange Children* (1951), and *The Malefactors* (1956)—do both. These books are set against the history of the South, like their predecessors, but only indirectly. And their mode is finally Christian comedy rather than tragedy. With the complexity of subject comes a new boldness of technique. The novels are more Jamesian than the earlier ones: the point of view is more strictly maintained. But they also draw more extensively on the resources of poetry, such as *The Waste Land*, important to *The Women on the Porch*, and Dante's *Purgatorio*, which informs *The Malefactors*. Gordon's converion to Roman Catholicism also made a difference in these novels. *The Malefactors*, especially, makes the highest demands on her talent; in it she dramatizes the actual experience of a religious conversion in her poet-hero, Tom Claiborne.

These eight novels and the short stories (finally brought together in the *Collected Stories* published just before Gordon's death) compose a genuine oeuvre. Using the materials accessible to her (her own life, the history of her family, the history of her region), she has created an impressive image of Western man and the crisis that his restlessness has created. We can see one instance in Rion Outlaw and his dream of infinite space, but there are hardly any institutional forms to restrain him. Chapman, the sophisticated historian in *The Women on the Porch*, is the latest version of Rion Outlaw, and *his* dream of infinite space becomes nightmare. Most of Gordon's heroes (and many of her heroines) are fleeing from some kind of historical ruin. In *The Strange Children*, which deals so candidly with the Tates' life at Benfolly, we see the futility (or at least the irony) of the effort to perpetuate a history already ruined. In it, and even more in *The Malefactors*, Gordon seems to be saying that redemption must lie in another order of existence, and she finally points to Christian faith.

The Glory of Hera (1972) is a remarkable novel about Heracles, and the author's treatment of a subject that lies outside history is bold. She was long interested in Heracles as a character; her first story, "Summer Dust" (1929), reveals this interest, and in 1961 her revision under the title of "The Dragon's Teeth" emphasized the association. (The revised story was given the title "One Against Thebes" when it was reprinted in *Old Red and Other Stories*, 1963.) Why Heracles? Howard Baker, Gordon's best critic at this late stage in her career, puts it well: "Heracles, in his many sacrifices of himself for the benefit of mankind, foreshadows the Christ of the Christian religion. Yet he is always something of a Kentuckian in his bearing, something of the stubborn, undaunted, naturally gallant frontiersman." But this re-creation of a great myth, as Gordon explained it, was to have been only the "lower pattern" of events in a larger work of fiction, in which the author herself and her ancestors were to occupy the "upper pattern." The upper pattern of this book was never finished, but her life's work has an extraordinary unity even without it.

SURVEY OF CRITICISM

Although there is no full-length account of Caroline Gordon's life and work, Ann Waldron and Veronica Makowsky are writing biographies. Recently Sally Wood (Mrs. Lawrence Kohn), one of Gordon's oldest friends, published *The Southern Mandarins*, a collection of Gordon's letters that run from 1924 to 1937. Most of these letters were written from Benfolly after 1930 and are the best source of information about the Tates and their friends during that period. Wood herself contributed valuable notes on the letters, and Andrew Lytle wrote the foreword to the book. Sally Fitzgerald, the biographer of Flannery O'Connor and editor of her letters, plans to publish the correspondence between Gordon and O'Connor under the title *The Master Class*. A section of this correspondence was published in the *Georgia Review* in 1979.

So far there have been two book-length critical studies of Gordon's work. William J. Stuckey's book in the Twayne series (1972) is short but still useful for a student who is taking up this author for the first time. *Caroline Gordon as Novelist and Woman of Letters* (1984), by Rose Ann C. Fraistat, is not much longer, but in some ways it is more ambitious. Her title points toward the fact that Gordon was more than a novelist. Unlike George Eliot, Virginia Woolf, and Rebecca West, who started out as reviewers and critics, Gordon turned to criticism relatively late. Married to a prominent poet-critic, she perhaps felt no need to assert her ideas about her art in public. But after World War II she wrote several pieces that certainly affected literary opinion, notably her long reviews of *The Portable Faulkner* and Ford's *Parade's End* in the *New York Times Book Review*. The reviewer soon became the essayist, and after 1950 she wrote extensively on O'Connor and others. Eventually her scattered critical essays should be collected and published. *The House of Fiction*, a large anthology on which she collaborated with Allen Tate in 1950, and *How to Read a Novel* (1957) are well-known, at least in academic circles, and are related to her role as teacher.

As usual, some of the best criticism about Gordon is found in essays that are uncollected and probably forgotten. Gordon was fortunate in having several first-rate pieces written about her work. She was never a popular writer, and no doubt it was important for her to be recognized by critics whom she respected. In 1931 Ford wrote a review essay of *Penhally* under the title "A Stage in American Literature." It appeared in the influential *Bookman*, alerting the public to the presence of a Southern novelist of considerable talent. Ford had been close to Hemingway, Glenway Wescott, and other Midwestern writers in the Paris of the 1920s, and he saw that Gordon, Elizabeth Madox Roberts, and Katherine Anne Porter were part of a new phase of American literature that was located in the South.

In 1949 an important essay came out in the *Sewanee Review*, Andrew Lytle's "Caroline Gordon and the Historic Image." Gordon had published six novels (most recently *The Women on the Porch*) and her first collection of stories, *The Forest of the South*, and it was possible to assess her work in large terms. Lytle's thesis was that, like Flaubert, she had a vision of a historic concept of society that controlled her imagination and allowed her to render different phases of history, including the contemporary, each within its own terms. Lytle's essay has many implications for Gordon's work and is, as Robert Fitzgerald has said, a classic piece of criticism.

In 1973, following the publication of *The Glory of Hera*, Howard Baker, the California poet-critic, wrote a remarkable long essay called ''The Stratagems of Caroline Gordon; or, The Art of the Novel and the Novelty of Myth.'' More than a major consideration of *The Glory of Hera*, it is an account of how Gordon's work, beginning with her first story, ''Summer Dust'' (published in a magazine coedited by Baker), evolved through a kind of ''mythic consciousness'' that emerges fully in this last novel. Baker knew the Tates during the old days in Paris, when she was writing *Penhally*, and although not a Southerner himself, had an unusual sensitivity to the issues that Southern history presented to her. His essay is also partly reminiscence, a valuable account of the Tates and their friends, including Ford and Hemingway. There have been many other essays on Gordon, but those by Lytle and Baker are outstanding.

BIBLIOGRAPHY

Works by Caroline Gordon

Penhally. New York: Scribner's, 1931.

Aleck Maury, Sportsman. New York: Scribner's, 1934. Reprinted with an Afterword by Caroline Gordon. Carbondale: University of Southern Illinois Press, 1980.

The Garden of Adonis. New York: Scribner's, 1937.

None Shall Look Back. New York: Scribner's, 1937.

Green Centuries. New York: Scribner's, 1941.

The Women on the Porch. New York: Scribner's, 1944.

The Forest of the South. New York: Scribner's, 1945.

The House of Fiction: An Anthology of the Short Story with Commentary. Ed. with Allen Tate. New York: Scribner's, 1950; rev. ed. 1960.

The Strange Children. New York: Scribner's, 1951.

The Malefactors. New York: Harcourt, Brace, 1956.

How to Read a Novel. New York: Viking Press, 1957.

''A Narrow Heart: The Portrait of Woman.'' *Transatlantic Review*, n.s., 3 (1960): 7–19.

A Good Soldier: A Key to the Novels of Ford Madox Ford. Davis: University of California Library, 1963.

Old Red and Other Stories. New York: Scribner's, 1963.

''Cock-Crow.'' *Southern Review*, n.s., 1 (1965): 554–69.

''Always Summer.'' *Southern Review*, n.s., 7 (1971): 430–46.

The Glory of Hera. Garden City, N.Y.: Doubleday, 1972.

''A Visit to the Grove.'' *Sewanee Review* 80 (1972): 509–54.

''A Master Class: From the Correspondence of Caroline Gordon and Flannery O'Connor.'' Ed. Sally Fitzgerald. *Georgia Review* 33 (1979): 827–46.

The Collected Stories of Caroline Gordon. Introduction by Robert Penn Warren. New York: Farrar, Straus & Giroux, 1981.

The Southern Mandarins: Letters of Caroline Gordon to Sally Wood, 1924–1937. Ed. Sally Wood. Foreword by Andrew Lytle. Baton Rouge: Louisiana State University Press, 1984.

Studies of Caroline Gordon

Alvis, John. "The Miltonic Argument in Caroline Gordon's *The Glory of Hera.*" *Southern Review*, n.s., 16 (1980): 560–73.

Baker, Howard. "The Stratagems of Caroline Gordon; or, The Art of the Novel and the Novelty of Myth." *Southern Review*, n.s., 9 (1973): 523–49.

Cheney, Brainard. "The Serpent's Coils: How to Read Caroline Gordon's Later Fiction." *Southern Review*, n.s., 16 (1980): 281–98.

Cowan, Louise. "Nature and Grace in Caroline Gordon." *Critique* 1 (1956): 11–27.

Cowley, Malcolm. "The Meriwether Connection." *Southern Review*, n.s., 1 (1965): 46–56.

Fraistat, Rose Ann C. *Caroline Gordon as Novelist and Woman of Letters*. Baton Rouge: Louisiana State University Press, 1984.

Ford, Ford Madox. "A Stage in American Literature." *Bookman* 74 (1931): 371–76.

Heilman, Robert B. "Schools for Girls." *Sewanee Review* 60 (1952): 299–309.

Landess, Thomas H., ed. *The Short Fiction of Caroline Gordon: A Critical Symposium*. Irving, Texas: University of Dallas Press, 1972.

Lytle, Andrew. "Caroline Gordon and the Historic Image." *Sewanee Review* 57 (1949): 560–86.

McDowell, Frederick P. W. *Caroline Gordon*. Minneapolis: University of Minnesota Press, 1962.

Porter, Katherine Anne. "Dulce et Decorum Est." Review of *None Shall Look Back*. *New Republic*, 31 March 1937, pp. 244–45.

Rocks, James E. "The Mind and Art of Caroline Gordon." *Mississippi Quarterly* 21 (1968): 1–16.

Squires, Radcliffe. "The Underground Stream: A Note on Caroline Gordon's Fiction." *Southern Review*, n.s., 7 (1971): 467–79.

Stuckey, William J. *Caroline Gordon*. New York: Twayne, 1972.

Thorp, Willard. "The Way Back and the Way Up: The Novels of Caroline Gordon." *Bucknell Review* 6 (1956): 1–15.

Warren, Robert Penn. "The Fiction of Caroline Gordon." *Southwest Review* 20 (1935): 5–10.

PAUL SCHLUETER

Shirley Ann Grau
(1929–   )

Although sometimes considered as merely one more local color writer of Southern fiction, Shirley Ann Grau, youngest of the fifteen women to win the Pulitzer Prize at the time she received that award in 1964, is a regional writer akin to Sarah Orne Jewett and Willa Cather, not a writer who uses "Southern" atmosphere, characters, and settings for superficial local color narratives.

BIOGRAPHY

Shirley Ann Grau was born in New Orleans on 9 July 1929, one of two daughters born to Adolph E. Grau, a dentist, and Katherine (Onions) Grau, both of whom died in 1961. Grau's background is of mixed German Lutheran, Scottish Presbyterian, and Louisiana Creole (French-Spanish) strains; she had a paternal grandfather who left Prussia in time for the U.S. Civil War, though he disapproved of militarism, and a maternal grandfather—the standard mixture of English, Scotch, and Irish—who came from a family of farmers and riverboat men. Different branches of her family were traced to North Carolina and Virginia in the 1700s and to Rhode Island and Massachusetts even earlier. Hence, she combines the two distinct traditions of earlier American settlement, New England and Southern. As a child, she lived with her family in both New Orleans (to please her mother) and Montgomery (to please her father), where she attended Booth School, a now-defunct finishing school that offered a solid nineteenth-century curriculum. Since Grau intended to go to college, she had to graduate from an accredited high school; so she spent her senior year at Ursuline Academy in New Orleans, a Roman Catholic boarding school chosen not only because it was accredited but also because it had strong offerings in classical languages.

Women at the time were allowed into Tulane University only in its women's division, Sophie Newcomb College. Grau attended Newcomb from 1946 to 1950, graduating with honors in English; she was elected to Phi Beta Kappa in her senior year, the same year she served as an editor of the campus literary magazine, where her first stories were published. One story originally written for a creative writing class was subsequently published in revised form in the *New Mexico Quarterly*, her first professional publication. She took a year of graduate study in English at Tulane but did not finish her master's degree; instead, she began writing stories in earnest and in short order sold several to such markets as *New World Writing* and the *New Yorker*.

In 1955 Grau, then twenty-six, married James Kern Feibleman, then fifty-one, chairman of the Tulane philosophy department and a widely published writer on numerous subjects as well as a friend of such figures as Faulkner, Einstein, and Sherwood Anderson and father of the novelist Peter Feibleman. The Feiblemans have four children and divide their time between Metairie, a suburb of New Orleans, and Chilmark, on Martha's Vineyard, Massachusetts.

MAJOR THEMES

Grau has received primary recognition for her eight published books, three collections of stories and five novels. When *The Black Prince and Other Stories* appeared in 1954, the entire first printing sold out in two weeks' time, and critics vied with each other to find hyperbolic comparisons for this new sensation. Grau's world, however, differs greatly from other writers' worlds. She has often declared her displeasure at being labeled a "Southern" writer. Although some of the elements in her work are similar to those of other Southerners—black-white relations, for example—many critics of her work failed to see that her South is no more monolithic and homogeneous than are the Souths depicted by other "Southern" writers. In fact, both blacks and whites have objected to some of Grau's portrayals of people from these ethnic categories, although Grau points out accurately that the books so criticized—notably *The Keepers of the House*— are really more about such basic questions as the nature of evil than they are about race.

Indeed, for most of her career Grau has emphasized sin and evil, especially the forms of evil and individual ways of handling evil. There is, she says, something that is "esthetically satisfying" in the "shape of sin" and in redemption; she points out that although these concepts are identified with fundamentalism, they are in fact basic human impulses and therefore must be faced regardless of theology or setting. As her career has developed, Grau has become considerably more subtle in her ability to suggest evil in human behavior, particularly as this results from modern man's dual greed for money and power and in the pathetic ways in which love itself can be perverted into evil.

Critics praised Grau's first book, *The Black Prince and Other Stories* (1954), excessively and compared her to Styron, Capote, Chekhov, Mansfield, Warren, and even Salinger, in addition to the major Southern women writers—Welty, O'Connor, and McCullers. Although this book is on balance a mature, craftsmanlike effort, it also contains stereotyped, unconvincing, and contrived touches that would be bound to make hyperbolic comparisons somewhat embarrassing in retrospect. Grau handles rural characters, notably blacks and primitives, especially well, as she does the regional setting and the seeking after power, wealth, and love; she is less persuasive in much of her fiction in probing into urban characters and in developing her themes and plots. Most of the characters in this collection are seen in perspective against the natural world, and Grau's lush style serves her well as she explores a sense of place on the humid Gulf Coast below New Orleans. The nine stories in *The Black Prince* often focus on black protagonists, sometimes with echoes of myth annd folklore. "White Girl, Fine Girl," for example, is a finely evocative rendering of biblical and mythic parallels, as is the title story (about the fall of Lucifer as personified in a mysterious black man) and "The Girl with the Flaxen Hair" (with overt fairy-tale elements). Adolescent coming-of-age is emphasized in some of the stories, as in "The Way of a Man" (about a boy's killing his father to assert his "manhood"), "One Summer," and "Joshua." At their best, these stories are distinguished accounts of life in the region Grau knows best, with the mythic overtones adding considerable richness. Although some early critics were bothered by Grau's "pseudo-folk" characterization, most reviewers found her intuitive grasp of behavior and motivation persuasive, her style meditative, her ear for dialogue acute, and her human understanding unsentimental, respectful, and not at all patronizing.

Grau's first novel, *The Hard Blue Sky* (1958), deals less with the nature of evil than do her subsequent works, but her talent as a sensitive, acute observer of life in the Mississippi Delta region is as great. This heavily atmospheric novel focuses on some 30 Cajun fishermen on an isolated island below New Orleans, almost to the Gulf of Mexico, and to a lesser extent on some Slavic fishermen on another island. Although these characters can be called primitives, Grau is concerned not with creating case studies of the downtrodden and semiliterate, but with suggesting ways in which setting and climate create potential for either destruction or survival. Her characters endure stoically whatever life brings them, with little surprise at human or natural disaster; only that which breaks the pattern of monotony in their lives is meaningful. And outsiders coming to the island become the catalyst by which some of the islanders' lives are altered, although for the majority life goes on as always. After a wealthy couple drop off their sloop in the island's harbor, their one-man crew, relatively sophisticated compared to the islanders, pairs off with an island girl and leaves the island with her just before a hurricane, paralleling a similar elopement of a Cajun boy and a Slavic girl. It is the storm, however, that dominates the book. Often predicted and increasingly imminent, the storm when it comes is catastrophic, its ferocity paralleling mankind's; those who are not directly affected by the violence of man or of nature merely sit and wait for one more of life's troubles to pass them by. Indeed, their passive acquiescence in the face of nature's activity is the same as it is about man's behavior; all of life is a continuum of sameness, with little qualitative difference between home and no home, child or no child, island or no island, life or no life. Grau is especially effective in handling character in this novel, notably in the case of the girl who leaves with the one-man crew; she has been a bundle of conflicts and opposing urges, tied in with family disruption, religious obsession, frustrations on several levels, seclusion, daydreaming, and reading.

Grau's 1961 novel, *The House on Coliseum Street*, is admittedly of lesser stature than her first one, though in her fairly straightforward presentation of Joan, a neurotic young woman, Grau is successful in probing deeply into depression and guilt. Engaged to one man and impregnated by another, Joan has an abortion, and after her return home becomes obsessed with vengeance against her impregnator. Living as she does in a New Orleans house full of women (her mother and her four sisters, each sister by a different stepfather), Joan finds herself alone in introspection, conscience, remorse, and guilt. Although she knows her fiancé is a "safe" choice for a husband, her betrayer is more "dangerous"—and appealing—but after the abortion she is intent on hurting the former and destroying the latter, at first through spying and then, deeply paranoid, through telling the administration in the school where he teaches of his behavior. Joan's introspection leads her to knowing and doing what is necessary for a new life for herself, even if her lover is destroyed in the process, for just as she had to "dispose" of his child, so must she dispose of him, and then she can start to build positively again. At the novel's end, she tries futilely to enter her family's locked house, studies the fountain outside that her own father had built, notices the sun rising, and adopts a fetal position. Presumably out of the chaos of her old life, the new day promises happiness. Hence, the novel ends on an emotional upbeat, with the symbolic tableau at the novel's end implying rebirth and redemption; in this psychic struggle against self-destruction, Joan is a memorable, somewhat contrived character.

The reception given Grau's third novel, *The Keepers of the House* (1964), was enthusiastic and brought her the Pulitzer Prize for fiction, winning out over such contenders as Bellow's *Herzog* and Auchincloss's *The Rector of Justin*. Grau's evocative handling of racial tensions in the Deep South was so free of polemics, so emotionally probing, so richly sensuous in language and balanced in handling potentially explosive materials that it remains her best book. The potential for sensationalism is remarkably restrained, especially as Grau threads her way through two distinct plot strands: one about the last Will Howland, in a dynasty of men with that name, who represents the archetypal conflict of the natural man against the civilized world, and the other about his granddaughter, Abigail, who eventually dominates the book as she does the area in which she lives, utterly thwarting the forces of repression and ignorance. Like Faulkner's *Absalom, Absalom!*, the novel is concerned both with dynastic manipulations and degeneration and with the creation of an entire mythical society. Successive generations of a clan profoundly aware of their destiny dominate the book, and

ultimately the struggle for racial justice argued in the book must be considered
in moral terms.

The moral imperatives presented in the novel are based on the black-white
dichotomy, and much of the force—and controversy—of the novel is the result
of Howland's marriage to a black housekeeper. Rather than being a mere sensational novel about miscegenation, this novel presents the varying ways in which
the offspring of Howland and the housekeeper resolve their various racial identities, and Grau explores the way in which racial unrest reveals evil. Besides the
complex manner in which the Howland clan relates to the changing attitudes in
the South, through Abigail's morally probing narrative Grau comments omnis-
ciently on all events in the novel, not only those passed down from earlier
generations but even more those related to the events in Abigail's own life,
where her awareness of the meaning of events is more limited. In college, for
instance, she meets and later marries a man who becomes a successful racist
politician; love is not enough to maintain the marriage, for Abigail's quiet,
genteel world ends when her grandfather's marriage is revealed publicly and her
husband chooses career over marriage. Abigail's sole concern thereafter is to
"keep" the "house" of Howland, even against raging mobs intent on "revenge"
for the racial outrage.

The scale of this novel is mythic, even tragic. The biblical source for the
novel's title implies both residence and lineage, and it is lineage especially that
makes grandfather and granddaughter seem like giants among pygmies, and the
black housekeeper comes to be as indomitable and proud as the family she joins,
almost a mythical "earth mother." Grau's profound sense of the problem of
evil as manifested in prejudice and power seeking, affecting and infecting an
entire region for over a century, makes the work more than a mere plea for racial
understanding; Grau's theme is carefully integrated into a convincing account
of character and values, and she is surely correct in describing this work as her
"most ambitious."

Grau intended to create characters of a similar magnitude in *The Condor
Passes* (1971), but this novel is much less convincing than *The Keepers of the
House*. Although Grau maintains careful control over her characters and probes
effectively the pernicious effects of power, *The Condor Passes* as a whole—
because it treats a family of criminals—was dismissed unfairly and inaccurately
as a poor imitation of Mario Puzo's *The Godfather*. But this book is less about
the world of crime than it is about the perversions of love that are possible when
money is the only catalyst. The book is narrated by a sequence of narrators in
and around the family of Thomas Henry Oliver, who near his death at ninety-
five reflects upon his long family history, his rise from poverty, and his family's
inability to express love. Oliver rose by attaching himself to a corrupt family in
New Orleans, and at age forty-two he married a seventeen-year-old by whom
he had two daughters: Anna, who is masochistically religious and who marries
a bright, promiscuous Cajun boy, and Margaret, who eventually takes over the

empire. Neither has offspring who can succeed Oliver; hence the dynasty so carefully built up expires. Although he epitomizes success, Oliver seems too weak a character to have succeeded as well as he has; he seems no more a financial wizard than he does a crime chieftain: so Grau's attempt to depict him in epic terms does not succeed. Oliver seems one-dimensional, identifiable as one more example of the rags-to-riches success story typical in earlier accounts of the American dream.

By contrast with Grau's first collection of stories, *The Wind Shifting West* (1973) seems less gifted and less distinguished. Of the eighteen stories in this collection, two were expanded into major portions of *The Condor Passes* and her later novel, *Evidence of Love*. Most of the stories deal with isolation and displacement; the protagonists are usually isolated women; and one unusual story is an effective end-of-the-world narrative. Few of the stories have the emotional range and impact of *The Black Prince and Other Stories*, and some of the tales are too dated or otherwise slight. "Homecoming" is a good attack on senti-mentality, as it tells of a dead youth whose survivors exaggerate the "love" that ostensibly existed between the boy and a girl who barely knew him. Several of the stories are similar in their handling of death, sometimes in relation to Vietnam. "The Last Gas Station" offers an unnamed catastrophe and its effects on an isolated family running the gas station, with only silence left at the end of the chillingly apocalyptic story. Grau's professionalism in these stories is evident, but few are superior examples of the genre.

Evidence of Love (1977) is set wholly outside the South, her first book to be so located. The several members of a family once again find it impossible to show any real "evidence of love" toward each other or toward others. An aged father, Edward Milton Henley, tells his story in the first and last sections of the novel, and his son and daughter-in-law narrate the two middle sections. As in *The Condor Passes*, the elder man dominates, and his complete indifference to others except in monetary terms is in sharp contrast to his rational, emotionless son, a Unitarian clergyman who lives stoically and cheerlessly serving others. His son's wife, Lucy, by contrast, is a vital woman with far greater emotional range and depth than her ascetic husband or amoral father-in-law. Lucy is some-where between the two men, more balanced, more alive in the fullest sense; she alone can understand death without self-pity, and she simply goes along trying to change those things in life that she can. She and her dying father-in-law can see each other clearly and without illusion; each knows the other's weaknesses and strengths; each has lived a full and varied life; each is essentially secure in a chaotic world, though Lucy's life is far less "wasted" than his. Narcissism is therefore no more valid than asceticism, since both extremes are ultimately self-defeating. Various kinds of "love" are rejected by the characters; only Lucy seems able, for example, to join the spiritual and the physical, for she is neither hedonist nor rationalist but rather a warm, loving person who has learned to subordinate some of her feelings in her marriage.

Grau has published no further novels since *Evidence of Love*, though she was reported a few years ago to be embarked on a novel considerably more experimental than her earlier work. In 1986 publication of *Nine Women*, nine stories about women at points of crisis, showed Grau at the top of her form. The stories are more in keeping with contemporary expectations for the short stories than were the heavily symbolic tales of her first collection or the more realistic ones of her second. The common theme among the new stories is the consequence of isolations, of being at the end of a stage in life. Mary Rohrberger discusses two of these stories in "Shirley Ann Grau and the Short Story," cited in the bibliography.

Grau's major themes often are so tightly tied in with her plots and characters that it is difficult to distinguish among them. Chief among these themes, at least for her earlier works, is the sense of region. Fully aware of her area's deep conflicts and unrest, Grau probes sensitively into the inner conflicts, especially those concerned with love and money and power, that lead so many of her characters to depths of personal and social unrest. Few of these works, however, necessarily *have* to be located in the South; for insofar as character development is concerned, the moral imperatives that govern her characters' lives are universal ones. She is particularly effective in delineating the way in which her Southern characters—especially blacks and primitives—move easily through settings which could appear as mere local color, picturesque settings with all the usual Southern gothic trappings. Since she has a strong sense of place, her best work remains that which has grown out of her long exposure to and affection for the hot, humid Gulf Coast below New Orleans.

Most of Grau's characters do seem incapable, however, of a mature, balanced acceptance of the role such forces as love and power have in normal lives. Too often they reject what seems to them to be a naive balance of love, mature handling of power, and normal control over the possibilities for evil but instead yield to such impulses as hatred, depravity, and hunger for power, commitments Grau explicitly denounces as sterile, futile, and ultimately self-defeating. Her characters rarely become as complex as they could be, almost as if she takes an easy way out in creating characters who rarely grow in the reader's mind so as to become fully persuasive; all too often they simply exist, lacking anything other than their basic urges. One would, for example, especially anticipate more complex portraits in her last two novels, where the advantage of long, dissolute lives should have given the old men who serve as narrators a complex, varied perspective. Even in Grau's best novel, *The Keepers of the House*, the basic conflicts seem ultimately to be good against evil, the forces of reason and tolerance against all the darker impulses popularly attributed to Southerners.

Indeed, Grau's seeming satisfaction with the superficial in some of her characters' lives is disappointing simply because too much is left on the surface. Grau has observed that she "has no cause and no message," meaning that her characters sometimes serve primarily to support plots that are contrived rather than that end satisfactorily. Her works often simply end, as with a protagonist's death or with a character falling into a fetal position at a moment of crisis. She is more of a stylist than a careful builder of plots, and the sometimes lush sensory stimuli presented in her works inadequately supplant carefully worked-out plots. From the reader's perspective, this means that though we are fully able to visualize the settings in which the characters move, we are not always sure that we can tell what motivates them or what causes them to relate to other characters as they do; we yearn, therefore, for a greater sense of engagement in her characters' actions and motives as these are borne out in the structure. Only in *The Keepers of the House* do the characters rise to the level of the truly tragic, as if to suggest that Grau only in this novel surpassed the level of competence reflected in her other work. Her newest short stories reveal a mature perspective and understanding of older women. The power and honesty of these stories is impressive.

SURVEY OF CRITICISM

Despite Grau's long career and wide publication history, the disappointing lack of substantial, even of sympathetic, criticism is astonishing. No doubt the excessive praise given her first book is responsible to some extent for the subsequent diminution of commentary, but this fails to explain the consistent, even perverse misunderstanding she has received. True, her first book was not so good as early reviewers claimed, but her subsequent books are not so weak as many reviewers have made them out to be.

From the start, reviewers have singled out such strengths as Grau's handling of sensory and atmospheric details, her sense of style, her handling of dialogue, and her lack of sentimentality. Characterization, however, has received everything from excessive praise to excessive denunciation, with *The House on Coliseum Street* merely the first of her books to be damned by some reviewers for the unpleasantness of the characters. Only *The Keepers of the House* was accorded consistent praise, especially for Grau's handling of elemental forces at work on humanity. *The Condor Passes*, by contrast, received almost exclusively antagonistic commentary, partly because of alleged parallels with *The Godfather*, partly because of the clichéd formula quality of the book. Perhaps to avoid the hyperbole earlier accorded to *The Black Prince*, the reviewers of Grau's second collection of stories, *The Wind Shifting West*, criticized the work's lack of emotional power and lasting relevance rather than mere topicality; despite acknowledging Grau's professionalism and competence, few reviewers of this volume probed more deeply than to say that it was "disappointing." And even though Grau was sometimes criticized earlier in her career for being tied too closely to the South, when she finally wrote a novel wholly set outside that region, the criticism centered on her alleged lack of familiarity with the North! *Evidence of Love* thus received mixed reviews, with the more perceptive reviewers singling out the emotionally sterile relationships to be found in the book. Ironically, Grau's careful control over her characters received both praise and criticism, suggesting that critics bring more than objective tools to their craft. More than many recent novels, this one illustrates quite well the extremes of opinion.

But all such commentary falls in the review category; Grau has received a singular lack of substantial criticism. Mary Rohrberger remains one of the few critics who have written about more than one of Grau's books; while not blind to Grau's faults, she has been more able than most critics to focus on Grau's lasting accomplishments. She noted, for example, that the "search for love" in *Evidence of Love* turns out to be a "quest for order and understanding." Rohrberger's essay on Grau's stories is by all odds the finest single essay thus far done on her work; it is sympathetic, astute, and free of polemics in its easy movement over Grau's career as a writer of short fiction.

Other essay-length appreciations include Alwyn Berland's 1963 essay. Published after only three of Grau's books were issued, it offers little insight into Grau's larger scope or the varied promise found in the later books, though it does offer reasonably accurate readings of the first three books. Ann Pearson's 1975 essay, by contrast, posits a valid thesis for Grau (i.e., that "nature is the vision"); this essay remains a valuable though limited analysis. Essays written for reference books include Chester E. Eisinger's patronizing summary and Jean W. Ross's more expansive, balanced piece. Frederick J. Hoffman in his *The Art of Southern Fiction* discusses all of Grau's career but with an emphasis on *The Keepers of the House*; he notes the book's virtues but comments that Grau is not "the master strategist of Southern history." Louise Y. Gossett, by contrast, not only treats Grau's "straightforward" style with understanding, she also observes that Grau tends to "oversimplify human relationships," with violence seen as a function of her characters' primitive natures. Finally, the only book-length study of Grau to date is Paul Schlueter's Twayne volume; covering all of Grau's career and based in part on interviews, it also provides in-depth analyses of all the novels and collections of short stories published in book form, except for *Nine Women*.

Grau's career has changed directions more than once, and there is every reason to believe that she will surprise her readers once again. As a writer still in her fifties, Grau is far from written out—and therefore one can legitimately anticipate even more careful, probing analyses of her work than have appeared thus far, particularly as her entire career can be seen in critical perspective.

BIBLIOGRAPHY

Works by Shirley Ann Grau

The Black Prince and Other Stories. New York: Knopf, 1954.
The Hard Blue Sky. New York: Knopf, 1958.
The House on Coliseum Street. New York: Knopf, 1961.
The Keepers of the House. New York: Knopf, 1964.
The Condor Passes. New York: Knopf, 1971.
The Wind Shifting West. New York: Knopf, 1973.

Evidence of Love. New York: Knopf, 1977.
Nine Women. New York: Knopf, 1986.

Studies of Shirley Ann Grau

Berland, Alwyn. "The Fiction of Shirley Ann Grau." *Critique* 6, no. 1 (1963): 78–84.
Coles, Robert. "Mood and Revelation in the South." *New Republic* 150 (18 April 1964): 17–19. [on *The Keepers of the House*]
DeBellis, Jack. "Two Southern Novels and a Diversion." *Sewanee Review* 70 (1962): 691–94. [on *The House on Coliseum Street*]
Donaghue, Denis. "Life Sentence." *New York Review of Books* 17 (2 December 1971): 28–30. [on *The Condor Passes*]
Eisinger, Chester E. "Grau, Shirley Ann." *Contemporary Novelists*. Ed. James Vinson. New York: St. Martin's, 1972, pp. 514–16.
Going, William T. "Alabama Geography in Shirley Ann Grau's *The Keepers of the House*." *Alabama Geography* 20, no. 1 (1967): 62–68.
Gossett, Louise Y. *Violence in Recent Southern Fiction*. Durham, N.C.: Duke University Press, 1965, pp. 177–95.
Hoffman, Frederick J. *The Art of Southern Fiction*. Carbondale: Southern Illinois University Press, 1967, pp. 106–09.
Pearson, Ann. "Shirley Ann Grau: Nature Is the Vision." *Critique* 17, no. 2 (1975): 47–58.
Rohrberger, Mary. "Shirley Ann Grau and the Short Story." *Southern Quarterly* 21, no. 4 (1983): 83–101.
———. " 'So Distinct a Shade': Shirley Ann Grau's *Evidence of Love*." *Southern Review* 14 (1978): 195–98.
Ross, Jean W. "Shirley Ann Grau." *Dictionary of Literary Biography, II: American Novelists Since World War II*. Ed. Jeffrey Helterman and Richard Layman. Detroit: Gale Research, 1978, pp. 208–15.
Schlueter, Paul. *Shirley Ann Grau*. Boston: Twayne, 1981.
Williams, Thomas. "Ducks, Ships, Custard, and a King." *Kenyon Review* 24 (1962): 184–88. [on *The House on Coliseum Street*]

———————— LAURENCE G. AVERY ————————

Paul Green
(1894–1981)

Folk and *symphonic* are the labels usually applied to Paul Green's plays, but another less frequently used term, *people's theater*, catches more of his aspiration and achievement. It is a useful term for exploring his career because it suggests all areas of his thought about the drama: its proper subject, form, and audience, and the purpose of the playwright. During his career Green worked out first one aspect, then another, of his idea of a people's theater.

BIOGRAPHY

Born on 17 March 1894, Paul Green grew up on his family's farm near Lillington, North Carolina. After graduation from Buies Creek Academy, he served as principal of the country school in Olive Branch. He entered the University of North Carolina (UNC) in 1916, but left after one year to serve in the army engineers. After two years with the American army in France (1917–19), he came back to the university and took a B.A. in 1921, then did graduate work in philosophy at Cornell. On 6 July 1922 he married Elizabeth Lay. They had four children. He returned to Chapel Hill in 1923 as a member of the university's department of philosophy, in which he taught until helping to found the department of dramatic arts in 1937. When Emily Clark relinquished the editorship of the *Reviewer* in 1924, the little magazine founded in Richmond in 1921, Green became editor, and the magazine moved to Chapel Hill, where it lived but a year. Although Green traveled extensively and although he worked sporadically for various companies in Hollywood, he always returned to Chapel Hill, where he taught in dramatic art through 1944. He died in Chapel Hill on 4 May 1981.

Active in the cause of blacks from the 1920s onward, prominently involved in organizations such as the Federal Theatre Project and the National Theater

Conference, and after World War II serving in several capacities with UNESCO, Green was always first a writer. When he returned from France in 1919, Frederick Koch had begun to establish the Carolina Playmakers. According to Green, Koch "believed that everybody was a playwright more or less, and the amazing thing was that he got the folks around him to believe it." By the time he graduated from UNC, Green had written perhaps a dozen short plays, five of them performed by the Playmakers, and he had found his real profession. The University of North Carolina recognized the contributions of Green to its programs and to dramatic literature by naming a new theatre (1978) the Paul Green Theatre.

MAJOR THEMES

Green's ideas about material for the drama were fostered by Koch, who urged on his playwrighting students a concern "with folk subject matter, with legends, superstitions, customs, . . . and the vernacular of the common people." When Green began to articulate his own ideas about the drama, it was this element of subject matter that he stressed. In 1925, in the first issue of the *Reviewer* under his editorship, he predicted a renaissance of Southern literature because, "If there is a section [of the country] containing an abundance of crude, unshaped material of art, it is [the South]." The fullest statement of his beliefs concerning the proper material for the drama came in an essay of 1934, "Drama and the Weather." He wrote folk plays, he said, because "the 'folk' are the people who seem to matter most to me," and in explaining why that was true he placed himself in the tradition of ideas stemming from Jeffersonian agrarianism through Wordsworth down to the Abbey Theatre movement of Yeats, Synge, and Lady Gregory. In that tradition "the outside natural world is the fountain of wisdom." Cut off from nature, city dwellers at best exhibit specialized concerns, at worst become demoralized or depraved. Rural people, on the other hand, take their habits and ideas from nature, and have "a consciousness of the great eternal Presence by which men live and move and have their being, and without which they die." The folk—these rural people—are animated by concerns common to all human beings and, when powerfully imagined, can be made to represent "man alone with his God and his destiny."

Green first attracted national attention with *In Abraham's Bosom: The Biography of a Negro*, which won the Pulitzer Prize in 1927. The play ends with the shooting of the central character by his Klan-like neighbors, and Green's real achievement was that he made it not a simplistic protest play but a complex folk tragedy. He did that by unfolding the character of his protagonist.

Abraham McCranie, a mulatto raised as a Negro in North Carolina of the late nineteenth century, has a thirst for learning. As a young man he struggles with borrowed books to educate himself. Then his vision expands, and he dreams of building a school for the black children of the area. Practicing a speech, he proclaims: "Looking over the country, ladies and gentlemen, we see eight million [black] souls striving in slavery, yea, slavery, brethren, the slavery of ignorance. And ignorance means being oppressed, both by yourselves and by others— hewers of wood and drawers of water. . . . We want our children and our grand- children to march on towards full lives and noble chareckters, and that has got to come, I say, by education. We have no other way." Against the realization of that inspiring vision two forces contend. One, the racial prejudice at the heart of Abe's society, is vividly presented. The highly charged opening scene shows his white father beating Abe to save him from worse treatment for hitting a white man, and other instances of humiliation abound. The other force is decisive, however, and it is Abe's own "chareckter." He sees himself as savior of the black race, and in his messianic fervor he alienates his own people: first his mother, most painfully his son, the other blacks of the community, and finally his wife. At the end he is shot for killing his bigoted white half-brother, but by then he is a leader with no following, a visionary who failed. That is the tragic realization with which he meets his death: black folk are "asleep, asleep, and I can't wake 'em! . . . But they'll wake up, they'll wake—a crack of thunder and deep divided from deep—a light! A light, and it will be!"

The House of Connelly, last of Green's early folk plays, is historically the most interesting. Conceived in 1926, it is the earliest work of imaginative lit- erature to forge that picture of the South later used in one version or another by William Faulkner, Lillian Hellman, Margaret Mitchell, and Tennessee Williams: a South whose aristocrats go back in memory to a time when social power and enlightened values coincided in their family but who in the present lack the ability to act and find themselves threatened with extinction. *Connelly* is also the play that launched the Group Theatre, until the Federal Theatre the most vital development in the theatre of the 1930s. In the play Will Connelly is incapacitated by guilt: about his family back through the generations, whose behavior showed they did not accept the humanity of blacks; also about himself, a dutiful son driven to renounce his family. "There's something to search for," he believes, "a way to act right and know it's right. [But] Father and Grandfather didn't [find] it, and we're paying for it. All the old Connellys have doomed us to die. Our character's gone." Last of the family line, his plantation in decay, and himself incapable of action, Will is correct at that point in his prophecy of doom. But to the plantation comes a tenant girl whose character is *not* gone. Unburdened by the past, Patsy Tate is full of energy, common sense, and decency. Although Will cannot undo injustices of the past, with Patsy's support he gains the strength to expose and free himself from them. And his marriage to her, in the version produced by the Group Theatre in 1931, signals his salvation. "The dead and the proud have to give way to us—to us the living," she says for the two of them. "We have our life to live and we'll fight for it to the end." Its final point of interest, however, is that *The House of Connelly* exists in two versions. In the second, Patsy does not revitalize the Connelly line. Two black maids of the Connelly household, spirits of the past, cannot accept her marriage to Will and conclude the play by smothering Patsy to death. This bleak version Green put into *Out of the South*, a collection of his plays published in 1939.

In 1928–29 Green and his family spent sixteen months in Berlin and London on a Guggenheim Fellowship. Until then his plays on folk subjects had remained, in their formal elements, largely within the bounds of lifelikeness associated with the realistic play since Chekhov. But a play should fully express the nature of its subject, Green thought, and several powerful means of expression lay beyond the bounds of probability as judged by the way things happen in life. Before leaving for Germany he vented his discontent and outlined the theatre of his dreams. At present its elements were scattered, but were suggested by "the true make-believe of marionettes," "dance, music, religious ritual, spectacle, the circus and stadium, the written and spoken word, the movies" [where "Charlie Chaplin walks so exquisitely between two worlds"]. "Some day," he prophesied, the means of expression suggested by that list "will receive their proper fusion in the New Theatre, the theatre of imagination, of lofty commmonsense." In Europe the only plays to excite him were those put on by Alexis Granowsky's Moscow Jewish Academy Theatre, then visiting Berlin. Using music, pantomime, farce, fantasy, masks, dance, and acrobatics, Granowsky's productions showed he "had deliberately meant to fuse all the elements of theatre art into one." During the 1930s one of Green's chief goals was to achieve such a fusion himself. The kind of play that resulted he called *symphonic drama*, "a 'sounding-together' in the true meaning of the Greek word."

In the late 1920s and 1930s Green incorporated elements of farce and fantasy into several plays and experimented with what he called "energized properties," such as the singing cannons in *Johnny Johnson*. He also began to use "mental speech"—choral passages or electronic equipment to convey the thoughts of characters. The new means of expression he concentrated on, however, were music, rhythmic movement, and the role of narrator or chorus. Music was the most important. Expressing a character or situation requires historical authenticity. If characters were on the chain gang, their music should consist of actual convict work songs; if sixteenth-century Englishmen, music known in sixteenth-century England. And Green used music for a variety of particular purposes, from establishing tone or theme to telescoping action. Rhythmic movement often involved music and proved useful in two areas: particular scenes, in which movements of characters were choreographed as strictly as a dance; and over a whole play, where intermissions were dropped and, with lights and music, one scene was made to slide imperceptibly into the next with no break in impression as the play built to a climax. Narrator and choral characters, sometimes both in the same play, acknowledged the existence of the audience and through commentary and narrative guided an audience in its relationship to the play.

The first play to which Green applied his new label was *Potter's Field: A Symphonic Play of the Negro People*, published in 1931. As a student, he had gotten interested in a Negro shantytown near the university, and in 1928 when he planned his play about it, he focused not on an individual but on the community, as Elmer Rice would do the next year in *Street Scene*. His aim of expressing the life of the group determined his setting (a boardinghouse on a summer evening where all might gather) and his characters (ones "representative of a cross-section of Negro life"). In writing the play, he says, he felt like "a composer driving forward his composition," with characters equivalent to musical instruments in a symphony. And its organization he saw as an expression of "the inner natural form" of the subject.

A long opening speech foreshadows the action. An old man broods on the boardinghouse porch, his thoughts projected through speakers to the audience. He begins: "After a life of fun and sweet momma from Louisville to Mobile, this swinging a pick in a ditch for two bucks a day and all the manhood gone out of you is a hell of a way to end. And then too them white men stand round in their collars and tell you what to do—Jesus!" Other characters are introduced, some admirable, others pathetic or humorous or frightening, and their stories come forward and recede, first one, then another, frequently with musical motifs, until woven together as the fabric of community life. Some of the characters work on a construction project, a "white man's" highway that is headed straight for the Negro tenement, and the boom of the blasting, far away at first, gets closer as the play proceeds. One of the stories, a triangular love affair, has a potential for violence, which erupts with a fight between the two men, then the shooting of one by the other. That scene is the climax of the action. The blasting is now so near it shakes the ground of the tenement. Over the speakers, so loud it rattles the building, comes the voice of the white man's law: "Heigh! I say heigh there!" And a wind rises and collapses the rickety boardinghouse. Music and lights modulate the scene. As the dust clears, the audience sees the new highway arching over the debris and two of the black men, now in striped convict clothes, as part of a chain-gang crew at work on the highway, their movement designed as a tortuous dance. One of the men, who had killed his rival, collapses, his spirit broken, then lashes out at the prodding of a guard and is shot. The other, far from broken in spirit, leads the crew in its pick-swinging dance off toward the sun.

Emerging from *Potter's Field* is an unsentimentalized picture of a black shantytown, rich in its own life but powerless in the white world, which is oblivious of the shantytown until disturbances occur there, then quick and sweeping in its destructive response. Honest and beautifully imagined, the play, perhaps in its shorter form, *Roll, Sweet Chariot* (1935), may become that unusual thing, a play better known a hundred years later than at the time it was written.

Johnny Johnson gave Kurt Weill his first opportunity in the American theatre. Newly arrived in this country, Weill, according to Cheryl Crawford of the Group Theatre, wanted to work with an American, and she put him in touch with Green. Green and Weill wrote the musical during the summer and fall of 1936, and it was produced that November by the Group Theatre. Johnny is a "natural" whose simplicity and goodness make absurd the world's complexity and evil.

In France because enlisting was the only way to keep the respect of his girlfriend, he learns that American soldiers do not hate or wish to kill Germans, and, ingeniously capturing a German, he discovers the same attitude in the "enemy." So he does the impossible and stops the war. Quickly, however, the generals save the day by having Johnny declared insane: "one of those naturals born into the world at rare intervals. You recall my monograph on St. Francis of Assisi, the rural prophet and will-less egocentric—same type, same type." Kept in an asylum for ten years, Johnny organizes the inmates into a League of Nations that works, then does not want to be released. The world around him seems crazy, personified as it is by a boyhood friend too cowardly in 1916 to go off to war but now a politician beating the drum for military preparedness. Sometimes funny, sometimes grim, always committed to brotherhood within a unified world order, *Johnny Johnson* satirizes competition between nation-states and the individuals who lead people into war.

By taking half-pay, Green and the Group kept *Johnny Johnson* running for nine weeks. *Roll, Sweet Chariot* ran for only one because the theatre owner, deciding the production would not make money, leased his building to another company. *Tread the Green Grass*, optioned by the Provincetown Players, then by Francis Fergusson's Lab Theater, finally had no professional production, as both organizations fell to the Depression. By the middle 1930s Green was despondent about his prospects as a playwright. To succeed on Broadway meant first to make money. And show business success required plays suited to the tastes of Broadway audiences. Disinclined to accommodate what he considered the interests of sophisticated city dwellers, Green needed an alternative theater to escape silence. In 1937 such a theater came about on Roanoke Island off the coast of North Carolina. On the site of Sir Walter Raleigh's colonies in the 1580s, the theater represented local, state, and national interests brought together by a wish to celebrate the 350th anniversary of the colony that vanished without trace. Beginning to work on *The Lost Colony* in January 1937, Green had a script for rehearsal late in the spring. The production opened on 4 July that year and ran until Labor Day. Except for four years during World War II, it has played on the island every summer since 1937.

The occasion of *The Lost Colony*, a historical celebration, called for a play more faithful than most to the historical record, and in his outline Green invented only the fate of the colony, about which the record is silent. Within the outline, however, Green devised a plot that deals with the meaning of the New World experience. The central character, John Borden, a tenant farmer in Raleigh's Devonshire, shows early in the play the debilitating result of life in a stratified society. Despite admirable personal qualities, he has no way of rising above tenancy in England, nor can he marry the woman he loves, Eleanor White, because her father, governor-to-be of the colony, has contracted a more advantageous marriage for her with Captain Dare. Before joining Raleigh's expedition, Borden is on the way to becoming a bitter cynic. In the New World, however, class distinctions fall under pressures of frontier life. Borden's worth in the eyes of the community comes to depend on his demonstrated ability. When Governor White returns to England, he leaves Borden in charge. During the trying final months Borden devotes himself to protecting the colony against Indian attack and supporting the sick. At the end, rather than accept easy terms of surrender from attacking Spaniards, he leads a march inland because, having come for freedom, they must not let themselves be enslaved. A humorous subplot echoes the theme of New World freedom and its consequences on democratic assumptions, a dual sense of self-respect and social responsibility.

For Green's generation Romain Rolland's *The People's Theatre* (trans. 1918) gave currency to the title phrase and the audience it implied. Immediately concerned with the working class of Paris, Rolland broadened the concept through historical treatment going back to Rousseau so that *the people* emerged as the common people of the nation, a loose term embracing all but the social elite. That democratic notion moved easily to America, where many were inspired by the idea of carrying the theatre beyond our few theatre districts, particularly in New York City, to the population at large. Ideas and aspirations associated with a "people's theatre" sprinkle the pages of *Arena*, Hallie Flanagan's account of the Federal Theatre Project, and she and her colleagues were enthusiastic about *The Lost Colony* especially because it cultivated a large regional, then national, audience. Easily debased, art for the masses can be of a high order, and Green carefully considered the nature of his play. Its hold on an audience is rooted in a common experience: on the spot of memorable events, being swept away in wonder and reflection about them. To stimulate such reverie, *The Lost Colony* opens with a reminder that the events behind its action unfolded where the audience now sits. Then as the audience watches and listens, the play interprets the events as the first experience of ideals central to the American heritage. People leave the theater, Green hoped, at least with a more vivid historical memory, at best with a refreshed sense of the country's democratic tradition.

In 1940–41 in his dramatization of *Native Son*, Green dealt again with a failure to realize the nation's democratic ideals. He read Richard Wright's novel shortly after its publication in the spring of 1940 and found it vivid and powerful. For his part, Wright welcomed Green's offer to dramatize the novel because of Green's sensitive treatment of blacks in his own plays. Wright visited Chapel Hill for a few days in June, when he and Green worked out a story line for the play. Then they drafted it during another visit in July and August. Over the winter Green revised the script for its moderately successful Broadway production, which opened in March 1941 under the direction of Orson Welles.

In ten brief scenes, sharply focused and done without intermission, the play follows Bigger Thomas from his tenement home in Chicago's Black Belt to his death cell on the day he is executed for murder. Early scenes show the suffocating conditions of Bigger's life and Bigger's violent rebellion against restraints, social as well as personal. Then as a chauffeur he is taken into the home of a rich white family noted for its social conscience, and the central problem of the play is vividly dramatized. The two worlds, Bigger's and the Daltons', though physically adjacent, are in experience so far apart that inhabitants of one find the other incomprehensible. Efforts by the Daltons to treat him as an equal only make Bigger "feel like a dog. . . . In their big house I was all trembling and afraid." Forced one night to take the daughter to her bed because she is too drunk to walk, Bigger panics at the approach of her mother, fearing the consequences of being caught in the bedroom, and smothers the girl to insure silence. His reaction to the killing is, in part, exhilaration. Effects have always flowed from the white world to him; now for the first time he has done a thing that causes whites to react. Fear also sets in, and he is caught and brought to trial. His lawyer's defense is a moving indictment of American society for failing to achieve its ideals of freedom and equality, but the defense fails. In his cell Bigger struggles toward an understanding of himself and his behavior in relation to others. Then he closes the play by going unaided into the electrocution chamber.

Before turning to *Native Son* Green had staged a second play in his drive to create a people's theater. First performed in Fayetteville, North Carolina, in November 1939, *The Highland Call* focuses on the large Scottish community along the Cape Fear River and its difficulties as Loyalists during the Revolution. After its second year *The Highland Call* was halted by World War II. The war also delayed *The Common Glory*. Written to be produced by the Federal Theatre, then adopted by Colonial Williamsburg after Congress terminated the Federal Theatre in June 1939, *The Common Glory* deals with Jefferson's struggle to formulate the social ideals of the Revolution. Held in abeyance during the war, the play ran annually in Williamsburg from 1947 to 1974. By 1981 when he died, Green had written fourteen additional plays for his people's theater and staged them from the east to the west coast and from Ohio to Florida. Five were still running in 1985. *Wilderness Road*, about the tensions generated by the Civil War in the emerging community of Berea, opened in Berea, Kentucky, in June 1955. *The Stephen Foster Story*, on the life of the composer, opened at Bardstown, Kentucky, in June 1959. *Cross and Sword*, on the founding of St. Augustine, opened in St. Augustine, Florida, in June 1965. *Texas*, on the settling of the panhandle, opened in Palo Duro Canyon, Texas, in July 1966. And *The Lone Star*, about Texas's struggle to win independence from Mexico, opened in Galveston, Texas, in June 1977.

Beginning his career as a teacher of philosophy, Green thought in traditional categories: the True, the Good, and the Beautiful. Much of his energy went to projects in the second, expressive of his strong sense of social justice. As early as the 1920s, when such efforts were hardly popular, he worked to secure fair treatment and opportunities for blacks. From the 1930s onward, thinking the death penalty unfair in its application to the poor and especially blacks, he was a leader in the movement to abolish capital punishment. People in that movement today hold rallies entitled "Lone Vigil" in memory of Green's practice of standing outside the state prison in solitary protest during an execution. But Green was first a playwright, a worker as he understood it in the field of the Beautiful. A fine achievement of his life was remaining faithful to that calling.

He could have taken prominent jobs that left little time for writing. Or as a writer he could have drifted from his vision: probably he could have succeeded on Broadway's terms; certainly as a screen writer he could have gotten rich; and—most tempting of all, given his social conscience—he could have reduced many of his plays to works of social protest. He chose to do none of those. For him a play was essentially an opportunity to discover the inner nature of his subject and display it for the pleasure of an audience—pleasure of the kind derived from an enlargement of understanding. His career was an exploration of the artistic possibilities inherent in that purpose.

SURVEY OF CRITICISM

Biographical studies began to appear early in Green's career. Barrett Clark's *Paul Green* (1928) sketches Green's youth, places his early plays in the context of his life, and discusses his aims as a writer. Agatha Boyd Adams's *Paul Green of Chapel Hill* (1951) is a chatty book useful mainly as a reflection of Green's standing among friends and colleagues where he lived. In 1978 *Pembroke Magazine* devoted an issue to Green (#10), which includes several discussions of his life and plays. *The Paul Green I Know* (1978), by Elizabeth Lay Green, is full of family lore. The society in which Green was raised is depicted in Henry Grady Owens, "The Social Thought and Criticism of Paul Green" (Ph.D. diss., New York University, 1945). As background for Green's ideas, Hegel's work on art and the drama is essential, and Charles Carroll Everett's *The Science of Thought* (rev. ed., 1890), an Hegelian exposition, influenced Green during his formative college years.

Book-length critical studies of Green so far are few. In "Form and Structure in Paul Green's Tragedies" (Ph.D. diss., Indiana University, 1967) Philip Lee Devin considers the tragedies in the context of Green's dramatic theory. Walter S. Lazenby, Jr., in *Paul Green* (1970), provides a sensitive reading of the plays and calls attention to the similarity of function among Green's Little Bethel country, Faulkner's Yoknapatawpha, and Hardy's Wessex. The strength of Vincent S. Kenny's *Paul Green* (1971) is its extended treatment of the outdoor historical plays after World War II; Kenny calls attention to such fine works as *Wilderness Road: A Parable for Modern Times*. A helpful list of the outdoor plays, along with an analysis of one, is Eleanor Anne Ponder's "A Bibliography of Paul Green's Symphonic Outdoor Dramas and a Study of the Artistry of *Trumpet in the Land*" (M.A. thesis, UNC, 1973). Fred Alan Eady deals with the relation of Green's plays to his social world in "Paul Green: Folk-Dramatist, Social Critic" (Ph.D. diss., Michigan State University, 1974). Green's own essays convey the situations in which he wrote and discuss his aims. The essays are collected in *The Hawthorn Tree* (1945), *Dramatic Heritage* (1953), *Drama and the Weather* (1958), and *Plough and Furrow* (1963).

A good way to see Green is through the eyes of his contemporaries. In *The Human Image in Dramatic Literature* (1957) Francis Fergusson provides a thoughtful survey of the American theater between the two world wars and concludes that Green and O'Neill were the most important playwrights to come from the noncommercial theater of the 1920s and that during the 1930s the most significant developments were the Group Theatre and the Federal Theatre Project. The Carolina Playmaker years when Green got his start are represented by Frederick H. Koch, *Carolina Folk-Plays* (1941). Harold Clurman, a founder of the Group, describes its development and Green's contribution in *The Fervent Years* (1945), as does Cheryl Crawford, another of the founders, in *One Naked Individual* (1977). Even more than the Group, the Federal Theatre matched Green's aspirations, and Hallie Flanagan, its director, tells the story of the Project in *Arena* (1940) and makes clear how Green and *The Lost Colony* embodied its aims. The Federal Theatre took shape in the context of hopes for a national theater. Kenneth Macgowan gives an early account of the work in support of that hope in *Footlights across America* (1929). A decade later, in *Advance from Broadway* (1941), Norris Houghton assessed the progress of the movement and found that "among all the artists of the theatre with whom I talked throughout the country, none had greater vision or wisdom than Paul Green." Ideas underlying the drive for a national theater had found recent expression in Rolland's *The People's Theatre* (trans. 1918) and go back to Wordsworth's 1802 "Preface" to *Lyrical Ballads* and Rousseau's *Letter à d'Alembert* (1758).

Nothing else conveys a sense of Green's personality and experience as vividly as his letters, an edition of which is underway. Most of the basic scholarship on Green, however, is yet to be done. He revised nearly every time he republished a piece. Thus, in order to know which state of a text is in hand, readers need a bibliography that charts the course of each text through the years. Also needed is editorial work on several of his plays. None of the others exists in states as different as *The House of Connelly*, but several were revised extensively over the years, among them *In Abraham's Bosom*, *Johnny Johnson*, *The Lost Colony*, *Native Son*, and the short plays "The No Count Boy" and "Hymn to the Rising Sun." And few aspects of Green's career have been adequately explored. He played an important role in launching the black drama movement during the early decades of the century. He was a leader in the Renascence of Southern literature during the 1920s and 1930s, and has a definable position in the controversy between agrarians and progressives. His outdoor historical plays, usually called symphonic dramas, constitute a distinctive kind of drama, a kind he invented. His works project a vision of life rich in possibilities for exploration. These and other tasks await able workers.

BIBLIOGRAPHY

Works by Paul Green

The Lord's Will and Other Carolina Plays. New York: Holt, 1925.
Lonesome Road: Six Plays for the Negro Theatre. New York: McBride, 1926.

The Field God and In Abraham's Bosom. New York: McBride, 1927.
In the Valley and Other Carolina Plays. New York: Samuel French, 1928.
Wide Fields. New York: McBride, 1928.
The House of Connelly and Other Plays. New York: Samuel French, 1931.
The Laughing Pioneer. New York: McBride, 1932.
Roll, Sweet Chariot. New York: Samuel French, 1935.
Shroud My Body Down. Iowa City: Clio Press, 1935.
This Body the Earth. New York: Harper, 1935.
Johnny Johnson, with Kurt Weill, composer. New York: Samuel French, 1937.
The Lost Colony. Chapel Hill: Univeristy of North Carolina Press, 1937.
The Enchanted Maze. New York: Samuel French, 1939.
Out of the South. New York: Harper, 1939.
The Highland Call. Chapel Hill: University of North Carolina Press, 1941.
Native Son, with Richard Wright. New York: Harper, 1941.
Forever Growing. Chapel Hill: University of North Carolina Press, 1945.
The Hawthorn Tree. Chapel Hill: University of North Carolina Press, 1945.
Salvation on a String and Other Tales of the South. New York: Harper, 1946.
The Common Glory. Chapel Hill: University of North Carolina Press, 1948.
Dog on the Sun: A Volume of Stories. Chapel Hill: University of North Carolina Press,
    1949.
Peer Gynt, adapted from Ibsen's play. New York: Samuel French, 1951.
Dramatic Heritage. New York: Samuel French, 1953.
Wilderness Road. New York: Samuel French, 1956.
The Founders. New York: Samuel French, 1957.
Drama and the Weather. New York: Samuel French, 1958.
The Confederacy. New York: Samuel French, 1959.
Wings for to Fly: Three Plays of Negro Life. New York: Samuel French, 1959.
The Stephen Foster Story. New York: Samuel French, 1960.
Five Plays of the South. Ed. John Gassner. New York: Hill & Wang, 1963.
Plough and Furrow. New York: Samuel French, 1963.
Cross and Sword. New York: Samuel French, 1966.
Texas. New York: Samuel French, 1967.
Home to My Valley. Chapel Hill: University of North Carolina Press, 1970.
The Honeycomb. New York: Samuel French, 1972.
Trumpet in the Land. New York: Samuel French, 1972.
The Land of Nod and Other Stories. Chapel Hill: University of North Carolina Press,
    1976.

Studies of Paul Green

Adams, Agatha Boyd. *Paul Green of Chapel Hill*. Chapel Hill: University of North
    Carolina Press, 1951.
Atkinson, Brooks. "Founding Fathers." *New York Times*, 15 August 1937, sec. 10,
    p. 1.
Carmer, Carl. "Paul Green: The Making of an American Dramatist." *Theatre Arts
    Monthly* 16 (1932): 995–1006.
Clark, Barrett. *Paul Green*. New York: Robert M. McBride, 1928.
Clark, Emily. *Innocence Abroad*. New York: Alfred Knopf, 1931, pp. 253–70.

Clifford, John. "A True American Artist: Paul Green." *Players: Magazine for American Theatre* 48 (1973): 201–15.

Dusenbury, Winifred L. *The Theme of Loneliness in Modern American Drama*. Gainesville: University of Florida Press, 1960, pp. 149–54.

Fagin, N. Bryllion. "In Search of an American *Cherry Orchard*." *Texas Quarterly* 1 (1958): 132–44.

Green, Elizabeth Lay. *The Paul Green I Know*. Chapel Hill: North Caroliniana Society, 1978.

Ilacqua, Alma A. "Paul Green—In Memoriam: A Bibliography and Profile." *Southern Quarterly* 20 (1982): 76–87.

Isaacs, Edith J. R. "Paul Green: A Case in Point." *Theatre Arts Monthly* 25 (1941): 488–98.

Kenny, Vincent S. *Paul Green*. Boston: Twayne, 1971.

Lazenby, Walter S., Jr. *Paul Green*. Austin: Steck-Vaughn, 1970.

Long, Richard A. "The Outer Reaches: The White Writers and Blacks in the Twenties." *Studies in the Literary Imagination* 7 (1974): 65–71.

Malone, Andrew E. "An American Folk Dramatist." *Dublin Magazine* 4 (1929): 31–42.

McCalmon, George and Christian Moe. *Creating Historical Drama*. Carbondale: University of Southern Illinois Press, 1965, pp. 286–87, 377–80.

Pearce, Howard D. "From Folklore to Mythology: Paul Green's *Roll, Sweet Chariot*." *Southern Literary Journal* 3 (1971): 62–78.

Sievers, W. David. *Freud on Broadway*. New York: Hermitage House, 1955, pp. 311–21.

Walters, Thomas N. "Paul Green's Transcendent Theater of the Imagination: *In Abraham's Bosom*." *Interpretations* 13 (1981): 48–58.

Young, Stark. *Immortal Shadows*. New York: Charles Scribner's Sons, 1948, pp. 88–90, 127–31, 223–26.

———————— JACOB H. ADLER ————————

Lillian Hellman
(1905–1984)

Lillian Hellman was, after Tennessee Williams, the most important dramatist to come from the South and to write about it. Although from the 1930s to the 1960s she was frequently dismissed as unimportant (in spite of many Broadway awards and honors), it has become increasingly clear she was one of the two or three most important pre–World War II American playwrights, and that her first two volumes of memoirs are as distinguished as her best plays.

BIOGRAPHY

Lillian Hellman, an only child, was born in New Orleans on 20 June 1905. Her father, also a New Orleans native, was the son of German Jewish immigrants. Her mother was from a wealthy Jewish family long established in Demopolis, Alabama, which, after brief sojourns in Cincinnati and New Orleans, moved, early in Hellman's life, to New York. In financial straits, her parents also moved to New York; thereafter, Hellman, through her childhood and early adolescence, spent six months of each year in New Orleans and six in New York, staying, as her parents apparently did, with her father's two sisters in the one city and her mother's family in the other. Hellman reports in her memoirs that she modeled the Hubbards on her mother's family. Her mother was the model for Birdie in the two Hubbard plays and, more precisely, for Lavinia in *Another Part of the Forest*; her paternal aunts were at least somewhat the models for the sisters in *Toys in the Attic*. Obviously her family, for better or worse, influenced her strongly. Her black childhood nurse Sophronia also exerted a formative influence.

As revealed in her memoirs, Hellman experienced numerous traumatic childhood experiences, including an attempted rape by a psychotic cousin; serious quarrels with her father, after one of which she ran away; the shock of learning that her father had a mistress; and the similar shock of learning that a young maternal great-aunt was a morphine addict and the mistress of her black chauffeur—this last instance being the model for Albertine Prine in *Toys in the Attic*. Her childhood also made her aware of a variety of extreme violence besides the attempted rape, a fact that may partially account for the violence in her plays: suicide in *The Children's Hour*, murder in the next three plays, a severe beating in *Toys in the Attic*, and the symbolic violence of blackmail in five of the six major plays. Additionally, Hellman's two French adaptations involve extreme violence.

Hellman graduated from high school in New York and spent three years at New York University, deliberately choosing not to finish her degree, though she later took some work at Columbia. She then read manuscripts for Horace Liveright and met, in those early years, many people who later became famous in literature and drama. In 1925 she married one of them: Arthur Kober, a budding dramatist. She became an occasional book reviewer for the New York *Herald-Tribune*, spent some time in Paris with Kober, and from 1927 to 1930 read plays for Herman Shumlin. In 1930 she and Kober moved to Hollywood, where she soon became a scenario reader for MGM and met, among others of the famous or to-be-famous, Dorothy Parker, who became her lifelong friend, and Dashiell Hammett, who became her lifelong (though with interruptions) companion. She and Kober divorced but remained friends, Hellman later being matron of honor at his second marriage. With useful criticism from Hammett setting a pattern that would continue, she wrote *The Children's Hour*, which Shumlin directed, as he did her next four plays. Dedicated to Hammett, the play seems to have been strongly considered for the Pulitzer Prize but was rejected because of its treatment—frank for its time—of homosexuality.

Hellman returned to Hollywood for a time as a scenario writer and began writing the film script for *The Children's Hour*, to be called *These Three*. In accordance with Hays Office rules, the play's homosexual triangle was changed to a traditional triangle. (Much later, in 1962, *The Children's Hour* was filmed in its original form.) Late in 1936, her next play, *Days to Come*, opened on Broadway and quickly failed. She later went to Europe, where she visited Russia. She also visited Spain to show her support for the Loyalists during the Spanish Civil War.

Involved in more traveling and various work in Hollywood, Hellman found time in the next few years to write *The Little Foxes*, which she dedicated to Kober. Produced in 1939, it was a popular and critical success; it remains Hellman's best-known play. In the same year, she bought a farm in Westchester County, where she and Hammett spent much of their time, though from 1943 to 1969 she also owned a home in the city.

Before the United States entered World War II, in 1941, *Watch on the Rhine*, a play based on the horror and danger of Nazism, opened to receptive audiences and won Hellman the Drama Critics Circle Award. In 1943 her film *The North Star* was produced; it concerned Russian hardship during the war. In 1944 her play *The Searching Wind*, based on American diplomatic failures in the historical prewar crises, won great acclaim, although it drew part of its success from its relevance to the war years. Since that time, the play has not been regarded as one of her best. Also in 1944, she went on a cultural mission to Moscow at the request of the United States government—ironically, in view of her later political troubles—and visited the Polish front. In 1946 *Another Part of the Forest* was produced, with Hellman directing it herself. Previously considered less successful than *The Searching Wind*, it is now regarded more highly.

Hellman's political troubles began in 1948 when she learned that she was on a secret Hollywood blacklist. Her adaptation of Emanuel Roblès' *Montserrat* was produced in 1949 and ran for about two months; in the same year, Marc Blitzstein's opera based on *The Little Foxes* had an almost equal run. In 1951 *The Autumn Garden*, her own favorite, had only slightly more success, although it too is now considered one of her best plays.

Shortly afterward, Hellman's political problems became grave. Summoned before the McCarthy Committee, Hammett refused to testify and was sentenced to six months in prison for contempt. The next year Hellman herself was called before the House Un-American Activities Committee. She was dismissed from testifying without penalty, but was openly blacklisted. She was forced to sell her farm and was, she said, sufficiently damaged financially that she had to work in a New York department store under an assumed name, although her poverty was apparently short-lived. She published in 1955 an edition of Chekhov's letters (her last two original plays are more Chekhovian than, as the earlier ones were, Ibsenian), and her adaptation of Jean Anouilh's *The Lark* was produced successfully. During the same year, she bought a home on Martha's Vineyard. In 1956 a musical version of Voltaire's *Candide*, for which Hellman wrote the libretto, ran for two or three months—not a commercial success, despite the collaboration of such luminaries as Dorothy Parker, Richard Wilbur, and Leonard Bernstein.

Toys in the Attic opened in 1960 to the longest run of any Hellman play since *The Children's Hour* and won her a second Drama Critics Circle Award. But any joy over this event was dimmed by Hammett's failing health. He died early in 1961, and as a soldier in both world wars, he was buried in Arlington Cemetery.

Hellman moved in 1962 to another house on Martha's Vineyard, her home until her death. Her last play, *My Mother, My Father, and Me*, adapted from Burt Blechman's novel *How Much?*, quickly failed.

Over her remaining years, Hellman taught at various universities, won many honorary degrees, and was elected to membership in several prestigious organizations. She also continued to be politically active and to travel. But until her first book of memoirs appeared (*An Unfinished Woman*, 1969), her only literary endeavors were an adaptation of Horton Foote's novel *The Chase* as a movie script (1966), and an edition, *The Big Knockover* (1966), of Hammett's short stories and short novels.

With *An Unfinished Woman* (which won the National Book Award), Hellman's literary career took on added luster that increased with the publication of three additional volumes of memoirs, especially the second, *Pentimento* (1973). The first volume is reasonably chronological, though with many significant hiatuses. As its subtitle indicates, the second is primarily *A Book of Portraits*, depicting such persons as two weird relatives and the famous Julia. (It also includes portraits of Dorothy Parker, Hammett, and Hellman's black maid Helen.) The next volume of memoirs, *Scoundrel Time* (1976), considerably shorter than the first two, is devoted to Hellman's problems with the House Un-American Activities Committee and other related circumstances. The final volume, *Maybe* (1980), still shorter and by far the least prominent of the four, is subtitled *A Story*; one is unclear as to how much is fact, how much (as Hellman herself says) is unreliable memory, and how much (if any) is fiction. It is concerned primarily with a childhood friend who again and again came mysteriously into and out of her life.

Remaining surprisingly active until her last year, Hellman spent more and more of her time at her home on Martha's Vineyard, until she died of heart failure on 30 June 1984.

MAJOR THEMES

Three of Hellman's statements expressive of her outlook and ideas are famous:

1. I am a writer. I am also a Jew. I want to be quite sure that I can continue to be a writer and that if I want to say greed is bad or persecution worse, I can do so without being branded by the malice of people who make a living by that malice. (from *Twentieth Century Authors*)

2. I long ago came to the conclusion that I was not a political person and could have no comfortable place in any political group. (also from *Twentieth Century Authors*)

3. I am most willing to answer all questions about myself. I have nothing to hide from your Committee and there is nothing in my life of which I am ashamed. . . . But . . . I am not willing, now or in the future, to bring bad trouble to people who, in my past association with them, were completely innocent of any talk or any action that was disloyal or subversive. I do not like subversion or disloyalty in any form and if I had ever seen any I would have considered it my duty to have reported it to the proper authorities. But to hurt innocent people whom I knew many years ago in order to save myself is, to me, inhuman and indecent and dishonorable. I cannot and will not cut my conscience to fit this year's fashions. . . . (from her letter to the Chairman of the House Committee on Un-American Activities, 1952)

Hammett had been a Communist Party member, but there is apparently no evidence to indicate that Hellman was, although it is possible to feel that at least for a time in her earlier years she was insufficiently aware of the horrors of Soviet rule. She has also been criticized for writing the script of *The North Star*, a movie about the Russian people during World War II, yet one must remember that Russia and the United States were then allies, and the horrors inflicted on the Russian people by the German armies are indisputable. In any case, Hellman's political views, as reflected in her life and work, remained controversial until her death.

What her plays seem principally to reflect is that "greed is bad and persecution worse." In *The Children's Hour* the psychotically malicious Mary Tilford is guilty of a form of persecution in her false accusation of homosexual activity between the two headmistresses of the boarding school at which she is a student, as well as in her blackmailing another student into supporting the accusation. Her grandmother is unintentionally guilty of persecution in believing her granddaughter and convincing her friends to remove their children from the school. The result is the school's ruin and the suicide of one of the headmistresses, Martha, who, after they have lost a slander suit against the grandmother, cannot bear the realization of homosexual feelings toward her friend. Martha's aunt, who had taught at the school, fails to return from abroad to testify at the slander trial, when her testimony would undoubtedly have resulted in her niece's vindication. Mary's grandmother learns, too late, that the accusation was false; she gains some comfort from persuading the surviving headmistress, Karen, to accept a large financial gift, but her decision to keep her psychotic granddaughter at home rather than in an institution insures that she herself will be a victim of "persecution" for the rest of her life.

In the two Hubbard plays, *The Little Foxes* and *Another Part of the Forest*, the greed and persecution are central and obvious. Already very well-to-do, Ben and Oscar Hubbard and their sister Regina Giddens, the wife of a banker, seek to become wealthy by joining with a Northern entrepreneur in establishing cotton mills in their Alabama town at a time (1900) when cotton mills were still centered in New England. Regina and Ben are brilliant, personable, and almost totally evil. Equally evil, Oscar and his son Leo are stupid, repellent, and in Oscar's case a petty persecutor of blacks, a member of the Klan. Regina needs money from her husband, Horace, in order to join with her brothers as the majority stockholders in the firm. Horace, seriously ill with heart trouble, refuses her the money, not wishing to add to the already serious exploitation of blacks and poor whites in the region. In a moment of crisis, Regina withholds heart medicine from Horace, allowing him to die. Meanwhile, Leo, who works at Horace's bank, has, with the connivance of his father and uncle, stolen bonds from Horace's safe deposit box. These bonds can be used as collateral for the brothers to get enough money without Regina's contribution, thus cutting Regina out. But Regina learns of the theft from Horace before he dies and blackmails her brothers into giving her a commanding share of the business, being, as she says, perfectly willing to take the other course and report their theft to the police if necessary. At the end, Ben becomes aware that Regina may be responsible for Horace's death, and the play closes with the possibility that he will, in time, learn enough to blackmail Regina.

But as the play concentrates on the persecutors, it also deals with the victims. The victims among the lower classes are always a part of the background, but

Regina's two black servants make us directly aware of Oscar's treatment of blacks, and of their desperately low place in the community. Horace is an unwitting victim, intelligent and wealthy, but still, after twenty years of marriage, not adequately aware of his wife's capacity for evil. Birdie, a dependent Southern aristocrat and an alcoholic, is dominated and physically abused by her husband, Oscar; but she has the courage at least once to rebel and warn Regina's daughter Alexandra when she learns that there may be a plan to force Alexandra to marry Leo. Alexandra herself, at the end of the play, has the courage to plan to walk out on her mother, by whom she has previously been dominated, and, she says, fight the evil that the family represents—although Hellman herself commented that she did not believe that Alexandra would succeed. At any rate, Hellman displays compassion for the victims. It is possible to view the play, as some critics have, as anticapitalistic, but there are wealthy characters in other plays whom she presents favorably, such as Horace in *The Little Foxes*. Viewed as a whole, her plays show that wealth and poverty do not make the absolute difference. Persecutors can be rich or poor, victims can be rich or poor, those who fight persecution can be rich or poor.

Another Part of the Forest, set in 1880, shows how the Hubbards got to be so despicable; once again we find the pattern of societal and familial persecution, of cold and malicious blackmail within the family, and of victims—especially Lavinia, the siblings' mother—presented sympathetically. But there is one new aspect in the pattern. In *The Little Foxes* Horace and Birdie have cultural interests, but the Hubbards decidedly do not. In *Another Part of the Forest*, their father, a financial and paternal tyrant who in the end becomes a victim of Ben, has strong cultural interests (the only one of Hellman's greedy persecutors to display this pattern) and hence is perhaps the most complex character in any of her plays.

Watch on the Rhine, set near Washington on the estate of a wealthy matriarch, Fanny Farrelly, and her son David, has hovering over it the aura of the Nazis, the ultimate representatives of persecution. The year is 1940. Fanny's daughter Sara is visiting with her husband Kurt and her three children. Kurt is a member of the German underground. Also visiting is the daughter of an old family friend and her husband, a penniless Rumanian count, eager to get money and status by ingratiating himself with the Nazis. He discovers Kurt's underground identity and attempts blackmail: Hellman's almost inevitable symbol of greed and persecution. The family would provide it, but Kurt realizes that the count cannot be trusted, that, blackmail received or not, he will go to the German embassy with the story, and that he will thus endanger not only Kurt and his underground friends but the very goals of the underground. And so Kurt, a man who advocates peace and nonviolence, kills the count as an act of war, and the family, awaking to the Nazi danger, supports Kurt in his escape to Mexico, from where he will return to Germany. Oddly but successfully, the form of the play is comedy of manners, and there is much humor in it, as well as a display of genuine love and genuine heroism to be matched in no other Hellman play, and indeed in few plays anywhere in modern drama. It reveals, as *The Children's Hour* does, great skill in the characterization of children.

The Farrellys come to understand the Nazi horror and hence, within the limits of possibility, to combat it. The characters in Hellman's next play, *The Searching Wind*, in a world of pre–World War II diplomacy where realization might have saved destruction, did not realize in time and thus failed.

Hellman's last two original plays, *The Autumn Garden* and *Toys in the Attic*, are involved only minimally with persecution and greed. What both seem primarily to say is that most people do not want what they think they want and do not like it if they get it. It is not, as in *Watch on the Rhine*, that some characters have misunderstood the *world*, but that most of them fail to understand *themselves*; and if they learn to do so, as a few do in each play, the understanding will not affect their lives. Thus, in the summer-vacation boardinghouse on the Gulf Coast in *The Autumn Garden*, a retired general learns that he does not want the divorce and freedom he had long thought he wanted, but that knowledge simply means that he will go on, as he has for many years, enduring a miserable marriage. And the two sisters in the family home in New Orleans in *Toys in the Attic* learn that they do not want money to travel as they long thought they did, and they do not want their brother to succeed as they had always assumed they did; so life will continue in its dreary, monotonous pattern.

But the idea of persecution is not completely gone. In *The Autumn Garden*, Nick—a weak, unpleasant, but somewhat pathetic character—victimizes his wife and makes some attempt to victimize others, apparently a regular pattern in his life; and the half-French niece of the proprietress, who wants desperately to return to France where she grew up, insists on blackmailing to obtain the money to do so even though it was offered to her as a gift. In *Toys in the Attic*, the ne'er-do-well brother obtains a hundred thousand dollars in a legal but exploitative fashion, and, by giving his sisters some of the money, attempts to control their lives. And the sister who is especially unable to bear the idea of her brother's independence successfully maneuvers his loss of the money, endangering his life in the process.

The two plays Hellman adapted from the French, Emanuel Roblès's *Montserrat* and Jean Anouilh's *The Lark*, both involve the battle against the persecution of foreign rule, in the person of an ally of Simón Bolívar in the first and of Joan of Arc in the second.

Another aspect of most of the plays is nonconformity. Hellman's life and memoirs indicate that she was a lifelong nonconformist, beginning in her childhood. A major example from *An Unfinished Woman* is her insisting that her black nurse Sophronia sit with her in the front of the bus in New Orleans, causing a tremendous ruckus. A famous example from her adulthood (although some have questioned the veracity of the story) was her dangerous trip into Nazi Germany to aid her friend Julia. Her plays display an admiration for nonconformists, such as Kurt; and because Ben and Regina and their father are certainly not conformists, the two Hubbard plays convey a certain humorous admiration for them (along with intense revulsion), a combination Hellman indicated she felt toward her Uncle Jake, on whom Ben was modeled. Toward the *weak* persecutors (Oscar and Leo Hubbard, the count in *Watch on the Rhine*, Nick in *The Autumn Garden*) Hellman displays mainly contempt. And she displays admiration for the more or less helpless victims who want to fight back, and hence be nonconformists, such as Addie, the black maid in *The Little Foxes*, and in *Another Part of the Forest* even the Hubbard's mother Lavinia, who has wanted to leave home and devote her life to the blacks and be part of their religious culture, and who will finally, perhaps, be able to do so.

The other examples are less clear-cut. The independent, wealthy grandmothers in *The Children's Hour*, *Watch on the Rhine*, and *The Autumn Garden* are viewed respectively with pity, humorous admiration, and neutrality. The half-French niece is viewed, at best, neutrally also, although she is certainly nonconformist. The intensely nonconformist Albertine Prine in *Toys in the Attic* can hardly be admired for her lack of concern for her daughter, but Hellman's final stance seems ambivalent.

Finally, there are in Hellman's plays set in the South, and in her memoirs, various insights into the Southern world, past and present: the attitude toward blacks and "poor whites," the beginnings of industrial development, the strong sense of family, the special world of New Orleans and the bayous, the effects of the Civil War. Hellman's plays reveal at least as much about the South as do those of Tennessee Williams; in some respects, such as the historical backgrounds and the presentation of blacks, they reveal more.

SURVEY OF CRITICISM

Since the publication of her volume of memoirs and the revival of a number of her plays (and possibly also because she had become almost the only survivor among important playwrights of the 1930s), scholarly and critical publication about Hellman has burgeoned. Jacob H. Adler's *Lillian Hellman*, a monograph (1969), was the first work of more than article length. Preceding the memoirs, it analyzes the plays.

Three important books have subsequently appeared: Richard Moody's *Lillian Hellman: Playwright* (1972), Doris N. Falk's *Lillian Hellman* (1978), and Katherine Lederer's *Lillian Hellman* (1979). Moody's book is important primarily because he had Hellman's assistance in gathering biographical information (although he also relies considerably on *An Unfinished Woman*); because he provides useful information about the earlier drafts of her plays (to be found in the collection at the University of Texas); and because he provides summaries of the critics' views of each play. In a sense a biography, the book actually concentrates on the plays. Moody's summaries of Hellman's plots at times contain small inaccuracies, and he is inclined to overemphasize Freud as an influence. Otherwise, his judgments are usually sound and well expressed, although they rarely open up new ground.

Falk's book concentrates on what she regards as two types of Hellman's plays: the "despoiler" plays (*Little Foxes, Another Part of the Forest, Watch on the Rhine*) and the "bystander" plays (*Searching Wind, Autumn Garden, Toys in the Attic*). The despoiler-bystander division seems for the most part illuminating and accurate. The Hubbard plays, for example, concentrate on the Hubbards, the despoilers, although there are also bystanders, such as Birdie, Lavinia, and possibly Horace. In *The Autumn Garden*, on the other hand, all the characters are bystanders who let things happen to them, except the two strong characters, the grandmother and the half-French niece, and except Nick, who is an interferer constantly damaging people's lives; but the play concentrates on the bystanders. The one play in which Falk's categorization seems doubtful is *Watch on the Rhine*. The Rumanian count in the play attempts unsuccessfully to be a despoiler, and the Nazi power in Europe looming over the play is despoiler in the extreme. But the play concentrates on Fanny and David, who have been bystanders and learn not to be, and on Kurt and his family, who have been fighting the despoilers and will go on doing so, even, if necessary, unto death. Falk deals effectively with the first three volumes of memoirs. Although there are a few errors in her book and some of her judgments and opinions seem dubious, the book is primarily sound and insightful.

Lederer's book seems, on the whole, the best of the three. It is built to a considerable extent on her good use of the categories in Robert Boies Sharpe's *Irony in the Drama*, although as Lederer says, irony cannot be used as an approach to *Watch on the Rhine*, because in that play the major characters live in accordance with what they believe, and the naive characters, lifted out of their naivete, learn to live, and act, in accordance with proper beliefs. But a play such as *The Little Foxes* is filled with a variety of irony, and this approach enables Lederer to see what many other critics have not seen: Hellman's work frequently contains a good deal that is funny and views sympathetically those characters who are not open to irony, even if they are weak. Lederer's plot summaries are effective, as are her criticisms and analyses. But the definitive book on Hellman, a larger-scale book exploring more thoroughly and deeply her life, her work, and her place in the world of drama, past and present, has yet to be written.

Another indication of the revival of interest in Hellman is that within two years (1979–80), three book-length bibliographies were published: those by Mark W. Estrin, Mary Marguerite Riordan, and Steven H. Bills. The three vary greatly in format, content, and, to a certain extent, accuracy and completeness. Estrin's is especially valuable for its thorough and discerning introduction, and for the simplicity, completeness, and apparent accuracy of its format and content: an astonishingly lengthy annual listing of writing about Hellman, 1934–79, all with annotations ranging from suitably brief to needfully extensive. Riordan's book is especially valuable for her year-by-year chronology of Hellman's adult life, 1922–78, with many interesting sidelights. Within the bibliography itself, her division of items into various categories is sometimes confusing, and there is an occasional error; but the book is on the whole very useful. Bills's format is different from either Estrin's or Riordan's, and once again it provides some material that the others do not. His long section on reviews of the plays is probably the most useful, although it contains some serious errors.

Other works deserving special mention include (1) Bernard F. Dick's *Hellman in Hollywood*, which deals in illuminating detail with the production and value of all of Hellman's plays turned into films (whether by Hellman or others); Hellman's original film script, *The North Star*; with works by others (such as Sidney Kingsley's *Dead End*) that she adapted for the screen; and with the movie *Julia*, taken from her story in *Pentimento*. (2) Margaret Case Harriman's "Miss Lily of New Orleans: Lillian Hellman" (3) Thomas Meehan's "Miss Hellman, What's Wrong with Broadway?" (4) John Phillips and Anne Hollander's "The Art of the Theatre: Lillian Hellman, An Interview." Finally, certain standard works on modern drama are important with regard to Hellman, including Winifred L. Dusenbury's *The Theme of Loneliness in Modern American Drama* and (within the limits of the approach) David W. Sievers's *Freud on Broadway*. Books surprisingly not important regarding Hellman, or which ignore her altogether (and thereby may illustrate some critics' disregard or dislike of her), include Robert B. Heilman's *The Iceman, The Arsonist, and The Troubled Agent: Tragedy and Melodrama on the Modern Stage* (1973); Ruby Cohn's *Dialogue in American Drama* (1971), which does not even mention Hellman; and Thomas E. Porter's *Myth and Modern American Drama* (1969) (likewise).

BIBLIOGRAPHY

Works by Lillian Hellman

The Children's Hour. New York: Alfred A. Knopf, 1934.
Days to Come. New York: Alfred A. Knopf, 1936.
The Little Foxes. New York: Random House, 1939.
Watch on the Rhine. New York: Random House, 1941.
Four Plays, with an introduction by the author. New York: Random House, 1942.
The North Star. New York: Viking Press, 1943.
The Searching Wind. New York: Viking Press, 1944.
Another Part of the Forest. New York: Viking Press, 1947.
Montserrat, an adaptation from the French play by Emanuel Roblès. New York: Dramatists Play Service, 1950.
The Autumn Garden. Boston: Little, Brown, 1951.
The Selected Letters of Anton Chekhov, translated by Sidonie K. Lederer, edited by Hellman, with an introduction. New York: Farrar, Straus, 1955.
The Lark, adapted from the play by Jean Anouilh. New York: Random House, 1956.
Candide. A Comic Operetta Based on Voltaire's Satire. Book by Lillian Hellman, score by Leonard Bernstein, lyrics by Richard Wilbur, other lyrics by John Latouche and Dorothy Parker. New York: Random House, 1957.
Six Plays, with an introduction by the author. New York: Modern Library, 1960.

Toys in the Attic. New York: Random House, 1960.

My Mother, My Father, and Me, based on Burt Blechman's novel *How Much?* New York: Random House, 1963.

"The Art of the Theatre: Lillian Hellman, An Interview," with John Phillips and Anne Hollander. *Paris Review* 33 (Winter-Spring, 1965): 64–95. Reprinted in George Plimpton, ed., *Writers at Work*. Third Series. New York: Viking, 1968.

The Big Knockover: Selected Stories and Short Novels of Dashiell Hammett. Edited and with an introduction by Hellman. New York: Random House, 1966.

An Unfinished Woman—a Memoir. Boston and Toronto: Little, Brown, 1969.

The Collected Plays. Boston and Toronto: Little, Brown, 1972.

Pentimento, A Book of Portraits. Boston and Toronto: Little, Brown, 1973.

Scoundrel Time, with an introduction by Garry Wills. Boston and Toronto: Little, Brown, 1976.

Three [An Unfinished Woman, Pentimento, Scoundrel Time]. Boston: Little, Brown, 1979.

Maybe, A Story. Boston and Toronto: Little, Brown, 1980.

Studies of Lillian Hellman

Adler, Jacob H. *Lillian Hellman*. Southern Writers Series, No. 4, Austin, Texas: Steck-Vaughn, 1969.

———. "Miss Hellman's Two Sisters." *Educational Theatre Journal* 15 (May 1963): 112–17.

———. "The Rose and the Fox: Notes on the Southern Drama." *South: Modern Southern Literature in its Cultural Setting*. Ed. Louis D. Rubin, Jr., and Robert D. Jacobs. Garden City, N.Y.: Doubleday, 1961, pp. 349–75.

Bills, Steven H. *Lillian Hellman: An Annotated Bibliography*. New York and London: Garland, 1979.

Clark, Barrett H. "Lillian Hellman." *College English* 6 (October 1944): 127–33.

Dick, Bernard F. *Hellman in Hollywood*. Madison, N.J.: Fairleigh Dickinson University Press, 1982.

Downer, Alan S. *Fifty Years of American Drama, 1900–1950*. Chicago: Henry Regnery, 1951.

Dusenbury, Winifred L. *The Theme of Loneliness in Modern American Drama*. Gainesville: University of Florida Press, 1960.

Estrin, Mark W. *Lillian Hellman: Plays, Films, Memoirs: A Reference Guide*. Boston: G. K. Hall, 1980.

Falk, Doris V. *Lillian Hellman*. New York: Frederick Ungar, 1978.

Felheim, Marvin. "*The Autumn Garden*: Mechanics and Dialectics." *Modern Drama* 3 (September 1960): 191–95.

Gould, Jean. *Modern American Playwrights*. New York: Dodd, Mead, 1966.

Harriman, Margaret Case. "Miss Lily of New Orleans: Lillian Hellman." *Take Them Up Tenderly*. New York: Alfred A. Knopf, 1945, pp. 94–109.

Holman, Lorena Ross. *The Dramatic Works of Lillian Hellman*. Uppsala: Almqvist and Wiksell, 1973.

Krutch, Joseph W. *The American Drama Since 1918*. New York: G. Braziller, 1957.

Lederer, Katherine. *Lillian Hellman*. Boston: Twayne, 1979.

Meehan, Thomas. "Q: Miss Hellman, What's Wrong with Broadway? A: It's a Bore." *Esquire* 58 (December 1962): 140, 142, 235–36.

Moody, Richard. *Lillian Hellman, Playwright*. New York: Pegasus, 1972.

New York Theatre Critics' Reviews, annual volumes.

Riordan, Mary Marguerite. *Lillian Hellman: A Bibliography: 1926–1978*. Metuchen, N.J.: Scarecrow Press, 1980.

Sievers, W. David. *Freud on Broadway: A History of Psychoanalysis and the American Drama*. New York: Hermitage, 1955.

Triesch, Manfred, comp. *The Lillian Hellman Collection at the University of Texas*. Austin: University of Texas Press, 1966.

Weales, Gerald. *American Drama Since World War II*. New York: Harcourt, Brace and World, 1962.

Zora Neale Hurston
(1891–1960)

For more than a decade after her death in 1960, Zora Neale Hurston was an all-but-forgotten writer. Although she was a major writer of the Harlem Renaissance and a pioneer among black folklorists and anthropologists, she did not win in her lifetime great recognition or wealth. Rediscovered in the early 1970s, her life and writings have attracted the attention of scholars, critics, and general readers. Her importance is now firmly established.

BIOGRAPHY

Zora Neale Hurston was born 7 January 1891 in Eatonville, Florida, an all-black town. Her father, John Hurston, was a Baptist preacher, and her mother, Lucy Potts Hurston, was a former teacher who encouraged Zora in her schoolwork and in the development of a strong self-image. Growing up in a small community of self-governing black people profoundly affected Zora's perspective, making it difficult for her to grasp the full impact of racism on the lives of other black Americans. As Robert E. Hemenway, Hurston's biographer, suggests, she used her own childhood experiences in Eatonville as the standard for measuring the quality of all black life in America.

The most significant event in Hurston's youth was the death of her mother, which shattered her secure and supportive homelife. After his wife's death, the Reverend Hurston soon remarried and sent Zora to Jacksonville, Florida, to live with an older brother and his family. Unwilling to quit school to work as maid and baby-sitter for her brother, constantly in disagreement with her stepmother and therefore unwelcome in her father's home, Zora took a job as a wardrobe mistress with a traveling Gilbert and Sullivan Repertory Company to earn money for her education. When the tour ended eighteen months later in Maryland,

Hurston enrolled in Morgan Academy (now Morgan State University), where she completed her high school studies.

In 1918 Hurston moved to Washington, D.C., where for five years she was a part-time student at Howard University. During summer 1918 she worked as a waitress at an exclusive nightclub and later obtained a job as a manicurist in a black-owned barbershop serving whites only. In *Dust Tracks on a Road*, her autobiography, she describes her reactions to a black man's bold attempt to integrate the shop. Afraid that such challenges to the status quo would drive away white customers and jeopardize her job, Hurston was outraged by the man's action, calling him a troublemaker who deserved to be thrown out of the shop when he refused to leave voluntarily. Hurston's negative response to the man's defiant stand against Jim Crow is consistent with her lifelong abhorrence of overt social protest and her tendency to accept racism as an inevitable part of American life.

At the end of the summer, Hurston enrolled in the Howard Prep School and successfully completed requirements that permitted her to enroll in Howard's college division; she planned to be an English major. An intermittent student, she completed a year and a half of college work in her years at Howard, 1919–24. Howard Academy granted her an associate degree in 1920. Financial problems and at least one serious illness contributed to her failure to complete her B.A., but she enjoyed Howard and was active in its life.

At Howard, Hurston met two men who became important in her life, Herbert Sheen and Alain Locke. Hurston and Sheen fell in love, but Sheen left Howard in 1921 to pursue his dream of becoming a physician. Although Hurston and Sheen lived in different cities for several years, their love for each other remained strong, and they were married in 1927. But Hurston's refusal to give up her career as writer and folklorist and become a full-time housewife, as Sheen desired, caused the marriage to fail. They were divorced in 1931, but maintained a cordial relationship until her death, nearly 30 years later.

Dr. Alain Locke, a professor of philosophy at Howard and promoter of black artists during the Harlem Renaissance, recognized Hurston's potential as a writer and published her first short story, "John Redding Goes to Sea," in *Stylus*, the school's literary magazine. A highly respected literary critic, Locke introduced promising black artists to patrons of the emerging Harlem Renaissance. Hurston was almost certainly one of the young writers who benefited from Locke's influence on the New York City literary scene in the 1920s.

By January 1925 Hurston's worsening financial situation and her growing desire to devote more time to her writing prompted her to drop out of Howard and to move to New York City, where the Harlem Renaissance was in full flower. Charles S. Johnson, noted black sociologist and editor of *Opportunity* magazine, had urged Hurston to come to New York after he read some of her short fiction, probably at the request of Locke. Johnson was so impressed with Hurston's early work that he published her short story "Drenched in Light" in the 20 December 1924 *Opportunity*. Shortly after her arrival in New York City, destitute but characteristically optimistic about her future, Hurston became aware of the relationship between young artists and influential patrons. To bring the artists and their potential supporters together, Johnson organized writing contests and awards dinners sponsored by *Opportunity*.

When Hurston's story "Spunk" (1925) won second prize in the first *Opportunity* contest, Zora met Fannie Hurst, a well-known novelist of the period and one of the contest judges. Hurst hired her as a live-in secretary; however, Hurst soon discovered that her new employee possessed neither the clerical skills nor the temperament of an efficient secretary. But captivated by Hurston's wit and ebullient personality, Hurst retained her as companion and chauffeur. This new arrangement apparently worked well, for Hurston writes warmly of the association.

Hurston also met Mrs. Annie Nathan Meyer at one of the *Opportunity* dinners. Mrs. Meyer, a novelist and cofounder of Barnard College, arranged for Hurston to attend Barnard on a scholarship, thus making it possible for Hurston to earn a college degree. She received her B.A. from Barnard in 1928.

Despite the demands of college life, Hurston continued to write, publishing "Muttsy" in *Opportunity* (1926), "The Eatonville Anthology" in the *Messenger* (1926), and *Color Struck: A Play in Fire!!* (1926). In 1927 Hurston published another play, *The First One*, in *Ebony and Topaz*, edited by Charles S. Johnson. Although these Renaissance publications are not among Hurston's best work, they are a significant record of her early attempts to find her voice as a writer and of her first efforts to weave folklore and her own Eatonville experiences into the fabric of her art. Hurston's Renaissance writings suggest her reluctance to confront racial issues and reveal her fascination with the marriage relationship and its capacity to survive a crisis.

But it was Hurston's personality, not her writing, that made her the most colorful and memorable figure of the Renaissance. Wallace Thurman's satiric portrait of Hurston in his novel *Infants of the Spring* (1928) captures the essence of Zora's personality, as many of her fellow Renaissance artists perceived it. Sweetie Mae Carr, Thurman's fictional representation of Hurston, is a short-story writer who is more noted for her wit and charisma than for her skill as a writer. Sweetie Mae, like Hurston, is a master raconteur who delights in sharing her enormous store of folktales with her friends. Moreover, Sweetie Mae shamelessly curries the favor of white patrons by deftly playing the role of the "primitive Negro" so popular with whites during the Renaissance. To be sure, Thurman's satiric portrayal of Hurston correlates well with nonfictional accounts of her behavior during the Renaissance. For example, Langston Hughes presents a similar picture of Hurston in his autobiography, *The Big Sea*. But Hughes and other Renaissance artists who knew Zora also recognized many positive aspects of her personality, the most significant being her strong sense of racial pride, unyielding self-esteem, irrepressible sense of humor, and her stubborn will to succeed.

Although Hurston quickly established herself as a dominant personality on the Harlem literary scene, entertaining some people and offending others, she also seriously pursued her interests in anthropology and Afro-American folklore. Studying with Columbia University's famed anthropologist Dr. Franz Boas, she shifted her efforts from creative writing to the scientific study of folklore. She discovered a fascinating new way in which to view the folk materials that she had absorbed so thoroughly during her childhood in Eatonville and shared so zestfully with her Renaissance friends. As an anthropologist, Hurston came to regard the vast body of folklore available for study in black communities throughout the South as a national treasure, a rich cultural heritage that should be preserved.

Encouraged by Boas and supported financially by a research fellowship, Hurston returned to the South in 1927 on her first folklore collecting trip, confident that her Southern background would facilitate her research. But as Hurston notes in her autobiography, her efforts to collect folklore in a familiar Southern setting failed dismally. In *Dust Tracks* she admits that informants were unresponsive to her requests for folk materials because she had unwittingly created a barrier between herself and them by approaching them as a "proper talking" college student, rather than as an insider, one of the folk. Hurston did not repeat this mistake on subsequent folklore collecting trips, and the results are impressive.

Funded by Mrs. Rufus Osgood Mason, a wealthy patron of Renaissance artists, Hurston returned to the South on her second trip to collect folklore in December 1927. Presenting herself as an ordinary member of the black folk community, she was warmly received in lumber camps, turpentine camps, and "jook joints" across rural Florida; and she collected an incredibly rich variety of folk materials. But the frequently wild, violent social atmosphere so common to the rural labor camps and jook joints made Hurston's fieldwork exciting and dangerous. Her easy manner and popularity with male informants aroused jealousies among the women, causing some of them to threaten her with knives and guns. In her autobiography Hurston describes several frightening encounters with jealous, irate women, and insists that her friend, Big Sweet, a large, fearless woman, protected her from physical assaults. Unwilling to subject herself to further risks and satisfied with the results of her collecting efforts, Hurston moved on to the safer, more familiar environment of Eatonville and vicinity.

When Hurston was ready to collect folklore dealing with hoodoo and conjure, she traveled to New Orleans, where she studied with some of that city's leading "two-headed doctors." Determined to get the most authentic material available, she immersed herself in the world of hoodoo and conjure, participating in strange ceremonies and assisting the "doctors" with the preparation of medicines and charms. Her courage and patience enabled her to collect a great deal of material on her subject. When she returned to her sponsor in New York, she took with her an impressive body of research that she later edited and published as *Mules and Men* (1935).

Although Hurston is known primarily as a novelist and folklorist, she was also a prolific journalist, publishing articles on a variety of topics in some of the nation's most widely read magazines and newspapers. Between 1942 and 1945, for example, she published six articles in the *American Mercury*, four in *Negro Digest*, and one in the *Saturday Evening Post*. Hurston's journalism from this period illustrates her keen sensitivity to the expectations of her audience and her ability to meet those expectations in finely crafted personal essays. In articles written for the *American Mercury* and its predominantly white audience, Hurston assumes the persona of a wise, friendly expert, offering white readers an insider's perspective on Afro-American life and culture. The articles are usually accommodating in tone. But in articles written specifically for *Negro Digest* and its predominantly black audience, Hurston drops that tone and views American society with a more critical eye.

"The 'Pet' Negro System," published in the *American Mercury* (June 1943), and "My Most Humiliating Jim Crow Experience," published in *Negro Digest* (June 1944), illustrate Hurston's ability to adapt subject and tone to fit the expectations of her audience. In the first article, she tells her readers that the "pet" Negro system, a long-standing Southern custom allowing whites to grant special privileges to their favorite black "pets," while denying them to the majority of blacks, created opportunities for black progress and achievement within the framework of the Jim Crow system. Moreover, she claims that Northern journalists unfamiliar with the "pet" Negro system portrayed most black Southerners as poor, illiterate, exploited sharecroppers. To correct that misconception, Hurston assures her readers that the special assistance of influential white friends has produced "many Negroes of opulence and education," and that "these comfortable, contented Negroes are as real as the sharecroppers." Although there is some truth to Hurston's argument, her attitude indicates a lack of social awareness, an unwillingness to confront reality.

In contrast, "My Most Humiliating Jim Crow Experience" reveals a marked social consciousness. Eager to challenge the notion that blacks could escape Jim Crow by moving to the North, Hurston locates her Jim Crow experience in New York City, symbol of the promised land for many black Southerners. According to Hurston's account, one of her white friends arranged for her to see an eminent stomach specialist to treat a recurring digestive ailment. When Hurston discovered that the doctor planned to examine her in a linen closet filled with soiled towels and uniforms, she considered leaving the office in protest. But sensing an opportunity to have a little fun at the doctor's expense, Hurston "stayed to see just what would happen, and further to torture him more." Describing her exit after the examination was completed, Hurston writes: "I got up, set my hat at a reckless angle and walked out, telling him that I would send him a check, which I never did." Hurston's black audience could readily understand her way of handling this discrimination.

In the 1950s Hurston's journalism focused primarily on political issues. For example, her involvement with the 1950 Florida senatorial primary race between Claude Pepper, the liberal candidate, and George Smathers, the conservative candidate, prompted her to write an article in which she accuses Miami's black voters of selling their votes to the Pepper campaign. The article, "I Saw Negro Votes Peddled," was rejected by the *American Mercury* and the *Saturday Evening Post* before the *American Legion Magazine* agreed to publish it. Hurston's unsubstantiated allegations of voter fraud are a result of her indignation against voters who overwhelmingly rejected her candidate, Smathers, in favor of Pepper. Another example of Hurston's political writings from the 1950s is "A Negro Voter Sizes Up Taft," published in the *Saturday Evening Post*. The distinguishing feature of these articles is their conservative tone; Hurston attempts to persuade liberal black voters to accept a conservative political philosophy.

With her income limited mostly to small fees earned from the sale of journalistic pieces, Hurston worked faithfully on her last book, a novel based on the life of Herod the Great, even though all attempts to interest a publisher in it had failed. Destitute and in poor health, she was placed in the St. Lucie County Welfare Home in Ft. Pierce, Florida, in 1959. She died there on 28 January 1960. Her grave remained unmarked until 1973, when Alice Walker placed a marker there. Walker explains that Hemenway's research on Hurston's life and her own sense of duty "as a black person, a woman, and a writer" inspired her to find and mark Hurston's grave.

MAJOR THEMES

In more than 30 years as a writer, Hurston produced a canon impressive both for its volume and its variety. She wrote novels, short stories, plays, essays, her autobiography, journalistic pieces, book reviews, and musical reviews. She was also an important folklorist. A new generation of readers is discovering especially her four novels.

Jonah's Gourd Vine (1934) is an excellent first novel. The central characters, the Reverend John Pearson and his wife, Lucy, are loosely based on Hurston's parents. The plot focuses upon the minister's inability to control his lust for women. John Pearson—a mulatto whose mother, stepfather, and siblings eke out a meager living as sharecroppers—meets Lucy Potts, whose family own their land and command the respect of the black community. After a brief courtship, John and Lucy are married despite her mother's objections. John subsequently moves his family to Florida, where he receives the call to the ministry. Under Lucy's guidance, John rises to power and prominence in the church. But his promiscuity threatens to destroy his career when church officials attempt to oust him from his pulpit. Lucy, who is also aware of John's sexual exploits, helps him to defeat the challenge of the disgruntled church members. But after Lucy's death, John is turned out of his church.

The novel explores the conflict between John's religious commitment and his carnal desires, while examining the effects of a negative self-concept upon his career and marriage. Mrs. Potts's vehement opposition to John's marriage to her daughter made him feel painfully unworthy of Lucy. He lacked the moral strength to overcome his sense of inadequacy. Through her portrayal of John

Pearson, Hurston helps her readers to see that preachers are only human, that they are heirs to the same weaknesses that afflict other men and women.

Hurston's second novel, *Their Eyes Were Watching God* (1937), is her finest achievement. It has influenced many contemporary black women writers. Paying a very high tribute to *Their Eyes*, Alice Walker insists, "There is no book more important to me than this one. . . . " And Sherley Anne Williams confesses that after reading *Their Eyes*, "I became Zora's for life." Hurston's classic novel is usually read as a love story, focusing on Janie Crawford's search for a meaningful love relationship. Although Janie's search for love is a dominant theme in the book, an equally significant theme examines Janie's quest for self-definition, the right to explore her unique personhood. Three characters in the novel, Nanny Crawford, Logan Killicks, and Jody Starks, attempt to define Janie's identity for her. The novel's main action focuses upon Janie's rejection of false identities and her determined search for a relationship which allows her to know and to express her inner sense of self.

To insure Janie escapes the hard work and sexual exploitation that many unmarried and unprotected black women experience, Nanny, Janie's grand-mother, arranges a marriage between Janie and Logan Killicks, an old man who owns 60 acres and a comfortable home. Although Nanny's intentions are good, her insistence upon the marriage amounts to a violation of Janie's personhood, a transgression against Janie's right to chart the course of her own life.

Janie's first husband, Logan Killicks, sees her as a work horse and expects her to share his devotion to the 60 acres and the neatly furnished home. Convinced that she cannot accept the role of the mindless drudge her husband demands, Janie runs away to Eatonville with Jody Starks, a man she meets near the Killicks farm. Janie marries the ambitious Starks, but she soon discovers that he too intends to reshape her identity to suit himself. Jody becomes the mayor of Eatonville and imposes severe restrictions on Janie's participation in the life of the community. Determined that his wife should not be treated like an "ordinary" woman, the proud Mayor Starks forces Janie onto a pedestal, making it impossible for her to assert her true sense of self.

After Jody's death, Janie meets Vergible Woods, called Tea Cake. She falls in love with him and marries him, even though he is much younger than she. Janie realizes that Tea Cake, unlike her other husbands, has no desire to force an identity upon her, that he respects her individuality. At last Janie's inner self is allowed to blossom in an environment full of love and sharing.

Their Eyes Were Watching God is a brilliantly executed story of a black woman's search for love, but it is also a compelling study of a woman's quest for selfhood. For like Edna Pontellier, the dissatisfied wife and mother who rejects identities her husband and society try to impose upon her in Kate Chopin's *The Awakening*, Janie Crawford insists upon the right to define herself.

Hurston's third novel, *Moses, Man of the Mountain* (1939), has received less acclaim than has *Their Eyes*, but may rival it in power. Unlike most critics of Hurston's work, Darwin T. Turner argues that "Miss Hurston's most accomplished achievement in fiction is *Moses, Man of the Mountain*,'' citing her superb handling of satire, irony, and dialect as the grounds for his assessment. In *Moses* Hurston explores the Moses legend in terms of its African roots, the image of Moses as a great hoodoo man. In Hurston's version of the story, the Hebrews speak black dialect and generally reflect the Afro-American slave experience and folk culture. Hurston invests the story with a wonderfully authentic folk humor that humanizes the Hebrews, making them resemble black characters in her previous novels.

The humor relieves the serious tone associated with the Hebrews' exodus from Egypt, but it never degenerates into burlesque or farce. Whether it is Moses' wife pestering him to declare himself king so that she may be his queen or the Hebrews complaining about the order to pack quickly for the escape out of Goshen, Hurston's humor is appropriate and effective. Moreover, the central themes of the novel, the importance of sustaining hope in the midst of despair, and the destructive nature of jealousy and vanity, lend weight and power to Hurston's treatment of the Moses legend.

Seraph on the Suwanee (1948), Hurston's last published novel, is her least successful, commercially and artistically. Unlike the central characters in her other novels, the main characters in *Seraph on the Suwanee* are white; several minor black characters appear as farm laborers or in other traditional occupations. The plot centers on Arvay Henson's awakening to her sense of self-worth. Like John Pearson in *Jonah's Gourd Vine*, Arvay feels unworthy of her spouse, and much of the novel explores the conflicts that her negative self-concept creates in her marriage. Jim Meserve, Arvay's husband, comes from a family of Southern planters, although the family wealth was lost before his birth. Arvay, who thinks of herself as a backwoods ''cracker,'' feels inferior to Jim and cannot understand why he chooses to marry her when so many prettier, more socially prominent girls are eager to be his wife. Arvay's inner conflict makes it impossible for her to express her love for Jim. But, by the end of the novel, she realizes her own personal worth and strength and feels secure enough to return her husband's love. Thus, Arvay's story reflects a universal truth, the notion that one must learn to love and accept himself or herself before he or she can truly love others.

Despite its universal theme, *Seraph on the Suwanee* did not sell well, probably because the white characters lack depth and authenticity, and because some situations in the novel are excessively melodramatic. The novel does, however, make effective use of language, humor, and Hurston's strong sense of place, her familiarity with the folklore of white Southerners.

Hurston's wide knowledge of folklore informs all of her novels, but her folklore collections, *Mules and Men* (1935) and *Tell My Horse* (1938), best demonstrate her achievement as folklorist and anthropologist. *Mules and Men* is generally held to be a classic text in Afro-American folklore. The distinguished folklorist Alan Lomax calls it ''the most engaging, genuine and skillfully written book in the field of folklore.'' Hurston organized the book into three sections; the first two deal with Florida folktales and Louisiana hoodoo, respectively, and the third presents a brief survey of Negro folk songs. The tales provide insights into the ways folklore functions in the black community. But the omission of tales of social protest is perhaps the book's one serious weakness.

In the second section Hurston individualizes the hoodoo doctors, noting their peculiar personality quirks and providing detailed accounts of the sights and sounds of the secret initiation ceremonies. Hurston also captures the mystery and drama of folk magic, placing it in a realistic context for her readers. We see the uses of hoodoo in the black community when Hurston describes "doctors" who promise their clients success in love or anonymous revenge against their enemies. Because hoodoo addresses such basic human concerns as love, hate, and the desire for money and power, it continues to be a strong force in many black communities. Hurston's brilliant research into Louisiana hoodoo gives readers a rare insider's perspective on the work of the hoodoo man.

Despite the absence of standard scholarly apparatus and critical commentary by the author, *Mules and Men*, with its superbly rendered tales, its highly authentic treatment of hoodoo, and its valuable selection of folk songs ranks among the finest collections ever assembled by an American folklorist.

Of Hurston's seven published books, *Tell My Horse* is probably the least well-known. Supported by two Guggenheim Fellowships, Hurston collected folklore in Jamaica and Haiti and then reported her research. *Tell My Horse* is a fascinating mixture of travelogue, folklore, and political commentary. Although the travelogue and folklore are effectively presented to complement each other, the political commentary is too often superficial and naive. In her discussion of Haitian politics, Hurston praises the American occupation of Haiti in 1915 for its restoration of stability in the midst of political upheaval, but she fails to mention the racism and fiscal mismanagement the Haitians suffered at the hands of the Americans. Other political commentary in the book is similarly incomplete.

The most richly descriptive part of the book deals with voodoo practices in Haiti. Avoiding "staged" ceremonies performed for tourists, Hurston waits patiently to experience authentic, nonpublic voodoo customs and rituals. She records in vivid details the rites she witnessed, re-creating the sights and sounds. *Tell My Horse* is informative and enjoyable reading for general audiences, as well as for specialists in the field.

Few people read *Tell My Horse*, but Hurston's autobiography, *Dust Tracks on a Road* (1942), is perhaps her most widely read nonfiction work. Winner of the Anisfield-Wolf Award for its contribution to race relations, *Dust Tracks* was a commercial success, especially with white readers. Many black readers, however, deplored the book's accommodationist tone. Hurston's autobiography continues to be one of her most popular books, as the recent publication of a second edition suggests, but perceptive readers now view it as an interesting, although often unreliable, text. Alice Walker addresses this concern when she observes, "After the first several chapters, it rings false." Mary Helen Washington argues that "Zora used all sorts of manipulative and diversionary tactics in the autobiography to avoid any real self-disclosure." Those chapters focusing on Hurston's childhood experiences in Eatonville are convincing, but sections detailing her adult life are evasive and problematic. Furthermore, the newly established fact that Hurston was born in 1891, not 1901, as she had said, will have a profound effect on the way readers approach *Dust Tracks*.

SURVEY OF CRITICISM

Darwin T. Turner was among the first critics of the 1970s to assess Hurston's life and work. He devotes a chapter to her in *In a Minor Chord* (1971), but the strong anti-Hurston attitude that permeates the chapter frequently overwhelms Turner's fine critical acumen. Alice Walker and Mary Helen Washington were also at the forefront of the Hurston revival. Both have published articles on Hurston, and Walker has edited a Hurston reader, *I Love Myself When I'm Laughing*, featuring Washington's excellent introduction, "Zora Neale Hurston: A Woman Half in Shadow."

In 1977 Robert E. Hemenway published his carefully researched study, *Zora Neale Hurston: A Literary Biography*. Hemenway examines Hurston's life in detail, correcting many errors and misconceptions found in earlier accounts. In addition to the biographical information, Hemenway writes astute critical commentary on most works in the Hurston canon. Three years after Hemenway's book appeared, Lillie Pearl Howard published *Zora Neale Hurston* (1980). Although Howard's book adds nothing new to the Hurston biography, it offers insightful analyses of Hurston's major work.

A Rainbow Round Her Shoulder (1982), a collection of essays edited by Ruthe T. Sheffey of Morgan State University, is another valuable source of Hurston criticism. The collection consists of papers presented at a symposium on Hurston's life and work held at Morgan State University in October 1981. Several important Hurston scholars, including her biographer, contributed essays to the collection.

Daryl C. Dance's bibliographical essay on Hurston is also an essential research tool. Published in *American Women Writers: Bibliographical Essays* (1983), Dance's essay is a well-written, thorough survey of texts treating Hurston's life and works. Included in the essay are sections covering primary works, biography, manuscripts, letters, and criticism.

Increasingly, Hurston's work is treated in journal articles, doctoral dissertations, and feminist criticism. But much work in Hurston studies remains to be done. A standard edition of her works is needed, and her short fiction and nonfiction writings, especially the journalism, deserve much more attention from critics and scholars than they are now receiving. Zora Neale Hurston is undoubtedly a major figure in Afro-American literature, and her reputation will continue to grow, as her life and works become more widely known.

BIBLIOGRAPHY

Works by Zora Neale Hurston

Jonah's Gourd Vine. Philadelphia: J. B. Lippincott, 1934.
Mules and Men. Philadelphia: J. B. Lippincott, 1935.
Their Eyes Were Watching God. Philadelphia: J. B. Lippincott, 1937.
Tell My Horse. Philadelphia: J. B. Lippincott, 1938.
Moses, Man of the Mountain. Philadelphia: J. B. Lippincott, 1939.
Dust Tracks on a Road. Philadelphia: J. B. Lippincott, 1942.
Seraph on the Suwanee. New York: Charles Scribner's Sons, 1948.

Studies of Zora Neale Hurston

Byrd, James W. "Zora Neale Hurston: A Novel Folklorist." *Tennessee Folklore Society Bulletin* 21 (1955): 37–41.

Dance, Daryl C. "Zora Neale Hurston." *American Women Writers: Bibliographical Essays*. Ed. Maurice Duke et al. Westport, Conn.: Greenwood Press, 1983.

Giles, James R. "The Significance of Time in Zora Neale Hurston's *Their Eyes Were Watching God*." *Negro American Literature Forum* 6 (Summer 1972): 52–53, 60.

Hemenway, Robert E. *Zora Neale Hurston: A Literary Biography*. Chicago: University of Illinois Press, 1977.

Howard, Lillie Pearl. *Zora Neale Hurston*. Boston: Twayne, 1980.

Lupton, Mary Jane. "Zora Neale Hurston and the Survival of the Female." *Southern Literary Journal* 15 (Fall 1982): 45–54.

Rayson, Ann. "*Dust Tracks on a Road*: Zora Neale Hurston and the Form of Black Autobiography." *Negro American Literature Forum* 7 (Summer 1973): 42–44.

Sheffey, Ruthe T., ed. *A Rainbow Round Her Shoulder: The Zora Neale Hurston Symposium Papers*. Baltimore: Morgan State University Press, 1982.

Smith, Barbara. "Sexual Politics and the Fiction of Zora Neale Hurston." *Radical Teacher* 8 (May 1978): 26–30.

Turner, Darwin T. *In a Minor Chord*. Carbondale: Southern Illinois University Press, 1971.

Walker, Alice. "In Search of Zora Neale Hurston." *Ms. Magazine*, March 1975, pp. 74–79, 85–89.

Wall, Cheryl A. "Zora Neale Hurston: Changing Her Own Words." *American Novelists Revisited: Essays in Feminist Criticism*. Ed. Fritz Fleischmann. Boston: G. K. Hall, 1982, pp. 370–93.

Washington, Mary Helen. "Zora Neale Hurston: A Woman Half In Shadow." Introduction to *I Love Myself When I'm Laughing*. Ed. Alice Walker. Old Westbury, N.Y.: Feminist Press, 1979.

Willis, Miriam. "Folklore and the Creative Artist: Lydia Cabrera and Zora Neale Hurston." *CLA Journal* 27 (September 1983): 81–90.

Randall Jarrell
(1914–1965)

Now recognized as a major American poet in the second generation of modern-ism, Randall Jarrell emerged as a poet under the influence of several Vanderbilt Fugitives. Dramatic poems containing a diversity of American characters draw upon war experiences, fairy-tale settings, and European backgrounds, as well as scenes of middle-class American life. Jarrell's achievement also includes his roles as critic, novelist, author of children's stories, translator, editor, and college teacher.

BIOGRAPHY

The cupbearer of the gods, Ganymede, sits in bas-relief on the west pediment of Centennial Park's Parthenon in Nashville, Tennessee. He holds a cup of ambrosia; a female figure rests beneath him. Randall Jarrell, at about the age of eleven, posed for the figure, his childhood behind him. It had hardly passed in the company of the gods. Born in Nashville on 6 May 1914, Jarrell and his family moved to Long Beach, California, when he was only a few months old. There, the parents separated when the boy was nine. His father, a photographer, went his own way; his mother and the two sons returned to Nashville. Young Randall went back to California for about a year with his paternal grandparents in 1926. The chronicle of that childhood world of Hollywood movie sets, boys' adventure stories, and his extended family is set out in two late poems, "The Lost World" and "Thinking of the Lost World," both told from the child's point of view. Even this artificial world could not last, and against his protes-tations, Jarrell was summoned back to Nashville, where he and his brother were often surrounded by his mother's relatives.

Jarrell attended Nashville's Hume-Fogg High School, where his widow re-members, "he played on the tennis team, edited the literary magazine, starred in some plays, and headed the Honor Roll.'' From there he enrolled in Vanderbilt University and began to be a poet. He benefited from exceptional instructors. John Crowe Ransom, one of them, remembers, ''I knew him when he was a child, almost, a sophomore and *enfant terrible* in my writing class at Vanderbilt. But even then, when you came to read what he had written, you knew that he had to become one of the important people in the literature of our time.'' Allen Tate was not an instructor but also knew Jarrell at Vanderbilt: ''Although he seemed as an undergraduate to have read all English poetry . . . he was I believe a psychology major almost to the time of his graduation. . . . It struck all his older friends at that time that his technical knowledge of verse must have come to him without labor: an early poem, 'A Description of Some Confederate Soldiers,' had a formal mastery that I, nearly fifteen years older, could not have equaled.'' Donald Davidson and Robert Penn Warren were also his instructors there. Jarrell was editor of a humor magazine, *Masquerader*. Graduating in 1935, Jarrell stayed on for an M.A. in English under the direction of Ransom, though Davidson became his adviser when Ransom moved on to Kenyon College. Jarrell's thesis on A. E. Housman was completed in 1939.

Jarrell followed Ransom to Kenyon. Even though his M.A. thesis was incomplete, he became an instructor at the Ohio college and shared a room for a while with the younger Robert Lowell in Ransom's house. Ian Hamilton, Lowell's biographer, recounts the influence of Jarrell: ''Jarrell was the exciting older brother: possibly the first person of more or less his own generation that Lowell genuinely held in awe. Not all the late-night chat . . . was about Henry James or Homer; a good deal of it was about Jarrell—his tennis, the girlfriend he had in town, his sometimes scathing view of Ransom, and also his conceit, his intransigence, his primness.'' Peter Taylor was another student there at the time. His lifelong friendship with the poet began with his enrollment in Jarrell's American literature class. ''To Randall's friends there was always the feeling that he was their teacher. To Randall's students there was always the feeling that he was their friend. And with good reason in both cases,'' recalls Taylor.

From Kenyon, Jarrell went on to teach at the University of Texas in Austin from 1939 to 1942. He married a colleague there, Mackie Langham, in 1940. In the same year, twenty of his poems appeared under the title ''The Rage for the Lost Penny'' in *Five Young American Poets*. His first complete volume, *Blood for a Stranger*, dedicated to Tate, followed two years later.

Jarrell is regarded today as one of the major American poets of World War II. Yet his years in the armed forces never took him to the European theater. He ''washed out'' of a pilot training program in Austin and became a private in the Air Force. He was stationed at bases in Wichita Falls, Texas; Rantoul, Illinois; and, finally, Tucson, Arizona, where he was a celestial navigation instructor. The military experience figures prominently in his next volume, *Little Friend, Little Friend* (1945).

After the war Jarrell taught for a year at Sarah Lawrence College and was literary editor for the *Nation* in New York City. In 1947, through the intercession of Peter Taylor, Jarrell and his wife were offered teaching positions at Woman's College of the University of North Carolina at Greensboro. The campus and city became Jarrell's permanent home.

His marriage ended in divorce in 1952, and later in the same year he married Mary von Schrader, whom he had met at a writer's conference in Boulder, Colorado. "To be married to Randall was to be encapsulated with him," she remembers in a 1967 memoir. "We took our three meals a day together, every day. I went along to his classes and he went along on my errands. I watched him play tennis and he picked out my clothes. Sometimes we were brother and sister 'like Wordsworth and Dorothy.' " Jarrell also became stepfather to Mary's two daughters from a previous marriage, Alleyne and Beatrice.

Jarrell's skill and patience as a teacher occupied the greater part of his life. His colleague Robert Watson at Greensboro recalled, "Student after student told me that Mr. Jarrell seemed to know ten times better than they what their poems and stories were about. He never tried to impose any rules or any system. The best teachers of writing, he always claimed, were the best works of the best writers." In 1948 he taught at the summer seminar in American civilization at Salzburg. Two other trips to Europe followed in 1958 and 1963. He taught at Princeton in 1951–52 and was consultant in poetry at the Library of Congress from 1956 to 1958.

All the while, poems, reviews, essays, translations, children's books, and a novel appeared. His third volume of poetry, *Losses*, was published in 1948, followed by *The Seven-League Crutches* three years later. Important and influential essays on Frost, Ransom, Stevens, Moore, Williams, and others appeared in *Poetry and the Age* (1953). His *Selected Poems* was issued in 1955, but two more volumes succeeded it: *The Woman at the Washington Zoo* (1960), earning the National Book Award, and *The Lost World* (1965). His novel, *Pictures from an Institution*, was published in 1954. Other collections of criticism also followed: *A Sad Heart at the Supermarket* (1962), *The Third Book of Criticism* (1969), and *Kipling, Auden & Co., Essays and Reviews 1935–1964* (1980). *The Complete Poems* was published in 1969. An edition of his letters edited by Mary Jarrell appeared in 1985.

Honors and recognition surrounded him at the end, including an honorary degree from Bard College. The O. Max Gardner Award for that member of the faculty from the consolidated University of North Carolina who is judged to have "made the greatest contribution to the welfare of the human race" was presented to Jarrell in 1962. There was time, too, for his hobbies, a favorite cat, professional football on television, the opera, tennis, and a Mercedes 190 SL. "Randall didn't join things," his wife recalls, "unless you count Phi Beta Kappa, the National Institute of Arts and Letters, and the Army."

The final year of Jarrell's life was perhaps his most difficult. From February to May of 1965 he was a patient at Memorial Hospital in Chapel Hill after suffering a nervous breakdown. The following October he was back in the hospital at the physical therapy center under the care of an orthopedist. Jarrell was fond of walks, and on the evening of the fourteenth, he was walking on a road about a mile south of the hospital in Chapel Hill. The report of the investigating officer describes the occasion: "As the vehicle came abreast of the pedestrian [Jarrell] he lunged into the side of the vehicle, striking the left fender of the vehicle, his head striking the windshield, killing him instantly." He was fifty-one years old. Almost exactly four years earlier, 18 October 1961, Jarrell had been in Chapel Hill to be honored by the University of North Carolina Press and the Historical Book Club of North Carolina. Over a thousand people attended the tribute. His teacher from Vanderbilt days, Robert Penn Warren, praised Jarrell for the "way of pity, warmth, and appreciation, in which his poem[s] would round the world."

MAJOR THEMES

In the year before the appearance of his first volume, Jarrell published in the *New Republic* an early major poem, "90 North." In many ways it anticipates themes to which the poet would return repeatedly for the next quarter century. There is a quest for "meaning"; the vehicle is dream; the character is child-as-adult; the setting is dramatic; the conclusion is discovery. The poem begins as a young boy "clambered to bed" only to enact through sleep and dream a polar exploration and arrival at the North Pole: "My world spins on this final point / . . . of cold and wretchedness: all lines, all winds / . . . End in this whirlpool I at last discover." At this tip of the world there is only emptiness and solitude ("my companions lay frozen"). The region is correlative of his interior "North," a state "Where I die or live by accident alone." His knowledge is revealed as ignorance:

> nothing comes from nothing,
> The darkness from the darkness. Pain comes from the
> darkness
> And we call it wisdom. It is pain.

The poem eschews simple assuagements. *As* a poem, however, Jarrell's statement perdures as a challenge to meaninglessness, an artifact thrown back against the chaos it describes. Even its title names and makes an order.

For Jarrell the problem of human mortality and pain would find no resolution in religion or earthly meliorism. The early poems in particular stress a naturalism of necessity that governs indifferently all human fate. The only constant is change, as "Children Selecting Books in a Library" makes clear. Still, for Jarrell, in spite of persistent pain, life comes to mean more than victimization.

A later poem, "Seele im Raum," again depicts pain, this time that of a housewife who finds herself distanced in love from her husband and children. She is befriended at her dinner table by an imaginary eland, a phenomenon that eventually leads to her hospitalization. The animal is successfully banished; the housewife returns home. But the imaginary figure is restored as her son describes an eland in the newspaper one morning and as she discovers the meaning of the German word *elend*: wretched. The woman's dilemma is not presented as pathology but as pathos: " 'To own an eland! That's what I call life!,' " says the lonely woman. Her imagination, in the end, is her lifeline:

> This is senseless?
> Shall I make sense or shall I tell the truth?
> Choose either—I cannot do both.

The "truth" of human sorrow may be senseless and unreal, but its imaginary properties, corresponding to the needs of the heart, are true and have their own sense. Through art, as Jarrell says in "Children Selecting Books in a Library," "we live / . . . By trading another's sorrow for our own."

Jarrell's own poetic elands often emerge through the fantasy of fairy tales and folk legends. A mythic escape into the world of childhood occurs where good and evil, life and death, fear and courage, innocence and experience, desire and reality all contend—at times in violence and cataclysm, at times in miracle and resurrection. The simplicity and starkness of these narratives served Jarrell's poetic ends uniquely, and he turned to the tales of Jacob and Wilhelm Grimm, Hans Christian Andersen, and others, especially in the poems of the second half of his career. (He also translated some of the tales.) Perhaps the best known of these is "The Märchen," drawing upon the Hansel and Gretel story. Other such poems include "A Soul," "A Quilt-Pattern," "The Night before the Night before Christmas," "The Sleeping Beauty: Variation of the Prince," "La Belle au Bois Dormant," "Hohensalzburg: Fantastic Variations on a Theme of Romantic Character," "Cinderella," "The House in the Wood." Jarrell chose other kinds of literary sources in the poems, such as *Robinson Crusoe* for "The Island," Kipling's story "They" for "The Lost Children," or Pushkins's *Eugene Onegin* for "A Girl in a Library." All these sources function in a similar fashion in that they furnish reverberations rather than allusions for the poem. The narratives provide a setting and tone. They contribute not so much plot as *mythos*—childlike fantasies or dream states in which characters act out dramas of human success and failure. The technique is one T. S. Eliot had also appropriated in such poems as *Ash Wednesday* and *Four Quartets*, and Jarrell, though he developed the technique more elaborately, may well have begun with Eliot's example.

Jarrell is often acknowledged as America's foremost poet of World War II. Yet, though he served for four years in the Air Force during the war, he saw no military action himself, and in his poems the experience of war is another metaphor for the movement toward insight into the larger condition of human suffering. The poems include the plight not only of soldiers who are war's first victims but the other victims as well: the widow and mother, the prisoners of war, the wounded, the veterans. Most of Jarrell's war poems appear in *Little*

Friend, Little Friend, published in the year before his discharge, and *Losses* (1948). "The Death of the Ball Turret Gunner" is perhaps Jarrell's best-known poem:

> From my mother's sleep I fell into the State,
> And I hunched in its belly till my wet fur froze.
> Six miles from earth, loosed from its dream of life,
> I woke to black flak and the nightmare fighters.
> When I died they washed me out of the turret with a hose.

The paradoxical state of birth that is death in a B–17 or B–24 is accompanied by imagery that is appropriate to both states ("hunched in its belly," "wet fur froze," "hose"). The short and undiscursive compression of imagery into five lines is not typical of Jarrell's other war poems, but like many of them it treats the soldier as a child. "The secret of his war poems," says Helen Vendler, "is that in the soldiers he found children; what is the ball turret gunner but a baby who has lost his mother?" The young and innocent soldier doomed by war reappears in the best of Jarrell's war poems: "Eighth Air Force," "Mail Call," "Second Air Force," "Losses," and "Pilots, Man Your Planes."

Asked to select a favorite poem for the *Poet's Choice* anthology in 1962, Jarrell chose "Eighth Air Force" with this explanation: "I don't have any favorite single poem. Perhaps if I were choosing one poem for people to read it would be 'The End of the Rainbow,' but that is too long for use in your book. 'Eighth Air Force' expresses better than any other of the poems I wrote about the war what I felt about the war."

All of Jarrell's poems consistently confront defeat, pain, and death. The greatest pathos of war, for example, may belong to the survivor. In "Burning the Letters" a young woman, widowed and embittered by her husband's death in the war, turns sardonically away from the consolation of religion: "The dying God, the eaten Life / Are the nightmare I awaken from to night." Jarrell's poems, nonetheless, do not easily surrender in the search for transcendence. His very fondness for the fantasy world of fairy tale and legend encourages such a groping. A reunion between an otherworldly mermaid and a man during which the latter ("My poor soul") seems momentarily and supernaturally rescued from being "lost" occurs in "A Soul." In "The Night before the Night before Christmas" an adolescent girl whose mother is dead rejects belief in God but seems unable to escape a belief in and yearning for life after death. Like angels, she and her brother at death "look down over the earth . . . / Home, home, whispers the wind." The speaker in "Nestus Gurley" imagines the newsboy of the poem's title as a voice calling from the dead "When I lie coldly . . . / . . . In the grave that is not lit by anything / . . . Except our hope." Jarrell's larger "hope" for transcendence and immortality remains little more than that, however. His poems advance no systematic program of human salvation.

Jarrell's greatest strength as a poet lies in his creation of human characters who may metamorphose into various guises, like Nestus Gurley, but who are rooted in their simple humanity, a newsboy from Greensboro. The poems of Jarrell, in fact, give as comprehensive a portrait of America at mid-century as Browning gave of the Italian Renaissance or Sherwood Anderson gave of small-town America earlier in the century. In his partiality for ordinary lives—women as well as men, young as well as old, uneducated as well as cultivated, typically middle-class but often lower-class as well—Jarrell displays an expansive portraiture that one might, in a different way, associate with Whitman. In this sense, Jarrell is a far less personal poet than Roethke, Lowell, Bishop, or other of his contemporaries: it is not the episodes of the poet's individual and personal life that are documented. The poems are not lyrics in the conventional sense but dramatic narratives, stories in which the characters are defined and come to knowledge themselves or are agents in conveying it to others. Although such personages appear in virtually all his poems, the range of their humanity is wide: a woman government worker in "The Woman at the Washington Zoo," a guard in an art gallery in "In Galleries," a football hero in "Say Good-bye to Big Daddy," an aging housewife in "Next Day," a dead black child in "Lady Bates," a Southern black prisoner of war in "New Georgia," a psychiatrist in "Jerome," or a young girl who has fallen asleep over her books in "A Girl in a Library." Of the latter, Jarrell says what might be said of all these characters and the others, "You are very human."

Jarrell's poetry, beginning around 1940, represents the second wave of modernism. Cleanth Brooks is correct when he says of Jarrell that he "fully assimilated the poetry that came to prominence in the 1920's." The achievement of Jarrell, however, is his own: a consolidation of the gains made by modernism reformed into his own original voice.

SURVEY OF CRITICISM

Ten years before Jarrell's death, Sister M. Bernetta Quinn published a long essay on Jarrell in *The Metamorphic Tradition in Modern Poetry*. By placing the poet in the company of Pound, Stevens, Williams, Eliot, Crane, and Yeats, she helped establish his reputation as a major poet. Here was the first study to dwell extensively on Jarrell's use of fairy tales and other folk material in the metamorphosis of character and action in the poems. Her later book, *Randall Jarrell* (1981), in the Twayne series, is a competent general introduction to the works of Jarrell, but some of the biographical details are inaccurate.

The most detailed and useful study of the poetry is *The Poetry of Randall Jarrell* (1971), by Suzanne Ferguson. Close readings of all the major poems with careful attention to sources and allusions provide excellent introductory material. The book is ordered chronologically around major themes as they emerge in each succeeding volume. Helen Hagenbüchle's *The Black Goddess: A Study of the Archetypal Feminine in the Poetry of Randall Jarrell* (1975) is a

Swiss publication and, as a result, somewhat less accessible. Her thesis is that the tragedy of Jarrell's world is traceable to a conflict with a mother figure, who includes parent, the archetypal Great Mother, the muse, as well as house, pond, cave, forest, and other similar images. The book discloses Freudian and Jungian readings of Jarrell, but the view of the work is highly specialized and somewhat fragmentary. M. L. Rosenthal's *Randall Jarrell* (1972) appeared in the university of Minnesota Pamphlets in American Writers series. This introduction is necessarily sketchy: Rosenthal traces Jarrell's career as an attempt ''to make a European of himself'' through his interest in Rilke, the German *Märchen*, and in the ''neglected European heritage of Americans.'' He sees Jarrell as only partially successful in this ambition. Jerome Mazzaro's *Postmodern American Poetry* places Jarrell in the company of Auden, Roethke, Ignatow, Berryman, Plath, and Bishop. Jarrell is seen as a neo-Arnoldian in his value of poetry as a substitute for religion, one who embraces Freud's notion of art as ''a balance between emotion and idea or id and superego.'' That balance, says Mazzaro, is to be found most readily for Jarrell in the poets themselves (Goethe, Arnold, Auden).

The critical readings of Jarrell are still pioneering and preliminary. Comprehensive assessments, building on the work of Ferguson, remain to be completed. Ferguson's gathering of essays in *Critical Essays on Randall Jarrell* (1983) is a crucial first step toward a larger overview. Major reviews, as well as essays on the poetry, criticism, fiction, and translations of Jarrell, help to establish the poet's versatility and breadth.

Biography must still be culled from various essays, memoirs, and other fragments. A comprehensive life does not exist. The most useful book for insights into the poet's personality is *Randall Jarrell 1914–1965*, edited by Robert Lowell, Peter Taylor, and Robert Penn Warren and published shortly after Jarrell's death. Essays by Ransom, Tate, Lowell, Eleanor Ross Taylor, Peter Taylor, Robert Watson, and others bring Jarrell to life in various stages of his 51 years. Most valuable of all is Mrs. Randall Jarrell's ''The Group of Two,'' a reprint of a memoir appearing in *Harper's* in 1967. Mary Jarrell's other introductions and essays are also valuable. She has published in *Shenandoah* (Winter 1977) an affectionate memoir on Jarrell and Peter Taylor entitled ''Peter and Randall.'' Her review of Jarrell's *The Complete Poems* in the Fall/Winter 1976 issue of *Parnassas* has revealing comments about the origins of poems for Jarrell, especially his use of her own dream in ''The Lost Children.'' Her ''Reflections on Jerome'' in *Jerome: The Biography of a Poem* (1971) provides much background for the making of ''Jerome.'' ''Faust and Randall Jarrell,'' her afterword in Jarrell's translation of *Goethe's Faust, Part One* (1976), shows the American poet's special affinity with the German. Jarrell's letters, edited by Mary Jarrell, appeared in 1985.

Two useful but somewhat difficult to locate special issues on Jarrell are the Spring 1966 issue of *The Alumni News* of the University of North Carolina at

Greensboro and the Spring 1964 issue of *Analects*. The former contains memoirs by former students and literary colleagues; the latter is a collection of critical tributes.

BIBLIOGRAPHY

Works by Randall Jarrell

"The Rage for the Lost Penny," in *Five Young American Poets*. Norfolk, Conn.: New Directions, 1940. (Twenty poems by Jarrell.)

Blood for a Stranger. New York: Harcourt, Brace, 1942.

Little Friend, Little Friend. New York: Farrar, Straus & Giroux, 1945.

Losses. New York: Harcourt, Brace, 1948.

Poetry and the Age. New York: Vintage Books, 1953.

Pictures from an Institution. New York: Knopf, 1954.

The Seven-League Crutches. New York: Harcourt, Brace, 1957.

The Woman at the Washington Zoo: Poems and Translations. New York: Atheneum, 1960.

The Golden Bird and Other Fairy Tales of the Brothers Grimm, translated and introduced by Randall Jarrell. New York: Macmillan, 1962.

The Rabbit Catcher and Other Fairy Tales of Ludwig Bechstein, translated and introduced by Randall Jarrell. New York: Macmillan, 1962.

A Sad Heart at the Supermarket: Essays and Fables. New York: Atheneum, 1962.

The Bat-Poet. New York: Macmillan, 1964.

The Gingerbread Rabbit. New York: Macmillan, 1964.

The Animal Family. New York: Pantheon Books, 1965.

The Lost World. New York: Macmillan, 1965.

Selected Poems. New York: Atheneum, 1965.

The Complete Poems. New York: Farrar, Straus & Giroux, 1969.

The Third Book of Criticism. New York: Farrar, Straus & Giroux, 1969.

The Three Sisters by Anton Chekhov, translated by Randall Jarrell. London: Macmillan, 1969.

Snow-White and the Seven Dwarfs. A Tale From the Brothers Grimm. New York: Farrar, Straus & Giroux, 1972.

The Juniper Tree and Other Tales from Grimm. New York: Farrar, Straus & Giroux, 1973. (Four tales translated by Jarrell.)

Fly by Night. New York: Farrar, Straus & Giroux, 1976.

Goethe's Faust Part I: An English Translation by Randall Jarrell. New York: Farrar, Straus & Giroux, 1976.

A Bat is Born, from *The Bat-Poet* by Randall Jarrell. New York: Doubleday, 1977.

Kipling, Auden & Co., Essays and Reviews 1935–1964. New York: Farrar, Straus & Giroux, 1980.

Randall Jarrell's Letters: An Autobiographical and Literary Selection. Ed. Mary Jarrell. Boston: Houghton Mifflin, 1985.

Studies of Randall Jarrell

Beck, Charlotte H. *Worlds and Lives: The Poetry of Randall Jarrell*. Port Washington, N.Y.: Associated Faculty Press, 1983.

Ferguson, Suzanne. *The Poetry of Randall Jarrell*. Baton Rouge: Louisiana State University Press, 1971.
———, ed. *Critical Essays on Randall Jarrell*. Boston: G. K. Hall, 1983.
Hagenbüchle, Helen. *The Black Goddess: A Study of the Archetypal Feminine in the Poetry of Randall Jarrell*. Bern: Francke Vergal, 1975.
Hoffman, Frederick J., ed. *The Achievement of Randall Jarrell: A Comprehensive Selection of His Poems with a Critical Introduction*. Glenview, Ill.: Scott, Foresman, 1970.
Lowell, Robert, Peter Taylor, and Robert Penn Warren, ed. *Randall Jarrell 1914–1965*. New York: Farrar, Straus & Giroux, 1967.
Mazzaro, Jerome. "Between Two Worlds: Randall Jarrell." *Postmodern American Poetry*. Urbana: University of Illinois Press, 1980, pp. 32–58.
Quinn, Sister M. Bernetta. "Randall Jarrell: His Metamorphoses." *The Metamorphic Tradition in Modern Poetry*. New Brunswick: Rutgers University Press, 1955.
———. *Randall Jarrell*. Boston: Twayne, 1981.
Rosenthal, M. L. *Randall Jarrell*. Minneapolis: University of Minnesota Press, 1972.
Weisbert, Robert. "Randall Jarrell: The Integrity of His Poetry." *Centennial Review* 17 (Summer 1973): 237–56.

James Weldon Johnson
(1871–1938)

James Weldon Johnson was not a prolific writer, especially not of belles lettres. His primary works include only one novel, three volumes of poetry, and his autobiography, along with two anthologies of spirituals, an anthology of black poetry, a social-cultural history of blacks in Manhattan, and one book of social commentary. Yet his literary achievement is important because of the focus of his novel, the quality of his poetry (especially *God's Trombones*), and his significant influence on the subject matter and attitudes of other writers of his time, both black and white.

BIOGRAPHY

James Weldon Johnson was born James William Johnson in Jacksonville, Florida, on 17 June 1871. His home provided more stability and more cultural emphases than did most other homes in Jacksonville, black or white. As a child he was introduced early to the pleasures of books and music; emphasis on education marked his childhood and his career as well as that of his younger brother, the composer Rosamond Johnson. Their home had a cosmopolitan flare, partly because of Jacksonville's Latin immigrants and its tourist business, but more so from his parents' respect and longing for the cultural life of both New York and Nassau, where both of them had lived earlier. As a child and young man Johnson visited friends and relatives in both places. This background and Johnson's natural inclinations led to his early development of the somewhat aloof, detached personality he cultivated and became noted for. During his active years as a leader of his race through his work with the National Association for the Advancement of Colored People, he and others viewed his even and calm personality as a distinct asset for all that he was trying to accomplish.

During the years of Johnson's childhood, Jacksonville was seen as a progressive city and a good place for blacks to live. Johnson's mother taught in the Stanton School, the city's largest elementary school for blacks, from which James graduated in May 1887. Already he had begun to write stories and poems. In fall 1887 he entered Atlanta University, for both secondary and college work, graduating in 1894 as a leader in his class. During 1888–89 a yellow fever epidemic had kept him in Jacksonville, where he worked for Dr. Thomas O. Summers, a local white physician of exceptional culture and experience, who had a lasting influence upon him. While he was enrolled at Atlanta, his horizons broadened greatly. The concern with the issue of race pervasive at the university was new to him, and his employment as a teacher in rural Georgia during the summers of 1891 and 1892 gave him his first real experience and awareness of the difficulties faced by most American blacks. Also, during the summer of 1894 he toured New England as a member of the university's quartet, thereby gaining increased appreciation for black music. In summer 1893 he had worked at the World's Columbian Exhibition in Chicago, where he heard both Frederick Douglass and Paul Laurence Dunbar; and he began there a continuing friendship with Dunbar, under whose influence he began to write black dialect verse. During his Atlanta years he greatly improved as a speaker, and he wrote about 30 poems, most of them not racial in emphasis. Four of them appeared in university publications.

During his college years Johnson developed what was to remain one of his firmest beliefs, that blacks must take the initiative in improving their status. This view informed his goals as he served as principal of Stanton School (1894–1902), to which he had returned after graduation from Atlanta; and he extended its curriculum to include the high school grades. In 1895 he also founded a newspaper for Jacksonville blacks, the *Daily American*, which he edited until its demise in 1896. That same year he met W.E.B. Du Bois in Atlanta, and in 1898 he met Booker T. Washington in Jacksonville. Johnson read law, and in 1898 became the first black lawyer admitted to the bar in Duval County; he and Douglas Wetmore formed a partnership. Wetmore had passed for white at the University of Michigan Law School and later helped to inspire Johnson's novel. In 1900 James and Rosamond Johnson wrote "Lift Every Voice and Sing," which eventually became known as "the Negro national anthem." Johnson continued to write poetry, and in 1900 *Century Magazine* published his poem "Sence You Went Away."

Circumstances in Jacksonville and the great appeal of New York combined to lead him to move to New York in 1902, where he again joined his brother and Bob Cole to continue their success in writing popular songs for stage and home, usually with Negro themes, probably the best known of which was "Under the Bamboo Tree." The three were called "Those Ebony Offenbachs" and were Broadway successes. They also organized a song and dance act, famous for several years both in Europe and America. The Johnsons collaborated on over two hundred songs, and James then considered himself firmly a New Yorker. During this period, he also studied literature at Columbia University and discussed with his teacher, Brander Matthews, the novel he had begun. In addition, his interest in Republican politics, which had begun while he edited his Jacksonville newspaper, now took root in New York. He became active in the Colored Republican Club, headed by Charles W. Anderson, a confidant of Booker T. Washington. Also, the Johnsons and Cole wrote two songs for the 1904 campaign of Theodore Roosevelt. This involvement, and his knowledge of Spanish, led to his being offered the post of U.S. consul at Puerto Cabella, Venezuela, which he assumed in March 1906. In 1908 he was promoted to the consulship at Corinto, Nicaragua, a position he took in April 1909. He returned to New York to marry Grace Nail on 10 February 1910. In December 1912 the Johnsons moved back to the United States, and he resigned his consular post in 1913 in the wake of Woodrow Wilson's election as president.

While in Latin America, Johnson had completed his novel and had continued to write poetry, publishing such poems as "O Southland" in the *Independent* in 1907 and "O Black and Unknown Bards" in the *Century* in 1908. In mid–1912 his only novel, *The Autobiography of an Ex-Colored Man*, was published anonymously in Boston. Both its subject and its authorship caused some curiosity, but it was not widely noticed. When his poem "Fifty Years" appeared on the editorial page of the *New York Times* on 1 January 1913, it was immediately and widely praised on all sides; and he began to renew the idea of following a literary career. One immediate result of his decision was changing his middle name. After settling the estate of his father in Jacksonville, Johnson returned to New York. In the fall of 1914 he began writing editorials and a column called "Views and Reviews" for the *New York Age*, the oldest and most influential black newspaper in the city—giving him wide visibility and the opportunity to expound and develop his views on the social and political difficulties, opportunities, and goals of American blacks. He also worked hard for the presidential campaign of Charles Evans Hughes in 1916. Meanwhile, he had published several poems in the *Crisis*, and in 1917 his first volume of verse, *Fifty Years & Other Poems*, was published in Boston. Like his novel, it received sparse notice.

On the other hand, he had begun an affiliation in December 1916 that was to take most of his time, energy, and attention for the next fourteen years and thrust him upon the national scene as nothing else had or would. He joined his future to that of the then seven-year-old National Association for the Advancement of Colored People (NAACP), becoming its first field secretary. His efforts at organizing new chapters around the country, particularly in the South, were very successful, but also demanding. He said that everything in his life seemed to have been pointing him toward this work. Soon he was appointed acting secretary in the national office in New York, and with his new assistant, Walter White, began the many years of vigorous antilynching campaigns. In 1918 he returned to his work as field secretary, only to become the actual secretary in November 1920, a post in which he served with extensive involvement, genuine satisfaction, great effectiveness, and increasing respect, until his resignation in December 1930. During his NAACP years he published many articles and essays related to his work and the causes he espoused, but he took pains to keep alive also his creative inclinations and interests.

In 1922 Harcourt, Brace published *The Book of American Negro Poetry*, with Johnson's significant introduction. (A revised edition was published in 1931.) It was the first anthology of black poetry from a major American publisher. In 1925 Viking published *The Book of American Negro Spirituals*, with a long introduction by Johnson and musical arrangements by his brother. Its success led to their compilation of *The Second Book of Negro Spirituals*, published the following year. In 1930 Knopf published Johnson's *Black Manhattan*, an informal history (1626–1930), with its strong emphasis on the cultural achievements of blacks. He had completed this history while holding a Rosenwald Fellowship. Johnson's most significant literary achievement of the 1920s was his Negro sermons in verse. He wrote the first of these, "The Creation," in 1918, and it was published in the *Freeman* in 1920. "Go Down, Death" appeared in the *American Mercury* and "Judgment Day" in the *Century* in 1927, the year in which Viking also brought out *God's Trombones*, with all seven sermons and with illustrations by Aaron Douglas. In terms of quality, this book was the capstone of Johnson's literary career. His increased visibility and reputation as a writer also led to Knopf's reprinting his novel in 1927, with an introduction by Carl Van Vechten. (This time it was more widely noted.) His various literary work in the 1920s, his residence in Harlem, and his encouragement of and numerous associations with both black and white writers who wrote well on black themes made Johnson a significant part of the Harlem Renaissance of the 1920s (a phenomenon he preferred to think of as a flowering rather than a rebirth).

Early in 1932 Johnson began his duties as Adam K. Spence Professor of Creative Literature and Writing at Fisk University in Nashville, Tennessee, entering a less strenuous and more literarily focused period of his life than had been possible earlier. He had to be in residence only from January to June of each year. Although he had a house on the campus, he also retained a residence in Harlem and in Great Barrington, Massachusetts, and he continued to be an adviser to the NAACP and a national lecturer. Each fall from 1934 to 1937 he also taught courses on black literature and culture at New York University. For Johnson and his wife the 1930s were relatively happy years, years which also produced his somewhat mellow autobiography, *Along This Way*, published by Viking in 1933, and very favorably and widely received. The next year Viking published *Negro Americans, What Now?*, a statement of the basic attitudes and positions, especially favoring racial integration, which he had maintained and practiced during his NAACP years. In 1935 Viking published his *St. Peter Relates an Incident*, a satirical poem about racial segregation, which had been published for private distribution in 1930 and now was combined with many of his earlier published poems for general sale.

Tragically, Johnson was killed on 26 June 1938 in Maine when the car in which he was riding was stuck by a train. His funeral in Harlem on 30 June was attended by over 2,000 persons. He was buried in Brooklyn's Greenwood Cemetery, at his request wearing formal trousers and a lounging robe, a copy of *God's Trombones* in his hand.

MAJOR THEMES

James Weldon Johnson was born and grew up in the South, yet he did not think of himself as a Southern writer, nor did he want others to do so. He emphasized that his interest was in all black Americans, about whom he had well-formed, firm, and consistent beliefs, which are reflected in his writing and were the basis for all of his endeavors. He believed that American blacks had given a great deal to American life. To American folk culture they had with great imagination contributed music and tales that were enduring and that had influenced America's whole culture. He also felt that blacks had made genuinely worthwhile contributions to American literature, especially in poetry. He emphasized that in these achievements blacks could and should take great pride; they should think of themselves as Americans and should take the initiative to work with determination to better their standing in every aspect of American culture and life. Although he advocated pride in race, it was not to obscure an equal awareness of American pride and participation. If blacks were to improve their position, they must work toward standards as high as those aspired to by anyone else, and any unfairly discriminatory or prejudicial obstacles, especially legal ones, should be rigorously assaulted through political and legal channels. He was not for separatism, but for integration in all facets of culture, with full equality and opportunity. He believed this would be possible if blacks cultivated self-respect and if white Americans could be led to understand better the accomplishments, contributions, and importance of blacks in American society. He believed that the logic of such an approach would prevail because Americans on the whole were reasonable and were ready to accept the truth when it was made obvious to them. Johnson worked very hard, even to exhaustion, in his various vocations to apply these beliefs. His reserved, cautious, but urbane and self-confident personality surely led others to share his beliefs. Johnson always considered writing one of his important vocations, even when he was not devoting much time to it; and both his works and his encouragement of other writers, both black and white, were important in providing literary impetus, emphasis, and direction, particularly during the Harlem Renaissance.

Although his first book, *The Autobiography of an Ex-Colored Man*, suffers as a novel from inadequate development of plot and characterization and at times tends to lapse into sociological reporting and analysis, it did help its readers understand better the anguish and frustrations of blacks, particularly talented, intelligent, sensitive blacks, in a prejudiced and largely segregated society. The vicissitudes of its light-skinned protagonist, which finally lead him in desperation to pass for white, were intended to give the book's readers unprecedented insights, and Johnson rightly presumed that a first-person narrator would assist his goal. White readers left it better informed and more prepared to accept blacks as fellow human beings, without prejudice. Such responses encouraged greater opportunity for blacks. Reprinted in 1927, the novel had a wider audience and was more influential socially and literally. Carl Van Vechten's new introduction said it was like a composite picture of the Negro race in the United States in modern times, and it encouraged those writing with similar themes and purposes.

In many of its sections Johnson's novel was more propagandistic in tone than he usually advocated or generally practiced. His approach to poetry was, however, more indirect, less obtrusive, and probably more effective. Clearly his most notable poetic achievement is *God's Trombones*. Although there is some unevenness among the seven Negro sermons in verse, the book's overall quality is excellent. Especially fine are the sermons on the creation, on death, on the prodigal son, and on the judgment day, and the introductory prayer; the book was relatively free of propaganda. In keeping with his major goals, however, Johnson's preface made clear an intention other than poetic, though his free verse was full of impressive rhythms and wonderful imagination. Johnson says that his primary purpose was to capture and preserve the essence of the old-time rural black ministers who, through their magnificent and moving sermons, served as eloquent instruments of God, God's trombones. His preface also provides a brief treatise on black preaching, and the book served to illustrate permanently and dramatically an area of significant and noble contribution by blacks to American folk culture.

Johnson's other published poetry is not extensive, including only 24 poems published in periodicals, all but five of them included in the three volumes of his poetry. *Fifty Years & Other Poems* contains 49 nondialect poems and sixteen "Jingles & Croons" in dialect, and all except five of the poems in the later collection, *Saint Peter Relates an Incident*, had been in *Fifty Years*, though he did slightly modify some of the reprinted poems, including the titles of five of them. Together his published poems total 75. Although Johnson generally believed that good art and direct social concerns could not be joined successfully, some of his poems do attempt to do that, and sometimes succeed, as in "Brothers." Most of his best poetry, however, does not attempt such joining, and his overriding concerns instead are invested obliquely, through illustration of types, events, and general human concerns, and by good writing, not by blatant didacticism. Although Johnson was attracted to overt and traditional poetic forms, his best poetry tends to be in free verse. Despite a number of truly successful poems (such as "O Black and Unknown Bards" and "The White Witch"), too many of his poems are trapped and strangled in forms not suited to their intended vitality and do little to enhance his stature as a poet. Although he wrote poetry during most of his life, much of it—except for *God's Trombones*—is thin in overall quality. Yet, as a writer, Johnson is rightly destined to be known primarily as a poet, especially for *God's Trombones*.

Behind and informing his autobiography, two collections of spirituals, an anthology of poetry by American blacks, and *Black Manhattan* lay his persistent concern with demonstrating, providing ready access to, and elucidating the cultural contributions to America by black people, including himself—and each of these books was significantly succesful in this regard. He saw his autobiography, intended for both blacks and white, as an exhibit of a life that demonstrated one way to apply the principles he espoused and also the success of doing so. Therefore, he tried to write it with the same detachment he brought to most of his works. The book received wide and immediate acclaim from blacks and whites, often with emphasis on his remarkable accomplishments in the face of racial difficulty; its own success was another example of what it was portraying.

The spirituals, black poetry, and *Black Manhattan* provided not only rich cultural evidence and resource material, but also focuses in the directions of Johnson's general concerns regarding black people and America. In *Black Manhattan* the emphasis on the significance of their contributions, especially to music and drama, is interwoven throughout its text. The three collections have important prefaces. Johnson sounded the main theme early in the 42-page preface for *The Book of American Negro Poetry*: "The status of the Negro in the United States is more a question of national mental attitude toward the race than of actual conditions." He then outlined what he believed to be the accomplishments and influence of blacks through folk stories, spirituals, dance, ragtime and its successors in popular music, and especially poetry. Although some of his own early poetry had been in Negro dialect and although in this preface he acknowledged the appropriateness of dialect, he also saw it as too limited and its range too narrow, calling attention to the need for using language that showed the breadth and variety of black life and interests, particularly in the urban context. He said that what was needed was also "a form that is freer and larger than dialect, but which will hold the racial flavor. . . . " This he hoped he had accomplished later in *God's Trombones*. The devaluation of dialect and call for new forms is repeated in his preface to *God's Trombones* and in *St. Peter Relates an Incident*. He himself did not publish dialect poems after 1917, although eight earlier ones were included in his last selection of poetry in 1935, including the poignant gem, "Sence You Went Away."

Despite the variety of his publications, Johnson constantly hoped they would assist in realizing his aspirations for black Americans. In its own way, his work was as successful in this regard as was his remarkable work with the NAACP, and it added some significant works to American literature and American cultural history.

SURVEY OF CRITICISM

As Robert E. Fleming has pointed out in the introduction to his helpful reference guide, Johnson fared better with the critics during his lifetime than did many other black writers, especially after he gained a wider reputation and more visibility in the 1920s, during and after which his books were reviewed not only favorably but also widely. This was especially true for *God's Trombones* (1927) and *Black Manhattan* (1930); and after *Along This Way* (1933) he clearly established his literary reputation, despite some disappointment with the last collection of his poems in 1935. After the flurry of activity following his death in 1938, critical attention to Johnson waned until the 1960s, when there developed a renewed interest in black culture in general. By the middle of that decade Johnson's works were widely available, and criticism about them was increasing. There was some falling off in the first years of the 1980s (the *MLA Bibliography* had no entries for Johnson for 1981 and 1982).

From the period of renewed interest in Johnson a number of things are of significance, but of special help has been the focus on Johnson biography, capped by the excellent, balanced, and thorough work by Eugene Levy published in 1973. This interest is seen in various scholarly articles too, and in books about him for young people in 1965, 1967, 1971, and 1974 offering for emulation Johnson and his ideas and his success. In 1971 special issues of both the *Crisis* (June) and *Phylon* (Winter) appeared to mark the centennial of Johnson's birth, and they contained valuable critical and biographical articles focusing on various facets of his career. The 1970s and 1980s have seen increased interest in Johnson as artist, particularly in his novel and its use of irony. Most critics of Johnson's poetry recognize his genuinely significant poetic accomplishments, especially in *God's Trombones* and its attempt to use a new approach to black speech in poetry; at the same time they point out the lack of overall quality in his poetry and caution against grandiose and indiscriminate praise of it. More critical attention needs to be given to Johnson's poetry, especially because his continuing status as a literary figure will probably depend on the place assigned to it.

In the 1970s scholars also began to try to place Johnson and his works in broader contexts. Houston A. Baker, Jr., and Fleming observe, for example, the influence of his novel on later black writers, particularly Ralph Ellison, and various studies of the Harlem Renaissance attempt to gauge his place in that. Several doctoral dissertations have also used a comparative approach. More recently Ladell Payne has attempted to place Johnson within the traditions of Southern literature; and Robert B. Stepto and Nicholas Canady study his novel in the traditions of black autobiography and biography respectively. It would be valuable to have an in-depth study of Johnson's own autobiography in those same contexts.

BIBLIOGRAPHY

Works by James Weldon Johnson

The Autobiography of an Ex-Colored Man. New York: Sherman, French, 1912. Reprinted as *The Autobiography of an Ex-Coloured Man*. New York: Knopf, 1927.
Fifty Years & Other Poems. Boston: Cornhill, 1917.
The Changing Status of Negro Labor. New York: National Council of Social Work, 1918. A pamphlet.

The Book of American Negro Poetry. Ed. with an introduction by Johnson. New York:
    Harcourt, Brace, 1922. Revised ed., 1931.
The Race Problem and Peace. New York: NAACP, 1924. A pamphlet.
The Book of American Negro Spirituals. Ed. with J. Rosamond Johnson. New York:
    Viking Press, 1925.
The Second Book of Negro Spirituals. Ed. with J. Rosamond Johnson. New York: Viking
    Press, 1926.
Native African Races and Culture. Occasional Papers No. 25. Charlottesville, Va.: John
    F. Slater Fund, 1927.
God's Trombones: Seven Negro Sermons In Verse. New York: Viking Press, 1927.
Black Manhattan. New York: Knopf, 1930.
St. Peter Relates an Incident. Private ed. New York: Viking Press, 1930.
Along This Way: The Autobiography of James Weldon Johnson. New York: Viking Press,
    1933.
Negro Americans, What Now? New York: Viking Press, 1934.
Saint Peter Relates an Incident: Selected Poems by James Weldon Johnson. New York:
    Viking Press, 1935.
"Letters to a Friend: Correspondence from James Weldon Johnson to George A. Towns."
    Ed. Miles M. Jackson, Jr. *Phylon* 29 (Summer 1968): 182–98.

Studies of James Weldon Johnson

Baker, Houston A., Jr. "A Forgotten Prototype: *The Autobiography of an Ex-Colored
    Man* and *Invisible Man.*" *Singers of Daybreak: Studies in Black American Lit-
    erature.* Washington: Howard University Press, 1974, pp. 17–31, 95–96.
Canady, Nicholas. "*The Autobiography of an Ex-Colored Man* and the Tradition of Black
    Biography." *Obsidian* 6 (Spring-Summer 1980): 76–80.
Collier, Eugenia. "The Endless Journey of an Ex-Coloured Man." *Phylon* 32 (Winter
    1971): 365–73.
Crisis (James Weldon Johnson Centennial Issue) 78 (June 1971): 111–41.
Fleming, Robert E. "Contemporary Themes in Johnson's *Autobiography of an Ex-Col-
    oured Man.*" *Negro American Literature Forum* 4 (Winter 1970): 120–24, 141.
———. "Irony as a Key to Johnson's *The Autobiography of an Ex-Coloured Man.*"
    American Literature 43 (March 1971): 83–96.
———. *James Weldon Johnson and Arna Wendell Bontemps: A Reference Guide.* Boston:
    G. K. Hall, 1978.
Garrett, Marvin P. "Early Recollections and Structural Irony in *The Autobiography of
    an Ex-Coloured Man.*" *Critique: Studies in Modern Fiction* 13 (December 1971):
    5–14.
Levy, Eugene. *James Weldon Johnson: Black Leader, Black Voice.* Chicago: University
    of Chicago Press, 1973.
Long, Richard A. "A Weapon of My Song: The Poetry of James Weldon Johnson."
    Phylon 32 (Winter 1971): 374–82.
Payne, Ladell. "Themes and Cadences: James Weldon Johnson, 1871–1938." *Black
    Novelists and the Southern Literary Tradition.* Athens: University of Georgia
    Press, 1981, pp. 26–37.
Phylon (James Weldon Johnson Centenary Issue) 32 (Winter 1971): 330–402.

Ross, Stephen M. "Audience and Irony in Johnson's *The Autobiography of an Ex-Coloured Man.*" *CLA Journal* 18 (December 1974): 198–210.

Skerrett, Joseph T., Jr. "Irony and Symbolic Action in James Weldon Johnson's *The Autobiography of an Ex-Coloured Man.*" *American Quarterly* 32 (Winter 1980): 540–58.

Stepto, Robert B. "Lost in a Quest: James Weldon Johnson's *The Autobiography of an Ex-Coloured Man.*" *From Behind the Veil: A Study of Afro-American Narrative.* Urbana: University of Illinois Press, 1979, pp. 95–127.

Vauthier, Simone. "The Interplay of Narrative Modes in James Weldon Johnson's *The Autobiography of an Ex-Colored Man.*" *Jahrbuch für Amerikastudien* 18 (1973): 173–81.

Wagner, Jean. "James Weldon Johnson." *Black Poets of the United States: From Paul Laurence Dunbar to Langston Hughes.* Trans. Kenneth Douglas. Urbana: University of Illinois Press, 1973, pp. 351–84.

MARK T. LUCAS

Andrew Lytle
(1902–   )

His name a byword in Southern circles for discipline, integrity, and high seriousness in the service of letters, Andrew Nelson Lytle's career has seen him in
many roles—biographer, Agrarian, literary critic, teacher, editor, memoirist—
but it is in his role as novelist that he is most deeply to be found.

BIOGRAPHY

Murfreesboro, in the bluegrass region of middle Tennessee, was Andrew
Lytle's birthplace, on 26 December 1902. His parents, Robert Logan Lytle and
Lillie Belle Nelson, were both from respected and deep-rooted Tennessee families, Murfreesboro itself having been founded on land donated by a Lytle fore-
bear. Young Andrew's upbringing in Murfreesboro and North Alabama took
place within the thick webwork of family connection, as *A Wake for the Living*,
Lytle's family history, elegiacally attests. The world of his and his sister's
childhood, peopled by Nelson and Lytle kin, was rich in tradition and marked,
he has said, by a deep sense of community. Lytle's father, a landowner involved
in cotton farming and timber production, was also a celebrated raconteur and
repository of family lore, a fact that helped keep the Southern past vividly alive
for his son. Even without words, though, this past was apparent enough to the
boy in the image of his grandmother Nelson's perpetual scarf, worn to cover
the scar left in childhood by Yankee sniper fire.

At age thirteen Lytle went for his secondary schooling to Sewanee Military
Academy, from which he graduated as valedictorian in 1920. Then, studying
for entrance to Oxford, he spent a year in France with his mother and a tutor.
He was subsequently admitted to Exeter College, Oxford, but summoned home
upon the death of his grandfather, he entered Vanderbilt University instead,
where he formed friendships crucial in shaping his later career. A talented college

actor, Lytle also distinguished himself in the creative writing class of Vanderbilt English professor and poet John Crowe Ransom. During Lytle's Vanderbilt years, 1921–25, he became friends as well with two others of the Nashville Fugitive group: professor Donald Davidson and fellow student Robert Penn Warren. Lytle himself published one poem in the *Fugitive*, but he was not a formal member of the group meeting fortnightly nor a serious aspirant in the field of poetry. (He genially took the hint when Ransom suggested that his poetry was like a fiddler playing expertly, but on one string only.) Play writing, not poetry or fiction, was his growing literary interest in these years.

Receiving his Vanderbilt B.A. in 1925, Lytle headed to Cornsilk, his father's cotton farm near Guntersville, Alabama, and ran the farm for a year. But despite his love of the land, his desire to be a playwright soon found him in George Pierce Baker's School of Drama at Harvard. Here Lytle studied in 1927 and 1928, and though he would later turn novelist, it was not time misspent; Baker taught him, Lytle has said in tribute, how to write a scene. Further, Baker gave him the good advice to write about the life he knew, Southern people in Southern settings, though Lytle, following this advice, would soon be deeply dissatisfied with the New York theater world's resistance to anything but caricatures of the South.

The fledgling playwright went to New York to support himself acting, but his off-hours were to find him hunched over yellowing military annals in the New York Public Library, at work on a biography of the Confederate hero Nathan Bedford Forrest. A recently acquired friendship was part of the reason. Lytle had called at Allen Tate's Greenwich Village apartment in the spring of 1927, and the two North-wandering Southerners had hit it off well. They quickly fell to discussing the "Monkey Trial" in Tennessee, Lytle has said, as part of liberal hostility to their traditional inheritance. Thus was a lifelong friendship begun with Tate and his wife Caroline Gordon—and soon the friends were touring Civil War battlefields together. Lytle had experienced a smoldering unease in the metropolitan Northeast and had come to see a Faustian materialism and power worship as the prevailing American pattern. He was ready, when he saw the way, to turn to his Southern heritage for images of a life to be reaffirmed. Tate, himself at work on a biography of Stonewall Jackson, secured a publishing agreement with Minton-Balch for Lytle's projected work on Forrest. With his research for the Civil War biography, Lytle took the first step of a sustained exploration, stretching over nearly a decade, of the history of his region.

When Lytle came back to the family steadings in Tennessee and north Alabama in 1929, he had returned South for good. His time outside the South had clarified his sense of himself as a Southerner. Increasingly, he saw what was distinctive about his region imperiled; the traditional, agrarian South was poised danger-ously, he felt, at the edge of the modern urban-industrial vortex. Thus he was more than ready to join forces with his Vanderbilt friends and others of like mind when Donald Davidson wrote to enlist him in the project that became *I'll Take My Stand* (1930). Lytle threw himself into the Agrarian venture with ferocity, and while the symposium was in the planning stage, he met frequently with Davidson and Ransom, the three of them beginning to discuss a credo to send to contributors. "The Hind Tit," Lytle's impassioned contribution to the symposium, addressed the Southern farmer, pushed back to the hind tit of the national economy. A jeremiad against the dangers of uncurbed industrial capitalism, the essay sketched the history behind the farming South's crisis, painted a deliberately idealized portrait of the small-farm agrarian's culture, then charted the ruin of the old culture when the farmer makes concessions to the ever-escalating demands of a money economy. In the rhetoric not of an economist but of an artist, Lytle declared, "A farm is not a place to grow wealthy; it is a place to grow corn"; the South should resist "the tumble-bellied prophets" of Progress and "dread industrialism like a pizen snake."

After he wrote "The Hind Tit" in the summer of 1930, Lytle drove hard toward completion of the Forrest biography. Living primarily at Cornsilk until 1938—and helping with the farm's management—he was also much at Benfolly, the Tate's recently acquired home north of Nashville (where he met and learned from Ford Madox Ford). There he completed *Bedford Forrest and His Critter Company* (1931). Portraying Forrest as perhaps the greatest military commander in the Confederacy, Lytle saw him as a man who summed up all that was best in his class, the Southern plain folk. In doing so, Lytle delineated not a moonlight-and-magnolias Brahmin ideal of the Old South but a hearthside-and-hominy yeoman ideal, the same ideal invoked in "The Hind Tit." The book's narrative strategy and feeling for the vivid scene were signs of the incipient novelist. Further, Lytle's research for *Bedford Forrest*—interviewing veterans, retracing Forrest's maneuvers, and reading diaries, letters, and battle reports—was an immersion in the folk culture of the upland South, the fictional milieu of a great part of his work.

Lytle remained active in the Agrarian cause until the movement dissipated in the late 1930s. He contributed "The Small Farm Secures the State" to *Who Owns America?* (1936), the quasi-sequel to *I'll Take My Stand*, and he wrote essays in appreciative reappraisal of John Taylor of Caroline, Robert Barnwell Rhett, John C. Calhoun, and other historical figures. The most significant of his Agrarian forays in these years was a wide-ranging meditation on the meaning of the pioneer backwoodsman, "The Backwoods Progression," published in the *American Review* in 1933. This Spengler-influenced essay reflected Lytle's widening perception of Western cultural decay and his construction of a whole superstructure of history in which to place his feelings about the South; Agrarianism broadened to a defense, as he would later put it baldly, of what was left of Christendom.

In the meantime Lytle recognized fiction, rather than drama, to be his métier, and he published his first story, "Old Scratch in the Valley," in 1932. This was followed by "Mr. MacGregor" in 1935 and "Jericho, Jericho, Jericho" in 1936, both of them acccomplished short stories (the latter in part a reworking of one of Lytle's play manuscripts). *The Long Night*, Lytle's first novel, was published by Bobbs-Merrill in 1936. A tale told Lytle by Frank Lawrence Owsley was its genesis. In 1933, visiting Cornsilk, Lytle's friend and fellow Agrarian had told the story of his great-uncle, a man who had devoted himself to a lifetime of vengeance against the gang of conspirators who murdered his father—and who, at the end of his life, had wished to pass what remained of the task to Frank's father. This was the germ of Lytle's revenger's tragedy of antebellum Alabama. The essentially heroic oral tale became, in Lytle's hands, a sprawling, violent, densely textured story of the moral ambiguities of revenge. Pleasant McIvor's humanity shrivels in the darkness of his long night until his will to revenge begins to give way before new allegiances during the Civil War.

The Long Night had the best sale of all his books—going into three printings in 1936, a little over 10,000 copies—but it was far from the popular success he had hoped for, and he was sternly indifferent to matters of commercial success or failure ever after. His chosen vocation showed little promise of making his living; thus things such as a history position at Southwestern University in 1936, successive Guggenheim Fellowships in 1940 and 1941, and a stint as managing editor of the *Sewanee Review* in 1942–43 were a necessary help in this period. Also, his responsibilities had increased. He married Edna Langdon Barker in 1938: a happy match, lasting until her death from cancer in 1963. (Although Lytle was raised a Methodist, he and his wife were Episcopalians. His strong Christian belief has been an important fact in his career.)

Lytle and his bride went to live in a log house in the mountaintop summer resort village of Monteagle, Tennessee. There he worked on the story that "chose him," he has said, when he was reading in Albert Pickett's *History of Alabama* a passage describing de Soto's Spaniards arriving on the coast of Florida in 50-ducat breastplates, only to flee the continent in animal skins four years laters. This became *At the Moon's Inn*, published in 1941. Exhaustively researched—making use of the accounts of Ranjel, Biedma, the Fidalgo of Elvas, and others—this ambitious book took the further step, as Lytle has insisted serious historical fiction must do, of wresting from a fragment of history "its intrinsic meaning." De Soto's ill-fated expedition into the Florida territory comes to represent, as Lytle put it in a letter to his Bobb-Merrill editor, D. L. Chambers, "the mind of Christendom . . . on its dance of death." His next work was the novella *Alchemy* (published in the *Kenyon Review* in 1942 and later one of the selections in *A Novel, A Novella, and Four Stories*). It is the tale of Pizarro's conquest of the Inca, a conquest so productive of gold that, to the conquistadors, some alchemy seemed to be at work in the New World. Originally intended to be a flashback segment of *At the Moon's Inn*, the story was so long and so self-contained that, at the advice of the Tates, Lytle removed it entirely. He has since wished it back in *At the Moon's Inn*, as prologue.

In 1943 Lytle moved to land he had bought near Portland, Tennessee, and he threw himself into the task of restoring the old house and regenerating the neglected farm. He named it Cornsilk, after the family farm that had become the floor of a TVA lake in 1940 ("Since that time," Lytle has said, "I have felt in exile''). Although all his hope for the new Cornsilk did not turn out— the area was no longer a place of true community and farming was too time-consuming to allow him enough freedom to write—his next novel, to some degree, battened on the experience. The only one of Lytle's novels whose scene is contemporary, *A Name for Evil* (1947) is narrated by a man wrestling with the difficulties of restoring a ''throwed-away'' Tennessee farm. A Jamesian ghost story in which the narrator gradually reveals himself as a madman, the book is obviously far from autobiography. But it is nonetheless a deep meditation on the perplexities of a backward-looking allegiance, a very interesting thing for a former Agrarian to undertake. This complex novel was begun as an experiment with the form of *The Turn of the Screw* but soon became something distinctively Lytle's as it told the story of Henry Brent's struggles with the ''presence'' of his ironic double, the ancestor who had perfected the farm then consigned it to ruin three quarters of a century earlier. Lytle's other entry in fiction in the last half of the 1940s was the short story ''The Guide'' (later entitled ''The Mahogany Frame''), published in the *Sewanee Review* in 1945.

Between 1946 and 1948 Lytle taught some terms at the University of Iowa School of Writing, and this was the beginning of another important strand of his career: mentor of young writers. Flannery O'Connor, a student at Iowa, was the first of many exceptionally talented writers to study under Lytle during his nearly three decades of teaching. In 1948 he went to the University of Florida at Gainesville to head its creative writing program, and in addition to beginning the eight years' labor that would go into his last and best novel, he began to write the penetrating literary criticism that has become a cornerstone of his reputation as man of letters. Tolstoy, Crane, Joyce, Ford Madox Ford, Caroline Gordon, and especially Flaubert and Faulkner—these have been principal subjects of Lytle's essays in criticism since the first of his influential studies of Faulkner was published in 1949.

Lytle has said the inception of his last novel, *The Velvet Horn* (1957), was his impulse ''to resuscitate a dead society,'' the latter-nineteenth-century South at a ''turning point'' between traditional ways and modernity. He was well prepared for the task. Not only had he spent his young manhood immersed in the history of his region, but through all the thinking that had gone into *At the Moon's Inn* and two recent essays on the historical novel, he had worked out for himself a highly sophisticated approach to historical fiction (''Caroline Gordon and the Historic Image'' appeared in 1949, ''The Image as Guide to Meaning in the Historical Novel'' in 1953; both are collected in *The Hero with the Private Parts*). Also, he had begun reading in archetypal psychology—in Jung's *Psychology and Alchemy*, Erich Neumann's *The Origins and History of Consciousness*, Heinrich Zimmer's *The King and the Corpse*—and a deep interest in the mythic patterns of human experience became part of the conscious craft of *The Velvet Horn*. Such were the diverse energies that converged in what has remained Lytle's favorite of all his works. A difficult novel employing multiple perspectives, frequent dislocations of time sequence, and a challenging symbolism, *The*

Velvet Horn is a powerful evocation of the tragic past of the Cropleigh family. Lucius Cree, his energetic and admired father having committed suicide, is forced to confront the torturous mystery of his mother's, and her three brothers', past. The book was well-reviewed, repeatedly declared major, but it soon went out of print and remained so for 25 years. Its reputation as a work of great depth and seriousness remained alive, however, and it has recently been republished (University of the South, 1983).

With *The Velvet Horn* Lytle had shifted to a new publisher, the firm of McDowell-Obolensky, and under the sympathetic editorship of David Mc-Dowell, Lytle published in the next year a collection of his shorter works, *A Novel, A Novella, and Four Stories*, then in 1960 a reissue of *Bedford Forrest and His Critter Company*. In 1961 he moved with his wife and three daughters back to Monteagle, to become editor of the *Sewanee Review* and to teach at the University of the South until retiring in 1973. After the publication in 1966 of a collection of his criticism, *The Hero with the Private Parts*, he edited, in 1971, a collection of short stories drawn from the quarterly that had first begun publishing fiction when he was managing editor 29 years earlier: *Craft and Vision: The Best Fiction from "The Sewanee Review."* Most significant, he began working in the latter half of the 1960s on the project that David McDowell was the first to urge on him: a book of family memoirs that would include some of the rambunctious anecdotes friends had long loved to hear him tell. Chronicling the family history of Nelsons and Lytles from colonial days to the modern South as late as 1942, this was published in 1975 as *A Wake for the Living: A Family Chronicle*.

After retiring from the *Sewanee Review*, Lytle lived for a time on a farm in central Kentucky, but he returned to the log house in Monteagle, where he lives currently and continues to write his highly organized essays, both critical and retrospective.

MAJOR THEMES

Although Lytle's oeuvre is small, his canvas has been large. His fictional world extends from Charles V's Spain to Atahualpa's Peru, from pioneer Alabama to modern Tennessee, from de Soto at Mauvilla to Johnston at Shiloh. As novel has followed novel at intervals of five, six, then ten years, each has been strikingly different from the preceding one in setting and treatment. Nonetheless, there are deep thematic continuities in Lytle's work, continuities reflective of his particular image not only of Southern but of Western history in general.

It bespeaks not only a character's private deficiency but Lytle's over-arching view of Western history when, at the conclusion of *The Velvet Horn*, Legrand says lamely to his stepson, "Money can help. I'm always behind you." Symbolized by his ledgers, Legrand the entrepreneur is, significantly, "such a man as multiplied." He is one figuration of modernity in this novel whose enveloping action depicts a clash of conflicting worldviews, one reverencing traditional values, the other exalting material ends as the only reward for action. In contrast to Legrand is such a man as Joe Cree, described as "the balance wheel in this county," who astounds small-time swindlers by putting them on their honor. Cree, however, commits suicide, while the newcomer Legrand prospers in league with the shiftless Rutters swarming out of the backwoods. This disintegration of an older order, in Lytle's judgment, is a phenomenon far from endemic to the postbellum South. Rather, the Western world has been in spiritual decline ever since the Renaissance and the breakup of Christian feudalism. The sad consequence of the medieval polity's collapse—so goes Lytle's concept—was a secular state founded solely on money and property. From the rise of the bourgeoisie to the defeat of the Confederacy, Western history since the Middle Ages has seen Faustian secularism and materialism go from success to success.

The aggressive, will-swollen man, the modern who impiously views the world as a possession ready to his exploiting designs—he, in Lytle's view, has been the cultural corrosive, the juggernaut of the world drama. In richly complex, fully human form, Pete Legrand is one such figure in Lytle's fiction. In *At the Moon's Inn*, the book next in stature to *The Velvet Horn*, Hernando de Soto is another one. Less complex than Legrand as a character, de Soto is deliberately more clear-cut as an emblem. Obsessed by hope of such gold as he had known in Peru, the relentless de Soto drives his diminishing army across *La Tierra Florida*, but instead of gold he finds his own spiritual destruction. In the central symbolic action of the book, de Soto is confronted at Mass by his priest, who holds aloft the Host and calls out, "By this God, whom I hold here in my hands, I warn, I beseech, I command that you now do that which you have not wished to do, which in your stubborn avarice and pride you have refused—Go out of this land!" When de Soto spits back his refusal, Tovar, the story's central narrator, sees exactly what it means: that de Soto has wrenched free from spiritual discipline and that from here "it is only one step further to supplant God's will by man's and call it divine—man made God, man with all his frailties and pride setting up the goods of the world over the good of heavenly grace." Thus it is that Lytle locates in de Soto the prototypal modern, the epitome of the Faustian strain of Western history.

Pleasant McIvor in *The Long Night* is less broadly representative in historical terms, but he too is an example of the condition of "unlimited will." The novel strongly implies that Pleasant's self-appointment to the role of divine avenger is an enormous piece of presumption. He calls himself "God's judgment" and quotes Old Testament vindictiveness, but it is clear that he would do better to ponder the New Testament. When in pitch blackness he finally confronts Tyson Lovell, the gang leader behind his father's murder, Pleasant is mistaken for his own assassin, an irony that speaks volumes. After Lovell knows whom he faces, he asks with point, "What will you do, Sonny, when I'm dead and gone?" Pleasant has indeed become nothing more than his one purpose and, in answering evil with evil, has inevitably suffered a moral rot.

Just as Pleasant comes to personify what he professedly abhors, so does Henry Brent in *A Name for Evil*, for he is the creature far more than he realizes of the tradition-razing modernism he deplores. Like his ancestor at The Grove who in "vanity and by will" had refused to submerge his ego in the continuities of family on the land, Henry is not the man to submerge his imperious sense of self in anything. This he quickly proves by reducing his attempted restoration of the place to an absurdly competitive war of egos with his long-gone relative. This egotism shared with his double, the Major, is what prevents Henry from being the traditional man he professes to be. Truly to possess the traditional sensibility that Lytle reveres is to discipline the raw ego within inherited patterns of conduct—ritual, manners, and institutions, especially the institution of the family. Henry, however, feels a subterranean recoil from tradition and the checks it would place on his ego. In that flicker of prescience of the mad, he briefly recognizes the destructive innocence of his motives at The Grove: "How was I to know that I had put myself in way of the past and future, bemused by the mad fancy that I could reach into history and regenerate, a function proper only to a god? . . . was not my idea the obverse of Major Brent's act . . . ?" It is true: Henry's willful attempt to regenerate the past is the obverse of the Major's willful attempt to proscribe the future. The Major's egomaniacal destruction of his posterity, an adumbration of the impious modern's arrogation of godlike license, finds its twentieth-century echo when Henry ends up scaring his pregnant wife into her grave.

In ultimate terms, all of these characters—Legrand, de Soto, McIvor, Henry Brent—in some way affront Lytle's Christian sense of the divine scheme. In his essay "The State of Letters in a Time of Disorder," Lytle writes that "the crimes which great literature exhibits are acts against the divine order of the universe. These crimes have to do with the disobedience by man of God's will, or the substitution of his own will for the divine will." Such have been the crimes portrayed in his own highly ambitious work, deeply informed as it is by moral and theological concerns. For Lytle, man is decidedly not self-defining, perfectible, or the measure of all things. Instead, this is a fallen world; attempts to go beyond human limitations are shot through with destructive hubris and typically end in catastrophe. "Sorrow," as Jack Cropleigh says in *The Velvet Horn*, "is the one thing we don't have to take on faith." It is a view essentially Augustinian in its powerful awareness of evil and in its perception, as Lytle once put it, of "The City of God as the end of the drama" (Foreword to *A Novel, A Novella and Four Stories*).

Lucius Cree, in *The Velvet Horn*, is the best example in Lytle's work of a character who wins through to a workable compromise with life. Learning bitterly that he is his mother's "woods colt," a bastard, Lucius is tempted to run away to the West, to try to escape plainly confronting his fall into the human condition. Ultimately, however, he comes to understand what his Uncle Jack says Job heard in the whirlwind: that a man cannot flee what he is (which is bound up with certain people in a certain place). Says Jack,

Job sat down in his ashes and rent the last suit of clothes left him. He complained, and who wouldn't half naked and running with boils. . . . But did Job run away? He didn't.

He sat there with the pus from his boils gumming up the ashes, naked enough to show his corruption common to all, defending himself against man and God, in his own neighborhood, before his own wife. (p. 357)

Should Lucius run away, he would be disregarding "all the conventions and institutions," continues Jack, "everything that constrains the natural man and makes him aware of his neighbors, and so aware of himself and his peril." Lucius does not run; rather, at novel's end he is sawing up the oak that killed Joe Cree—for boards "to raise a small house to bring his wife to." When Jack Cropleigh sacrifices his own life to save his nephew's, Lucius finally absorbs the truth of his uncle's words, and in Uncle Jack's version of Job can be heard values pervasive in Lytle's work, values ultimately rooted, for Lytle, in reverence before the mystery and power of the Divine.

SURVEY OF CRITICISM

The story of Lytle criticism to date is one of relative neglect. Outside of the gathering of essays edited by M. E. Bradford, *The Form Discovered: Essays on the Achievement of Andrew Lytle* (1973), Lytle has as yet received no full-length critical study. A heartening sign, however, is the fact that at least two books of criticism are presently in preparation. Another encouragement is the reappearance in print of several of Lytle's works in the last few years: *The Velvet Horn* (University of the South, 1983), *Bedford Forrest and His Critter Company* (Green Key Press, 1984; C. Elder, 1984), and *Stories: Alchemy and Others* (University of the South, 1984). Further, study of Lytle has recently been served well by bibliographical scholarship. Between Stuart Wright's *Andrew Nelson Lytle: A Bibliography 1920–1982* (1982) and Victor Kramer's chapter in *Andrew Lytle, Walker Percy, Peter Taylor: A Reference Guide* (1983), the student of Lytle has everything he could want in the way of bibliography—except more critical items to be put *in* bibliographies. Kramer's offering is valuable for its annotated secondary bibliography, chronologically arranged, 1931–80. Also listing secondary material, although without annotation, Wright's meticulous book gives special attention to bibliographical descriptions, according to standard formulas, of primary material.

Among general essays on Lytle, Robert V. Weston's "Faulkner and Lytle: Two Modes of Southern Fiction" is the best. Criticism on Lytle's early career, "The Hind Tit" through *The Long Night*, is scant. Of the handful of essays on Lytle's first novel, Robert Penn Warren's "Andrew Lytle's *The Long Night*: A Rediscovery" stands out. No book or article has taken a sustained look at Lytle's role in the exchange of ideas that led to *I'll Take My Stand*, at his Agrarian essays, or at the relationship between his early social criticism and his career in fiction after 1931 (although Mark Lucas's forthcoming book on the Southern roots of Lytle's work promises to do so). Lytle's short fiction has come in for some good criticism, especially Madison Jones's essay on "Mister MacGregor,"

Sidney Landman's on "Jericho, Jericho, Jericho," Edward Krickel's on "The Mahogany Frame," and M. E. Bradford's on *Alchemy*. All four of these essays are in the "Andrew Lytle Issue" of *Mississippi Quarterly*, 23 (Fall 1970) and are reprinted in *The Form Discovered*. In editing the Lytle issue of *Mississippi Quarterly* and then culling the best of those essays plus others into *The Form Discovered*, M. E. Bradford has been the chief advocate of Lytle's achievement.

Relatively little has been written about the major fiction from the 1940s on, but much of that little is quite good. Robert Benson's "The Progress of Hernando de Soto in Andrew Lytle's *At the Moon's Inn*," *Georgia Review*, 27 (Summer 1973), 232–44, is a good starting point for study of that novel, as is, for the next novel, Charles C. Clark's "*A Name for Evil*: A Search for Order," *Mississippi Quarterly*, 23 (Fall 1970), 371–82 (both of these are in *The Form Discovered* as well). An excellent entering wedge for study of *The Velvet Horn* is Lytle's own essay on its composition, "The Working Novelist and the Myth-making Process," collected in *The Hero with the Private Parts*. After that, of greatest interest are the Frenchwoman Anne Foata's "La Leçon des Ténèbres: The Edenic Quest and Its Christian Solution in Andrew Lytle's *The Velvet Horn*"; Thomas Landess's "Unity of Action in *The Velvet Horn*," *Mississippi Quarterly*, 23 (Fall 1970), 349–61 (in *The Form Discovered* also); and Clinton W. Trowbridge's "The Word Made Flesh: Andrew Lytle's *The Velvet Horn*."

Continuing to invite critical attention are the Lytle manuscript collections at Vanderbilt and the University of Florida, as well as Lytle's correspondence housed at Vanderbilt. Also of strong interest are his letters to Allen Tate, part of the Tate Papers at Princeton. These resources have as yet been little used. Indeed, systematic commentary is called for in many areas. Lytle biography, the development of Lytle's aesthetic, Lytle's uses of myth and history—these and other topics remain open to full-length scrutiny.

BIBLIOGRAPHY

Works by Andrew Lytle

"The Hind Tit." *I'll Take My Stand: The South and the Agrarian Tradition* by "Twelve Southerners." New York: Harper and Brothers, 1930, pp. 201–45.
Bedford Forrest and His Critter Company. New York: Minton, Balch, 1931.
"Old Scratch in the Valley." *Virginia Quarterly Review* 8 (April 1932): 237–46.
"The Backwoods Progression." *American Review* 1 (September 1933): 409–34.
The Long Night. Indianapolis and New York: Bobbs-Merrill, 1936.
"The Small Farm Secures the State." *Who Owns America?* Ed. Herbert Agar and Allen Tate. Boston: Houghton Mifflin, 1936, pp. 237–50.
At the Moon's Inn. Indianapolis and New York: Bobbs-Merrill, 1941.
A Name for Evil. Indianapolis and New York: Bobbs-Merrill, 1947.
The Velvet Horn. New York: McDowell-Obolensky, 1957.
A Novel, A Novella and Four Stories. New York: McDowell-Obolensky, 1958.

The Hero with the Private Parts: Essays by Andrew Lytle. Baton Rouge: Louisiana State
    University Press, 1966.
Craft and Vision: The Best Fiction from "The Sewanee Review." Ed. and with a foreword
    by Andrew Lytle. New York: Delacorte Press, 1971.
"The State of Letters in a Time of Disorder." *Sewanee Review* 79 (Autumn 1971): 477–
    97.
A Wake for the Living: A Family Chronicle. New York: Crown, 1975.

Studies of Andrew Lytle

Bradford, M. E., ed. *The Form Discovered: Essays on the Achievement of Andrew Lytle.*
    Jackson: University and College Press of Mississippi, 1973.
Foata, Anne. "La Leçon des Ténèbres: The Edenic Quest and Its Christian Solution in
    Andrew Lytle's *The Velvet Horn." Southern Literary Journal* 16 (Fall 1983): 71–
    95.
Kramer, Victor A., et al. *Andrew Lytle, Walker Percy, Peter Taylor: A Reference Guide.*
    Boston: G. K. Hall, 1983.
Trowbridge, Clinton W. "The Word Made Flesh: Andrew Lytle's *The Velvet Horn.*"
    Critique 10 (1967–68): 53–68.
Warren, Robert Penn. "Andrew Lytle's *The Long Night*: A Rediscovery." *Southern
    Review* 7 (Winter 1971): 130–39.
Weston, Robert V. "Faulkner and Lytle: Two Modes of Southern Fiction." *Southern
    Review* 25 (Winter 1979): 34–51.
Wright, Stuart. *Andrew Nelson Lytle: A Bibliography 1920–1982.* Sewanee, Tenn.: Uni-
    versity of the South, 1982.

Carson McCullers
(1917–1967)

Although critics frequently describe Carson McCullers as a writer of the gothic and the grotesque, her most popular and acclaimed work is *A Member of the Wedding*, where those elements are minimal. Whether or not she is a major writer, critics still debate. Most agree, however, that her significant literary accomplishments add up to a major achievement, and that readers will continue to find her work timely.

BIOGRAPHY

Carson McCullers was born Lula Carson Smith on 19 February 1917, in Columbus, Georgia, a mill town perched on the edge of the Chattahoochee River across from Phenix City, Alabama. Touted by her mother for her precocity and curried for genius, she was the daughter of Marguerite Waters Smith, a descendant of Irish settlers in South Carolina before the Revolutionary War, and her husband, Lamar, a small-town jeweler from Alabama. The first of three children, Lula Carson was recognized as a brooding, solitary child with a predilection for music, books, and games of make-believe. Reared on tales of her kinsmen who fought and died in the Civil War and the strong-willed women they left behind, she was both repelled and attracted by the paradoxes of life in the South.

She dropped Lula from her name at thirteen and answered only to Carson (or ''Sister,'' as she was known to the family) and announced that she would be a concert pianist, an obsession that gave way to writing. In her mid-teens she set down stories and plays in a Blue Chief notebook. Among these juvenile attempts were ''The Faucet'' and ''The Fire of Life''—which she described as ''thick with incest, lunacy, and murder,'' both imitative of the plays of her idol, Eugene O'Neill. She presented a number of such plays at home for family and friends. They were never published. The first short story she was proud enough to show her parents was "Sucker," which she wrote in longhand, then laboriously typed on her new typewriter, a gift from her father when she was seventeen. "Sucker" remained unpublished until 1963.

Encouraged by her mother and supported by funds from the sale of an heirloom diamond and emerald ring, she went alone to New York City in 1935, supposedly to study at Juilliard School of Music, but enrolled, instead, in creative writing classes with Dorothy Scarborough and Helen Rose Hull at Columbia University. After one semester, she returned to Columbus for the summer to write at home and worked briefly as a reporter on the local newspaper. In July she met a young soldier from Wetumpka, Alabama, who was stationed at nearby Ft. Benning, and they fell in love, a courtship promoted by her mother. Reeves McCullers also wanted to be a writer, and as soon as he could buy himself out of the Army joined Carson in New York City, where she returned in the fall to study at New York University with Sylvia Chatfield Bates. She studied at Columbia University, too, with Whit Burnett, editor of *Story* magazine. In December 1936 Burnett chose "Wunderkind," a story Carson had written for Bates, and published it to launch their protégée. He also purchased a second story, "Like That," but failed to publish it. The tale appeared for the first time in *The Mortgaged Heart*, a posthumous collection edited by her sister, Margarita G. Smith, in 1971.

The young writer was twenty when she married Reeves McCullers in fall 1937 in her parents' home at 1519 Starke Avenue. The marriage surprised almost everyone in Columbus who knew her, for she had always been shy, unpopular with her peers, eccentric in appearance, and often diffident; and they were impressed that her groom was handsome, athletic-looking, and personable. Reeves, twenty-four, took his bride to Charlotte, North Carolina, where he worked for eight months as a credit investigator, the only happy period of their marriage. Their plan was to alternate roles as writer and breadwinner, but it was soon apparent that Carson's creative life would always come first.

She began work on "The Mute," her first novel (retitled after it was in galley proofs at the insistence of her editor as *The Heart Is a Lonely Hunter*), on her honeymoon and finished it after their move to Fayetteville, North Carolina, a town she thoroughly disliked. On the basis of an outline and six chapters, she had placed second in a literary contest sponsored by Houghton Mifflin as a means of discovering new talent and was awarded a contract and $500. While awaiting its publication on 4 June 1940, she dashed off a second novel in barely two months. "Army Post" (published in 1941 as *Reflections in a Golden Eye*) had as its fictional setting Ft. Bragg, North Carolina, located just outside Fayetteville, and Ft. Benning, the post she had visited often while taking piano lessons from the wife of the commanding officer of the infantry school there.

The 1940s were Carson McCullers's most productive years. Determined never again to live in the South, she and her husband moved to New York City practically on the eve of the publication of *The Heart Is a Lonely Hunter*. Later, she admitted that she had to return South periodically to renew her "sense of horror." The novel received rave notices, and at twenty-three she was hailed a "wunderkind" and declared the "publisher's find of the decade." Reveling in the critical acclaim by the nation's major reviewers and cashing in on her instant popularity, she told reporters that *The Heart Is a Lonely Hunter* was subtle parable about facism, a gripping topic on the eve of World War II.

Her marriage had begun to disintegrate before she left the South, and once in New York, she fell in love almost immediately with a beautiful, neurotic Swiss writer, Annemarie Clarec-Schwarzenbach, to whom she dedicated *Reflections in a Golden Eye*. Her love unrequited, she found solace in Louis Untermeyer at Bread Loaf Writers' Conference, a relationship described by Untermeyer as "platonic with some not so platonic embraces." In the fall, separated from Reeves and desperately lonely (her Swiss friend had returned to Europe), she moved into a brownstone in Brooklyn Heights at 7 Middagh Street with George Davis and W. H. Auden. Soon there was an eccentric ménage in the old Victorian house that included Gypsy Rose Lee, Paul Bowles, Richard Wright, Benjamin Britten, Peter Pears, Oliver Smith, Golo Mann, Marc Blitzstein, and countless other kindred spirits who stayed for weeks or months at a time, all under the tutelage of Auden. Visitors agreed that it was the most extraordinary and electrically creative atmosphere of twentieth-century America. McCullers's several stays there were brief, but she insisted that the experience was the most important of her life. An essay published in *Vogue* in 1941, "Brooklyn Is My Neighborhood," provides keen insight into her abandonment of provincial Southern roots for what she saw as a more glamorous life in the urban North. Yet she returned South again and again to recuperate from the ill health that beset her in the North.

Since 1939 McCullers had been struggling with a nebulous plot conceived during one such bout with illness and was anguishing to find the heart of the book, which she referred to as "The Bride and Her Brother," when she had an incisive moment of illumination while chasing a fire engine in her Brooklyn neighborhood with Gypsy Rose Lee. She caught her friend's arm and shouted for her to stop. "Frankie is in love with her brother and the bride and wants to become a member of the wedding," she exclaimed. Her book's focus had sharpened at last, but it went through countless drafts until its publication on 19 March 1946 as *The Member of the Wedding*, which she dedicated to Elizabeth Ames, executive director of Yaddo Artists Colony, a literary haven for McCullers many times. During this period she was supported, also, by grants from the Guggenheim Foundation and the American Academy of Arts and Letters. When the writing went poorly, she worked on other things. Especially notable were "A Tree. A Rock. A Cloud," which was named an O. Henry Prize Story in 1942, and the novella, *The Ballad of the Sad Café*, which Louis Rubin hailed as one of the "most intense short stories of the twentieth century." Both tales are treatises on McCullers's concept of unrequited love.

Considered her best work by many critics, *The Member of the Wedding* was more widely reviewed than the first two novels. Most of the criticism was positive, reviewers being taken by her brilliant style, more normal subject matter, and sensitive portraiture. Soon after its publication, she met Tennessee Williams. With his encouragement and nurturing—the beginning of a lifelong friendship—she adapted it for the stage despite a crippling stroke. It was directed in 1950 by Harold Clurman and won for her the New York Drama Critics Circle Award, the Donaldson Award, and the Gold Medal of the Theatre Club, as the best playwright of the year. A film version (with most of the original cast) reinforced the popularity of both the novel and the play.

In 1950 *Reflections in a Golden Eye* was reissued by New Directions with a preface by Tennessee Williams, who called the book ''one of the purest and most powerful of those works which are conceived in that Sense of the Awful which is the desperate black root of nearly all significant modern art.'' Williams's remarks triggered the beginning of serious McCullers criticism in contrast to occasional insightful reviewing. His insights were echoed often in the outpouring of critical writing that followed the 1951 publication of the omnibus volume of her work entitled *The Ballad of the Sad Café and Other Works*, a collection that won universal acclaim from the critics. At this point McCullers was on the crest of her popularity, having established herself as a formidable writer. Her works were being translated into many foreign languages.

Meanwhile, in spring 1945, she remarried Reeves McCullers, who had returned to the Army in 1942, took a commission, and was a company commander of a U.S. Ranger outfit. He returned from World War II with three bronze stars, a silver star, and a purple heart, his combat injuries forcing him to accept a medical discharge with full disability benefits. A born leader, Reeves felt stymied living in his wife's shadow, yet devoted himself to her care rather than pursuing his own creative outlets. They spent winter 1946–47 in Paris, where she was enthusiastically received, but both were flown home ill on stretchers in December 1947, Reeves suffering from delirium tremens and Carson from two additional strokes. Their eight-year second marriage was fraught with countless separations, reconciliations, and great heartache. Reeves often threatened suicide, begged Carson to join him in a double suicide, and finally killed himself on 19 November 1953 in a hotel room in Paris while she was visiting Lillian Smith in Clayton, Georgia, seeking solace and trying to decide if she should divorce him. To her, in a sense, he was already dead, yet she suffered trauma by the knowledge of his death (Reeve's three siblings also committed suicide).

Most critics thought that her later works did little to support the accolades earned by the omnibus volume. A second play, *The Square Root of Wonderful*, opened on Broadway in 1957, ran for 45 performances, and folded. Some thought its chief merit was its title. Those who knew her saw it as an incoherent and fragmented attempt to overcome the psychic scars of her life with Reeves and his suicide, and her grief over the death of her mother, on whom she had been inordinately dependent, in 1955.

Despite pre-release publicity of her fifth novel (and final one) emphasizing her courage and relentless struggle against pitiable ill health, *Clock Without Hands* received harsh criticism and was a major disappointment to most reviewers. Irving Howe's review in the *New York Times* faulted the book's weak structure (particularly its lack of symmetry between the Judge Malone and Jester Clane strands of the plot), its unreal portrait of the contemporary South, and the author's lack of "inner conviction and imaginative energy." Howe and other critics saw *Clock Without Hands* as evidence that McCullers's power as a writer had waned significantly.

The *New York Times* quoted her as saying, "Sometimes I think God got me mixed up with Job. . . . But Job never cursed God, and neither have I. I carry on." On 15 August 1967, she suffered a massive brain hemorrhage. Comatose for 47 days, she died on 29 September without regaining consciousness. She was fifty.

MAJOR THEMES

In her fiction as in her life, Carson McCullers—like Frankie Addams in *The Member of the Wedding*—sought repeatedly her "we of me." In 1957 she wrote: "I suppose my central theme is the theme of spiritual isolation. Certainly I have always felt alone." Beginning with *The Heart Is a Lonely Hunter*, she posed the existential dilemma that beset all of her major characters. Repeatedly she adroitly exposed the confinement of the soul and the futility and ultimate betrayal of what she saw as the "human hymn" called hope.

A predominantly pessimistic view of life and a sense of frustration about the South served as a compelling background to the introspective, taciturn quality of McCullers's fiction, which she peopled with characters whose amputated consciousnesses, irreversible physical deformities, and acute psychological dysfunctions rendered them spiritually autistic. When criticized for the freakishness and grotesqueness of her characters, McCullers replied: "One cannot explain accusations of morbidity. A writer can only say he writes from the seeds which flower later in the subconscious. Nature is not abnormal, only lifelessness is abnormal. Anything that pulses and moves and walks around the room, no matter what thing it is doing, is natural and human to the writer." Significantly, only McCullers's "androgyns" are allowed to attempt to break out of their spiritual confinement. Those characters whose sexuality is explicit are doomed to estrangement both from themselves and society. No matter how hard they seek genuine intercourse with others, their efforts are never rewarded. Such was man's plight and his destiny, thought McCullers. Throughout her career, it remained her central and controlling concern. In her fiction she laid bare many poorly shaped plaintiffs who crave congenial communion with others. Yet in their attempt to connect, they form aberrant attachments that ultimately destroy them, or further entrap them. Although her stories and novels do not deal directly with physical imprisonment, her characters are "caught" both symbolically and literally in a variety of ways.

Mick Kelly and Frankie Addams, her young protagonists in *The Heart Is a Lonely Hunter* and *The Member of the Wedding*, are apt metaphors for expressing such entrapment as each character attempts to create a whole new insular world. Mick, who fears she will become a freak because at thirteen she already is five feet, six inches tall, retreats to her "private" room of music and a hatbox of secrets (she keeps in it, among other things, an incongruously constructed home-made violin). John Singer, the deaf-mute to whom she attaches herself, also is a private room for Mick, for she believes that he shares her appreciation of music. Paradoxically, he cannot hear the music and cannot intellectually conceive any such notion. Entrapped, Mick quits school to go to work at Woolworth's to help support the family. She hopes vaguely that someday she may be able to buy her own piano. Her job and the impossibility of fulfilling her yearnings frustrate and embitter her. Unable to connect with Mick and unaware of her adoration, even, Singer is thwarted by the death of his chosen one, the fat Greek, Antonapoulos, whose cretinous mentality does not allow him to perceive Singer's devotion. Upon learning of his friend's death in a mental asylum, Singer can communicate with no one, not even the other deaf-mutes, and calmly puts a bullet through his head, his suicide understood by no one. Every character in the novel feels that he has been "left out on a limb"—his hopes and best intentions dashed, with no single person to blame, merely his caught condition of life. As Mick expressed it, "It was like she was cheated. Only nobody cheated her. So there was nobody to take it out on. However, just the same she had that feeling. Cheated."

Klaus Mann wrote in his diary upon meeting McCullers, having just read *The Heart Is a Lonely Hunter*: "What astounding insight into the ultimate incon-solability and incurability of the human soul! . . . Uncannily versed in the secrets of all freaks and pariahs, she should be able to compose a revealing tale of exile." Most readers would agree that every book she wrote fit Mann's description.

In *The Member of the Wedding*, Frankie Addams yearns to be included in a purpose, be it big or small, but meets an impasse at every turn. Like Mick, she fears that her rapid growth will turn her into a freak. Estranged from family, friends, the town, even trees and flowers, Frankie struggles to break from the confines of her kitchen, the backyard, and her ambivalent self. Her solution to the problem, which would allow her the membership she craves, is destined to fail. By falling in love with "the wedding" and the shattering of the unstable singular pronoun "I," which has plagued her, for the contiguous, unshakable plurality of "we," Frankie sees the configuration of her "we of me" in her brother and his bride. Similarly, her dream of becoming a "member of the whole world" remains a figment of her immature imagination. Of course, the bride and groom do not take her with them, and she is dragged in hysterics from the honeymoon car. Yet the book ends on an affirmative note. Frankie has evolved from the "F. Jasmine" of her fantasy world to Frances—her real name—and is seen embarking on a new life that promises membership in her own peer group. Mick, too, is seen at the end of *The Heart Is a Lonely Hunter* grasping at a straw, unwilling to accept defeat: "Maybe she would get a chance soon. Else what the hell good had it all been—the way she felt about music and the plans she had made in the inside room? It had to be some good if anything made sense. And it was too and it was too and it was too and it was too. It was some good. All right! O.K.! Some good.'' Berenice Sadie Brown, like William Faulkner's Dilsey, accepts what she cannot change: ''We all of us somehow caught. We born this way or that way and we don't know why. . . . Me is me, you is you, and he is he.'' Because Berenice is black, she tells Frankie that she is caught ''worse than you is.''

A few other characters are seen in an affirmative stance, too, as is the cuckolded tramp in ''A Tree. A Rock. A Cloud.'' In a tawdry café, he accosts a young newsboy, a stranger, and declares, ''I love you.'' He is not a deviant attempting a homosexual encounter, but a man reconciled to his ''science of love.'' Yet it is a sterile life, a safe life. Having loved a woman who deserted him, the tramp concluded that love is a ladder and that most men make the mistake of beginning at the top rung by loving a woman. After years of fruitless search, he developed a new strategy. He bought a goldfish and loved it, then ''graduated to one thing and another. . . . I am a master, Son. I can love anything. . . . a bird . . . a traveler on the road. All strangers and all loved!'' But he pales when the newsboy asks if he had fallen in love with a woman again. ''No. . . . I go cautious. And I am not quite ready yet.'' Ironically, the old man is still isolated and lonely because of his science, not in spite of it. It has not only failed to warm his heart; it has also alienated any possible human recipient of love because of his monomania to explain it. Moreover, his tale is incomprehensible to the youngster. The embittered, stingy Leo who runs the café chooses not to enlighten the newsboy. McCullers seems to be saying that the child has to find his own way, existentially.

She also explores the futility of love in *The Ballad of the Sad Café*. Here the archetypal pattern of love is presented in its clearest and simplest form. Each character is successively a lover and a beloved, each a slave and a tyrant depending upon whether he loves or is being loved. In her often-quoted thesis of love from this novella, McCullers wrote:

Love is a joint experience between two persons—but the fact that it is a joint experience does not mean that it is a similar experience to the two people involved. There are the lover and the beloved, but these two come from different countries. Often the beloved is only a stimulus for all the stored-up love which has lain quiet within the lover for a long time. And somehow every lover knows this. He feels in his soul that his love is a solitary thing. He comes to know a new, strange loneliness and it is this knowledge which makes him suffer. So there is only one thing for the lover to do. He must house his love within himself as best he can; he must create for himself a whole new inward world—a world intense and strange, complete in himself. . . . Most of us would rather love than be beloved. . . . And the curt truth is that, in a deep secret way, the state of being beloved is intolerable to many. The beloved fears and hates the lover, and with the best of reasons. The lover craves any possible relation with the beloved, even if this experience can cause him only pain.

The theme of a fallible Creator who had "withdrawn His hand" too soon, in the words of Berenice Sadie Brown, is evident in *Reflections in a Golden Eye*. Through its pages parades the greatest assortment of freaks and half-people in all of McCullers's fiction. In this novel there are no psychologically sound people. All are seen as grotesque aberrations reflected in the golden, distorted eye of a ghastly green peacock. In fact, distorted vision is the malady that afflicts each of the grotesque creatures in this work. Each character is desperate to establish some substantial bond with another, yet his effort leads to death either by extinction or utter negation. The message here, as in her other works, is that human beings are not whole. It is as if a capricious Creator had suddenly become more interested in something—or someone—else than His creative task at hand. Rather than fashioning man in a mirror image of Himself who will behold Him with love and adoration, He becomes distracted by a love object already created and existing on a higher plane whom He, in turn, may worship and adore.

The Maker of McCullers's world of blighted creatures seems to have erred once more in His creation of Sherman Pew, the handsome, blue-eyed, black youth in *Clock Without Hands*. A foundling abandoned in a church, Sherman has one black parent and one white parent, but does not know which. His mysterious parentage obsesses him, and he yearns to know his mother and to be acknowledged by her. But she had died while giving birth to him, and his quest for identity leads to a dead end, his loneliness acute in the drag of time.

Throughout her career, McCullers developed and perfected a blueprint of the solitary soul, a poignant portrait of the twentieth-century human condition that reveals the disjunction between the isolated grotesque and the world in which he lives, and obliquely, between the hapless freak and his imperfect Creator.

SURVEY OF CRITICISM

McCullers's critical reputation presents a complicated and curious pattern. She was highly acclaimed for her first novel in 1940, yet her subsequent books were less well received. The stage version of *The Member of the Wedding* in 1950 solidified her popular success, but not her critical reputation. The publication of her omnibus volume earned her, along with the usual popular reviews, her first academic criticism. Notable are Dayton Kohler's and Oliver Evans's thematic studies that served as the impetus for the general consensus of McCullers's fiction.

In the decade between the success of the omnibus edition and the failure of *Clock Without Hands*, academic critics continued to confirm the importance of McCullers's early achievement. During these years her work elicited a generally positive response in foreign language criticism; unfortunately, however, this writing is for the most part introductory, simplistic, and repetitive. Some of the more important American academic considerations include Frank Baldanza's influential article, "Plato in Dixie" (*Georgia Review*, Summer 1958), and Ihab Hassan's fine essay, "Carson McCullers: The Alchemy of Love and the Aesthetics of Pain," which appeared first in *Modern Fiction Studies* (Winter 1959). Portions of this essay have been reprinted at least eight times, indicating the importance of Hassan's view of McCullers's work.

Her ensuing silence, caused by her prolonged, serious illnesses, somewhat weakened her critical reputation, which was not enhanced by the publication of her play, *The Square Root of Wonderful*, in 1957, and her novel, *Clock Without Hands*, in 1961. Since her death in 1967 and the posthumous publication of *Carson McCullers: The Mortgaged Heart*, criticism has treated her more favorably, comparing her with other important writers of the Southern Renascence. Notable in this barrage of critical articles from a social point of view is Leslie Fiedler's influential study, *Love and Death in the American Novel* (1960).

The 1960s marked the decade of critical retribution following the negative reception of *Clock Without Hands*. Alfred Kazin made judicious observations on McCullers in his article "Bright Book of Life: American Storytellers from Hemingway to Mailer." (1973). Another notable chapter on McCullers was Irving Malin's study of her gothic characteristics (in contrast to the gothic in works of Capote, Hawkes, Salinger, Purdy, and O'Connor) in *New American Gothic* (1962). Louise Gossett's *Violence in Recent Southern Fiction* (1965) effectively contrasted McCullers's use of violence with O'Connor's. Mark Schorer's "McCullers and Capote: Basic Patterns" in *The World We Imagine* (1968) examined the "lyrical and mythical transcendence of the social realities of McCullers' books," in the words of Margaret B. McDowell, whose full-length study *Carson McCullers* (1980) takes advantage of recent biographical and critical writings to provide a fine general introduction to the author. It is the most recent book on McCullers.

Lawrence Graver's *Carson McCullers* (1969), Dale Edmonds's *Carson McCullers* (1969), and Richard Cook's *Carson McCullers* (1975) are three succinct studies, each providing good basic biographical and critical material.

The first book on McCullers was Oliver Evans's *Carson McCullers: Her Life and Work* (1965), followed by an American edition, *The Ballad of Carson McCullers* (1966). Researched with the author's cooperation (yet somewhat unreliable in its biographical details), Evans's study is a fair and appreciative introduction to McCullers's life and major works. Earlier, Evans published several fine articles inviting a reevaluation of McCullers's reputation.

Virginia Spencer Carr's *The Lonely Hunter: A Biography of Carson McCullers* (1975) is the only comprehensive biography to appear since the author's death. The introduction, "Some Words Before," is by Tennessee Williams.

Several distinct strands of McCullers criticism have appeared since the posthumous *The Mortgaged Heart*. One is the feminists' acclaim of her muted but powerful rendition of her androgynous adolescents and their troubled lives. Among the notable articles in this vein are Patricia S. Box's "Androgyny and the Musical Vision: A Study of Two Novels by Carson McCullers" (*Southern Quarterly*, January 1978) and Margaret Bolsterli's " 'Bound' Characters in Porter, Welty, and McCullers: The Pre-Revolutionary Status of Women in American Fiction'' (*Bibliotheque Universelle et Revue de Geneve*, 1978). Both articles deal with McCullers's female characters and their entrapment in the roles dictated by society. Claire Kahane's ''Gothic Mirrors and Feminine Identity'' (*Centennial Review*, 1980) provides a psychoanalytic and feministic perspective of andro-gyny in McCullers's writings, which Kahane claims ''has become a core sym-bol for contemporary women.'' Other articles that consider the psychological and social realism in McCullers's works include Joseph R. Millichap's fine study, ''The Realistic Structure of *The Heart Is a Lonely Hunter*'' (*Twentieth-Century Literature*, January 1971), and Irving Buchen's Freudian reading of her writing in ''Carson McCullers: The Case of Convergence'' (*Bucknell Review*, Spring 1973).

Another trend in McCullers criticism is her view of the South and the significant role it played in her fiction. Important in this context is Delma Eugene Presley's ''Carson McCullers and the South'' (*Georgia Review*, Spring 1974), which argues cogently that McCullers's genius was Southern in origin and that it declined when she cut herself off prematurely from her Southern roots. Important to the study of her short fiction is Robert Phillips's ''Freaking Out: The Short Stories of Carson McCullers'' (*Southern Review*, Winter 1978). Louis Rubin's ''Carson McCullers: The Aesthetic of Pain'' (*Virginia Quarterly Review*, Spring 1977) is also significant. Critical examinations of her short stories of note include Dale Edmonds's '' 'Correspondence': A 'Forgotten' Carson McCullers Short Story'' (*Studies in Short Fiction*, Winter 1972), James Grinnell's ''Delving 'A Domestic Dilemma' '' (*Studies in Short Fiction*, Summer 1972), and Laurence Perrine's ''Restoring 'A Domestic Dilemma' '' (*Studies in Short Fiction*, Winter 1974). Her short works are being anthologized increasingly.

A number of graduate dissertations and festschrift articles in recent years confirm scholarly interest in McCullers, and foreign language criticism is in-creasing, too. Alicia Cervantes Leal's ''Los Elementos Grotescos en la Narrative de Carson McCullers'' (*Kanina*, 1980) and Marzenna Raczkowska's ''The Pat-terns of Love in Carson McCullers' Fiction'' (*Studia Anglica Posnaniensia: An International Review of English Studies* [Poland], December 1980) are notable cases in point.

Although article continues to beget article (an average of four per year in the past decade), there is a need to redefine the McCullers canon. Although gothic and grotesque elements pervade much of McCullers's fiction, the critics have repeated such studies to the point of distraction. It is time for new approaches, for more feminist and social studies of her work, for structuralist and semiotic readings, for connections with other literary and intellectual traditions, and for comparisons with other art forms. The renewed interest in women writers and the Southern Renascence promises continued developments in these direc-tions. Overall, the body of McCullers criticism has improved since her death in 1967.

BIBLIOGRAPHY

Works by Carson McCullers

The Heart Is a Lonely Hunter. Boston: Houghton Mifflin, 1940.
Reflections in a Golden Eye. Boston: Houghton Mifflin, 1941.
The Member of the Wedding. Boston: Houghton Mifflin, 1946.
The Ballad of the Sad Café and Other Works. Boston: Houghton Mifflin, 1951.
The Member of the Wedding (Play). New York: New Directions, 1951.
The Square Root of Wonderful. Boston: Houghton Mifflin, 1958.
Clock Without Hands. Boston: Houghton Mifflin, 1961.
Sweet as a Pickle and Clean as a Pig (Poems). Boston: Houghton Mifflin, 1964.
The Mortgaged Heart, ed. Margarita G. Smith. Boston: Houghton Mifflin, 1971.

Studies of Carson McCullers

Bixley, George. "Carson McCullers: A Bibliographic Checklist." *American Book Collector*, n.s. 5 (January–February 1984): 38–43.
Carr, Virginia Spencer. *The Lonely Hunter: A Biography of Carson McCullers*. New York: Doubleday, 1975; London: Peter Owen, 1976; New York: Carroll & Graf, 1985 (paperback reprint).
Carr, Virginia Spencer and Joseph R. Millichap. "Carson McCullers." *American Women Writers: Fifteen Bibliographic Essays*. Ed. Maurice Duke, Jackson R. Bryer, and M. Thomas Inge. Westport, Conn.: Greenwood Press, 1981, pp. 297–319.
Cook, Richard. *Carson McCullers*. New York: Ungar, 1975.
Edmonds, Dale. *Carson McCullers*. Austin: Steck-Vaughn, 1969.
Evans, Oliver. *Carson McCullers: Her Life and Work*. London: Peter Owen, 1965; American edition published in 1966 by Coward-McCann, retitled *The Ballad of Carson McCullers*.
———. "The Theme of Spiritual Isolation in Carson McCullers." *New World Writing* 1 (April 1952): 297–310.
Fiedler, Leslie. *Love and Death in the American Novel*. New York: Stein and Day, 1960.
Gossett, Louise. *Violence in Recent Southern Fiction*. Durham, N.C.: Duke University Press, 1965.
Graver, Lawrence. *Carson McCullers*. Minneapolis: University of Minnesota Press, 1969.
Kazin, Alfred. "Bright Book of Life: American Novelists and Storytellers from Hemingway to Mailer." *Contemporaries*. Boston: Little, Brown, 1973.
Kiernan, Robert F. *Katherine Anne Porter and Carson McCullers: A Reference Guide*. Boston: G. K. Hall, 1976, pp. 95–169, 185–94.
Kohler, Dayton. "Carson McCullers: Variations on a Theme." *College English* 13 (October 1951): 1–8.
McDowell, Margaret B. *Carson McCullers*. New York: Twayne, 1980.
Malin, Irving. *New American Gothic*. Carbondale: Southern Illinois University Press, 1962.
Shapiro, Adrian M., Jackson R. Bryer and Kathleen Field. *Carson McCullers: A De-*

scriptive Listing and Annotated Bibliography of Criticism. New York: Garland, 1980.

Schorer, Mark. "McCullers and Capote: Basic Patterns." *The World We Imagine*. New York: Farrar, Straus, and Giroux, 1968.

Wikborg, Eleanor. *The Member of the Wedding: Aspects of Structure and Style*. Gotenberg, Sweden: Acta Universitatus Gothoburgensis, 1975; paperback reprint, Atlantic Highlands, N.J.: Humanities Press, 1975.

————— FRED HOBSON —————

H. L. Mencken
(1880–1956)

One of America's greatest essayists and stylists and one of the most original, irreverent, and fearless of American social critics, H. L. Mencken profoundly affected the Southern Renascence. During the 1920s, when his influence as literary critic was greatest, he spent a great deal of his time "Southwatching." He goaded the South even as he gave encouragement to new writers who helped shape the Renascence.

BIOGRAPHY

Henry Louis Mencken was born on 12 September 1880 in Baltimore, Maryland, the son of Anna Abhau and August Mencken. His father was a prosperous cigar manufacturer, a high tariff Republican, an authoritative parent, a practical joker, and a religious skeptic. When Henry Mencken was three years old, his family moved to a comfortable red brick row house in west Baltimore, and there Mencken lived virtually all of his life. Baltimore was always the center of his universe; although he later worked in New York, he kept his residence in Baltimore by "the great protein factory" of the Chesapeake Bay. The city meant to Mencken the good life—good food, drink, music, and camaraderie. It was, he believed, one of the few civilized places to live this side of the Atlantic.

Mencken's grandfather, Burkhardt Mencken, had emigrated from Germany in 1848, and in the late nineteenth century the Menckens were still keenly aware and proud of their German heritage. They were also aware of their place within the large German-American community of Baltimore. They were not among the poor Germans or political radicals who had flocked to America in the mid–nineteenth century. Rather, the Menckens were a family of scholars and, more recently, successful merchants. Direct ancestors had been professors in the universities of Leipzig and Wittenberg. One of them, Johann Burkhardt Mencken, had become famous as the author of *De Charlataneria Eruditorium* (1715), a satire on scholarly frauds.

It was from his grandfather that Mencken absorbed most of his German consciousness; his father was a practical man, more concerned with the here and now than with the past. Young Henry attended a German primary school, apparently at his grandfather's suggestion, and was attracted to books at an early age. He read Shakespeare, Thackeray, and other English authors, but the American Mark Twain became his favorite novelist and *Huckleberry Finn* his favorite novel. At first, he was destined for something other than a life in letters. At age twelve he entered the Baltimore Polytechnic School, an institution that stressed science and vocational skills. Upon graduating he rejected the idea of university education and dutifully went to work in his father's cigar factory.

What Mencken wanted to be from his teens onward was a newspaperman, but his father thought journalism an unworthy pursuit. Mencken toiled in frustration in his father's factory, wondering when and how he could make the break and go his own way. The break came in a way totally unexpected: in 1899 his father died at age forty-four of a kidney infection. August Mencken was buried on a Sunday. On Monday, Mencken later wrote, he showed up at the Baltimore *Morning Herald* and applied for a job.

His rise in the rough and tumble world of Baltimore journalism was meteoric—from reporter to feature writer to columnist to Sunday editor of the *Morning Herald*. In his early twenties he became the youngest city editor of an urban American newspaper. In 1906, after the *Morning Herald* folded, he became Sunday editor of the respectable Baltimore *Sun*, the newspaper for which he was to write for most of the rest of his life. But Mencken's interests also turned to literature. He became drama critic for the *Sun*, and he himself wrote plays, poems, and short stories, as well as books on George Bernard Shaw (1905) and Friedrich Nietzsche (1908). In 1908 he became literary critic for a New York magazine, the *Smart Set*.

It was at the *Smart Set* that Mencken first gained widespread national attention. He served as literary critic until 1914, when he became coeditor with drama critic George Jean Nathan. Between 1914 and 1924 he and Nathan made the *Smart Set* the slickest, most influential literary publication in the country, and in his columns Mencken became a literary and cultural force. In particular, he took dead aim at the genteel tradition, that Anglo-American tradition of literature that Mencken believed was overly polite, overly optimistic, sentimental, and life-denying—in short, dishonest. The American writers he championed—Theodore Dreiser, James Branch Cabell, Sinclair Lewis, and Sherwood Anderson among others—were themselves rebelling against that tradition, and Mencken played a role greater than that of any other critic in bringing them to the fore.

Mencken's reasons for attacking the genteel tradition lay in his background and early reading. As a German-American, he resented any tradition that prized the English roots of American writing to the exclusion of all others. As an irreligious freethinker, he resented any literature that was grounded in Christian morality, particularly a rigid Victorian morality. As something of a hedonist (or so he considered himself, although in fact he was usually a proper Victorian gentleman), he resented American puritanism—"the haunting fear that someone, somewhere, may be happy"—which be believed shaped the literature of the genteel tradition. And as an early admirer of Mark Twain, he detested any literature that did not tell the *truth*; like Mark Twain, he believed unmasking frauds was the primary task of any writer or critic.

Mencken's opinions—his prejudices, he called them—were reinforced during World War I. His pro-German, anti-British positions were articulated so vigorously that the Sunpapers silenced him for a time. One can hardly underestimate the effect of World War I on Mencken. The anti-German propaganda that flowed from American newspapers, the glorification of the English—combined with the grand abstractions uttered by that latter-day Puritan, Woodrow Wilson—caused him to look even more harshly at America than he had before. The Mencken of the 1920s—the cynic, the iconoclast, the antidemocrat, the enemy of puritanism and of that stronghold of Anglo-Saxons, the American South—had roots in an earlier Baltimore, but the American response to the war in Europe also played a great role in shaping America's most famous and influential social and literary critic of the 1920s.

No one can deny that fame and influence. During his heyday, from the end of World War I until the start of the Great Depression, Mencken was (as the *New York Times* called him) "the most powerful private citizen in America"; or, as Walter Lippmann wrote, "the most powerful personal influence on this whole generation of educated people." He was not simply an editor, writer, and essayist: he was the spokesman for a generation, capturing and articulating the spirit of that segment of postwar America that was, at one and the same time, both disillusioned and exuberant. He attracted followers in New York (although he was always somewhat critical of the Greenwich Village writers), but mainly he gained apostles in the provinces. Through such essays as "Puritanism as a Literary Force" and "The Sahara of the Bozart," he declared war on the old and the traditional—on puritanism and Victorianism. From the Middle West, writers such as Dreiser, Lewis, and Anderson flocked to his banner, but it was in the American South that his influence was particularly strong. In "The Sahara," that eloquent indictment of the late, lamented Confederacy, he blasted the South as a cultural and literary desert, and although he became the leading target of a hundred editors throughout Dixie, he also became the idol of a number of young Southern writers, including Thomas Wolfe, Paul Green, W. J. Cash, Gerald W. Johnson, and (for a time) Allen Tate. He responded to the letters he received from the South and Midwest, encouraged regional writers, and published their stories and poems. No literary arbiter—not even the editors of *Scribner's Monthly*, the *Atlantic Monthly*, and the *Century*, who encouraged local colorists in the late nineteenth century—had ever done so much for an honest regional American literature as H. L. Mencken.

Much of this work was done in his capacity as editor of the *American Mercury*, the magazine that he and Nathan began to edit when they gave up the *Smart Set* in 1923. The *Mercury* became, within a year or two of its founding, the most famous, most widely quoted, most notorious magazine in the United States, and Mencken's editorial columns, book reviews, and general remarks about life in America further increased his influence.

It is often assumed that Mencken's influence lasted only through the 1920s, that with the 1930s his power seriously declined. That assumption is generally correct, and the reasons for the decline are revealing. In fact, Mencken's influence as a literary critic had waned before the Depression: by the mid–1920s he had lost his earlier interest in literature and had turned increasingly to broader social and political issues. By 1929 he had so lost touch with the American literary scene that he virtually ignored such works as Faulkner's *The Sound and the Fury* and Thomas Wolfe's *Look Homeward, Angel*, although both Faulkner and Wolfe had earlier felt his influence.

In the 1930s Mencken's interest in politics completely overshadowed his literary interest. After Roosevelt's election in 1932, Mencken began to direct his attention—and increasingly his invective—toward "Roosevelt II." He had always been critical of the occupant of the White House, regardless of political party—Wilson, Harding, Coolidge, and Hoover had all felt his wrath—but the attack he unleashed against Roosevelt was unequaled by his assault on any other political figure, save perhaps William Jennings Bryan. Not only was Mencken out of touch with mainstream politics in America in the 1930s, but when he showed any interest at all in literature he was out of the mainstream too: he disliked reigning proletarian fiction. In a larger sense, however, Mencken lost influence because the 1930s was not a decade for satire, debunking, smartness, and his brand of iconoclasm. It was a decade for social and economic reform; and reformers—"do-gooders"—were a breed Mencken had always detested.

But his diminished role in the national life allowed him more time to write books. Since his early works on Shaw and Nietzsche, most of his works had been collections of essays he had earlier written for the *Smart Set*, the *American Mercury*, and other magazines. His *Book of Prefaces* (1917) and the six volumes of *Prejudices*, published between 1919 and 1927, contain in many respects the essential Mencken. But the works of the 1930s hang together better as books. In *Treatise on the Gods* (1930) he attempted to trace the origins of man's need for religion and the development of religion up to his day. In *Treatise on Right and Wrong* (1934) he focused on ethics. In the mid–1930s he undertook a series of articles about his youth and young manhood in Baltimore, articles that first appeared in the *New Yorker* and later became part of his superb work of reminiscence, *Happy Days* (1940), *Newspaper Days* (1941), and *Heathen Days* (1943). In the 1930s he also returned to the study of the American language that he had begun as a young newspaperman in Baltimore and that fascinated him throughout his career. The first edition of *The American Language* had been published by Alfred A. Knopf in 1918, and revised editions had appeared in 1921 and 1923, but Mencken's frantic pace in the 1920s prevented him from giving much time to his study for more than a decade. In the early 1930s he was able to return to the project in earnest, and in 1936 he issued a rewritten and greatly expanded edition of *The American Language*. From the beginning Mencken had been struck by the extent to which American English differed from the variety spoken in Great Britain, and he attempted to capture the color and vitality of American speech in his most scholarly work.

Mencken settled down to a quieter life as his influence waned. In 1930 he had married Sara Haardt of Montgomery, Alabama, one violet he had found in the "Sahara," and the long-time bachelor left the Mencken home in West Baltimore, took an apartment downtown, and found great happiness in marriage until his wife's death in 1935. After that he moved back into the family home where he lived for the remainder of his life with his brother, August. He continued to berate Roosevelt, to protest the growth of government under the New Deal, and noticed—at first with more amusement than alarm—the rise to power of Adolph Hitler in Germany. Again, Mencken's German loyalties—and his distaste for the British—made it difficult for him to acknowledge the German threat to world peace. When war came, he refrained from political commentary, continued to work on his reminiscences for the *New Yorker* and on *The American Language*, continued to see old friends from the Sunpapers, and kept a close eye on the state of his own health. An amateur student of medicine, Mencken had always been aware of his own ailments, real and imaginary.

What afflicted Mencken in 1948, however, was all too real. On the evening of 23 November he suffered a massive stroke, and although he survived, he never recovered. He lost the capacity to read and write, the two activities that had given meaning to his life. He lived more than seven more years, confused and depressed and often wishing for death. On 29 January 1956 he died. His ashes were deposited in the Mencken family plot in Baltimore.

MAJOR THEMES

Although Mencken was more a synthesizer than an originator of ideas, it was evident in the 1940s that American society had never seen anything like him. His intellectual forebears were Voltaire and Swift and, in America, Mark Twain, but he possessed a courage and a devotion to truth that even Mark Twain lacked. Mark Twain, after all, eventually caved in to the genteel tradition and, in the long run, was so careful of his reputation that he did not allow his bitterest works to be published in his own lifetime. Mencken never was governed by caution: he was outspoken, often caustic (one thinks of his obituary of William Jennings Bryan), and he refused to let anything—institutional loyalties or personal friend-ship—stand in the way of his honest expression of ideas.

With Mencken, however, the ideas sometimes seem to be overwhelmed by the style. For as a prose stylist he had no equal, although some of his Southern apostles, particularly Gerald W. Johnson and W. J. Cash, came close. The Mencken style was characterized by a heavy dose of metaphor and hyperbole, a sense of the ridiculous, and a love of colloquial American speech. But if Mencken and his readers reveled in his style, he was nonetheless a consistent thinker—and most of his ideas were formed by the time he was twenty years old.

With Mencken, one suspects that the opinions—the "prejudices"—came first, and the writers who are presumed to have "influenced" him did not in fact shape him so much as simply give him a system and vocabulary to express those strongly held opinions. He was a Shavian before he read Shaw, a Nietzschean before he read Nietzsche, a Darwinian before he read Darwin. But in those three writers, as well as Thomas Henry Huxley and James Gibbons Huneker, he found if not intellectual influences at least kindred spirits, and he paid homage to them (with the exception of Shaw) for the rest of his days.

Early, he was drawn to Shaw's iconoclasm and to Huxley's agnosticism. Or, rather, as he later wrote, "Huxley gave order and cohesion to my own doubts and converted me into a violent agnostic." Similarly, Herbert Spencer and William Graham Sumner taught him what he already felt: that Darwin's theory of natural selection could be applied as well to society—that social and economic competition was the essence of life in the modern world. Mencken, thus, was a Social Darwinist before he knew the meaning of the term.

Nietzsche and Huneker were somewhat later influences. Nietzsche's attacks on religion, conventional morality, and the mass of men—his emphasis on superior men who rise above the herd—all appealed to the son of a German-American skeptic who himself felt superior to most of the people around him. And Huneker influenced Mencken's literary criticism more than any other writer, largely because Huneker was one American critic who did not conform to the genteel tradition in letters. Huneker's view of literature was nonprovincial and aesthetic. He was an iconoclast who championed rebels. He was completely different, Mencken believed, from dull academic critics.

Indeed, academic critics—the "professor-doktors," Mencken called them—always bore the brunt of Mencken's criticism. In this case, too, one might contend that Mencken's point of view was shaped in part by his own situation: that is, not only was he not a "professor-doktor," but he had never even attended a university. There were other reasons as well for his criticism of professors. The academy seemed to be a sheltered place to Mencken the reporter, who had seen life in the raw—the city jail and the morgue—at age eighteen and nineteen. Furthermore, academic literary critics were more accurately literary *historians* whose interest seemed to lie only in the past. Not only did most of them appear uninterested in contemporary literature, they refused to acknowledge its existence—except when a writer like Dreiser made so much noise he could not be ignored, and then the academic critics, Stuart Sherman in particular, dismissed the new naturalists as barbarians. It was this attitude that led to Mencken's war with the New Humanists, that group of academic critics led by Sherman, Irving Babbitt, and Paul Elmer More, who made literature a branch of morality, an extension of puritanism.

Mencken's primary ideas about literature were set forth in a series of essays written between 1915 and 1920. In "Puritanism as a Literary Force" (1917) he maintained that the legacy of puritanism prevented America from realizing a great literature: puritanism could not recognize beauty or acknowledge the need for pleasure, and puritanism, which Mencken equated with censorship and repression, shied away from sex, from any explicit reference to the human body, thus from much of life itself. If Mencken sometimes confused "puritanism" with Victorianism, so did other American social critics of the 1920s; but the fact remains that he, more than any other American of his time, is responsible for giving puritanism the bad name it possesses today.

Other essays—"Criticism of Criticism of Criticism" (1917) and "The Natitonal Letters" (1920)—set forth other aspects of Mencken's position, but when one takes his critical philosophy as a whole, one finds a critical stance remarkably similar to that professed by Matthew Arnold, with whom Mencken violently disagreed on many matters. Arnold had written in his essay "The Function of Criticism at the Present Time" (1864) that a major role of the literary critic as well as the social critic was to "create an intellectual situation of which the creative power can profitably avail itself." The bold critic should introduce a new "order of ideas," should cause a "stir and growth everywhere," out of which would come "the creative epochs of literature." "Criticism first," Arnold had written, "a time of true creative activity, perhaps . . . hereafter, when criticism has done its work." In American literature from 1905 to 1925 Mencken filled precisely the role Arnold had described. He was, first and foremost, the bold critic, exposing old, outmoded forms, introducing a "new order of ideas," clearing the way for Dreiser, Lewis, Anderson, and their descendants.

But any study of Mencken's ideas and themes must go beyond literature since, from 1920 on Mencken saw himself as primarily a social and political commentator and intellectual historian and only secondarily as a literary critic. He was the most relentlessly honest social critic America has ever seen, writing with little allegiance to the nation itself (other than that of a man who enjoyed seeing an endless "carnival of buncombe"), seeing America nearly from a European point of view, except for his distinctly American exuberance. In *Notes on Democracy* (1926) he contended that democracy amounted to little more than mob rule, with mediocrity triumphing over superior men and principles. In *Treatise on the Gods* (1930), which he considered his best book, he approached religion skeptically but was, at the same time, fascinated by any phenomenon that had so occupied man from his beginning. All religions, he contended, stemmed from a common need, although that need was diminishing as science came to explain more and more of life's mysteries. In *Treatise on Right and Wrong* (1934) he maintained that certain standards of morality, like religious beliefs, were nearly universal: nearly all humans in all civilizations had agreed that acts such as murder and theft are wrong. Mencken considers various origins of the ethical impulse—in religion, in philosophy (he particularly admired Aristotle), in self-protection, and in social sanction. In this book, as in his others, it is clear that Mencken, although well grounded in intellectual history, was no theologian or philosopher. But if he was not an altogether original thinker, in these books and even more in his social and literary criticism he became something even more important for his time and place: as William H. Nolte has remarked, he was *himself* an original.

SURVEY OF CRITICISM

Mencken has been one of the most widely discussed of American authors, although the writing about him has been decidedly uneven. Most early studies of his life and thought, studies written during his lifetime, are among the least objective, largely because the authors tend to be either strongly pro-Mencken or, in one notable instance, anti-Mencken. Many of the books appearing before his death in 1956 were written by journalists or by his friends or associates. Most of those books were of a general nature. Since 1960 scholars—the dreaded "professors-doktors"—have largely taken over the field and have focused on more specialized aspects of Mencken's life, writing, and influence. An irony over which Mencken would surely chuckle is that they have treated him well indeed. Academic critics and historians have been aided greatly by the collections of Mencken letters and manuscripts in the New York Public Library, the Enoch Pratt Free Library of Baltimore, and other repositories. The 1971 opening of a large body of Mencken correspondence in the New York Public Library proved to be a particular bonanza for Mencken scholars.

The earliest book-length studies of Mencken appeared in 1925 when their subject was a mere forty-five years old. In that year a Mencken admirer, Isaac Goldberg, produced *The Man Mencken: A Biographical and Critical Survey*, an uneven but valuable study for which Mencken himself provided a great deal of information about his family background. The same year Mencken's friend, Ernest A. Boyd, produced *H. L. Mencken*, a slender volume that is a generally astute assessment of his thought.

Although Mencken was lauded and analyzed in books in the mid–1920s, he had to wait a quarter of a century for further book-length studies—perhaps a sign of his waning influence. His career was over when Edgar Kemler and William Manchester, both with help from Mencken himself, undertook biographies. Kemler's *The Irreverent Mr. Mencken* (1950) is a rather critical look at Baltimore's Sage. Manchester, like Goldberg earlier, was a young Mencken admirer, and he set out in his *Disturber of the Peace* (1950) to make a favorable case for his subject. Despite his partisanship, Manchester's book is in some respects the best Mencken biography, engagingly written and characterized by a deep understanding of what Mencken represented in American life. Six years after this work, Charles Angoff wrote a book that was as harsh toward Mencken as Manchester had been kind. Angoff had worked under Mencken at the *Mercury*, had served as the butt of his humor, and was out to even the score in his *H. L. Mencken: A Portrait from Memory* (1956). His was, as one reviewer noted, a "mean and vengeful book."

The three decades since Mencken's death have seen an explosion of scholarly studies of Mencken as writer, critic, editor, and cultural force. Carl Bode in *Mencken* (1969) wrote the biography that is, to this point, most nearly definitive, but Bode is stronger on presentation of fact than on interpretation. Guy J. Forgue's *H. L. Mencken: L'Homme, L'Oeuvre, L'Influence* (1967) is a perceptive biographical and critical study, although it has yet to be translated into English. Sara Mayfield in *The Constant Circle: H. L Mencken and His Friends* (1968) made no pretense of scholarship. A close friend of Mencken's and particularly of his wife, Mayfield wrote a delightful and charming memoir.

Three other books published in the 1960s focused more on Mencken the editor and critic than Mencken the man—although their authors fully realized that those identities could hardly be separated. Marvin K. Singleton's *H. L. Mencken and the "American Mercury" Adventure* (1962) and Carl R. Dolmetsch's *"The Smart Set": A History and Anthology* (1966) dealt with Mencken as editor and literary arbiter in the second and third decades of the century, and William H. Nolte in *H. L. Mencken, Literary Critic* (1966) provided a valuable and well-written account that focused on Mencken in the years between 1908 and 1925, the period of his most serious interest in literature.

Most recent studies have been concerned with specific aspects of Mencken's literary career. Charles Scruggs in *The Sage in Harlem* (1984) treats admirably Mencken's interest in and connections with black writers in the 1920s. Edward A. Martin in *H. L. Mencken and the Debunkers* (1984), a valuable if not well-written book, sees Mencken in relation to other American iconoclasts, particularly Sinclair Lewis, Don Marquis, and Ring Lardner. Fred Hobson in *Serpent in Eden: H. L. Mencken and the South* (1974) treats Mencken's love-hate affair with Dixie and his role in the Southern literary Renascence of the 1920s. Other recent works have dealt with Mencken's thought and influence in more general terms. The best of these are Douglas C. Stenerson's *H. L. Mencken: Iconoclast from Baltimore* (1971) and Charles A. Fecher's *Mencken: A Study of His Thought* (1978). Fecher's study, a product of love, is somewhat more impressive in intention than in execution. Other, less valuable works on Mencken's thought are W.H.A. Williams's *H. L. Mencken* (1977) and George H. Douglas's *H. L. Mencken: Critic of American Life* (1978).

A final irony by which one is struck in surveying Mencken scholarship is that this journalist-critic—who is generally considered such a lowbrow that he is not usually taught in American literature courses—has in fact attracted more scholarly attention than all but three or four American writers of the twentieth century. Not only has he been the subject of the biographies and monographs mentioned above—and numerous articles in the sort of scholarly journals he once debunked—but several collections of his letters and critical essays have also appeared, as well as other collections of essays on Mencken. And with more Mencken papers and letters being released for scholarly use each decade—the next haul will be in 1991 in the New York Public Library—the end of the Mencken industry is hardly in sight.

BIBLIOGRAPHY

Works by H. L. Mencken

Ventures into Verse. Baltimore: Marshall, Beek and Gordon, 1903.

George Bernard Shaw: His Plays. Boston: J. W. Luce, 1905.

The Philosophy of Friedrich Nietzsche. Boston: J. W. Luce, 1908; rev. ed., 1913.

Men versus the Man, with Robert Rives La Monte. New York: H. Holt, 1910.

The Artist: A Drama Without Words. Boston: J. W. Luce, 1912.

Europe after 8:15, with George Jean Nathan and Willard Huntington Wright. New York: Lane, 1914.

A Book of Burlesques. New York: Lane, 1916.

A Little Book in C-Major. New York: Lane, 1916.

A Book of Prefaces. New York: Alfred A. Knopf, 1917.

Damn! A Book of Calumny. New York: Goodman, 1918.

In Defense of Women. New York: Alfred A. Knopf, 1918.

The American Lanugage: A Preliminary Inquiry into the Development of English in the United States. New York: Alfred A. Knopf, 1919; rev. eds., 1921, 1923, 1936; supplements, 1945, 1948.

Prejudices, First Series through *Sixth Series*. New York: Alfred A. Knopf, 1919, 1920, 1922, 1924, 1926, 1927.

The American Credo, with George Jean Nathan. New York: Alfred A. Knopf, 1920.

Notes on Democracy. New York: Alfred A. Knopf, 1926.

James Branch Cabell. New York: McBride, 1927.

Menckeniana: A Schimpflexicon. New York: Alfred A. Knopf, 1928.

Treatise on the Gods. New York: Alfred A. Knopf, 1930.

Making a President. New York: Alfred A. Knopf, 1932.

Treatise on Right and Wrong. New York: Alfred A. Knopf, 1934.

Happy Days, 1880–1892. New York: Alfred A. Knopf, 1940.

Newspaper Days, 1899–1906. New York: Alfred A. Knopf, 1941.

Heathen Days, 1890–1936. New York: Alfred A. Knopf, 1943.

A Christmas Story. New York: Alfred A. Knopf, 1946.

A Mencken Chrestomathy. New York: Alfred A. Knopf, 1949.

Minority Report. New York: Alfred A. Knopf, 1956.

The Bathtub Hoax and Other Blasts and Bravos from the Chicago Tribune. New York: Alfred A. Knopf, 1958.

Letters of H. L. Mencken. Ed. Guy J. Forgue. New York: Alfred A. Knopf, 1961.

H. L. Mencken's "Smart Set" Criticism. Ed. William H. Nolte. Ithaca: Cornell University Press, 1968.

The Young Mencken: The Best of His Work. Ed. Carl Bode. New York: Dial Press, 1973.

The New Mencken Letters, Ed. Carl Bode. New York: Dial Press, 1977.

Studies of H. L. Mencken

Adler, Betty. *The Mencken Bibliography*. Baltimore: Johns Hopkins University Press, 1961.

Angoff, Charles. *H. L. Mencken: A Portrait from Memory*. New York: Yoseloff, 1956.

Bode, Carl. *Mencken*. Carbondale: Southern Illinois University Press, 1969.

Boyd, Ernest A. *H. L. Mencken*. New York: McBride, 1925.

Dolmetsch, Carl R. *"The Smart Set": A History and Anthology*. New York: Dial Press, 1966.

Dorsey, John, ed. *On Mencken*. New York: Alfred A. Knopf, 1980.

Douglas, George H. *H. L. Mencken: Critic of American Life*. Hamden, Conn.: Archon Books, 1978.

Fecher, Charles A. *Mencken: A Study of His Thought*. New York: Alfred A. Knopf, 1978.

Forgue, Guy J. *H. L. Mencken: L'Homme, L'Oeuvre, L'Influence*. Paris: Minard, 1967.

Goldberg, Isaac. *The Man Mencken: A Biographical and Critical Study*. New York: Simon and Schuster, 1925.

Hobson, Fred. *Serpent in Eden: H. L. Mencken and the South*. Chapel Hill: University of North Carolina Press, 1974.

Kemler, Edgar. *The Irreverent Mr. Mencken*. Boston: Little, Brown, 1950.

Manchester, William. *Disturber of the Peace: The Life of H. L. Mencken*. New York: Harper, 1950.

Martin, Edward A. *H. L. Mencken and the Debunkers*. Athens: University of Georgia Press, 1984.

Mayfield, Sara. *The Constant Circle: H. L. Mencken and His Friends*. New York: Delacorte, 1968.

Nolte, William H. *H. L. Mencken: Literary Critic*. Middletown, Conn.: Wesleyan University Press, 1966.

Scruggs, Charles. *The Sage in Harlem: H. L. Mencken and the Black Writers of the 1920s*. Baltimore: Johns Hopkins University Press, 1984.

Singleton, Marvin K. *H. L. Mencken and the "American Mercury" Adventure*. Durham, N.C.: Duke University Press, 1962.

Stenerson, Douglas C. *H. L. Mencken: Iconoclast from Baltimore*. Chicago: University of Chicago Press, 1971.

Wagner, Philip. *H. L. Mencken*. Minneapolis: University of Minnesota Press, 1966.

Williams, W. H. A. *H. L. Mencken*. Boston: Twayne, 1977.

Margaret Mitchell
(1900–1949)

In *Gone with the Wind* Margaret Mummerlyn Mitchell provided the world the standard measure for a fictional South. She created scenes, characters, and language that live with uncommon vividness for a vast readership. Her Pulitzer Prize–winning work belongs almost as much to folklore and mythology as to literature. So does its author. Before her death at forty-eight in 1949, she had become the stuff of lore and legend. The Mitchell cult survives even as her novel remains among the most widely known fictions in history.

BIOGRAPHY

Born on 16 November 1900, Mitchell grew up in Atlanta, Georgia, where her family had lived for four generations. Intensely active and physical as a child, she relished rough play and sports of every kind. School held fewer attractions. Although raised a Catholic, she attended public schools until she was twelve, and was graduated from a fashionable finishing school, Washington Seminary, in 1918. She achieved only a mediocre academic record there, but she polished her reputation as a writer and rebel. The summer she completed high school, she accepted an engagement ring from a young army officer, Lt. Clifford Henry, a wealthy, serious-minded, poetry-quoting, Harvard-educated, silk-stockinged New Yorker. Two months after their secret betrothal, he died in the final German offensive of the war.

Mitchell enrolled at Smith College in Northampton, Massachusetts, that fall, but she aborted her education after two terms to keep house for her father, widowed in January 1919. Spending the next three years as a Southern flapper, she debuted in 1920–21. In these years, men and courtship filled her life. As she approached her twenty-third birthday, with neither training, career, nor husband, she surrendered to the social pressure for marriage.

Berrien Kinnard Upshaw personified the aggressive Southern male. Although he had established a reputation for instability, this did not deter his lady; his type even attracted her. They married in September 1922, and less than three months later, Upshaw deserted her. Returning in the spring, he beat her and dragged her to the bedroom for rape. The 1924 divorce was uncontested.

This explosion of her private life liberated Mitchell's old ambition for a career in journalism. Her byline appeared for the first time on 22 December 1922, in the Atlanta *Journal's* Sunday "Magazine." Until she resigned in May 1926, she produced 130 verifiable articles, stories, and reviews. If a career satisfied old ambitions, the job dissatisfied her: the pay exploited, the misogyny galled, the literary limitations rankled, the inexorable deadlines pressured her relentlessly. The work whetted her ambitions even as it confined her. She reached a professional turning point at the same time she was redefining her private life.

Her domestic considerations hinged on her second husband, John Marsh. He first entered her life in 1920–21 as the mercurial Upshaw's roommate. After working as a copy editor in Atlanta, he settled permanently by 1924 as an advertising subaltern. After Upshaw departed, Marsh pressed his suit again by tendering friendship and professional support to the novice journalist.

Mitchell struggled with the decision to marry again. She disliked sexual intimacy and treasured her freedom, but she craved the security of a legitimizing male. The wedding date of 4 July 1925 suggested Mitchell's ambivalence and hopes for the union. Marsh did not disappoint her. Devoid of Upshaw's passion or Henry's poetry, he offered brotherly sympathy and dogged loyalty. Among *Gone with the Wind*'s masculine archetypes, if the willowy Clifford Henry found a voice in Ashley Wilkes and "Red" Upshaw in the wife-raping Rhett, then John Marsh is reflected in the long-suffering Frank Kennedy.

For all Marsh's indulgences, Mitchell returned her husband's loyalty measure for measure. In the spring of 1926, his promotion obviated the financial excuse for her employment. Feeling a dead end at work, she decided to honor her husband's ego and resign. The decision weighed heavily on her, and she floundered. Her social isolation grew; indeed, it formalized when a hurt ankle mysteriously failed to heal, and she took to bed. Confined to her room in the late fall and early winter of 1926, she began her novel.

From late 1926 through 1929, Mitchell worked steadily on her epic, sometimes up to eighteen hours a day. A highly meticulous craftsman, she constantly drafted and redrafted. In one case—Frank Kennedy's death—and probably others, she created full-blown alternative versions. The original manuscript also contained additional scenes and episodes in chapters dropped from the final text. She said that only one section stood finally as she originally wrote it: the part beginning with Scarlett's return to Tara after Atlanta's destruction and ending with the protagonist's determination to shoulder her load. She essentially completed the work by 1930 when she was twenty-nine years old. It lacked only a first chapter and final polishing.

In 1935 Mitchell submitted her manuscript for publication. That act is symbolically as well as practically important. On the one hand, publishing a novel was the logical conclusion towards which her life had tended. As early as age eighteen she documented her ambition to write professionally. Her whole career testifies to this purpose. She created plays and stories from the time she could hold a pencil, and she produced a novel when she was sixteen and a novella when she was twenty-one. On the other hand, contrary impulses pulled her in the opposite direction. She created her novel as a profoundly private, even intimate act, revealing the story to John Marsh alone and allowing only him access to her copy. By nature almost pathologically secretive, she had grown more insular in the 1930s. Closemouthed about her work and disguising her craftsmanship behind a giddy, belle-ish persona, Mitchell convinced most people of her lack of seriousness as a writer; paradoxically, this public attitude increased her motive to prove herself after all. Indeed, the casual comment of a friend that she lacked the requisite seriousness to produce a book precipitated the furious reaction to release her manuscript in 1935. In keeping with her ambivalence, she later wired the Macmillan editor to return her novel.

Despite the chaos of the manuscript, the editor kept it; he liked it enormously. So did the world. Its sales and popularity had no precedent in literary history. The hoopla concentrated unequaled attention on the author.

The fame overwhelmed Mitchell. Her response, however, was mixed. While she decried the disorder, she rejected structural changes in her life that might have reduced the attention. Indeed, her actions often generated the opposite effect. She insisted on her literary innocence and dismissed suggestions of her professional skill and ambitions; she repeated constantly that she was only a lucky housewife. Such claims fired the Mitchell legend.

Attention flagged with American entry into World War II. Her voluminous correspondence fell off sharply, and she filled her time with dedicated war work. Protecting her copyrights, she committed great energy to legal battles. Physical illness, personal and familial, sapped her too. Always accident-prone and frequently ill, Mitchell suffered especially from back problems in the war years. Her father's health deteriorated steadily from the late 1930s until his death in 1944. Her husband's massive coronary soon after her father's death allowed her no relief. Tending Marsh as she did her father, she also wrangled bitterly with physicians about what constituted proper care. Rancor and bitterness also colored her politics, as she sulked privately about regional liberals, and encouraged the anticommunist columnist Westbrook Pegler.

Threatened by fame, preoccupied with managing her estate, overwhelmed with personal and family illnesses, Mitchell never published anything after *Gone with the Wind*. She did, however, write. In truth, throughout her life she seems to have channeled more time and energy into personal correspondence than into writing fiction. From her adolescence she wrote incredible numbers of letters, often of remarkable length, ten to twenty typed pages being unexceptional. These constitute their own genre. Containing separate narratives and dialogue, they generally work like small short stories. They function as serial narratives from her own literary biography, cut, honed, and elaborated so as to delight and entertain.

Other than these remarkable letters, she wrote nothing else. Near her forty-eighth birthday, the same age her mother died, Mitchell made a will. Within the year, on 11 August 1949, an automobile struck her as she walked from her apartment with John Marsh to see a movie, *The Canterbury Tales*. She died on 16 August. She left no children.

To a remarkable degree, myth and folklore still surround Mitchell's life. Intellectual as well as practical explanations account for this phenomenon. For her friends and correspondents, she created a whole cabinet of conflicting personae. Maintaining such contrary images nurtured the Mitchell legend while she lived; it fostered a cult after her death. The numerous popular accounts of her life continue to blur the distinctions between fact and fiction. More practically, the destruction of her papers and manuscripts has complicated the problem, as has her family's limitation of access to her still vast archive.

MAJOR THEMES

Mitchell matured in the half-light world of regional romance when mythology and tradition exercised great power in the South. She responded naturally to the mythic and primitive, not least as embodied in the oral tradition. She grew up on regional oratory—of stump speeches and sermons. She listened well and cultivated a keen ear for the spoken word. She absorbed both the form and content of the tales repeated by her elders. She perpetuated the tradition. Even as a child, she won a reputation as a rare storyteller; as an adult, friends insisted that no one matched her ability as a talker and raconteur.

The Mitchells had been one of the richest, best-placed, and politically important families in the city, especially in the generation of the author's baronial grandfather, Russell Crawford Mitchell, who died in 1905. Yet dour evangelicalism, or the family's residual Methodist piety perhaps, soured family ambitions, especially for Eugene M. Mitchell, the author's father, a narrow, humorless, highly conservative real estate lawyer. His wife remained Eugene Mitchell's one real passion, yet she reemphasized his alienation: he was a Spencerian, lapsed Methodist; May Belle Stephens was a devout Irish Catholic. Mrs. Mitchell's biting wit, aggressive intelligence, and daring personality contrasted with her husband's stodginess. With their religious differences, they represented opposites joined.

As suggested in the otherwise eccentric decision to make *Gone with the Wind*'s protagonists Irish, Catholic, and immigrants, the author's maternal line dominated her imagination. Mrs. Mitchell shaped her daughter's values and motives more directly and thoroughly still. Full of paradoxes herself, she provided her children the most contradictory models. She embodied the most austere ideal of ladyhood, yet she plunged into the woman's suffrage movement and the Catholic Layman's Association at the height of the Tom Watson era. She constantly goaded her offspring to excel, but as she allowed tenderness or approval with difficulty, she established the hardest goals, especially for her daughter.

Psychologically, Mrs. Mitchell left a divided legacy. This problem, however, overlapped with cultural and political ones. If her mother goaded her to success even while rigidly defining proper feminine spheres, a regional patriarchal system did much the same thing. Holding women as the sacred essence of the Southern social order, it nevertheless denied them initiative and legitimacy on their own. This divided feminist consciousness consistently influenced both the form and content of Mitchell's art. Judging by her adolescent fiction, she wrestled with this divided consciousness by age fifteen at least.

This feminist literary dilemma militated against a final definition of character. Mitchell met the problem by making a virtue of play, change, and disguise. She jested with the nature of reality in plays about plays, and she stretched the meaning of language itself as she built on double and even triple meanings of words. Her juvenilia offers telling biographical clues, too. In one surviving play, the protagonist, named "Margaret Mitchell," is the star; she is also the villain, paradoxically described as a "sanctified cherub." At the same time, this protagonist provides the dramatic action by fighting for the female part even while this "shero" represents the mute, abused, passive victim of the drama. Two published short stories from her high school days work similarly. Both revolve around the destruction of homelife and domestic unity; in one, the loss means life and liberation; in the other, death and anomie for the female protagonists. Such antagonistic endings suggest Mitchell's personal ambivalence about home and family, men and society.

Mitchell's epic spins the tale of Scarlett O'Hara, a Georgia belle during the Civil War and Reconstruction. Artfully combining various themes, plots, and subplots, it chiefly chronicles the heroine's frustrated pursuit of her aristocratic neighbor, Ashley Wilkes, and Rhett Butler's similarly blighted love for Scarlett herself. By this measure, frustration simmers at the novel's core, and along with it, misunderstanding, cross-purposes, and irony. Writing the last chapter first, Mitchell steered the whole narrative towards the unhappy ending. Indeed, it dominated her artistic conception. Thus, while she formally surrendered any influence over the film, she was adamant in private that David Selznick not brighten the ending.

The novel relates to the plantation romance as developed between 1880 and World War I. Thus, for example, Ashley Wilkes reminisces in a letter from the front about the moon, magnolias, and happy darkies singing in the quarters. She used conventions and forms of "the gentle Confederate novel," too, as she called it, among them the noble patriarch, loyal slaves, strutting freedmen, and highly charged rape scenes. While drawing on the genre, Mitchell radically altered its meanings. Thus, Ashley Wilkes's nostalgia is his alone, not the narrator's; indeed, confining his prettiest sentiments to letters within the text (which the recipients also fail to understand) underlines their isolation from the narrative flow. Mitchell's use of the rape illustrates still more graphically her distance from the plantation romance. The old form hinged on the interracial rape. It symbolized the work's most essential themes and motives, such as the idealization of women's innocence and vulnerability, black men's evil, corrupting lust, and the white male's heroic, redemptive political action. By making the shantytown rapists white as well as black, Mitchell blasts these conventional usages. While white male redemption lacks any clear political frame at all, it misses heroism, too, as the Ku Kluxers blunder into an ambush and escape only through the semicomic intervention of the local madam and her house of ill repute. Much more critical to the dramatic narrative line, the rape scene between Rhett and Scarlett illuminates most starkly of all the radically different meaning Mitchell applied to the old convention. Here rape represents personal, psychological, and sexual confrontations for themselves and underlines the novel's ultimate theme of frustration and missed fortune. Mitchell's realism also grossly undercuts the old romanticism. Her insistent focus on the bourgeoisie and petit bourgeoisie adds a whole new dimension to her work. Except for the Wilkeses, she skimped cavaliers and ladies for a rough and tumble mélange of familyless hustlers, Irish immigrants, and frontier yokels made good. As she celebrated bourgeois values even in the antebellum South, Atlanta's centrality in the prewar and postwar sections is, then, thoroughly appropriate. In keeping with glorifying the yeomanry and diminishing the aristocracy, Mitchell also transformed the cavaliers' slave cohort. Black characters figure significantly in her novel; race does not.

In such ways, Mitchell rewrote regional history along lines thoroughly compatible with her generation of fellow Southerners—W. J. Cash, William Faulkner, Erskine Caldwell, Frank Owlsley, and the host of other participants in the Southern cultural awakening of the interwar years. As with these, Mitchell was lured by the past, the old way, and tradition, but modernity pulled her too. No less than Faulkner or Cash, she adopted Freudian insights to understand her social order. If she liked escapist literature herself, she deeply appreciated the somber, pessimistic prose and poetry of the post–World War I years that described the darkness she would flee. She told old tales in a modern voice. This technique affirmed and denied simultaneously. It appealed to traditionalists on the one hand, while it attracted modernists on the other. Without resolving the contradictions, she unified them in a coherent, dramatic structure. That remains her most significant, if confusing and misapprehended, achievement.

SURVEY OF CRITICISM

When *Gone with the Wind* first appeared in 1936, reviewers lavished praise upon it. They compared it to the great novels of the nineteenth-century European tradition, especially those of Dickens, Tolstoy, and Thackeray. They especially praised Mitchell's ability to master a great dramatic structure and to weave many divergent characters and episodes into a tight narrative line. They admired, too, her talent of creating figures who lived and breathed in the imagination. Their chief criticism centered upon her language, a lack of elegance and style. Yet even the most favorable critics also singled out issues of sentimentality, melodrama, amorality or nihilism, and excessive focus upon women for condemnation. Although the tide ran overwhelmingly positive, a countercurrent did exist. Marxists anathematized the novel primarily on racial grounds. Leftist liberal opinion objected on other grounds—excessive Southernism, moral ambiguity, inadequate realism, and feminine biases.

The novel's overwhelming popularity also galled many critics; Mitchell's apparent casualness about her talent and achievement aggravated the rancor. The film, however, marked the real watershed in critical opinion. The production itself solidified these various antipathies and sealed the book's fate for over a generation. The filmmaker David Selznick edited out Mitchell's yeomen and exaggerated the cavalier tradition (to Mitchell's own vast amusement). In his effort to avoid the adverse politics greeting *Birth of a Nation* twenty years before, Selznick also heightened the roles of blacks and slaves in the movie. This, ironically, stepped backward towards a more romantic tradition of local color for the movie. He also excised Mitchell's pessimism and irony. By exaggerating the force of external evil and minimizing internal conflict in the characters or in the South itself, he effectively justified or even glorified the protagonist's most vicious, self-serving, antisocial actions.

Even before the film appeared, readers had often focused on the work's romanticism; afterward, this bias held the field. Even among scholars, *Gone with the Wind* became the touchstone of the plantation romance. Thus identified with regional mythology and, by extension, racial chauvinism and reaction in general, the novel fell still further in critical estimation after World War II, especially as the South itself declined in social and political prestige.

Between about 1940 and the late 1960s or early 1970s, the novel generated almost no critical opinion at all. Robert Drake's thoughtful essay in 1957 in the *Georgia Review* remained anomolous and isolated. Mitchell and her novel in these years belonged almost exclusively to journalists, popular writers, and occasional memorialists.

Critical opinion reached its nadir between 1970 and 1973 in two profoundly negative evaluations by regional literary scholars, Floyd Watkins and James Boatwright. By that time, however, the tide had quietly turned. Although calculated for a popular audience, Finis Farr's 1965 biography benefited from access to Mitchell's vast manuscript collection, still held privately. It remains trustworthy for its objectives. With Perry Carlton Lentz and his incisive Vanderbilt dissertation, a new generation of graduate students in the late 1960s rediscovered the novel on their own and independently of each other. Their work broke new ground, even if their work went mostly unpublished.

By the mid–1970s, *Gone with the Wind* acquired new luster as a popular subject of ''nonfiction,'' as two books on the film attracted new attention to the phenomenon. Simultaneously, well-known academics legitimized the novel for scholarly research. Like the Farr biography, Richard Harwell's 1976 edition of Mitchell's letters was both cause and effect. In 1977 the premier scholar of the

Southern literary Renascence, Louis D. Rubin, Jr., compared Mitchell and Faulkner. In 1976, then again in 1979, Leslie Fiedler also analyzed the novel. Although beginning her work much earlier, the historian Willie Lee Rose of the Johns Hopkins University also published her research in 1979.

Younger scholars have tended to follow Rubin's lead towards a detailed analysis of the novel itself rather than fitting it more generally into American culture. Harold K. Schefski's essay (1980) developed the comparisons of Tolstoy's work with *Gone with the Wind*; Merlin G. Cheney's 1966 master's thesis compared Mitchell and Thackeray. Dawson Gaillard and Anne G. Jones offered the most useful, if contradictory, analyses of the fiction as a feminist work in 1974 and 1981. Their contradictory conclusions speak to a fundamental idea in the criticism that Perry Lentz noted as early as 1970 (and that John Peale Bishop had condemned in 1936): of a basic dualism within the epic. In this regard, Blanche Gelfant (1980) makes the very broadest claims for the novel by arguing that Mitchell's mysterious reconciliation of opposite desires offers a key to understanding all great literature. Similarly, Dieter Meindl (1981) argues that *Gone with the Wind* stands on its own artistic merits and that scholarly opinion distorted the work in the careless urge to fit it into the plantation romance; he linked the novel to the pessimism of the 1920s and the literary milieu of *A Farewell to Arms* (one of Mitchell's favorite novels). Evelyn Scott and Belle Rosenbaum had made similar observations in their 1936 and 1937 reviews, but critics failed to take their cue. The author herself has attracted almost no sustained scholarly inquiry except from Jones. If Farr remains limited but useful, Anne Edwards's biography (1983) adds little new and actually distorts standard data in a novelistic rendering.

Within this welter of inquiry, little cross-fertilization or cross-reference occurs. No center or focus has developed, much less a canon of criticism. Taken together, two anthologies impose some order on the field: Richard Harwell's *"Gone With the Wind" as Book and Film* (1982) offers a critical miscellany of essays, reviews, prefaces, articles, memoirs, and scholarly critiques. *Recasting: "Gone With the Wind" in American Culture*, ed. Darden Asbury Pyron (1983), gathers thirteen essays under three headings. The first group presents the critical setting; the second group discusses the novel as art; the last group, the novel as history.

If a scholarly center to this work solidifies, the novel, the author, and the *Gone with the Wind* phenomenon still lend themselves to sensationalism and exploitation. The fiftieth anniversary of the novel and film might encourage broader and deeper investigation; that anniversary might just as easily provide the occasion to stir the waters of Mitchell legend one more time.

BIBLIOGRAPHY

Works by Margaret Mitchell

Gone with the Wind. New York: Macmillan, 1936.
Margaret Mitchell's "Gone with the Wind" Letters, 1936–1949. Ed. Richard Harwell. New York: Macmillan, 1976.

A Dynamo Going to Waste: Letters to Allen Edel, 1919–21. Ed. Jane Bonner Peacock. Atlanta: Peachtree Publishers, 1985.

Studies of Margaret Mitchell

Adams, John Donald. "A Fine Novel of the Civil War." *New York Times Book Review*, July 5, 1936, p. 1.

Atlanta Historical Bulletin. *Margaret Mitchell Memorial Issue*, 9 (May 1950).

Atlanta Journal Magazine. *Margaret Mitchell Memorial Issue*, December 18, 1949.

Baldwin, Faith. "The Woman Who Wrote *Gone with the Wind*." *Pictorial Review*, March 1937, pp. 5, 69–71.

Bargannier, Earl. "The Myth of Moonlight and Magnolias." *Louisiana Studies* 15 (Spring 1976): 5–20.

Bishop, John Peale. "All War and No Peace." *New Republic*, July 15, 1936, p. 301.

Boatwright, James. "Reconsideration: Totin' de Werry Load." *New Republic*, 1 September 1973, pp. 29–32; see also Harwell, *Book and Film*, pp. 211–17.

Chalfant, Fran. "Mirror of Vanities and Virtues: A Reappraisal of *Gone with the Wind*." *West Georgia College Review* 4 (1971): 15–26.

Cheney, Merlin G. "*Vanity Fair* and *Gone with the Wind*: A Critical Comparison." M.A. thesis, Brigham Young University, 1966.

Conrad, Peter. "In Praise of Profligacy." *Times Literary Supplement* (London), September 10, 1976, p. 1094.

De Voto, Bernard. "Fiction and the Everlasting If." *Harper's Magazine* 77 (June 1938): 42–49.

———. "Fiction Fights the Civil War." *Saturday Review*, 18 December 1937, pp. 3–4, 15–16.

Drake, Robert Y. "Review." *Resources for American Literary Study* 7 (Spring 1977): 98–101.

———. "Tara Twenty Years After." *Georgia Review* 12 (Summer 1957): 142–50.

Edwards, Anne. *Road to Tara*. New Haven and New York: Ticknor & Fields, 1983.

Farr, Finis. *Margaret Mitchell of Atlanta*. New York: William Morrow, 1965.

Fiedler, Leslie. "Fiction of the Thirties." *La Revue des Langes Vivant: U.S. Bicentennial Issue* (1976): 93–104.

———. *Inadvertent Epic: From "Uncle Tom's Cabin" to "Roots."* New York: Simon and Schuster, 1979.

Fox-Genovese, Elizabeth. "Scarlett O'Hara: The Southern Lady as New Woman." *American Quarterly* 33 (Fall 1981): 391–411.

Gaillard, Dawson. "*Gone with the Wind* as 'Bildungsroman' or Why Did Rhett Butler Really Leave Scarlett O'Hara?" *Georgia Review* 28 (Spring 1974): 9–28.

Gelfant, Blanche. "*Gone with the Wind* and the Impossibilities of Fiction." *Southern Literary Journal* 13 (Fall 1980): 3–31.

Harwell, Richard. *"Gone with the Wind" as Book and Film*. Columbia: University of South Carolina Press, 1982.

Jones, Anne G. *"Tomorrow Is Another Day": The Woman Writer in the South, 1859–1936*. Baton Rouge: Louisiana State University Press, 1981.

Jones, Marian Elder. " 'Me and My Book,' Margaret Mitchell's *Gone with the Wind*." *Georgia Review* 16 (1962): 180–87.

Lentz, Perry Carlton. "Our Missing Epic: A Study in the Novels about the American Civil War." Ph.D. dissertation, Vanderbilt University, 1970.

Margaret Mitchell of Atlanta. Atlanta Public Library Memorial Publication, 1954.

May, Robert. "*Gone with the Wind* as Southern History: A Reappraisal." *Southern Quarterly* 17 (Fall 1978): 51–64.

Miendl, Dieter. "A Reappraisal of Margaret Mitchell's *Gone with the Wind.*" *Mississippi Quarterly* 34 (Fall 1981): 414–34.

Myrick, Susan. *White Columns in Hollywood*. Ed. Richard Harwell. Macon: Mercer University Press, 1982.

O'Brien, Kenneth. "Race, Romance and the Southern Literary Tradition," in Pyron, *Recasting*, pp. 153–66.

Pyron, Darden Asbury. "Margaret Mitchell: 'First or Nothing.' " *Southern Quarterly* 20 (Spring 1982): 19–34.

———, ed. *Recasting: "Gone with the Wind" in American Culture*. Gainesville: University of Florida Presses, 1983.

Ransom, John Crowe. "Fiction Harvest." *Southern Review* 2 (1936–37): 407–08.

Rose, Willie Lee. *Race and Region in American Historical Fiction*. Oxford: Clarendon Press, 1979.

Rosenbaum, Belle. "Why Do They Read It?" *Scribner's* 99 (1937): 23–24, 69–70.

Rouse, Blair. "*Gone with the Wind*—But Not Forgotten." *Southern Literary Journal* 11 (September 1978): 173–79.

Rubin, Louis D., Jr. "Scarlett O'Hara and the Two Quentin Compsons." *The South and Faulkner's Yoknapatawpha: The Actual and the Apocryphal*. Ed. Evans Harrington and Anne J. Abadie. Jackson: University Press of Mississippi, 1977, pp. 168–94. See also Pyron, *Recasting*, pp. 81–103.

Schefski, Harold K. "Margaret Mitchell's *Gone with the Wind* and *War and Peace.*" *Southern Studies* 19 (1980): 243–60. See also Harwell, *Book and Film*, pp. 229–43.

Scott, Evelyn. "War Between the States." *Nation*, July 4, 1936.

Shavin, Norman and Martin Sharter. *The Million Dollar Legends: Margaret Mitchell and "Gone with the Wind."* Atlanta: Capricorn, 1974.

Stern, Jerome. "*Gone with the Wind*: The South as America." *Southern Humanities Review* 7 (Winter 1972): 5–12.

Wade, John Donald. "Romance Permitted." *Virginia Quarterly Review* 12 (December 1936): 618–20.

Watkins, Floyd. "*Gone with the Wind* as Vulgar Literature." *Southern Literary Journal* 2 (Spring 1970): 86–103. See also Harwell, *Book and Film*, pp. 198–210.

MARTHA STEPHENS

Flannery O'Connor
(1925–1964)

A writer who worked slowly and with great care for detail, often under very difficult circumstances, Flannery O'Connor is widely recognized as one of the great short-story writers of her time. She is a writer of rich comic gifts, but there is a fundamental high seriousness about everything she wrote. A fierce and uncompromising Christian belief informs her stories and her two novels.

BIOGRAPHY

Flannery O'Connor was born in Savannah, Georgia, on 25 March 1925 and lived there until she was twelve, when the family moved to Milledgeville. "Mary Flannery," as she was called at home, was the only child of Catholic parents of considerable social standing. In Savannah she was sent to Catholic grade schools, and then in Milledgevile to what she later described wryly as a "progressive high school," run by the local college; she had little regard for any of her early schooling and liked to say in later years that she was happy to have been blessed with "total non-retention."

The move to Milledgeville came about when Mr. O'Connor fell ill with disseminated lupus. Milledgeville was Mrs. O'Connor's home and the home of her forebears on both sides of the family. The first Mass in Milledgeville had been said in her maternal grandfather's apartment in 1847, and her grandmother had later given the plot of ground for the church. Many relatives of Regina O'Connor's were still well-known citizens of the town and provided a rich—if for the author often comic—family setting for her life there, both as an adolescent and later as a writer and semi-invalid.

When O'Connor was fifteen, her father died of his disease at age forty-four. After high school she enrolled in the local college, Georgia State College for Women (now a coeducational school called Georgia College). She liked college and worked as a cartoonist for the newspaper and during her last year as the editor of the literary magazine. (One of her linoleum-cut cartoons depicts two fish, one saying to the other, "You can go jump out of the lake.") Her interest in writing was taken seriously enough at the college for one of her teachers to help her get a fellowship to the Writers' Workshop at the University of Iowa.

This proved to be a profound stroke of good fortune for O'Connor and in fact launched her on a literary career of unusual smoothness. This in spite of the fact that her early work was not especially precocious; six rather mild and conventional short stories were submitted for her master's degree at Iowa—they can be read today in the *Collected Stories* brought out some years after her death. But the individuals she met at Iowa—for instance, Paul Engle, John Crowe Ransom, and Robie Macauley, and through them people like Andrew Lytle and Caroline Gordon—were in positions to help her win prizes and find publishers; become a guest at Yaddo Artists Colony, Saratoga Springs, New York; gain the attention of the best-known quarterlies; and be chosen for important grants and fellowships. In short, they were able to provide ready entry for her into a profession that has proved to be for most of its practitioners—even for William Faulkner—a notoriously resistant medium. Few writers have had less struggle to put their work before the public, and this was true in spite of the fact that her stories were of a special character, not of the kind ever likely to be widely popular or to make large profits.

After Iowa, she spent nearly a year at Yaddo. There she met the not always mentally balanced Robert Lowell, and became involved in an incident in which he tried to have the Yaddo board dismiss the colony's director, Elizabeth Ames, for sponsoring a guest said to be a Communist. O'Connor, Lowell, and Elizabeth Hardwick left Yaddo in protest, but most of their fellow artists in the New York area came to the rescue of Ames, and she kept her position.

In 1949, during a five-month period in which she worked on her writing in New York, living in a YWCA on 134th Street, O'Connor met through Macauley a couple who would become lifelong friends and supporters of her work, Robert and Sally Fitzgerald. During that summer the Fitzgeralds bought a house in the Connecticut countryside, and O'Connor became a boarder in a room over their garage. She had published a story in the *Sewanee Review* about a character named Hazel Motes and now began writing a novel about Motes, a more than peculiar young man—a Christian *malgré lui*, as she later styled him in a brief preface to this book—who gives up in the end his fierce, though often broadly comic, struggle for un-belief.

She had been living with the Fitzgeralds for over a year and was typing out the first draft of *Wise Blood* when she noticed a heaviness in her arms. The ailment feared by the local doctor was rheumatic arthritis, but when O'Connor went home for Christmas, she became seriously ill on the train, and she spent that winter and spring in Emory Hospital in Atlanta, too ill even to write to friends. Her disease was not arthritis but the related disease that had killed her father, lupus—a degenerative and often crippling disease in which the body forms antibodies to its own tissues and which can affect any part of the body. At the time her father had contracted it, "there was nothing for it but the undertaker," she later reported, but by her own time it was often controllable with steroids. The lupus, she wrote to Lowell, "comes and goes, when it comes I retire and when it goes, I venture forth. . . . I have enough energy to write with and as that is all I have any business doing anyhow, I can with one eye squinted take it all as a blessing. What you have to measure out, you come to observe closer, or so I tell myself. . . . I have bought me some peafowl and sit on the back steps a good deal studying them." Mrs. O'Connor had inherited a farm on the outskirts of Milledgeville, and when Flannery left the hospital, it was to this farm they had gone to live. O'Connor lived there until her death at thirty-nine.

Although there was at the time of its onset virtually no complaint in her letters about her illness, much later on O'Connor conceded to friends that she had felt severely frightened by these unlooked-for events, and had believed she would not be able to continue to live the life of a writer under her mother's commanding care in this town she had set out to escape.

And yet as life on the farm took shape, she quickly set about to see *Wise Blood* through the press and then to compose some of her most successful stories, some of the best of them dark but very funny religious comedies about a domineering and self-righteous farm woman and her sullen daughter ("Circle in the Fire," for instance, and "Good Country People"). Nine of these stories were collected in *A Good Man Is Hard to Find* in 1955.

What may have seemed to many to be a life of strange reclusiveness, pain, and discontent was seen in fact to be something on the whole quite different from that when O'Connor's letters appeared in 1979—a large volume titled *The Habit of Being*, edited by Sally Fitzgerald. Mother and daughter, it became clear, were in certain ways extremely irritating to each other—Mrs. O'Connor was not in the least literary but nevertheless had opinions about everything and sometimes infuriated her daughter with her views about writing and especially about Flannery's own, which she did not really understand; but in other respects the two women were alike and compatible—both were determined, unsentimental women with none of the childlike feminity sometimes associated with Southern women of their class.

A life that in the early years seemed much too circumscribed, and that seems to have brought O'Connor's native streak of contrariness and her powers of mockery to full perfection, came to seem to her more and more endurable and finally to be simply the right life for a person of her particular gifts and temperament. She had not really liked city life when she had been able to live it, and she also came to feel that a Southern writer did best to remain in the South. She even took to counseling the other young Southern writers she corresponded with to come back home where they "belonged" for the sake of their writing. With careful doctoring, her health stabilized after the first severe attack of the disease and was in what could almost be called remission for most of her life;

her worst problem was with the bones in her hips, and after 1955 she could get about only on crutches. Still, she was able to fly away on trips around the country to speak and to read her work—at first mostly at Catholic colleges, but as time went on, at many other schools as well.

The farm also bore witness to a mounting stream of visitors. O'Connor was a more sociable person than she appeared to be in public, and she liked seeing both friends and passers-by at Andalusia. People who had read about her wrote and called and stopped in, and sometimes became friends. Literary and church friends came from all over and often stayed—the writer Caroline Gordon, for instance, an early friend and adviser who continued to read and critique in detail virtually all O'Connor stories as they were composed.

The farm had a special attraction for many; unusual flocks of fowl had always been O'Connor's special interest. She had peafowl and peachickens, ducks and geese and swans—and of course her famous peacocks. She once gave her mother a burro as a birthday present. Their animals were in demand for Christmas pageants and mangers, and schoolchildren, scout troops, and various church groups were continually being brought to them for country outings.

As for O'Connor's writing, possibly the glummest years were the seven years she worked on *The Violent Bear It Away*. She never felt great confidence in this work. If there is a flaw in her career as a writer, it may well be the fact that she did not realize that she could achieve a reputation and carry out her intentions simply by writing short stories, but she did not have her own example before her as young writers do today; it is understandable that she would have felt that to be taken seriously as a writer she had to write novels, and she labored hard to write one that satisfied her. After *The Violent Bear It Away*, she worked off and on for several years on another large-scale piece, *Why Do the Heathen Rage?*, which never fully engaged her and was left unfinished when she died.

The other aggravation she suffered was the persistent misunderstanding of her religious themes. Most readers thought that she was writing contemptuously about religious fanatics and could not grasp the fact that the sympathies of such a serious writer could lie with a half-crazy backwoods "prophet" like old Tar-water in *The Violent Bear It Away*. It seemed that no one could be counted on but other discriminating Catholics to know what she was actually expressing and that her work was really a study in faith and belief. Her closest literary friends and associates remained people who were also in the church and interested in the same religious questions she was. Much of her correspondence is taken up with dialogues with these friends about works in theology and religious thought, a literature in which O'Connor was widely read and in which she took almost a scholarly interest.

It was, indeed, her special good fortune to live a life of unusual integration: she had her work and her religious life and the two were really one—she felt she had a mission to write stories that testified to her faith and instructed the faithless, and that is what she set out to do in story after story.

It was discovered in the winter of 1964 that O'Connor, who had become weak and anemic, might have to be operated on for a fibroid tumor, even though her doctor feared a reactivation of the lupus. By that spring it was no longer possible to delay; "if they don't make haste and get rid of it," O'Connor wrote, "they will have to remove me and leave it." The lupus was in fact reactivated by the operation, and there ensued a serious kidney infection. O'Connor was in and out of hospitals in Atlanta and Milledgeville all spring and summer; when she was at home she was permitted to move the few feet from bed to typewriter for only an hour at a time. Still, she went ahead with her plans for a new volume of short stories; she had wanted to revise certain of the already published stories she was including ("The Lame Shall Enter First," for instance, and "The Enduring Chill'), but she now decided not to attempt that task but to concentrate simply on bringing to satisfactory completion two new ones, "Parker's Back" and "Judgement Day." She continued her long-time habit of typing out copies and sending them to friends for comments. She had also written "Revelation" during the earlier part of this last year, and these last three stories are three of the best she ever wrote. The last two were finished just before her death. Her almost daily correspondence, already reduced to handwritten scrawls, ceased entirely six days before her death on 3 August 1964. Her new collection, *Everything That Rises Must Converge*, was published the following year to wide admiration and even, at last, almost uniform understanding of its religious themes.

MAJOR THEMES

The O'Connor short stories are widely respected today, perhaps especially among other writers, as models of the well-made story. O'Connor knew above all how to keep a story on track, how to make it dramatic from beginning to end and to make every detail count, and she said that to do this she just followed her nose like an old hound dog. There was no secret to her technique, she liked to say, but the secret of "taking pains."

One of the reasons she was able to keep so firmly to her purposes in story after story was that unlike most of her contemporaries, she was never in doubt as to what her purposes were. She often said that for her the Eucharist was the center of existence and that what she saw in the world she saw in relation to that. Such firmness of belief is unusual in modern times and in some ways a considerable advantage for a writer; she knew almost from the beginning exactly what she wanted to tell. The doctrine of original sin was deep and instinctual with her, and she wanted to write about the fallen state of mankind—but also about the sudden appearance of grace in the lives of the prideful and forsaken.

She once wrote to a friend: "All human nature vigorously resists grace because grace changes us and the change is painful," and it is possible to see virtually all her tales as tales about a painful descent of grace. These stories show us prideful, self-congratulatory individuals suddenly being brought low in some ironic way by such agents as escaped convicts or stray bulls or simply some fundamental blow to their self-esteem. In "Revelation" a stout country wife who prides herself on her good disposition and likeability has a book thrown at her—and a terrible epithet—by a college girl enraged by her pieties. In "Good Country People" a smug, young female intellectual suffers a rude shock in an encounter with a much more knowing Bible salesman. In "The Artificial Nigger" an old countryman, proud of his knowledge of city ways, takes his nephew on a visit to the city and is himself "burned clean" by a sudden insight into his own childlike ignorance.

That many readers saw O'Connor's harrowing tales as simply malevolent always baffled her, but is perhaps no more than the measure of the distance in belief between herself and her non-Catholic readers. Her characters are generally so contemptible, so physically repugnant, and their comeuppance at the end of the stories described in so comic and seemingly unpitying a way, that many readers have found it hard to realize that their narrator also felt sympathy and affection for them, and that the usually violent—often fatal—visitation of grace she caused them to suffer was portrayed as something to be rejoiced in, as almost a gift from the Almighty. When a young reader asked why a certain character was made so "ugly," one of O'Connor's friends replied, "because Flannery loves her"; O'Connor found this exchange very pleasing.

She naturally felt that no one could be exempted from the taint of evil and of original sin, and she did not except herself; the sullen and egoistical grown-up children in her stories do resemble the author herself in certain ways, and it will be remembered that when she set out to paint her self-portrait, she painted her face disfigured by the medicines she took and alongside the ugly staring head of a pheasant. Yet she was not completely without personal vanity and could complain that photographers made her look worse than she did. She said about the pictures made for the jacket of *Wise Blood*: "The one I sent [back to them] looked as if I had just bitten my grand-mother and that this was one of my few pleasures. . . . "

O'Connor liked action stories and was not much interested in the fluid interior forms that have engaged other modern writers; what she preferred was a highly colored plot where something climactic happened in the end, and she wanted everything to move toward this climactic action—usually a vivid and in some way disastrous event that causes a character finally to see himself as he really is or simply to realize the Lord's purpose for him.

In her first novel, *Wise Blood* (1952), Hazel Motes tries desperately to prove to himself that he is not a Christian. He moves to the city and takes up with a prostitute and a whole gallery of cartoonlike nonbelievers. But he cannot seem to escape his fate as a preacher and is soon starting his own street-corner church, "The Church without Christ." He is portrayed as having had all along the supreme virtue of being able to act on his beliefs, and once he becomes convinced—by a queer trail of events climaxed by the pushing of his old Essex off a cliff by a policeman—that there is a Jesus after all, he loses interest in all worldly pleasures and pursuits, enters into a life of contemplation, wears barbed

wire under his shirt, and in fact begins his penance by blinding himself with a
bucket of lime, to the astonishment of his landlady. When she tells him that
what he's doing isn't normal anymore, that people have quit doing it, he says
simply, "They ain't quit doing it as long as I'm doing it." Hazel wanders away
on a cold rainy night and is found in a ditch, casually beaten to death by
policemen. As in her second novel as well, and many of her short stories,
O'Connor abandons her blunt, unadorned style of narration at the very end of
the story and allows Motes a moment of lyric pathos—and the landlady a moment
of unmocked religious insight: "She had never observed his face more composed
and she grabbed his hand and held it to her heart. . . . She sat staring with her
eyes shut, into his eyes, and felt as if she had finally got to the beginning of
something she couldn't begin, and she saw him moving farther and farther away,
farther and farther into the darkness until he was the pin point of light."

In spite of this final scene, *Wise Blood* was taken by most reviewers to be a
comic parody of Southern fundamentalism. Perhaps the author's intentions
strictly within the novel ought to have been clearer, but in any case her later
statements about it leave no room whatever to doubt that in spite of the book's
broad farce, she was deadly serious about the religious quest of Hazel Motes.
"Let me assure you," she wrote to a friend, "that no one but a Catholic could
have written *Wise Blood* even though it is a book about a kind of Protestant
saint."

She could have said very nearly the same thing about one of her best-known
short stories, "A Good Man Is Hard to Find," written not long after *Wise Blood*.
It was one of her own favorites and the one she liked best to read aloud. An
escaped convict and two companions waylay a vacationing family of five and
lead them off two by two to the woods to be shot. The grandmother of the family
is the last to die; she is suddenly shot by the Misfit as she reaches out to touch
him, saying, "Why you're one of my own children!"—a line that has been
interpreted in many different ways but which O'Connor herself said was the sign
that the grandmother had realized her connection to all men and suddenly grown
in grace in this last moment of her life. The Misfit the author saw as a man
capable of a heroic life for either good or evil; she said that if he were ever able
to believe that Jesus Christ did truly live and die for mankind, he would become
a great man, in effect a saint.

A Good Man Is Hard to Find contains at least four other stories that have
continued over the years to interest readers and anthologists: the two stories
mentioned above, "Good Country People" and "The Artificial Nigger"; as well
as "The Life You Save May Be Your Own," a very funny story in a tall-tale
style reminiscent of Mark Twain and Faulkner; "The River," a story about the
drowning of a young boy trying to find Jesus in the river in which he had been
baptized; and "A Circle in the Fire," possibly the masterpiece among O'Connor's short stories. In this very carefully built-up tale, three youngsters from the
city show up at a farm where one of them had once lived, bringing a reign of
exquisite terror to the proud mistress of the estate.

The writing of her second novel, *The Violent Bear It Away*, was a labor that was often frustrating. She said it was like "escaping from the penitentiary" to turn from time to time to a short story. This second novel has almost exactly the same narrative pattern as *Wise Blood*—a primitive true believer tries to throw off, in very dramatic and often comical ways, his Christian beliefs, but finally is unable to. In *The Violent Bear It Away* a boy who has grown up in the wilderness with a fanatical great-uncle tries to decide, on the day of the uncle's death, whether or not to accept the mantle of prophecy his uncle said would be his legacy. The great strength of the book is the long opening section set in the clearing called "Powderhead," where the boy remembers, on this fateful day, the dramatic scenes of his life there with his stormy old uncle. In the latter half of the book young Tarwater sets out to defy his uncle's charge by going to the city. He means to live with a younger uncle, Rayber, a school psychologist and nonbeliever despised by the old man, and a character O'Connor never really "got right," as she herself realized. Inevitably, the boy, too, comes to despise Rayber's life—in effect, its sterile secularism—and in the end returns to Powderhead and to the acceptance of his Christian destiny.

In the posthumous volume *Everything That Rises Must Converge*, there is a group of stories O'Connor was not satisfied with and probably would not have included if she had lived to write more tales. There should perhaps now be issued a one-volume *Selected Stories* that would add to the eight best tales of *A Good Man Is Hard to Find* five equally good ones from *Everything That Rises*; the three last stories she wrote, noted above, as well as "Greenleaf" (another tale about a self-satisfied woman who runs a dairy-farm), and the title story, "Everything That Rises Must Converge," which describes a bizarre conflict on a city bus between a white woman of class and an angry black woman—the black woman wallops the white woman over the head with her pocketbook. This is such a deep shock to the white woman's sense of "who she is"—this unbearable contempt shown her by a lowly black person—that it leads to her collapse and death as she gets off the bus. This skillful tale is the only one O'Connor wrote about "that issue," as she called it, and for many readers it is one of her clearest and most successful stories. Still, O'Connor never very heartily endorsed the civil rights movement and rarely seemed to be able to find very much of dramatic interest in the lives of blacks other than willful resistance to taking good care of white people. But it must be understood that she was not interested in social reform of *any* kind—to one who believed so strongly in a transfigured life to come in which the last might well be first and the first last, it did not seem of any great importance to rearrange the social conditions of this life. She seemed to feel, almost like the Christians of medieval times, that in this unimportant earthly life people had their assigned, their predestined "places," and it was their duty to make the best of them. Again we note her wide divergence on these fundamental questions from other educated people of her own time; it is a profound difference in outlook that may continue to deny her the full emotional harmony with serious readers that might have gained her an even more lasting place in the literary tradition of her country, a country which is not very Catholic after all, nor even deeply religious. She did not like being termed "a Catholic writer"—she felt that she expressed, not "the truth of the church," but simply "the truth," but for many readers there is a higher truth completely different from hers, the tragic truth that man is alone, knows nothing of a divine purpose for himself or of any saviour who lived and died for his redemption, and it remains to be seen what difference in the long run her stern and literalistic religious beliefs will make to the continuing assessment of her as an artist.

SURVEY OF CRITICISM

Book-length studies of O'Connor began to appear after her death, and in general it can be said that interest in her work has remained high. A number of critical volumes have been brought out by university presses, though few of these are of any real significance. An early monograph by Robert Drake (*Flannery O'Connor*, 1966) remains a good short introduction. Another volume that appeared just after the writer's death, *The Added Dimension* (edited by Melvin J. Friedman and Lewis A. Lawson), is a useful tool for study of her work: it contains ten critical articles and well-chosen excerpts from her essays, speeches, and interviews, as well as a number of excellent bibliographies, including a comprehensive list of reviews for each of the four O'Connor volumes. In the light of the rather long public struggle for understanding of her work, reviews of her books in newspapers and magazines make particularly interesting reading.

Certain parts of *The Added Dimension* have been superseded by a volume titled *Mystery and Manners: Occasional Prose* (1969), edited by Robert and Sally Fitzgerald, a collection of the author's complete speeches, essays, and reviews.

Students of her work in Milledgeville issue a journal called the *Flannery O'Connor Bulletin*; some of the critical pieces in this journal lean rather too much in the direction of the pious homily, but it has also published some interesting work on O'Connor's local sources.

The main caretakers of O'Connor's literary career have been Sally Fitzgerald and her ex-husband, Robert Fitzgerald. As has been noted, O'Connor lived with them for over a year when she was starting out as a writer and still writing *Wise Blood* and just before she became ill. They were the first people she went to visit when she could leave Milledgeville after she began to recover, and although they lived abroad for considerable periods during her lifetime, she never lost touch with them or ceased to be a close friend. They often read and commented on her manuscripts in draft form and worked to advance her career in every way they could. They are Catholics as she was (Sally Fitzgerald is also a Southerner) and were no doubt among the first readers to understand what her work was saying. Robert Fitzgerald's introduction to *Everything That Rises Must Converge* is an expressive commentary on her life and death, the best biographical piece presently available.

The Fitzgeralds were the editors of *Mystery and Manners*, the nonfiction writings, and Sally Fitzgerald brought out, in 1979, a large volume of O'Connor letters, *The Habit of Being*. There turned out to be a great many more of these letters than had been known to exist, and Fitzgerald has told an interesting tale about the long labor of finding and editing them, and her difficult conjunction with Regina O'Connor, in an edition of the *Radcliffe Bulletin* for 1982. "As the contract was written the volume was to be in a sense a collaboration between the mother and myself. As it turned out, my collaborator interpreted this to mean that I would do the legwork, assemble the results, and she would disapprove of the outcome." Perhaps it was only to be expected that a book of letters published only twelve years after an author's death, and that death at so young an age, would contain many references to living people that would have to be pared— not only, in O'Connor's case, by her mother (with regard to Milledgeville friends and relatives), but also no doubt by Fitzgerald herself (with regard to the literary world of the East, for instance). Even so, this kind of editing seems to have done no great damage to the life-record the letters provide; they constitute a remarkably readable volume in themselves, a deep and very witty book always satisfyingly personal and expressive.

Fitzgerald has been at work for some time on an O'Connor biography; as time goes on it will no doubt become less difficult to make public a full and accurate record. But in any case there is no reason to believe that the main contours of O'Connor's life, and a great deal of the detail, have not already been made available through the letters themselves and the detailed notes Fitzgerald sometimes attaches to them in *The Habit of Being*.

BIBLIOGRAPHY

Works by Flannery O'Connor

Wise Blood. New York: Harcourt, Brace, 1952.

A Good Man Is Hard to Find. New York: Harcourt, Brace, 1955.

The Violent Bear It Away. New York: Farrar, Straus and Cudahy, 1960.

Everything That Rises Must Converge. New York: Farrar, Straus and Giroux, 1965.

Mystery and Manners: Occasional Prose. Ed. Sally Fitzgerald and Robert Fitzgerald. New York: Farrar, Straus and Giroux, 1969.

The Complete Stories of Flannery O'Connor. New York: Farrar, Straus and Giroux, 1971.

The Habit of Being: Letters of Flannery O'Connor. Ed. Sally Fitzgerald. New York: Random House, 1979.

Studies of Flannery O'Connor

Browning, Preston M. *Flannery O'Connor*. Carbondale: Southern Illinois University Press, 1974.

Coles, Robert. *Flannery O'Connor's South*. Baton Rouge: Louisiana State University Press, 1980.

Drake, Robert. *Flannery O'Connor*. Grand Rapids: William B. Eerdmans, 1966.

Driskell, Leon V. and John T. Brittain. *The Eternal Crossroads*. Lexington: University of Kentucky Press, 1971.

Eggenschwiler, David. *The Christian Humanism of Flannery O'Connor*. Detroit: Wayne State University Press, 1972.

Espirit 8 (Winter 1964). Special issue on O'Connor at the time of her death.

Feeley, Sister Kathleen. *The Voice of the Peacock*. New Brunswick: Rutgers University Press, 1972.

Fitzgerald, Robert. Introduction to *Everything That Rises Must Converge*. New York: Farrar, Straus and Giroux, 1965.

The Flannery O'Connor Bulletin. Biannual. Ed. Rosa Lee Walston. Milledgeville, Georgia.

Friedman, Melvin J. and Lewis A. Lawson, *The Added Dimension: The Mind and Art of Flannery O'Connor*. New York: Fordham University Press, 1966.

Hayman, Stanley Edgar. *Flannery O'Connor*. Minneapolis: University of Minnesota Press, 1966.

Hendin, Josephine. *The World of Flannery O'Connor*. Bloomington: Indiana University Press, 1969.

Martin, Carter. *The True Country*. Nashville: Vanderbilt University Press, 1969.

Orwell, Miles. *Invisible Parade*. Philadelphia: Temple University Press, 1972.

Stephens, Martha. *The Question of Flannery O'Connor*. Baton Rouge: Louisiana State University Press, 1973.

Walker Percy
(1916–   )

In his December 1977 *Esquire* self-interview, "Questions They Never Asked Me," Walker Percy objected to being labeled a Southern writer: "I'm fed up with the subject of southern writing. Northern writing too, for that matter. I'm also fed up with questions about the state of the novel, alienation, the place of the artist in American society, race relations, the Old South. . . . Of all the things I'm fed up with, I think I'm fed up most with hearing about the New South." As for the South's "strong sense of place, of tradition, of rootedness, of tragedy," he says, "I've read about that. Actually I like to stay in motels in places like Lincoln, Nebraska, or San Luis Obispo" (p. 170).

Far from disqualifying Percy from inclusion in this volume, such comments emphasize the variety and diversity of contemporary Southern writing celebrated by C. Hugh Holman in his "No More Monoliths, Please: Continuities in the Multi-Souths" (*Southern Literature in Transition*, ed. Philip Castille and William Osborne, 1983). Percy's comments also highlight both his major concerns and his major mode, an irony honed to such razor sharpness that, as with a paper cut, the reader is sliced before the cut is felt. His irony operates at his own expense as well: in the same self-interview, he compared the "very minor trick" of writing to a high school acquaintance who, "due to an anomaly of his eustachian tubes, could blow smoke out of both ears. He enjoyed doing it and it was diverting to watch. Writing is something like that" (p. 184).

BIOGRAPHY

Although Walker Percy resembles his protagonists—middle-aged, supersensitive, alienated white males—in important ways, it is a mistake to identify him with his characters, as too many critics do. He was born in Birmingham, Alabama, on 28 May 1916. When Percy was eleven, his father committed suicide, and two years later his mother was killed in an automobile accident. Percy and his two brothers were then adopted by William Alexander Percy, a lawyer, poet, and landowner. First cousin to Percy's father but called "Uncle Will" by the Percy boys, he was best known as the author of a memoir, *Lanterns on the Levee* (1941); and life at his home in Greenville, Mississippi, was that of a traditional Southern patrician, with regular visitors, including William Faulkner.

When Percy went to the University of North Carolina at Chapel Hill, for his freshman diagnostic theme he submitted a rambling Faulknerian passage and was promptly assigned to a remedial class. Few Faulknerian mannerisms survive in his mature fiction. He received a B.A. in premed chemistry from Chapel Hill in 1937, and at his Uncle Will's urging went on for his M.D. at Columbia University's College of Physicians and Surgeons. He received the degree in 1941, but while interning the following year at Bellevue Hospital, he contracted pulmonary tuberculosis and had to enter Trudeau Sanatorium in the Adirondacks. Released in 1944, he returned to Columbia to teach pathology but soon suffered a relapse and entered another sanatorium in Connecticut.

During his extended illness Percy recognized that he would not be able to practice medicine, and turned to the extensive philosophical reading that informs his novels' critique of humanism and of the limits of the scientific method. Perhaps the strongest influence on his later work was his reading of Kierkegaard, but he was also drawn to Jaspers, Heidegger, Marcel, Sartre, and Camus. These European existentialists, rather than the writers of the American South or the subject of the Civil War, formed Percy's literary themes and techniques. His application of those themes and techniques to the very subjects he disparaged in the self-interview cited above—the state of the novel, alienation, the place of the artist in American society, race relations, the Old and New South—makes Percy an important novelist and a Southern novelist. As Louis D. Rubin, Jr., notes in "The Boll Weevil, the Iron Horse, and the End of the Line": "The details of the southern heritage are deeply embedded in Percy's imagination, and in taking on the continuing human problems of self-definition, belief, good and evil, man's place in society from the perspective of a changed set of social and historical circumstances, Percy is doing what every major southern author before him has done. . . . Far from representing an end to the so-called traditional southern literary mode, *The Last Gentleman* is a redefinition of it, one that is necessary if it is to continue to have any significance" (218–19).

With the death of William Percy in 1942, Percy was financially independent, able to devote the rest of his outwardly uneventful life to his reading, his writing, and his family. On 7 November 1946, he married Mary Bernice Townsend and moved to Sewanee, Tennessee. About six months later, they both moved to New Orleans and converted to Roman Catholicism, another strong influence on his work, although he may have some trouble getting an imprimatur. In 1950 they moved to Covington, Louisiana, across Lake Pontchartrain from New Orleans, where they have since lived. The Percys have two daughters, Mary Pratt and Ann Boyd.

Percy writes both fiction and essays on linguistics and philosophy, and the interconnectedness of the two has not yet been fully explored. Percy's first mature published work was the essay "Symbol as Need" (1954), which was collected, along with fourteen other essays written over the next 21 years, in *The Message in the Bottle* (1975). Although all of them have direct bearing on Percy's fiction, the most important ones are the title essay (1959), "The Loss of the Creature" (1958), "The Man on the Train" (1956), and "Notes for a Novel about the End of the World" (1967–68).

As important and entertaining as his essays are, they would be largely unread were it not for his fiction. Much to the surprise of the author and his publisher, Percy's first novel, *The Moviegoer* (1961), won the 1962 National Book Award. Unsuccessfully trying to immerse himself in "the most ordinary life imaginable, a life without the old longings," Binx Bolling wakes up one day to "the search," "what anyone would undertake if he were not sunk in the everydayness of his own life." Even though he characterizes himself as a "castaway," alienated from his neighbors and their pursuits, he recognizes in Kierkegaardian fashion that "To become aware of the possibility of the search is to be onto something. Not to be onto something is to be in despair." Despite some cumbersome cerebral baggage, the novel is both entertaining and provocative, and a harbinger of better things to come.

The Last Gentleman (1966), a runner-up for the National Book Award, recounts Will Barrett's odyssey from New York City to the deep South and on to the southwestern desert. Carrying ruins to ruins, Will, like Binx, is looking for something the nature of which is ineffable. Observing his countrymen, he asks himself, "Is it not true that the American Revolution has succeeded beyond its wildest dreams of [Mad Anthony] Wayne and his friends, so that practically everyone in the United States is free to sit around a cozy fire in ski pants? What is wrong with that? What is wrong with you, you poor fellow?" This "last gentleman" is a watcher, a wanderer, whose problem finally boils down to "how to live from one ordinary minute to the next on a Wednesday afternoon." Percy's philosophical interests and vocabulary ("immanence" and "transcendence") remain very strong, but this novel's characters are better realized and the humor is more biting than its predecessor's.

With *Love in the Ruins* (1971), Percy's talent came to full flower. Dr. Tom More's ambition is to cure his age's malaise—the separation of body and spirit—by means of his invention, the lapsometer, "a caliper of the soul." The electric charge of Percy's cerebral themes is well grounded in his narrator, Tom More, who announces early, "I believe in God and the whole business but I love women best, music and science next, whiskey next, God fourth, and my fellow man hardly at all." In this novel Percy weaves his moral and philosophical concerns into a hilarious, ironic dystopia.

Percy followed that achievement with *Lancelot* (1977), an ambitious and penetrating book, a monologue delivered from a prison hospital cell by its insane title character to a friend/physician/confessor named Percival. Percy has disarmingly called it "a small cautionary tale," his "involuted sexual-theological number" ("Questions They Never Asked Me," 188). A savage indictment of a culture in moral ruins, *Lancelot* strips away much of Percy's familiar humor and language play to attain a searing intensity. Language itself is so worn out that Lance tries to communicate with another patient by tapping on the wall. Although Percy maintains his distance from the title character's perspective, its power is so compelling that Lancelot's voice dominates and the novel's harsh tone overwhelms most readers with its bitterness.

Having exorcised the demon, Percy abruptly changed directions again in *The Second Coming* (1980), returning to the character of Will Barrett some twenty years older and a lawyer now instead of an "engineer." In this tender and delightful love story, Will, still searching, discovers Allie, a sanatorium escapee with problems of her own and language that is always right yet at the same time a bubble or two off center. Will's despair, his ludicrous Pascalian wager designed to provoke God into revealing His existence once and for all, and his coming to terms with good and evil, faith and uncertainty, are all conveyed in an engaging, ear-popping language. Combining Will's outsider's perspective with Allie's Rip Van Winklish return to society, the novel is in Percy's own words "a breakthrough": "It has a feeling of affirmation, of celebration. I've never done this before.... And I think this is the first time I've actually seen a way out of this predicament" (Henry Kisor, "Dr. Percy on Signs and Symbols," *The Critic*, 11 September 1980, p. 5).

His publishers decided to reward him by bringing out *Lost in the Cosmos: The Last Self-Help Book* (1983), an amusing but overextended parody of self-help manuals and a cartoon version of the themes of his novels.

MAJOR THEMES

In varying proportions and with varying degrees of success, Walker Percy's writings combine three major qualities: an ethical and moral philosophy, a well-developed aesthetic sense of language and craft, and humor laced with irony. Any writer with one of these characteristics would be regarded as an interesting if minor figure. Having two of them, he would command some critical attention as an important figure. Displaying all three establishes Percy as a dangerous genius or an eccentric fool, and each of his books must be judged on its ability to combine these traits in some harmony or proportion.

Percy's ethical and moral philosophy contains what is often called "theme," but it has stronger overtones of informed discourses, more especially concerned with crucial issues of twentieth-century philosophy and religion than is the work of most novelists. Percy reads like an existential writer at times, and at other times like an Old Testament prophet, especially Jeremiah. His moral and metaphysical themes combine righteous wrath with hope for reconciliation both here and hereafter.

Percy is a self-confessed "philosophical Catholic existentialist"; his major theme is the predicament of modern man in the world, a state of alienation, but with a characteristic torque: "Clearly we are talking about a species of alienation, the traditional subject matter of psychiatrists, the original alienists. But notice that the novelist is raising a Copernican issue and standing the question on its head. Who is alienated? And from what? And is one better off nowadays alienated or unalienated?" ("The State of the Novel," *Michigan Quarterly Review* 16 [1977]: 367). Percy's protagonists are alienated, abstracted, dislocated. But their despair is their good fortune. According to Percy's Christian view, man is *supposed* to feel alienated, dislocated in this world, a strange land that Percy as often as not calls "Ohio." Knowing one is in despair is the first step in coming to terms with that alienation. Percy's displaced protagonists critique "Ohio" with their uniquely "Martian view."

Binx labels his various solutions "ordeal," "repetition," "rotation," and "return," but to avoid cumbersome definitions each can be explained as a means of defamiliarizing the familiar so that it can actually be seen and appreciated, concretely rather than abstractly. The anonymity and artificiality of Will Barrett's room at the Y, for instance, are underlined in its description: the room "was furnished with a single bed and a steel desk varnished to resemble wood grain," and later the TV room is described as "a room done in Spanish colonial motif with exposed yellow beams and furniture of oxidized metal." Barrett escapes by way of that quintessential American environment, the mobile home—"the Trav-L-Aire, glittering and humped up and practical, yet somehow airy and light on its four brand-new Goodyear jumbo treads," in which he feels "mobile yet at home, . . . in the world yet not of the world, sampling the particularities of place yet cabined off from the sadness of place." From such a vehicle, described with biblical echoes tinged with irony, he can occasionally step down "from the zone of the possible to the zone of the realized," escaping if only momentarily his dis-ease.

That dis-ease is the modern age's disease, a schism, typically rendered in Percy's novels in dualistic terms, and in such either-or extremes that both choices are vitiated: Binx's refusal to choose between Stoicism and Christianity and his view that "all the friendly and likable people seem dead to me; only the haters seem alive"; Sutter Vaught's carnality or transcendence; Will Barrett's "gentleman's" view of women as whores or virgins; Tom More's diagnosis of the angelism-bestialism syndrome; Lancelot Lamar's Louisiana vs. Los Angeles; and Will Barrett's hilarious attempt to force God Himself into an either-or proof of His existence.

As healthy as it is to be alienated from such a world, in *Lancelot* the separation of spirit and body reaches homicidal proportions. Lance's abstraction is so great that even in committing a murder he is totally objective and unfeeling: "What I remember better than the cutting was the sense I had of casting about for an appropriate feeling to match the deed . . . and not finding one." His drive to resolve the conflicts between appearances and realities takes the form of sexuality—carnal knowledge, supposedly, will beget angelic knowledge, epistemology and sex intertwined in an orgy of "knowing." Driven to such extremes, he has become a homicidal maniac, clearly not an authorial persona. Percy's characters' desire for an "Everlasting Yea" or, failing that, at least a "No! in thunder," is set against the torturous uncertainty of life itself at four o'clock on an ordinary Wednesday afternoon.

The ineffability of religious insight and the extreme mundanity of what one does at four o'clock on a Wednesday afternoon have driven Percy to a self-conscious artistry. Art helps us to make contact with others and with our locale, so that we can be, in Binx's terms, someones somewhere, not anyones anywhere. Unlike the scientist with his interest in types, according to Percy's essay "State of the Novel" (1977), art deals with "what it is like to be an individual, to be born, live and die in the twentieth century." Tom More's scientific lapsometer cannot render his crucial insight; "Dear God, I can see it now, why can't I see it other times, that it is you I love in the beauty of the world and in all the lovely girls and dear good friends, and it is pilgrims we are, wayfarers on a journey, and not pigs, nor angels." As Percy has directly stated, "It is the artist who at his best reverses the alienating process by the very act of seeing it clearly for what it is and naming it, and who in this same act establishes a kind of community" ("State of the Novel," p. 372).

Percy is fully aware, however, that "You don't have a thesis and then illustrate it." As he told John Carr, "What you do is put a man down in a certain situation and see what happens." Percy is thus sharply aware of the demands of fiction, and he has a well-developed aesthetic sense of language and craft. He has written scholarly essays on language theory and signs, as well as other nonfiction ranging from parables to bemused jokes. Several of his essays directly address the questions of craft and of the place of the artist in society, yet another subject he claims to be "fed up with." Despite Percy's pervasive irony, his serious commitment to his craft is clear: "My main assumption is that art is cognitive, that is, it discovers and knows and tells, tells the reader how things are, how we are, in a way that the reader can confirm with as much certitude as a scientist taking a pointer-reading" ("State of the Novel," p. 360). In a more characteristic tone, he writes in "Why I Live Where I Live" for *Esquire*, "My own suspicion is that many American writers secretly envy writers like Solzhenitsyn, who get sent to the Gulag camps for their writings, keep writing on toilet paper, take on the whole bloody state—and win. The total freedom of writers in this country can be distressing. What a burden to bear, that the government not only allows us complete freedom—even freedom for atrocities like *MacBird!*—but, like 95 percent of Americans, couldn't care less what we write. Oh, you lucky Dostoevskys, with your firing squads. . . . Mailer and Vidal write books reviling the establishment—and make main selection of Book of the Month" (April 1980, p. 35).

The results of Percy's careful craftsmanship, and its evolution over time, are difficult to describe and, because his effects are dependent on context, impossible to excerpt. A few examples, at least, can be briefly cited: his ability to handle tender love scenes, such as Binx's encounter with Kate on the "dark little mezzanine" in *The Moviegoer* and the developing affection between Will and Allie that takes up most of the second half of *The Second Coming*; Barrett's memories of his father's suicide in *The Last Gentleman* and his discovery, in *The Second Coming*, that his father had tried to murder him before taking his own life; and the use of the naive yet profound faith of children, such as Lonnie in *The Moviegoer*, Jamie Vaught in *The Last Gentleman*, and Tom More's daughter Samantha, to approach ineffable moments of recognition. Each of Percy's novels demonstrates an increasing awareness of characterization, narrative technique, and tone, as well as a novelistic sense of place. Most important, however, has been Percy's single-minded commitment to dealing with fundamental human concerns, however mundane and difficult to realize they may be. Despite his ironic dismissal of the questions of alienation and of the place of the artist, Percy clearly deems the subject more important than the ability to blow smoke out of one's eustachian tubes.

Even so, Percy's humor is perhaps the most important quality behind his success. As it defuses the heavy-handed moralizing and brings the philosophical ideas into human terms, it also disengages the material from the dangerous slough of sentimentality that mars so much "moral fiction." Without it, Percy sounds like Mark Twain when Colonel Sherburn steals Huck Finn's novel for a few pages. In spite of his indignant rage at the mores of the twentieth century, Percy's point is usually embedded in a polished humor that ranges from parody to hilarity to razor-sharp irony.

Out of context the humor loses much of its effect, but some examples are needed. Parodies include his concise demolition of the radio series "This I Believe" in *The Moviegoer*, his masterful use of Bill Cullen's "grateful Los Angeles TV studio audience laughter" on "Strike It Rich" to defuse any hint of sentimentality as Barrett comes to terms with his father's suicide in *The Last Gentleman*, and his mocking treatment of the Southern ideal of an artificial return to agrarianism with his movie-set Tara in *Love*.

A biting humor laces all of Percy's novels, even the bitter *Lancelot*, whose title character asks, "Which is worse, to die with T. J. Jackson at Chancellorsville or live with Johnny Carson in Burbank?" Only this character's desperate alternatives finally repel us. The pervasive humor of *Love* is a key to the novel's success. In a particularly good sustained scene, Dr. More applies his lapsometer to the apparently senile and mute Mr. Ives, who reveals the true source of his antisocial behavior: "How would you like it if . . . you had been pestered without letup by a bunch of chickenshit Ohioans?" At the beginning of *The Second Coming*, we immediately sympathize with Will Barrett's alienation from "the most Christian nation in the world" when he lists the ten churches he passes on the main street of "the most Christian town in North Carolina" and notes signs for the African Methodist Episcopal Church and Starlight Baptist Church, both "down in the hollow," and another for St. John o' the Woods Episcopal Church, six blocks away on "a pine grove on the ridge."

Percy's irony turns savage, as well, as in the extended passage in which Lance describes the New Southerner as "Billy Graham on Sunday and Richard Nixon the rest of the week." The very premise of *Love in the Ruins* is that the world is near its end, a premise convincingly if humorously rendered in the opening description of the chaos from the vantage point of the narrator, pinned down by a sniper in a ruined Howard Johnson motel waiting for the Early Times bourbon to run out and the buzzards circling above to descend. The American Catholic Church's major feast is Property Rights Sunday, and divorced priests and nuns are seeking the right to remarry. Nor is fiction spared: "American literature is not having its finest hour. The Southern gothic novel yielded to the Jewish masturbatory novel, which in turn gave way to the WASP homosexual novel, which has nearly run its course. The Catholic literary renascence, long awaited, failed to materialize. . . . Gore Vidal is the grand old man of American letters."

Percy has, then, the elements of greatness, if in actual practice they sometimes lack proportion. "Novel writing," he notes in "Questions They Never Asked Me," "is a serious business in which the novelist is out both to give joy and to draw blood." He does both for his careful readers, whom he knows constitute a sharp minority: "All serious writers and readers constitute less than one percent of the population. The other ninety-nine percent don't give a damn. They watch *Wonder Woman*." His eccentricities are disconcerting as well as entertaining, and his ironies can mislead as well as slice through to the bone. Dangerous genius as well as eccentric fool, however, with his cool irony and warm humanity, this Southern writer presents his serious readers with a disquieting joy, with a truth that must be acted upon.

SURVEY OF CRITICISM

If, as Percy claims, serious readers and writers are only one percent of the population, he can hardly pretend to have been neglected by that minority. Since his "discovery" in 1962 by Jean Stafford, a judge for the National Book Award, Percy has been the subject of three books, two collections of essays (*The Art of Walker Percy*, ed. Panthea Reid Broughton, 1979; and *Walker Percy: Art and Ethics*, ed. Jac Tharpe, 1980), and literally hundreds of articles and dissertations. Some of it is insensitive, and a good deal of it is repetitive, but I pass over such in silence and, indeed, must omit many good studies in this rapid survey. The beginner would do well to consult Jac Tharpe's *Walker Percy* (1983) for a good basic introduction, although Tharpe's neglect of Percy's essays on language is disappointing.

Percy's philosophical ideas and influence have received much attention. Martin Luschei's *The Sovereign Wayfarer* (1972) presents a clear, distinguished discussion of Percy's complex ideas and his reading of Kierkegaard and Marcel. Often imitated and more often merely repeated, this study is rarely improved upon by the many later essays on these topics. Other noteworthy treatments include Lewis Lawson's "Walker Percy's Indirect Communications," one of the early studies of Percy's use of Kierkegaard, and Cleanth Brooks's "Walker Percy and Modern Gnosticism" (in Broughton), a discussion of Percy's work in terms of Eric Voegelin's *Order and History* with convincing applications to both *Love in the Ruins* and *Lancelot*. John F. Zeugner's "Walker Percy and Gabriel Marcel: The Castaway and the Wayfarer" aggressively dissects not only Marcel's influence but also Percy's "method of inculcation by irony and indirection," which Zeugner calls "a kind of Jesuitical literariness." Preferring *The Moviegoer* among Percy's novels, Zeugner judges *Love in the Ruins* harshly: "the gleam of condescension, always present in Percy's work, has become the sun."

Percy's Southernness is the subject of Lawson's "Walker Percy's Southern Stoic," Brooks's "The Southernness of Walker Percy," Lewis P. Simpson's "The Southern Aesthetic of Memory," and Louis D. Rubin, Jr.'s thoughtful personal essay "The Boll Weevil, the Iron Horse, and the End of the Line." Lawson's "William Alexander Percy, Walker Percy, and the Apocalypse," in his *Another Generation*, illustrates Percy's concern "with the fatal ease with which the Southern ideal becomes a gnostic nightmare."

Percy's theory of language is the topic of one of the most recent books on Percy, Patricia Lewis Poteat's *Walker Percy and the Old Modern Age: Reflections on Language, Argument, and the Telling of Stories* (1985). Other discussions on the topic include J. P. Telotte's "Charles Peirce and Walker Percy: From Semiotic to Narrative" (in Tharpe) and his "Walker Percy's Language of Creation"; James Walter's opposing view in "Spinning and Spieling"; Charles P. Bigger's "Walker Percy and the Resonance of the Word" (in Tharpe); and two essays in Broughton, Weldon Thornton's "Homo Loquens, Homo Symbolificus, Homo Sapiens: Walker Percy on Language" and William H. Poteat's "Reflections on Walker Percy's Theory of Language." Peter S. Hawkins does a commendable job of linking Percy's language to his religious themes in *The Language of Grace*.

Percy's literary craftsmanship is the particular concern of Richard Pidell's "Basking in the Eye of the Storm" and of Mark Johnson's "The Search for Place in Walker Percy's Novels" and "*Lancelot*: Percy's Romance." With sensitive, very detailed readings, Simone Vauthier applies structuralist analytical techniques in her "Narrative Triangulation and Triple Alliance: A Look at *The Moviegoer*" and "Narrative Triangulation in *The Last Gentleman*" (in Broughton). Michael Pearson's "Art as Symbolic Action" (in Tharpe) discusses Percy's aesthetic theory.

General cultural perspectives include Mary Thale's "The Moviegoer in the 1950's," Edward J. Cashin's "History as Mores: Walker Percy's *Lancelot*," and Ted R. Spivey's "Walker Percy and the Archetypes" (in Broughton). Robert Coles's *Walker Percy: An American Search* (1979) is a ruminating appreciation of Percy's work and its influence on the well-known author and child psychiatrist.

This well-informed, thoughtful discussion of Percy's essays and fiction in personal terms does not pretend to be literary criticism, though Coles is familiar with the criticism even when he does not cite it.

Too numerous to mention, studies of the individual novels are listed by Weixlmann and Gann (see below). A final important resource is Percy's many interviews, always amusing even if they have to be read, like the fiction, with one's guard up.

BIBLIOGRAPHY

Works by Walker Percy

The Moviegoer. New York: Alfred A. Knopf, 1961.
The Last Gentleman. New York: Farrar, Straus and Giroux, 1966.
Love in the Ruins. New York: Farrar, Straus and Giroux, 1971.
The Message in the Bottle. New York: Farrar, Straus and Giroux, 1975.
Lancelot. New York: Farrar, Straus and Giroux, 1977.
"The State of the Novel: Dying Art or New Science?" *Michigan Quarterly Review* 16 (Fall 1977): 359–73.
The Second Coming. New York: Farrar, Straus and Giroux, 1980.
Lost in the Cosmos: The Last Self-Help Book. New York: Farrar, Straus and Giroux, 1983.

Studies of Walker Percy

This selective bibliography omits many good essays. The most comprehensive Percy bibliography, listing both primary and secondary work and including the interviews, is by Joe Weixlmann and Daniel H. Gann, in *Southern Quarterly* 18, no. 3 (1980): 137–57, and reprinted in *Walker Percy: Art and Ethics*, listed below. *Andrew Lytle, Walker Percy, Peter Taylor: A Reference Guide*, by Victor A. Kramer, Patricia A. Bailey, Carol G. Dana, and Carl H. Griffin (Boston: G. K. Hall, 1983), annotates its listing of works about Percy up to 1980, but it does not include Percy's interviews and uncollected essays.

Brooks, Cleanth. "The Southernness of Walker Percy." *South Carolina Review* 13 (1981): 34–38.
Broughton, Panthea Reid, ed. *The Art of Walker Percy: Stratagems for Being*. Baton Rouge: Louisiana State University Press, 1979.
Cashin, Edward J. "History as Mores: Walker Percy's *Lancelot*." *Georgia Review* 31 (1977): 875–80.
Coles, Robert. *Walker Percy: An American Search*. Boston: Little, Brown, 1979.
Hawkins, Peter S. *The Language of Grace: Flannery O'Connor, Walker Percy, & Iris Murdoch*. Cambridge: Cowley, 1983.
Johnson, Mark. "*Lancelot*: Percy's Romance." *Southern Literary Journal* 15, no. 2 (1983): 19–30.
———. "The Search for Place in Walker Percy's Novels." *Southern Literary Journal*, 8, 1 (1975): 55–81.

Lawson, Lewis. *Another Generation: Southern Fiction Since World War II*. Jackson: University Press of Mississippi, 1984.

―――. "Walker Percy's Indirect Communications." *Texas Studies in Literature and Language* 11 (1969): 867–900.

―――. "Walker Percy's Southern Stoic." *Southern Literary Journal* 3, no. 1 (1970): 5–31.

Luschei, Martin. *The Sovereign Wayfarer: Walker Percy's Diagnosis of the Malaise*. Baton Rouge: Louisiana State University Press, 1972.

Pindell, Richard. "Basking in the Eye of the Storm: The Esthetics of Loss in Walker Percy's *The Moviegoer*." *Boundary* 2, no. 4 (1975): 219–30.

Poteat, Patricia Lewis. *Walker Percy and the Old Modern Age; Reflections on Language, Argument, and the Telling of Stories*. Baton Rouge: Louisiana State University Press, 1985.

Rubin, Louis D., Jr. "The Boll Weevil, the Iron Horse, and the End of the Line: Thoughts on the South." *A Gallery of Southerners*. Baton Rouge: Louisiana State University Press, 1982.

Simpson, Lewis P. "The Southern Aesthetic of Memory." *Tulane Studies in English* 23 (1978): 207–27.

Telotte, J. P. "Walker Percy's Language of Creation." *Southern Quarterly* 16 (1978): 105–16.

Thale, Mary. "The Moviegoer in the 1950's." *Twentieth Century Literature* 14 (1968): 84–89.

Tharpe, Jac. *Walker Percy*. New York: Twayne, 1983.

―――. ed. *Walker Percy: Art and Ethics*. Jackson: University Press of Mississippi, 1980. First published as *Southern Quarterly* 18, 3 (1980).

Vauthier, Simone. "Narrative Triangle and Triple Alliance: A Look at *The Moviegoer*." *Les Americanistes: New French Criticism on Modern American Fiction*. Ed. Ira Johnson and Christiane Johnson. Port Washington, N.Y.: Kennikat, 1978.

Walter, James. "Spinning and Spieling: A Trick and a Kick in Walker Percy's *The Moviegoer*." *Southern Review* 16 (1980): 574–90.

Zeugner, John F. "Walker Percy and Gabriel Marcel: The Castaway and the Wayfarer." *Mississippi Quarterly* 28 (1974–75): 21–53.

————— JOAN GIVNER —————

Katherine Anne Porter
(1890–1980)

Katherine Anne Porter's reputation rests on her *Collected Stories*, rather than on the best-selling novel *Ship of Fools* that she labored 30 years to finish. In spite of her limited output, because of her style (personal as well as literary) she was an important influence on a younger generation of Southern writers such as Eudora Welty, Carson McCullers, Flannery O'Connor, and Truman Capote.

BIOGRAPHY

Katherine Anne Porter was born on 15 May 1890 in Indian Creek, Texas, the fourth of five children of Mary Alice and Harrison Boone Porter, both Methodists. Her mother died before she was two, and the four surviving children were raised by Porter's grandmother in Kyle, Texas. The grandmother, Catherine Anne Porter, celebrated in Porter's fiction, died in 1901 and left the family emotionally and financially destitute, since the father seemed incapable from the time of his wife's death of caring for his family.

The only effective education Porter had was a year or possibly two at the Thomas School, a private nonsectarian girls' school in San Antonio, which Porter persuaded her father to let her attend so that she could train to be an actress. Equipped with that training, she and her sister subsequently supported themselves by running a little class in elocution, singing, and dramatic arts in a rented room in Victoria, Texas. The necessity of earning a living was removed when Porter married shortly after her sixteenth birthday. Her first husband, John Henry Koontz, a railway clerk in Louisiana, was a member of a prominent ranching family from Inez, Texas. The Koontzes moved back from Louisiana to Houston and then to Corpus Christi, John Koontz having taken a job as a salesman for a wholesale grocery firm. Porter left Koontz in 1914 to go to Chicago to try to make a career for herself in the movies. The nine-year first marriage ended in divorce in 1915.

The movie work proved too strenuous for Porter, who returned to Louisiana to support her sister during a collapsing marriage and a difficult childbirth. In order to help support the sister, Porter made herself a costume and performed a song and drama routine on the Lyceum circuit in small towns in Louisiana. Once the sister regained her health, Porter went off to start life anew in Dallas. She was almost immediately felled by tuberculosis and spent the next year in sanatoriums in Texas.

In the Carlsbad Sanatorium she met Kitty Barry Crawford, a journalist who influenced her next choice of work. When she recovered her health, Porter worked first on the Fort Worth paper run by Crawford's husband and subsequently on the *Rocky Mountain News* in Denver. The year in Denver was highly productive. Not only did Porter become a successful journalist, but her experiences (including near-death in the influenza epidemic of 1918) provided the material for "Pale Horse, Pale Rider." She left Denver for Greenwich Village, determined to write fiction. At first she supported herself by writing publicity copy for a movie company, but she also published some children's stories and did a ghost-written book, *My Chinese Marriage*. She left New York for Mexico in 1919 and arrived there in time to witness Obregon's inauguration as president. For the next six months, she did a variety of writing and teaching jobs and met the revolutionaries, artists, and bandits who provided material for her early stories. During the next years she traveled several times between New York and Mexico.

In the mid–1920s she made a second brief marriage to Ernest Stock, an Englishman and aspiring artist. After the marriage ended, she returned to New York to work on the biography of Cotton Mather for which she had a contract with Horace Liveright. Under the pressure of work and an unhappy love affair, her health collapsed, and in 1929 friends raised money to send her to Bermuda. The five months there were highly productive; even though she did not finish the biography, she conceived some of her finest stories. In late 1929 she finished "Flowering Judas," which gave proof that she was an exceptional writer. The next year Harcourt, Brace published a limited edition of *Flowering Judas and Other Stories*. It was so successful that a second edition was published a few years later.

In 1930 Porter returned to Mexico for her longest period of residence in that country. There she met Eugene Pressly and also spent a week on the movie set of Eisenstein's *Que Viva Mexico*, a visit that resulted in the story "Hacienda." In the fall of 1931 she sailed with Pressly on the S.S. *Werra* from Veracruz to Bremerhaven in Germany, a voyage that provided the basis for *Ship of Fools*. Porter spent the next months in Berlin while Pressly went to a job at the American Embassy in Madrid. She left Berlin in early 1932 and visited Madrid and Paris and later settled in Basel to be near Pressly, who was working in Geneva. When he was posted to Paris, she returned there, and the two were married in spring 1933. The next three years were relatively settled and productive ones in a life that was usually neither. This security ended when the couple returned to the United States in 1936. After her arrival, Porter spent several weeks in an inn in Doylestown, Pennsylvania, where the work of the past years culminated in completed versions of "Noon Wine," "Old Mortality," and a version of "Pale Horse, Pale Rider."

Separated from Pressly, she moved to New Orleans where she met Albert Erskine. They were married in spring 1937, as Porter received her divorce from Pressly. The marriage to Erskine was unhappy almost from the first day, when during the marriage ceremony Erskine learned to his dismay that Porter was twenty years his senior.

During the late 1930s marital difficulties and literary successes came together. With the publication of her second collection, *Pale Horse, Pale Rider*, Porter was acclaimed by the critics and compared to Milton, Hawthorne, and Henry James. Yet her literary powers were waning. In the introduction to the Modern Library edition of *Flowering Judas and Other Stories*, she declared that she was not one of those who could flourish in the conditions of the past two decades. Nevertheless, she was describing her most productive period. At fifty, she was faced with financial insecurity, rootlessness, writing difficulties, and the sense that with the end of her fourth marriage, any hope of domestic happiness had gone forever.

She spent some time at the artists' colony in Yaddo, New York, established a home for herself in nearby Saratoga Springs, got her divorce from Erskine, and tried to finish the many works for which she had signed contracts. In 1944 her final short story collection, *The Leaning Tower*, appeared, a disappointment to her publishers, who were hoping for a novel. Thereafter she departed for Hollywood, hoping that the substantial salary she could earn as a scriptwriter would put her on sounder financial footing.

Never able to meet deadlines or work to order, she quit after thirteen weeks but remained in California. She did another stint as scriptwriter and then taught at Stanford, her first of many university positions. At the end of the decade she returned east and settled in New York, hoping to finish *Ship of Fools*. Soon, however, she was tempted away by teaching offers and the lure of a steady income. In the next decade she taught at the University of Michigan; at the University of Liege, where she had to resign because of ill-health; and at Washington and Lee University, besides doing other shorter stints in many universities.

At the end of a decade of teaching, she settled in Washington, D.C., determined to finish her novel. *Ship of Fools* was triumphantly published in 1962, bringing her at seventy-two the financial security that had eluded her all her life. The novel was a best-seller and a successful movie, but this time critical acclaim was withheld. The novel was seen, on balance, to be a fundamentally flawed work. Nevertheless, in the next years her *Collected Stories* was published and awarded both the National Book Award and the Pulitzer Prize. *The Collected Essays and Occasional Writings* was published when she was eighty.

With her newly acquired fortune, her last years were fairly happy. She lived first of all in a lavish house that she rented in Spring Valley and then in smaller, more convenient places in College Park, Maryland. The University of Maryland set up a Katherine Anne Porter Room, to be the main repository of her papers, books, and personal memorabilia, and she gained much satisfaction from making ceremonial visits there. She died after a series of strokes on 18 September 1980, at the age of ninety.

MAJOR THEMES

One important fact to be borne in mind in evaluating Porter's work is that her period of creativity was brief. She published a few scattered and somewhat uncharacteristic stories in the early 1920s, but it was not until 1928 that she mastered her métier and began to write her best fiction. By 1941 she had finished "The Leaning Tower" and was already struggling with the novel that became *Ship of Fools*. From this time on she published no new fiction and finished only a few stories already begun. Her creative life lasted, in effect, for little over twelve years. Linked to this fact, not surprisingly, is a second important one— that her basic theme changes very little throughout her work. She admitted as much herself in the *Paris Review* interview done by Barbara Thompson in 1963:

It's astonishing how little I've changed: nothing in my point of view or way of feeling. I'm going back now to finish some of the great many short stories that I have begun and not been able to finish for one reason or another.

Perhaps even Porter herself did not realize, and she certainly did not acknowledge, the first appearance of her theme. It occurs in the dramatic criticism she wrote in 1919 when she worked for the *Rocky Mountain News* and reviewed plays (often crude melodramas) performed in the local theaters. There she confessed to a long-standing fascination with villains. She declared that the real villain deserves some admiration because it takes imagination and courage to be villainous. Recognizing the positive qualities in villains, she transferred her attention to the virtuous, passive heroines.

The shift of Porter's attention from the villain to the saintly heroine was not a temporary change of focus but a permanent one, and her attitude toward the virtuous heroine eventually formed the cornerstone of her moral philosophy. The main tenet of this philosophy is that the evildoers are not the most reprehensible people in the world, because they at least have the courage of their convictions. Nor are they the most dangerous people, since they can be easily recognized. The people who really need to be watched are the so-called innocents who stand by and allow others to perpetrate evil. Porter was to express repeatedly the opinion that the innocent bystanders allow the activity of evildoers, not merely because of fear and indifference, but because they gain vicarious pleasure from seeing others perform the wicked deeds they themselves wish but fear to perform.

She came eventually to see the passive, virtuous people as guilty of promoting evil even when they do not consciously do so.

This theory about the relationship between saints and evildoers and their collusion in evil became her lifelong gospel, the subject of numerous informal talks, the message she preached from political platforms, and the basis of her interpretation of current events. After the publication of *Ship of Fools*, she gave this account of some of the events of the twentieth century:

. . . the collusion in evil that allows creatures like Mussolini, or Hitler, or Huey Long or McCarthy—you can make your own list, petty and great,—to gain hold of things, who permits it? Oh, we're convinced we're not evil. We don't believe in that sort of thing, do we? And the strange thing is that if these agents of evil are all clowns, why do we put up with them? God knows, such men are evil, without sense—forces of pure ambition and will—but they enjoy our tacit consent. (*College English* 24 Feb. 1963)

The same theory informed all her fiction. An early, spare version of her theme appears in the short story "Magic." Here a maid, hoping to relax her mistress as she brushes her hair, tells a story of a villainous madam who cheats and bullies the prostitutes in a New Orleans brothel. The point of the story is that the madam's activity is made possible by those around her—the male clients, the police, and the cook—who do nothing. Not only are these people as guilty as the one who perpetrates the violence, but so too are the woman and the maid who relish the story. The woman sniffs scent (a detail suggesting her desire to hide unpleasant realities), stares at her blameless reflection in the mirror, and urges the storyteller to continue whenever she pauses. Lest there be any doubt about the equation of guilt between both madams and both maids, they resemble each other so closely as to invite confusion. When the storyteller describes the cook of the brothel, she might be describing herself: "she was a woman, colored like myself with much French blood all the same, like myself always among people who worked spells. But she had a very hard heart, she helped the madam in everything, she liked to watch all that happen" (*Collected Stories*, p. 41). The theme of the story echoes Porter's words that the evil of our time is not an accident but a total consent.

A fuller version of the theme appears in "Flowering Judas," which, like many of Porter's stories, has a triangular arrangement of characters, consisting of villain, victim, and "heroine." Braggioni, like all Porter's villains, is pure caricature and looms in the story like a grotesque Easter egg in shades of mauve and purple and yellow. A hideous creature with the eyes of a cat and the paunch of a pig, he embodies each of the seven deadly sins.

The implication of the story is that if Braggioni is a self-serving, self-indulgent villain, he has not always been so. Once he was a young idealist in both politics and love. It is Laura and people like her who have caused him to change from idealist to opportunist, and the main focus of the story is upon her and upon her motivation. She neither loves nor opposes Braggioni, because she is basically indifferent to him as she is to most people. She has trained herself to remain uncommitted in her relationships with others and has developed a principle of rejection: ". . . . the very cells of her flesh reject knowledge and kinship in one monotonous word. No. No. No. She draws her strength from this one holy talismanic word which does not suffer her to be led into evil. Denying everything she may walk anywhere in safety, she looks at everything without amazement" (*Collected Stories*, p. 197). It is the death of Eugenio in which she has conspired with Braggioni that causes her finally to become aware of her guilt, and then only in a dream. As she falls asleep, she receives a message from her own depths warning her of motives and the meaning of her acts.

Porter's longest treatment of her theme is, of course, *Ship of Fools*. She described her intentions in the novel in a 1946 letter to Josephine Herbst. She said that her book was about the constant, endless collusion between good and evil. She said that she believed human beings to be capable of total evil but thought that no one had ever been totally good, and that gave the edge to evil. She intended not to present any solution, but simply to show the principle at work and to demonstrate that none of us had an alibi in the world. She said that her plan and conclusion had been worked out ten years before and that nothing had happened since to change her mind—indeed, everything confirmed her old opinion.

Again, in the novel the villains are depicted in caricature. Herr Rieber is piglike; and the Zarzuela Company—a group of thieves, pimps, and prostitutes who stop at nothing—is described as a flock of crows or other quarreling, thieving birds.

The pivotal character who corresponds with Laura of "Flowering Judas" is Dr. Schumann. He is well qualified by his superior intelligence and by his professional training to be influential, but he has developed a detachment that distances him from the others. When he first appears in the novel, he is standing above the other characters, watching them come aboard. As he looks down from his elevated position, his interest is clinical, aloof. The hunchback stirs his interest as a case of extreme malformation; Jenny excites his disapproval as an immodest woman; and Mrs. Treadwell with her bruise arouses his worst, and as it turns out, totally unfounded suspicions. Typically, he soon loses interest, and it is apparent that his physical weakness of the heart is symptomatic of a corresponding spiritual weakness. He is a professional helper of mankind who gives help automatically but is incapable of love or involvement. When the Captain asks his advice on what to do about the Zarzuela Company, his reply, "Do nothing at all," marks his kinship with Laura. Like her, he eventually experiences a moment when the implications of his acts become apparent, even to himself: "The Doctor suffered the psychic equivalent of a lightning stroke, which cleared away there and then his emotional fogs and vapors, and he faced his truth, nearly intolerable but the kind of pain he could deal with, something he recognized and accepted unconditionally" (*Ship of Fools*, p. 373).

The theme is made explicit in a discussion that takes place at the Captain's table of the *Vera*. The guests are discussing the activities of the Spanish dancers, and Frau Rittersdorf expresses the opinion that they are "dangerous criminals." The Captain disagrees because "it requires a certain force of character to be really evil." (His remark has the special interest of being almost word for word what Katherine Anne Porter wrote in 1919 in her editorial on the villains of the Denver stage.) Dr. Schumann elaborates on the Captain's statement:

I agree with the Captain, it takes a strong character to be really evil. Most of us are too slack, half-hearted or cowardly—luckily, I suppose. Our collusion with evil is only negative, consent by default you might say. I suppose in our hearts our sympathies are with the criminal because he really commits the deed we only dream of doing. (*Ship of Fools*, p. 294)

In the last years of her life, Porter completed a number of stories and essays that she had started earlier, among them an account of her participation in the movement protesting the execution of Sacco and Vanzetti in Boston in 1927. Her publication of her essay, *The Never Ending Wrong*, 50 years after the event made it the work with the longest gestation period, twenty years longer than that of *Ship of Fools*.

Reactions to the book were mixed. Others who were involved in the Sacco-Vanzetti case felt that the writers who flocked to Boston did so seeking grist for conversations in such gathering places of the literati as the round table of the Algonquin. One reviewer felt that the essay was an inconsequential work that told too little about the case and too much about how Porter felt on every occasion of human betrayal. Only Porter's friend Eudora Welty pointed out the close thematic link between the essay and the fiction. In fact, the theme of the essay is exactly that of the stories and the novel, the arrangement of characters in a triangle of villain, victim, and not-so-innocent hero/heroine, the same that appears in all her work.

The villains have all the recognizable porcine, complacent traits of such other villains as Braggioni and Herr Rieber. They are Governor Fuller, Judge Thayer (who is reported to have said while playing golf, "Did you see what I did to those anarchistic bastards?"), and the Judges who presided over the trial of the picketers.

Arrayed against these representatives of corrupt authority are all those who wish to help the victims and protest their unfair trial. On close inspection, however, they turn out like other of Porter's blameless people to be secretly allied with the villains and conspiring toward the same end. Chief among these are the Communists, represented by Rosa Baron. When Porter expressed the wish that the victims might be saved, she was astonished to hear Rosa Baron reply, "Why, what on earth good would they be to us alive?" And there are other protesters of dubious intention, notably the journalists who profit from the scenes of high emotion when the members of the victims' families appear. One journalist gloats that they arranged the whole show. The victims, of course, are not saved, and they die, like Eugenio of "Flowering Judas" and Echegaray of *Ship of Fools*, with dignity and resignation, gazing steadfastly at death.

Students of Porter's work have assumed that she is another writer whose philosophy developed out of her reaction to the rise of Nazism. The assumption is a logical one, for she had more reason than most writers to be affected by that phenomenon, since she witnessed it at first hand. The experiences in Mexico and Germany, however, did not produce new opinions so much as they confirmed and strengthened already existing ones. Porter's journalism shows that her philosophy was already shaped before she went to Mexico and that it developed out of her attempt to write criticism of contemporary theater.

SURVEY OF CRITICISM

The excesses of the early critics of Porter's work are well indicated by two 1938 reviews of *Pale Horse, Pale Rider*. Paul Rosenfeld, writing for the *Saturday Review of Literature*, asserted that "Katherine Anne Porter moves in the illustrious company headed by Hawthorne, Flaubert and Henry James." Glenway Wescott, writing for the *Southern Review* a piece entitled simply "Praise," compared "Noon Wine" to Milton's *Paradise Lost*. This tendency to exaggerated praise never entirely disappeared.

At the same time more astringent criticism began to appear. Lodwick Hartley's first essay on Porter appeared in the *Sewanee Review* in 1940. Over the years he proved the most balanced of Porter's critics, admiring her as an artist yet remaining fully aware of her limitations.

The turning point in the critical assessment of Porter's work came after the publication of *Ship of Fools*. The early reviews of that novel were, for the most part, as adulatory as the early reviews of the stories had been. Mark Schorer, reviewing the book on the front page of the *New York Time Book Review* 1 April 1962, began by saying:

This novel has been famous for years. It has been awaited through an entire literary generation. Publishers and foundations, like many once hopeful readers, long ago gave it up. Now it is suddenly, superbly, here. It would have been worth waiting for for another thirty years if one had had any hope of having them. It is our good fortune that it comes at last still in our time. It will endure, one hardly risks anything in saying, far beyond it, for many literary generations.

He ended by saying that it should be compared not with the works of Sebastian Brandt or Richard Hughes but with George Eliot's *Middlemarch*. Schorer's praises, echoed by other critics, were soon followed by equally immoderate attacks.

The most devastating of these, "*Ship of Fools*: and the Critics" by Theodore Solotaroff, appeared in *Commentary* 24 October 1962. After attacking Porter's "fretful and trifling caricature of Jews that is a hallmark of genteel anti-Semitism,'' Solotaroff went on to show that the treatment of Lowenthal ''is only one example of Miss Porter's compulsive tendency to simplify and close her characters and issues, to look down upon life from the perspective of towering arrogance, contempt, and disgust.'' (Solotaroff's review and Mark Schorer's are reprinted in *Katherine Anne Porter: A Collection of Critical Essays*, edited by Robert Penn Warren.)

Not surprisingly, in view of the uniformly unpleasant portrayal of the German characters in the book, the reception in Germany was cold. English criticism was also unfavorable, causing Porter to comment that the old taste for blood sports was in full hue and cry. An anonymous reviewer in the *Times Literary Supplement* in November 1962, granted the book moments of great power and compassion but thought that the achievements were those of a great short-story writer. They glittered like passages of subtle, concentrated brushwork on a canvas too thinly composed. He thought the novel lacked a dramatic center and added:

One cannot help wondering whether she *knows* enough—of German history, of the sources of modern anti-Semitism, of European middle-class speech and values—or whether that knowledge has penetrated the exquisite but very special range of her feelings.

One of the few favorable English reviews appeared in the *Spectator* in the same month. Sybille Bedford concluded that the Great American novel had appeared and that ironically it turned out to be a great universal novel. At the end of an otherwise approving review, she wondered if the book might have been even more stunning if it had been less bulky, and she also felt that the grotesque might have been done more lightly. ''Did the only Jew on board have to be such an utter wretch?'' she asked. She concluded that the most serious flaw in the novel was its static nature and the fact that the characters move on tramlines towards crescendos, showing no development, arriving at no crossroads and experiencing no turning points.

The completion of the novel signaled the appearance of more ambitious critical studies of her entire oeuvre. They include theses, dissertations, pamphlets, collections of critical essays, and book-length studies.

The first pamphlet was Harry John Mooney, Jr.'s *The Fiction and Criticism of Katherine Anne Porter* (1957); a revised edition with a chapter on *Ship of Fools* was published in 1962. Ray B. West, Jr.'s *Katherine Anne Porter* came in 1963, with a revised edition following in 1968 after Porter informed West that his statements about her Catholic girlhood were incorrect. Winfred S. Emmons's *Katherine Anne Porter: The Regional Stories* appeared in 1967.

Of the early book-length studies the weakest are M. M. Liberman's *Katherine Anne Porter's Fiction* (1971), a series of disconnected essays, described with some accuracy by one of the first reviewers as ''an exercise in superficiality,'' and William L. Nance's *Katherine Anne Porter and the Art of Rejection* (1964). Originally written as a doctoral dissertation, Nance's book suffers from a thesis-ridden approach.

George Hendrick's *Katherine Anne Porter* (1965) and John Edwards Hardy's *Katherine Anne Porter* (1973) remain sound guides to Porter's work. Although neither book attempts to break new critical ground, each provides sound synopses and balanced interpretations.

Of the collections of critical essays *Katherine Anne Porter: A Critical Symposium*, edited by Lodwick Hartley and George Core (1969), is the most useful guide to Porter's work. It contains an important interview with Porter, a collection of the best critical essays, and a useful bibliography. A second collection of critical essays, *Katherine Anne Porter*, edited by Robert Penn Warren, appeared in 1979. The justification for this book is hard to imagine. It consists of eighteen essays, seven of which appeared in *Katherine Anne Porter: A Critical Symposium*, four of the ecstatic reviews of *Ship of Fools* and, for balance, the unfavorable *Commentary* review. Perhaps the most misleading feature of the book is the introduction, which besides biographical errors has other factual mistakes, such as an inaccurate publication date for *Ship of Fools*. The conclusion is inescapable that the book was intended not so much as a scholarly tool as a tribute to Porter herself. Certainly there could be no objection to such a tribute, but since the volume is part of a series habitually used by students, it seems to have been made at their expense.

Over the years, a persistent problem with Porter criticism has been the inaccurate biiographical record, often falsified by Porter herself. She gave out erroneous information about her name, birthdate, education, and marriages. Most misleading, however, were her statements that she was not the daughter of an impoverished dirt farmer (which she was) but a "member of the guilt-ridden white-pillar crowd" raised in decaying mansions with well-stocked libraries and servants who were former slaves. These fabrications led Mark Schorer and other critics to praise her ability in stories such as "Noon Wine" to go beyond her own class to portray realistically the members of another class, that of the plain people. In fact, the characters of "Noon Wine" were based on members of her own class and own family. The imaginative leap took place when she described the background of Miranda Gay in her stories.

These and other biographical problems were clarified in 1982 when Joan Givner's biography, *Katherine Anne Porter: A Life*, appeared. In spite of the existence of an accurate record, however, the old errors persist. Jane DeMouy, whose critical work *Katherine Anne Porter's Women* appeared in 1983, completely ignored the need for careful research. She made no effort to check facts in the extensive Porter archive, nor did she wait to check facts in the biography. Her book is, therefore, riddled with errors of every kind—wrong publication and composition dates for stories, wrong assumptions about Porter's class and culture. Her inaccuracies suggest a thesis worked out ahead of the evidence and willfully maintained in spite of it. The *Norton Anthology of Literature by Women* (1985), although the biography has been available for three years, contains totally misleading and inaccurate information on Porter's life.

The future of Porter criticism, however, is not completely bleak. George

Hendrick is preparing a revised edition of his 1965 study, and it should provide an indispensable tool for students. Darlene Unrue's *Truth and Vision in Katherine Anne Porter's Fiction* (1985) traces the controlling images in the fiction, based on a thorough study of Porter's essays, letters, and unpublished sources. It is to be hoped that these books will herald a new era in Porter studies.

BIBLIOGRAPHY

Works by Katherine Anne Porter

Flowering Judas and Other Stories. New York: Modern Library, 1940.
The Leaning Tower and Other Stories. New York: Harcourt, Brace, 1944.
Pale Horse, Pale Rider: Three Short Novels. New York: Modern Library, 1949.
The Days Before. New York: Harcourt, Brace, 1952.
Ship of Fools. Boston: Little, Brown, 1962.
The Collected Stories of Katherine Anne Porter. New York: Harcourt, Brace & World, 1965.
The Collected Essays and Occasional Writings of Katherine Anne Porter. New York: Delacorte Press, 1970.
The Never-Ending Wrong. Boston: Little, Brown, 1977.

Studies of Katherine Anne Porter

DeMouy, Jane Krause. *Katherine Anne Porter's Women: The Eye of Her Fiction*. Austin: University of Texas Press, 1983.
Emmons, Winfred S. *Katherine Anne Porter: The Regional Stories*. Austin: Steck-Vaughn, 1967.
Givner, Joan. *Katherine Anne Porter: A Life*. New York: Simon & Schuster, 1982.
Hardy, John Edwards. *Katherine Anne Porter*. New York: Frederick Ungar, 1973.
Hartley, Lodwick and George Core, eds. *Katherine Anne Porter: A Critical Symposium*. Athens: University of Georgia Press, 1969.
Hendrick, George. *Katherine Anne Porter*. New York: Twayne, 1965.
Kiernan, Robert F. *Katherine Anne Porter and Carson McCullers: A Reference Guide*. Boston: G. K. Hall, 1976.
Krishnamurthi, M. G. *Katherine Anne Porter: A Study*. Mysore, India: Rao and Raghaven, 1971.
Liberman, M. M. *Katherine Anne Porter's Fiction*. Detroit: Wayne State University Press, 1971.
Mooney, Harry John, Jr. *The Fiction and Criticism of Katherine Anne Porter*. Pittsburgh: University of Pittsburgh Press, 1957; rev. ed., 1962.
Nance, William L. *Katherine Anne Porter and the Art of Rejection*. Chapel Hill: University of North Carolina Press, 1964.
Unrue, Darlene. *Truth and Vision in Katherine Anne Porter's Fiction*. Athens: University of Georgia Press, 1985.
Walsh, Thomas. "Identifying a Sketch by Katherine Anne Porter." *Journal of Modern Literature* 7 (1979): 555–61.

Walsh, Thomas. "Xochitl: Katherine Anne Porter's Changing Goddess." *American Literature* 52 (1980): 183–93.

Warren, Robert Penn, ed. *Katherine Anne Porter: A Collection of Critical Essays*. Englewood Cliffs, N.J.: Prentice-Hall, 1979.

West, Ray B., Jr. *Katherine Anne Porter*. Minneapolis: University of Minnesota Press, 1963, 1968.

EUGENE CURRENT-GARCIA

William Sydney Porter [O. Henry] (1862–1910)

William Sydney Porter, better known the world over by his pen name O. Henry, was already famous in New York before his first book was published in 1904; and though he lived only six more years after that event, his fame as America's premier short fiction writer doubled and redoubled as eight more volumes of his stories appeared before he died. These nine collections, however, contained only about half of the nearly 300 stories he had written for a variety of magazines and newspapers during his relatively brief career; the other half appeared in seven posthumous volumes published between 1910 and 1939. Yet notwithstanding the worldwide popularity that O. Henry's stories soon achieved and still enjoy, at his death few really knew who he was, and fewer still were aware of what he had been as Will Porter, the poor Southern youth who had become in his forties the darling spokesman for Manhattan's voiceless millions. And even now the paradox of O. Henry's appeal to a global reading public as opposed to the shadowy career of his alter ego is no less intriguing than it must have been 75 years ago.

BIOGRAPHY

Significant facts regarding Will Porter's life are well-known and can be quickly summarized, as they fill four distinct segments of his experience. But exactly how each of these segments affected the psyche of Porter the man and what each contributed, for better or worse, to the art of O. Henry the writer are not so readily assimilable. Porter was born near Greensboro, North Carolina, on 11 September 1862, the second son of Dr. Algernon Sidney and Mary Jane (Swaim) Porter. Will's initial readjustment to a problematic world began when he was three, when his mother died shortly after the birth of her third son. Coupled with the strain of overwork at the war's end in a defeated South, this private loss devastated Will's father, "Dr. Al," the town's most popular physician; he gave up his home and his practice, moved into his widowed mother's house, and soon abandoned the discipline of his two little boys, Shirley and Will (the youngest, David, died in infancy), to his mother and his maiden sister, Evelina. The father of Will's earliest memories, wrote a family friend years later, "was a man who had already lost his grip."

Still, Will Porter's childhood and youth were otherwise normal. His contacts with people and events in Greensboro furnished abundant resources that his fertile imagination later transformed into fiction. The two strongest influences shaping his mind and character at this stage were the formal schooling he received from his aunt, Miss Lina, and the apprenticeship he served in his Uncle Clark's pharmacy. Evelina inculcated in the young boy a passion for English and American literature and a desire to emulate the standard authors from Chaucer to Henry James, particularly in their rhetorical mastery of diction and imagery; she also encouraged his childish efforts to express himself in both verbal and pictorial forms. He developed these skills further during the three years he worked in his uncle's pharmacy, becoming a teenaged celebrity for his amusing cartoons while simultaneously absorbing enough knowledge of the pharmacopoeia to secure a state license to practice pharmacy and more than enough awareness of community attitudes and individual oddities in dress, mannerisms, and modes of speech to fashion a host of lifelike fictional characters and events. Such well-known stories as "A Municipal Report," "A Blackjack Bargainer," and "The Rose of Dixie" clearly reveal Porter's deftness in recapturing the essence of Old South nostalgia that permeated the Reconstruction era.

At the age of twenty Porter blithely left Greensboro for Texas, where during the next fifteen years his awareness broadened and his responses to life's joys and sorrows deepened dramatically. Among the many new experiences he encountered in this totally different world, the most important ones that affected his personality and his professional career occurred first during the two years he spent as a guest at one of the great cattle ranches near the Mexican border, where his sensitive eyes and ears captured and recorded the distinctive cultural peculiarities of Hispanic behavior and speech. Next, Porter's longer residence in Austin, which included four years' employment as a draughtsman in the Texas Land Office as well as his marriage to Athol Estes Roach in 1887 and the birth of their two children, extended his friendships and social contacts in the booming young capital. For him these were relatively happy years despite such personal misfortunes as the loss of a firstborn infant son and the anxiety over Athol's declining health after the birth of their daughter, Margaret, in 1889. Besides enjoying his work Porter was writing steadily; and when political exigencies wiped out the Land Office job in 1891, he soon obtained another as teller in the First National Bank, one that afforded him time—even during banking hours—to keep up his sketching and skit writing for three more years. But it was a job that brought disaster as well as local fame. For although Porter was apparently doing his work satisfactorily, toward the close of 1894 he was indicted on the charge of having embezzled over $5,000 of the bank's funds. The money, presumably, had been borrowed surreptitiously to help meet the printing costs of his first publishing venture, the *Rolling Stone*, a weekly humor magazine he had begun in March and kept alive for a full year, largely with anecdotes and sketches of his own composition.

These writings had again made Porter a local celebrity, but notwithstanding the generosity of his father-in-law and the offers of other friends to rectify his defalcation, banking examiners in Washington ordered him to stand trial the following year. Having been obliged to leave the bank, Porter while awaiting trial took a feature-writing job on the Houston *Post*, where he again drew favorable attention to his humorous writings by conducting a daily column entitled "Some Postscripts." Here in embryo, as in the pieces he had written for the *Rolling Stone*, Porter incorporated many of the themes, plots, and situations that reappeared later, elaborated and polished, in some of O. Henry's most famous stories. But as the deadline approached for his trial in July 1896, Porter panicked; instead of returning to Austin he fled to New Orleans and from there to Honduras, where he stayed until the end of the year. His lonely sojourn there, like the earlier ones in New Orleans and Houston, provided abundant new material for his later fiction, hilarious tales of revolutionary escapades in the imaginary banana republic of Anchuria in *Cabbages and Kings*. But whatever plans he may have had for bringing Athol and little Margaret to live with him were doomed: in January Porter learned that Athol was dying, and with borrowed funds he returned home to face not only his trial but possibly the grimmest year of his life.

Ironically, this was also the year that presaged Porter's future literary renown: in December the McClure Company accepted his first full-length story, "The Miracle of Lava Canyon." But Athol did not survive to share this good fortune; she died on 25 July, having firmly kept faith to the end in both her husband's innocence and his ultimate success. Out of deference to the family's plight the court had postponed the trial until February 1898; yet when it opened, Porter, although still protesting his innocence, had not prepared an adequate defense to counteract the evidence against him. He was convicted but given the lightest possible sentence the law permitted: a five-year term (which good behavior would cut to three years) to be served beginning in April at the Ohio Penitentiary in Columbus. For Porter's pride, this was a bitter finale to his Texas experience, despite the auspicious foreshadowing of future literary triumphs and the blessed support of the Roaches, who not only believed in him but also stood ready to care for Margaret during his absence.

Porter then entered prison with two fixed ideas uppermost in mind: to blot out the past and, while guarding his anonymity, to develop and perfect his fictional techniques. Although he kept up a matter-of-fact correspondence with his mother-in-law, to spare his child's humiliation he concealed his whereabouts from her in a charmingly disguised series of letters. As a model prisoner he was admired for his helpfulness, wit, and quiet dignity, but he declined to expose in reportorial muckraking the inhumane prison conditions he knew of or heard about from his fellow inmates. Instead, he stuck to his fiction, blotting out the bitterness of his prison experiences by the same process of transformation he had already applied and would later apply to so many other experiences.

In this way, too, "O. Henry," the alter ego, was literally born during Porter's three-year stretch in prison. Although the precise origin of the pseudonym itself is still unknown, the fourteen stories written and published as O. Henry's during these years (beginning with "Georgia's Ruling" in 1900) were not the sole products of his incarceration. Many others published later—such as the Jeff Peters stories in *The Gentle Grafter* and those dealing with frontier outlawry, fraud, violence, and banditry in *Heart of the West, Roads of Destiny*, and still other volumes—came originally from yarns and anecdotes picked up from fellow prisoners. Many of these prison-oriented stories, including "A Retrieved Reformation," the most famous of all, develop what appears to be an artfully concealed autobiographical element that, Gerald Langford suggests, sets forth the same basic idea: "the vindication of a character who has in some way forfeited his claim to respectability or even integrity . . . and the plot invariably turns on the regeneration of an admitted delinquent, not on the vindication of a character who is blameless." However accurate this judgment may be, it shows how fully Porter's craftsmanship matured during his imprisonment. He entered the Ohio Penitentiary an amateur but emerged three years later as O. Henry, the professional literary artist.

When Porter left prison in 1901, he had only nine more years to live, a period destined to bring him spectacular success as New York's O. Henry, the self-anointed Caliph of Bagdad-on-the-Subway. But they would also be years of anguish, loneliness, want, and guilt-ridden fear, as he strove vainly to elude the shadow of his past and to secure financial independence through exhausting literary effort. Before going to New York in the spring of 1902, Porter spent nearly a year in Pittsburgh, residing in modest hotel rooms and working for the *Dispatch* to support himself and Margaret, now a girl of twelve still living with her grandparents. He was also writing stories at a furious pace during these months, having published ten of them in *Ainslee's* and *McClure's* by the end of the year and, under various pseudonyms in other magazines, about five or six more shortly afterwards. At this point Porter was already earning about $150 a month, he told his friend Al Jennings; but always fearful of being recognized as an ex-convict in Pittsburgh, he was anxious to preserve his anonymity among New York's faceless masses, yet he also wished to write stories and have them published in that more exciting, more lucrative marketplace. In both literary and financial terms, his expectations were soon richly rewarded: he belonged to New York, fitting it snugly like a hand in a glove.

By the end of 1902 the O. Henry byline had become more and more familiar as stories bearing the name appeared, sometimes simultaneously, in nearly a dozen monthly magazines. More than 25 were published that year, including such favorites as "A Retrieved Reformation," "Roads of Destiny," and "While the Auto Waits." Yet Porter had barely begun to exploit the manifold riches that New York spread before him. As he prowled the city's crowded streets and glittering nightspots, excitedly savoring the varied color and texture of its life, the ever-shifting shapes of its human scene offered him a cornucopia of sights and sounds with which to delight a cosmopolitan audience, eager to see themselves mirrored in such sympathetic ambience.

Thus Porter's big break came in the fall of 1903, when he signed a contract with the *Sunday World* to supply that newspaper with a story each week for $100 apiece. With its circulation of nearly half a million, the *World* now rewarded Porter with what he had always coveted: a prodigious number of faithful readers and, in his roseate view, an opulent income enabling him at last to live lavishly at 55 Irving Place near Gramercy Park. On that vantage ground, Robert H. Davis and Arthur B. Maurice noted, he could "establish himself in what he called 'the business of caliphing,' and . . . indulge in the vagaries and extravagances appropriate to the generous handed role." Given the sharp contrasts between such respectable places at one extreme as the Westminster Hotel, where Dickens had stayed, and bawdy houses, saloons, and honky-tonks like McGlory's and Tom Sharkey's at the other; and given, too, Porter's talent for appreciating such kaleidoscopic scenery, one can accept the avowal of Davis and Maurice that "from 1904 to 1907, O. Henry was Haroun [Al Rashid] in his golden prime."

During the two years that Porter served the *World*, seldom missing his weekly deadline, he wrote for that newspaper 113 tales (syndicated throughout the United States) and 25 longer ones, which were published in such monthly magazines as *Everybody's*, *McClure's*, and *Munsey's*. The demand for his stories from competing editors was now so great that he could not have met it, a friend exclaimed later, even if he had turned them out two at a time with both hands all day long. As a result, by 1905–6 Porter was making more money than ever, over $600 a month, and spending it faster than he made it. By this time he had also begun the new venture that would bring lasting fame to his memory and fabulous profits to the publishing firm of Doubleday and Company: that of having all his stories reissued in book collections. At Witter Bynner's suggestion, he and Bynner had cut and stitched, combined and restructured most of his Central American stories to produce a simulated novel, *Cabbages and Kings*, which McClure, Phillips and Company published in November 1904. The book sold well enough to justify the experiment: within two more years, following the publication of *The Four Million* in April 1906, the popularity of O. Henry's second book showed that his works would not soon be forgotten.

A collection of 25 stories drawn mostly from the *World*'s files, *The Four Million* contained such top favorites as "An Unfinished Story," "The Cop and the Anthem," "The Gift of the Magi," and "The Furnished Room." Each of these dramatized in a slightly different way Porter's assertion that the nameless "little people" comprising New York's four million souls were as well worth writing about as were the elite "400" in Ward McAllister's social register. This was a claim that not only won the hearts of the average New Yorker but also appealed to the democratic instincts of people everywhere. Accordingly, *The*

Four Million soon drew favorable reviews even from serious literary critics, who began comparing Porter to Maupassant and other eminent writers, indicating thereby that further volumes of his stories would be promptly noticed.

They followed in an orderly procession during Porter's last years and after his death: in 1907–08, *The Trimmed Lamp* and *The Voice of the City*, adding 50 more New York stories in book form; and in the same period, *Heart of the West* and *The Gentle Grafter*, containing stories based primarily on Porter's experiences in Texas and in prison. Before he died three more volumes appeared: *Roads of Destiny* and *Options* in 1909 and *Strictly Business*, containing 22 more New York stories, in 1910. Later the same year came the first posthumous volume, *Whirligigs*, followed by *Sixes and Sevens* in 1911, *Rolling Stones* in 1912, *Waifs and Strays* in 1917, and *O. Henryana* in 1920. Most of these later volumes contained a mixture of overlooked New York stories along with other fugitive pieces reflecting earlier categories of Porter's experience. In 1939, finally, came the important collection of his Houston *Post* writings, *O. Henry Encore*, edited by Mary Sunlocks Harrell.

By 1908 when *The Voice of the City* appeared, Porter had indeed become "Haroun in his golden prime." He had reached the pinnacle of his spectacular climb from penury and shame and was earning an income of about $14,000 for the 29 new stories he wrote that year. But it had been a costly climb, comparable in physical and emotional stress to the final stages of a Mt. Everest ascent. As early as 1905 the steady routine of churning out his stories day after day had begun to damage Porter's health; his ferocious pace slackened as the demand for his stories intensified, and his output began falling off perceptibly. Compared to the 120 new stories he produced in 1904–5, in 1906 he published nineteen and in 1907, only eleven. Moreover, having drifted into an ill-advised second marriage in November 1907, he needed money even more than before, and he drove himself mercilessly during the following year to earn it. Yet the $14,000 income was not enough to support the opulent life-style he was accustomed to, and his morale suffered all the more.

From the start Porter had led a reclusive existence in New York, stealthily preserving his anonymity, making few friends among his magazine associates, and rarely extending his full confidence even to them. And though he obviously enjoyed casual contacts with waitresses, shopgirls, cancan dancers, and demimondaines whom he met in Broadway crowds and Bowery vaudeville houses, his relations with women above their social level remained stiff and awkward. Apart from Margaret and her aunt Nettie Roach, neither of whom he saw very often, Porter enjoyed easygoing friendships only with Anne Partlan, a young writer whom he met occasionally; with Mabel Wagnalls, a publisher's daughter; and with one or two others of his own class. Thus it was typical that in seeking another wife he proposed to Sara Lindsay Coleman, a spinster of thirty-seven from Greensboro with whom he had played as a child 25 years before. Their marriage was virtually predestined to fail. It was difficult enough for the couple to adjust to each other's fixed habits, and when Margaret also joined the family, the strains imposed by increased demands on Porter's diminishing creative energy became unbearable. By summer 1909 the attempt to maintain a normal family life was abandoned: Sara returned to Asheville, North Carolina, for a long visit, Margaret was sent to another private school in New Jersey, and Porter reverted to his old bachelor habits at the Hotel Caledonia.

As his health deteriorated during these final months, Porter grew morbidly dissatisfied with his stories and tried his hand at other forms of literary expression. He talked of doing a long, serious novel on the theme of the Old South versus the New and even drew sizable cash advances for writing it from Doubleday, Page and Company. But that work was never written. Instead, Porter worked with Franklin P. Adams on the musical comedy *Lo!*, based on "He Also Serves," one of the last few stories he had written in 1908. *Lo!* folded even before reaching the New York stage, but its road tryouts brought Porter an offer from George Tyler, another theatrical producer, to subsidize a dramatic version of his much earlier tale, "A Retrieved Reformation." Had Porter followed through with this commitment during the long rest cure he undertook while visiting Sara in Asheville, he might have reaped the bonanza that he so desperately needed. But once again his aberrant behavior undid him: instead of writing the play Tyler wanted, he delayed and equivocated and finally sold the impatient producer the dramatic rights to the story for $500. It was promptly turned over to another writer, Paul Armstrong, who soon transformed "A Retrieved Reformation" into *Alias Jimmy Valentine*, one of the hits of the season, which earned Armstrong over $100,000 in royalties by the end of its first run.

Porter had gone to North Carolina under the delusion that the "neurasthenia" that had baffled his New York physicians for over a year could be cured with hill climbing and fresh mountain air, as told in one of his most poignant posthumous tales, "Let Me Feel Your Pulse." But when he returned to New York and the Caledonia in March 1910, he was finished and doubtless knew it, despite the bravado that his creative faculties were unimpaired. Virtually an invalid during his final weeks, Porter could barely summon up energy enough to do any writing at all: he refused company, rarely emerged from his room, and kept himself alive mainly with whiskey until his collapse on the evening of 3 June. Among the last to see him still conscious were Anne Partlan and her physician, Dr. Charles Hancock, who took him to the Polyclinic Hospital. Two days later he died there from an advanced stage of cirrhosis of the liver, and after a brief funeral service at the Little Church Around the Corner, his body was taken to Asheville for burial.

Porter's end, like his beginning, was fraught with sadness and irony. Owing thousands of dollars advanced to him by his publishers, friends, and relatives, he died a pauper, unknown, unrecognized, perhaps unmourned by all but his family and the handful of literary folk who attended his funeral service. Yet Porter had given pleasure to millions and had made the name "O. Henry" an indelible symbol in American life.

MAJOR THEMES

Embryonic forms of the typical O. Henry story—its plotting, characters, situations, and style—can be found in both the skits and anecdotes that Porter concocted for the *Rolling Stone* and in the 35 longer tales and sketches he composed for his column in the Houston *Post*. In these latter pieces, for example, one sees his facility for ringing changes on the familiar O. Henry themes of mistaken identity, false pretense, misplaced devotion, nobility in disguise, and the bitter irony of fate. Here, too, one finds such sentimental types as the sensitive tramp, the ill-starred lovers, the starving artist, and the gentle grafter or con man. Thus, nearly two decades before New Yorkers rhapsodized over such stories as "The Enchanted Kiss," "While the Auto Waits," "The Caliph and the Cad," and "Mammon and the Archer," Porter had been shaping the basic structure of these stories.

One of many examples showing how Porter's *Post* offerings provided the germ for his well-known later ones is a slight four-page tale entitled "An Unknown Romance." Developing the theme of disparity between wealth and poverty through the device of mistaken identity, this early version concerns two wealthy young Americans who fall in love while vacationing in the Alps; as they mistake each other's peasant garb for the real thing, they discard the planned marriages of convenience arranged by their families, only to discover that they are destined for each other. Variations of the identical situation are worked out in "A Night in New Arabia" and "Lost on Dress Parade"; with roles reversed in "Transients in Arcadia" and "The Caliph and the Cad"; and again with a double reversal in "While the Auto Waits." The disguise or impostor motif, coupled with the idea that destiny, or fate, imposes inescapable roles on the individual, is a dominant theme that recurs in many forms throughout all of O. Henry's writing; its treatment, both serious and comic, can be seen in his earliest work.

Regardless of whether O. Henry's protagonists are threadbare Southern ladies like Azalia Adair or impoverished shopgirls like Dulcie in "An Unfinished Story," Mexican desperados like the Cisco Kid or philanthropic New York caliphs like Carson Chalmers in "A Madison Square Arabian Night," a fundamental attitude toward the human predicament pervades the situations he prepares for all of them to confront. Life, he appears to suggest repeatedly, is an adventure that tests the individual's courage and integrity; its rigors cannot be evaded, nor can its rewards be taken for granted, for they are always subject to misdirection or revocation. Thus, the basic themes dramatized in his stories are much the same whether their settings are laid in New York, the Old South, or the raw West; four of them recur again and again, sometimes singly, but more often in combination and in varied forms. These major themes are (a) pretense and the reversal of fortune, (b) discovery and initiation through adventure, (c) contrast and adversity as stimuli to the imagination, and (d) the yearning for self-fulfillment in all human nature.

The theme of pretense—an urge to pose for what one is not, if only for a few moments and notwithstanding the price exacted—is probably O. Henry's most persistent one, as variations of it appear in a great many stories from the first to the last few he left unfinished at his death. His ironic treatment of the theme dramatizes in some stories the pathos of lost opportunities suffered by either men or women because of their bent toward one-upmanship; whereas in other stories the same treatment focuses on amusing situations in which profit rather than loss accrues to one or more of the characters involved. Thus, with his assortment of technical shifts and devices O. Henry could develop the pretense theme effectively in many different ways. In "The Social Triangle," for example, he employed ironic contrast to expose the pretentiousness of three different levels of New York society; and, changing his approach through several other contrivances, he juxtaposed the pretenses of different social levels as well as the effects of pretense among members of the same social class in at least a dozen other stories, such as "The Poet and the Peasant," "The Country of Elusion," and "Past One at Rooney's." In virtually all of them, his carefully crafted surprise ending cuts off further exploration of the particular problem displaying the theme.

Although the two themes of pretense and discovery through adventure often unfold concurrently in O. Henry's stories, they are not invariably yoked together or mutually dependent. The idea of eagerly confronting the unknown, with or without the protective coloration of a disguise, seems to have excited O. Henry throughout his life, especially toward the end. The sort of adventurer he admired is his hero Rudolph Steiner in "The Green Door," eager to find "what might lie just around the next corner" and willing to pay the toll charged for following up a lead, even though aware that it may come high. There are many others like Steiner in O. Henry's stories, and not always men. They may be winsome adventurers like Katy Dempsey, heroine of an absurd but charming tale, "A Philistine in Bohemia"; or like Daisy, the ignorant little shopgirl whose daring in "Psyche and the Pskyscraper" shows that both awareness and simplicity are as essential as courage in pursuing an adventurous life. And their discoveries, like Big Jim's in "Dougherty's Eye-Opener," prove that the adventure itself need not be a sensational one, but merely the simplest departure from routine behavior to yield rich rewards.

O. Henry's most poignant treatments of the adventure and discovery theme, however, occur in "The Venturers," published a few months before his death, and in the posthumous "Let Me Feel Your Pulse." Although both clearly express what C. Alphonso Smith, his first biographer, identified as his "revolt against the calculable," on a deeper level these two stories may also harbor a veiled commentary on the misgivings Porter felt toward his second marriage. True or not, they reveal unmistakably his deep-seated conviction, the result of painful experience, that one cannot escape one's destiny regardless of the road taken; that it is better, therefore, to accept willingly the chances that come than to try to manipulate one's fate. The essence of the adventurous life lies in confronting and accepting its proffered risks; for even though these may lead to sad ends, the ends themselves are unforeseen. Hence satisfaction can only be derived from the kind of race one runs.

O. Henry's adventure theme is sometimes hard to distinguish from either or both of the other two themes that portray contrast or adversity and human yearning as stimuli toward imaginative or heroic action. The reason is that these latter are pervasive rather than pointedly specific; they appear in scattered passages, hints, and overtones, not as the predominant motif of entire stories; and one becomes aware of them in O. Henry's frequent use of contrasting viewpoints or attitudes as a standard device. He is reported to have said that every house in every street in New York "has a drama in it." To grasp what he meant by drama here, one need only consider two of the stories that still head the list of O. Henry favorites: "The Gift of the Magi" and "The Furnished Room." Representing the polar opposites of joy and despair in the lives of average New Yorkers, these two have not lost their original popular appeal because they dramatize, albeit tritely, what the world knows to be of fundamental value in ordinary family life. Unselfish love shared is repeatedly set forth as a criterion in O. Henry's fictional treatment of domestic affairs—not just among New Yorkers but also among many others in his Southern and Western stories. If such love is at hand, life can be a great adventure transcending all drabness; if absent, nothing else can take its place. Hence the warm glow of "The Gift" and the utter bleakness of "The Furnished Room."

Because the many-faceted drama of New York's four million persons became the primary stimulus for O. Henry's imagination, the city as a unit can be seen as an objective correlative that vivifies his broadest theme. As the source of more than half of his total output of short fiction, Manhattan's masses dramatize the idea of oneness at the heart of things in human society. This is a typically romantic approach to life, a throwback to Whitman and Wordsworth, that tends to minimize or blur subtle distinctions between the good and bad, rich and poor, strong and weak, in order to focus attention on the ideal goals for which we all strive. Nevertheless, it is also an approach we cherish and cling to, and it explains O. Henry's hold on his vast reading public. His readers know that things seldom work out in the world of fact as they do in his world of the imagination, but at heart we would like to believe they might. We would like to believe that all brides are beautiful; that all bums and con men, even all millionaires, are alike redeemable. O. Henry's stories about fictive New Yorkers, Southerners, West-erners, and Latin Americans are thus part of a vast literature that has always fed this basic human hunger: "the search for those common traits and common impulses" whose ultimate theme, C. Alphonso Smith wisely concluded, "is your nature and mine."

SURVEY OF CRITICISM

During the decade following his death, O. Henry's works approached the zenith of their public acclaim from leading literary critics as well as the reading public at large. By 1920 nearly five million copies of his books had been sold in the United States, many of them in sleek deluxe printings of allegedly complete editions. Many copies were also being sold abroad in other English-speaking countries, and foreign language translations of the stories were soon prepared to meet a growing demand for them in France, Russia, Scandinavia, and the Spanish-speaking countries. Thanks to such widespread acceptance both at home and abroad, O. Henry's image quickly overshadowed all others in the field of short fiction writing; thus, when an annual series of volumes containing the year's best stories was inaugurated in 1919, his name was the inevitable choice for its title. The *O. Henry Memorial Award Prize Stories* clearly implied that his works represented the highest standard of artistry in short story form.

In America critical support for such an exalted reputation before 1920 came from several essayists whose formal discussions in the *Bookman, Nation, North American Review*, and other literary journals treated O. Henry's work with growing respect. The leading figure in this group was Porter's boyhood chum, Professor C. Alphonso Smith, whose *O. Henry Biography*, published in 1916, strengthened its subject's claim to rank among America's major authors. Smith's book was well received, but his high praise also evoked strong rebuttals from more fastidious academic critics such as F. L. Pattee and H. L. Mencken, who dismissed O. Henry's stories as specious journalization void of serious substance.

Throughout the 1920s this adverse view gradually took hold. As the critical pendulum swung the other way, Mencken's puritanical sneer at O. Henry's "smoke-room and variety-show smartness" led to Sherwood Anderson's condemnation of his mechanized, "poison" plots; and this, in turn, to the apparent critical oblivion signalized in A. H. Quinn's haughty pronouncement that upon rereading the stories he could find scarcely a dozen in the entire canon that might be called "first rate." Thus, by the 1930s the falling off of O. Henry's reputation among literary critics in the United States became nearly as swift and precipitous as its original ascent. The "new" fiction, embodied in Anderson's *Winesburg, Ohio* tales and in Hemingway's *In Our Time* and *Men Without Women*, had gained so much respect that O. Henry's style of writing no longer seemed important enough to notice, even unfavorably.

Scholarly interest in O. Henry during the next 30 years reflected this sharp decline in critical esteem. Throughout the entire United States in the 1930s scarcely a dozen master's theses were written about his work, and the only other important critical material (aside from a few bits of personal reminiscence) included several articles in the *South Atlantic Quarterly* and the *Southwest Review*. One other important essay in *American Literature* by P. S. Clarkson clarified the composition of O. Henry's first book, and the same author's *A Bibliography of William Sydney Porter*, though incomplete, was perhaps the most significant piece of American scholarship devoted to him in the 1930s. But slight as such critical concern may seem, it was abundant compared with the almost total neglect that O. Henry's reputation suffered in the United States during the 1940s and most of the 1950s. Except for a few more theses, a single published dissertation, and several articles that reexamined the facts of his embezzlement trial and the use of classical allusions in his stories, O. Henry was virtually dismissed as unworthy of any further serious consideration. "The world of O. Henry is an intellectual Sahara," concluded George F. Whicher in *The Literature of the United States*, ed. Arthur Hobson Quinn (1951); *A Literary History of the United States*, ed. Robert Spiller (1953), scarcely bothered to mention his name at all.

Meanwhile, as in the past, foreign critics and literary scholars had been exhibiting a more perceptive awareness than their American counterparts of O. Henry's significant role in the art of short fiction. Just as it took a Baudelaire to reverse unfavorable American attitudes toward Poe in the 1850s, in 1919 another Frenchman, Raoul Narcy, displayed similar objectivity in summing up the important artistic qualities in O. Henry's fiction: its compactness, order, economy of specific detail, particularly its "abounding *verve* [and] . . . intelligence armed with irony," as well as its welcome avoidance of moral preachments. Equally objective and more comprehensive, "O. Henry; or, the Literary Trick," by the Italian scholar Cesare Pavese, was published originally in 1932, though not in an English translation until 1970. But 60 years ago perhaps the most thoroughgoing foreign criticism of O. Henry's work was the Russian scholar B. M. Ejxenbaum's "O. Henry and the Theory of the Short Story," published originally in 1925 but available in English only since 1968.

Formalist critics such as Pavese and Ejxenbaum, who could appreciate the purely literary innovations of O. Henry's short fiction without becoming enmeshed in conventional attitudes toward his moral or social limitations, foreshadowed the more balanced assessment of his work that has characterized the criticism of a few American scholars since the 1960s. Seeing him as a regionalist whose inherent good humor and extraordinary command of assorted dialects and speech patterns enabled him to capture the intonations and imagery of many levels of American society with fidelity and grace, these scholars are more inclined than those of the 1930s to give O. Henry "his rightful place in American literature" as a *minor* classic who is here to stay. Millions of unpretentious readers here and abroad, of course, have known that all along.

BIBLIOGRAPHY

Works by O. Henry

Cabbages and Kings. New York: McClure, Phillips, 1904.
The Four Million. New York: McClure, Phillips, 1906.
Heart of the West. New York: McClure, 1907.
The Trimmed Lamp, and Other Stories of the Four Million. New York: McClure, Phillips, 1907.
The Gentle Grafter. New York: McClure, 1908.
The Voice of the City: Further Stories of the Four Million. New York: McClure, 1908.

Options. New York and London: Harper and Brothers, 1909.
Roads of Destiny. New York: Doubleday, Page, 1909.
Strictly Business: More Stories of the Four Million. New York: Doubleday, Page, 1910.
Whirligigs. New York: Doubleday, Page, 1910.
Sixes and Sevens. New York: Doubleday, Page, 1911.
Rolling Stones. New York: Doubleday, Page, 1912.
Waifs and Strays: Twelve Stories by O. Henry, Together with a representative selection of critical and biographical comment. New York: Doubleday, Page, 1917.
O. Henryana. Seven Odds and Ends. New York: Doubleday, Page, 1920.
Letters to Lithopolis, from O. Henry to Mabel Wagnalls. New York: Doubleday, Page, 1922.
Postscripts by O. Henry. Ed. with introduction by Florence Stratton. New York: Harper and Brothers, 1923.
O. Henry Encore: Stories and Illustrations by O. Henry, Usually Under the Name the Postman. Discovered and Edited by Mary Sunlocks Harrell. New York: Doubleday, Doran, 1939.

Studies of O. Henry

Arnett, Ethel Stephens. *O. Henry From Polecat Creek*. Greensboro, N.C.: Piedmont Press, 1962.
Brown, Deming. "O. Henry in Russia." *Russian Review* 12 (October 1953): 253–58.
———. *Soviet Attitudes Toward American Writing*. Princeton, N.J.: Princeton University Press, 1962, pp. 230–38, passim.
Clarkson, Paul S. *A Bibliography of William Sydney Porter (O. Henry)*. Caldwell, Idaho: Caxton Printers, 1938.
———. "A Decomposition of Cabbages and Kings." *American Literature* 7 (May 1935): 195–202.
Current-Garcia, Eugene. *O. Henry*. New York: Twayne, 1965.
Ejxenbaum, B[oris] M[ixhailovich]. *O. Henry and the Theory of the Short Story*. Translated with notes and postscript by I. R. Titunik. Ann Arbor: University of Michigan Press, 1968.
Gallegly, Joseph. *From Alamo Plaza to Jack Harris's Saloon: O. Henry and the Southwest He Knew*. The Hague: Mouton, 1970.
Harris, Richard C. *William Sydney Porter (O. Henry): A Reference Guide*. Boston: G. K. Hall, 1980.
Kercheville, F. M. "O. Henry and Don Alfonso: Spanish in the Work of an American Writer." *New Mexico Quarterly Review* 1 (November 1931): 367–88.
Langford, Gerald. *Alias O. Henry: A Biography of William Sydney Porter*. New York: Macmillan, 1957.
Long, E. Hudson. *O. Henry: The Man and His Work*. Philadelphia: University of Pennsylvania Press, 1949.
———. "O. Henry as a Regional Artist." *Essays on American Literature in Honor of Jay B. Hubbell*. Ed. Clarence Gohdes. Durham, N.C.: Duke University Press, 1967, pp. 229–40.
Millstein, Gilbert. "O. Henry's New Yorkers—and Today's." *New York Times Magazine* (9 September 1962): 36–37, 132, 134, 135.

Narcy, Raoul. " 'O. Henry' Through French Eyes." *Littell's Living Age* 303 (11 October 1919): 86–88.

O'Connor, Richard. *O. Henry: The Legendary Life of William S. Porter.* Garden City, N.Y.: Doubleday, 1970.

Pattee, F. L. "The Journalization of American Literature." *Unpopular Review* 7 (April-June 1917): 374–94.

————. "O. Henry and the Handbooks." *The Development of the American Short Story.* New York and London: Harper and Brothers, 1923, pp. 357–79.

Pavese, Cesare. "O. Henry; or, The Literary Trick." *American Literature: Essays and Opinions.* Ed. Edwin Fussell. Berkeley: University of California Press, 1970, pp. 79–90.

Sartin, Howard. "Margaret and 'The Unknown Quantity.' " *Southern Humanities Review* 10 (Winter 1976): 1–18.

Smith, C. Alphonso. *O. Henry Biography.* New York: Doubleday, Page, 1916.

Voss, Arthur. "O. Henry." *The American Short Story: A Critical Survey.* Norman: University of Oklahoma Press, 1974, pp. 121–26, passim.

Reynolds Price
(1933–   )

In 1970 Reynolds Price received an Award in Literature from the American Academy and the National Institute for Arts and Letters. Accompanying the presentation is a citation that reads: "His gifts are a vigorous intelligence, a strongly individual perception of the nature—both physical and psychological—of a given time and place, of the variety in kind and intensity of human relationships. Over all his prose fiction there is a poet's daring and control."

BIOGRAPHY

Reynolds Price was born on 1 February 1933 in Macon, North Carolina. It was a difficult birth both for the child and for the mother, Elizabeth Rodwell Price—so difficult, in fact, that William Solomon (Will) Price promised God that if the mother and child were spared he would give up drink, a promise he was incapable of keeping. Will, an appliance salesman, saw his son into the world in the midst of the Great Depression. Life was difficult for the family, who moved from one North Carolina town to another as Will sought to provide for his family, often only barely managing to do so. Perhaps the lowest point in the family's financial odyssey was reached when the Price family had to give up their home because Will could not come up with a $50 payment.

Against this background of poverty and uncertainty punctuated by his father's constant predilection for drink, and by his father's series of financial failures, and finally by his father's slow and agonizing death from cancer, Price's childhood at first seems to be the nightmare from which so many Americans have labored to escape, but as Price's fiction so often instructs us, a man's life or childhood is much more complex than simple environment. Although he was eight years older than the next Price sibling and often lacking for playmates, young Reynolds was provided with a strong and nurturing sense of warmth and belonging through the family's strong ties with aunts, uncles, and cousins. This extended family, much given to loquaciousness and to reading, developed in Price an ear for speech and a love of literature and made him an accomplished teller of stories as well. "Absolutely hopeless in sports," the adolescent Price sought first to be a singer and then a painter and produced some juvenile poetry and plays. His early intention of writing continued when he entered Duke University in 1951. At Duke he threw himself completely into his studies and, as a result, was awarded a Rhodes scholarship. In his senior year he had the opportunity to show his first adult story, "Michael Egerton," to Eudora Welty, who was visiting Duke to give a lecture entitled "The Place of Fiction." Out of this meeting came the encouragement that he needed as a young writer and the beginning of a friendship between Price and Welty that continues today. Upon graduation, Price attended Merton College of Oxford University and during these three years of study (1955–58) completed his thesis on Milton and finished several stories.

Upon his return from England, Price accepted a faculty position at Duke University, where he has regularly taught Milton and writing. In 1961 he completed his first novel, *A Long and Happy Life*, which was enthusiastically received by critics and which was published in its entirety a year later in *Harper's* magazine. The *Harper's* publication, the favorable critical reception of the novel, and the Faulkner Foundation Award for a first novel brought Price's literary reputation into the first rank of Southern fiction writers. In 1963 Price returned to England for a brief visit; that same year *The Names and Faces of Heroes*, a collection of stories that includes "Michael Egerton" as well as the often anthologized stories "The Warrior Princess Ozimba" and "Uncle Grant," was published. In 1966 his second novel, *A Generous Man*, another story of the Mustian family of *A Long and Happy Life*, followed. *A Generous Man* also was greeted with acclaim. Price met his first mixed response from the critics in 1968 with *Love and Work*, a novel about a somewhat neurotic and consciously intellectual professor. Price's experimentation both with form and with the intersection of fact, autobiography, and fiction is continued in many of the stories of *Permanent Errors* (1970). After the publication of a collection of essays, *Things Themselves* (1972), Price's longest and perhaps most ambitious novel *The Surface of Earth* (1975) appeared. It was followed by a sequel, *The Source of Light* (1981). Although the reviews of these two novels were again mixed, the enthusiasm many critics brought to their judgment has insured Price's continuing and growing reputation. In 1983 the Mustian saga—"A Chain of Love," *A Generous Man*, and *A Long and Happy Life*—was reissued under the single title *Mustian*. Although he has abjured the label himself, many critics consider Price one of the preeminent stylists in modern American prose.

A distinguished essayist and novelist, Price has also been honored as a poet and playwright. Numerous poems have appeared in journals and magazines; they have been collected in *Vital Provisions* (1982) and in several limited edition collections. His play *Early Dark*, based on *A Long and Happy Life*, appeared in 1977. He has also written *Private Contentment*, a play for television. Price has also turned his hand to adaptation; he achieved his greatest acclaim in this mode with *A Palpable God* (1978), modern translations from the Old and New Testament.

Price has received awards from the Guggenheim Foundation and from the National Endowment for the Arts. He has also been the recipient of an Award in Literature from the American Academy and the National Institute of Arts and Letters. He has received several honorary degrees, and during his brief absences from Duke University, where he is a James B. Duke professor, he has held positions as writer-in-residence at both the Chapel Hill and Greensboro campuses of the University of North Carolina, as well as at the University of Kansas and Washington and Lee University.

Price, who has never married, lives near Durham, North Carolina, where he invariably writes several hours a day, six days a week, 52 weeks a year. Despite suffering from a rare spinal cancer in the 1980s, he has kept his active writing schedule. His most recent novel, *Kate Vaiden*, was published to critical acclaim in 1986.

MAJOR THEMES

Price has often been compared to Faulkner, partly for the complexity of his style and for the intricate structures of his later novels, and partly because many of his works, the Mustian and Mayfield sagas, form the fictional history of a place. At least one critic has openly taken Price to task for trying to put on the "Mantle of Faulkner," declaring that "one Yoknapatawpha county is enough." Price himself denies the importance of such a claim, asserting that he is chiefly influenced by "the writers most literate people admire and return to—Tolstoy, Milton, the Bible." Certainly Eudora Welty and Flannery O'Connor must be added to this list and, to a lesser extent, as Price discusses in an essay in *Things Themselves*, Ernest Hemingway. As other critics have pointed out, Price's serpentine style is more Miltonic than Faulknerian.

Because Price has not been reticent to discuss his life and his work, both in interviews and in his essays, the many autobiographical elements of his work have often been the subject of discussions of his fiction. Although he has protested any such oversimplification of his work as a parallel to his life, he has consistently declared that experience and style are as much the forces behind fiction as is imagination. In two works in particular, *Love and Work* and *Permanent Errors*, autobiography becomes inextricably interwoven into the fabric of the fiction; yet one easily believes the result to be of the realm of the symbolic and metaphoric rather than of the smaller sphere of one man's life. The interweaving of experience and fiction is consistent with one of the central ideas of Price's work— family as an emotional and "chemical predispositioning," family as the "irreducible fact of human life," family as "the institution which affects or *has* most affected the whole spectacle of human history." Price has stated that

"Southern writers have an extraordinary sense of the power of family over the individual." By these uses of family, Price means not only the immediate influence of a circle of blood relations but also the cumulative and generational influence of the past upon the present—family as destiny.

Much of Price's fiction narrates the fortunes of two families. One family, the Mustians, is the focus of the story "A Chain of Love" and of *A Long and Happy Life* and *A Generous Man*. Price's later novels, *The Surface of Earth* and *The Source of Light*, take the Kendal-Mayfield families through four generations. In these later works especially, the idea of hereditary determinism is affirmed and reaffirmed as the Mayfield males, in varying degrees, make the same mistakes their fathers made, show the same tendencies away from love and toward isolation, and make the same desperate attempts to escape from the pattern of their lives only to will themselves back into the same pattern. The social characteristics of the fathers and sons are similar even though the sons are raised away from the fathers and the biological fate of the clan is portended in the high infant and mother mortality rate in both novels.

Although the Mustian saga is not as outwardly deterministic as Price's later novels, the character of the family is nevertheless affirmed as the children grow to resemble increasingly their parents and each other. The promise for Milo Mustian's life in the ending of *A Generous Man* is undercut by the previously published *A Long and Happy Life*, in which Milo is presented as an agonizingly isolated character trapped within an unhappy marriage and a pattern of life he despises. The promise for Rosacoke's marriage and life at the ending of *A Long and Happy Life* is undercut by the falseness of the promise for Milo in *A Generous Man*, for the possibility is raised that, no matter how upbeat the ending, Rosacoke's marriage may turn out to be as unhappy as her brother's. Thus, the two novels, each a substantial achievement on its own, reflect upon each other and enforce the idea of familial determinism.

Even the relations of the families with servants and associates—a sort of extended family—take on the same characteristics and exert the same influence generation after generation. Price's contention seems to be that, if not the sins of the fathers (and mothers and relatives), some *sense* of the fathers is a compelling and often overwhelming force from generation to generation.

Coupled with this idea of hereditary determinism is Price's other theme "that man has free will, that he suffers from and is blessed by free will." This theme is accompanied by the Christian idea of Original Sin, namely that man "has certain burdens that are upon his shoulders simply as a result of being born, of being a human being." Thus, many of Price's characters, though burdened with "fate" or "sin," have the possibility and often the responsibility to break with their destiny through the exercise of free will.

The theme of Original Sin is particularly addressed in *The Surface of Earth* and *The Source of Light*, in which the Mayfield progeny seek to expiate the guilt and isolation passed on to them from their Kendal and Mayfield predecessors. But if the Mayfields are perhaps the most prominent examples, Price's other works abound with his modern retelling of Original Sin—that is, "permanent errors," mistakes of free will that can be forgiven but never rectified or eliminated. Rosacoke's desertion of her brother at the height of his despair over the death of his newborn son in *A Long and Happy Life*, a misunderstanding that ends a relationship in "Waiting at Dachau," the suicides (one attempted and one accomplished) of wives in "Good and Bad Dreams" and in "Walking Lessons," the simple burning of a deceased parent's papers and memorabilia in *Love and Work*—all of these are examples of "sins," errors permanent and unforgettable that cannot be changed and that predestine, in one way or another, the lives of Price's characters, unless those characters learn to accept and then to embrace the "sin."

These themes of familial destiny and determinism, of free will and Original Sin, and of "permanent errors" and the acceptance of the past, merge together in much of Price's work as the complex literature of a man who seems at once a biological and environmental determinist, a dogmatic Christian, a Christian existentialist, and a Southerner. In *Reynolds Price*, Constance Rooke has suggested that the Southern past, Original Sin, and familial destiny all combine in Price's work as different versions of the same design. Original Sin "has its counterpart in the history of the South" and in the history of a family. Each version—the story of Adam, the history of the South, and the saga of a family—is a working out of the same pattern on different scales.

In Price's work, the reader is usually presented with dialectical complexity—the Christian doctrine of Original Sin and the Christian optimism that through free will man can make that sin a blessing; the determining factor of family and the responsibility of the individual for his own life; the fate of the past and the free possibilities of the future. The intention of this dialectic is one of a secular wonder at unfathomable mystery, a wonder akin to that in the works of those from whom Price borrows his epigrams—Dante, Swedenborg, Augustine. Like Flannery O'Connor, Price is able to expose these paradoxes to the reader without disarming the mystery. Like Hemingway, Price often finds his fullest expressions couched within the simplest of events. In "The Names and Faces of Heroes," a young boy has an epiphanic experience while riding home from summer camp with his father. Rosacoke Mustian, in "A Chain of Love," learns the value of unrequited giving in the expression of grief on a stranger's face in a hospital. Charles Tamplin of "The Happiness of Others" experiences the overwhelming fullness of his isolation from others as he watches a shepherd herd his sheep across an English country road. In these and other stories and in instances of the novels, an ineffable occurrence is described, but the mystery inherent within the occurrence is left intact.

At other times, Price is richly symbolic. In *A Generous Man*, adolescent Milo, named for the Greek wrestler, comes briefly into his manhood while pursuing a huge snake named Death. In *A Long and Happy Life*, Rosacoke Mustian, secretly pregnant, resolves, as she plays the role of the Virgin in a Christmas pageant, to marry the father of her unborn child. Throughout *The Surface of*

Earth and again in *The Source of Light*, the misfortunes of the Mayfield males are linked by the circulation of a gold wedding band returned by a wife as she deserted her husband. As these examples show, the effectiveness of Price's symbolism derives in part from the fact that it is often coupled with irony and so turns back upon itself, doubling its resonances. Rosacoke not only *is* the Virgin, she also is decidedly *not* the Virgin at the same time, nor *a* virgin; thus, Price's symbol extends meaningfully in both directions. It is precisely this sense of irony, and often double irony, that makes his recurrent use of the supernatural effective. Milo Mustian, in *A Generous Man*, meets a ghost who clubs him over the head with a real tire iron. In *Love and Work* the excrement left by vandals on the kitchen floor is more terrifying to Thomas Eborn than the ghosts of his parents (an implied joke, certainly), and though Eborn is fascinated by the ghosts, they exclude him from their concern—an ironic inversion of the "ghost story."

The paradoxes of Price's work and their inherent mystery, the symbolism expanded by irony and often humor, all lead him to an essentially comic vision—comic in the sense of Dante's *Commedia*, the idea that man is himself an absurd and often ludicrous being who can nonetheless both raise himself above or sink himself below his human condition. Price has said of *A Long and Happy Life* that the central idea—"temptation" and "sin"—is tragic, but the last term, "redemption," is comic, a happy ending or the possibility of one. Price's message is perhaps that the ultimate and restorative comedy is that which is snatched out of tragedy. Ultimately, according to Price, and as his fiction shows, the aim of literature is in itself comic and that aim is "to *educate*, to lead out of the lonely and desperate self into the wider world of other like and unlike beings." In other words, to pull human lives from the tragic into a realm of greater possibility. Price's latest novel, *Kate Vaiden*, conveys the same affirmation. In a review of that novel, W. Kenneth Holditch compares Price with Graham Greene, Flannery O'Connor, Walker Percy, and John Updike—writers of, in the best sense, religious novels. He calls Kate Vaiden's life "a moral fable of sorts in which the author comments on the obligations of the human being to herself and to others."

SURVEY OF CRITICISM

Until Constance Rooke's 1983 *Reynolds Price*, no book-length study of Price's work had been published. A volume in Twayne's United States Authors Series, Rooke's study attempts to see Price's individual works as woven threads of an entire fabric, a task she accomplishes admirably. Drawing upon all Price scholarship to date, Rooke integrates criticism, interviews, and reviews into this ground-breaking investigation and includes a complete and annotated bibliography.

Perhaps the most valuable sources of information for the student of Price's fiction are contained in the interviews with Price conducted by Rooke, Wallace Kaufman, and William Ray. All of these interviews give unusual and useful perspectives of the author's relationship to his work, but Ray's "Conversations: Reynolds Price and William Ray," five interviews published in an entire issue of the *Bulletin of Mississippi Valley Collection*, is the richest source for those interested in Price's literature.

Frederick Hoffman's chapter in *The Art of Southern Fiction* (1967) in which he examines the work of Truman Capote, Walker Percy, and Reynolds Price was, for much of the academy, an announcement that Price was a Southern writer to be reckoned with. Hoffman's defense of Price against the charge of imitating Faulkner and Hoffman's brief linking of Price with O'Connor and Welty have provided the initial directions for the routes that later scholars have chosen to follow. Of particular interest to students of Price are the reviews of Price's work, especially the almost notorious "Mantle of Faulkner" essay by John Wain in the *New Republic*.

There is much inquiry yet to be made on Price's work. Each individual work and the works as a whole are still rich lodes for scholarly mining and, with only one dissertation written on the subject, for doctoral examination. Those studying Price's work will welcome a new reference guide, *Reynolds Price: A Bibliography, 1949–1984*, edited by Stuart Wright and James L. West, III. Periodical references in this work quote from and comment upon articles.

BIBLIOGRAPHY

Works by Reynolds Price

A Long and Happy Life. New York: Atheneum, 1962. London: Chatto & Windus, 1962.
The Names and Faces of Heroes. New York: Atheneum, 1963. London: Chatto & Windus, 1963.
A Generous Man. New York: Atheneum, 1966. London: Chatto & Windus, 1967.
"A Conversation with Reynolds Price," ed. Wallace Kaufman. *Shenandoah* 17 (Summer 1966): 3–25. Expanded in "Notice, I'm Still Smiling," in *Kite Flying and Other Irrational Acts*, ed. John Carr. Baton Rouge: Louisiana State University Press, 1972, pp. 70–95.
"An Interview with Reynolds Price on Writing, Readers, Critics," ed. Eugene Moore. *Red Clay Reader* 3 (1966): 18–26.
Late Warning: Four Poems. New York: Albondocani, 1968.
Love and Work. New York: Atheneum, 1968. London: Chatto & Windus, 1968.
Permanent Errors. New York: Atheneum, 1970. London: Chatto & Windus, 1971.
Things Themselves: Essays and Scenes. New York: Atheneum, 1972.
Presence and Absence: Versions from the Bible. Columbia: Bruccoli and Clark, 1974.
The Surface of Earth. New York: Atheneum, 1975.
"Conversations: Reynolds Price & William Ray," ed. William Ray. *Bulletin of the Mississippi Valley Collection* 9 (Fall 1976): 8–82.
Early Dark: A Play. New York: Atheneum, 1977.
Lessons Learned: Seven Poems. New York: Albondocani, 1977.
Oracles: Six Versions from the Bible. Durham, N.C.: Friends of Duke University, 1977.

"On Women and His Own Work: An Interview with Reynolds Price," ed. Constance Rooke. *Southern Review* 14 (Autumn 1978): 706–25.

A Palpable God: Thirty Stories Translated from the Bible with an Essay on the Origins and Life of Narrative. New York: Atheneum, 1978.

Nine Mysteries (Four Joyful, Four Sorrowful, One Glorious). Winston-Salem, N.C.: Palaemon Press, 1979.

A Final Letter. Los Angeles: Sylvester & Orphanos, 1980.

The Annual Heron. New York: Albondocani, 1980.

The Source of Light. New York: Atheneum, 1981.

Vital Provisions. New York: Atheneum, 1982.

Mustian: Two Novels & A Story. New York: Atheneum, 1984.

Private Contentment: A Play. New York: Atheneum, 1984.

House Snake. Northridge, Calif.: Lord John, 1986.

Kate Vaiden. New York: Atheneum, 1986.

Studies of Reynolds Price

Davenport, Guy. "Doomed, Damned and Unaware: *Permanent Errors*." *New York Times Book Review*, October 11, 1970, p. 4.

Eichelberger, Clayton L. "Reynolds Price: 'A Banner in Defeat.' " *Journal of Popular Culture* 1 (1967): 410–17.

Freeman, Anne Hobson. "Penetrating a Small Patch of *The Surface of Earth*." *Virginia Quarterly Review* 51 (Autumn 1975): 637–41.

Gilman, Richard. "A Mastodon of a Novel, by Reynolds Price." *New York Times Book Review*, June 29, 1975, p. 4.

———. "This Is the Way It Happened." *New York Times Book Review*, June 30, 1963, p. 4.

Hicks, Granville. "Country Girl Burdened with Love." *Saturday Review*, March 10, 1962, pp. 17–18.

———. "In Pursuit of a Snake Named Death." *Saturday Review*, March 26, 1966, pp. 27–28.

Hoffman, Frederick. *The Art of Southern Fiction*. Carbondale: Southern Illinois University Press, 1967, pp. 137–45.

Oates, Joyce Carol. "Portrait of the Artist as Son, Lover, Elegist." *New York Times Book Review*, April 26, 1981, pp. 3, 30.

Rooke, Constance. *Reynolds Price*. Boston: Twayne, 1983.

Shepherd, Allen. "Love (and Marriage) in *A Long and Happy Life*." *Twentieth Century Literature* 17 (January 1971): 20–35.

———. "Notes on Nature in the Fiction of Reynolds Price." *Critique: Studies in Modern Fiction* 2 (1970): 83–94.

Solotaroff, Theodore. "The Reynolds Price Who Outgrew Southern Pastoral." *Saturday Review*, September 26, 1970, pp. 27, 29, 46.

Stevenson, John W. "The Faces of Reynolds Price's Short Fiction." *Studies in Short Fiction* 3 (1966): 300–06.

Vauthier, Simone. "The 'Circle in the Forest': Fictional Space in Reynolds Price's *A Long and Happy Life*." *Mississippi Quarterly* 28 (Spring 1975): 123–46.

Wain, John. "Mantle of Faulkner." *New Republic*, May 14, 1966, pp. 31–33.

———. "Puppeteers." *New York Review of Books*, August 22, 1968, p. 35.

Wolff, Geoffrey. " 'Murder Your Darling.' " *New Leader*, June 17, 1968, pp. 14–15.
Woiwode, Larry. "Pursuits of the Flesh, Adventures of the Spirit." *Washington Post Book World*, April 26, 1981, p. 5.
Wright, Stuart and James L. West III. *Reynolds Price: A Bibliography, 1949–1984*. Charlottesville: University Press of Virginia, 1986.

John Crowe Ransom
(1888–1974)

The literary reputations of most writers included in this volume rest on their achievements in a particular genre—poetry, drama, or fiction. Many have demonstrated considerable skill in more than one genre. But few have acquitted themselves so admirably in so many roles as John Crowe Ransom, and even fewer approach his rank in literary influence or leadership. As poet, critic, editor, and teacher, Ransom is arguably among the three or four most important literary figures in twentieth-century American letters.

BIOGRAPHY

Born in Pulaski, Tennessee, on 20 April 1888, John Crowe Ransom spent his childhood years in the small villages and towns of middle Tennessee where his father, a Methodist minister, held pastorships. Because his family moved so often, he was educated at home until age ten, when he first enrolled in public school in Nashville. In 1903, when he was fifteen, he was admitted to Vanderbilt University by special waiver, largely on the strength of his exceptional performance on the entrance examinations.

His college education was interrupted at the end of his sophomore year by a two-year stint teaching secondary school, during which he saved money to complete his degree. Upon graduation from Vanderbilt in 1909, Ransom returned briefly to teaching before enrolling at Christ Church College, Oxford, as a Rhodes scholar, from 1910 to 1913. He earned a degree in humanities from Oxford, where his studies in the classics, philosophy, history, and literature were enriched by summer vacations in Europe. After finishing his Oxford studies, Ransom spent a year teaching at the Hotchkiss School in Connecticut. In autumn 1914 he joined the English faculty at Vanderbilt, where he remained for nearly a quarter of a century, and where Donald Davidson, Allen Tate, Robert Penn

Warren, Andrew Lytle, Randall Jarrell, and Peter Taylor were among his students.

As an undergraduate at Vanderbilt, Ransom had been an active participant in a literary discussion group called the Calumet Club, and he had founded a similar group at Oxford known as the Hermit Crabs. Hence he was delighted upon returning to Vanderbilt to be invited to join a discussion group of faculty members and students where he could test the aesthetic theories he was then developing. His lack of formal postgraduate training in English literature led him to prepare carefully for his classes by reading extensively both primary and secondary sources. Out of this study came the foundations of the critical theories he would devote much of his life to exploring.

The Vanderbilt group disbanded in 1917 when most of its members left to serve in World War I, but reunited in fall 1920, with many old members and some new ones. Ransom gradually became the recognized, though unofficial, intellectual leader of the group, and the discussions increasingly centered on the craft of poetry, in part owing to his growing interest in the form, and in part to the interests of two new members—Donald Davidson and Allen Tate. Ransom had published his first volume of poetry, *Poems About God*, in 1919, had studied the French Symbolists during his service tour in France, and had found matching enthusiasm for poetry in both Davidson and Tate.

By 1922 the group had adopted a name—the Fugitives—and decided to publish a journal of poetry and ideas. During its three years of publication, Ransom contributed steadily to the *Fugitive*, including several essays that foreshadowed the concerns of his later aesthetic theories. Stimulated by the interchange the fugitive group provided, he experienced a spurt of creative activity, and over a three-year period wrote the best poetry of his career. He published his second and third volumes of poetry, *Chills and Fever* and *Grace After Meat*, in 1924. These poems were vastly superior in style and subject to his early verse, and led Tate to observe that Ransom had "suddenly" found his true poetic voice. By 1926, however, he had given up writing poetry to pursue the formal study of poetry as a unique art form. He was trying to arrive at a theory of aesthetics that would satisfactorily define the genre and identify the peculiar quality of poetry that distinguished it from all other modes of discourse.

In 1926, while on a sabbatical in Colorado, Ransom worked hard on a book of theoretical criticism, under the working title *The Third Moment*, which he never published. He wanted to distinguish between the immediacy of sensory perception (the First Moment), the intellectual apprehension and manipulation of that perception (the Second Moment), and the effort to reconstitute the original experience through the union of image and idea in art (the Third Moment). Although the manuscript has not survived, a summary contained in a letter to Allen Tate demonstrates clearly that Ransom was building the foundation for much of his future critical theory. During this same period, he finished work on *Two Gentlemen in Bonds*, his fourth volume of poetry, which appeared early in 1927 to widespread critical acclaim.

About this time, Ransom and several of the former Fugitives became actively involved in defending Southern culture against attacks from leading Northern intellectuals, and against the inroads being made by what they saw as a godless (and artless) industrial capitalism. Partly to counter the notoriety resulting from the 1925 Scopes "Monkey Trial" in Dayton, Tennessee, and partly in response to the general attitudes of H. L. Mencken, who sneeringly described the South as the "Sahara of the Bozart," and of Mencken's followers, Ransom and the other Agrarians, as they came to be known, undertook a concerted campaign of lectures, debates, articles, editorials, and reviews in defense of their native region.

Ransom wrote dozens of short and long newspaper and magazine articles and reviews defending Agrarian principles. To the Agrarian symposium *I'll Take My Stand* he contributed the "Introduction: A Statement of Principles" and the lead essay, "Reconstructed but Unregenerate." And his first book of prose, *God Without Thunder: An Unorthodox Defense of Orthodoxy* (1930), is concerned with many of the cultural and social issues underlying the Agrarian movement. This book, although roundly scoffed by critics and reviewers, in fact contains a discussion of myth that is crucial to a full understanding of Ransom's later work.

During a Guggenheim Fellowship in 1931–32, Ransom worked on an economic treatise entitled *Land!*, but after publishing two essays from the manuscript, abandoned it in 1932 as "nearly a total loss." Although political and economic matters dominated his public energies during the early 1930s, Ransom nonetheless continued to publish critical essays. The seminal article in terms of his later work was "Poetry: A Note in Ontology," which synthesized most of his thinking since his Oxford days on the uniqueness of poetry as a mode of discourse and cognition.

By 1936, however, Ransom had decided he would "write no more economic essays," and turned his full attention to literature once again. Under the title *The World's Body*, in 1938 he published fifteen essays that had appeared over the previous five years. This collection coincided with his 1937 move from Vanderbilt to Kenyon College, a move he made with the intention "to work at literature a little more single-mindedly than I have been doing." The proof of that intention was not long in coming, for almost as soon as he arrived at Kenyon, Ransom undertook to found and edit a quarterly review—on the eve of his fiftieth year. Over the next twenty years, as editor of the *Kenyon Review* from 1939 to 1959, Ransom established it as one of the leading literary journals in America and extended his influence widely as a leading man of letters.

In 1941 he published *The New Criticism*, a book whose title was misappropriated by a younger generation of students and scholars to declare their independence from traditional historical literary criticism. In fact, the book only explained further what for over 25 years had been Ransom's general critical approach: a focus more on the poem itself and less on its historical context. In the final essay, "Wanted: An Ontological Critic," Ransom once again developed at length his aesthetic theory of poetry, and argued for a critical approach that focused on the special kind of knowledge poetry offers. In more than twenty critical essays published in the *Kenyon Review* and elsewhere over the next four years, he demonstrated by example how he believed an "ontological" critic should approach his task.

In 1945 Ransom published *Selected Poems*, comprising 39 existing works, nearly all of them revised, and five new ones. As the proportion indicates, Ransom had not spent much time writing poetry since the mid–1920s; always a "tinkerer" with his verse, he revised his poetry with each new collection. Between 1945 and 1950 Ransom did little writing; his time was occupied teaching, editing the *Review*, and developing other projects in pursuit of his goal of promoting the humane study of letters in a culturally hostile world.

In 1947 he founded the Kenyon School of English with a grant from the Rockefeller Foundation. With a dozen established critics and men of letters as fellows, the school exposed graduate students during summer terms to the best literary minds of the times. Although it was transferred to Indiana University in 1950 as the School of Letters, Ransom remained on its board until the program was terminated in 1972. From 1953 to 1958, in another program conceived under his leadership, the Kenyon Review Fellowships were established to provide promising new poets, fiction writers, and critics the freedom to pursue their craft free from financial concerns.

The 1950s were the period of Ransom's greatest influence and active reputation. He routinely accepted twenty or more speaking engagements a year, and resumed an active writing schedule. He also received many tributes, including in 1951 the Bollingen Award in Poetry and the Russell Liones Award in Literature. He edited *The Kenyon Critics* that same year, and issued *Poems and Essays* in 1955. The most sigificant essays of this period were two articles on "The Concrete Universal" in 1954–55, in which he once again sought to define the uniqueness of poetry.

Although he retired from his editorship in 1959, Ransom continued to write and lecture until his health prevented it. He edited a selection of Hardy's poetry in 1961, and was awarded an Academy of American Poets Fellowship in 1962. He published his *Selected Poems* twice more, in 1963 and 1969. Although the 1963 collection received the National Book Award in poetry, the 1969 collection showed evidence of too much tinkering and revision. His final book of essays, *Beating the Bushes*, appeared in 1972. Ransom died on 30 July 1974 and was buried in Gambier, Ohio.

MAJOR THEMES

In criticism and in poetry, in theory and in practice, all of Ransom's major themes and arguments proceed from his fundamental view of man. Ransom saw modern man as hopelessly apart from but inescapably a part of the natural world, and he saw art, and poetry in particular, as the sole but partial means of recovering a sense of wholeness between man and his world. Although Ransom was not a religious man in the traditional sense of the term, the division between man and nature, and the function of myth and poetry in restoring man's integrity with the world's body, were major and continuing subjects in all his writings.

At one time, Ransom believed, before man's excessive reliance on reason led him to place ultimate faith in the abstractions of science, there was harmony between the intellectual and sensory aspects of man's being. Man understood the limits and uses of both sensory experience and rational knowledge. But in modern times man's faith in his rational powers resulted in discontinuity between man and his "contingencies" (a favorite Ransom word). The result of this dissociation of sensibility was a hopeless confusion that left man unable to function in the modern world, torn between body and spirit, between head and heart, between the real and the ideal. Although Ransom was equally mistrustful of the Romantic exaltation of emotion and feeling, his sympathies lay more with sensibility than with reason, and he consistently favored the concrete particularity of the world over the intellectual abstractions of science.

In his poetry, Ransom's dualistic view of man informs his explorations of the paradoxes, ironies, and ambiguities that result from the tension between reason and the senses, between human consciousness and the bodily existence that sustains it. *Poems About God* reveals the beginnings of these concerns in its satiric treatments of romantic idealism and in its rejection of abstractions and generalizations. But Ransom's subsequent reading of the Symbolists and his participation in the Fugitive discussions sharpened both his technique and his themes. The poem that seems most clearly to mark this change in his poetic practice is "Necrological," which, when it was presented at a Fugitive meeting, caused Tate to remark that Ransom had found his poetic voice.

"Necrological," like all Ransom's mature poems, is a work of great artifice, carefully contrived and balanced. "One has the sense," John Stewart observes, "of powerful internal forces precisely poised and counterpoised within the hard, crystalline style and structure." Indeed, in their richly allusive verbal surfaces and in their use of sympathetic yet detached observers as personae, Ransom's poems have great energy and tension. In tone they typically exhibit that energy in a tighty maintained ironic balance between mawkishness or sentimentality on the one hand, and excessive cleverness on the other. It is almost as if Ransom enjoyed the danger of writing so close to the edge of disaster.

This tension in poetic form advances and mirrors Ransom's major themes. He is concerned with the transitoriness of all human endeavor in the face of death, repeatedly demonstrating in such poems as "Necrological" that while battles may be won, the war is already lost, that death subsumes all. Man often appears in Ransom's poetry as a foolish yet complex and sublime creature, foolish because of his belief in abstractions or in his own sufficiency, yet sublime nonetheless for his ability to dream.

Ransom's concern—some would say preoccupation—with death often merged with another of his favorite themes, that of innocence and experience. In "Bells for John Whiteside's Daughter'' Ransom contrasts the reality of a young girl's death with the image of her youthful liveliness to portray the theme of mortality. And in ''Janet Waking'' he turns that awareness around to a child's first apprehension of death and the irrecoverable loss of innocence that results.

In his treatment of human love Ransom's concern with mortality often led him to portray love as an essentially destructive force. With an almost Romantic sense of fatalism, he saw death lurking precisely at the point of the most extraordinary human experience or accomplishment. Hence in ''The Equilibrists,'' one of his best poems, the lovers are doomed forever to a ''torture of equilibrium'' in which they can neither consummate their passion nor still their desire. The culprit, as Ransom observes here and in ''Vaunting Oak'' and ''April Lovers,'' is man's overly developed consciousness. He can be comfortable in neither the natural world nor his own human society.

Ransom did not find in the ironic vision of his poetry a desirable state of being; he did insist, however, that man could not fully understand his condition and its contingencies except through poetry. Hence, while his poetry was devoted to capturing and communicating that condition, his criticism insisted that poetry represented a special order of knowledge. Poetry, he once wrote, was the means ''by which we must know that which we have arranged that we shall not know otherwise.'' In one form or another, this definition of poetry informs all Ransom's criticism.

It is possible, indeed desirable, to see the fundamental continuity of Ransom's critical thought from his earliest writings to his last. A major weakness in his aesthetic theory, however, is a somewhat distorted view of science. Science, in his view, pursued abstraction too assiduously, preferring that to the cluttered ''contingency'' of the real world. Ransom appeared not to allow for any but the most manipulative of motives on the part of scientific research. But however mistaken, this mistrust of abstraction, whether Platonic or scientific in character, sprang from and informed Ransom's fundamental view of modern man.

His bias against abstraction comes through also in his notion of the ''Third Moment,'' the moment when the artist or poet attempts to reconstitute an experience. Ransom believes that artistic reconstitution is inevitably adulterated by the play of memory (the Second Moment) in recording the experience (the First Moment). The purity of the original experience can never be recaptured; what art does in the Third Moment is to invest the intellectual record of an experience with something of its original sensory context. In doing so, art uses the concrete particularity of words, images, and events to suggest as far as possible the richness of the original experience and to convey its significance in a way no abstract statement can.

This stress on the aesthetic function of poetry—indeed of all art—is at the core of Ransom's theory of poetics. In ''Forms and Citizens'' (1938) he notes that poetry is one of a series of humanizing disciplines he calls ''aesthetic forms'' or ''play forms.'' Poetry restrains the artist's ''natural'' impulse to seize or acquire an object and induces in the poet the aesthetic impulse to explore its significance in a formal way. Poetry forces the artist to "taste and enjoy" and experience instead of "gulp[ing] it down"; hence it is an indispensable civilizing influence on the scientific tendency toward abstraction.

These ideas are given more detailed analysis in "Poetry: A Note in Ontology" (1934), where Ransom differentiates between three types of poetry: "physical poetry," which attempts to present "things in their thingness" and excludes ideas altogether; "Platonic poetry," which uses images solely to "decorate" ideas; and "metaphysical poetry," which fuses ideas and images into an inseparable whole that is superior in every respect to the partial knowledge provided by science.

In "Wanted: An Ontological Critic" (1941) Ransom again returns to the special nature of poetry, describing its unique union of "structure" and "texture": "We sum it up by saying that the poem is a loose logical structure with a good deal of local texture." In arguing for the essential ontological nature of poetry, Ransom goes beyond his earlier explorations of the function of poetry to analyze further the difference between "scientific symbols," which "are abstract and refer to abstract concepts," and "aesthetic icons," which "recall whole concrete objects."

In his last major pronouncements on poetic theory, Ransom wrote in two essays entitled "The Concrete Universal" (1954–55) that he was unhappy with his former structure/texture formulation, and described a poem as an organism with three "speaking" parts: a head, which speaks in an intellectual language; the heart, which speaks in an affective language; and the feet, which speak in a rhythmical language. According to Ransom, the three voices all speak at once, although we are attentive to them in varying degrees of intensity. In the second essay, Ransom returns to Kant, his acknowledged mentor, for an explication of the essential continuity between Kant's view of poetry and his own lifelong view of poetry as a dynamically informing competition between ideas and images.

SURVEY OF CRITICISM

Over the past decade there has been a renewal of critical interest in the Fugitive and Agrarian movements, connected in part with the fiftieth anniversary of *I'll Take My Stand*. Ransom's leading role in both movements has received general recognition in recent scholarship, but the original accounts of these movements contain highly informative treatments of his activities and influence from 1920 to 1935. Louise Cowan's *The Fugitive Group* (1959) is a definitive history that emphasizes Ransom's intellectual leadership, while John M. Bradbury's *The Fugitives: A Critical Account* (1958) and John L. Stewart's *The Burden of Time* (1965) concentrate on Ransom's writings and critical theories in relationship to those of other group members. Stewart's analysis also extends to include the Agrarian period in Ransom's career.

The personal accounts and recollections of Allen Tate, Donald Davidson, and Robert Penn Warren, scattered throughout their letters and writings, provide invaluable sources for studying Ransom's personality, his involvement with the Fugitives and the Agrarians, and the dynamics of these groups. But the fullest, most informative treatment of Ransom's life and work is Thomas Daniel Young's authorized biography, *Gentleman in a Dustcoat* (1976). In addition to a detailed account of Ransom's life, Young's biography traces the essential continuity of Ransom's thought from his Oxford days to his death. This book and Young's many shorter studies of Ranson's life and writings constitute the most authoritative body of research and commentary on Ransom and his work.

Most critical attention to Ransom's writings has focused on the poetry, with Robert Buffington's careful study *The Equilibrist* (1967) having benefited from Karl F. Knight's *The Poetry of John Crowe Ransom* (1964), the first book-length treatment of Ransom's poetic practices. Miller Williams's *The Poetry of John Crowe Ransom* (1972) focuses on the poet's use of irony and ambiguity and studies Ransom's chief metaphors. Louis D. Rubin, Jr.'s account of Ransom's poetic career in *The Wary Fugitives* (1978) concludes with an analysis of why Ransom ceased writing poetry.

Vivienne Koch's story survey of Ransom's career tends to reduce his complex and often refractory themes to a simplistic few, whereas Isabel Gamble MacCaffrey argues convincingly that Ransom's poetry is a nearly perfect mirror of his time. In early and late studies of Ransom's poetry, Robert Penn Warren evaluates Ransom's poetic career and identifies Ransom's dualistic view of man as a recurrent theme that underlies many others.

Ransom's critical writings have unfortunately received less attention than they deserve. William J. Handy's *Kant and the Southern New Critics* (1963) explores Kant's influence on Ransom, Tate, and Brooks, and James E. Magner, Jr.'s *John Crowe Ransom: Critical Principles and Preoccupations* (1971) analyzes the philosophical bases upon which Ransom's critical theories rest. The best analysis of Ransom's unique prose style is Marcia McDonald's "The Function of Persona in Ransom's Prose."

But apart from Young's studies, there have been too few efforts to measure the origins, development, and influence of the "New Criticism" and Ransom's work in laying its foundations, as well as his role as an editor and promoter of letters. It is a field that calls for new and original views, and one that promises rich rewards. The recent publication of Ransom's letters and essays, including many previously unavailable articles, should provoke further study in the work of this remarkable man of letters.

BIBLIOGRAPHY

Works by John Crowe Ransom

Poems About God. New York: Henry Holt, 1919.
Chills and Fever. New York: Alfred A. Knopf, 1924.
Grace After Meat. London: Hogarth Press, 1924.

Two Gentlemen in Bonds. New York: Alfred A. Knopf, 1927.

God Without Thunder: An Unorthodox Defense of Orthodoxy. New York: Harcourt, Brace, 1930.

Topics for Freshman Writing: Twenty Topics for Writing with Appropriate Materials for Study. New York: Henry Holt, 1935.

The World's Body. New York: Charles Scribner's Sons, 1938.

The New Criticism. Norfolk, Conn.: New Directions, 1941.

A College Primer of Writing. New York: Henry Holt, 1943.

Selected Poems. New York: Alfred A. Knopf, 1945; rev. 1963, 1969.

The Kenyon Critics, ed. Cleveland: World, 1951.

Poems and Essays. New York: Vintage Books, 1955.

Selected Poems of Thomas Hardy, ed. New York: Macmillan, 1961.

Beating the Bushes: Selected Essays 1941–1970. Norfolk, Conn.: New Directions, 1971.

The Selected Essays of John Crowe Ransom. Ed. T. D. Young and John Hindle. Baton Rouge: Louisiana State University Press, 1984.

The Selected Letters of John Crowe Ransom. Ed. T. D. Young and George Core. Baton Rouge: Louisiana State University Press, 1985.

Studies of John Crowe Ransom

Bradbury, John M. *The Fugitives: A Critical Account*. Chapel Hill: University of North Carolina Press, 1958.

Buffington, Robert. *The Equilibrist: A Study of John Crowe Ransom's Poems, 1916–1963*. Nashville, Tenn.: Vanderbilt University Press, 1967.

Cowan, Louise. *The Fugitive Group: A Literary History*. Baton Rouge: Louisiana State University Press, 1959.

Handy, William J. *Kant and the Southern New Critics*. Austin: University of Texas Press, 1963.

Knight, Karl F. *The Poetry of John Crowe Ransom: A Study of Diction, Metaphor and Symbol*. The Hague: Mouton, 1964.

Koch, Vivienne. "The Achievement of John Crowe Ransom." *Sewanee Review* 68 (Spring 1950): 227–61; reprinted in *John Crowe Ransom: Critical Essays and a Bibliography*, ed. Thomas Daniel Young, pp. 115–42.

MacCaffrey, Isabel Gamble. "Ceremonies of Bravery: John Crowe Ransom." *South: Modern Southern Literature in Its Cultural Setting*. Ed. Louis D. Rubin, Jr., and Robert D. Jacobs. Garden City, N.Y.: Doubleday, 1961.

McDonald, Marcia. "The Function of Persona in Ransom's Prose." *Mississippi Quarterly* 30 (Winter 1976–77): 87–100.

Magner, James E., Jr. *John Crowe Ransom: Critical Principles and Preoccupations*. The Hague: Mouton, 1971.

Parsons, Thornton H. *John Crowe Ransom*. New York: Twayne, 1969.

Rubin, Louis D., Jr. *The Wary Fugitives: Four Poets and the South*. Baton Rouge: Louisiana State University Press, 1978.

Stewart, John L. *John Crowe Ransom*. University of Minnesota Pamphlets on American Writers. Minneapolis: University of Minnesota Press, 1962.

———. *The Burden of Time*. Princeton, N.J.: Princeton University Press, 1965.

Warren, Robert Penn. "Notes on the Poetry of John Crowe Ransom on His Eightieth Birthday." *Kenyon Review* 30 (1968): 319–49.

————. "John Crowe Ransom: A Study In Irony." *Virginia Quarterly Review* 40 (January 1940): 93–112, in *John Crowe Ransom: Critical Essays and A Bibliography*, pp. 24–40.

Williams, Miller. *The Poetry of John Crowe Ransom.* New Brunswick, N.J.: Rutgers University Press, 1972.

Young, Thomas Daniel. *Gentlemen in a Dustcoat: A Biography of John Crowe Ransom.* Baton Rouge: Louisiana State University Press, 1976.

————. *John Crowe Ransom.* Southern Writers Series, No. 12. Austin, Texas: Steck-Vaughn, 1970.

————, ed. *John Crowe Ransom: Critical Essays and A Bibliography.* Baton Rouge: Louisiana State University Press, 1968.

OWEN GILMAN

Marjorie Kinnan Rawlings
(1896–1953)

Marjorie Kinnan Rawlings always sensed she was born to write, and her life was made full by writing. Yet, had Rawlings not discovered the north central region of Florida—a place no other writer had claimed—she would probably be little known today. The peculiar South of the Florida hinterlands was her salvation, her deliverance. This exotic land and the backwoods people who struggled to survive in harmony with it became the key to her success as a writer. Her story, then, is one of fateful discovery.

BIOGRAPHY

The road to Florida and a measure of literary renown was not a direct one for Marjorie Kinnan Rawlings. Born on 8 August 1896, the daughter of Arthur F. Kinnan and Ida May Traphagen Kinnan, she grew up in suburban Washington, D.C., where her father was an attorney for the U.S. Patent Office. She and her younger brother Arthur often spent time with their father at a farm he owned in nearby Maryland. This early taste of rural life would figure powerfully in her heartfelt embrace of the Florida landscape during her middle years, for she had warm memories of youthful days in the countryside. She gained an instinctive feel for the enduring quality of the land, perhaps even a notion that it could be simultaneously rejuvenating and obdurate, and it is certainly no accident that her best work, *The Yearling* (1938), involves the experiences of a youth in nature. As a writer, she completed a circle with that novel, fusing memory with present experience.

She began writing at the age of six. By the age of eleven, she was published, winning a $2.00 prize for a story entered in a *Washington Post* contest. In 1912 she won second prize in *McCall's* Child Authorship Contest for ''The Reincarnation of Miss Hetty,'' a story published that year in the August *McCall's*. These accomplishments confirmed her ambition to be a writer, a commitment that kept her busy until December 1953, when she died of a cerebral hemorrhage. She was then at work on a biography of Ellen Glasgow.

When Arthur Kinnan died in 1913, his daughter was deeply shaken. Evidence of an abiding affection for her father appears throughout her fiction; many of her narratives include a sympathetic portrait of a man whose essential identity is as father. Likewise, her fiction suggests she felt some tension in her relationship with her mother, for the mother figures in story after story are distant, sometimes even hostile. Marjorie Kinnan herself never had children, and so she chose to concentrate in her writing on the parent she had known most truly and warmly.

In 1914 Mrs. Kinnan moved the family to Madison, Wisconsin, and Marjorie matriculated at the University of Wisconsin that year. An English major, she distinguished herself as a student, making Phi Beta Kappa in her junior year, taking an active role in the campus dramatic society, and writing for the Wisconsin *Lit*, a campus literary magazine. She and her fellow editors prided themselves on being familiar with the latest literary trends, including the emergence of radically new poetic styles. It was also through this effort that she met her future husband, Charles Rawlings, who was preparing for a journalism career.

This heady immersion in college literary affairs may have contributed to the difficulties Marjorie Kinnan Rawlings had getting her fiction published throughout the 1920s. Although a rich background in literature can be indispensable for a writer, reading experience is not the same as lived experience. The creative writing Rawlings produced in her first decade out of college inclined toward an excess of fancifulness, and she collected a daunting series of rejection slips before she found her true voice.

After graduation she went to New York City. She soon located a position doing editorial work at the headquarters for the national YWCA. Then, in 1919, she married Charles Rawlings and moved to Rochester, New York, where the couple established their home. While her husband began immediately his own writing career, Rawlings played a supportive role, although she did journalistic work for the Louisville *Courier-Journal*, the Rochester *Journal*, and the United Features Syndicate. At the same time, a series of her poems, published under the general heading of "Songs of the Housewife" in the Rochester *Times-Union* and other newspapers, revealed a part of her life that would later be featured in her long fiction; her novels are liberally sprinkled with descriptions of lavish and hearty feasts. As Rawlings declared in the chapter "Our Daily Bread" of *Cross Creek* (1942), her autobiographical account of life in Florida, "I hold the theory that the serving of good food is the one certain way of pleasing everybody." So it is not surprising that the occasional peaceful moments in her stories typically coincide with festive breaking of bread. Just as the land can hold promise for mitigating the torments of human life, so too can the simple pleasure of sharing a meal lovingly prepared.

Yet Rawlings's writing was not going well in Rochester, and the future looked dim. Then in the spring of 1928, she and Charles visited Florida. She was enchanted by what she saw there and instinctively knew that such a place would be good for her work. By late summer, they owned a tract of land that included a fairly large stand of citrus trees, pecan trees, chickens, acreage for planting other crops, a farmhouse, and a tenant residence. She and Charles moved to the South in November. Almost immediately, she began to write, recording as many of her first impressions as she could.

Because Rawlings was an outsider, much was noteworthy. She looked with the wonder of fresh discovery upon the vegetation, the wild creatures, and the human inhabitants of this new place. What she saw fascinated her—especially the "Florida Crackers," those plain, earthy folks whose resilience was magnified by the challenge of an engulfing wilderness. They knew the land. They bore their frustrations with dignity; it seemed the land taught them this lesson. They lived from harvest to harvest, from hunt to hunt, and they affirmed their essential humanity through the stories they swapped. Rawlings listened raptly to their talk, the seamless accounts of encounters with nature. She listened and she wrote. She had found the materials of her craft.

Rawlings's interest in Florida soon began paying dividends. "Cracker Chidlings," a set of short pieces on the ways of the backwoods folk of Florida, was bought by *Scribner's* magazine in March 1930. Later that year *Scribner's* also purchased *Jacob's Ladder*, a short novel published in the April 1931 issue. This story sparked the interest of Maxwell Perkins, and Rawlings subsequently benefited from his devoted editorial work.

Rawlings explains the title of *Jacob's Ladder* in *Cross Creek*. Ladders were an essential part of the fruit harvest, thus providing a material index to life in Florida. More important was the allusion to the powerful black spiritual, which suggested a key component in Rawlings's emerging philosophy: life's adversities are best countered with quiet resignation. This fatalism bears the stamp of the Old Testament, and it led her, at the close of her career, to attempt a modern rendering of the story of Job. Such a view mandated narratives filled with trials and tribulations, episode after episode of unwarranted suffering, and for a nation caught in the throes of economic depression, her fiction provided an apt mirror. Moreover, it proved the virtue of endurance.

Rawlings often depended on real people and events to spark her imagination. Two families in particular contributed to her fiction in the 1930s, each time involving a visit by her to the Big Scrub, a region of inhospitable land calling for the utmost in endurance and fortitude. For three months in late summer and early fall 1931, Rawlings lived with the Fiddia family—an old woman and her moonshiner son who became Piety Lantry (*piety* having both a religious connotation and the sense of dutiful regard for one's parents) and her son Lant Jacklin in *South Moon Under* (1933), which was a Book-of-the-Month Club selection. Then in July 1933, she went again to the Big Scrub to live with Cal Long and his family; the impressions of this visit soon were making their way through Rawlings's imagination toward an appearance in *The Yearling*, the best-selling, Book-of-the-Month Club novel (and subsequent MGM movie) which gave Rawlings a national reputation and assured her of a place in twentieth-century American literature.

Before Rawlings began to develop her most widely read fiction, she devoted two years to *Golden Apples*. This novel, sold in 1934 to *Cosmopolitan* in a condensed version, proved a misstep; Rawlings tried to introduce an international theme to her meditations on Southern life by featuring an Englishman who is exiled by his family to a Florida plantation. Although the conflicts between this foreigner and the indigenous people are natural enough, his characterization and the machinations of the plot seem shallow and false. Rawlings did not possess the dexterity and structural subtlety of Henry James in working out the conflict between natives and an outsider.

Nevertheless, following election to the National Academy of Arts and Letters in January 1939, a Pulitzer Prize for *The Yearling* in May of that year, and publication of *When the Whippoorwill* (1940), a collection of her 1930s short fiction, which included "Gal Young Un," an O. Henry Award winner, Rawlings tried again to treat the experiences of an outsider in a new land. This time she dispensed with the artifice of fiction and simply told her own story. Unlike *Golden Apples*, *Cross Creek* satisfies, mainly because it reveals honestly how an outsider can come to know and appreciate a discovered place, even while maintaining a sense of objectivity impossible to the lifelong resident. *Cross Creek* soon became another best-seller for Rawlings, and it was followed in August 1942 by *Cross Creek Cookery*.

By this time Rawlings had arrived as a writer, but her accomplishments were not without cost. Her marriage to Charles Rawlings had ended in divorce in 1933, largely as a consequence of her success and independence. By 1941 she was ready to try matrimony again, marrying Norton Sanford Baskin, who managed the Castle Warden Hotel in St. Augustine. This marriage survived because each partner had a separate career. The next personal challenge came in 1943, when Zelma Cason, whom Rawlings had met on her very first visit to Florida and who had introduced her to the Florida backwoods, filed a $100,000 libel suit against Rawlings. Cason felt that her portrait in *Cross Creek* was maliciously uncomplimentary. In the next four years this case went through several reversals in the Florida courts. First, the state Supreme Court ruled that the case would have merit as invasion of privacy, not libel. Then in a circuit court trial in 1946, Rawlings won—only to have Cason appeal to the state Supreme Court. In May 1947 the lower court ruling was reversed, but damages of only one dollar and payments of costs were stipulated. Rawlings counted this as a moral victory.

Offsetting this adversity, she had seen *The Yearling* appear in 1946 on the screen with Gregory Peck and Jane Wyman as Jody Baxter's parents and an unknown youth, Claude Jarman, Jr., in the role of Jody. The movie, while altering the novel's sense of Jody's parents, was nevertheless a box office success. Meanwhile, Rawlings continued to write fiction, but only with fair success. *The Sojourner* (1953) was the result of ten years of effort. This novel, chronicling three generations of the Linden family, was based on her maternal grandfather's farming background. The setting was upstate New York, to which Rawlings moved in 1947 to understand better the land that would be featured in *The Sojourner*. Rawlings also published *Mountain Prelude*, which was serialized in the *Saturday Evening Post* in 1947, but this story did not arouse her enthusiasm, and it has scant literary merit.

The Sojourner appeared to mixed reviews, but was a Literary Guild selection, clearly indicating that Rawlings was still held in high regard by the publishing community in the third decade of her career. The book is ambitious, an effort to break from the cast of regionalism and adolescent fiction, categories to which Rawlings was frequently assigned, and its sense of despair and frustration pervades. Rawlings envisioned the book as a capstone achievement for her life's work, but even though the book has had many readers who remember it well, it seems excessive and indulgent, as if the writer tried too hard to make the story significant. At the close of her life, Rawlings had slipped back into the extravagance of her youthful days as a writer, and her death on 14 December 1953 made one more circle complete.

MAJOR THEMES

The thematic concerns of Marjorie Kinnan Rawlings are best approached through *Cross Creek*, which was reintroduced to the American public in a 1983 movie starring Mary Steenburgen in the role of Rawlings. In *Cross Creek* it is easy to discern Rawlings's preoccupation with the land. People who take their sustenance directly from the land have special significance for her; they may not all be virtuous, but most seem to possess a fundamental decency. *Cross Creek* also indicates that Rawlings was in awe of nature. She understood human fragility in the context of forces of nature; every season has both its beauty and its challenge. In the chapter on "Winter," Rawlings details the threat of cold to the fruit that represents economic survival; the metaphor used to convey the gravity of the struggle is that of war, and a woman—Rawlings herself—takes the role of general. She seems determined to show, through an account of her own experience, that essential decisions in the struggle for existence can be made equally well by women. Throughout *Cross Creek* Rawlings assumes the guise of a prototypical feminist, but because she makes her case with subtlety, her feminism has not been widely recognized.

Her autobiography is carefully crafted, with signals throughout that it is to be read as part of a specific literary tradition. When she declares in the first chapter, "We need above all, I think, a certain remoteness from urban confusion . . ." (3), we are meant to hear echoes of Thoreau's *Walden*, especially "Where I Lived and What I Lived For." In fact, *Walden* serves as an appropriate model for the whole text, though Rawlings's act of self-isolation still allows for many lively interpersonal encounters, certainly more than in Thoreau's case.

Rawlings also drew upon Genesis to assert the primacy of the earth, declaring:

We were bred of earth before we were born of our mothers. Once born, we can live
without mother or father, or any other kin, or any friend, or any human love. We cannot
live without the earth or apart from it, and something is shrivelled in a man's heart when
he turns away from it and concerns himself only with the affairs of men. (3)

These sentiments shape all of Rawling's fiction of the South. She proved to be
as much a conservative in spirit as any of the contributors to the 1930 Agrarian
manifesto *I'll Take My Stand*.

In the chapter "Hyacinth Drift" of *Cross Creek*, Rawlings aligned herself
with another critic of civilized life, Mark Twain. When Rawlings found her life
turning nightmarish, she needed a solution, and that solution came in the form
of a long trip down the St. John's River on its obscure route through marshes
and lakes toward entry into the Atlantic near the Georgia-Florida border. Her
companion was another woman, so Rawlings gives a feminist twist to the adventures Mark Twain had shaped around river rafting and steamboating for his
male protagonists—including himself, as a youth, in *Life on the Mississippi*.
Soon the women are lost in a maze of channels. Map and compass, the man-
made instruments of navigation, prove to be no help. Instead, they find they
must learn to read the signs of nature. They discover that by watching the floating
hyacinths they can catch hints of the river's current. Rawlings concludes:

It was very simple. Like all simple facts, it was necessary to discover it for oneself. We
had, in a moment, the feel of the river; a wisdom for its vagaries. When the current took
us away that morning, we gave ourselves over to it. There was a tremendous exhilaration,
an abandoning of fear. (347)

For every major character in Rawlings's fiction, the greatest challenge is to
discern some true sense of the river of life—and to accept it on its own terms.
Ironically, freedom is found in this acceptance, and so is peace.

Cross Creek concludes with a meditation on land ownership. Rawlings emphasizes the transitory nature of human life. People struggle through their al-
lotment of days, endure best by being responsive to the land, and then leave the
land to others:

But we are tenants and not possessors, lovers and not masters. Cross Creek belongs to
the wind and the rain, to the sun and the seasons, to the cosmic secrecy of seed, and
beyond all, to time. (368)

The structure of Rawlings's narratives is episodic, with set-piece scenes strung
together to make a skein of life. Although the emotional life of her characters
is sometimes given with maudlin sentimentality and the psychological battles of
her people may sometimes seem paramount, it is always the place, the land,
that binds everything together. Her fiction is ultimately a study in how we must
accommodate ourselves in reverence to the world that will survive us.

Jacob's Ladder turns on this point, but it also concerns survival of love between a man and a woman. The story begins with a problem: a young woman, Florry Leddy, falls in love with another "rabbity" youth, Mart, and because Florry's father is abusive to her and determined that she spend her days serving him, the young couple flees. Together they move from one place to another, trying a succession of jobs (working on a Yankee's orange grove, lake fishing, fishing in the Gulf of Mexico, moonshining, trapping in the Palmetto scrub), but each effort fails, and they are inexorably brought closer and closer to doom. At each waystop they try to extend the resources of their love to something else (a pet pig on one occasion, a racoon on another), and during the lake fishing period, they have a child. Their hardships are enormous, and each attachment of the heart ends in heartbreak: the pets have to be abandoned, and the child dies in infancy. The pathos attending these losses is overbearing, and in many ways, this Rawlings story is more akin to the sentimental fiction of the nineteenth century than to the naturalistic realism of so much modern writing. The couple's odyssey ends on a positive note, however. Having reached a nadir of suffering, Florry and Mart determine to return to the region of their origins. Despite the grave threat of a hurricane, they succeed in returning home, and it seems that this home will be a sanctuary for their love. *Jacob's Ladder* schematically represents the absolute need to honor one's roots. Flight from one's heritage is pointless, perhaps even lethal.

"Gal Young Un" similarly comments on rootlessness. Once again love is put in a crucible, and the limits of loving are discovered in this story. Mattie Styles, a confident and independent widow, falls prey to the amorous advances of a worthless man about town, Trax Colton. She marries him and accepts him into her country home. Yet the man remains a wandering scoundrel, leaving often to peddle the product of the moonshining operation he has established on Mattie's property, violating her respect for the land. Eventually he becomes brazen enough to bring home a young girl to serve as his mistress. Mattie grows increasingly uncomfortable with her husband's abuses, and at the conclusion of the story, she obliterates her husband's still, his car, and his romantic claim on her. But even as she icily sends him on his way, she opens her heart to the wastrel girl. This particular narrative establishes a firm place for Rawlings in the canon of American feminist literature. Mattie proves a woman can be both independent and loving.

The pain that comes with love is given even deeper and finer consideration in *The Yearling*. The narrative centers on the maturation of a youth, Jody Baxter. In contrast to more recent explorations of the trauma of adolescence (*The Catcher in the Rye; Goodbye, Columbus*; several of Judy Blume's novels), Rawlings did not feel obligated to focus on sexual experiences. She was not skittish about sex, as her other books confirm, but she chose to present Jody's coming to terms with adult reality in other contexts. Her choice seems delightfully old-fashioned, and *The Yearling* seems light-years from the 1980s regarding the pervasiveness of sex as an anchor for literary seriousness.

Jody moves from childhood innocence to adulthood by surviving emotional hardship. He is the only child of Penny and Ora Baxter, who have been sorely tested by the loss of many children in childbirth or infancy. To Jody's need for affection, Penny responds generously, often at his own expense, for he depends on Jody to help in the work of farming and hunting. Yet Jody needs more, and since his mother does not readily show affection, he strikes up a friendship with another youth who is similarly sensitive toward the world of nature. Fodderwing Forrester, however, does not live long; a cripple, he is poorly suited to the rigors of life in the backwoods. His family is meant to represent the coarser strains of humanity often found among the Florida Crackers. By the time Fodderwing dies, Jody has convinced his family to let him adopt a fawn that has lost its mother in a hunt. Jody's fancy is that the fawn can become part of his world, on the family's terms. Of course, that is not possible. Jody finally learns that animals from the wild must live on their own terms, and those terms are fundamentally incompatible with the order necessary for successful cultivation of the land.

Penny Baxter is a determined romantic, willing to place his yearning for independence and closeness to nature above convenience. His determination, often not appreciated by his wife, is successfully conveyed to Jody. Penny and his son have several sublime moments together, often as they are engaged in the ritual of a hunt. One such hunt, for a marauder bear, Old Slewfoot, compares favorably with the initiation theme that Faulkner built into "The Bear" section of *Go Down, Moses*. Rawlings had previously spotlighted the spiritual union of modern man with his darkest origins by portraying Lant Jacklin's hunting prowess in *South Moon Under*. Lant has an instinctive feel for nature—and a strong instinct for survival, as shown in the kill-or-be-killed confrontation between Lant and his nemesis Cleve near the end of the story—and this is reflected in Lant's skill as a reader of signs. Here, Rawlings's efforts correlate well with the extended lore of the hunt in American culture, ranging from Cooper's Leatherstocking to the character Mike in Michael Cimino's movie *The Deer Hunter*.

For Jody Baxter, it is an ingrained respect for his father and the resources of nature that brings him back home after a climactic flight from the tormenting anguish that comes when he is obligated to kill his yearling deer, Flag. Jody returns to be his father's understudy, but now more a man than a boy.

The resolution of suffering for Ase Linden in *The Sojourner* is considerably more muted. Ase is the second son of Amelia Linden, born after she has come to hate her husband. As a consequence, all her love is bestowed on her firstborn, Benjamin. Ase is rejected, and throughout the story he is subject to constant humiliation and pain by his mother, even though he remains at home to care for the family farm and his mother. Ase marries Ben's sweetheart when Ben heads west to find his fortune—a quest that is fruitless. As the years pass, Ase demonstrates unbelievable tolerance toward his mother. Meanwhile, her malevolent influence extends to all his children, making horrible materialists out of most of them, but also destroying his beloved daughter Doll, whose death by freezing is caused by Amelia.

Amelia's will conveys to Ben title to the family homestead. Ase realizes that none of his children will honor the traditional use of the land for farming—that they will yield to the temptation of commercial development—and his final achievement comes when he convinces his dying brother to sign over the title of the land to a tenant family that has worked on the farm for years. Rawlings strove in this last work to affirm the primacy of the land, even when there is great cost attached. Ase dies while ascending heavenward in a plane. His final rest is guaranteed to be peaceful, a clear reward for his steadfastness.

SURVEY OF CRITICISM

Studies of Rawlings's work are few. But she has been served well by those who have read her thoroughly. Aside from reviews, Rawlings was not subjected to much scrutiny until after her death. The first major study, Gordon E. Bigelow's *Frontier Eden: The Literary Career of Marjorie Kinnan Rawlings* (1966), did much to rectify this neglect. Bigelow carefully consulted the large University of Florida collection of Rawlings correspondence and papers, and he talked with many people who had known her. He articulates well Rawlings's stance in the American tradition of seeing the frontier as a symbolic Eden where the quality of innocence is tested again and again. Moreover, his comments on her relationship with other writers of her time (Hemingway, Fitzgerald, Frost, Wolfe, Cabell, Glasgow, Hurston) are useful. With Laura V. Monti, Bigelow has more recently edited the *Selected Letters of Marjorie Kinnan Rawlings* (1983), which should stimulate productive new considerations of her work.

The only other comprehensive survey, Samuel I. Bellman's *Marjorie Kinnan Rawlings* (1974) in the Twayne series, complements Bigelow's analysis with a discussion of the psychological forces at work in her fiction as a consequence of the fact that she did not have children, a thesis that works best in relationship to *The Yearling*. Bellman also finds existential qualities in Rawlings's fiction, but this philosophical reading raises more questions than it answers.

Several shorter studies have been fruitful in clarifying the nature and range of Rawlings's writing. Because Rawlings wrestled with the problem of how to represent backwoods talk in a book for a national audience, M. H. Figh's "Folklore and Folk Speech in the Works of Marjorie Kinnan Rawlings" (1947) is valuable. The symbolic tendencies in Rawlings's fiction, particularly in connection with the meaning of rivers, have been illuminated in two essays within the last decade: Lamar York's "Marjorie Kinnan Rawlings's Rivers" and John Cech's "Marjorie Kinnan Rawlings' *The Secret River*: A Fairy Tale, A Place, A Life." Given Rawlings's stature as a writer of fiction about the passage from childhood to adulthood, Jean Kelty includes her in a general discussion about "The Cult of the Kill in Adolescent Fiction."

Still, much about Rawlings's writing remains unexamined. Little attention has been paid to the structural qualities of her fiction, and surprisingly, the feminist issues in her work have not been studied. There is clearly more to be discovered about Marjorie Kinnan Rawlings.

BIBLIOGRAPHY

Works by Marjorie Kinnan Rawlings

South Moon Under. New York: Charles Scribner's Sons, 1933.

Golden Apples. New York: Charles Scribner's Sons, 1935.

The Yearling. New York: Charles Scribner's Sons, 1938.

When the Whippoorwill. New York: Charles Scribner's Sons, 1940.

Cross Creek. New York: Charles Scribner's Sons, 1942.

Cross Creek Cookery. New York: Charles Scribner's Sons, 1942.

Jacob's Ladder. Miami: University of Florida Press, 1950; previously published in *Scrib-*
     ner's 89 (April 1931), 351–66, 446–64, and in *When the Whippoorwill*.

The Sojourner. New York: Charles Scribner's Sons, 1953.

The Secret River. New York: Charles Scribner's Sons, 1955.

Selected Letters of Marjorie Kinnan Rawlings, Ed. Gordon E. Bigelow and Laura V.
     Monti. Gainesville: University of Florida Press, 1983.

Studies of Marjorie Kinnan Rawlings

Bellman, Samuel I. *Marjorie Kinnan Rawlings*. New York: Twayne, 1974.

———. "Marjorie Kinnan Rawlings: A Solitary Sojourner in the Florida Backwoods."
     Kansas Quarterly 2 (Spring 1970): 78–87.

———. "Writing Literature for Young People: Marjorie Kinnan Rawlings' 'Secret River'
     of the Imagination." *Costerus* 9 (1981): 19–27.

Bigelow, Gordon E. *Frontier Eden: The Literary Career of Marjorie Kinnan Rawlings*.
     Gainesville: University of Florida Press, 1966.

———. "Marjorie Kinnan Rawlings' Wilderness." *Sewanee Review* 73 (Spring 1965):
     299–310.

———, ed. "Marjorie Kinnan Rawlings' 'Lord Bill of the Suwanee River.' " *Southern
     Folklore Quarterly* 27 (1963): 113–31.

Cech, John. "Marjorie Kinnan Rawlings' *The Secret River*: A Fairy Tale, A Place, A
     Life." *Southern Studies* 19 (1980): 29–38.

Figh, M. H. "Folklore and Folk Speech in the Works of Marjorie Kinnan Rawlings."
     Southern Folklore Quarterly 11 (September 1947): 201–09.

Kelty, Jean. "The Cult of the Kill in Adolescent Fiction." *English Journal* 64 (February
     1975): 56–61.

York, Lamar. "Marjorie Kinnan Rawlings's Rivers." *Southern Literary Journal* 9 (Spring
     1977): 91–107.

—————— WILLIAM H. SLAVICK ——————

Elizabeth Madox Roberts
(1881–1941)

Ford Madox Ford, speaking in 1935 of Southern writing, observed: "With Miss Roberts the whole complexion of your literature changed; the local became the universal." Earlier, he had called *The Time of Man* (1926) "the most beautiful individual piece of writing that has yet come out of America," a judgment shared by Yvor Winters, "almost" by Hart Crane. Upon reading that novel, Sherwood Anderson wrote her, "No one in America is doing such writing."

But with the allegorical *He Sent Forth a Raven* (1935), which appeared in the middle of the Depression, her audience drifted away and by her death six years later had all but disappeared. Despite the frequent reappearances of *The Time of Man* and new editions of other of her works, the general forgetting of Elizabeth Madox Roberts, save by a coterie of Southern academics, ranks next to the half-century forgetting of Herman Melville as the most notable lapse of literary memory on the American scene. For those who have remembered, her achievement continues to rank high: on the occasion of the Roberts Centenary in 1981, Robert Penn Warren called *The Time of Man* a "masterpiece." Lewis P. Simpson counts her among those—Faulkner, Warren, Welty, Porter, Lytle, and Wolfe—who attempt "to arrest the disintegration of memory and history" through a search for "images of existence which will express the truth that man's essential nature lies in his possession of the moral community of memory and history."

BIOGRAPHY

Elizabeth Madox Roberts was born in Perryville, Kentucky, 30 October 1881, to Simpson and Mary Brent Roberts. After coming over Boone's Trace, her maternal forebears settled at Blue Spring Cove in Hart County, then in Three Springs. Her maternal grandfather had served in the Union army. After seeing his father cut down by Union recruiters, Roberts's father at age sixteen had joined Bragg's Army. In 1868 he was graduated from Eminence College in Henry County.

The growing Roberts family soon moved from Perryville to Willisburg, where her parents taught, finally to Springfield, seat of Washington County, a sleepy town of 1,000. Her father ran a store, surveyed and engineered for the railroad, and farmed. Elizabeth was a quiet child in a family of five brothers and a sister. She imagined a family about which she and her siblings made up stories and heard stories of Greece and Troy from her father and of pioneer days from a grandmother. Her frailty, sensitivity, and interest in literature appear to have won her special consideration in her family.

After attending Covington Institute in Springfield, she went to high school in Covington, a town of 42,000 across the Ohio from Cincinnati, living with her Grandmother Brent. Then she taught intermittently over the next ten years, first in Springfield, where the folklorist Stith Thompson was a colleague, then in one-or two-room schools in nearby Mooresville-Maud and Pleasant Grove, where she met the rural folk she portrays in *The Time of Man*. But teaching overtaxed her; she gave up teaching school for long walks, buggy rides, and music (she gave lessons). Apparently anemic, in 1910 she was discovered to have tuberculosis and went west, staying with her brother Charles in Lakespur in the Pike's Peak region of Colorado or in California. In 1915 her first book was published, *In the Great Steep's Garden*, a small volume of seven poems about Rocky Mountain flowers. "But that other country is mine," she wrote, and later she spoke of returning to Kentucky "with a rush that carried me deep and deep."

Elizabeth had been admitted to the University of Kentucky in 1900 but apparently never attended; she had sat in on classes there and at Colorado College— with little satisfaction. Finally, at age thirty-five, in December 1916 she began the spring term at the University of Chicago on a scholarship. Soon she was a central figure in the Poetry Club, a small group of serious students half her age, and made lifelong friendships with Yvor Winters, Janet Lewis, Glenway Wescott, Maurice Lesemann, Monroe Wheeler, Gladys Campbell, and Pearl Andelson Sherry. Through Wescott and Winters, she encountered the work of Yeats, Pound, Eliot, Stevens, H. D., and Williams.

In her classes, Roberts began writing memories; in her summer letters to her friends she discussed the "Little Country" that foreshadowed her first novel, already gestating in her imagination. Then, suddenly, came a succession of "child poems," as she called them, beginning with "The Butterbean Tent," that comprised *Under the Tree*, published by B. W. Huebsch in 1922, a year after her graduation with a B.A. in philosophy.

Back in Springfield, Elizabeth missed her college friends, but she was soon at work on *The Time of Man* (1926). By 1923 her sister, Lel, was married and far away; her brothers were dispersed; and her sense of isolation and lack of appreciation in Springfield, coupled with severe headaches, had virtually stalled work on the novel. Recognizing her situation, Winters and Janet Lewis collected a fund from her friends to allow her to spend the late fall at Riggs Foundation in Stockbridge, Massachusetts. It was probably here that she developed considerable familiarity with modern psychology. Stockbridge may well have saved *The Time of Man*, which quickly won her notice as a Book-of-the-Month Club selection; it also initiated several years of relatively good health, during which she completed *My Heart and My Flesh* (1927), the fantasy-satire *Jingling in the Wind* (1928), and *The Great Meadow* (1930), along with several short stories, including the 1930 O. Henry second-prize selection, "The Sacrifice of the Maidens," and the idyll, *A Buried Treasure* (1931).

Returning to Springfield after she finished *The Great Meadow*, she built a large brick two-story wing on the family home on upper Walnut Street, to which the family had moved in 1904, and named it Elenores. But even with central heating, she found cold weather painful and regularly wintered in Orlando, Florida. Occasionally, she went to New York; sometimes she stayed in Louisville.

In 1932 *The Haunted Mirror* was published. *He Sent Forth a Raven*, a World War I period story in which the forces of pride, faith, rationalism, and collectivism contend, followed in 1935. B. W. Huebsch justified its publication on grounds of loyalty; Eleanor Clark found the characters argument racks.

By then Roberts's health was an increasing preoccupation—she carried drinking water with her and sunbathed as a cure-all. A throat disorder required an operation she found traumatic. In 1936 her skin condition and anemia turned into Hodgkins disease, which gradually enveloped the lymph glands.

Now the awards came—honorary degrees and membership in the National Academy of Arts and Letters. The completion of *Black Is My Truelove's Hair* in 1938, the story of a young woman's restoration of life and respect after a brief affair and encounter with death, exhausted her. Thereafter, she worked intermittently at an epic novel about the 1937 Louisville flood and published a volume of poems, *Song in the Meadow* (1940), and a second collection of stories, *Not by Strange Gods*, which appeared just after her death. During the late 1930s her books netted her virtually no royalties.

On 13 March 1941, in Orlando, she died. An obituary observed that critical and commercial success had eluded her, but in fact, by 1930 she had won a solid reputation and achieved financial security.

MAJOR THEMES

Beginning with the poems of *Under the Tree*, in which the title poem recounts the effort of the child, standing on the hill and looking down at her backyard, to see "how it looks when I am there," Elizabeth Roberts's work seeks to understand "how it is" and to discover a meaningful order in that experience. In these poems, she catches the child's momentary mood, orders that perception, and utters it in the natural rhythms of the child. "The little girl, myself, the 'I' of the verses," discovering order and mystery, is a forerunner of the older central consciousnesses in the novels to come. The novels represent Roberts's determination, as she began *Time of Man*, to "order the chaos about me and the apparent chaos that is myself." The existentialist search for identity is her central theme: an expanding consciousness ("Life is from within," she wrote) leads to a recognition of the order and mystery of existence, psychic individuation, and completion in love.

For her the journey was uncertain because reality did not exist until properly perceived by the mind; this was one way of explaining the working of consciousness. But her aim was clear:

Somewhere there is a connection between the world of the mind and the outer order— it is the secret of the contact that we are after, the point, the moment of union. We faintly sense the one and we know as faintly the other, but there is a point where they come together, and we can never know the whole of reality until we have these two completely.

Berkeley argued that the order the mind discovers is an apprehension of God, and Ellen Chesser's creation of her world in a Berkeleyan discovery of design in reality would give "evidence of an unseen power at work." But, Lewis Simpson argues convincingly, Roberts struggled with the modern replacement of a transcendent community by the rational imagination's awareness of history as "the reference for human imagination of the truth of existence"—in her fiction, a struggle between "the act of thought that was, and is, Kentucky" and the consciousness of her heroine who would transcend history.

The first pages of *The Time of Man* reveal that Roberts would meet that challenge as a Modernist, employing the mythic method—using symbolism and mythology to order experience and to shape an inner, psychic journey to rebirth, transformation, and a harmonious existence. Everywhere there are extraordinary correspondences between man and nature, mind and landscape. Ellen Chesser is the first in a series of feminine "cerebro-sensual interpretations or interpreters" at the center of the story who descends into the depths of the soul to find wholeness and a mystical sense of oneness with life. Throughout the novel, there is a complex interweaving and repetition of images, motifs, and experience characteristic of Modernism. Like Yeats, Pound, Eliot, and Joyce, Roberts creates her world, a style, and a voice that allow her to discover an order in the chaos. "Poetic realism," she called it—reality, the perception of the truth of things, heightened by poetry.

In *The Time of Man*, Roberts presents "the sweet soil . . . and white sun mystically braided in life form, all life, which is Ellen." She would, she once explained, "bring the physical world close to the mind so the mind rushes out to the edge of sense, like Emily Dickinson." So Ellen's journey is in large part discovery of the myriad symbolic correspondences of man and nature. Out of the rite of farming, folk wisdom and speech, and Ellen's imaginative experiences of nature, Roberts fashions a symbolic harmony. "A white clover of thought" passes through Ellen's mind; emotions find physical reflections. She discovers in nature "those structures which seemed everlasting and undiminished within herself." The rocks she wonders about are emblems of the time of man but also of Ellen's time, of the order she sees in the autumn equinox and the monks' routine and the mysteries she and Jasper acknowledge humbly with an exclamation, "God knows."

Roberts saw "the wandering tenant farmer" of the region as "offering a symbol for an Odyssey of man as a wanderer buffeted about by the fates and weathers." As that representative wanderer, Ellen is a Demeter-Persephone figure, pastoral, close to the earth, aware of its mystery and sacredness and communing with it, often a solitary, lonely wanderer, immersed in the cycles of sowing and harvesting, birth and death, strongly maternal, even a matriarch.

That journey is also the unique story of Ellen Chesser Kent's personal progress to what Jung calls integration of personality, the radiance in harmony with life that Luke Wimble recognizes in repeating, "She's got the honey of life in her heart." Ellen journeys from self-identification and capture of the physical world to an experience of pain, evil, and rejection that leads to a withdrawal from society and self, and then to a "flowering out of stone" that reveals the strength and harmony she has found in life, and to the generosity of love—of life, the physical world, Jasper, and her children. It is "necessary love for the self to live," Earl H. Rovit observes. "Life and herself, one, comprehensible and entire," she realized, and "a sense of happiness surged over her."

"I tried to achieve a form in which the uses of poetry and prose were identical," Roberts wrote afterward. She describes *The Time of Man* as "a symphony brought into words." The highly individualized prose style she developed to serve Ellen's reflective expressions of "the points where poetry touches life" is marked by an "agreeable monotony," which critics see accomplished by rising and falling sentence rhythms, repetition of sentence patterns, word and phrase repetition, piled-up *and*'s and compound sentences, frequent use of the "would" tense, and a falling-away phrasing that creates rhythms close to verse. She, too, had learned much from Pound about poetic composition. And like J. M. Synge, who found in Anglo-Irish speech a rich resource, Roberts fashioned a language to serve her purposes out of her knowledge of medieval, Elizabethan, and frontier speech, "strong old utterance," and often ungrammatical colloquialisms caught by her perfect ear. The poetry is lyrical; her objective was a language "as being some essence from the roots of life." Ellen incarnates the highest virtues of her land in the epic struggle of Henry Chesser's phrase, "the time of man." But the folk song she lives is not "Bangum rode to the boar's den," which she once thought real; it is one reflecting the common experience of man—"But now I know better how the world is, a little"—as she renews her hope for "a strong house that the wind couldn't shake and the rain couldn't beat into."

The marks of Roberts's prose style and this "striving backward" toward dignity and peace are on all the fiction that followed. *The Time of Man* had come out of the "little country" surrounding Springfield. *My Heart and My Flesh* (1927) came out of the artist's struggle to find herself. She began it in 1923, the year of her sojourn to Stockbridge. Theodosia Bell's dark and even more lonely journey is from aristocratic innocence and a disturbing emptiness through a series of deprivations into the nightmare fears of her unconscious, to near death at Aunt Doe's, and then to rebirth. The account of her travail prompts comparisons of this novel with Faulkner and Dostoevsky, and Winters's claim that, like Melville, she "possibly comes closer to involving the whole consciousness than does the more perfect . . . Henry James." The series of unworthy suitors, her father's incestuous interest, and her mulatto siblings' sexuality and violence support Simpson's reading of Theodosia's artistic handicap as emblematic of the "deformation of Theodosia's consciousness by the crude sexuality of the demythologized historical society in which she strives for her identity as an artist."

Roberts wrote of Theodosia's "rebirth in union with the simple and uncomplicated earth." Theodosia desperately wants the fullness of life, and the book teems with life until she reaches the nadir of her fortunes. But it falters in realizing her transformation: contemplating suicide, she reaches for a word to which she can hold—"tomorrow" is a substitute for it. Then she recognized "pride in life and joy"—Simpson calls it an orgasmic spiritual ecstasy—and the next thing we know her fear is gone and she is an Aphrodite fertility goddess figure capable of love and of union with Caleb, nature, and the community.

While writing her first two novels, Roberts was also at work on *Jingling in the Wind* (1928), "a sort of relief or recreation." Jeremy, a rainmaker, is, in his pride, closed to love, and his beloved, Tulip Tree McAfee, is immersed in the cultural confusion and decadence of the city. The satire that follows through Jeremy's frustrations and a series of Chaucerian tales is good-natured, but it reflects Roberts's profound concern about the historical discontinuity of the age, the growing commercial spirit, the corruption of the human spirit, and the inadequacy of Christianity, which she found to be a "treeless, barren waste" in her region, to meet these challenges. Finally, love prevails, if as a ghost in the modern heart.

As a prologue to *My Heart and My Flesh*, Roberts had introduced an archetypal city and Luce, whose need to discover the sources of life would occasion a series of novels spanning Kentucky's history. With *The Great Meadow*, Roberts continued—and abandoned—her plan. Diony Jarvis, in Albemarle, utters a Berkeleyan wish: "Oh, to create rivers by knowing rivers, to move outward through the extended infinite plane until it assumed roundness. Oh, to make a world out of chaos." The westward journey is for her, then, a journey of her mind ever inward. Like Ellen, her sensibility and imagination lead to the identification of inner and outer worlds. Her marriage to Berk Jarvis, the Boone type, joins his physical power to her domestic power, "lateral" and "enduring"—civilizing. As Jo Reinhard Smith demonstrates, it is the epic journey of Aeneas to establish an old culture in a new land.

Later, in Berk's absence, Diony feels lost, allied in some mysterious way "to the distant crying of wild turkeys." Her "sense of the hostility of the forest life, of the horror of the indefiniteness of the outside earth," brings her to see "another way of knowing" than Berkeley's, which she can define only as mystery. Her choice of Berk over Muir when Berk returns after her remarriage reflects godly power, like that of her Greek namesake, Dione, but Diony is modest. In the end, her weaving a metaphor for the order she would make, she finds "a little harmony which men are able to make with one another or with a few kinds."

In *A Buried Treasure*, a kettle of gold coins Andy and Philly Blair find leads to the emergence of Andy's individuality and Philly's awareness of herself "as being lovely both without and within"—and to their recognition of the treasure of love they have amassed. The shadowy figure, Ben Shepherd, come to the community to learn of his family's past and so of himself, is a figure of the past witnessing the human comedy. The idyll ends in a midsummer night ring dance: drawn by the power of sex and love, in harmony with the rhythms of the earth, "The great wheel turned, making ready a world, a world of mankind living all together. . . . "

In *He Sent Forth a Raven* (1935) Roberts offers a World War I fragment of what would have been another part of the Book of Luce. Stoner Drake's blasphemous vow that he will "never set foot on earth again while time lasts" unleashes a torturous conflict in which Drake, who takes fate as a personal affront, and a mechanistic carpenter, Sol Dickon, are arrayed against Jonnie Briggs, who preaches the inevitability of the seasons and the wrath of God, and Logan Treer, the young visionary and life force who preaches the collective man. The disorder represented by the war crowds in upon Wolflick. The raven of the title is the dauntless spirit of man trying to go it alone—the Ahab-like Drake, worn out by hatred; his niece Jocelle; and also Treer. After being raped, Jocelle, like Persephone, finds life again, among her hens, in what appears to be a middle way of "communal sharing" and in "the lonely will . . . to believe . . . to divide hate from love . . . to love God the Creator."

"Dena's story is the story of Man—not me—as are all my stories," Roberts wrote of *Black Is My Truelove's Hair*. But into it is woven as well her struggle with death and resignation to it. Death appears in Will Langtry, an empty, rootless man with whom Dena has eloped and who would possess and use her. The Glen, a Catholic community, is the Edenic scene of her sin and return to grace. Nat Journeyman, the orchardist, is the ambiguous power of nature and love. Cam Elliott figures nature, life, and love. Dena herself is an Everyman claiming a right to life, and in time, the sun, and through confession and true love she is reborn. The lost thimble of purity becomes, in her rebirth, the grail Sir Galahad recovers.

Although Roberts spoke of the short story as an "unsatisfactory form" and doubted that anything "very good can be done with it," many of the stories in her two volumes demonstrate a mastery of what Eudora Welty calls "the lyrical impulse"—the orderly realization of a substantial world through the magic and mystery of language. Leon V. Driskell has shown how "Love by the Highway" manifests what Welty calls "beauty of order imposed." "The Haunted Palace" has a unique place in Roberts's work as a reverse image of the harmony with nature and affirmation of the novels: Hubert and Jess befoul a mansion in a will to destroy what lacks utility; Jess is herself the haunted palace. "Death in Bearwallow," Dave Nally's reflections on an earlier wake while at another, traces the growth in spiritual awareness that marks several stories. Roberts's gift for realizing place is found throughout the stories, but often her artifice is conspicuous, and her achievements in the form are modest beside her novels.

Roberts always saw herself as a poet, but her plans to publish another or several further volumes of poems after *Under the Tree* did not materialize until *Song in the Meadow* appeared in 1940—a collection ranging from child poems to love songs, ballads, poems about folk-tale figures and her fictional heroines, to a Hopkinsesque celebration and several philosophical and contemplative poems. Many rise out of Kentucky experience—a feeling and a scene that express what Paul Goodman called a "happy love." A small collection of 38 previously unpublished poems, including several "butterbeans," *I Touched White Clover*, appeared in 1981.

The Roberts canon is completed by her unpublished papers and over 500 extant letters, many beautiful accounts of life in the "little country" or incisive discussions of her work, which are now being edited for publication.

SURVEY OF CRITICISM

With three book club selections early in her career, Elizabeth Madox Roberts's work did not want for the attention of reviewers. Even *Under the Tree* received good notices, including perceptive assessments by Yvor Winters, Maurice Lesemann, and, later, William Jay Smith.

During her lifetime several journal evaluations appeared. Wescott provided a "Personal Note." J. Donald Adams compared her work favorably with that of Glasgow, Cather, Woolf, Dostoevsky, and Hemingway. In a long essay, F. Lamar Janney contrasts the affirmation of Roberts's spiritual vision learned from life and the scientific reductions of Bertrand Russell and Joseph Wood Krutch echoed in the sense of futility in Millay, Jeffers, and Dreiser. Mark Van Doren discusses the special "substance" of her prose style in relation to her heroines' minds. Donald Davidson's notice of "how people are extensions of things" and vice versa in *A Buried Treasure* reflects the usefulnes of his insights regarding all of her fiction. Alexander M. Buchan distinguishes the various techniques Roberts employs to make "narrative poems" marked by a "sharp difference in almost every phrase, and for a purpose" and requiring the kind of rigorous attention poetry commands.

The first dissertation, by Andrew Beeler, appeared a year before Elizabeth Roberts's death. Critical monographs by Lucy Young Fisk, Edward F. Foster, and William Slavick followed a decade later. The most valuable of the earlier academic work is Woodridge Spears's 1953 dissertation, "Elizabeth Madox

Roberts: A Biographical and Critical Study,'' particularly for its examination of her growth as a literary artist.

The explosion of criticism in America in the 1950s brought new attention to her work, beginning with Edward Wagenknecht's judicious reevaluation in *Cavalcade of the American Novel*, which balances high praise with questions about narrative method and style. Three book-length studies followed. The first, *Elizabeth Madox Roberts: American Novelist* by Harry Modean Campbell and Ruel E. Foster (1956), includes a substantial biography and many citations of Roberts's comments and notes on her art; it associates her work with much of the current critical and literary scene, occasionally awkwardly but often provocatively. A more rigorous critical study, Earl H. Rovit's *Herald to Chaos: The Novels of Elizabeth Madox Roberts* (1960), emphasizes the symbolic and structural nature of her art, her contemporary themes, and her poetic style, and examines her portrayal of ''the epic consciousness of the American experience.'' Frederick P. W. McDowell's *Elizabeth Madox Roberts* (1963) is an especially useful study in its critical analysis, appreciation of the psychological dimensions of the fiction, examination of her style, and placement of her work in the Southern Renascence. All three studies rank her fiction high.

Probably more influential than these studies was Robert Penn Warren's introduction to *The Time of Man* (1963), first published in the *Saturday Review of Literature*. Warren sees Ellen's odyssey as a spiritual journey of ''the self toward the deep awareness of identity which means peace'' and ''inner victory''—a ''journey by which one may learn to convert the wound into wisdom.'' Warren identifies the special quality at the center of Ellen's consciousness as wonder and, beyond that, ''a sense of life as ceremony, as ritual,'' seen in the characters' telling and language. He notes ''the subtle way the language of the outer world is absorbed into the shadowy paraphrase of Ellen's awareness'' and the ''sober actuality of her language.''

Other studies from the 1960s include Willard Thorp's assessment and Louis Auchincloss's chapter in *Pioneers and Caretakers*. Auchincloss sees Roberts expressing the pioneer American tradition in epic terms without Glasgow's and Cather's solemn hymning to the land. Herman E. Spivey's essay alludes to handicaps greater than Roberts ''understood or was able to overcome.'' She lived, like Woolf, in ''an ambience of ideality''; her work lacked external action, subsidiary characters, and mastery of technical experiments.

Between 1969 and 1981 Roberts received little attention save by Ph.D. candidates. The most important study of this period is Christopher Hayes's 1978 dissertation examination of Roberts's mythic method. Her novels reveal the patterns of nature deeply embedded in the human psyche and reflected in the mythic consciousness ''that unites men with one another and unplumbed mystery.'' The search for order in her novels involves ''weaving a network of literary and mythic symbols (*mythos*) into an archetypal life-death-rebirth pattern (*epos*) which affords a controlling structure for the [life] of each heroine and for the narrative design of each novel" that "yields for the protagonist a pattern of rational values (*logos*)" and affords harmony and wholeness.

The 1981 Roberts Centenary occasioned a special Roberts number of the *Southern Review* (October 1984). The issue includes memoirs by Janet Lewis, Gladys Campbell, Maurice Lesemann, and Pearl Andelson Sherry, and a selection of letters (1919–20) to Janet Lewis. William Slavick's discussion of the papers and letters helps fill in some of the biographical holes. Victor A. Kramer's essay sees Roberts's journey to peace, living in and of the order of existence, as involving a dependence upon language that reveals "the essence of her consciousness as it became aware of itself," and a recognition that "the mystery of being—sharing or not sharing, giving and expending . . . is ultimately beyond language in the silence of contemplation."

The major product of the Centenary, however, is Lewis P. Simpson's seminal essay "The Sexuality of History." Simpson examines the implications of Berkeleyan subjectivity of history in Roberts's work and finds her burdened, like Faulkner, with the consciousness of history that stands between the self and society, nature, and God—with the "experience of a constant tension between the self and history." The mythic consciousness she creates is an act of mind, of the artist's self-consciousness, not a reflection of the transcendent order of things. Her major heroines are all surrogates, representing the mind of the artist as the crux of the relation between self and history. Ellen is "an earth goddess displaced in history," a "symbol of the isolation of the poetic self in history." Simpson sees the female spider that would eat its mate in *Jingling in the Wind* as reflecting feminine aggression against masculine will, the separation of mind and spirit, and possibly "the death of love." Throughout Roberts's work, the self-consciousness that is history comes between idea and action. The tension between the artist's and God's creation is a "struggle with history" in which she is the peer of Faulkner, Allen Tate, and Warren.

Simpson's essay, new editions, publication of the letters and papers, a Roberts newsletter, and discovery of her by feminist criticism, however tardily that comes, are likely to result in a substantial increase in the current renewal of interest.

BIBLIOGRAPHY

Works by Elizabeth Madox Roberts

In the Great Steep's Garden. Colorado Springs: Goudy-Simmons, 1915.

Under the Tree. New York: B. W. Huebsch, 1922. enl. ed. New York: Viking Press, 1930. With afterword by William H. Slavick. Lexington: University Press of Kentucky, 1985.

The Time of Man. New York: Viking Press, 1926. With Introduction by Robert Penn Warren, the Compass edition, 1962. With Introductions by William H. Slavick and Robert Penn Warren. Lexington: University Press of Kentucky, 1982.

My Heart and My Flesh. New York: Viking Press, 1927.
Jingling in the Wind. New York: Viking Press, 1928.
The Great Meadow. New York: Viking Press, 1930. With an Afterword by Willard
    Thorp. New York: New American Library, 1961.
A Buried Treasure. New York: Viking Press, 1931.
The Haunted Mirror. New York: Viking Press, 1932.
He Sent Forth A Raven. New York: Viking Press, 1935.
Black Is My Truelove's Hair. New York: Viking Press, 1938. With an Introduction by
    Elizabeth Hardwick. New York: Arno Press, 1977.
Song in the Meadow. New York: Viking Press, 1940.
Not by Strange Gods. New York: Viking Press, 1941.
I Touched White Clover. Ed. with essay, "The Poetry of Elizabeth Madox Roberts," by
    William H. Slavick. *Kentucky Poetry Review* 17 (Fall 1981).

Studies of Elizabeth Madox Roberts

Adams, J. Donald. "Elizabeth Madox Roberts." *Virginia Quarterly Review* 12 (January
    1936): 80–90.
Auchincloss, Louis. *Pioneers and Caretakers: A Study of Nine American Women Nov-
    elists*. Minneapolis: University of Minnesota Press, 1965.
Buchan, Alexander M. "Elizabeth Madox Roberts." *Southwest Review* 25 (July 1940):
    463–81.
Campbell, Harry Modean and Ruel E. Foster. *Elizabeth Madox Roberts: American Nov-
    elist*. Norman: University of Oklahoma Press, 1956.
Davidson, Donald. "Analysis of Elizabeth Madox Roberts' *A Buried Treasure*." *Creative
    Reading* 6 (December 1931): 1235–49.
Janney, F. Lamar. "Elizabeth Madox Roberts." *Sewanee Review* 45 (October-December
    1937): 388–410.
Kramer, Victor A. "Through Language to Self: Ellen's Journey in *The Time of Man*."
    Southern Review 20 (Fall 1984): 774–84.
McDowell, Frederick P. W. *Elizabeth Madox Roberts*. New York: Twayne, 1963.
Rovit, Earl H. *Herald to Chaos: The Novels of Elizabeth Madox Roberts*. Lexington:
    University of Kentucky Press, 1960.
———. "Recurrent Symbols in the Novels of Elizabeth Madox Roberts." *Boston Uni-
    versity Studies in English* 2 (Spring 1956): 36–54.
Simpson, Lewis P. "The Sexuality of History." *Southern Review* 20 (Fall 1984): 785–
    802.
Slavick, William H. "Taken With a Long-Handled Spoon: The Roberts Papers and
    Letters." *Southern Review* 20 (Fall 1984): 752–73.
Smith, Jo Reinhard. "New Troy in the Bluegrass: Vergilian Metaphor and *The Great
    Meadow*." *Mississippi Quarterly* 22 (Spring 1969): 39–46.
Smith, William Jay. *The Streaks of the Tulip: Selected Criticism*. New York: Delacorte
    Press/Seymour Lawrence, 1977.
Spivey, Herman E. "The Mind and Creative Habits of Elizabeth Madox Roberts." *All
    These to Teach: Essays in Honor of C. A. Robertson*. Ed. Robert A. Bryan, Alton
    C. Morres, A. A. Murphee, and Aubrey L. Williams. Gainesville: University of
    Florida Press, 1965.

Thorp, Willard. *American Writing in the Twentieth Century*. Cambridge: Harvard University Press, 1960.

Van Doren, Mark. "Elizabeth Madox Roberts." *English Journal* 21 (September 1932): 521–28.

Wagenknecht, Edward. *Cavalcade of the American Novel*. New York: Henry Holt, 1952.

Elizabeth Spencer
(1921–)

In her early novels Elizabeth Spencer portrays the twentieth-century South, showing the forces of family and community that both support and compromise the hero intent upon making his separate way. In later work, Spencer broadens her settings and themes, frequently writing of contemporary women who face intense but problematical challenges as they balance the conflicting demands of self and society.

BIOGRAPHY

Elizabeth Spencer was born on 19 July 1921 in Carrollton, Mississippi, the second child of James Luther Spencer and Mary James McCain Spencer. Both her parents came from families who had lived and farmed in rural Carroll County for nearly a century. She has given accounts of her childhood in a number of interviews and essays, noting particularly her memories of growing up happily and securely in an agrarian society, her close attachment to her immediate and extended family, and the shared enjoyment many members of the family took in reading and talking about books.

Her father was a businessman whose various enterprises included the Carrollton Chevrolet agency, the Standard Oil franchise, a farm, and some stores. Given the hard times of the Depression and the small size of the town, it was not, according to Spencer, until later in life that he achieved "any kind of affluence." Her mother, a piano teacher before her marriage, was a lover of books and frequently read aloud to her daughter. Writing of her childhood in "Emerging as a Writer in Faulkner's Mississippi," Spencer noted, "It was no interruption in small town social life, or family life or church-going or hunting or fishing, to have your mother read to you every night out of Greek and Roman myths, the story of the Bible, Robin Hood, Arthurian legend, Uncle Remus,

Hawthorne, Aesop, Grimm, Robert Louis Stevenson, George MacDonald, Louisa May Alcott, and all those others, who followed naturally after Mother Goose and Peter Rabbit.''

As a child, Spencer was also particularly close to her maternal grandfather, John Sidney McCain, who is the model for the characters Daniel Armstrong in her first novel, *Fire in the Morning*, and the grandfather in the story "A Christian Education." A lifelong resident of the area and a former sheriff, McCain passed on to Spencer a rich knowledge of the region's stories; she drew upon them especially in her first three novels. Another significant association of her childhood was her love of the nearby family plantation. She frequently visited the place, which bore the Choctaw name for "tall pines"—Teoc Tillala. It lay just at the edge of the rich delta land that extended further westward, near the great estate of Malmaison, the home of the Choctaw chieftain, Greenwood Leflore.

In "Emerging as a Writer in Faulkner's Mississippi," Spencer has given a detailed portrait of her youth in Carrollton, a town lying about 60 miles southwest of William Faulkner's Oxford. Carrollton was chosen as the site for the filming of Faulkner's *The Reivers* because the town had changed so little over 50 years—unlike Oxford—and thus made a more credible "Jefferson." Spencer describes the Carrollton of the 1920s and 1930s when she was growing up as a sleepy town, but one that maintained a complicated relationship with its sister town, North Carrollton. "North Carrollton got mad at Carrollton once, back in the mists of time, or Carrollton got mad at North Carrollton, I forget which. At any rate, we had, between us, never more than 1,000 souls, but two separate 12-year high schools, two separate post offices, two mayors and boards of aldermen, and any number of separate reasons to feel different and superior, each to the other." In her depiction of Tarsus in *Fire in the Morning* and Lacey in *The Voice at the Back Door*, Spencer clearly draws upon her experience and knowledge of Carrollton.

Despite the town's smallness, Spencer received an impressive literary education in the public school. In the seventh grade she began the study of Latin, and in high school she studied Shakespeare under the tutelage of a Peabody graduate who had the class read the plays aloud. Spencer recalls their "sitting around an iron stove with our knees toasting and our backs cold and hunks of plaster threatening to fall down on our heads, taking parts in *Romeo and Juliet*, *The Merchant of Venice*, or *As You Like It*, building up to grade 12," when they moved "full-scale into *Macbeth*." During these years many forces were forming and furnishing Spencer's literary imagination. Her reading at home and at school, her early attempts at writing, which she has said began when she was quite young, and her wide exposure over time to a rich, settled culture all helped shape the fiction writer she would become.

In 1938 Spencer left Carrollton to attend Belhaven College, a small Presbyterian college for women in Jackson, Mississippi. She had wanted to attend the University of Mississippi in Oxford, but her strongly religious family insisted upon Belhaven. She graduated in 1942, cum laude, having served as class president, editor of the school paper, and president of the literary society. It was through the literary society that she most seriously pursued her writing, and one year she won second place for the short story at the Southern Literary Festival. It was also through the society that she first met Eudora Welty, whose home stood just across the street from the college. Spencer called upon Welty to invite her to speak to the group, an occasion that Welty recalled in her 1981 foreword to *The Stories of Elizabeth Spencer*. "I met then a graceful young woman with a slender, vivid face, delicate and clearly defined features, dark blue eyes in which, then as now, you could read that Elizabeth Spencer was a jump ahead of you in what you were about to say. . . . But the main thing about her was blazingly clear—this girl was serious. She was indeed already a writer." The friendship that began in the early 1940s continued through the years, with Spencer's dedicating her first collection of short stories, *Ship Island and Other Stories*, to Welty, and Welty's writing the foreword to Spencer's collected stories.

In the fall of 1942 Spencer left for Vanderbilt, where she had a fellowship to begin an M.A. in English. There she studied with Donald Davidson and wrote a thesis on "Irish Mythology in the Early Poetry of William Butler Yeats." The next year she taught English at a junior college in Mississippi, but returned to Nashville in 1944 to teach in a private school for girls. During this time she enrolled in a class in short-story writing taught by Raymond Goldman at the Watkins Institute, and she submitted her story "The Little Brown Girl" to the *New Yorker*. The magazine rejected the work in 1945, but later, in 1957, published it.

In 1945–46 Spencer worked as a reporter for the Nashville *Tennessean*, but finally in the summer she quit the job to devote herself full-time to her first novel. With the encouragement of Donald Davidson, Robert Penn Warren, and others, she submitted portions of the manuscript to David M. Clay, an editor with Dodd, Mead, who read the work and recommended its publication. In 1948 the novel appeared to strong critical acclaim, although many reviewers commented upon similarities between it and works by Faulkner, Warren, and Hellman. In general, however, critics admired Spencer's originality and praised her handling of plot and delineation of strong, vital characters.

The comparisons with Faulkner continued to arise in the reviews of her next two novels, *This Crooked Way* and *The Voice at the Back Door*. In some ways the works do reflect Faulkner's influence, which is not surprising given the fact that Spencer came to read Faulkner during her graduate school days at Vanderbilt. Furthermore, although her early novels were very much products of her own experience, drawn from the people and places she had known growing up in Carroll County, the proximity to Faulkner's Lafayette County led inevitably to reminders of Yoknapatawpha.

Faulkner's achievement has been an intimidating one for many of the second generation of writers of the Southern Renascence. Flannery O'Connor, Eudora Welty, and many others have written of the looming power of Faulkner's fiction and have noted the pressure upon Southern writers coming after him to establish a separate, original voice. Spencer doubtless felt the pressure of this influence, but she also found Faulkner's example galvanizing—someone from her own neck of the woods had come to be the preeminent writer of the United States. In the fall of 1948 Spencer moved to Oxford to join the English faculty at the University of Mississippi. At a literary festival on campus the following spring, she visited with John Crowe Ransom and Stark Young, who was a distant relation of hers. At a party given for Young, Spencer met Faulkner for the first time.

During the next few years Spencer visited Italy, began to publish short stories, and continued to work on *This Crooked Way*, which was published in 1952. The novel brought Spencer an award from the National Institute of Arts and Letters. In 1953, with a Guggenheim Fellowship, she left Mississippi for an extended stay in Italy. While in Rome she met John Arthur Blackwood Rusher (b. 1920), a young language instructor from England. She returned to Mississippi briefly in 1955 and then took up residence in New York while she completed *The Voice at the Back Door*. With its publication in 1956, she went to England to marry Rusher. The ceremony was held, with his family in attendance, on 29 September 1956 at St. Colomb Minor in Cornwall, England.

As in the two earlier works, Spencer set *The Voice at the Back Door* in the twentieth-century South. The novel dealt principally with racial relations and appeared at a time of mounting tensions following the *Brown vs. Board of Education* decision. In an introduction to a Time-Life reissue of the book in 1965, Spencer says that as she was writing the novel in Italy it had seemed to her still possible that the South might find peaceful ways of reaching some kind of racial harmony. When she returned to Mississippi in 1955, however, shortly after the infamous Emmett Till murder, she realized that during her absence "a precipitate moment had come and gone," that the local scene she had portrayed, "with its many ramifications in love and blessing," had vanished. Nonetheless, she stuck to her story, having written it from her own direct knowledge of the South.

With the publication of *The Voice at the Back Door* Spencer moved beyond apprenticeship and any residual Faulknerian influence to create a mature, original portrait of Southern life. The novel received excellent reviews, and subsequently Spencer received the Rosenthal Award of the American Academy of Arts and Letters and a Kenyon Review Fellowship. In 1958 she and her husband moved to Montreal, where they lived for over twenty-five years. The Canadian residence represented something of a compromise between England and the United States, she has said on occasion. Through the years she has maintained close ties with her native state, often visiting family and using extended trips to gather details for her writing. And, in 1986, she and John Rusher moved to Chapel Hill, North Carolina.

The greatest commercial success of any of Spencer's novels to date occurred with the publication of *The Light in the Piazza* in 1960. It is the story of an American woman who travels to Italy with her daughter, a beautiful young woman who has unfortunately suffered an accident in youth that has left her with the intelligence of a ten-year-old. At the heart of the work are the moral and psychological deliberations that the mother undergoes before finally deciding to promote the marriage of her daughter to a young Italian man who has fallen in love with her. Like *The Voice at the Back Door*, the book was widely and favorably reviewed. The novella appeared originally in the *New Yorker*, which has published many of Spencer's stories, and it was later dramatized in a film by MGM. The work marked Spencer's first departure from the Southern locales of her earlier novels and the beginning of her fiction with international settings. In the introduction to *The Stories of Elizabeth Spencer*, she discussed this period of her life and the effect that leaving the South had had on her work: "For me it meant the breaking up of those long tides of existence in one locale that have yielded up countless novels, out of which the novel seems to unfurl so naturally, so rhythmically, so right. My experience was now broken into pieces, no less valid, perhaps no less interesting—perhaps even more relevant, I was tempted to speculate, to the restless life of the world?" For several years she concentrated upon short fiction, which she said seemed to her more suited to themes of the "restless life of the world."

In 1965 Spencer published another novella set in Italy, *Knights and Dragons*, a work with a densely symbolical, psychological texture that many critics faulted for its obscurity and static quality. The protagonist is a young American woman who slowly and deliberately comes to free herself from the emotional domination of a former husband. Spencer creates a similar protagonist in the character of Catherine Sasser in her next novel, *No Place for an Angel* (1967). In this work, set in Italy, New York, Texas, Massachusetts, and elsewhere, Spencer portrays a group of five central characters who variously embody the rootlessness and restlessness of modern life.

The decade of the 1960s, an extremely productive one for Spencer, saw the publication not only of the two novellas and the new novel but of a number of short stories. Two stories, "First Dark" and "Ship Island," won O. Henry prizes. In 1968 Spencer published these two plus eight others in the collection *Ship Island and Other Stories*. During the late 1960s she also continued to work on a long novel that she had begun about the time she first started *No Place for an Angel*. The new novel, *The Snare*, came out in 1972 to generally favorable, though mixed, reviews.

Set in New Orleans, *The Snare* traces the journey of Julia Garrett from her comfortable life with her aunt and uncle, who are respectable, well-to-do residents of the Garden District, to the exotic, menacing world of musicians and drug dealers in the French Quarter. Although Spencer uses a Southern locale for the setting of the novel, *The Snare* differs markedly from the earlier Mississippi novels. Its preoccupations are mainly psychological, focusing upon the haunted protagonist who deliberately seeks out the underside of life in her attempt to free herself from banality and emptiness.

In an interview with E. P. Broadwell and R. W. Hoag, Spencer called the book a "study of evil," saying, "I do believe that evil is incurable; but I wanted to show that, even in such a climate, life can persist and perhaps grow into a kind of sainthood. The lesson Julia learns is that she has to make a place for herself in the world of *The Snare*." Although the novel reflects the societal tensions and confusions of the 1960s, it has at its center the figure of a lonely, separate heroine, a woman who renounces passivity and self-destructiveness for autonomy and self-acceptance. Stylistically, it is Spencer's most subtle and experimental work.

Throughout the 1970s Spencer continued to write, concentrating mainly on short fiction. The illness and death of her parents in Mississippi made heavy claims on her time and emotional energies, however, and she did not publish another novel until 1984. Her short fiction during this period represents some of her strongest work—stories like "I, Maureen" and "The Girl Who Loved Horses," both of which present rich psychological studies of character. In 1981 the publication of *The Stories of Elizabeth Spencer* brought together the ten stories of *Ship Island*, 22 other stories previously published but not collected, and the novella *Knights and Dragons*. In the same year the University Press of Mississippi separately published three of the stories from the collection in the slender volume *Marilee*. The stories share a central protagonist, Marilee Summerall, an engaging Southerner whose narrator's voice reveals Spencer's mastery of idiomatic speech.

Spencer's most recent novel, *The Salt Line* (1984), was well reviewed, although it did not elicit the widespread critical attention that had marked such earlier works as *The Voice at the Back Door* and *The Light in the Piazza*. In many ways the new book represents a thematic sequel to *No Place for an Angel* and *The Snare*, for the situation of the central character, Arnie Carrington, parallels that of Julia Garrett and Catherine Sasser at the end of the earlier novels. He has withstood tempestuous storms, literally and metaphorically, surviving the loss of his professorship at an upstate university during the campus confusions of the 1960s, the killing hurricane Camille in 1969 on the Mississippi Gulf Coast, and finally the lengthy illness and death of his wife. In his struggle to persevere as he grows old in a confused and diminished world, he embodies one of Spencer's most suggestive and representative characters. Although the affirmations embodied in *The Salt Line* are somewhat muted and ambiguous, the novel gives finally a hopeful reading of life's possibilities.

During the years Spencer resided in Montreal, she gave readings and traveled widely in the United States. She has continued to visit Italy and has used European as well as American settings for her fiction. Only in a few of the more recent stories has she employed a Canadian locale. She has taught creative writing at Concordia University in Montreal from 1976 through 1986, and on a number of occasions she has agreed to serve short appointments as writer-in-residence on U.S. university campuses. In 1983 she was awarded the Merit Medal for the Short Story by the American Academy and Institute for Arts and Letters, and in 1985 she was elected to membership in the Academy. In 1986 she accepted a teaching position at the University of North Carolina at Chapel Hill.

MAJOR THEMES

In the early novels set in Mississippi, Spencer explores with great sympathy and subtlety the way the legacy of the past—the "burden of history"—affects an individual's attempt to establish a separate life. The protagonists of *Fire in the Morning* and *The Voice at the Back Door* are sensitive, moral men who find it almost impossible to act responsibly and justly and at the same time honor the traditions of the family and community. In her handling of this theme, Spencer shows that an ignorant or arrogant dismissal of these traditions just as surely leads to wrongful actions. Both Kinloch Armstrong and Duncan Harper confront the issue of how one opposes evil in the community, whether the evil is land greed or racial oppression, without hurting innocent people. Spencer suggests no easy solutions, only the inescapability of compromising entanglements with the past.

In her second novel, *This Crooked Way*, she explores a slightly different version of the theme of the search for selfhood and integrity. Amos Dudley bears the mark of the past in his radical religious vision, which he takes as a clear sign from God that he is to succeed in this world. His single-minded pursuit of wealth, which he rationalizes as his God-willed destiny, leads to hurt and violence for his family. Only by giving up his sense of special destiny and seeing himself as a family man, bound to his parents and siblings and wife and children, is he able to find the fulfillment he has sought for a lifetime. Accepting his place as an ordinary man before an unfathomable God, he finds what happiness and satisfaction are available on this earth.

In the novellas *The Light in the Piazza* and *Knights and Dragons*, Spencer depicts two female protagonists who are caught, as are the earlier male protagonists, between opposing needs and obligations. In the case of Margaret Johnson and Martha Ingram, as with subsequent heroines, Spencer shows that for these women the ultimate challenge is to become free, self-sustaining individuals. Whereas the chief quest for Spencer's male protagonists seems to be the recognition and respect of the other, the challenge for the female protagonists is the acknowledgment and acceptance of the separate self. In Spencer's vision, the free woman stands inevitably apart from the world, specifically, apart from her husband and family. Margaret Johnson acts in defiance of her husband to secure the future of her daughter, and her action has the effect of securing Margaret's own future freedom and self-possession. Similarly, Martha Ingram finally makes a livable life for herself when she frees herself from obsessive memories and guilts that bind her to her former husband.

In *No Place for an Angel* Spencer greatly expands the canvas upon which she draws contemporary men and women in search of habitable lives—lives in which there is a healthful blend of regard for the self and regard for the other. In this novel, however, the overweening self-centeredness of four of the five major characters, as well as most of the minor characters, makes such a harmony impossible. Only Catherine Sasser, who enters the adult world as a self-effacing, dependent, frightened girl, shows evidence that life may embody at least a minimal decency and nobility, if not spirituality. In this rich, problematic, realistic novel, Spencer portrays the social and psychological tensions that afflict contemporary society. She shows, for example, how our pride and power quickly give way to disillusionment, which we sustain with an ironical, contemptuous view of life. Catherine Sasser's gentle goodness suggests an alternative, but Spencer's portrait of Catherine, vulnerable and haunted, is at best a tenuous sign of hopefulness.

In an interview with Broadwell and Hoag, Spencer discussed the theme of her fiction in talking about *The Stories of Elizabeth Spencer*, a collection that spans 33 years of writing. "I think many of the stories are about liberation," she said, "and the regret you have when you liberate yourself. You see, however much you might want to, you cannot both hold on and be free. And that's the crux in a lot of those stories." In many ways the theme of *The Snare* is also centered on the issue of liberation: Julia Garrett discovers and accepts a dark, demonic world that cannot be avoided if one fully and freely confronts life. Unlike characters in *No Place for an Angel*, however, Julia Garrett resists disillusionment and ultimately draws strength from her encounter with the "snare" that is the world. She forges an independent identity for herself, but in the end her independence is modified by her acceptance of responsibility for her child. In very much the same vein, Arnie Carrington of *The Salt Line* chooses a life that involves him in the welfare of others.

In *The Salt Line*, as in her fiction of the late 1960s and 1970s, Spencer suggests the dire consequence for humanity of radical individualism, a dominant strain in the American mind, and of unremitting self-consciousness, the characteristic mode of modernism. She shows that the autonomous will devoted solely to the separate self will not sustain life. She portrays a Western society battered by social tensions, lacking any sustaining tradition, a sterile, even morbid society that has largely abandoned family and community. If the balance once weighed more heavily on the side of tradition and family, it has now shifted, she implies. It is necessary for youth to establish independence, to be sure, but if life is to be continued, the adult man and woman must accept responsibility for the nurture of others. Implicit in the conclusion of both *The Snare* and *The Salt Line* is the characters' acceptance of such responsibility.

SURVEY OF CRITICISM

The first book-length study of Spencer's fiction is that by Peggy Whitman Prenshaw (1985). A volume in the Twayne United States Authors Series, Prenshaw's book surveys Spencer's work through *The Salt Line* (1984). Laura Barge compiled an invaluable bibliographical guide for "An Elizabeth Spencer Checklist, 1948 to 1976." The numerous and widespread reviews of Spencer's fiction, dating from 1948, are listed. Nash K. Burger wrote a thematic analysis of the early novels in "Elizabeth Spencer's Three Mississippi Novels," and John Malcolm Brinnin gave a retrospective review of *The Voice at the Back Door* in a revealing analysis of the social themes of the novel. There have been several master's theses written; one of the best of them is by Regina Nichols Johnson on Spencer's depiction of the sense of community. Some of the most acute and helpful commentaries on the fiction are those furnished by Spencer herself in various interviews that have been published in recent years. Although there are some excellent brief analyses to be found among the reviews, some of which are written by major critics, overall the paucity of serious, detailed critical studies is striking. Given the richness and artistry of Spencer's fiction, the negligence by the academic literary establishment is puzzling.

BIBLIOGRAPHY

Works by Elizabeth Spencer

Fiction

Fire in the Morning. New York: Dodd, Mead, 1948.
This Crooked Way. New York: Dodd, Mead, 1952.
The Voice at the Back Door. New York: McGraw-Hill, 1956.
The Light in the Piazza. New York: McGraw-Hill, 1960.
Knights and Dragons. New York: McGraw-Hill, 1965.
No Place for an Angel. New York: McGraw-Hill, 1967.
Ship Island and Other Stories. New York: McGraw-Hill, 1968.
The Snare. New York: McGraw-Hill, 1972.
Marilee. Jackson: University Press of Mississippi, 1981.
The Stories of Elizabeth Spencer. New York: Doubleday, 1981.
The Salt Line. New York: Doubleday, 1984.

Selected Essays and Articles

"Valley Hill." *Delta Review* 1 (Autumn 1964): 18–23.
"On Writing Fiction." *Notes on Mississippi Writers* 3 (Fall 1970): 71–72.
"Storytelling, Old and New." *Writer* 85 (January 1972): 9–10, 30.
"Emerging As a Writer in Faulkner's Mississippi." *Faulkner and the Southern Renaissance.* Ed. Doreen Fowler and Ann Abadie. Jackson: University Press of Mississippi, 1982, pp. 120–37.
"Writers' Panel." *E. M. Forster: Centenary Revaluations.* Ed. Judith Scherer Herz and Robert K. Martin. Toronto: University of Toronto Press, 1982, pp. 288–307.

Interviews with Elizabeth Spencer

Broadwell, Elizabeth Pell and Ronald Wesley Hoag. "A Conversation with Elizabeth Spencer." *Southern Review* 18 (Winter 1982): 111–30.

Bunting, Charles T. " 'In That Time and at That Place': The Literary World of Elizabeth Spencer." *Mississippi Quarterly* 28 (Fall 1975): 435–60.

Cole, Hunter McKelva. "Elizabeth Spencer at Sycamore Fair." *Notes on Mississippi Writers* 6 (Winter 1974): 81–86.

Haley, Josephine. "An Interview with Elizabeth Spencer." *Notes on Mississippi Writers* 1 (Fall 1968): 42–55.

Jones, John Griffin. "Elizabeth Spencer." *Mississippi Writers Talking*. Jackson: University Press of Mississippi, 1982, pp. 95–129.

Studies of Elizabeth Spencer

Anderson, Hilton. "Elizabeth Spencer's Two Italian Novellas." *Notes on Mississippi Writers* 13 (1981): 18–35.

Barge, Laura. "An Elizabeth Spencer Checklist, 1948 to 1976." *Mississippi Quarterly* 29 (Fall 1976): 569–90.

Brinnin, John Malcolm. "Black and White in Redneck Country." *Washington Post Book World*, 15 May 1983, p. 10.

Burger, Nash K. "Elizabeth Spencer's Three Mississippi Novels." *South Atlantic Quarterly* 63 (Summer 1964): 351–62.

Cole, Hunter McKelva. "Windsor in Spencer and Welty: A Real and an Imaginary Landscape." *Notes on Mississippi Writers* 7 (Spring 1974): 2–11.

Evoy, Karen. "*Marilee*: 'A Permanent Landscape of the Heart.' " *Mississippi Quarterly* 36 (Fall 1983): 569–78.

Johnson, Regina Nichols. "The Sense of Community in the Fiction of Elizabeth Spencer." M.A. thesis, University of Alabama–Huntsville, 1977.

Park, Clara Claiborne. "A Personal Road." *Hudson Review* 34 (Winter 1981–82): 601–05.

Prenshaw, Peggy Whitman. *Elizabeth Spencer*. Boston: Twayne, 1985.

Pugh, David G. "*The Voice at the Back Door*: Elizabeth Spencer Looks into Mississippi." *The Fifties: Fiction, Poetry, Drama*. Ed. Warren C. French. Deland, Fla.: Everett, Edwards, 1970, pp. 103–10.

RUEL E. FOSTER

Jesse Stuart
(1906–1984)

After becoming a nationally known writer, Jesse Stuart later suffered a sense of displacement. He felt he was neither a Southern writer nor a Northern writer. Where did he belong? By writing *Taps for Private Tussie*, a novel selling over two million copies, and some of the best short stories in American literature, Stuart did much to bring Appalachian literature into the national consciousness. He died in 1984, conscious that he had a literary home—the Appalachian region.

BIOGRAPHY

Jesse Stuart was born on 8 August 1906, the first of seven children, in the somber hills of eastern Kentucky in Greenup County. Heeding an old adage, he chose his hardy mountain parents well. His father, Mitchell, was tough as whit-leather but had an extraordinary eye for the beauty of nature, a sense he passed on to Stuart. His mother, Martha Hilton Stuart, who was part Cherokee Indian, gave to her son her physical vigor, a strong ethical sense, and an immense love.

The place was a log cabin in W-Hollow; the life and culture were in a number of ways unchanged from what life had been in 1806 in this region. In 1906 W-Hollow was still "the land that time forgot," in Horace Kephart's phrase. Dark and forbidding as this land and life were, they left an indelible mark on Stuart and on his writing. Although later he traveled over the world and into more than 70 countries, he made W-Hollow his lasting home, living and dying there.

Stuart's success in poetry, fiction, and expository prose is partially traceable to a series of unusual mentors he had beginning with Mrs. Harriet Hatton in high school and including Harry Kroll at Lincoln Memorial Institute, where Stuart received his B.A. in 1929, and ending with Donald Davidson at Vanderbilt University. (Stuart left Vanderbilt after one year, his master's uncompleted.) All three mentors recognized his verbal gift, but Davidson was most important, providing a tutelage and friendship that guided and shaped Stuart right up to Davidson's death in April 1968.

Stuart set out to be a writer early; his idol was Robert Burns. Stuart's father could neither read nor write, but both he and his wife cherished education and instilled the desire for it in their son. After he graduated from Lincoln, Stuart began a career in public education, but he abandoned the commitment to writing that he began in high school only when his first stroke in 1980 made writing physically impossible.

Stuart often said "Writing is my life," and he meant it. The physical act of writing gave him pleasure even if it was no more than a grocery list. As a beginning writer, he was like a powerful motor needing to be geared up. He heeded the advice of Harry Kroll at Lincoln Memorial Institute, who told him, "Write as you talk. Turn it on and pour it out." His most important advice came from Davidson at Vanderbilt. Davidson returned a sheaf of Stuart's early derivative poems with the remark, "Don't be a pretty boy, Jesse." When Stuart left Vanderbilt, Davidson told him, "Stick to your hills, Jesse, and write about the people you know, the sheriffs and constables you hate. Write of your country as Yeats is writing of his native Ireland. Your country is your material." Stuart considered this the most significant writing advice he ever received.

On 14 October 1939 when Stuart married Naomi Deanne Norris, he had four books in print and was becoming well-known in both popular and serious literary circles. His first published book was a thin volume of poems, *Harvest of Youth*, which he subsidized himself in 1930. This effort drew no particular attention, and Stuart felt so chagrined with the book that he refused to keep a single copy himself. Although quite derivative, this book does present the rough, natural rhythms that characterize his best poetry.

Man with a Bull-Tongue Plow, a collection of 703 sonnets published in 1934, was Stuart's second volume. It was a robust mountain work, earthy and masculine. Eastern critics hailed him as the "American Robert Burns." The book remains the best of his poetic works.

In 1936 *Head O'W-Hollow* appeared, the first of many subsequent collections of short stories. *Beyond Dark Hills* (1938) was an autobiography carrying Stuart's life up to his departure for Scotland on a Guggenheim Fellowship.

By the time of his marriage, Stuart had rejected offers of jobs in London and in Hollywood. He was committed to living in W-Hollow. He bought land bit by bit, year after year, until he owned over 1,200 acres—all of W-Hollow. He supported himself by lecturing throughout the United States and by writing. From time to time he taught because he loved to do so and because he felt needed.

In 1940 his first novel, *Trees of Heaven*, a story of landowners versus squatters, was published. It was a satisfying and acute representation of a now-vanished mountain way of life. Other novels followed as Stuart pursued his anatomizing of the mountain life, but *Trees of Heaven* remains one of his best novels.

By 1941 Stuart's literary work began to receive acclaim that lasted throughout his life. In that year he received the $500 award of the American Institute of Arts and Letters for his contribution to literature in the preceding year. During 1941 *Men of the Mountains*, a second collection of short stories, was published.

His novel *Taps for Private Tussie* (1943) proved to be the most popular of all of his works. By 1980 over 2,000,000 copies of *Taps* had been sold. Hollywood purchased the movie rights but never made the movie. For his work Stuart received the $2,500 Thomas Jefferson "Southern Award" for the best Southern book of the year. In one respect a boisterous ballad of lolling reliefers and inherited indolence, the novel is, in a lesser key, a sad-comic pastorale of a family caught in the turbulence of acute social change yet not realizing the cause of the turbulence.

Like most of his mountain kin, Stuart was patriotic. With the United States in World War II, he felt that he should be too. On 12 July 1944 he was commissioned Lieutenant (jg) in the U.S. Naval Reserve. Because of his success as a writer, he was assigned to a Naval Writing Division to work on material for the *Naval Aviation News* and similar publications. In the same year he published another volume of poems—*Album of Destiny*, the result of several years' labor. Its reception was modest. The war ended, and Stuart was discharged from the Navy on 31 December 1945. He packed his wife and daughter Jessica (born 20 August 1942, his only child) and a few belongings into his Plymouth and headed toward W-Hollow and home.

Stuart's writing colleagues in the Navy had laughed at some of his tall tales. They encouraged him to put them in a book. The result was *Foretaste of Glory* (1946). A comic masterpiece, it good-naturedly portrays the religious high jinks of a group of fundamentalist villagers who see a great display of the northern lights for the first time and feel that the Second Coming is at hand. Stuart was not prepared for the virulent reaction to his satire by the natives of Greenup. They denounced him and threatened physical violence. Although Stuart thought seriously of moving away, he did not, but some animus against him remained in Greenup for the rest of his life. Read today, *Foretaste* remains full of exuberant life and fun, a literary analogue to a Brueghel the Elder painting such as "Peasant Wedding" or "Peasant Dance."

In 1949 *The Thread That Runs So True*, an account of Stuart's teaching career, was published. Dr. Jay Elmer Morgan, founder and president of the National Education Association, considered *The Thread That Runs So True* "the best book on education written in the last fifty years." It is a dramatic, pungent, inspirational account of a young man who loved teaching and was a superb success in a series of difficult teaching assignments in mountain schools in Kentucky. But after nine years of selfless teaching, Stuart found that he had endured a series of bitter personal attacks and was averaging $100.30 a month, not enough to support him and his wife. He wrote: "[Teaching] is the greatest profession under the sun. . . . I still love it. But I'm leaving it because it's left me.'' His book remains an interesting, caustic assessment of the teaching profession in general and of the Kentucky educational wastelands of the 1920s and 1930s in particular.

Stuart, always deeply committed to his family, was profoundly moved by the unexpected death of his mother. It was an omen to him of other tragic changes soon to alter his life irretrievably. On 8 October 1954 he suffered a massive heart attack, and his attending physician told Mrs. Stuart that her husband had only one chance in a thousand of surviving. Because of his enormous willpower, Stuart survived, but it was a year later before he could return to a semblance of the life he had known. For the remainder of his life, his health was troubled. Several repeated heart attacks eventually caused his death.

In December 1954, two months after Stuart's first heart attack, his father died, increasing the deep melancholy that descended on Stuart during his physical recuperation. Stuart's family—his wife, daughter, and siblings—rallied around him and supported him and encouraged his will to live. But the signs of mortality were very strong to him, and he underwent a spiritual change during the ensuing year. All of this he discusses in *The Year of My Rebirth* (1956).

As energy and life returned to Stuart, so did the desire to write. He turned to the short story, his favorite art form. *Plowshare in Heaven*, a volume of short stories whose title story is an agrarian tribute to his dead mother, was published in 1958. Stuart's vigor was such that in 1960 he accepted an invitation to teach for a year at the University of Cairo in Egypt. He and his family enjoyed their sojourn there but were bedeviled by bureaucratic restrictions. He railed at them in a secret journal; it has never been published.

Also in 1960, *God's Oddling*, one of Stuart's finest autobiographical works, was published. It recounts the story of Stuart's fiercely independent, idiosyncratic father. The book is a ''Life with Father'' suffused with humor and touched with the somberness of the hard life of the hills. Although his father was illiterate, Stuart praises him as the greatest earth poet he had ever known.

In 1961 Stuart found that the world increasingly appreciated his work. Still in Egypt, he received notice that he had been given the Academy of American Poets Award, with it a $5,000 stipend. The twelve judges of the Academy included W. H. Auden, Marianne Moore, Randall Jarrell, and Frederick A. Pottle. Stuart was gratified to have his poetry honored by so distinguished a group.

Stuart returned to W-Hollow in 1961 to resume his writing and lecturing, pausing long enough in 1962 to make a goodwill tour overseas for the State Department. In the same year he published another volume of poetry, *Hold April*, which is more subdued in tone and more religious than his previous work— a note of acceptance of the burdens and vagaries of life had crept in. With *Save Every Lamb* (1964), a volume of short stories wherein every story had something to do with animals, Stuart now had close to 400 short stories in print, and he began to organize his short-story volumes around central motifs, a practice he continued until his death. In 1965 *Daughter of the Legend*, Stuart's novel about the evils of racial segregation, was published. Stuart could not understand the cool critical reception the novel received.

From 1966 till his death Stuart showed evidence of his physical weakening, accompanied by a loss of spontaneity in his writing. His health gradually worsened, and he was increasingly distracted by travel, talks, visitors, and many miscellaneous requests for his services in public or charitable duties. For years he wrote over 4,000 letters and cards per year.

Despite the flagging of his literary powers, he managed to publish some excellent works during these twilight years. As late as 1977, he pointed out that he had a good reserve of publishable manuscripts (like a deep bench in baseball, he said) and could continue for ten years to have a book a year published without his writing another word. He came close to doing just that with these collections of short stories: *Save Every Lamb* (1964); *My Land Has a Voice* (1966); *Come Gentle Spring* (1969); *Come Back to the Farm* (1971); *Dawn of Remembered Spring* (1972); *32 Votes Before Breakfast (1974)*; and *The Best-Loved Short Stories of Jesse Stuart* (1982). These works represent Stuart at a high level of his talent.

But his last years were difficult. On his seventy-first birthday, he wrote in his journal, "What do I have to live for? The best is over." He set about preparing for death. The Jesse Stuart Foundation was set up to preserve W-Hollow and his home as a public preserve in perpetuity. "Whitman was grass; I am land," he said. He suffered his first stroke in spring 1980. He recovered slowly but could no longer write. Naomi and nurses cared for him in W-Hollow. Then on 10 May 1982 he suffered his second stroke; it left him mute and comatose. He was never again able to speak but lived until 17 February 1984. He was buried in the Plum Grove Cemetery with his mother and father and two brothers who had died in infancy.

MAJOR THEMES

Open any book by Stuart and you will find that a fine mist of nature blows from it. The most important theme in his vast work is devotion to nature. His love for his mountains and the earth is the theme that unifies his major works. In *Man with a Bull-Tongue Plow*, his first important book, Stuart begins the first sonnet with the line "I am a farmer singing at the plow," and he hymns the pleasures of tilling the soil as Virgil and Horace had done almost two millennia ago. Stuart is no gentleman farmer—"I'm just a dirt-colored man," he observed vehemently. For centuries the primitivist has declared that life close to the soil is the good life and that man finds happiness by following the norms of nature. Stuart agreed with this doctrine unequivocally—"Live right down against the soil. Be envious of the snake because it rubs the soil closer than you. . . . from the bitterness of life among the hills, there is the greatest sweetness in the world."

Like other primitivists, Stuart had his discontent with civilization. He praised the old-time music and the old mountain ballads and many of the old mountain

ways, and he revealed his discontent with civilization by creating several characters in the mold of the "Natural Man" of romantic primitivism. Sparkie in
Hie to the Hunters is such. Sparkie is untutored in books and the sophisticated
knowledge of the cities, but he loves the land and forests, and he has to some
degree the "knowledge carried to the heart" which Allen Tate has found more
domesticated in agrarian than in urban culture. Another "Natural Man" was
Stuart's father, Mitch Stuart, celebrated in *God's Oddling*. He loved to pick up
a handful of freshly plowed earth and fondle and sniff it. He could sit for hours
in the woods looking at a clump of violets by a rotten log. Another "Natural
Man" is Anse Bushman of *Trees of Heaven*. Anse is a patriarch who loves the
outdoors so much that he cannot stay indoors when the great equinoctial storms
come. Barefoot and clad only in a nightgown, he plunges into the night and
walks unprotected up and down his fields, soaking up the water, enjoying thunder
and lightning in an ecstasy of communion. Into this same category would come
Op Akers, the protagonist of the novel *The Good Spirit of Laurel Ridge*. Op is
a "child of nature" who lives as a squatter on Laurel Ridge—"He's [the owner
of the land] got the deed on paper. I've got the deed for it in my heart," says
Op in a thoroughly Thoreauvian statement. Op lives completely in accord with
nature's norms—"There are still pockets of the earth left as God made 'em. . . .
Fruit, nuts and wild game left as they must have been in the beginnin'." Moreover, a beneficent God shapes this rural Eden: "There's a weed a-growin on
Laurel Ridge for every ailment of the body. The Old Master has a purpose fer
every weed and flower he's created!"

Stuart's primitivism grew naturally out of his way of life. It is not a romantic
escape from life, inculcated by reading Rousseauesque books on the delights of
untrammeled nature. Until his death, he was about as honest a primitivist as we
could find in this country. He knew the grimness and tragedy of life on the
mountain soil. He practiced what the Vanderbilt Agrarians preached.

Stuart was not an ideologue; he did not write his poetry and fiction to prove
debaters' points. He had about as strong and active a love of life as one could
find in a writer, and he wrote about the life he had seen and the drama and
ambivalences of that life. In *Daughter of the Legend* he attempted to write a
thesis novel attacking racial segregation. The cause was laudable, but the novel
failed badly. His best works do advance themes and do so rather skillfully, but
they are themes intrinsic to the work, themes that grow naturally from his own
life experience.

Such a theme in his early work is his obsession with death. The death theme
is paramount in his first important book, *Man with a Bull-Tongue Plow*, so much
so that it could well bear a woodcut of a death's head or some other medieval
emblem of death on the flyleaf. Something in Stuart's personal experience—his
two brothers buried young on lonely mountain eminences, his paternal grandfather bludgeoned to death by an enemy feudist, the frequent mountain-born
babies who died in the first few days of their life, often preceded in death by
their mothers—ingrained far more deeply in him than in the average person the

constant awareness that death conquers all. Sonnet 387 mourns men killed by the feudists—"And long for them the bull-tongue plows will wait"—echoing Housman's *A Shropshire Lad*. Sonnet 390 views young lovers and their ultimate end when they "would sleep together the night through / This bridegroom never turning to the bride."

There are many parallels in this work to the death obsession of Edgar Lee Masters's *The Spoon River Anthology*, though Stuart denied any conscious influence. "I actually got the idea for the death section of *Man with a Bull-Tongue Plow* from Plum Grove Cemetery. There is a stone there that gave me the idea." Wherever it came from, the death theme meanders throughout the majority of the 703 sonnets that make up the work and is the primary subject of the last section of the book, "Preface for After Death," which ends with sonnet 703 and its concluding couplet: "Now if there is a Resurrection Day / I shall be one that's taken by surprise."

The death aura so prevalent in Stuart's poetry is sprinkled generously through his short stories also. In *Plowshare in Heaven* (1956) violent death is a major subject. There are two fatal shootings over women in "A Land Beyond the River"; two murders and five hangings in "Sunday Afternoon Hanging"; a death by natural causes and one from a broken heart in "The Reaper and the Flowers"; a death and a grand family fistfight in the graveyard at the burial of grandpa in "Death and Decision"; a mountain wake in "Plowshare in Heaven." Stuart moves easily and familiarly among the artifacts of death and gets striking effects—some grisly, some comic, some pathetic. His variations on the theme convey the harshness of mountain life in the late nineteenth and early twentieth centuries.

Like his persona of sonnet 703, the young, brash Stuart seemingly doubted resurrection, but as he aged he looked with more and more certainty to the promise of an afterlife. One of his chief testaments on this theme was *The Year of My Rebirth*, written after his near fatal heart attack in 1954: "There was never a time when I doubted the resurrection of Christ. . . . I have faith—that when man, the seed of God, is planted in the ground, though his husk will go back to the earth, he will be resurrected into a new life, for this is the law of God." Shortly before his last stroke Stuart spoke to his wife: "Isn't it wonderful to have another life? That promise of eternal life? . . . I can't wait to go." Later he told her, "The greatest trip I'll ever take will be the last one. . . . I will visit God and be judged, and I'm not afraid of that. . . . I will visit with my old friends. . . . It will be a great day."

Stuart's achievement is rooted in his fictional creation of W-Hollow, now lodged firmly in the literary imagination of America. Stuart never apologizes for the Appalachian background of his stories. It is significant that Stuart's writing has been the catalyst for the current Appalachian renaissance in literature. The life of the Southern Appalachians has been in American literature for a long time (William Byrd wrote about it in the 1720s), but it has not been classified as "Appalachian." It either floated in a critical limbo or was vaguely and obscurely thought of as "Southern." The body of Stuart's work, of which the short stories are the finest portion, represents the most significant work of any Appalachian writer.

How to sum Stuart up? He is primarily a *maker*, a *poet*. He says "yes" to life in his poems, stories, and novels. "Yes" in spite of sickness, injustice, and death; "yes" to the bone-deep sweetness and diversity of life. His work teaches us that life is grievous, hard, and mixed, but ultimately comes from God. His characters accept and affirm life with all its suffering and deep joy. Life is worth it—as Stuart phrases it, "A good seed dropped upon a fruitless land" that miraculously brings a lasting sweetness from the most barren soil.

SURVEY OF CRITICISM

Stuart's literary reputation has endured several twists of fortune. He first came to the attention of a general audience in 1934 with *Man with a Bull-Tongue Plow*. Reviewers liked the "primitivist poet" from the Kentucky mountains. As Stuart's work in other genres appeared, he received attention also in academic journals. Although many granted that he was a talented primitivist, they complained that he wrote too much. The "new critics" faulted him because he lacked irony and subtle nuances and because he had not "aged in these intellectual disciplines," as advocated by their mentor, John Crowe Ransom. Although Stuart had studied for a year at Vanderbilt and knew all of the important Fugitive and Agrarian writers there, he never felt himself to be one of them, even though his views epitomized their doctrines. Increasingly, critics turned from his poetry and looked to his short stories, novels, and autobiographical prose works. But for the most part Stuart felt himself the victim of critical neglect.

The process of saving Stuart from the overadulation of newspaper reviewers and the too finicky judgments of the quarterlies began with a master's thesis by Lee Oly Ramey at Ohio University in 1941. Ramey's was the first in a long line of theses and dissertations assessing the quality of Stuart's work. The first comprehensive bibliography of Stuart's writing was published in 1960: Hensley C. Woodbridge's *Jesse Stuart: A Bibliography*. Woodbridge continued his bibliographical coverage of Stuart with a supplemental bibliography in 1965. The bibliography is updated regularly in the *Jack London Newsletter*, which Woodbridge edits at Southern Illinois University at Carbondale.

The earliest full-length bio-critical book on Stuart was Everetta Love Blair's *Jesse Stuart, His Life and Work* (1967). Blair quotes extensively from newspaper reviewers and literary critics, but does not proffer any particularly new critical insights. She was a good friend of Stuart and received a warm accolade from him in the foreword.

In *Jesse Stuart* (1968) Ruel E. Foster argues that Stuart should be considered a regional writer from the Southern Appalachians, with accent on "Appalachians." Foster finds that although Stuart was haunted by the specter of the poet he might have been, Stuart was best with fiction, especially the short story.

Foster concedes that Stuart wrote too much and that his early work is better than his later, but he is still one of the great and original regional writers.

The most authoritative treatment of the folk element in Stuart's writing appears in Mary Washington Clarke's *Jesse Stuart's Kentucky* (1968). Clarke explores the hill man's religion, folklore, pleasures, and schools. Her work is a valuable adjunct to any serious student of Stuart's work.

In 1971 Dick Perry's *Reflections of Jesse Stuart on a Land of Many Moods* appeared. It was put together from eight days of steady talk with Stuart. Rambling, anecdotal, opinionated, it is of interest because it uncovers background material about Stuart's writing, such as the genesis of certain stories, the source of characters, and commentary on Stuart's friends and enemies. Perry is not really concerned with critical evaluation. An important move forward in Stuart criticism was marked by the publication of *Jesse Stuart: Essays on His Work*, edited by J. R. LeMaster and Mary Washington Clarke (1977). There are essays by ten of the most knowledgeable Stuart critics assessing a prolific writer's half century of literary activity.

H. Edward Richardson's *Jesse: The Biography of an American Writer, Jesse Hilton Stuart* was published in 1984. It is the authorized biography for which Jesse and Naomi granted many interviews. It provides much detail and much new material. It will undoubtedly be the standard biography for a long time although there are massive numbers of Stuart's letters still to be covered and digested and synthesized by future students. Richardson was Stuart's long-time friend, and his biography is "friendly." It does not go into the difficult question of Stuart's relationship to his hometown. Stuart felt antipathy toward him exuding from his hometown and county. What was the cause? This is still to be dealt with. The Richardson biography, nevertheless, remains a fine and helpful work.

For the future there is still work to be done, both critical and biographical. The question of Stuart's alienation from his home turf needs to be dealt with before all the living witnesses die. There are a number of extremely influential friendships in his life with strange ups and downs. These need to be plumbed. They include his friendships with Don West, Elizabeth Hall, James Still, Robert Penn Warren, and Donald Davidson. (Ruel Foster is currently working on an edition of the voluminous Stuart-Davidson correspondence for future publication.) Stuart's knowledge and use of folklore and dialect were massive, and further study of these subjects is in order. Extensive work is also needed on Stuart's use of humor, a central characteristic of his work. Stuart's Vanderbilt period and his continued association with members of the Fugitive and Agrarian groups needs to be assessed much more thoroughly. A comparative study of Stuart and his fellow Appalachian writer James Still would also be valuable. A number of these tasks are already underway. The Jesse Stuart Foundation and the University Press of Kentucky have reprinted in the last few years ten of Stuart's books. The Foundation will be instrumental in maintaining a national interest in Stuart's work. Stuart's reputation seems to be in good hands.

BIBLIOGRAPHY

Works by Jesse Stuart

Harvest of Youth. Howe, Okla.: Scroll Press, 1930.

Man with a Bull-Tongue Plow. New York: E. P. Dutton, 1934.

Head O'W-Hollow. New York: E. P. Dutton, 1936.

Beyond Dark Hills. New York: E. P. Dutton, 1938.

Trees of Heaven. New York: E. P. Dutton, 1940.

Men of the Mountains. New York: E. P. Dutton, 1941.

Taps for Private Tussie. New York: E. P. Dutton, 1943.

Album of Destiny. New York: E. P. Dutton, 1944.

Mongrel Mettle. New York: E. P. Dutton, 1944.

Foretaste of Glory. New York: E. P. Dutton, 1946.

Tales from the Plum Grove Hills. New York: E. P. Dutton, 1946.

The Thread That Runs So True. New York: Charles Scribner's Sons, 1949.

Clearing in the Sky. New York: McGraw-Hill, 1950.

Hie to the Hunters. New York: Whittlesey House, 1950.

Kentucky Is My Land. New York: E. P. Dutton, 1952.

The Beatinest Boy. New York: Whittlesey House, 1953.

The Good Spirit of Laurel Ridge. New York: McGraw-Hill, 1953.

A Penny's Worth of Character. New York: Whittlesey House, 1954.

Red Mule. New York: Whittlesey House, 1955.

The Year of My Rebirth. New York: McGraw-Hill, 1956.

Plowshare in Heaven. New York: McGraw-Hill, 1958.

God's Oddling. New York: McGraw-Hill, 1960.

Huey the Engineer. St. Helena, Calif.: James E. Beard, 1960.

The Rightful Owner. New York: Whittlesey House, 1960.

Andy Finds a Way. New York: Whittlesey House, 1961.

Hold April. New York: McGraw-Hill, 1962.

A Jesse Stuart Reader. New York: McGraw-Hill, 1963.

Save Every Lamb. New York: McGraw-Hill, 1964.

Daughter of the Legend. New York: McGraw-Hill, 1965.

A Jesse Stuart Harvest. New York: Dell, 1965.

My Land Has a Voice. New York: McGraw-Hill, 1966.

Mr. Gallion's School. New York: McGraw-Hill, 1967.

Come Gentle Spring. New York: McGraw-Hill, 1969.

To Teach, To Love. Cleveland: World, 1970.

Come Back to the Farm. New York: McGraw-Hill, 1971.

Dawn of Remembered Spring. New York: McGraw-Hill, 1972.

The Land Beyond the River. New York: McGraw-Hill, 1973.

32 Votes Before Breakfast: Politics at the Grass Roots as Seen in Short Stories by Jesse Stuart. New York: McGraw-Hill, 1974.

My World. Lexington: University Press of Kentucky, 1975.

Up the Hollow from Lynchburg, with photographer Joe Clark. New York: McGraw-Hill, 1975.

The Seasons of Jesse Stuart: An Autobiography in Poetry 1907–1976, sel. by Wanda Hicks. [Danbury, Conn.]: Archer Editions Press, 1976.

Dandelion on the Acropolis: A Journal of Greece. [Danbury, Conn.]: Archer Editions Press, 1978.
The Kingdom Within: A Spiritual Autobiography. New York: McGraw-Hill, 1979.
Lost Sandstones and Lonely Skies and Other Essays. [Danbury, Conn.]: Archer Editions Press, 1980.
The Best-Loved Short Stories of Jesse Stuart. Ed. H. Edward Richardson; Introduction by Robert Penn Warren. New York: McGraw-Hill, 1982.
Land of the Honey-Colored Wind. Ed. Jerry A. Herndon. [Morehead, Ky.]: Jesse Stuart Foundation, 1982.

Studies of Jesse Stuart

Blair, Everetta Love. *Jesse Stuart: His Life and Works.* Columbia: University of South Carolina Press, 1967.
Clarke, Mary Washington. *Jesse Stuart's Kentucky.* New York: McGraw-Hill, 1968.
Foster, Ruel E. *Jesse Stuart.* New York: Twayne, 1968.
Leavell, Frank Hartwell. "The Literary Career of Jesse Stuart." Unpublished Ph.D. dissertation, Vanderbilt University, 1966.
LeMaster, J. R. *Jesse Stuart: A Reference Guide.* Boston: G. K. Hall, 1979.
————. *Jesse Stuart: Kentucky's Chronicler-Poet.* Memphis: Memphis State University Press, 1980.
LeMaster, J. R. and Mary Washington Clarke, ed. *Jesse Stuart: Essays on His Work.* Lexington: University Press of Kentucky, 1977.
Perry, Dick. *Reflections of Jesse Stuart on a Land of Many Moods.* New York: McGraw-Hill, 1971.
Ramey, Lee Oly. "An Inquiry into the Life of Jesse Stuart as Related to His Literary Development and a Critical Study of His Works." Unpublished M.A. thesis, Ohio University, 1941.
Richardson, H. Edward. *Jesse: The Biography of an American Writer, Jesse Hilton Stuart.* New York: McGraw-Hill, 1984.
Woodbridge, Hensley C. *Jesse Stuart: A Bibliography.* Harrogate, Tenn.: Lincoln Memorial University Press, 1960.
————. *Jesse and Jane Stuart: A Bibliography.* Murray, Ky.: Murray State University Press, 1970.

See also the regular updatings in *The Jack London Newsletter*.

————————— MELVIN J. FRIEDMAN —————————

William Styron
(1925–   )

William Styron is probably the least parochial and least regional of major contemporary Southern writers. His broad and far-ranging sympathies make him an author of international scope and consequence, clearly of Nobel laureate stature. His fiction and essays have confronted the most complex and controversial themes of our time, with no trace of compromise.

BIOGRAPHY

William Styron was born in Newport News, Virginia, on 11 June 1925, the only child of William Clark Styron (whose roots were in the upper South) and Pauline Margaret Abraham (a Pennsylvanian). He maintained an abiding love for the Virginia Tidewater, which he characterized years later in *This Quiet Dust* as possessing "a unique unspoiled loveliness" and as being "distinctly Southern, adumbrated by the memory of a tragic past." His early sense of place indelibly marks his mature writing.

Styron was sent to Christchurch (an Episcopal boys' prep school near Urbanna, Virginia) in 1940, about a year after his mother's death. Following an unremarkable two years at Christchurch, characterized by what he later referred to as "my wretched grades," he entered Davidson College in North Carolina. He enlisted in the Marine Corps in the spring of 1943. His subsequent academic training, both during and after World War II, was at Duke University. Whereas his Marine Corps service proved rather uneventful—he was discharged in 1945 without seeing combat—his years at Duke were crucial in determining his career as a writer. There he studied with William Blackburn, serving a creative writing apprenticeship similar to that of many of his contemporaries—Flannery O'Connor, Robie Macauley, and W. D. Snodgrass. With encouragement from Blackburn, he applied for a Rhodes scholarship in his senior year and reached the interview stage in Atlanta, only to be denied at that point.

Styron graduated from Duke in 1947 and took a job at McGraw-Hill shortly thereafter. His six-month stint with this New York publisher, described with a fine satirical edge many years later in *Sophie's Choice*, was frustrating. During this period he also enrolled in Hiram Haydn's creative writing class at the New School for Social Research. Haydn served as mentor and editor during the next several years—which saw Styron's first novel, *Lie Down in Darkness*, pass through the presses at Bobbs-Merrill and receive acclaim from such reviewers as Malcolm Cowley, Howard Mumford Jones, Maxwell Geismar, and John W. Aldridge.

Styron turned to this novel virtually full-time in fall 1947 and completed it by April 1951 after a number of early false starts. One of the most productive periods for his work in progress was spent at Valley Cottage, a village near Nyack, New York, at the home of Sigrid de Lima (the author of *Carnival by the Sea*, *Oriane*, *Captain's Beach*, and other novels, to whom he dedicated *Lie Down in Darkness*). Styron's stay at Valley Cottage perhaps stands to his career as Flannery O'Connor's residence at the Connecticut home of Sally and Robert Fitzgerald stands to hers.

He was called back into the Marines following the completion of *Lie Down in Darkness* but was discharged after a few months, in time for the 10 September 1951 publication date of his first novel. Just as the negative McGraw-Hill experience offered him the substance for the first chapter of *Sophie's Choice*, so this frustrating, though abbreviated, second tour of duty supplied him with the basis for his novella *The Long March* and raw material for his current novel in progress, "The Way of the Warrior."

For *Lie Down in Darkness* Styron received the Prix de Rome in 1952. He left for Europe in the spring of that year to begin his *Wanderjahre*, which brought him briefly to England and Denmark; then to Paris for an extended stay; and finally to Rome, where he settled into the American Academy in October. The months in Paris (a city he has returned to on numerous occasions) were especially productive: there in the summer he wrote *The Long March* "with miraculous ease" and was also involved in founding the *Paris Review*. The lengthy residence in Rome was less memorable from a literary standpoint; it was highlighted, however, by his marriage on 4 May 1953 to the poet Rose Burgunder, whom Styron had met earlier at Elliott Coleman's writing seminar at Johns Hopkins University.

After a long stay in Ravello and travels about Italy, in October 1954 the Styrons settled in Roxbury, Connecticut, where they have lived ever since. Styron commented on the decision not to return to the South when he told Robert K. Morris: "I felt a far more cosmopolitan sense of direction, and I needed to get out of the South because it was no longer a deeply involved part of my psychic nature." By the time of the move to Connecticut after more than two years in Europe, Styron was into his third extended work of fiction, *Set This House on*

Fire. This novel took maximum advantage of a variety of settings its author felt close to: the Virginia Tidewater of his childhood, the France and Italy of his recent travels. Whereas *Lie Down in Darkness* profited immensely from Styron's reading of Faulkner, especially *The Sound and the Fury*, and of Robert Penn Warren's *All the King's Men* (for the second-person voice of the opening pages), *Set This House on Fire* seemed much closer to the F. Scott Fitzgerald of *The Great Gatsby* and *Tender Is the Night*. Styron's third novel was published on his seventh wedding anniversary, by Random House, the publisher that had brought out a paperback edition of *The Long March* in October 1956—three and a half years after its appearance in the first number of *Discovery*. Styron moved from Bobbs-Merrill to Random House, along with Hiram Haydn, and remained with Random House, which has been bringing out his work for the past three decades.

Set This House on Fire fared less well with the reviewers than *Lie Down in Darkness* did. Although Charles Fenton's lengthy review in the Autumn 1960 *South Atlantic Quarterly* was unsparing in its praise, other established critics found much to be unhappy and perplexed about. In France, however, following its appearance in Maurice-Edgar Coindreau's elegant translation in February 1962, *Set This House on Fire* (*La Proie des flammes*) was roundly applauded and helped place Styron among an elite gathering of American writers who have been virtually canonized by the French. (Flannery O'Connor commented on this in a letter dated 3 November 1962 in *The Habit of Being*: "M. Coindreau tells me that Styron's book, *Set This House on Fire*, was a great success in France . . . and that the French think Styron is the greatest thing since Faulkner.")

In the years following the publication of *Set This House on Fire*, Styron became something of an expert on the literature and historiography of slave revolts as he began his novel about the Nat Turner slave insurrection. During this period his nonfiction writing for magazines such as the *New York Review of Books* (he contributed to its inaugural issue in 1963), the *New York Times Book Review*, *Harper's*, and *Esquire* placed him in a Gallic tradition of *engagement*, a tradition that includes Sartre, Malraux, and Camus. Styron, like these older French contemporaries, was confronting in his essays the larger subjects: capital punishment, American Negro slavery, the Holocaust, and the military. He began to assume in these journalistic pieces a polemical stance that served him well in his next two novels.

Although *The Confessions of Nat Turner* was not published until October 1967, Styron spoke about his novel in progress in the July 1963 *Esquire* ("Two Writers Talk It Over") in a conversation with James Jones. He discussed it in even more detail in the April 1965 *Harper's* ("This Quiet Dust"). Sections of the novel were serialized in *Partisan Review*, *Life*, and *Harper's*. Word was out, surely, in advance of the appearance of *Nat Turner* that Styron was at work on an extended work of fiction about a slave insurrection—a rather daring enterprise during a period of so-called black power when whites were expected to avoid black subjects.

The early reviews in the prestigious weeklies were overwhelmingly favorable:

C. Vann Woodward in the *New Republic*, Philip Rahv in the *New York Review of Books*, and George Steiner in the *New Yorker*, for example, proclaimed its virtues. Eventually, however, charges of historical inaccuracy and of lack of sympathy and understanding in portraying Nat Turner were hurled at Styron. On 4 July 1968 Benson Press published *William Styron's Nat Turner: Ten Black Writers Respond*, a collection of ill-tempered essays accusing Styron, among other things, of having "a vile racist imagination" and of being "morally senile." Styron took on his critics in the *Nation* and the *New York Review of Books* in the next several years, as the polemical climate continued into the 1970s. The final judgment was doubtless rendered in Styron's favor when he was awarded the Pulitzer Prize in 1968 and the Howells Medal of the American Academy in 1970.

His only play to date, *In the Clap Shack*, was put on by Yale Repertory Theatre in December 1972 and brought out as a book by Random House in 1973, also the year of publication of Rose Styron's collection of poems, *Thieves' Afternoon*, by Viking, and of Styron's screenplay collaboration with John Phillips, "Dead!," in the December *Esquire*.

Styron's next large undertaking after *The Confessions of Nat Turner* was a novel, still unfinished, "The Way of the Warrior." Parts of it appeared in the September 1971 *Esquire* ("Marriott, the Marine") and the May/June 1974 *American Poetry Review* ("The Suicide Run"). He temporarily put this work aside for reasons he explained in his 1975 interview with James L. W. West III: "But there intervened, when I was fairly well along in the book—several hundred pages—together with a sense of confusion as to where I was going, there intervened this new vision which was so demanding: the novel that I'm now writing called *Sophie's Choice*." *Sophie's Choice* was published 11 June 1979, on Styron's fifty-fourth birthday. This novel flashes back and forth between fact and fable, blurring distinctions between the two, on the way to diagnosing the ills of a period in Western history that accommodated such atrocities as American Negro slavery and the Nazi concentration camps. Although there is much going on in this work, which reveals Styron's skills as an essay writer as well as a novelist, the central preoccupation is with the Holocaust. Styron seems to go beyond such Jewish writers as Elie Wiesel and Edward Lewis Wallant by making the phenomenon of the death camps "antihuman" rather than merely anti-Semitic.

There were rumblings here and there among Jews who felt that Styron was making an abstraction out of a concrete instance of the systematic attempt by the Nazis to annihilate the Jewish people. These voices, however, were not nearly as strident as those of the ten black writers who responded to *Nat Turner*; nor were those of a group of Polish American historians who questioned the authenticity of the Polish scenes in *Sophie's Choice* in the Spring 1983 number of *Polish American Studies*. The cinema version attracted a good deal of attention and earned an Academy Award for Meryl Streep. The *New Yorker*, which had dismissed the novel in its unsigned "Books Briefly Noted" (18 June 1979), was unencouraging also about the film: Pauline Kael expressed contempt for the movie based on what she called "William Styron's Holocaust Gothic" (27 December 1982).

In 1982 Styron collected his essays and reviews in *This Quiet Dust*. Stretching back over three decades, these pieces systematically mirror the development of his literary talent as well as the maturing of his public and historical consciousness. The volume possesses a unity absent from other recent gatherings of nonfiction by novelists, such as John Updike's *Hugging the Shore* and John Barth's *The Friday Book*.

Styron is apparently again at work on "The Way of the Warrior" and continues to write occasional essays and reviews. He has always been a painfully slow worker, as he has reminded all of his interviewers since his 1954 *Paris Review* interview. But as he told West, he still maintains that "very comfortable relationship with No. 2 pencils and these yellow sheets."

MAJOR THEMES

Styron has consistently dealt with the larger themes, the more demanding subjects. Even in his novella *The Long March*, he was able to enlarge the possibilities of a forced march in the Marine Corps and turn it into a tragedy of almost Sophoclean dimensions. He achieved this effect partly through allusion: "In the morbid, comfortless light they were like classical Greek masks, made of chrome or tin, reflecting an almost theatrical disharmony . . . " (p. 29). The Bible, Greek tragedy, the plays of Shakespeare, Mozart's operas, the philosophy of Kierkegaard, and other central texts of Western culture enlarge the frame of Styron's novels and carry their experiences beyond the quotidian. The ordinary in all of his works is expanded by symbol, myth, and allusion.

Styron's work is Southern, but not in the usual sense. In his interview with Robert K. Morris, he made the salient distinction: "I do not consider myself a southern writer in the sense that let us say, Eudora Welty might consider herself one. She is, and Flannery O'Connor is another, an almost perfect example of a fine 'regional' southern novelist. Basically, I guess, I am trying to make a distinction between southern regionalism (which can be a very strong, fine thrust in literature), and my own work, which is southern, but perhaps not regionally southern."

Styron is most recognizably a Southern writer in *Lie Down in Darkness*. Although set in the Virginia Tidewater of Styron's early years, it offers echoes and reminders of other places and events. Faulkner's Yoknapatawpha cycle of novels immediately comes to mind. Reviewers and critics connected Peyton's funeral procession with the burial expedition in *As I Lay Dying*, Peyton's lasciviousness with Temple Drake's in *Sanctuary*, and Peyton's suicide monologue with Quentin's in *The Sound and the Fury*. Indeed, one might say that *The Sound and the Fury* stands to *Lie Down in Darkness* in somewhat the same way that *The Odyssey* stands to Joyce's *Ulysses*, as offering a literary scaffolding.

Just as Joyce seemed to be acknowledging his lifelong fondness for Homer in using the *Odyssey* parallel, so Styron was staking out his position as a Southern writer when he persistently and creatively echoed *The Sound and the Fury*. Styron uses something akin to T. S. Eliot's "mythical method" in structuring *Lie Down in Darkness*.

The scaffolding is more elaborate in *Set This House on Fire*. The narrator is a Virginian and the backdrop of the novel is Southern, but much of the action occurs in Europe. The theme of the ingenuous American abroad, which we associate with Mark Twain, Henry James, and F. Scott Fitzgerald, is one of several myths Styron explores. Echoes from *The Great Gatsby* are sounded intermittently through Styron's text. There are also echoes of Kierkegaard ("I was very nearly sick unto death"), of Sartre ("as for being and nothingness"), and of E. E. Cummings ("he moved through dooms of love, through griefs of joy"), among other writers. There is even something of a running parallel between Styron's text and Sophocles's *Oedipus at Colonus*, which has been explained persuasively by another novelist who has skillfully cultivated myth, Michel Butor (in his preface, "Oedipus Americanus," to *La Proie des flammes*). *Don Giovanni* (which also threads its way through Leopold Bloom's thoughts in *Ulysses*) and *The Magic Flute* are frequently invoked in this richly textured novel.

The Confessions of Nat Turner more restrainedly contains literary references and echoes. Biblical quotations occur frequently in Nat's almost hymnal confession; they are drawn especially from the prophetic books of the Old Testament. They serve almost as subtexts as they enlarge the frame of Styron's narrative. Styron's novel is more than a historical rendering of a slave insurrection. It is "a meditation on history," as Styron calls it in his author's note, as well as an extended poetic statement about the possibilities of myth.

A number of myths converge in *Sophie's Choice*. Most of this novel takes place in New York, "amid the Kingdom of the Jews," as the displaced Virginian, Stingo, refers to it. Although the here-and-now events occur in Jewish Brooklyn, Tidewater Virginia keeps intruding; more important than either of these settings is the Poland of Cracow, Warsaw, and especially of Auschwitz. *Sophie's Choice* begins as a typical *Künstlerroman*, with a young Southern writer at work on his first novel, but it expands into a vastly complicated meditation on evil, with American Negro slavery and particularly the Holocaust as touchstones. (In his July 1963 *Esquire* exchange with James Jones, Styron had already brought the two events together: "The plantation slave . . . was brutalized spiritually in a way that the only analogy is to the victims of the Nazi concentration camps who *never revolted*.")

Sophie's Choice is surely Styron's most ambitious book, containing the seeds of the urban Jewish novel, with a nod to Philip Roth and Saul Bellow; the Southern novel, with frequent glances back at Faulkner and Thomas Wolfe; and the European novel of ideas of the kind written by Thomas Mann and André Malraux. Woven into the text are an elaborate series of documentary subtexts.

Styron, for example, culls from the formidable literature on the Holocaust bits and pieces from such works as George Steiner's *Language and Silence*, Richard Rubenstein's *The Cunning of History*, and Rudolf Hoss's *Commandant of Auschwitz*—which he reinforces at every turn with his own elegant commentary. The "mythical method" that operated on a small scale in *Lie Down in Darkness*, with its Faulknerian indulgences, swells to giant proportions in *Sophie's Choice*. Although Styron remains a Southern writer in his latest novel, he has eliminated any vestige of the regionalism that in his interview with Morris he attached to the works of Welty and O'Connor. His strongest ties here are with the European modernists such as Gide, Malraux, and Mann, especially with the way they secure everything in comfortably mythical terms.

Violence is another compelling force in each of Styron's works. *Lie Down in Darkness* moves circularly toward its moment of violence, Peyton Loftis's suicide. *The Long March*, with its division into five parts, has the spareness of Greek tragedy and an atmosphere of impending doom. We are reminded at one point of man's being hopelessly "astray at mid-century in the never-endingness of war." Violence occurs early and late in this novella; it starts with a graphic description of the accidental and unnecessary death of eight Marine recruits ("what was left of eight dead boys lay strewn about the landscape. . . . ") and ends with a reference to Captain Mannix, whose "drawn-down mouth was one of tortured and gigantic suffering." One of the last words describing Mannix is *endured*, a word that Faulkner used frequently.

Set This House on Fire, with even more circularity than *Lie Down in Darkness*, moves toward violence, this time rape and murder. The landscape of violence has shifted from Virginia to Sambuco, Italy. Through a mock-detective twist— something readers have come to expect from contemporary French writers such as Alain Robbe-Grillet and Michel Butor—Cass Kinsolving, the murderer of Mason Flagg, is granted absolution by the Italian policeman Luigi, who declares the death a suicide, and is permitted to return to his native South Carolina. Although *Lie Down in Darkness* and *The Long March* end in the falling apart of worlds, *Set This House on Fire* concludes with renewal and revitalization. Styron's third novel is his only tragicomedy.

In *The Confessions of Nat Turner* Styron enters American history to confront violence. In choosing his approach to the Nat Turner slave insurrection, Styron took the moderate position expressed in Stanley M. Elkins's *Slavery*, eschewing the extreme views of Herbert Aptheker's *American Negro Slave Revolts*. As in *Lie Down in Darkness* and *Set This House on Fire*, we are led through complex occurrences before the actual violence is reached—this time by the first-person voice of Nat himself, which weaves in and out of psychological and historical events. The insurrection is described in considerable detail, with Nat's murder of Margaret Whitehead (the only murder he is able to commit) presented in all its grim and shocking immediacy: "She crumpled to earth, limp, a rag, and as she fell I stabbed her again in the same place, or near it, where pulsing blood already encrimsoned the taffeta's blue." Violence is perhaps more graphically expressed here than in Styron's earlier fiction.

In *Sophie's Choice* Styron explores the Holocaust, a subject he eloquently characterized in *The Quiet Dust* as "so incomprehensible and so awesomely central to our present-day consciousness." He counterpoints his study of this most sustained and horrifying occurrence of violence in the twentieth century with reminders of Nat Turner's insurrection. These two instances of destruction offer, in a sense, forewarnings of the death of two of the central characters of Styron's novel, Sophie Zawistowska and Nathan Landau, through a double suicide. Collective and individual violence are both on display in *Sophie's Choice*.

Styron resembles his modernist forebears in the way he seems to delight in the suggestive possibilities of language, in the way that poetry mixes with prose— denying all classical distinctions between the two. His novels achieve much of their force and vitality through elaborate descriptions. His sense of place, often thought of as a special province of Southern writers, is everywhere apparent in his Baedeker-like appreciations of landscape: of the Virginia countryside in *Lie Down in Darkness* and *The Confessions of Nat Turner*; of the scenery of southern Italy in *Set This House on Fire*; of the angle shots of Poland in *Sophie's Choice*. In one brief section of *Sophie's Choice* (pp. 246–47), he brings Poland and the American South into compelling juxtaposition:

Poland is a beautiful, heart-wrenching, soul-split country which in many ways . . . resembles or conjures up images of the American South—or at least the South of other, not-so-distant times. It is not alone that forlornly lovely, nostalgic landscape which creates the frequent likeness . . . but in the spirit of the nation, her indwellingly ravaged and melancholy heart, tormented into its shape like that of the Old South out of adversity, penury and defeat.

Such passages, which abound in Styron's fiction, reveal a fondness for words equaled only by a very few of Styron's American contemporaries—John Hawkes and John Updike, for example.

SURVEY OF CRITICISM

Probably the best starting point for the scholar approaching Styron criticism is the work of James L. W. West III. Styron speaks of him appreciatively as his bibliographer in his "Note to the Reader" at the start of *This Quiet Dust*. West performed this function admirably in his *William Styron: A Descriptive Bibliography*, "a full-dress bibliography," which "charts Styron's literary career from his high school and prep school years to the present." The book also contains a short, admiring preface by Styron. This bibliography is a model of its kind: thorough, accurate, imaginative, and intelligently arranged for easy use.

West is also coeditor (with Arthur D. Casciato) of *Critical Essays on William Styron*, part of the distinguished, ongoing Critical Essays on American Literature series, under the general editorship of James Nagel. This volume offers an effective blend of biography, criticism, textual study, and literary reception. West's introduction, "William Styron in Mid-Career," is an admirably compressed biographical sketch, the best we have. The West-Casciato collection contains sections on all five of the author's extended works of fiction and his single play, as well as a concluding part entitled "Styron *en France*." Reviews mingle with lengthy critical essays. All but two of the sections contain statements by Styron himself. Important pieces by Roger Asselineau and Michel Butor appear here in English translation for the first time.

The Achievement of William Styron, edited by Robert K. Morris and Irving Malin and now in its second edition, is also useful. As I noted in my review of the first edition, "The nine essays in the Morris-Malin collection are generally of high quality, with the most distinguished being the reprinted pieces of Louis Rubin and of Seymour Gross and Eileen Bender. . . . Among the new essays, Malin's on *The Long March* and Morris' on *In the Clap Shack* are probably the best" (*Studies in American Fiction*, Autumn 1978). The second edition expands the collection to twelve essays, the most impressive addition being Richard Pearce's "Sophie's Choices."

Pearce is the author of one of the four pamphlets on Styron. His is No. 98 in the University of Minnesota Pamphlets on American Writers series and offers a balanced, critically sound appraisal of the work through *The Confessions of Nat Turner*. The other three—written by Cooper R. Mackin, Robert H. Fossum, and Melvin J. Friedman—are also series books and concentrate on Styron's first four novels. Friedman's study, longer than the others, ventures outside of the American scene and offers a chapter on French relationships.

Marc L. Ratner's *William Styron* (Twayne's United States Authors Series) is the longest sustained examination by a single critic. Individual chapters are devoted to each of the first four novels; these are framed by chapters with biographical and thematic orientations; and a final chapter, "Styron and the South," offers a useful context for the work. Ratner should consider bringing out a second edition of his valuable work. The second edition should add assessments of *In the Clap Shack*, *Sophie's Choice*, and *This Quiet Dust*.

Three other books deal largely with *The Confessions of Nat Turner*. *William Styron's "The Confessions of Nat Turner": A Critical Handbook*, edited by Melvin J. Friedman and Irving Malin, and *The Nat Turner Rebellion: The Historical Event and the Modern Controversy*, edited by John B. Duff and Peter M. Mitchell, are casebooks that offer broad perspectives on the novel and its backgrounds, mainly through reprinted material. The contributions to *William Styron's Nat Turner: Ten Black Writers Respond*, edited by John Henrik Clarke, have more than their share of anger and dissatisfaction, less than their share of literary analysis and considered judgment.

Two book-length bibliographies of the criticism appeared in 1978. Jackson

R. Bryer's *William Styron: A Reference Guide* is the work of perhaps the most accomplished bibliographer and editor of twentieth-century American literature. Bryer also supplied elaborate checklists of Styron material for both *William Styron's "The Confessions of Nat Turner": A Critical Handbook* and the two editions of *The Achievement of William Styron*. His introduction to *William Styron: A Reference Guide* is the best overview of the criticism. His annotations of the individual entries are models of compression and accuracy. Philip W. Leon's *William Styron: An Annotated Bibliography of Criticism* uses a quite different format. It fortunately complements rather than duplicates Bryer's efforts. The style of the G. K. Hall reference guide virtually prohibits critical judgments from intruding on the annotations. Leon works under no such handicap, as he often ventures opinions, both positive and negative.

Critique: Studies in Modern Fiction on two occasions offered issues with heavy concentrations of Styron criticism (Summer 1960 and Winter 1965–66). The first of these gatherings, which included Harold W. Schneider's bibliography (the first one published), seemed to launch the first wave of Styron commentary. All three of the essays in this Summer 1960 number expressed some disappointment with *Set This House on Fire*. Particularly scathing (and in large part unjustified) is Richard Foster's "An Orgy of Commerce: William Styron's *Set This House on Fire*," which begins with this overblown sentence: "The spirit of Hollywood looms and hovers over this absurd book like some Unholy Ghost, giving it its vast Cineramic shape, its hectic vulgar supercoloration, its hollow belting loudness of tone, and its ethos of commercial self-excitation." Negative soundings resurfaced in different forms in response to Styron's subsequent work. Most often they took on nonliterary aspects, as when black writers and certain American historians expressed outrage at *The Confessions of Nat Turner* and when a group of Polish American historians found fault with the Polish settings depicted and attitudes expressed in *Sophie's Choice*. Objections have also been raised to literary habits. Roy Arthur Swanson, in his "William Styron's Clown Show" (found in the Friedman-Malin *Critical Handbook*), quotes Richard Foster approvingly on his first page and proceeds to identify such things as "tired romantic prose." J. Mitchell Morse offers several pages on *The Confessions of Nat Turner* in his *The Irrelevant English Teacher* (Temple University Press, 1972), concluding that "it is very sloppily written" and "has no place in any college course concerned with literature or with writing."

But the critical commentary has been by all odds more positive than negative, especially when it has concentrated on aesthetic rather than political matters. Styron's work has indeed been praised by some of the most gifted critics of American literature, including Louis D. Rubin, Jr., Frederick J. Hoffman, Ihab Hassan, Malcolm Cowley, and Philip Rahv. Yet Styron remains a controversial writer in this country, while his French critics generally elevate him above any of his American contemporaries.

A new collection of Styron criticism appeared in *Delta* in 1985, under the guest editorship of André Bleikasten. This journal is the official organ of the

Centre d'Étude et de Recherches sur les Écrivains du Sud aux États-Unis at l'Université Paul Valéry à Montpellier. This anthology of essays reinforces the high regard with which Styron is held in France. The French taught us how to appreciate Faulkner; perhaps they will accomplish the same with Faulkner's worthiest heir.

BIBLIOGRAPHY

Works by William Styron

Lie Down in Darkness. Indianapolis and New York: Bobbs-Merrill, 1951.

The Long March. New York: Random House, 1956; Modern Library Paperback.

Set This House on Fire. New York: Random House, 1960.

The Confessions of Nat Turner. New York: Random House, 1967.

"Marriott, the Marine." *Esquire* 76 (September 1971): 101–104, 196, 198, 200, 202, 204, 207–208, 210.

"Dead!" *Esquire* 80 (December 1973): 161–168, 264, 266, 270, 274, 277–278, 280, 282, 286, 290; screenplay collaboration with John Phillips.

In The Clap Shack. New York: Random House, 1973.

"An Interview with William Styron," ed. Ben Forkner and Gilbert Schricke. *Southern Review* 10 (Fall 1974): 923–34.

"The Suicide Run." *The American Poetry Review* 3 (May/June 1974): 20–22.

"Shadrach," *Esquire* 90 (21 November 1978): 85, 87, 88–90, 92–93, 95–96; *Shadrach*. Los Angeles: Sylvester and Orphanos, 1979 [limited signed edition].

"An Interview with William Styron," ed. Valarie M. Arms. *Contemporary Literature* 20 (Winter 1979): 1–12.

Sophie's Choice. New York: Random House, 1979.

This Quiet Dust. New York: Random House, 1982.

Studies of William Styron

Aldridge, John W. "William Styron and the Derivative Imagination." *Time to Murder and Create: The Contemporary Novel in Crisis*. New York: McKay, 1966, pp. 30–51.

Baumbach, Jonathan. "Paradise Lost: The Novels of William Styron." *South Atlantic Quarterly* 63 (Spring 1964): 207–17. Reprinted in *The Landscape of Nightmare: Studies in the Contemporary American Novel*. New York: New York University Press, 1965, pp. 123–37.

Bryant, Jerry H. "The Hopeful Stoicism of William Styron." *South Atlantic Quarterly* 62 (Autumn 1963): 539–50.

Bryer, Jackson R. with Mary Beth Hatem. *William Styron: A Reference Guide*. Boston: G. K. Hall, 1978.

Casciato, Arthur D. and James L. W. West III, ed. *Critical Essays on William Styron*. Boston: G. K. Hall, 1982.

Clarke, John Henrik, ed. *William Styron's "Nat Turner": Ten Black Writers Respond*. Boston: Beacon Press, 1968.

Core, George. "*The Confessions of Nat Turner* and the Burden of the Past." *Southern Literary Journal* 2 (Spring 1970): 117–34.

Crane, John Kenny. *The Root of All Evil: The Thematic Unity of William Styron's Fiction.* Columbia: University of South Carolina Press, 1984.

Davis, Robert Gorham. "Styron and the Students." *Critique* 3 (Summer 1960): 37–46.

Duff, John B. and Peter M. Mitchell, ed. *The Nat Turner Rebellion: The Historical Event and the Modern Controversy.* New York: Harper & Row, 1971.

Fossum, Robert H. *William Styron: A Critical Essay.* Contemporary Writers in Christian Perspective. Grand Rapids, Mich.: William B. Eerdmans, 1968.

Foster, Richard. "An Orgy of Commerce: William Styron's *Set This House on Fire.*" *Critique* 3 (Summer 1960): 59–70.

Friedman, Melvin J. "The 'French Face' of William Styron." *International Fiction Review* 10 (Winter 1983): 33–37.

———. *William Styron.* Popular Writers Series No. 3. Bowling Green, Ohio: Bowling Green University Popular Press, 1974.

Friedman, Melvin J. and Irving Malin, ed. *William Styron's "The Confessions of Nat Turner": A Critical Handbook.* Belmont, Calif.: Wadsworth, 1970.

Friedman, Melvin J. and August J. Nigro, ed. *Configuration Critique de William Styron.* Paris: Lettres Modernes, 1967.

Galloway, David D. *The Absurd Hero in American Fiction: Updike, Styron, Bellow, Salinger.* 2d rev. ed. Austin: University of Texas Press, 1981.

Gossett, Louise Y. "The Cost of Freedom: William Styron." *Violence in Recent Southern Fiction.* Durham, N.C.: Duke University Press, 1965, pp. 117–31.

Gray, Richard. "Victims of History and Agents of Revolution: William Styron." *The Literature of Memory: Modern Writers of the American South.* Baltimore and London: Johns Hopkins University Press, 1977, pp. 284–305.

Hoffman, Frederick J. "William Styron: The Metaphysical Hurt." *The Art of Southern Fiction: A Study of Some Modern Novelists.* Carbondale and Edwardsville: Southern Illinois University Press, 1967, pp. 144–61.

Klotz, Marvin. "The Triumph over Time: Narrative Form in William Faulkner and William Styron." *Mississippi Quarterly* 17 (Winter 1963–64): 9–20.

Leon, Philip W. *William Styron: An Annotated Bibliography of Criticism.* Westport, Conn.: Greenwood Press, 1978.

Mackin, Cooper R. *William Styron.* Southern Writers Series No. 7. Austin: Steck-Vaughn, 1969.

Moore, L. Hugh. "Robert Penn Warren, William Styron, and the Use of Greek Myth." *Critique* 8 (Winter 1965–66): 75–87.

Morris, Robert K. and Irving Malin, ed. *The Achievement of William Styron.* 2d ed. Athens: University of Georgia Press, 1981.

O'Connell, Shaun. "Expense of Spirit: The Vision of William Styron." *Critique* 8 (Winter 1965–66): 20–33.

Pearce, Richard. *William Styron.* University of Minnesota Pamphlets on American Writers No. 98. Minneapolis: University of Minnesota Press, 1971.

Ratner, Marc L. *William Styron.* New York: Twayne, 1972.

Robb, Kenneth A. "William Styron's Don Juan." *Critique* 8 (Winter 1965–66): 34–46.

Rubenstein, Richard L. "The South Encounters the Holocaust: William Styron's *Sophie's Choice.*" *Michigan Quarterly Review* 20 (Fall 1981): 425–42.

Rubin, Louis D., Jr. "William Styron: Notes on a Southern Writer in Our Time." *The*

Faraway Country: Writers of the Modern South. Seattle: University of Washington Press, 1963, pp. 185–230.

Stevenson, David L. "Styron and the Fiction of the Fifties." *Critique* 3 (Summer 1960): 47–58.

Tischler, Nancy M., ed. *"The Confessions of Nat Turner*: A Symposium." *Barat Review* 6 (1971): 3–37.

Urang, Gunnar. "The Voices of Tragedy in the Novels of William Styron." *Adversity and Grace: Studies in Recent American Literature*. Ed. Nathan A. Scott, Jr. Chicago: University of Chicago Press, 1968, pp. 183–209.

West, James L. W., III. "A Bibliographer's Interview with William Styron." *Costerus*, n.s., 4 (1975): 13–29.

———. *William Styron: A Descriptive Bibliography*. Boston: G. K. Hall, 1977.

THOMAS DANIEL YOUNG

Allen Tate
(1899–1979)

Allen Tate is assured of a place among the most significant writers of his generation. The author of twelve books of poetry, two biographies, eight books of essays, a novel, and a book of memoirs, and editor of more than a dozen other books, he excelled in each of these genres. Tate's primary concerns are those of his age: (1) the dissociation of sensibility, (2) the search for a sustaining and continuing tradition, (3) the opposition to materialistic positivism, and (4) the necessity of man's finding a meaningful relationship to a universe from which the gods have disappeared.

BIOGRAPHY

Born on 19 November 1899 to John Orley and Eleanor Varnell Tate, in Winchester, Kentucky, Allen Tate believed until he was thirty, because his mother told him he was, that he was a Virginian. In his childhood Tate's family moved two or three times a year, "moving *away* from something my mother didn't like." His earliest memories are of residential hotels, watering places, and resorts visited yearly by his mother. In one of these places, Tate recalled years later, his mother told him: "Son, put that book down and go play with Henry. You are straining your mind and you know your mind isn't very strong." (Tate's head was abnormally large and he refers to it ironically in several poems as if he were a water head.)

Because his father early withdrew from social and economic activity, the responsibility of head of the family passed to Allen's older brother, Ben. Tate's early education was haphazard and irregular because his mother seldom stayed in one place long enough for him to complete a school year. In the twenty or so different schools he attended, for periods varying from a few weeks to a rare academic year, he was, he recalled later, always the "new boy.... I had to win my masculine standing at every new school by fist fighting the bully. I don't think I ever won, for if my mind was weak, my physique was weaker.''

One of the few schools he attended for an entire year was the Tarbox School in Nashville, where he lived with his mother while his two older brothers attended Vanderbilt University. Years later when Tate enrolled in Vanderbilt he found that although the passage from Latin he was given to translate as part of the admissions requirements was taken from a longer passage he had memorized, he needed a tutor to pass required mathematics. Having no idea that he had any literary ambitions, he enrolled in Greek and Latin, as well as in the classes of some of the most respected faculty members: in English, Walter Clyde Curry and John Crowe Ransom; in philosophy, Herbert Charles Sanborn; in Greek, Herbert Cushing Tolman. For Curry and Ransom he wrote his first poetry. Later, as a member of the Fugitive group, he continued to write poetry and published his first criticism.

Tate's first books to be published were biographies and poetry, which appeared after he moved to New York in the mid–1920s: *Stonewall Jackson: The Good Soldier* (1928) and *Mr. Pope and Other Poems* (1928). These were followed the next year by *Jefferson Davis: His Rise and Fall*. By this time he was earning his living by contributing reviews and essays to such journals as the *Nation*, the *New Republic*, and *Hound and Horn*. His first full-length critical essay, "Poetry and the Absolute," appeared in the *Sewanee Review* in 1927. In 1928 he received the first of two Guggenheim Fellowships, and before sailing to France, he contributed to *Fugitives: An Anthology of Verse* (1929), which included the first version of "Ode to the Confederate Dead." In 1930 he returned to Tennessee and moved into an antebellum farmhouse, where he could help plan *I'll Take My Stand* (1930), to which he contributed an essay, "Remarks on the Southern Religion."

Although he taught briefly at Southwestern at Memphis, North Carolina Woman's College, Princeton, St. Johns, Vanderbilt, and other institutions, his chief academic appointment was to the University of Minnesota, where he served for more than twenty years. In spite of his academic appointments, he always considered himself primarily a man of letters. For his creative and critical work he received many awards, including the Bollingen Prize, the *Medaglia d'Oro di Societa Italana di Dante Alighieri*, the Fellowship Award of the Academy of American Poets, and membership in the American Academy of Poets and the American Academy of Arts and Letters. He was married to the novelist Caroline Gordon (1924–59), the poet Isabella Gardner (1959–66), and Helen Heinz (1966–79). With Caroline Gordon he had a daughter, Nancy, and with Helen Heinz three sons: John Allen, Michael Paul (who died in childhood), and Benjamin Lewis Bogan. Tate died in Nashville on 9 February 1979.

MAJOR THEMES

In November 1921 Tate was invited to join the Fugitive group, a small coterie of faculty, students, and townspeople meeting at the home of James M. Frank, a local businessman, to discuss the writing of poetry and to criticize each other's verse. Tate's contributions to these meetings can hardly be overestimated. Although at this time he was not an accomplished poet and his verse was obviously that of an apprentice, he changed the nature and direction of the group's discussions. Rather than concentrating on Swinburne, Hardy, and the Imagists, who the most forward-thinking members of the group thought best represented modern techniques and attitudes in poetry, Tate introduced these young poets and would-be poets to the French Symbolists: Baudelaire, Valéry, Verlaine, Mallarmé, Remy de Gourmont, and Gerard de Nerval. Then he published a translation of Baudelaire's "Correspondences" in the December 1924 *Fugitive*, after explaining in the number for the previous April how Baudelaire assisted the modern poet's attempts to delineate his complex experiences by dressing up an idea out of one class of experience in the vocabulary of another. In this way the influence of the French on modern poetic theory and practice differed from that of both the English traditionalists and the Imagists. In his essay Tate had also, without mentioning the concept, prepared the group to receive Eliot's explanation of the same problem in his phrase "the objective correlative."

Although the poetry Tate wrote at Vanderbilt differs remarkably from his later verse, his associations with Ransom, Warren, and Davidson aided him in finding his subject—that is, contrasting a vital past with a purposeless present. Also, the intense criticism of his earliest poetic efforts by some of the most talented critics of the time profoundly influenced the search for his true poetic voice. Although he and Ransom disagreed on the nature and function of poetry—once their vastly differing opinions almost resulted in a permanent breach when Ransom reviewed unfavorably Eliot's *The West Land*—these sometimes violent discussions assisted both men in establishing their permanent positions on basic critical matters. Ransom argued that Tate's poetry was "obscure" because it lacked essential "structure" and placed too much emphasis on "seemingly irrelevant texture." The reason for Tate's intentional obscurity, Ransom speculated, was to avoid falling into the "moral-beautiful compound." Tate chose a "subject nearest to his own humanity, a subject perhaps of terrifying import; but in treating it" he stopped "short of all moral or theoretical conclusions, and confuse[d] his detail to the point where it [left] no positive implications."

Soon after Tate moved to New York in 1924, he began writing poetry markedly more finished than his earlier verse. On 2 September 1925 he published in the *Nation* "Mr. Pope," the title poem of his first collection three years later, *Mr. Pope and Other Poems* (1928). Along with allied subjects, the poem deals with the relations of the poet to society, not only Pope to the eighteenth century but any poet to any society. The sophisticated ladies in their sedans stare at the hideous shape of the poet:

> When Alexander Pope strolled in the city
> Strict was the glint of pearl and gold sedans.

Ladies leaned out, more out of fear than pity;
For Pope's tight back was rather a goat's than man's.

Tate points out, however, that the poet's misshapen body is merely temporal, but the poet "who dribbled couplets like a snake" belongs to the permanent world of art. Pope's use of traditional form and meter gives the form and order to his verse that his body, like the work of the modern poets, is denied. A carefully controlled poem is permanent and important, different from the help- lessly deformed creature who created it.

Shortly after the publication of this poem, Tate began working on "The Ode to the Confederate Dead," which carried a more emphatic statement of his concerns than any other poem he wrote before the 1940s: dissociation of sen- sibility, search for traditions, and opposition to positivism. The poem, as Tate points out in "Narcissus as Narcissus" (1938), is about narcissism, the belief that man creates the world in the act of perceiving it. A man stops at the gate of a Confederate cemetery. The season is autumn and the falling leaves, blown by the wind, "sough the rumor of mortality." Despite the desolation around him, he can only surmise that the "inexhaustible bodies" that lie in the graves beyond the stone wall are not "harbingers of spring," the promise of new life, because they are not part of the endless cycle of nature. They exist, if at all, because their decaying bodies have fed "the grass . . . row after rich row." His thoughts turn to "ambitious November . . . with a zeal for every slab." Novem- ber's only ambition, it would seem, is to destroy what April has produced. The decaying slabs stain "the uncomfortable angels that rot / On the slabs." As the man gazes transfixed, he is as impotent as those stone angels. Whatever ability to symbolize metaphysical reality they once possessed they have lost. The strophe ends with the man at the gate realizing that the stone wall really does separate him from the dead and what they represent. He is modern man who *knows* the grandeurs of the past but cannot participate in them. Like the blind crab, he has motion but no direction, energy but no purposeful world in which to use it.

As the poet moves into the antistrophe, the mood naturally changes. He turns to a consideration of the heroism that once characterized, his mind tells him, an entire society. Although he knows of Stonewall Jackson, the hero who gave his life for a cause, and the many battles in which others have done the same— Antietam, Malvern Hill, and Bull Run—his sensibility is unchanged. All he can perceive is that "the leaves / Flying, plunge and expire." He is left locked within his narcissistic self, "Cursing only the leaves crying / Like an old man lost in a storm." He has lost his creative imagination. He is bound to immanence. Unlike the Romantic poets, he cannot experience a "spot of time" or transcend his natural surroundings through the song of a nightingale. He is "The hound bitch / Toothless and dying, in a musty cellar."

Although the themes of "active faith" and "fragmentary chaos," as Hart Crane once characterized them, have struggled for ascendency throughout the poem, the winner is no longer in doubt:

We shall say only the leaves whispering
In the improbable mist of nightfall
That flies on multiple wing;
Night is the beginning and the end
And in between the ends of distraction
Waits mute speculation, the patient curse
That stones the eyes, or like the jaguar leaps
For his own image in the jungle pool, his victim.

Modern man, even he who has "knowledge / Carried to the heart," can only wait for death, or if he is too impatient to await his natural turn, he can *court* it.

Tate's essays of social and cultural criticism were of great significance to him as he struggled to find his own identity and place, as well as his function, in the modern world. Many of these essays were motivated by the same concerns that were the prime movers of the poetry appearing after 1928 and of his only novel, *The Fathers* (1938). In "Message from Abroad" (1929) he begins with an epigram from *Traveller to America* (1799): "Their faces are bony and sharp but very red. . . . " If these red-faced men are a part of his tradition, Tate can find no evidence of them in the expatriate society of the Left Bank; he is, therefore, very much aware of being an alien. Their feeling leads him to speculate on how a culture passes its traditions from one generation to another. He concludes that those cultures that have "poetry" and "statues" transmit naturally and easily their rites, rituals, ceremonies, myths, and manners. All cultural vestiges are lost, however, from those societies that do not have art.

A few weeks after he finished this poem, he began writing another, which at this time he was calling "Picnic at Cassis." He sent the poem to John Peale Bishop, who suggested major changes—some of which Tate adopted—and assured Tate that it "is not one of your best poems. It is your *best*." He also encouraged Tate to change the title to "The Mediterranean," for never "has the feeling of the Mediterranean from one of Northern blood . . . been so well expressed." That Tate wanted to retain this particular effect is indicated by his inclusion of some literal details of a picnic which he, Caroline Gordon, and perhaps fifteen others had attended with Ford Madox Ford: they had entered a small cove under perfect blue skies, where they ate "cocks boiled in wine and in great cauldrons a sumptuous bouillabaisse, a towering salad, a pile of cheese and fruit," all washed down with "61 bottles of wine." Ford remarked to Tate, according to Radcliffe Squires, "that it must have been in such a cove that Aeneas and his band had stopped to eat," a remark that sent Tate back to reread *The Aeneid*. That he wanted to expand on the remarks Ford had made is suggested by the fact that Tate supplied an epigraph from Book One of the epic. Venus is speaking to Jupiter, asking what has happened to Aeneas and his group. In translation her question is "What limit do you set to their pains, great king?" Or, as Tate has translated it: "What is the end of all this sorrow, great king?"

In the first stanza Tate suggests the three levels at which he wants the poem read. The first two lines are almost a direct statement of literal details:

> Where we went in the boat was a long bay
> A slingshot wide, walled in by towering stone—

The reference to the bay as being a "slingshot wide" foreshadows later metaphorical meanings that will be imposed upon the poem. The third line, "Peaked margin of antiquity's delay," reminds the reader that he will be asked to recall the flight of Aeneas from the fallen Troy, a landless wanderer seeking a new home. The fourth line, "And we went there out of time's monotone," reminds us of the comparison between Aeneas and his companions with the modern revelers that will thread its way throughout the poem. In "The New Provincialism" (1945) Tate reminds us in the phrase "time's monotone" that modern man is limited in time if not in space. He is a prisoner of time because he believes the present moment is unique. "He cuts himself off from the past and without the friend of traditional wisdom approaches the simplest problems . . . as if nobody had ever heard of them before." The modern picnickers do not realize that they are as homeless as Aeneas and his companions were. They too are seeking spiritual roots that will provide a center and purpose to their lives. In the third stanza the poet reminds us of the Aeneas myth: "And we made feast and in our secret need / Devoured the very plates Aeneas bore." Our secret need, of course, is an awareness of our traditions, not only of our Grecian heritage encompassed by the Aeneas myth but of our spiritual background suggested by the myth of the slingshot with which David slew the enemy of Jehovah.

But the westward movement of the modern world has carried us in a new direction, as our philosophy of acquisitive materialism has given us a new sense of values:

> What country shall we conquer, what fair land
> Unman our conquest and locate our blood?
> We've cracked the hemispheres with careless hand!
> Now, from the Gates of Hercules we flood
>
> Westward, westward till the barbarous brine
> Whelms us to the tired land where tasseling corn,
> Fat beans, grapes sweeter than muscadine
> Rot on the vine; in that land were we born.

In our search for material splendor, we have squandered our opportunities and fouled our nest; we must change our direction; we must make our journey eastward and find the traditional values that gave force and direction to the lives of such heroes as Aeneas and David. Nothing in the poem is as clear as the reminder of the lack of purpose and direction in the lives of modern men, but Tate's skillful use of image and metaphor to blend structure and texture makes it, in Radcliffe Squires's words, "the best of Tate's poems written before he was forty."

The basic attitudes of this poem are altered slightly in some of the later poems and the essays of cultural criticism written in the late 1930s and 1940s. In "The New Provincialism" he defines regionalism as "that consciousness or that habit of men in a given locality which influences them to certain patterns of thought and conduct handed to them by their ancestors." In "What Is a Traditional Society?" (1936), a revision of an essay given as the Phi Beta Kappa address at the University of Virginia, he remarks that "here within the walls of Mr. Jefferson's university there is a special tradition of realism in thinking about the nature of tradition." A little later in the same essay he asks what does this tradition of realism mean and how does it differ from the general American society of the present:

It means that in ages which suffer the decay of manners, religion, morals, codes, our indestructible vitality demands expression in violence and chaos; it means that men who have lost both the higher myth of religion and the lower myth of historical dramatization have lost the forms of human action: it means that they are no longer capable of defining human objectives.... [Such a man] is surrounded by the grandeurs of the past, but he does not participate in them; they do not sustain him.... Man in his plight lives in an untraditional society. For an untraditional society does not permit its members to pass to the next generation what it received from its immediate past.

Tate employs this distinction between the traditional and the untraditional society in his only novel *The Fathers* (1938), except in this work he speaks of the "classical" or "traditional" and the "romantic" or "untraditional" hero. The Posey family has given up their land and moved into town where all semblance of family ties has disappeared. Like the other Poseys, George is oblivious to tradition. He believes that every human act is intended for his own personal consumption. Buchan, the classical hero, can objectify his personal experiences—even the loss of his wife and the participation of his sons in a disastrous war—because he "can participate in the grandeurs of the past." He is able "to form a definite concept of [his] human role," and he can "function in every level of life."

R. K. Meiners believes "The Seasons of the Soul" is one of the most important poems of the twentieth century. In this poem, Tate is trying to present what one poet has called the "metaphysical present." The form of the poem is that of the dramatic monologue in which the speaker addresses each of the seasons. Because the seasons are personified, and even contain a part of the poet's (modern man's) personality (his wanton needs and fears), the mood of the poem is reverential.

Each of the four sections—Summer, Autumn, Winter, Spring—has six stanzas or 60 lines, and each section bears some resemblance to one of the four elements of ancient philosophy: summer—air; autumn—earth; winter—water; spring—fire. Its attention never wandering far from sin and salvation, the poem can best be experienced if one recalls the scene when Dante and Virgil reach the seventh circle where the violent reside and the speaker is blind and imprisoned. (One is reminded of Tate's often-repeated observation that modern man has a "locked in sensibility.") The reader should remember, too, that Beatrice had brought Dante to salvation; in that way he can get the full impact of Tate's protagonist's pursuit of Santa Monica. With his imprisoned sensibility and his faith destroyed by positivism, the protagonist wants her to convince him that he is not dying into nothingness.

The opening section (Summer), which traces the disintegration of the soul, opens with an epitaph from the *Inferno*: "Then I stretched forth my hand and pulled a twig from a large thorne and the trunk cried: 'Why do you tear me?' " This epigram sets the mood for the section, which is primarily concerned with man who is crippled by the imbalance between head and heart, and the poet's insistence that he must attain metaphysical (metaphorical) vision if he is to climb the stair toward salvation. To accomplish this feat he must regain the innocence of childhood and nature:

> Under the summer's blast
> The soul cannot endure
> Unless by sleight or fast
> It seize or deny its day
> To make the eye secure.
> Brothers-in-arms, remember
> The hot wind dries and draws
> With circular delay
> The flesh, ash from the ember,
> Into the summer's jaws.

The section ends with the poet's urging man to descend deeply into the inferno of self, for down there he finds, as Dante did, the wise centaur, the blend of human and animal.

The second section opens with the protagonist's realizing he is "down a well," in an empty grave, in an endless corridor with no means of escape. (Tate alludes to a scene of the thirty-third canto of the *Inferno*, where Dante descends into a cistern to view those destroyed by their own kind.) The overall feeling engendered by the section is that of the nightmare in which one dreams of his inability, despite his constant efforts, to reach a longed-for destination. (Tate tells of a recurring dream he had in which he could not escape from his material self.)

Section III is dominated by images of water.

> Goddess sea-born and bright,
> Return into the sea
> Where eddying twilight
> Gathers upon your people—

The protagonist obviously is attempting to escape from his rational self, to plumb to the depth of instinctive subconsciousness. The burned land he is trying to escape is that of the first section, a land destroyed by war and filled with the corpses of the dead, and he attempts to escape first into the realm of naturalistic sexuality.

The attempt to drown the conscious, rational self in sensuality is unsuccessful because the problem of the unfulfilled self is unassuaged. The poet moves, then, to the final section, Spring. The speaker remembers the pleasant land of his childhood and feels a faint stir of life and hope. Living in a time of turbulence and violence (the poem was written during World War II) and uncertain of his fate, the poet calls on the mother of silence:

> Speak, that we may hear;
> Listen, while we confess
> That we conceal our fear;
> Regard us, while the eye
> Discerns by sight or guess
> Whether, as sheep foregather
> Upon their crooked knees,
> We have begun to die;
> Whether your kindness, mother,
> Is mother of silences.

She does not respond, and the speaker's doubts remain. His ordeal is that of modern man, a fear of the spiritual disintegration of the world. Few other modern poets have expressed as well as Tate the essential tone of their age.

At his death he left unfinished a proposed poem of some length to be written in *terza rima*. The three parts of the poem he completed indicate that the poet's career was determinedly set in the direction indicated in *Seasons of the Soul*. Although literature is much the poorer because the poem was never finished, Tate wrote enough verse to convince us that few other writers have been as much concerned with the relationship of the artist to the traditions of the society that produced him. The literature of the Renascence, he warns us, is regional, but it is not local color. The Southern writer of the era he is writing about "takes the South as he knows it today or can find out about it in the past, and . . . sees it as a region with some special characteristics, but otherwise . . . offers it as an imaginative subject as it has been and will doubtless continue to be here and in other parts of the world." A man unaware of who he is and where he comes from, Tate concludes, is hardly human.

SURVEY OF CRITICISM

The authorized biography is being prepared by Robert Buffington. Until it is available the most reliable sources of information about Tate's personal life are Radcliffe Squires's *Allen Tate: A Literary Biography*, Ferman Bishop's *Allen*

Tate in the Twayne United States Authors Series, Louise Cowan's *The Fugitive Group* (for the Fugitive period), and Rob Roy Purdy's *Fugitives' Reunion*. The best available bibliography is Marshall Fallwell's *Allen Tate: A Bibliography*. The most helpful book-length critical studies are Louis D. Rubin, Jr.'s *The Wary Fugitives*; R. K. Meiner's *The Last Alternative: A Study of the Works of Allen Tate*; and the previously mentioned books by Squires and Bishop.

An illuminating insight into the regard Tate's contemporaries felt for him appears in *Allen Tate and His Work*, ed. Radcliffe Squires. Two monographs that give a perceptive insight into Tate's literary career are George Hemphill's *Allen Tate* in the University of Minnesota Pamphlets on American Writers and Melvin E. Bradford's *Rumor of Mortality*. Both Arthur Mizener in ''*The Fathers* and Realistic Fiction'' and Thomas Daniel Young in *The Past in the Present* emphasize the relationship between Tate's social and cultural criticism and *The Fathers*. The only two books of Tate's voluminous literary correspondence that have been published are *The Literary Correspondence of Donald Davidson and Allen Tate*, edited by John Tyree Fain and Thomas Daniel Young, and *The Republic of Letters in America: The Correspondence of John Peale Bishop and Allen Tate*, edited by Thomas Daniel Young and John Hindle. Tate's contributions to the Agrarian movement are presented in William C. Havard and Walter Sullivan, eds., *A Band of Prophets* (Baton Rouge: Louisiana State University Press, 1981) and Thomas Daniel Young, *Waking Their Neighbors Up: The Nashville Agrarians Reconsidered* (1982).

In the future it seems unlikely that Tate's career will attract as much attention as it has in the past. Fallwell lists more than 200 essays and dissertations. Only the most significant of these are listed in the selected checklist that follows this essay. Although there might be some attempt to balance the almost unrestrained adulation he has received in the past, it is certain that Tate has earned a secure and permanent place in Southern letters.

BIBLIOGRAPHY

Works by Allen Tate

The Golden Mean and Other Poems, with Ridley Wills. Nashville: Privately printed, 1923.
Mr. Pope and Other Poems. New York: Minton, Balch, 1928.
Stonewall Jackson: The Good Soldier. New York: Minton, Balch, 1928.
Jefferson Davis: His Rise and Fall. New York: Minton, Balch, 1929.
Poems: 1928–1931. New York and London: Charles Scribner's Sons, 1932.
The Mediterranean and Other Poems. New York: Alcestis Press, 1936.
Reactionary Essays on Poetry and Ideas. New York: Charles Scribner's Sons, 1936.
Selected Poems. New York and London: Charles Scribner's Sons, 1937.
The Fathers. New York: G. P. Putnam's Sons, 1938. Reissued as *The Fathers and Other Fiction* with introduction by Thomas Daniel Young. Baton Rouge: Louisiana State University Press, 1977.

Reason in Madness, Critical Essays. New York: G. P. Putnam's Sons, 1941.
On the Limits of Poetry, Selected Essays 1928–1948. New York: Swallow Press and
William Morrow, 1948.
Poems: 1922–1947. New York: Charles Scribner's Sons, 1948.
The Hovering Fly and Other Essays. Cummington, Mass.: Cummington Press, 1949.
Two Conceits for the Eye to Sing, If Possible. Cummington, Mass.: Cummington Press,
1950.
The Forlorn Demon: Didactic and Critical Essays. Chicago: Henry Regnery, 1953.
The Man of Letters in the Modern World, Selected Essays: 1928–1955. New York:
Meridian Books, 1955.
Collected Essays. Denver: Alan Swallow, 1959.
Poems. New York: Charles Scribner's Sons, 1960.
Essays of Four Decades. New York: William Morrow, 1968.
The Literary Correspondence of Donald Davidson and Allen Tate. Ed. John Tyree Fain
and Thomas Daniel Young. Athens: University of Georgia Press, 1974.
Memoirs and Opinions. Chicago: Alan Swallow, 1976.
Collected Poems, 1919–1976. New York: Farrar, Straus and Giroux, 1977.
*The Republic of Letters in America: The Correspondence of John Peale Bishop and Allen
Tate*. Ed. Thomas Daniel Young and John J. Hindle. Lexington: University Press
of Kentucky, 1981.

Studies of Allen Tate

Beatty, Richmond C. "Allen Tate as a Man of Letters." *South Atlantic Quarterly* 47
(April 1948): 226–41.
Bishop, Ferman. *Allen Tate*. New York: Twayne, 1967.
Blackmur, R. P. "*San Giovanni in Venere*: Allen Tate as Man of Letters." *Sewanee
Review* 67 (Autumn 1959): 614–31.
Bradford, Melvin E. *Rumors of Mortality: An Introduction to Allen Tate*. Dallas: Argus
Academic Press, 1969.
Brooks, Cleanth. "Allen Tate." *Poetry* 66 (September 1945): 324–29.
Cowan, Louise. *The Fugitive Group: A Literary History*. Baton Rouge: Louisiana State
University Press, 1959.
———. *The Southern Critics*. Irving, Texas: University of Dallas Press, 1972.
Cowley, Malcolm. "Two Winters with Hart Crane." *Sewanee Review* 67 (Autumn 1959):
547–56.
Fallwell, Marshall, ed. *Allen Tate: A Bibliography*. New York: David Lewis, 1969.
Foster, Richard. *The New Romantics: A Reappraisal of the New Criticism*. Bloomington:
Indiana University Press, 1962.
Havard, William C. and Walter Sullivan. *A Band of Prophets: The Vanderbilt Agrarians
after Fifty Years*. Baton Rouge: Louisiana State University Press, 1982.
Hemphill, George. *Allen Tate*. Minneapolis: University of Minnesota Press, 1964.
Kermode, Frank. "Contemplation and Method." *Sewanee Review* 72 (Winter 1964):
124–31.
———. "The Dissociation of Sensibility." *Kenyon Review* 19 (Spring 1957): 169–94.
———. "Old Orders Changing." *Encounter* 15 (August 1960): 72–76.
Meiners, R. K. *The Last Alternatives: A Study of the Works of Allen Tate*. Denver: Alan
Swallow, 1962.

Mizener, Arthur. "*The Fathers* and Realistic Fiction." *Accent* 7 (Winter 1947): 101–9.

Nemerov, Howard. "The Current of the Frozen Stream: An Essay on the Poetry of Allen Tate." *Furioso* 3 (February 1948): 50–61.

Purdy, Rob Roy, ed. *Fugitives Reunion: Conversations at Vanderbilt, May 3–5, 1956.* Nashville: Vanderbilt University Press, 1959.

Ransom, John Crowe. "*In Amicitia.*" *Sewanee Review* 67 (Autumn 1959): 528–39.

Rubin, Louis D., Jr. *The Wary Fugitives.* Baton Rouge: Louisiana State University Press, 1978.

Schwartz, Delmore. "The Poetry of Allen Tate." *Southern Review* 5 (Winter 1940): 419–38.

Spears, Monroe K. "The Criticism of Allen Tate." *Sewanee Review* 67 (Spring 1949): 317–34.

Squires, Radcliffe. *Allen Tate: A Literary Biography.* New York: Pegasus, 1971.

———, ed. *Allen Tate and His Work.* Minneapolis: University of Minnesota Press, 1972.

Vivas, Eliseo. "Allen Tate as Man of Letters." *Sewanee Review* 62 (Winter 1954): 131–43.

Young, Thomas Daniel. *The Past in the Present: Thematic Study of Modern Fiction.* Baton Rouge: Louisiana State University Press, 1981.

———. *Waking Their Neighbors Up: The Nashville Agrarians Reconsidered.* The Lamar Lectures 1980. Athens: University of Georgia Press, 1982.

_____ LYNN Z. BLOOM _____

Peter Taylor
(1917–   )

Peter Taylor is America's short-story writer par excellence. As critic Jonathan Yardley says, "Among American writers now living, only Eudora Welty has accomplished a body of fiction so rich, durable and accessible as Taylor's."

BIOGRAPHY

Although Peter Taylor's fiction does not appear to be conspicuously autobiographical, his heritage of place and family has contributed much to his work. As in many of his writings, the external events of Taylor's life are low-key. He was born on 8 January 1917, the youngest of the four children of Matthew Hillsman Taylor (1884–1965) and Katherine Baird Taylor (1886–1929). He lived for only seven years in his West Tennessee birthplace of Trenton, in old Chickasaw country and a county seat and trading center for the local cotton farmers. Albert Griffith identifies Taylor's hometown as "the obvious model for the fictional town of Thornton, the point of origin of numerous characters in about a dozen of Taylor's works," and a point of reference for many of the values they hold.

The history of Taylor's ancestors is intimately intertwined with the history and politics of the state. Both of his grandfathers, coincidentally named Robert Taylor, were lawyers and politicians. His mother's father, Robert Love, a Democrat from Happy Valley, Tennessee, served one term in Congress and three terms as state governor before being elected to the United States Senate in 1907, where he served until his death in 1912. Robert's Republican brother, Alf Taylor, had a comparable career that lasted until his death in 1931, when Peter was fourteen. Their practical jokes and tall tales greatly contributed not only to their political success but to the narrative skill and lore of Bob's daughter, Katherine. Indeed, Peter Taylor dedicated *Collected Stories* to his mother, "who was the best teller of tales I know and from whose lips I first heard many of the stories in this book.''

Taylor's own father, Hillsman, was also active in politics, serving as speaker of the Tennessee House of Representatives in 1909, just three years after graduating from Vanderbilt Law School. Although when Peter was born Hillsman Taylor was attorney general of the Thirteenth Judicial Circuit of Tennessee, in 1924 he left his country law office to move to Nashville, and in 1926 moved to St. Louis to become president of the Missouri State Life Insurance Company. There the Taylors lived in the enclaves of middle- and upper–middle-class homes bordering Forest Park, whose householders, imbued with a sense of family and of place, took it for granted that their children would attend such private schools as Miss Rossman's and St. Louis Country Day—as, indeed, Peter did from 1926 to 1932. This affluent, cultivated milieu is the setting of such stories as ''The Dark Walk,'' ''The Little Cousins,'' and ''The Promise of Rain''; the play *Tennessee Day in St. Louis*; and the ''long novelette,'' *A Woman of Means*.

When the Depression dictated a move, Hillsman returned to Tennessee, ''a State of Mind'' as his son was later to say, to business in Nashville. There Peter attended Memphis Central High School, of a status nearly comparable to that of a private school, from which he graduated in 1935 with a scholarship to Columbia University. That summer Taylor worked his way to England and back on a New Orleans freighter, but because of his father's objections did not attend Columbia. Instead, he dutifully enrolled in Southwestern at Memphis in spring 1936, where he took Allen Tate's English courses. When Tate left, Taylor transferred to Vanderbilt to study under John Crowe Ransom, and there became a friend of Randall Jarrell, in whose honor he later edited a volume of commemorative essays, *Randall Jarrell, 1914–1965*, with Robert Lowell and Robert Penn Warren (1967). When Ransom moved to Kenyon College in 1937, Taylor dropped out of college and sold real estate for a year before transferring to Kenyon and resuming his studies under Ransom. There, through aptitude and inclination, Taylor rejected the study of law and concentrated on literature; there, too, began his friendship with Robert Lowell. By the time of his graduation in 1940, Taylor had published two short stories, ''The Party'' and ''The Lady Is Civilized,'' in *River*, a little magazine emanating from Oxford, Mississippi, and a poem in the *Kenyon Review*.

Taylor then enrolled as a graduate student at Louisiana State University to study under Robert Penn Warren and Cleanth Brooks, but soon recognized his ultimate vocation, dropped his courses, and spent the year reading and writing fiction. Warren accepted ''A Spinster's Tale,'' ''Sky Line,'' and ''The Fancy Woman'' for the *Southern Review*, but Taylor's burgeoning literary career was interrupted by World War II. He enlisted in the United States Army in June 1941 and served at Fort Oglethorpe, Georgia (the setting of ''Rain in the Heart''), for two and a half years before assignment to the Rail Transportation Corps at Tidworth Camp, in England. He was honorably discharged in December 1945, having risen to the rank of sergeant.

Since that time, Taylor has lived what appears to be an unusually serene life, combining writing and college teaching, punctuated by occasional years abroad on fellowships. He married Eleanor Ross, a poet, on 4 June 1943, with Robert Lowell as best man; they have two children, Katherine Baird (b. 1948) and Peter Ross (b. 1955). Taylor taught at the Woman's College of the University of North Carolina in Greensboro (1946–48, 1949–52, and in 1963); he has also taught at Indiana University (1948–49), the University of Chicago (1952), Kenyon College (1952–57), Ohio State University (1957–63), and Harvard (1964). From 1967 to 1983 he was a Commonwealth Professor of English at the University of Virginia. Today the Taylors continue to live in Charlottesville.

In "1939," the story with the most conspicuous parallels to Taylor's life, the narrator portrays himself as a college teacher/writer "who has known neither [great] financial success . . . nor [an extravagant] reputation. Yet this man behind the lectern is a man who seems happy in the knowledge that he knows—or thinks he knows—what he is about." This is a fitting self-assessment by an author whose work has received nearly unanimous critical praise throughout his career, even as he continues to surpass his previous accomplishments. Robert Penn Warren early identified Taylor as a "very gifted writer"; the *Virginia Quarterly Review* later pronounced him "an impeccable stylist" who wrote "demonstrably superior work." Joyce Carol Oates called *Collected Stories* (1968) one of the major works of literature; Taylor is considered the equal of Chekhov and Joyce, "the greatest [short-story writer] writing in English today." Yardley accurately labels Taylor's four most recent stories, published in the last decade, as his finest, and singles out "The Old Forest" as "an American masterpiece." The other three are "The Captain's Son," "In the Miro District," and "The Gift of the Prodigal."

Many of Taylor's stories have been included in Martha Foley's *Best American Short Story* annuals; "Venus, Cupid, Folly and Time" won the 1959 O. Henry first prize. This storyteller's storyteller has received numerous awards: a Guggenheim Fellowship in 1950–51, a grant from the National Institute of Arts and Letters in 1952, a Fulbright in 1956, a Ford Foundation Fellowship in 1961, a Rockefeller Foundation grant in 1965–66, membership in the National Academy of Arts and Letters and that society's Gold Medal for Fiction in 1979, and a Senior Fellowship from the National Endowment for the Arts in 1984.

Nevertheless, despite Taylor's 45 years of continual publication, much of it in the *New Yorker*, his work remains, as Yardley says, "almost entirely unnoticed by the larger world of serious readers." His books have had modest sales; his one-act plays and the closet drama *Tennessee Day in St. Louis* are seldom produced. One reason may be that Americans equate size with significance and pay more attention to novels than to short stories. Another reason lies in Taylor's subject matter, epitomized in the original title of "The Little Cousins"—"Cousins, Family Life, Family Love, All That." Although these subjects are universal, Taylor's emphasis, as the narrator of "The Old Forest" says, is on "the binding and molding effect upon people of the circumstances in which they are born," rather than on the more sensational themes of sexual vagaries, psychological angst, violence, or, with the exceptions of "A Spinster's Tale" and "Venus, Cupid, Folly and Time," on the grotesque. Furthermore, Taylor's technique is subtle and understated; as Griffith says, "He is never brutal, coarse, shocking; but neither is he precious, coy, titillating. . . . [His voice] is essentially the voice of a gentlemen." The style echoes Taylor himself, cultured, urbane, and sensitive, but never flamboyant or self-aggrandizing.

MAJOR THEMES

Taylor's major themes are family and place. These are often interrelated through common history and heritage, through ties emotional as well as geographical. Both family and place are invariably affected, for better and for worse, by the passage of time and its inevitable changes.

Taylor's characters—middle- or upper–middle-class white (businessmen, lawyers, and well-kept housewives and society matrons) from Memphis, Nashville, or St. Louis, their black servants, and their country cousins—seldom exist in isolation. Only the social deviants, the shambling peripatetic alcoholic in "A Spinster's Tale" and the kept "Woman of Fancy," also an alcoholic, are without family, friends, and a supporting matrix of social and historical connections— and Taylor treats these characters, like the others, with his customary mixture of sympathy and irony. Yet even these characters have their "place"; tension and conflict occur when they are in the wrong place at the wrong time.

Happy Families Are All Alike, Taylor's 1959 collection of stories, implies through its provocative, doubly ironic title many of the complexities of the family relations in nearly all of Taylor's works. Taylor's happy families—full of grandparents, parents, and a great many more children than populate most modern fiction—are neither all alike nor always happy, though they have many common and binding ties. The Tolstoyean extension of this title, "every unhappy family is unhappy in its own way," is likewise both true and false in Taylor's stories; we have met his unhappy people, and they are us.

Most important, Taylor's families, and by extension the larger communities of which they are a part, are invariably Southern. They hail from the cities Taylor knows best, Memphis and Nashville and St. Louis (which Taylor treats as an extension of Southern, rather than Midwestern, culture), and from the country hamlet of Thornton (read Trenton), seat of Taylor's equivalent to Faulkner's Yoknapatawpha County. They share a common history and a common culture that value family and tradition, though the more perceptive characters continually reassess the relation of the old to the new, continuity to change. They are simultaneously burdened and buoyed by their heritage of "old country manners and . . . old, country connections," as in "The Old Forest," static only in memory, whose significance changes in response to the tides of the present. Indeed, as Jane Barnes Casey has noted, a recent story, "The Captain's Son," is "deliberately the caricature of all the elements associated with 'Southern' fiction—

complex family ties, historical skeletons in the closet, dark sexual problems. The villain . . . is snobbery in one form or another,'' as Tolliver, a member of the establishment, and his father-in-law silently collude in the corruption of Tolliver's bride, who quickly becomes as alcoholic as her husband. The men "want to preserve a way of life . . . but at the expense of life itself.''

Casual commentators have mistakenly tried to link Taylor with the Southern Agrarian movement, since three of its major leaders—Ransom, Tate, and Warren—were his teachers. Various of his characters wistfully refer to "the old ways and the old teachings'' and to the earlier "atmosphere of a prosperous and civilized existence'' in comparison with the present corruption of the "traditions and institutions.'' But these characters, who according to Griffith "might gladly rally with the Agrarians against the urban-industrial menace,'' are as often as not mistaken in their allegiance to a nonexistent or radically altered romantic ideal.

Conspicuous among these romantic Agrarians is Sylvia Harrison, the central character of "The Dark Walk,'' but she cannot stay that way forever. She handles with aplomb the many moves her husband, "a sort of 'efficiency vice-president' '' makes from bucolic Cedar Springs (near Thornton), Tennessee, to "Memphis, St. Louis, Detroit—everywhere.'' Not only does she transport her four children, a black servant couple from home, and pets, but, at a "tremendous expense,'' four reassuring "vans of furniture—almost everything in the way of furniture that her family or Nate's had ever owned.'' Indeed, the furniture transforms every house in which they live into a replica of the ancestral home, obscuring its individuality and locale. "None of these houses'' on their itinerary "was really home for them,'' for home "would always be Tennessee,'' where everything that was good in the noble past . . . [met] head on with everything that was exciting and marvelous about the twentieth century.'' To those "pleasant, prosperous, pastoral surroundings'' they will one day return, Sylvia reiterates with every move.

But when that day arrives, precipitated by Nate's sudden death in Chicago when Sylvia is forty-four, she realizes that she can't go home again. By agreeing to bear her husband's discards throughout their marriage, "she herself had become a widow . . . the day he asked her to marry him, in the Dark Walk.'' To become her own person she must trade in her burdensome legacy for "only what was new and useful and pleasing to the eye. . . . only what she herself had selected.'' She cannot walk into the light, her modern pilgrim's progress, without dispensing with "all that was old and useless and inherited.''

"The Old Forest'' explores with Taylor's characteristic finesse and subtle psychological understanding the impact of a single, quintessential event on the lives of its three major protagonists. Nat Ramsey, twenty-three, newly entered into his father's cotton-brokerage firm, is "still learning how to operate under the pecking order of Memphis's male establishment.'' Caroline Braxley, like her fiancé Nat a child of Memphis society, is wise beyond her years and her experience. She expects not only to have "a marriage and a family of the kind

[her] parents had had," but because of her establishment heritage inevitably to contend with "girls of another kind . . . who had no conception of what it was to have a certain type of performance expected of them." Caroline's unwitting nemesis is just such a "girl whose origins nobody knew anything about." Lee Ann Deerhart is a "dead attractive," intelligent young woman come from the country to earn her own living in the big city, freed from the doubly binding constraints and protection of generations of family that "girls like Caroline" enjoy.

A week before the wedding, on a snowy afternoon in 1937, Nat's car skids on the ice as he is on his way to study for a Latin test, and the resulting accident becomes "a calamitous thing to have happen—not the accident itself, which caused no serious injury to anyone, but the accident plus the presence of that girl," Lee Ann. She has gone along for the ride, as she has on other occasions gone with Nat to drink in roadhouses, although she is "perfectly decent" and their relationship is not sexual. Immediately upon impact, Lee Ann disappears into "the old forest in Overton Park," "an immemorial grove of snow-laden oaks and yellow poplars and hickory trees. . . . that men in Memphis have feared and wanted to destroy for a long time and whose destruction they are still working at" even some 40 years later as the aging Nat tells the story.

The old forest, Memphis's version of the forest primeval, is the site of an age-old conflict, literal and metaphorical, between men and women: "It has only recently been saved by a very narrow margin from a great highway that men wished to put through there—saved by groups of women determined to save this last bit of old forest from the axes of modern men." Women see as benign and sheltering what men see as sinister and destructive of the established order:

Perhaps in old pioneer days, before the plantation and the neoclassic towns were made, the great forests seemed woman's last refuge from the brute she lived alone with in the wilderness. Perhaps all men in Memphis who had any sense of their past felt this, thought they felt more keenly . . . that the forest was woman's greatest danger. Men remembered mad pioneer women, driven mad by their loneliness and isolation, who ran off into the forest, never to be seen again, or incautious women who allowed themselves to be captured by Indians.

Although the wedding cannot take place until Lee Ann is found, we know from the outset that she emerges from hiding four days later and that life goes on, superficially as usual, but deepened by the process of both the search and the discovery. Caroline, the levelheaded and magnificent representative of the old order, recognizes her precarious status in a "world where women [are] absolutely subjected and under the absolute protection of men," a world in which women "have to protect and use whatever strength [they] have" in order to survive within the boundaries the patriarchy permits.

Lee Ann represents both the threat and the freedom of the new order. She and her liberated women friends "treat men just as they please . . . and men like them better for it.'' They ''have learned to enjoy life together and to be mutually protective, but they enjoy a [communal] protection also . . . from the men who admire their very independence''—the police, the newspaper editors who shield their names from public notice, business and community leaders, the very fathers of the ''girls like Caroline [who] took seriously'' the forms and heritage of their closely regulated lives.

In this magnificent story Taylor explores many facets of his quintessential themes: the injustice of arbitrary power; the inevitability of social change; the fragility of social status; the complex ambiguity of relationships between parents and children, peers and subordinates, friends and lovers—with the women here, as in many other stories, far stronger than the men in personality and in character.

SURVEY OF CRITICISM

Each of Taylor's collections of stories has been greeted with superlative reviews by major commentators. John Leonard in the *New York Times* (7 April 1977) says, ''Peter Taylor makes stories the way Mercedes-Benz makes automobiles: to last.'' William Peden in the *Hollins Critic* explains, ''The drama of Taylor's stories tends to be internal. It exists in and flows from the inner lives of his people, inner lives which are only occasionally revealed in terms of dramatic external events or incidents. Character, indeed, *is* the story. The careful and knowing explorations of the nuances of the situation, the interrelationships of individuals, the revelation, usually quiet, of the essence of non-exceptional human beings confronted with non-exceptional situations, replaces the plot as such. It is difficult to think of any writer since James who depicts the nuances of such relationships more successfully.'' And in the *Saturday Review* (14 May 1977), Linda Kuehl concludes, ''I am tempted to say that Peter Taylor is the greatest living short story writer, but I shall be prudent and suggest he is the greatest one writing in English today.''

Nevertheless, Taylor's works have received scant critical attention: one book, two unpublished doctoral dissertations, ten critical articles—in 45 years. Reasons for this critical neglect have been offered above; they are certainly not shared by the authors of the generally admiring and perceptive critical commentary.

The only full-length work is Albert J. Griffith's *Peter Taylor* (1970), an exceptionally fine volume in Twayne's United States Authors Series. Employing the Twayne format, Griffith begins with a brief biographical chapter, followed by six chapters on Taylor's works, in order of publication, and concludes with a brief summary of Taylor's achievements. Griffith, a sensitive and careful reader, refuses to stereotype Taylor's themes, characters, or literary techniques, and indeed cautions his readers against doing so.

His analysis of Taylor's novella, *A Woman of Means*, is typical. Quint, the narrator, ''no Holden Caufield, no subjective adolescent'' but more like Melville's Redburn, reflects as a mature adult on his adolescent maturation that occurred during his widowed father's courtship and initially idyllic two-year marriage to Anna Lauterbach, an exceedingly charming and very rich St. Louis divorcée with two college-age daughters. The questions of whether she "is more attracted to the prospective son she envisions in Quint" than to her bourgeois businessman husband from rural Tennessee, whose economic rise and fall she witnesses, is never resolved, nor is the question of whether Gerald married her for her money. What is clear is the thoroughly nurturing effect of "a mother's love and solicitude lavished on [Quint] by his beautiful stepmother: 'I thought of the firmness with which I was established in her heart. Suddenly I had become the carefree hero of a wonderful adventure.' '' But as Quint's "burgeoning desire for adult independence asserts itself" as he rejects her "silent demand" to turn his middle school achievement award over to her, "she turns to fantasy and imagines herself to be carrying in her womb the son who will love her for herself"—a delusion that leads to her hospitalization and ultimately breaks up the marriage. Griffith aptly observes, "The characters do not fall into neat moral categories: there are no heroes or villains in this novel. Not a single character is completely unsympathetic and not a single character is without flaws." Nor are the characters merely symbols; "they are in this novel, as elsewhere, of primary importance as people truthfully re-created," "known and defined precisely by their interactions with other characters and with their environment."

Griffith's judgments accurately apply to works published after his volume was completed: "Peter Taylor's greatest achievement is probably his ability to create, within the restrictive confines of a short story, characters with a richness and complexity rarely found even in novels." Likewise, Griffith recognizes weaknesses in Taylor's plays, which suffer "from the loss of the chief strength of his fiction—the unifying presence of a narrative consciousness," that continue to prevail in his one-act plays published during the 1970s in *Presences*. Indeed, though Taylor said in an interview with Stephen Goodwin (1973), "I would like to spend most of my time writing plays," he has received little critical encouragement (mostly through inattention) to do so, and every reason to continue writing stories.

The most perceptive recent commentary is Jane Barnes Casey's "A View of Peter Taylor's Stories" (1978), which focuses on *In the Miro District* (1977). Casey first establishes that in Taylor's stories published before 1974 (the predecessors of those in *In the Miro District*) there is "conflict between the affectionate, civil society and chaos, regardless of whether the disorder is sexual, drunken, or natural," and that "disorder is associated with men trampling the social restraints enforced or represented by women."

In the earlier stories there was a "coincidence between strong women and unhappy men," which prevailed as long as Taylor "preserved the notion that women's domain was the house and family, while man's was the exterior one of commerce and politics. More precisely, this condition prevailed as long as Mr. Taylor accepted women as the carriers of the social conscience." By the mid–1970s, however, Taylor's stories reflect the passing away of one moral code—"based on the Southern woman's honor"—and its replacement by another, more egalitarian standard of behavior, where men and women owe each other, as well as members of their own gender, respect and trust.

"In the Miro District" illustrates this theme in three remembered instances of conflict and confrontation between Grandfather Manley, a Civil War veteran, and his teenage grandson who, in the course of coming-of-age in the 1920s, violates the old code by committing in the family home (when his parents are out) acts that a gentleman of an earlier era would have committed off the premises. On one occasion he gets drunk; on another he stages a sleep-in houseparty for four couples; on both occasions his disapproving but ultimately indulgent grandfather helps conceal the evidence.

The third time, however, Grandfather arrives "unheralded and unannounced," as is his habit, "And what he found . . . was not a clean-cut young boy whom he had watched growing up. . . . He found, instead, a disheveled, disreputable-looking young fellow of eighteen summers who was hardly recognizable . . . a boy who had just now frantically pulled on his clothes . . . [and] was keeping a young girl in the house with him." This time, Grandfather leaves in umbrage at the discovery, and instead of feeling shame or chagrin, the boy and girl "smiled at each other and kissed." Says Casey, "For both men, custom has not changed its essential reference to love. The woman who once had all values vested in her honor still represents all that's important. Once her importance was expressed by not acknowledging her passionateness, now the opposite is true."

The remaining Taylor criticism is limited by its restricted scope, either because it was written before much of Taylor's best work was published or because it pertains to a single work. This distinguished writer has received unstinting critical respect; now is the time for his carefully wrought works to receive sustained and thoughtful critical attention.

BIBLIOGRAPHY

Works by Peter Taylor

A Long Fourth and Other Stories. New York: Harcourt, Brace, 1948.

A Woman of Means. New York: Harcourt, Brace, 1950.

The Widows of Thornton. New York: Harcourt, Brace, 1954.

Tennessee Day in St. Louis: A Comedy. New York: Random House, 1957.

Happy Families Are All Alike: A Collection of Stories. New York: McDowell, Obolensky, 1959.

Miss Lenora When Last Seen and Fifteen Other Stories. New York: Obolensky, 1963.

Randall Jarrell 1914–1965. Ed. Robert Lowell, Peter Taylor, and Robert Penn Warren. New York: Farrar, Straus and Giroux, 1967.

The Collected Stories of Peter Taylor. New York: Farrar, Straus and Giroux, 1969.

"An Interview with Peter Taylor," ed. Stephen Goodwin. *Shenandoah* 24 (Winter 1973): 3–20.

Presences: Seven Dramatic Pieces. Boston: Houghton Mifflin, 1973.

In the Miro District and Other Stories. New York: Knopf, 1977.
The Old Forest and Other Stories. New York: Doubleday, 1985.
A Summons to Memphis. New York: Knopf, 1986.

Uncollected Stories and Drama

"Uncles." *New Yorker* 25 (17 December 1949): 24–28.
"Nerves." *New Yorker* 37 (16 September 1961): 38–41.
"The End of Play." *Virginia Quarterly Review* 41 (Spring 1965): 248–65.
"A Cheerful Disposition." *Sewanee Review* 75 (1967): 243–65.
"A Stand in the Mountains." *Kenyon Review* 30, no. 2 (1968): 169–264. [play]
"Tom, Tell Him." *Sewanee Review* 76 (Spring 1968): 159–86.
"The Early Guest." *Shenandoah* 24 (Winter 1973): 21–43. [play]

Studies of Peter Taylor

Blum, Morgan. "Peter Taylor: Self-limitation in Fiction." *Sewanee Review* 70 (Autumn 1962): 559–78.

Brown, Ashley. "The Early Fiction of Peter Taylor." *Sewanee Review* 70 (Autumn 1962): 588–602.

Casey, Jane Barnes. "A View of Peter Taylor's Stories." *Virginia Quarterly Review* 54 (Spring 1978): 213–30.

Cheney, Brainard. "Peter Taylor's Plays." *Sewanee Review* 70 (Autumn 1962): 579–87.

Griffith, Albert J. *Peter Taylor*. New York: Twayne, 1970.

Peden, William. "A Hard and Admirable Toughness: The Stories of Peter Taylor." *Hollins Critic* 7 (1970): 1–9.

Pinkerton, Jan. "The Non-Regionalism of Peter Taylor." *Georgia Review* 24 (Winter 1970): 432–40.

Schuler, Sister Cor Mariae [Barbara]. "The House of Peter Taylor." *Critique* 9, no. 3 (1967): 6–18.

Smith, James Penny. "Narration and Theme in Taylor's *A Woman of Means*." *Critique* 9, no. 3 (1967): 19–30.

Williamson, Alan. "Identity and Wider Eros: A Reading of Peter Taylor's Stories." *Shenandoah* 30 (Fall 1978): 71–84.

Yardley, Jonathan. "Peter Taylor: The Quiet Virtuoso." *Washington Post Book World*, 27 January 1985, p. 3.

Jean Toomer
(1894–1967)

As the imagination of writers, critics, and literary entrepreneurs in the 1920s created a Harlem Renaissance, the appearance of Jean Toomer's *Cane* in 1923 served as a sign of soulfully black art. Like the pastoral genre to which *Cane* is akin in its nostalgic projection of the concerns of sophisticated metropolitans onto a ''primitive'' subject, this narrative of a poet's return to his roots offered both the satisfaction of technically experimental art and an affecting representation of the conflict between an intuitive range of experience that could be idealized because it is heritage and the conditions of alienated urban life that seem to be the price of modernity as well as reason for self-conscious literary experimentation in the first place. Practically as soon as the book was published, its reputation became a phenomenon separate from the author. The legend of the 1920s made *Cane*, first, a precursor and, then, a historical classic of the Harlem Renaissance, while Toomer himself pursued a mission as writer and philosophical reformer that had little or nothing to do with the blackness of identity and culture that had inspired the lyricism of his masterpiece.

BIOGRAPHY

In the opening of ''Earth-Being'' (c. 1928–29), the first of several autobiographies on which we must depend for an outline of his life and the sources of his art, Jean Toomer establishes his birthdate as 26 December 1894. The same passage also provides a characteristic statement of self-perception. ''Some cells within my then small body,'' he writes, ''were indelibly impressed with the sensations experienced when, passing through a burning body, I was projected into this, the next larger world. . . . From one point of view it is difficult for me to dramatize the career of a tiny cosmic speck, even if that speck is myself. For all events in this universe . . . are local events important only if the observer has a local view or if he has a true view of the whole. . . . I have outgrown the local. I have not yet crystallized the universal. My consciousness swings in a wide arc between the two.'' Despite the philosophical self-justification Toomer intends by his language, the remark epitomizes his biography, for it is clear that he lived his life in ambivalent movement between a singular individualism and a yearning to immerse himself in a protectively comprehensive unity.

His mother, Nina, was the only daughter of P.B.S. Pinchback, a prominent figure in Louisiana Reconstruction politics who earned his reputation initially as an officer with the Corps d'Afrique in the Civil War and then served as both lieutenant governor and acting governor. Twice denied a seat in the United States Senate, he moved his family to Washington, D.C., when the Democrats returned to power. There Nina met and married Nathan Toomer, a Georgia planter of a similarly mixed ethnic background. Within a year of the birth of Nathan Eugene, as the future author was first named, his father returned to Georgia, and Nina Pinchback returned to her father's house, filing for divorce in 1898. The Toomer autobiographies record a single moment of intimacy between father and son, but specify in detail the uneasy relationship between Nina and Pinchback following her divorce and suggest an effort to suppress evidence of the failed marriage by the practice of calling the child Eugene Pinchback, the name by which he was known throughout his childhood.

Nina Pinchback remarried in 1906, to a man named Coombs, and took Eugene to Brooklyn and then New Rochelle to live. In June 1909 his mother died of appendicitis, and Eugene returned to Washington, unhappy with the tyranny he perceived in his grandfather's direction of his mother's life but sympathetic to his grandmother and deeply fond of his uncle Bismarck, who displayed a love of books and encouraged a degree of rebellion against the patriarchal P.B.S.

Putting the best face upon his childhood as preparation for maturity, Toomer characterized the world of childhood as ''a comparatively free and open world, subject to but few of the rigid conventions and fixed ideas which contract the human psyche and commit people to narrow lives ruled by narrow preferences and prejudices. . . . I was fortunate enough not to be victimized by the forms of insanity which induce people to believe that they love or hate entire classes, races, nations, religions.'' Freedom from such conditioned responses deserves approval, but Toomer's escape from lessons of prejudice derived from conditions in the household and a personal manner favoring isolation. Adults seem to have kept their distance from him, so that the other side of his personal freedom was fear of abandonment and a seige of psychosomatic illness he later understood as an unconscious attempt to secure maternal attention.

Resident with his grandparents, Toomer entered the M Street High School, later renamed Paul Laurence Dunbar High School, where he enjoyed his studies and took pleasure in a black environment. In his second year of high school, he was struck by ''acute emotional and sex problems,'' which continued into his third and final years of high school. He undertook a regimen of physical culture and willed self-control carried on without benefit of counseling and in ''almost complete isolation.'' Time after time he would briefly follow an enthusiasm, then enlarge upon a disappointing incident connected with his project, and then return home to Washington to live until a new plan for self-development formed itself. This pattern led Toomer to matriculate at the University of Wisconsin, where he studied agriculture for a semester; took him in fall 1915 to enroll at the University of Massachusetts, where a delay in the receipt of his transcript from Madison provoked his departure; caused him to enter the American College of Physical Training in Chicago in February 1916; generated an excited adoption of socialism, then Darwinism and atheism, followed by transfer of interest to sociology courses at New York University and City College of New York in 1917; created in him a wish to enter the Army to replace his earlier preference for staying out of the World War; and, when the military rejected him, brought him to momentary rest as a clerk in a grocery firm in New York City.

The intellectual explanation for each of the goals Toomer sought in this period of his life is illustrated by his remarks on discovering socialism: ''I had been, I suppose, unconsciously seeking . . . an intelligible scheme of things . . . a body of ideas which held a consistent view of life and which enabled one to see and understand as one does when he sees a map. Socialism was the first thing of this kind I had encountered. It was not so much the facts or ideas, taken singly, that aroused me . . . it was the *body*, the *scheme*, the order and inclusion.'' Later he saw the study of psychology the same way. He became ''convinced that herein, rather than in social theories, lay the key, and the one fundamental approach, to life.'' Yet the ephemerality of these serial enthusiasms for *the* fundamental explanation suggests a problem more emotional than intellectual. Toomer abandoned socialism for good after working in a shipyard where he found that real workers ''had two main interests: playing craps and sleeping with women.'' In other words, the comprehensive ideal faded because the workers for whom socialism is meant did not measure up.

The pattern of mood swings shows Toomer constantly searching to merge into a cause greater than himself, one that might provide him both the security of complete truth and a self-gratifying role as leader. Each failure, each swing from enthusiasm to insecure depression, follows upon an incident of disillusion where he found himself isolated and exposed, no longer a potential messiah.

For a brief period, however, there was sufficient unity of action and goal, stability of emotion, for art to emerge. This he called ''The *Cane* Years.'' Having begun to write in earnest in 1920, Toomer, who had earlier reclaimed his father's name and also begun to call himself Jean, eagerly read contemporary writers and made an acquaintance with the literary world through Lola Ridge, an editor of *Broom*, who introduced him to Waldo Frank. The material to stimulate his literary imagination Toomer found through brief service in 1921 as a substitute teacher at Georgia Normal and Industrial Institute in Sparta, where he encountered what he understood to be the folk culture of the black peasantry, people linked by a group spirit rather than atomized by twentieth-century individualism. Immediately upon his return from Georgia, he began composing the poems and sketches that would become part one of *Cane*, submitting them singly to little magazines, and filling out his book by composing a second set of sketches continuing his themes in a sequence of urban sketches and the dramatic piece "Kabnis." In the same period he also wrote the plays "Natalie Mann" and "Balo" as well as an autobiographical novel now lost. "Balo" was produced at Howard University in 1923–24; *Cane*, issued by Liveright in 1923, was received by critics as a harbinger of the vital new art of the Harlem Renaissance.

Later Toomer would describe *Cane* as the swan song of a folk spirit dying in a modern desert and, thus, a work that could not have a sequel. However true that might be as commentary on the themes of *Cane*, for the author of the book an extension of the lyric representation of black life became impossible because, for a complex of reasons, he abandoned Afro-American subjects and issues almost immediately after affirming them in one of the distinguished books of black literature. His new comprehensive map of reality he discovered in the mystical program of Georges Gurdjieff. Study at the Gurdjieff Institute in Fontainebleau, France, in 1924 and a personal mystical experience in 1926, reinforced by ardent teaching on behalf of the new vision, rendered racial designations irrelevant to Toomer and convinced him that to crystallize the "universal" was a nobler mission than to interpret the "local view."

Twice he married women associated with him in the program of spiritual renewal, and although he continued to write and hope for publication, works in the post-*Cane* style were too didactic in manner, too static in conception to achieve more than occasional publication. In the 1940s Toomer and his second wife, Marjorie Content Toomer, became members of the Society of Friends. Toomer wrote several articles for *Friends Intelligencer* and delivered the William Penn Lecture in Philadelphia in 1949. His health began to fail in 1950, and he eventually entered a rest home. Jean Toomer died 30 March 1967.

MAJOR THEMES

Toomer's masterpiece moved Langston Hughes to say it "contains the finest prose written by a Negro in America," ("The Negro Artist and the Racial Mountain," *Nation*, June 23, 1926) and led William Stanley Braithwaite to describe Toomer as the first black artist who "can write about the Negro without surrender or compromise of the artist's vision" (*Crisis*, September 1924). For other contemporary reviewers, and a good number of critics writing since 1923, *Cane* is a problematic work, for as Gorham Munson observed (*Opportunity*, September 1925), the book is as much a search for a suitable literary form as it is a representation of black life.

Whether or not the form Toomer devised qualifies *Cane* as a novel, or as some other genre, seems beside the point. What becomes clear to readers is that the collection of sketches, verse, and semidramatic pieces achieves unity through Toomer's use of imagistic statements representing the consciousness and unconsciousness of characters among whom the privileged viewpoint belongs to the presiding eye of the writer. In "Georgia Dusk" he observes a rural scene of working life through which moves a line of men singing "folk-songs from soul sounds." Carrying their African identity in their unconscious, the singers animate nature so that "pine trees are guitars" and the "chorus of the cane / Is caroling a vesper to the stars." The spontaneous expression of soul in folk song is potentially redemptive, bringing "dreams of Christ to dusky cane-lipped throngs." Coupling with this rendition of folk redemption is "Song of the Son," a lyric that promises redemption for the poet who may take from the ripened folk culture a seed that will become an "everlasting song, a singing tree, / Caroling softly souls of slavery, / What they were, and what they are to me."

The operative themes of these lyrics—acceptance of the racial past and spontaneous expression—become the goals for the search for identity throughout *Cane*. The poetic manner of the lyrics dominates the sketches as well, because Toomer conceives of self-discovery as an intuitive experience. The first of the three discrete sections of *Cane* contains six sketches, each set in rural Georgia and each centering on a woman's relationship to her instinctual sexual self. Male lust, caste taboos, repression, and jealousy frustrate full expression, but as in the case of "Fern," a type of the blessed virgin, it is evident that mystical unification hovers just beyond reach.

In the second part of *Cane* the redemptive promise lessens and disappears as Toomer follows the trail of history to consider characters who have migrated from the rural South to Washington, D.C., where an urban, materialistic culture represses instinctual feeling. In two of the sketches in this section Toomer develops the figure of a male savior for the females. In one, "Avey," the self-conscious narrator who has risen above Avey in social standing tries to stimulate her ambition but only succeeds in putting her to sleep, whereas in "Box Seat" the redeemer figure of Dan Moore cannot free his love Muriel from the trap of social respectability. Failed communion also serves as the theme for the evidently autobiographical "Bona and Paul," where the male protagonist hesitates to act upon his love because of uncertainty about the Southern-born white woman's acceptance of him as a mulatto.

The final section of *Cane* returns to rural Georgia for setting and again concerns a Northerner seeking to comprehend the life of black Southerners. Where the first part of the book employs impressionism, and the second exploits techniques of expressionism, the third uses a semidramatic form to move Ralph Kabnis through six scenes displaying movement from a mood of anguish through a period of guilt and finally to a condition of self-hate where he despairs of both personal and social redemption.

Despite the fragmentary substance of *Cane* and the evidence that Toomer deliberately filled out the collection of sketches and verse in order to produce a book that would be his passport to the literary world, the volume has a progressive unity. In the first section Toomer presents the waning possibility of redemption in the passing folk culture of the black South. The second part represents increased inhibition of spontaneous life as the characters become more self-repressing because of the values they adopt as guides in the society based upon economic classes. Although the poet narrator can respond to the promise of redemption in the instinctual women of the South, the characters in the second portion of the book are only distressed by the signs of instinctual life. Finally, in "Kabnis" Toomer presents a protagonist who cannot bear the feeling of a South animated by soul and deliberately closes his senses.

Cane earns its place in the Afro-American literary tradition as a narrative of immersion in the sources of black identity. In this respect it is thematically akin to W.E.B. Du Bois's *The Souls of Black Folk* (1903) and Ralph Ellison's *Invisible Man* (1952) among other works. Recalling the early reviews of *Cane*, however, we must recognize that reception of the book depended as much on its connection to contemporary literary experiments and association with the works classified as expressions of the *New* Negro as it did on its value as Afro-American writing. It is very largely the art of the work that quite properly gained its reputation.

In two plays written during the 1920s, Toomer continued to apply himself to the themes of black culture in an experimental mode. "Balo," a one-act play produced in 1923–24, parallels *Cane* in rendering the daily life of a rural black family actively adapting their folk spirit to conditions of economic hardship in which community integrity, and even a degree of understanding with white farmers, remains possible. In contrast to the folk drama, and reminiscent of the second section of *Cane*, is "Natalie Mann," an expressionistic three-act play written in 1922 but never produced. Characters include Natalie, a middle-class woman constrained by false morality; Etta, a spontaneous performer who is a friend of Nathan Merilh, a redeemer figure seen as synthesis of African and European culture who provides guidance to Natalie; Mertis, who is described as evading the prime urges of life; and a collection of black and white citizens who serve as the backdrop of deracinated bourgeois culture. Although the sympathy for the condition of Afro-American women seems genuine, it cannot be overlooked that the autobiographical figure of Nathan serves as the agent to release the impulses of Natalie; thus, Toomer's desire to be a messiah is symbolically enacted. Although it cannot account for the failure of the play to be produced, equally important as a limitation on its theme is the underlying conception of the play that opposes assimilation of middle-class conduct to natural living. Like other writers making up the avant-garde to which Toomer hoped to affiliate, he represents the resolution of a historical condition as a matter of individual choice of creativity over materialism when in fact education and economic security for blacks are available only in the context of the dominant American culture.

With the completion of "Balo" and "Natalie Mann," Toomer effectively ended his writing on Afro-America. Other works completed in the 1920s include "Easter" (1925), a symbolic story of the world awaiting spiritual rebirth in an atmosphere of surreal chaos; an unproduced drama, "The Sacred Factory" (1927), described by Toomer as a modern morality play, in which workers and the middle class play out their aimless, unfulfilled lives in separate chambers on stage; ''The Gallonwerps'' (1927), an unproduced satiric drama, later revised as fiction, concerning ''diking,'' or the art of manipulating events so that the manipulator is approved by his victims; ''Mr. Costyve Duditch'' (1928), a short story about compensatory devices adopted by man who lacks a coherent identity or will to accomplish his aims; ''York Beach'' (1929), another story about an unfulfilled woman and male contrasts; and ''Winter on Earth'' (1928), a return to impressionistic prose lyricism for a portrayal of the death in life resulting from loss of spiritual harmony. As the listing indicates, Toomer persisted in equating psychological identity with spiritual liberation and harmony while employing the advanced means of art to raise a conception of modern redemption to the highest level of generality that symbolism would permit.

Despite periods of exhaustion in adult life similar to the episodes of his childhood, Toomer seems never to have been unable to write. As he put it in ''Outline of an Autobiography'' (c. 1931–32), ''before I had even so much as glimpsed the possibility of writing *Cane*, I had written a trunk full of manuscripts. The phrase 'trunk full' is often used loosely. I mean it literally and exactly.'' Following the appearance of *Cane* and during the time when Toomer was a leader in the Gurdjieff movement, his energy was just as prolific of manuscripts as it had been before 1923. As the 1920s ended, he prepared a collection that included seven short stories besides already published pieces. In addition, he wrote a full-length novel titled ''Transatlantic,'' and later revised as ''Eight Day World'' (c. 1933), and a collection of aphorisms. None of these projects found a commercial publisher, so to share some part of his work with an audience Toomer issued the aphorisms privately (1931) under the title *Essentials*. In the 1930s his literary efforts were preoccupied with four of the autobiographical narratives in which he sought to explain himself; a novel ''Caromb,'' a reply to vicious racist charges leveled against an experimental community Toomer conducted in Portage, Wisconsin; and a long philosophical poem, ''The Blue Meridian.'' Finally, in the 1940s the nearly unquenchable drive to write, or to be discouraged by rejection, resulted in a collection of poems, ''The Wayward and the Seeking.'' It also failed to find a publisher.

The resolve illustrated by rehearsal of this record of unpublished works, and some insight into their crucial defect, may be suggested by two quotations from *Essentials*. In the first Toomer asserts that ''Human values are empowered in two ways: by force of beauty and by moral force.'' He who uses the force of beauty is an artist; ''he using moral force, is a teacher who himself speaks and directly works effects / Artist and teacher have common values and aims.'' That Toomer aims at something more than the traditional *dulce et utile* becomes clear a few passages later when he says of the artist: ''I count it good that any poet stops writing his own small verse, that any man stops doing his own small work, and becomes a student of the Great Work.''

Undeniably Toomer saw himself a student of the ''Great Work,'' and nothing makes the point clearer than the writing we turn to in addressing the chief critical problem in the study of Toomer: his views on race. Three publications are pertinent to this theme. The first is the essay ''Race Problems and Modern Society'' (1929). Here he cites the anthropological research of Melville J. Herskovits and others on syncretism to support his belief that in America a new race was emerging from the intermingling of black, white, and red. Second is the privately issued pamphlet *A Fiction and Some Facts* (1931), where he expands upon ideas expressed in his other autobiographical writings to explain that his grandfather Pinchback, despite his reputation, was not as a matter of fact black; no more so is his grandson, says Toomer, who goes on to characterize himself as biologically, racially, and sociologically an American who has never identified himself with any one branch of the tree of human life. Finally, there is the long poem ''The Blue Meridian'' (1936), which translates these sentiments, and no doubt, as Frederik L. Rusch contends, a good deal of feeling as a marginal citizen under the influence of Whitman, into an idealistic vision of racial plurality synthesized in a utopian future wherein the black and white meridians fertilized by the red will transmute into a balanced homogeneity.

Looking back to *Cane* from the perspective of Toomer's late poem, one finds consistency. Despite its reputation as exemplar of the New Negro in the Harlem Renaissance, the book is, much as Toomer suggested by terming it a swan song, thematically occupied with the end of a historical episode that could be sustained only through the literary invention of a nostalgically imagined folk. For other writers the next appropriate subject after the rural South of Afro-America would be the experience of developing black consciousness in urban conditions, but for Jean Toomer, disposed as he was to resist the demands of the specific and yearning for an overarching conception of life, universal spirit had first claim as the realm in which to seek identity and to prescribe it for others. His failure through more than two decades of writing to find an audience for his teaching about Being is sufficient answer to the critics, recalling *Cane*'s promise, who have asked, ''What became of Jean Toomer?''

SURVEY OF CRITICISM

Predictably, critical study of Jean Toomer has centered largely upon analysis of *Cane*, and most of the interpretations of form and theme appear in journal articles too numerous to note beyond the selected items at the end of this entry.

The most complete record of the first 50 years of critical comment is John M. Reilly's ''Jean Toomer: An Annotated Checklist of Criticism'' (1974). This may be supplemented by the entry on Toomer in Margaret Perry's *The Harlem Renaissance* (1928) and by the yearly entries on ''Black Literature'' in *American Literary Scholarship/An Annual*, edited by J. Albert Robbins, James Woodress, and Warren French (Durham, N.C.: Duke University Press). In general, the scholarly essays on *Cane* address the problems of unity, sources for the book's form, the blackness of the work, representations of female characters, and such themes as redemption and repression.

At the same time as it attracts the most critical attention, *Cane* constitutes a problem in literary study, because its fame and apparent uniqueness threaten to misrepresent an artist whose canon exists largely in unpublished manuscripts in a special collection at Fisk University Library. Darwin T. Turner's unsurpassed work in these unpublished materials has done great service in presenting a full picture. His examination of the plays written between 1922 and 1947 in "The Failure of a Playwright" (1967) alerted critics to Toomer's experiments in absurdist drama, and his section on Toomer for *In a Minor Chord* (1971) is an acute study in critical biography that includes both published and unpublished works in its scope. Turner is also responsible for the invaluable collection *The Wayward and the Seeking*, which weaves together the previously unpublished autobiographies into a single narrative, prints poetry from the unpublished collection that gives the volume its title, gives the texts of "Natalie Mann" and "The Sacred Factory," offers liberal excerpts from *Essentials*, and also presents the texts of the short stories "Mr. Costyve Duditch," "Winter on Earth," and "The Withered Skin of Berries," the latter never before published. The volume's apparatus discusses the Fisk materials and the problems associated with editing Toomer.

The earliest dissertation on Toomer was written in 1967 by Mabel Maryle Dillard (Ohio University), who also studied unpublished materials to describe the development of Toomer's aesthetics. In 1980 Dillard joined with Brian Joseph Benson to produce *Jean Toomer* for the Twayne United States Authors Series. Their book is especially valuable for its description of Toomer's views on transcendent American identity and for careful exposition of the circular structure of *Cane*. Even fuller treatment of *Cane* forms the central three chapters of the most recent book on Toomer, Nellie Y. McKay's *Jean Toomer, Artist: A Study of His Literary Life and Work, 1894–1936* (1984). This interpretive study of themes presents exposition of the biographical background by careful use of the autobiographies and a treatment of the literary apprenticeship as well as an exhaustive examination of *Cane* and interpretations of "The Blue Meridian" and the plays. The McKay and Benson and Dillard volumes and Turner's *In a Minor Chord* contain listings of primary works that will serve to guide critics until a complete register of Toomer's writings is prepared.

Naturally enough, Toomer figures prominently in general studies of black literature. Robert Bone's *The Negro Novel in America* (1958; rev. ed. 1965) accords *Cane* status equal to the fiction of Richard Wright, Ralph Ellison, and James Baldwin. Jean Wagner in *Black Poets of the United States* (1973) introduces to critical discussion affirmative interpretation of "The Blue Meridian." Greatly at odds with the earlier evaluations of *Cane* is Donald B. Gibson's chapter in *Politics of Literary Expression* (1981), which argues that the frustrations of Kabnis are those of Toomer himself, whose writing fiction rather than facing social reality displays strategies of evasion.

The real significance of the difference in critical views between earlier *Cane*-centered studies and Gibson's lies not so much in the change of opinion as it does in a shift from New Criticism. Toomer can no longer be studied ahistorically or without awareness of his biography. As a result, it now becomes necessary to return the remarkable book and the singular author to their context. Both literary history and our critical practice will be the better for the necessity.

BIBLIOGRAPHY

Works by Jean Toomer

This selective list does not include works incorporated into *Cane* or minor items printed in *The Wayward and the Seeking*.

"Banking Coal." *Crisis* 24 (1922): 65.
Cane. New York: Boni and Liveright, 1923; repr. New York: University Place Press, 1967; New York: Harper and Row, 1970; New York: Liveright, 1975.
"Gum." *Chapbook* no. 36 (April 1923): 22.
"Oxen Cart and Warfare." *Little Review* 10 (Autumn/Winter 1924–25): 44–48.
"Easter." *Little Review* 11 (Spring 1925): 3–7.
"Balo." *Plays of Negro Life*. Ed. Alain Locke and Montgomery Gregory. New York: Harper's, 1927, pp. 269–86.
"Mr. Costyve Duditch." *Dial* 85 (December 1928): 460–76.
"York Beach." *The New American Caravan*. Ed. Alfred Kreymborg, Lewis Mumford, and Paul Rosenfeld. New York: Macauley, 1928, pp. 12–83.
"Race Problems and Modern Society." *Man and His World*. Ed. Baker Brownell. New York: D. Van Nostrand, 1929, pp. 67–101.
"Reflections." *Dial* 86 (April 1929): 314.
Essentials: Definitions and Aphorisms. Private ed. Chicago: Lakeside Press, 1931.
A Fiction and Some Facts. Private ed., 1931.
"As the Eagle Soars." *Crisis* 41 (1932): 116.
"Brown River, Smile." *Pagany* 3 (January-March 1932): 29–33. First 125 lines of "The Blue Meridian." Also published in *The Adelphi* 2 (September 1931).
"The Hill." *America and Alfred Stieglitz: A Collective Portrait*. Ed. Waldo Frank, Lewis Mumford, Dorothy Norman, Paul Rosenfeld, and Harold Rugg. New York: Doubleday, Doran, 1934.
"Of a Certain November." *Dubuque Dial*, 1 November 1935.
"The Blue Meridian." *The New Caravan*. Ed. Alfred Kreymborg, Lewis Mumford, and Paul Rosenfeld. New York: W. W. Norton, 1936.
Living Is Developing. Private ed., 1937.
Work Ideas I. Private ed., 1937.
An Interpretation of Friends Worship. Philadelphia: Committee on Religious Education of Friends General Conference, 1947.
The Flavor of Man. Philadelphia: Young Friends Movement of the Philadelphia Yearly Meetings, 1949.
"Five Vignettes." *City in All Directions: An Anthology of Modern Poems*. Ed. Arnold Adoff. New York: Macmillan, 1969, p. 34.
"Blue Meridian." *The Poetry of the Negro, 1746–1970*. Ed. Langston Hughes and Arna Bontemps. New York: Doubleday, 1970, pp. 107–33. Third version of the poem.

The Wayward and the Seeking: A Collection of Writings. Ed. Darwin T. Turner. Washington, D.C.: Howard University Press, 1980.

Studies of Jean Toomer

Bell, Bernard. "A Key to the Poems in *Cane*." *CLA Journal* 14 (March 1971): 251–58.

———. "Portrait of the Artist as High Priest of Soul: Jean Toomer's *Cane*." *Black World* 23 (September 1974): 4–19, 92–97.

Benson, Brian Joseph and Mabel Mayle Dillard. *Jean Toomer*. Boston: Twayne, 1980.

Bone, Robert. *The Negro Novel in America*. New Haven: Yale University Press, 1958; rev. ed., 1965, pp. 80–89.

Fullinwider, S. P. "Jean Toomer: Lost Generation, or Negro Renaissance?" *Phylon* 27 (Winter 1966): 396–403.

Gibson, Donald B. "Jean Toomer: The Politics of Denial." *Politics of Literary Expression: A Study of Major Black Writers*. Westport, Conn.: Greenwood Press, 1981, pp. 155–81.

Gysin, Fritz. *The Grotesque in American Negro Fiction: Jean Toomer, Richard Wright and Ralph Ellison*. Bern: Franke Verlag, 1975, pp. 36–90, 276–79.

Innes, Catherine L. "The Unity of Jean Toomer's *Cane*." *CLA Journal* 15 (March 1972): 306–22.

Krasny, Michael J. "Design in Jean Toomer's *Balo*." *Negro American Literature Forum* 7 (Fall 1973): 103–4.

McKay, Nellie Y. *Jean Toomer, Artist: A Study of His Literary Life and Work, 1894–1936*. Chapel Hill: University of North Carolina Press, 1984.

Perry, Margaret. *The Harlem Renaissance: An Annotated Bibliography and Commentary*. New York: Garland, 1982, pp. 138–58.

Reilly, John M. "Jean Toomer: An Annotated Checklist of Criticism." *Resources for American Literary Study* 4 (Spring 1974): 27–56.

———. "The Search for Black Redemption: Jean Toomer's *Cane*." *Studies in the Novel* 2 (Fall 1970): 312–24.

Rusch, Fredrik L. "The Blue Man: Jean Toomer's Solution to His Problems of Identity." *Obsidian* 6, nos. i-ii (1980): 38–54.

———. "A Tale of the Country Round: Jean Toomer's Legend 'Monrovia.' " *MELUS* 7, no. ii (1980): 37–46.

Scruggs, Charles W. "The Mark of Cain and the Redemption of Art: A Study in Theme and Structure of Jean Toomer's *Cane*." *American Literature* 44 (May 1972): 276–91.

Turner, Darwin T. "The Failure of a Playwright." *CLA Journal* 10 (June 1967): 308–18.

———. "An Intersection of Paths: Correspondence Between Jean Toomer and Sherwood Anderson." *CLA Journal* 17 (June 1974): 455–67.

———. "Jean Toomer: Exile." *In a Minor Chord: Three Afro-American Writers and Their Search for Identity*. Carbondale: Southern Illinois University Press, 1971, pp. 1–59.

————. "Jean Toomer's *Cane*: A Critical Analysis." *Negro Digest* 18 (January 1969): 54–61.

Twombly, Robert C. "A Disciple's Odyssey: Jean Toomer's Gurdjieffian Career." *Prospects: An Annual of American Cultural Studies*, vol. 2. New York: Burt Franklin, 1976, pp. 437–62.

Wagner, Jean. "Jean Toomer." *Black Poets of the United States from Paul Laurence Dunbar to Langston Hughes*. Urbana: University of Illinois Press, 1973, pp. 259–81. Originally published in French. Paris: Libraire Istra, 1963.

Anne Tyler
(1941–   )

Since 1964, when her first book was published, Anne Tyler, who grew up in North Carolina, has continued to turn out sensitive and highly crafted novels and short stories. Although her reputation has been slow to reflect the quality of her fiction, she has gradually attracted a wide audience as well as the respect of discerning readers. With the success of *Dinner at the Homesick Restaurant* (1982) and then of *The Accidental Tourist* (1985), she has come to be recognized as an important writer of late twentieth-century America.

BIOGRAPHY

A Quaker heritage, a mostly Southern childhood, early marriage and motherhood: these are major facts in Anne Tyler's life and primary influences on her work. For the six years that followed her birth in Minneapolis on 25 October 1941, Tyler was "on the road," moved from one "commune-like arrangement" to another by parents trying to live by some "Emersonian ideal." She is one of four children born to her social-worker, later journalist, mother, Phyllis Mahon Tyler, and her chemist father, Lloyd Parry Tyler, parents she recalls as having "supported and encouraged anything their children did that was creative." When Anne was six, the Tylers joined what the author has described as "an experimental Quaker community in the wilderness," at Celo, North Carolina. Five years later, the family moved to Raleigh and took up an "ordinary middle class existence," that must have seemed very strange to an eleven-year-old who had never used a phone and who could "strike a match on the soles of [her] bare feet." At sixteen she graduated from Broughton High School in Raleigh, where she had benefited from Phyllis Peacock, an inspiring English teacher who several years earlier had taught and encouraged Reynolds Price. In the high school library, Tyler discovered Eudora Welty's stories and so learned that "literature could be made out of the ordinary things of life—Coca-Cola signs, and *crêpe de chine* bras, and all those other little objects George Eliot never heard of.''

On her seventeenth birthday, Tyler was already enrolled, on full scholarship, at Duke University, where she twice won the Anne Flexner Award for creative writing and was elected to Phi Beta Kappa. At Duke she was taught by twenty-three–year–old Reynolds Price, who, Tyler has said, ''turned out to be the only person I knew who could actually teach writing.'' She worked on the Duke literary magazine, the *Archive*, where she first published short stories, two of which were selected for an anthology of student writing entitled *Under Twenty-Five*. After graduating from Duke with a major in Russian, Tyler went to New York and completed the course work for an M.A. at Columbia before she was sidetracked, first by the urge to spend a summer in Maine and then by the desire to return to North Carolina.

On 3 May 1962, after nine months back in Durham spent working as bibliographer in Russian at the Duke University Library, Tyler married Taghi Mohammad Modarressi, an Iranian doctor at Duke as a resident in psychiatry. Two months after the wedding, the Modarressis moved to Montreal, where during six months ''unemployment'' Tyler wrote what was to be her first published novel. In 1963 three of her stories appeared in national periodicals, and in 1964 Alfred Knopf brought out *If Morning Ever Comes*. Tyler took a job at the McGill University Law Library, where she worked until a month before the birth of her first daughter, Tezh, born on 24 October 1965. By her twenty-fourth birthday, Tyler was wife, mother, and established writer.

The Tin Can Tree, Tyler's second novel, was issued by Knopf in 1965, the year her first child was born. A second daughter, Mitra, was born in 1967, after the Modarressis had moved to Baltimore; as Tyler cared for first one and then two children, the short stories continued to appear, but the novel written during this period, *Winter Birds, Winter Apples*, remains unpublished. *A Slipping-Down Life* appeared in 1970, and since then Tyler's novels have come out at regular intervals.

Since 1967 the Modarressis have lived quietly in Baltimore, and Tyler, writing ''between 8:05 and 3:30,'' has managed to maintain steady production of not only novels but also reviews, articles, and short stories. Since the early publications in the Duke *Archive*, Tyler's short fiction has appeared in a range of periodicals, both popular (*Seventeen, Mademoiselle*, and *McCall's*) and sophisticated (*Harper's, Southern Review*, and *New Yorker*, where eight of her stories were published between 1966 and 1977). Although a collected edition of Tyler's stories has yet to appear, her fiction has won inclusion in several anthologies, including the O. Henry Awards *Prize Stories* for both 1969 and 1972, and *The Best American Short Stories* for 1977. In 1983 she edited, with Shannon Ravenel, that year's collection of *Best American Short Stories* and in the introduction expressed continued allegiance to the genre and ''its special place,'' not as ''a truncated, ersatz sort of novel'' but ''an art form all its own.''

Because Tyler's priorities rule out the public appearances that promote sales and generate publicity, her reputation has been slow to grow. The acclaim that she has won is due solely to the quality of her work. She won a *Mademoiselle* award for writing as early as 1966 and an American Academy and Institute of Arts and Letters Award for Literature in 1977; the 1980 publication of *Morgan's Passing* brought her wide recognition and with it a Janet Heidinger Kafka Prize and nomination for an American Book Award. *Dinner at the Homesick Restaurant* (1982) won her a P.E.N./Faulkner Award for Fiction and more nominations, including one for a Pulitzer Prize. *The Accidental Tourist* (1985) was greeted with both critical and popular acclaim; it was awarded the National Book Critics Circle award as the most distinguished work of American fiction published in 1985. With the success of *Dinner at the Homesick Restaurant* and *The Accidental Tourist*, Tyler has at last been recognized as an important contemporary writer. "With each new novel . . . it becomes ever more clear that," as Jonathan Yardley put it in the *Washington Post Book World*, 25 August 1985, "the fiction of Anne Tyler is something both unique and extraordinary in contemporary American literature."

MAJOR THEMES

Tyler's first published novel, *If Morning Ever Comes* (1964), is a delicate, even fragile, story of a young man from Sandhill, North Carolina, who feels painfully responsible for his mother, grandmother, and five sisters. A law student at Columbia, not only is he chilled and displaced in New York; he is also obsessed with what is going on at home. Ben Joe Hawkes goes AWOL from law school and takes the train south to Sandhill, where he comes to terms with ironic facts: the women of his family are self-sufficient, and it is he who cannot let go of his ties with home. The novel closes with Ben Joe on the train back to New York, accompanied by a wife-to-be, an orphaned high-school sweetheart who from now on "would always be waiting for him, like his own little piece of Sandhill transplanted. . . . "

In 1965 Knopf released *The Tin Can Tree*, in which the author continues to explore separateness and connectedness and the tension between them, a theme of *If Morning Ever Comes* and one central to most of Tyler's later work. In this book, she introduces the dilemma of the artist whose creativity demands a self-centered solitude his humanity rejects: James Green is a photographer (photography as metaphor turns up later in *Morgan's Passing* and, notably, in *Earthly Possessions*). The plot of *The Tin Can Tree* centers on the effect the death of six-year-old Janie Rose Pike has on her bereaved family and the other occupants of a ramshackle, sun-baked, three-family dwelling perched on the edge of a tobacco field well away from the tree-shaded town. The house is described as an "ark," and the isolation and interdependence of its inhabitants justify the image. James is torn between responsibility to his petulant, self-declared invalid brother, and the girl he presumably loves, Joan Pike, cousin to Janie Rose and her brother. The book ends with James's private confusions unresolved, but with the image of the disparate inhabitants of the three-family house fixed into unity by the power of the lens:

The glass of the finder seemed to hold them there like figures in a snowflurry paperweight who would still be in their set positions when the snow settled down again. . . . whole years could pass, they could be born and die, they could marry or live out their separate lives alone, and nothing in this finder would change.

Evie Decker, teenage heroine of *A Slipping-Down Life* (1970), is at the book's beginning "a plump drab girl in a brown sweater that was running to balls at the elbows," whose chief companion was her radio. Evie's lethargic infatuation for a would-be rock singer, "Drumstrings" Casey, leads to the one remarkable event of her life: she emerges from the ladies' room at the Unicorn Club with "CASEY" carved raggedly in the flesh of her forehead. Drum himself is moved by such proof of devotion to take a wary interest in Evie, at first perhaps for publicity's sake but gradually out of a certain aimless fascination. They elope and take up residence in a tar-paper shack on the edge of town where Drum reveals a surprising yen for domesticity and biscuits made with bacon grease. Pregnancy and the death of her father shock Evie into a hitherto uncharacteristic "taking hold," and she moves back to the house she has suddenly inherited, having shed Drum and now focused on the baby who is to be born, her grief channeled into a "brief tearing sensation that lasted long after she had rolled out of the yard toward town."

In a July 1972 *National Observer* interview, Tyler disowned her first two novels but admitted abiding affection for *A Slipping-Down Life* as the one of her early books in which characters change. Evie, who has never had a real home, with either father or husband, has so changed by novel's end as to be able herself to make a home for a child. (Tyler has subsequently confessed to a desire to know how "Evie Decker's baby turned out.")

The action of *The Clock Winder* (1972) alternates between North Carolina, where the first three novels were set, and Baltimore, where Tyler has lived with her family since 1967. Elizabeth Abbott, the "clock winder," is a more defined character than Evie Decker, Joan Pike, James Green, or Ben Joe Hawkes—and one more in touch with physical realities. Elizabeth, a misfit in her own family, finds an unexpected niche among the Emersons of posh suburban Baltimore. Beyond the ups and downs of her interactions with the Emerson family (two of the sons fall in love with her, one of whom commits suicide), she manages over a span of years to reconstitute a home in a house that once seemed to have "outlived its usefulness."

Elizabeth cleans and fixes, tends and prunes, and around the nucleus of her "irritating" presence, a new family forms. The novel closes not only with an affirmation of the Emersons snugly barricaded against the plague of locusts without but also with the escape of Peter, Mrs. Emerson's youngest, who cannot survive within his birth family but rather must establish a new one with the

Georgia waitress he has married. "Bye," Peter's young nephew tells the fleeing couple, "as if every day of his life he saw people arriving and leaving and getting side-tracked from their travels."

In *Celestial Navigation* (1974) Tyler deals with older and still more formed characters in a narrowed and intensely focused setting. Jeremy Pauling, an agoraphobic artist, cannot bring himself to stray beyond his block in a shabby section of Baltimore, and spends his time in an upstairs studio creating, first collages, and later intricate three-dimensional paper sculptures. Even when he was a child, his vision was for detail. When his mother dies, Jeremy is cut adrift, and when Mary Tell, also adrift, takes a room in the house and with her child becomes part of the household, it is not long before the unlikely pair get together. To the reader's shcok, the apparently sexless Jeremy not only lives in apparent harmony with the beautiful young woman but fathers children as well, all the while going on with his art. The union gives way when Mary, absorbed by maternity and counting Jeremy as little more than another child needing nurture, goes to the hospital to give birth to their fourth baby without even waking him. Absolved and so deprived of the responsibility that is a necessary component of love, Jeremy withdraws from what is left, and Mary's realization of his withdrawal prompts her to leave him and home. When Jeremy at last bestirs himself to follow, it is too late. The novel ends with a glimpse of the unremitting isolation that will be Jeremy's future lot. Having opted, however passively, for the work, he is left with a husk of the life.

Searching for Caleb (1976), the story of a quest for a lost brother, is built around the metaphor of travel, a structure and theme important in several of Tyler's recent works. Sixty-one years before the book's opening, Caleb Peck had fled from the restriction imposed by his family and to his art—the music that afforded self-expression even if it brought no worldly success. Tyler lines up the generations of the Pecks for our inspection almost, on a small scale, as Galsworthy does the Forsytes. In Baltimore, as elsewhere, preserving property and tribal allegiance at all costs can lead to a drying up and a dying off. The most vital Pecks are those who get away: Duncan and Justine, cousins and man and wife, who live a life on the move, from one makeshift job to another, from one flimsy rented house to the next.

There are two conflicting motions in this novel, conflicting motions that operate in most of Tyler's work: the urge to nonattachment, irresponsibility, and freedom, and the counterurge to settling, gathering, and drawing together. Tyler does not cheat: the weight is evenly distributed before the tug-o'-war begins, and she convincingly conveys the paradoxical coexistence of the solid love between Duncan and Justine and the alliance between Justine and the grandfather who joins the vagabound household without relinquishing one whit of his quintessential Peckness. The impulses fuse, however, as Justine and her grandfather journey together in ostensible search for the defector Caleb. Daniel Peck does not live to see his long-lost brother once he is found, and Caleb, the artist, even in extreme old age, is one still compelled to "light out for the territory."

Earthly Possessions is a more consciously (too consciously, according to Doris Betts) structured book in which the contrary impulses are laid out with all but absolute symmetry. Tyler tells the story from the first-person point of view of her protagonist, Charlotte Emory, and Charlotte's narrative alternates neatly between present events and the memories of the past they provoke. Movement in space parallels movement in time, and Charlotte, taken halfheartedly hostage by a bumbling bank robber, travels away from her Maryland home and southward, at last to Florida. Thus she is compelled to make the journey she had longed to take and so temporarily escapes the demands of marriage and family and the accumulated clutter of a lifetime spent in one house. "My life," Charlotte claims, "has been a history of casting off encumbrances, paring down to the bare essentials, stripping for the journey." By the time she reaches Florida, Charlotte's reveries have brought her up to the moment she had finally determined to cut and run, to the morning she was abducted as she stood in line at the bank to get cash for her own flight. The novel concludes with Charlotte's realization that journeys in space are no longer necessary: "I don't see the need. . . . We have been traveling for years, traveled all our lives, we are traveling still. We couldn't stay in one place if we tried."

Morgan Gower is another character all but swamped by clutter. *Morgan's Passing* (1980) recounts its protagonist's struggle to hold out against the limitations of one life, to insist on living many lives. Masquerading as a doctor, Morgan delivers a baby and so comes into the lives of Emily Meredith, a creator of puppets, and her would-be actor husband, Leon. Morgan, like Elizabeth Abbott in *The Clock Winder*, is a misfit at home and a mainstay abroad. Morgan finally moves in with Emily and her children, the daughter he had delivered and the son he has fathered (Leon having conveniently agreed to go "home" to the bourgeois life he had once so vehemently renounced). Rather than achieving the stark economy he had admired in Emily's life, however, Morgan brings along the very clutter he yearned to escape: "Trunks and dress forms, a rusty birdcage, barrels containing a gigantic cup-and-saucer collection muffled in straw, stacks of *National Geographics*, Brendle's catalogs, Louisa's autograph book, a samovar, a carton of records, a lady's bicycle, a wicker elephant. And this was only what lined the hall. . . . " Whereas Morgan is perplexed by such an albatross of accumulation, "Emily loved it all." "You could draw vitality from mere objects," she comes to see, "from the seething souvenirs of dozens of lives raced through at full throttle."

Morgan takes up the puppet-master role that Leon abdicates, and the lives of all the characters go on, surprisingly undisturbed by dislocation and realignment. Driven by financial pressure to sign up the puppet show with the Holy Word Entertainment Troupe of Tindell, Maryland, Morgan takes up his new life under the name of Emily's husband, thus doing away with "Morgan Gower." He is nonetheless taken aback to read his own obituary, the whimsical revenge of the deserted mother of his seven daughters, who thus frees herself for a new love. Morgan realizes, however, that reclaiming his identity would be useless: people would only say, "Aren't you that fellow Meredith . . . ?" Characteristically, he quickly gets over the shock of "passing," and, indeed, comes to find in it an ultimate emancipation. As the book ends, Morgan is humming, and "everything he looked at seemed luminous and beautiful and rich with possibilities."

Dinner at the Homesick Restaurant (1982) recounts the history of the Tulls of Baltimore; through them Tyler said that she finally tells the "truth" about families. A dark vision informs this novel about a family abandoned by the father and cut off by circumstance and the mother's character from any sense of community. In the narrow Baltimore row house where Pearl Tull and her children accidentally alight—the father's wanderings go on—Pearl struggles incessantly to tighten, repair, and fortify. As in most of Tyler's novels, the material house is inseparable from those who live in it, leave it, or return to it. Pearl raises her two sons and daughter in an atmosphere without warmth. Jenny, the daughter, endures two unhappy marriages before meeting Joe St. Ambrose, whose first wife had left him with six children, and with him creating one of those "large, noisy families," that Tyler, perhaps somewhat wistfully, includes in her books. Cody—Pearl's handsome, aggressive, superficially successful son, who is frozen in a childhood jealousy that makes any triumph turn to ashes in his mouth—hates his gentle brother Ezra. Even stealing the girl Ezra loves does not free Cody from his obsession. Ezra, however, is not to be deterred from the pursuit of the dream that is his response to the emotional deprivation of the Tull children's youth, the dream of the Homesick Restaurant. "Ezra's going to have him a place where people come just like to a family dinner," explains a friend: "He'll cook them one thing special each day and dish it out on their plates and everything will be solid and wholesome, really homelike. . . . Really just like home." Working in an Italian restaurant and becoming surrogate son and heir to the owner, Ezra moves toward fulfilling his ambition, all the while "feverish" with ideas: "Of course! He'd cook what people felt homesick for—tacos like those from vendor's carts in California, which the Mexican was always pining after; and that wonderful vinegary North Carolina barbecue that Tood Duckett had to have brought by his mother several times a year in cardboard cups. He would call it the Homesick Restaurant."

Only after Pearl's death can the Tulls actually get through a meal; in Tyler's world as in the real world, gathering around the table at once affirms and severely tests the unity of family. But the steaming platters that emerge from the kitchen at the Homesick Restaurant are more than accoutrements of ordeal; they are also works of art. Tyler deals, here and elsewhere, with the creative impulse, and her strength is that she shows the various forms creativity can take. Elizabeth Abbott's woodcarvings, Emily Meredith's puppets, Charlotte Emory's photographs, and even Justine Peck's fortune-telling are art. Jeremy Pauling is an artist, but so too is Ezra Tull. In the kitchen, as nowhere else, Ezra "came into his own, like someone crippled on dry land but effortlessly graceful once he takes to water." His restaurant was his realized vision, and there he "circulated among the diners," urging upon them "his oyster stew, his artichoke salad, his spinach bisque and his chili-bean soup and his gizzard soup that was made with love.''

"Families'' has been suggested—and largely accepted—as a major Tyler theme, but left unqualified and unelaborated, the label could prove reductive. More precisely, her theme is connectedness and separateness, the tensions between them, and the myriad forms they can assume. Tyler is concerned with all the bonds: children and parents and grandparents; spouses and especially brothers; in-laws and former in-laws. (In *If Morning Ever Comes* and *Morgan's Passing*, mothers-in-law live with daughters-in-law after the son-husband who originally brought them together is gone.) The connectedness Tyler projects extends beyond even extended families to what might be called ''accumulated families,'' flesh-and-blood equivalents, perhaps, of the clutter of ''earthly possessions'' that can gather over years in old houses. The lodging house in *Celestial Navigation* shelters one such accumulated family; the Emorys' house in *Earthly Possessions* just takes people in:

Often Saul invited people for Sunday dinner. . . . Sometimes they stayed. We had an old lady named Miss Feather, for instance, up on our third floor—evicted from her apartment the spring of '63, just borrowing a room until she found another. Which she never did. Never will, I suppose. We had soldiers, hitchhikers, traveling salesmen—country people lonesome for their family churches. . . . And one Sunday, a bearded man in work clothes came to the mourners' bench while the congregation was singing "Just As I Am." . . . We took him home for dinner. . . . Then he went upstairs and claimed another of Alberta's old beds, and unpacked his cardboard suitcase into a bureau.

Are you keeping track? There were seven of us now, not counting those just passing through.

Opposed to the tendencies of accumulating and gathering in are the centrifugal forces of clearing out and moving on. Tyler's novels are full of departures and returns, and her characters speculate about changing places and switching families. As counterpoise to the accumulated households and rambling cluttered houses, Tyler explores the urge to travel and to travel light; to eliminate layers—of objects, people, attachments; to sand things down to the grain. Charlotte Emory responds to her life by discarding ''clothing, books, knick-knacks, pictures . . . aiming for a house with the bare, polished look of a bleached skull.'' Later she begins to discard people: ''I stopped answering the phone, no longer nodded to acquaintances, could not be waylaid in the grocery store. . . . I didn't want to be bothered. They were using up such chunks of my life. . . . '' Like Charlotte, Tyler herself, she tells us in ''Still Just Writing,'' is ''continually prepared to travel.'' ''It is physically impossible for me,'' she writes, ''to buy any necessity without buying a travel-sized version as well. I have a little toilet kit, with soap and a nightgown, forever packed and ready to go.''

Even more than in Tyler's other fiction, travel is the organizing motif in *The Accidental Tourist* (1985). The novel's protagonist, Macon Leary (like his creator devoted to travel-sized toiletries), journeys by car and cab, by train, and on planes, large and small; he is, all the same, a tourist who hates to travel. Leary of life, as his name suggests, Tyler's Macon dotes on appliance maintenance contracts, cannot make a purchase without consulting *Consumer Reports*, and keeps a file of detailed written directions without which he would go hopelessly astray in the city of his birth. The "geographic dyslexia" that renders Macon peculiarly unfit for journeys he must make, is a family trait, shared with his siblings, who (like Pearl Tull and the Pecks of *Waiting for Caleb*) belong to the "cautious half" of humanity. Finding himself alone after the violent death of his only son and the departure, a year later, of his wife of twenty years, Macon retreats more and more into agoraphobic eccentricity. Dressed in gray sweats that could be for day and night, eating popcorn for breakfast, doing his laundry as he showers to save water and electricity, Macon comes to dread going shopping, even on Tuesdays, "when the supermarket was least crowded with other human beings." Liberated at last by a broken leg that forces him to summon help, he is soon so securely encased in plaster—"sealed away from himself"— and so comfortably installed in the house of his youth that "he almost wondered whether, by some devious subconscious means he had engineered this injury . . . just so he could settle down safe among the people he'd started out with." Thus reunited, the Learys, three brothers and their sister, ignore the telephone (messenger from the outside world) and eat baked potatoes—"there was something about the smell of a roasting Idaho that was . . . well, *conservative*, was the way Macon put it to himself." They occupy themselves with a family card-game so deliberately complicated that no outsider can master the Byzantine intricacies of its "rules."

Macon, alone of the Leary brothers, doesn't put in his days at the family bottle-top business. He has been recruited to turn out travel guides that only he can write—books intended for people who hate to travel, reluctant or accidental tourists. "As much as he hated the travel," Macon "loved the writing—the virtuous delight of organizing a disorganized country. . . . " The books are anonymous, marked as his only by the logo of the winged armchair; "while armchair travelers dream of going places," his publisher explains, "traveling armchairs dream of staying put."

Enervated to the point that he finds it difficult even to set down his grudging instructions for "Trying to Eat . . . " or "Trying to Sleep . . . " in England or elsewhere, Macon dreads that day when he would be stripped of his cast and forced to resume his travels: "Sometimes he wished he could stay in his cast forever. In fact, he wished it covered him from head to foot. People would thump faintly on his chest. They'd peer in through his eyeholes. 'Macon? You in there?' Maybe he was, maybe he wasn't. No one would ever know."

The Accidental Tourist is a comedy, a comedy that, with due deference to verisimilitude, grows out of tragedy and grief. It is also a psychological novel (in the sense of Walker Percy's *The Second Coming*) that carefully traces the stages—measured in dreams, in dialogue, in moments of self-definition—of Macon's painful movement from numbness to affective rebirth. A traveler who habitually barricaded himself behind hand luggage, noncommittal grunts, and a thousand-page novel kept for the purpose, Macon emerges at the book's end as a man capable of plying a terrified octogenarian seat mate with sherry and reassurance. As his dreams and memories of his dead son move back in remembered time from the summer the boy was killed to the days of his infancy, as the dialogues he engages in develop from reluctant or desperate telephone calls to intense and personal encounters, the image he presents to himself and to others changes. Alone in his deserted house early in the novel, Macon, stooped and sloppy in his sweat suit, looks at himself in the mirror, and "his reflection reminded him of a patient in a mental hospital." A year later, however, after the companionable journey with frightened old Mrs. Bunn, Macon realizes that he has come to be perceived as "this merry, tolerant person": "only later, when he passed a mirror and noticed the grin on his face, did he realize that, in fact, he might not have been lying to Mrs. Bunn after all."

In his initial isolation and throughout his cure, Macon is not actually alone. In his successive states and abodes, Macon's constant companion is an irrepressible Welsh Corgi named Edward. Tyler's Edward, probably the book's most captivating character, is, however, more than a scene-stealer; he is the id in canine form. It is Edward who expresses the rage and confusion that Macon so carefully represses: "Can a dog have a nervous breakdown?" Edward, beloved of readers as he may be, does not endear himself to those obliged to live with his barks and bites, leaps and snarls; and more than one pronounces him "sick." Even the all but imperturbable "trainer," Muriel Pritchett, agent of Edward's cure and of Macon's, is driven to ask: "You want a dog that hates the whole world? Evil, nasty, *angry* dog? That kills the whole world?"

It is Muriel, the dog trainer—bony, tacky, undereducated—who brings Macon back to life; it is at her house on Singleton Street, a place he learns to find without direction, that he is brought to be a self he'd rather be: "in the foreign country that was Singleton Street," he knew himself as an "entirely different person," "never suspected of narrowness, never . . . accused of chilliness." Muriel, who has been nowhere, offers to travel with Macon so that she can show him "the good parts." And she manages to dispel at last the deep-seated distrust he feels for anything that strikes him as even faintly "foreign." Macon, through Muriel, comes to be reconciled to foreignness and so to otherness, to travel and so to the adventure of life. At the moment of decision, when he determines to make a life with Muriel, "he felt a kind of inner rush, a racing forward": "The real adventure, he thought, is the flow of time; it's as much adventure as anyone could wish."

As a critic, Anne Tyler is thorough, unpretentious, and as compassionate as her novels would suggest. Not only do her reviews inform readers of the *New Republic* (in the past she has reviewed regularly for the *National Observer*, *New York Times Book Review*, and the *Washington Post*); they also illuminate Tyler's values, her attitudes about literature and life. Her dedication to precision of construction lies behind objections to fragmentary structure, in the case, for instance, of Renata Adler's *Pitch Dark*. Her devotion to precision of language moves her to praise Elizabeth Hardwick's "crispness" of style; she goes on to note, however, that "mere aptitude of language . . . is not sufficient," that what makes *Bartleby in Manhattan* memorable is "the sense of the author's firm character." All the same she can accept the "distaste for his fellow human beings" revealed in Australian novelist Patrick White's autobiography because, she believes, it has "allowed him to view the world with that wary, obsessive, unblinking alertness that formed his memorable novels."

The criterion that stands out in Tyler's criticism, a primary value, is "truthfulness"; the closest she comes to contempt is provoked by what she sees as a "dishonest plot," and even a poorly structured work can be at least partially redeemed in her eyes by "reality." Aware as she is that truth-telling is essential to art, so is she aware that telling the truth exacts a price; she takes note of David Bradley's perception, recorded in *In Praise of What Persists*, that the cost of being a writer is the cost of telling the truth.

The truth that Tyler tells consists of a gentle but accurate rendering of common American life and of common American speech. She clearly conveys the lives and attitudes of the left-behind folk, at once unremarkable and eccentric, who people her fictional world. In this world, recipes are swapped and directions given in a flawlessly colloquial idiom lovingly rendered by an author who claims to have spent her adolescence "listening to the tobacco stringers." Tyler's people are, in any case, not consumers but characters—in a society that seems to run on credit cards and other plastic, they wear old clothes, drive old cars, pay cash for bus-station coffee, and buy Fritos out of machines. They either live in the same houses all their lives, struggling frantically to keep up with repairs—or abandoning the effort, they wind up in a trailer park. Tyler makes new the perennial American struggle with the conflicting claims of stability and freedom, the contrary urges to settle and to wander. Even in their restlessness, however, Tyler's characters seem passive and accepting. In a society marked by agitation, she penetrates the facade and gets back to the aimlessness and the drifting that actually rule the lives of most people. In a frantic age, Anne Tyler continues beautifully to evoke what Louis Rubin, writing of Eudora Welty, has termed the "bemusement of life."

SURVEY OF CRITICISM

Critical attention to Anne Tyler's work has been largely in the form of reviews, and her novels have passed muster with major reviewers, with such writer-critics as Gail Godwin, Joyce Carol Oates, and John Updike. Whereas Godwin (like Doris Grumbach writing in the *New Republic*) was struck by *Celestial Navigation*, a work Kathy Pollit in the *New York Times Book Review* described as "extraordinarily moving and beautiful," it was with *Searching for Caleb* that Tyler attracted real attention. Updike recommended *Caleb* to readers of the *New Yorker* (29 March 1976) as "a lovely novel, funny and lyric and true-seeming, exquisite in its details and ambitious in its design," and he dubbed Anne Tyler "*wickedly good.*" He expressed reservations, however, about *Morgan's Passing*; confronted with a heroine who is "fabricator of puppets" and a hero "whose life is a succession of poses, stuck in a thick beard and an array of funny hats and costumes," readers, Updike contended, can hardly avoid suspecting that they are being toyed with. "Still," he concluded, "what a magical puppeteer this writer remains." *Dinner at the Homesick Restaurant* allayed Updike's uneasy sense that something of Tyler's gift was "being withheld." He pronounced himself satisfied that no traces of the fey he had detected in *Morgan* tainted *Dinner at the Homesick Restaurant*. Noting elements of "literary foolery" and moments of what he felt constrained to call "precious diminishment" in *The Accidental Tourist*, Updike, in his *New Yorker* review of that novel, nonetheless reveals himself as sensitive as ever to Tyler's "generous empathy and distinguished intelligence." The lingering discomfort occasioned him by a worldview he perceives as perhaps suspiciously "benign" he is willing to ascribe to the contemporary loss of familiarity with "the comedic spirit." Thematically of a piece with its predecessors, *The Accidental Tourist*, in Updike's view, explores "more forthrightly" than any of them "the deep and delicate conflict between cosiness and venture, safety and danger, tidiness and messiness, home and the world. . . . "

Although Tyler's novels have been increasingly widely (and, for the most part, respectfully) reviewed, the academic world has been slow to pay her heed. (In Daniel Hoffman's *Harvard Guide to Contemporary American Writing* published in 1979, Tyler's short stories rate a single sentence, and her novels are not mentioned at all.) In a 1979 Louisiana State University doctoral dissertation, Stella Anne Nesanovich took note of the neglect and offered her own book-length study as something of a corrective. Nesanovich's treatment is thorough and sympathetic; she has collected and assimilated bibliographical and biographical material, elicited and recorded comments from the author about her work, and detailed careful readings and sympathetic critical perceptions. Nesanovich's analyses are focused on her identifications of the isolation of the individual within the family as Tyler's major theme. She correctly praises Tyler's "keen ear for . . . everyday speech," her humor, her lively prose and deft characterization. Although Nesanovich completed "The Individual in the Family" in 1979 and so did not consider the last three novels, she has nonetheless rendered important service in compiling a carefully researched record of Tyler's career up through *Searching for Caleb* and *Earthly Possessions*. The *Dictionary of Literary Biography*'s "Second Series" volume on *American Novelists Since World War II* includes a survey of Tyler's work through *Morgan's Passing*, written by Mary Ellen Brooks, and the *DLB* treatment is supplemented in the 1982 *Yearbook* with an assessment by Sarah English of *Dinner at the Homesick Restaurant* and the development it marks in Tyler's career.

In 1984 the University Press of Mississippi issued a volume on *Women Writers of the Contemporary South*, edited by Peggy Whitman Prenshaw, that includes

an interview with Tyler and a substantial critical essay on her work by Doris
Betts. "The Fiction of Anne Tyler," as befits a writer's piece on a writer,
examines Tyler's technical development, the evolution, as Betts sees it, of a
short-story writer into a novelist:

Anne Tyler's nine novels over seventeen years trace her own accommodation of the
methods of the short story, methods geared to change and revelation, until they become
adapted to her more novelistic conclusions about a Reality which changes very little, but
waits for its runaways to come home and learn at the dinner table how to tolerate even
their next-of-kin.

From the piercing of a moment in time in order to suggest the past, Betts observes,
Tyler gradually expands her scope in time and space, experiments with point of
view, and while still selecting temporal "entry points," "heads toward
magnitude."

Whereas Betts, in considering Tyler's thematic use of the "family as micro-
cosm," concentrates on her treatment of the tension between stay-at-home and
runaway, Mary F. Robertson examines Tyler's family theme as correlative to
her narrative techniques. In an essay entitled "Anne Tyler: Medusa Points and
Contact Points," published in *Contemporary American Women Writers: Narrative Strategies* (1985), Robertson seeks to rescue Tyler from underestimation.
Tyler's version of the family novel, Robertson argues, does not, in its stress on
the private life, threaten feminist conceptions of the properly public role of
women; rather, Tyler's narrative strategies "disrupt conventional expectations."
In her narrative emphasis on moments of missed connection at which neither
severance nor reconciliation quite materialize and in her transgressing of the
boundaries between insiders and outsiders, Tyler undercuts the traditional family
as touchstone of order. Thus the "assault on the notion of what is a proper
family" that Robertson infers from Tyler's fiction marks her as unexpectedly
close "in spirit" to stylistically radical postmodernists who more obviously
question the conventional distinctions that "we use to order our lives and
thought."

The vanguard critical work of Betts and Robertson, as well as the serious
attention accorded Tyler's work by John Updike, presages the end of academic
neglect of Anne Tyler's achievement. Scholars must inevitably recognize, as
critics and readers have already recognized, that she is not only one of the major
"writers of the contemporary South," but also an important American writer
whose highly crafted novels and short stories tell the truth about the little lives
people lead—and the large issues contained within those lives. In *The Accidental
Tourist*, Macon Leary, flying low over the landscape, has a crucial insight:

It came to him . . . that every little roof concealed actual lives. Well, of course he'd known
that, but all at once it took his breath away. He saw how real those lives were to the
people who lived them—how intense and private and absorbing.

BIBLIOGRAPHY

Works by Anne Tyler

If Morning Ever Comes. New York: Knopf, 1964.
The Tin Can Tree. New York: Knopf, 1965.
A Slipping-Down Life. New York: Knopf, 1970.
The Clock Winder. New York: Knopf, 1972.
Celestial Navigation. New York: Knopf, 1974.
Searching for Caleb. New York: Knopf, 1976.
Earthly Possessions. New York: Knopf, 1977.
Morgan's Passing. New York: Knopf, 1980.
"Still Just Writing." *The Writer on Her Work*. Ed. Janet Sternberg. New York: W. W. Norton, 1980.
Dinner at the Homesick Restaurant. New York: Knopf, 1982.
The Accidental Tourist. New York: Knopf, 1985.

Studies of Anne Tyler

Betts, Doris. "The Fiction of Anne Tyler." *Women Writers of the Contemporary South*. Ed. Peggy Whitman Prenshaw. Jackson: University Press of Mississippi, 1984.
Brooks, Mary Ellen. "Anne Tyler." *Dictionary of Literary Biography* 6 (1980): 336–344.
Brown, Laurie L. "Interviews with Seven Contemporary Writers." *Women Writers of the Contemporary South*. Ed. Peggy Whitman Prenshaw. Jackson: University Press of Mississippi, 1984.
English, Sarah. "Anne Tyler." *Dictionary of Literary Biography Yearbook 1982*: pp. 187–94.
Nesanovich, Stella Ann. "The Individual in the Family: A Critical Introduction to the Novels of Anne Tyler." Diss. Louisiana State University, 1979.
Olendorf, Donna. "Tyler, Anne." *Contemporary Authors*, Detroit: Gale Research, 1984. New Revision Series, 11: 510–13.
Robertson, Mary F. "Anne Tyler: Medusa Points and Contact Points." *Contemporary American Women Writers: Narrative Strategies*. Ed. Catherine Rainwater and William J. Scheick. Lexington: University Press of Kentucky, 1985.
Updike, John. "Family Ways." *New Yorker*, 29 March 1976, pp. 110–12.
———. "Imagining Things." *New Yorker*, 23 June 1980, pp. 94–101.
———. "Leaving Home." *New Yorker*, 28 October 1985, pp. 106–12.
———. "On Such a Beautiful Green Little Planet." *New Yorker*, 5 April 1982, pp. 189–97.

JAMES H. JUSTUS

Robert Penn Warren
(1905–   )

As a productive and influential writer, Robert Penn Warren for more than six decades has been a major figure in American letters. He began his career as a poet, one of the youngest members of the Fugitive group in the 1920s at Vanderbilt University, and he entered the 1980s with the often-repeated assertion that it is as poet that he wishes to be remembered; but in the intervening years Warren achieved distinction not only as a poet but also as a skillful practitioner of many modes—novel and short story, criticism, history, biography, journalism, pedagogy. As a man of letters, Warren ranks with the greatest twentieth-century American artists. Appropriately, in 1986 he was named U.S. Poet Laureate, the first to hold that honor.

BIOGRAPHY

Born, as he says, "at 7 a.m., April 24, 1905, in Guthrie, in southern Kentucky," Robert Penn Warren spent his youth in the small railroad town in Todd County near the Tennessee-Kentucky state line and, from 1911 to 1918, most of his summers at his maternal grandfather's place, a remote Trigg County farm. His early reading was encouraged by the examples of both his father, a businessman, merchant, and failed poet, and old Gabriel Penn, who had once ridden with Nathan Bedford Forrest in the Civil War and who delighted his grandson with re-creations of battles and recitations of Shakespeare, Burns, Byron, and Scott. With few childhood companions, Warren grew up exploring on his own the rolling farmlands and woodlands, becoming able, according to one informant, to "outswim, outrun, outwalk anyone in Guthrie." In 1921 Warren graduated from high school in Clarksville, Tennessee, twelve miles from Guthrie, and because an eye accident prevented his going to Annapolis where he had received an appointment to the U.S. Naval Academy, he entered Vanderbilt University.

Although he intended to study chemistry, he soon fell under the sway of Donald Davidson and John Crowe Ransom, English professors and poets, and his roommate Allen Tate, who persuaded Warren to join the Fugitives, a group of Vanderbilt poets and Nashville intellectuals who read and discussed each other's work. By the time Warren first published in the *Fugitive* in 1923, his apprenticeship had been under the aegis of the most rigorous communal criticism available anywhere in the 1920s.

He graduated summa cum laude in 1925 and earned his M.A. at the University of California (1925–27), where he studied Elizabethan drama and seventeenth-century poetry. He attended Yale University briefly (1927–28), and before going as a Rhodes scholar to New College, Oxford (B. Litt., 1930), he contracted to write a biography of John Brown, which as *John Brown: The Making of a Martyr* (1929) became his first book. In this unorthodox biography and in "Prime Leaf" (1931), a novella based on the Black Patch tobacco wars in the Cumberland Valley in the early years of the century, Warren dealt with many of the themes, images, and character types that would recur, sometimes obsessively, in his mature work: the ambiguity of truth, the conflict between father and son, the dialectical battles between the idealist and the pragmatist, the power of the past, the painful path to self-knowledge. While at Oxford, Warren also wrote "The Briar Patch" as his contribution to *I'll Take My Stand* (1930), the symposium initiated by Davidson and Ransom, former Fugitives turned Agrarian polemicists. Warren's essay was a dutiful assessment of the place of the Negro in the Southern economy, a subject about which he knew little.

Back in the United States, Warren married Emma Brescia in 1930 and spent the next decade teaching at Southern institutions: Southwestern University in Memphis (1930–31), Vanderbilt (1931–34), and Louisiana State University (1934–42), where with his old friend from Vanderbilt and Oxford, Cleanth Brooks, he helped to found the *Southern Review* (1935–42) and began collaborating on a series of pedagogical textbooks, the most influential of which, *Understanding Poety* (1938), revolutionized the teaching of literature in American classrooms. From this intensely productive period came Warren's first two volumes of poetry and his first published novel, *Night Rider* (1939), a reworking of "Prime Leaf." A Guggenheim Fellowship enabled him to go to Italy for the 1939–40 academic year where he began work on a verse play based on a Southern politician much like Huey Long of Louisiana; the figure of Willie Talos in "Proud Flesh" eventually became Willie Stark of *All the King's Men* (1946).

By the time Warren accepted a professorship of English at the University of Minnesota (1942–50), he was firmly associated with the New Criticism and the name of Warren as practical critic, editor, and pedagogue was considerably more widespread than that of Warren as poet and novelist. But in this decade, while solidifying his reputation as an innovator in pedagogical approaches to literature with *Understanding Fiction* (1943) and *Modern Rhetoric* (1949)—both coedited with Brooks—Warren published his second novel, *At Heaven's Gate* (1943), issued his first *Selected Poems* (1944), won a Pulitzer Prize for *All the King's*

Men (1946), and published his only volume of short stories, *The Circus in the Attic and Other Stories* (1947), and an elegant limited edition of his finest and most enduring piece of short fiction, *Blackberry Winter* (1946). During his year as consultant in poetry at the Library of Congress (1944–45), Katherine Anne Porter showed him an obscure bit of nineteenth-century Kentuckyana, *The Confession of Jereboam O. Beauchamp*, which eventually became the basis of his fourth and most ambitious novel, *World Enough and Time* (1950). Although Warren had become an important name in the literary world, he had not yet given up his earlier ambition to complete a satisfactory verse play, now titled *All the King's Men*, from among his several ongoing versions; the most successful was directed by Irwin Piscator in New York in 1948. His continued interest in play writing, though it proved to be his least comfortable mode, led him in 1950 to accept a position in the Yale Drama School. The move to New England marked a decisive phase in his life and career, just as had his earlier moves to Baton Rouge and Minneapolis. Although the experience in play writing produced nothing literarily more substantial than a reading version of *All the King's Men: A Play* (1960), his interest in the formal devices and distributed conflicts of drama can be seen in one of his greatest works, *Brother to Dragons* (1953; rev. 1979). This "Tale of Verse and Voices," which eludes generic classification, recounts the imagined effects on Thomas Jefferson of the brutal ax murder of a slave by his two nephews; when Warren finished with its ceremonial communal rite, unifying disparate needs and personalities, it had provided its author with a new sense of poetic release, out of which would come a freer lyric mood.

In 1952, after he and his first wife of twenty years were divorced, Warren married the writer Eleanor Clark. Although he published two more novels in this decade, *Band of Angels* (1955) and *The Cave* (1959), the 1950s is memorable in his career primarily because he returned with renewed vigor to the writing of poetry, occasioned in part, as he has suggested, by the happiness of his personal life. *Promises: Poems, 1954–1956* (1957) was to his lyric impulse what *Brother to Dragons* had been to his dramatic and dialectic impulse. The volume is a lyrical tribute to his past and his parents—a kind of poetic patrimony to his own children, Rosanna Phelps and Gabriel Penn, to whom it is dedicated. The primary texture of Warren's early verse is highly cerebral, in an idiom of clotted intensities, dignity, and metaphysical portentousness; the verse beginning with *Promises* moves away from the syntactical and stanzaic formalities and arcane diction that had made "Bearded Oaks" a favorite anthology piece of the 1940s into a looser, more variable, poetic line, with looping clauses and elliptical grammar, all in praise of the human animal and awe of the natural world in which he finds himself ambiguously placed. *Promises*, which earned Warren's second Pulitzer Prize as well as several other awards, was followed by *You, Emperors, and Others* (1960), which decisively confirmed poetry as his favorite and most congenial genre and which continued the more modulated and open form as his chosen poetic style. Especially after his second *Selected Poems* (1966), which received the Bollingen Prize, *Incarnations* (1968), and *Audubon:*

A Vision (1969), Warren was frequently spoken of as America's greatest living poet.

In addition to the steadily accruing volumes of poetry in his older years, Warren continued to be active as a general man of letters. His interest in the status of Southern blacks, growing from his personal evaluation of the effects of the 1954 Supreme Court decision against the South's two-track educational system in *Segregation: The Inner Conflict in the South* (1956), culminated in *Who Speaks for the Negro?* (1965), an analysis of the leading figures in the civil rights movement of the 1960s. In 1970 Warren received the National Medal for Literature. For an anthology of American literature, edited with R.W.B. Lewis and Cleanth Brooks, he undertook an intensive reading and rereading of classic and not-so-classic American texts, a project out of which came not only *American Literature: The Makers and the Making* (1973) but, on his part, a series of distinguished revaluations of Mark Twain, Nathaniel Hawthorne, Herman Melville, John Greenleaf Whittier, and Theodore Dreiser. These separately published essays and books were Warren's most sustained acts of literary criticism since 1958, when he had assembled *Selected Essays*, a miscellany of his previous reviews and essays that included his famous analysis of Coleridge's *The Rime of the Ancient Mariner*. In 1974, under the auspices of the National Foundation for the Humanities, he was chosen to deliver the Jefferson Lecture, published as *Democracy and Poetry* (1975).

Although in 1975 he retired from Yale, with which he had been associated for a quarter of a century, Warren continued as an active man of letters. When President Carter signed Joint Resolution 16 in 1978, returning citizenship to Jefferson Davis, the President of the Confederacy who died still disenfranchised in 1889, the ceremony that it provoked the following June in Todd County, Kentucky (Davis's birthplace), also became a catalyst for Warren. His meditation, *Jefferson Davis Gets His Citizenship Back* (1980), built upon a lifetime of interest in the Civil War, is a brilliant evocation of that event, which Warren has called our only "felt" history, interweaving biography, philosophy, historical fact, family legend, autobiography, and cultural artifact. Warmer in tone and more subtly structured than *The Legacy of the Civil War* (1961), *Jefferson Davis* is one of Warren's finest works.

MAJOR THEMES

Most of the aesthetic strengths in Warren's work derive from a constitutional unease in the comforts of single-minded ideologies. Many of his tragic characters are philosophical idealists who, when faced with the messy ruck of actuality, cannot endure the ambiguity of truth and the pragmatic approach to conduct. Nor do the scientific positivists in his work fare better: they frequently provide wit and cynical humor in their rhetorical battles with the idealists, but they tend to end their lives with suicide, whereas their opponents move on cautiously and painfully toward a moral integration. Expressions of naturalism thread their way compulsively through the earliest work, culminating in "The Ballad of Billie Potts" and *At Heaven's Gate*, Warren's own versions of Eliotic despair and Poundian disgust over a broken world. Warren's early vision is a compound of naturalistic reductiveness and orthodox Christian—actually, Calvinistic—suspicion of human beneficence. Warren's most perdurable subject is the soul in conflict with itself, a dialectical movement that constitutes the drama of most of the fictive protagonists and the personal quests undertaken in much of the poetry beginning with *Brother to Dragons*. The course of salvation in Warren's works is never very straight; the price of integration of self for the spiritual drifter Jack Burden (*All the King's Men*) and for the romantic monomaniac Jeremiah Beaumont (*World Enough and Time*) is a trail of active evil even as they search for ways out of the dark wood. Ultimately, Warren's naturalism merges with a Christian view of man as fallen but redeemable. "What poetry most significantly celebrates," Warren once said, "is the capacity of man to face the deep, dark inwardness of his nature and fate." This declaration is reflected in the anguish of such fictional characters as Ashby Wyndham (*At Heaven's Gate*) and Jed Tewksbury (*A Place to Come To*) and in the personae of "Original Sin," *Brother to Dragons*, *Audubon*, and dozens of scattered lyrics and poetic suites. It is the governing premise behind Warren's efforts in his revaluations of American history (*The Legacy of the Civil War*, *Jefferson Davis Gets His Citizenship Back*), in his analyses of contemporary American society (*Who Speaks for the Negro?*, *Democracy and Poetry*), and in his brilliant critical assessments of earlier American writers (*Homage to Theodore Dreiser*, *John Greenleaf Whittier's Poetry*).

Although Warren has always exercised his considerable knack for vivid portrayal of the world, perhaps most memorably in the political scenes of *All the King's Men* and *World Enough and Time* or in the quotidian details of the lives of poor whites, farmers, and blacks depicted in both his poetry and fiction, his real interest has always been the symbolic heightening of people, places, and things—of society generally—for essentially moral fables. One of the most compulsive of those is the son's rebellion against the father and the struggle to come to terms with him, a basic pattern enacted on many levels. The youthful difficulties with the biological parent are often linked to a rejection of the claims of the past in order to live in and by the present moment, but such a protagonist comes to learn that a rage to construct himself anew means alienation from others, not merely the father, and dissociation of the self. The bewildering pain of a floating identity unanchored to others drives him to another rage: to assert the primacy of a communal identity without which man is amorphous. The climax in the drama of the self comes with a recognition of the common frailty of man caught in webs of deceit, delusion, ignorance, and a murderous innocence demanding that an abstract ideal be translated into action at whatever cost. Hence, acknowledgement of universal imperfection leads the wandering son back to the father, at once the most actual and the most symbolic summation of community. The typical resolution is for the protagonist to see things as they are, to recognize that the world moves at its own pace and with its own purpose, that chaos and confusion are the human lot, and that father and son are alike bound to the commonality suggested by the phrase "the frail integument of flesh." This symbolic drama undergirds the varying narrative specificities of the fiction from *Night Rider* to *A Place to Come To*, and it lurks prominently in some of the major poems in the early volume *Thirty-Six Poems*, the pivotal *Brother to Dragons*, and through the more autobiographical volumes of the late 1970s.

In the early fiction Warren's intertwined themes of alienation, the rejection of and reconciliation with the father, self-knowledge, regeneration, and the presumptive good of community all find their most effective expression through the means of a single device: the interpolated story. This technique for widening and deepening theme through the use of alternative points of view also becomes a visible, dramatized need for verbalization of error, confession, and, to use the language of Protestant fundamentalists, witnessing. From *Night Rider* to *Band of Angels* Warren creates a vernacular storyteller functioning like Coleridge's Mariner as the spiritually aware man attempting to galvanize quiescent protagonists to moral attention. After 1955 Warren drops such a narrative device, perhaps because the overall shape of his later novels, which is more emblematic than realistic, makes such a device superfluous. *The Cave* has no real protagonist and no authoritative point of view, and a spatial area becomes both the unifying structural element and the orienting thematic focus; *Wilderness* uses the geographical setting of the Civil War Battle of the Wilderness as both literal place and metaphysical spiritual state; both *Flood* and *Meet Me in the Green Glen* are stories of the buried life rendered through a talismanic place soon to be flooded by waters created by new dams; *A Place to Come To* is both a literal town in Alabama and the final spiritual place for a tattered sensibility. This later fiction subordinates the solidly rendered circumstantiality of the actual world to bold, if not always successful, manipulations of caricature and stereotype, of artifice and rhetoric, of episodes that are more ceremonial and ritualistic than realistic, and of the author's own voice as authority.

The later personal voice, anticipated first in *Brother to Dragons*, in which "RPW" is both narrating voice and aggressive debater, bluntly affirms what the narratives enact: the necessity of all men to find a communal context, to acknowledge the linking of the innocent and the monstrous in order to heal the divided self. If one mode common to the Warren protagonist is the anguished search for the defining marks of his own uniqueness, another is the equally anguished drive to submerge that uniqueness, to temper individuality with community. Jack Burden is only the best known of these figures who proceed from a mechanistic view of people and things in their atomistic dispersion to a comprehensive vision of infinite and mutual responsibility. The emotional release that in the fiction comes from the acceptance of weakness as part of one's fate has its less mediated equivalents in the resolution of dozens of poems from *Promises* through *Audubon*, which, with different tonal effects, celebrate "joy," "heart-joy," "blessedness," "surprise," and "delight." In his later volumes—

Now and Then (1978), *Being There* (1980), and *Rumor Verified* (1981)—Warren
draws back from the customary habit of most aging poets to pontificate, to assert,
to give "affirmative" visions that will justify the long labor of a high and
passionate calling. While he still traces the contours of the difficult progress of
the self to a position of joy or celebration, this aging poet never succumbs to
the simplistic rounding-off that would make the earlier efforts less ambiguous,
even in those poems that are blatantly nostalgic. For Warren, imaginative return
is itself a kinetic act proceeding from a belief—or at least a hope—that to re-
see, re-play, re-construct, will be to understand. The best of these poems—"The
Red-Tail Hawk and Pyre of Youth," "Convergences," "Recollection in Upper
Ontario, From Long Before"—have as their actual subject the imagination's
anarchic energy; here the poet names its sources and its manifestations in icon-
ographic images that haunt and threaten the complacent daylight sensibility.
Because of his general disinclination to find satisfaction in the settled definitions
of Time, Self, Truth, Reality, the Word, joys are hard-earned. In his most recent,
like his earliest volumes, Warren's poetry of the *then* as well as the *now* constitutes an Inquiry Into rather than a Disquisition Upon.

SURVEY OF CRITICISM

Despite his earliest work in poetry, Warren's Fugitive verse and his first two
published volumes attracted scant readership and only modest critical praise.
From the first it was Warren the novelist who attracted critical attention—primarily because *Night Rider*, *At Heaven's Gate*, and *All the King's Men* seemed
to be at once vehicles for high-flown philosophical meditation and the raunchy
exploitation of sex and violence. Many of the reviewers traced Warren's characteristic style and subject matter to Faulkner's versions of "southern gothic,"
but the more perceptive critics saw that both the fiction and the poetry reflected
the despair and human fragmentation behind much Modernist writing; in 1944
his friend and mentor John Crowe Ransom believed that unrelieved naturalism
marred even Warren's best work. The first acute assessment of Warren as artist
came with Robert B. Heilman's often-reprinted review essay of *All the King's
Men* ("Melpomene as Wallflower," *Sewanee Review* 55 [Summer 1947], 154–
66) and Eric Bentley's examination of the first three novels ("The Meaning of
Robert Penn Warren's Novels," *Kenyon Review* 10 [Summer 1948], 407–24).
Despite the remarkably productive years from the mid–1940s to the mid–1950s,
in which Warren enjoyed great popular success and continued critical controversy, it was not until 1960 that this diversely talented writer received concentrated critical attention with a special number of *Modern Fiction Studies* and the
first book-length study to discuss and evaluate his work in its totality, Leonard
Casper's *Robert Penn Warren: The Dark and Bloody Ground*. Casper's book,
although it covered chronologically Warren's writing in all genres, was especially
valuable for its sensitive focus on Warren as poet. In 1963 a special number of
South Atlantic Quarterly featured fine separate essays on Warren in his varied

roles (William C. Havard on his historical writing, John Hicks on his criticism, Madison Jones on his fiction, and M. L. Rosenthal on his poetry). This growing recognition of Warren as master of many genres was reinforced by Charles H. Bohner's Twayne volume, *Robert Penn Warren* (1964; rev. 1981), which stressed the massive coherence of the work, and Paul West's graceful introduction in the University of Minnesota Pamphlets series, *Robert Penn Warren* (1964).

Perhaps the most useful of the early collections of miscellaneous pieces was John L. Longley, Jr.'s *Robert Penn Warren: A Collection of Critical Essays* (1965), arranged by theme and genre. The value of this volume, however, is now diminished because of two more recent anthologies of secondary materials: Neil Nakadate's *Robert Penn Warren: Critical Perspectives* (1981) and William Bedford Clark's *Critical Essays on Robert Penn Warren* (1981). A readable but often factually inaccurate account by John L. Stewart, *The Burden of Time: The Fugitives and Agrarians* (1965), devoted two long chapters to Warren in the contexts of his earlier intellectual and aesthetic associations. But the most important early study of Warren is Victor H. Strandberg's *A Colder Fire: The Poetry of Robert Penn Warren* (1965), a close study of the controlling imagery, the major themes, the influence of the Modernists (primarily Eliot), and the mythic continuities in the poetry through *You, Emperors, and Others*. Strandberg's second, totally different, book on Warren as poet, *The Poetic Vision of Robert Penn Warren* (1977), stresses the Jungian overtones of the theme of the undiscovered self and concentrates on "The Ballad of Billie Potts" as a crucial poem.

While the admiration for Warren's poetry grew steadily, culminating in the enthusiastic reception of *Audubon: A Vision*, and respect for his penetrating social and historical analyses soared, in the 1960s the reception of Warren's fiction became cooler and more hostile with the publication of each successive novel. The common complaints continued to be, paradoxically, his unhealthy fascination for sexual melodrama and overly portentous rhetoric as a substitute for dramatized narrative action. Many critics attributed the failure of *The Cave*, *Wilderness*, and *Flood* to the New Critic in Warren, with his talent for analysis and his penchant for finding meaning in unlikely or minimal details of form and structure. Those who defended the fiction tended to stress not the aesthetic effects but the author's philosophical coherence. In his *Robert Penn Warren and History: "The Big Myth We Live"* (1970), L. Hugh Moore, Jr., summarized the relationships between the author's view of history and his conception of man; and in *Web of Being: The Novels of Robert Penn Warren* (1975), Barnett Guttenberg investigated the compulsive presence of the fragmented self in Warren's work in terms of Heidegger's brand of existentialism. James H. Justus's *The Achievement of Robert Penn Warren* (1981) is an attempt to place the entire career in perspective, although it is clear that for a writer whose vigorous production continues into his eightieth year, no satisfactory overall assessment will be possible for several years. Warren has declared he will write no autobiography, but his papers and other materials, most of them housed in the Beineke Library of Yale University, with other relevant materials at the University of Kentucky, will provide the solid basis for a biography. A fine collection of interviews has been assembled by Floyd C. Watkins and John T. Hiers—*Robert Penn Warren Talking: Interviews 1950–1978* (1980). The full range of critical evaluation of Warren can be seen in Neil Nakadate's *Robert Penn Warren: A Reference Guide* (1977), a complete annotated listing of scholarship from 1925 to 1975; James A. Grimshaw, Jr.'s *Robert Penn Warren: A Descriptive Bibliography, 1922–79* (1981), replaces all earlier piecemeal bibliographies and checklists.

BIBLIOGRAPHY

Works by Robert Penn Warren

John Brown: The Making of a Martyr. New York: Payson & Clark, 1929.

Thirty-Six Poems. New York: Alcestis Press, 1935.

An Approach to Literature: A Collection of Prose and Verse with Analyses and Discussions, with Cleanth Brooks and John T. Purser. Baton Rouge: Louisiana State University Department of English, 1936; New York: F. S. Crofts, 1939; New York: Appleton-Century-Crofts, 1952, 1964; Englewood Cliffs, N.J.: Prentice-Hall, 1975.

Understanding Poetry: An Anthology for College Students, with Cleanth Brooks. New York: Henry Holt, 1938, 1950; New York: Holt, Rinehart and Winston, 1960, 1976.

Night Rider. Boston: Houghton Mifflin, 1939.

Eleven Poems on the Same Theme. Norfolk, Conn.: New Directions, 1942.

At Heaven's Gate. New York: Harcourt, Brace, 1943.

Understanding Fiction, with Cleanth Brooks. New York: F. S. Crofts, 1943; New York: Appleton-Century-Crofts, 1959; Englewood Cliffs, N.J.: Prentice-Hall, 1979.

Selected Poems, 1923–1943. New York: Harcourt, Brace, 1944.

All the King's Men. New York: Harcourt, Brace, 1946.

Blackberry Winter. Cummington, Mass.: Cummington Press, 1946.

The Circus in the Attic and Other Stories. New York: Harcourt, Brace, 1947.

Modern Rhetoric, with Cleanth Brooks. New York: Harcourt, Brace, 1949; repr. as *Fundamentals of Good Writing: A Handbook of Modern Rhetoric*, with Cleanth Brooks. New York: Harcourt Brace, 1950.

World Enough and Time: A Romantic Novel. New York: Random House, 1950.

Brother to Dragons: A Tale in Verse and Voices. New York: Random House, 1953.

Band of Angels. New York: Random House, 1955.

Segregation: The Inner Conflict in the South. New York: Random House, 1956.

Promises: Poems, 1954–1956. New York: Random House, 1957.

Remember the Alamo! New York: Random House, 1958.

Selected Essays. New York: Random House, 1958.

The Cave. New York: Random House, 1959.

The Gods of Mount Olympus. New York: Random House, 1959.

How Texas Won Her Freedom: The Story of Sam Houston & the Battle of San Jacinto. San Jacinto Monument, Tex.: Museum of History, 1959.

All the King's Men: A Play. New York: Random House, 1960.

The Scope of Fiction, with Cleanth Brooks. New York: Appleton-Century-Crofts, 1960.
You, Emperors, and Others: Poems 1957–1960. New York: Random House, 1960.
The Legacy of the Civil War: Meditations on the Centennial. New York: Random House, 1961.
Wilderness: A Tale of the Civil War. New York: Random House, 1961.
Flood: A Romance of Our Time. New York: Random House, 1964.
Who Speaks for the Negro? New York: Random House, 1965.
Selected Poems: New and Old, 1923–1966. New York: Random House, 1966.
Incarnations: Poems 1966–1968. New York: Random House, 1968.
Audubon: A Vision. New York: Random House, 1969.
Selected Poems of Herman Melville: A Reader's Edition. New York: Random House, 1970.
Homage to Theodore Dreiser, August 27, 1871–December 28, 1945, on the Centennial of His Birth. New York: Random House, 1971.
John Greenleaf Whittier's Poetry: An Appraisal and a Selection. Minneapolis: University of Minnesota Press, 1971.
Meet Me in the Green Glen. New York: Random House, 1971.
American Literature: The Makers and the Making, with R.W.B. Lewis and Cleanth Brooks. New York: St. Martin's Press, 1973.
Or Else—Poem/Poems, 1968–1974. New York: Random House, 1974.
Democracy and Poetry. Cambridge: Harvard University Press, 1975.
Selected Poems: 1923–1975. New York: Random House, 1976.
A Place to Come To. New York: Random House, 1977.
Now and Then: Poems 1976–1978. New York: Random House, 1978.
Being Here: Poetry 1977–1980. New York: Random House, 1980.
Robert Penn Warren Talking: Interviews 1950–1978, ed. Floyd C. Watkins and John T. Hiers. New York: Random House, 1980.
Rumor Verified: Poems 1979–1980. New York: Random House, 1981.
Chief Joseph of the Nez Perce: A Poem. New York: Random House, 1983.

Studies of Robert Penn Warren

Bedient, Calvin. *In the Heart's Last Kingdom: Robert Penn Warren's Major Poetry*. Cambridge: Harvard University Press, 1984.
Bohner, Charles H. *Robert Penn Warren*. New York: Twayne, 1964; rev. ed., 1981.
Bradbury, John M. *Renaissance in the South: A Critical History of the Literature, 1920–1960*. Chapel Hill: University of North Carolina Press, 1963.
Brooks, Cleanth. *The Hidden God: Studies in Hemingway, Faulkner, Yeats, Eliot, and Warren*. New Haven: Yale University Press, 1963, pp. 98–127.
Casper, Leonard. *Robert Penn Warren: The Dark and Bloody Ground*. Seattle: University of Washington Press, 1960.
Chambers, Robert H., ed. *Twentieth Century Interpretations of "All the King's Men": A Collection of Critical Essays*. Englewood Cliffs, N.J.: Prentice-Hall, 1977.
Clark, William Bedford, ed. *Critical Essays on Robert Penn Warren*. Boston: G. K. Hall, 1981.
Cowan, Louise. *The Fugitive Group: A Literary History*. Baton Rouge: Louisiana State University Press, 1959.
Edgar, Walter B., ed. *A Southern Renascence Man: Views of Robert Penn Warren by*

Thomas L. Connelly, Louis D. Rubin, Jr., Madison Jones, Harold Bloom, and James Dickey. Baton Rouge: Louisiana State University Press, 1984.

Gray, Richard, ed. *Robert Penn Warren: A Collection of Critical Essays.* Englewood Cliffs, N.J.: Prentice-Hall, 1980.

Grimshaw, James A., Jr. *Robert Penn Warren: A Descriptive Bibliography, 1922–79.* Charlottesville: University Press of Virginia, 1981.

Guttenberg, Barnett. *Web of Being: The Novels of Robert Penn Warren.* Nashville: Vanderbilt University Press, 1974.

Huff, Mary Nance. *Robert Penn Warren: A Bibliography.* New York: David Lewis, 1968.

Justus, James H. *The Achievement of Robert Penn Warren.* Baton Rouge: Louisiana State University Press, 1981.

Light, James F., ed. *The Merrill Studies in "All the King's Men."* Columbus, Ohio: Charles E. Merrill, 1971.

Longley, John L., Jr. *Robert Penn Warren.* Austin, Tex.: Steck-Vaughn, 1969.

————, ed. *Robert Penn Warren: A Collection of Critical Essays.* New York: New York University Press, 1965.

Moore, L. Hugh, Jr. *Robert Penn Warren and History: "The Big Myth We Live."* The Hague: Mouton, 1970.

Nakadate, Neil. *Robert Penn Warren: A Reference Guide.* Boston: G. K. Hall, 1977.

————, ed. *Robert Penn Warren: Critical Perspectives.* Lexington: University Press of Kentucky, 1981.

Rubin, Louis D., Jr. *The Wary Fugitives: Four Poets and the South.* Baton Rouge: Louisiana State University Press, 1978.

Stewart, John L. *The Burden of Time: The Fugitives and Agrarians.* Princeton, N.J.: Princeton University Press, 1965.

Strandberg, Victor H. *A Colder Fire: The Poetry of Robert Penn Warren.* Lexington: University Press of Kentucky, 1965.

————. *The Poetic Vision of Robert Penn Warren.* Lexington: University Press of Kentucky, 1977.

Walker, Marshall. *Robert Penn Warren: A Vision Earned.* New York: Barnes & Noble, 1979.

Watkins, Floyd C. *Then and Now: The Personal Past in the Poetry of Robert Penn Warren.* Lexington: University Press of Kentucky, 1982.

West, Paul. *Robert Penn Warren.* Minneapolis: University of Minnesota Press, 1964.

——————— JAMES A. BRYANT, JR. ———————

Eudora Welty
(1909–   )

No one today hesitates to call Eudora Welty Mississippi's greatest living writer, and many would call her the greatest living Southern writer. The magnitude of her achievement stands second only to Faulkner's, but the quality of her work is uniquely her own.

BIOGRAPHY

Eudora Welty was born on 13 April 1909. She is a first-generation Mississippian. Her father, Christian Webb Welty, was a schoolteacher who came south from Ohio by way of West Virginia, where he met and married another teacher, Chestina Andrews. The two made their home in Jackson, Mississippi, where Christian was associated with the Lamar Life Insurance Company. In time he became its president and remained in that office until his death in 1931. The Weltys' first child, a son, died in infancy; but they brought up three others in Jackson—Eudora, Edward, and Walter. All three attended Jefferson Davis Grammar School, presided over by an austere Miss Lorena Duling, whom Welty has brought to life more than once, she confesses, "in my perhaps inordinate number of schoolteacher characters." After that there was Central High for all three, and for Edward a career in architecture; for Walter, association with another insurance firm in Jackson. Both brothers have now died, as has Chestina Welty; Eudora Welty lives alone on Pinehurst Street in a brick and stucco house that her father built for them in 1925, just across from the Belhaven College campus.

Her childhood in Jackson was a happy blend of the normal and the extraordinary. In addition to the usual school experiences, she had, like other children in small Southern cities, the annual holidays, weekly Sunday school with Bible stories and hymns, Sunday afternoon rides, circuses in season, political speakings, itinerant evangelists (especially Gypsy Smith), and the silent movies—

Mary Pickford, Saturday westerns, Buster Keaton, Charlie Chaplin, Ben Blue, and the Keystone Kops. Books, however, were also essential in the Welty household, whether taken two at a time from the local Carnegie library or provided by the parents in an expanding collection at home. The latter included the works of such authors as Dickens, Scott, Mark Twain, and Ring Lardner as well as Stoddard's Lectures, the Victrola Book of the Opera, the Columbia Encyclopedia, Compton's Pictured Encyclopedia, the Lincoln Library of Information, and later the Book of Knowledge and the Britannica. Welty recalls that on her sixth or seventh birthday her parents gave her a ten-volume set of *Our Wonder World*, volume 5 of which was *Every Child's Story Book*. She wore out this volume with reading, and it left its mark on much of her writing.

Welty's undergraduate experience consisted of two years at Mississippi State College for Women and two at the University of Wisconsin, where she majored in English, began her formal study of literature, and decided to become a writer. When she graduated in 1929, Christian Welty advised her to learn in addition a profession that might be more marketable, so she studied advertising at the Columbia Business School for a year. The death of her father in 1931 brought her back to Jackson, where she remained for the next decade, serving as society correspondent for the Memphis *Commercial Appeal*, doing odd jobs at radio station WJDX, and from 1933 to 1936 working as Junior Publicity Agent for the Works Projects Administration. The last job required her to travel widely over the state, writing news stories, conducting interviews, and sometimes setting up information booths at county fairs. Along the way she indulged her interest in photography; a number of the pictures she took then were displayed subsequently in a "one-man show" given in 1936 by the Lugene Gallery, a small photography shop in New York. Thereafter she worked for a time writing copy and making photographs for the Mississippi Advertising Commission. In 1971 her photographs were published as *One Time, One Place: Mississippi in the Depression: A Snapshot Album*.

The year 1936 also marked the beginning of Welty's public career as a writer. Throughout her adventures in business she had continued to write, and she would spend two weeks a year in New York going from publisher to publisher, trying to place a collection of stories. Finally, a friend in Jackson suggested that she try John Rood at *Manuscript*. She did, and to her surprise and pleasure Rood accepted a story, "Death of a Travelling Salesman." Within the year she was sending stories to Cleanth Brooks and Robert Penn Warren at the *Southern Review*; in 1937 they published "A Memory" and "A Piece of News." In the same year *Prairie Schooner* published two more stories. Katherine Anne Porter was at Baton Rouge at the time; and it was she, Welty believes, who called her to the attention of Ford Madox Ford. In any event, Ford took an interest in the new writer and tried vigorously but unsuccessfully during his last years to find an English publisher for Welty's stories. Meanwhile, John Woodburn, an editor with Doubleday, Doran and Company, put her in touch with Diarmuid Russell, son of the Irish poet A. E., and in 1940 Russell officially became her agent.

Within a year he had placed stories in the *Atlantic Monthly*, *Harper's Bazaar*, and *Harper's*. After that, book publishers began to express interest, and in 1941 Doubleday published a collection of her stories entitled *A Curtain of Green*, with an introduction by Katherine Anne Porter.

The 1940s were lucky years for Eudora Welty—to use a term that she herself frequently applies to her successes. Two of her stories received a first prize and one a second prize in the annual O. Henry Memorial contests. Two novels appeared: *The Robber Bridegroom* in 1942 and *Delta Wedding*, which was first serialized in the *Atlantic Monthly*, in 1946. A second collection of stories, *The Wide Net*, came out in 1943, and in 1949 a third, *The Golden Apples*, which some readers persist in calling a novel but which by any name contains some of her best work. The decade also brought a Guggenheim Fellowship for 1942–43 and a renewal in 1949–50, which enabled her to travel to Italy, France, and England. At the invitation of Robert Van Gelder she joined in 1942 the staff of the *New York Times Book Review*, and, under the pseudonym Michael Ravenna, turned out amazingly expert reviews of World War II battlefield reports. In 1944 she received an award from the American Academy of Arts and Letters. Before the war ended, however, she put Michael Ravenna aside and returned to Jackson, where, except for excursions to Europe, visits to New York, and trips to lecture engagements, she has remained ever since.

The 1950s brought a widening of experiences for Welty and a widening of her recognition by others. Her third novel, *The Ponder Heart*, was published first in the *New Yorker* in 1953 and in book form the following year, when Random House also reprinted in its Modern Library Series her first two story collections as *Selected Stories*. During that decade she made two more trips to Europe, and on the second of these spent six weeks at Cambridge, where she had been invited to lecture. Some of her experiences abroad are reflected in the fourth collection of stories, *The Bride of the Innisfallen*, published in 1955. In addition to new pieces about Mississippi, it contains stories set in Italy, Ireland, and, imaginatively, on Circe's Isle of Aeaea. For about ten years after 1955, however, no major work appeared. Smith College published three critical essays on fiction in 1962, the year in which she held a William Allan Neilson professorship there; and *The Shoe Bird*, a book for children, came out in 1964. She traveled during these years, lecturing and receiving honors, among them the William Dean Howells Medal of the Academy of Arts and Letters, the Lucy Donnelly Fellowship Award from Bryn Mawr, an appointment as honorary consultant at the Library of Congress, and the Ingram Memorial Foundation Award in Literature. But these were also the years of Chestina Welty's terminal illness (she died in 1966), and for much of the time her daughter stood by, ministering, never away for long from Jackson, still writing but bringing less to completion. This devotion was a measure of the love and respect she felt for a woman whose presence and unselfish giving had enriched vastly the lives of her husband and children; and it eventually bore fruit in the novels of the 1970s, *Losing Battles* (1970) and *The Optimist's Daughter* (1972), most especially in the latter, which is rich in details reflective of Welty's own life and that of her mother. For *The Optimist's Daughter* she received a Pulitzer Prize.

Since 1972 Welty's publications have included *The Eye of the Story: Selected Essays & Reviews*, a gathering of most of her nonfiction pieces, including some written as early as 1942, the collection of her photographs, *One Time, One Place*, already mentioned, and an engaging book of reminiscence, *One Writer's Beginnings* (1984), part of which she gave to inaugurate the William E. Massey lectures series at Harvard. Harcourt Brace Jovanovich brought out *The Collected Stories of Eudora Welty* in 1980.

In addition to the honors already mentioned, Welty has received a total of four O. Henry first prizes for stories, the Hollins Medal, the Creative Arts Medal for Fiction from Brandeis University, the Gold Medal for the Novel from the National Institute of Arts and Letters, the National Medal for Literature, and the Presidential Medal of Freedom. A member of the American Academy of Arts and Letters, she has received honorary degrees from the University of the South at Sewanee, the University of North Carolina at Chapel Hill, Washington University at St. Louis, Smith College, the University of Wisconsin, Western College for Women, Millsaps College, Yale University, and Harvard University.

MAJOR THEMES

Any general discussion of Eudora Welty's work should begin with a reference to Mississippi, which constitutes the locus for all but a fraction of it. Welty's Mississippi includes most of the state, the rich delta, the hill country, all in between, and in addition New Orleans, which Mississippians sometimes claim. From time to time critics have argued that such a clear geographical identification ought to make her a regionalist, yet she properly rejects that term as "condescending." Every writer needs to stand somewhere, she declares in her essay "Place in Fiction," but the point of view thus established is "an instrument, not an end in itself, that is, useful as a glass, and not as a mirror to reflect a dear and pensive face." In short, place performs the same function for Eudora Welty that it does for some of the writers she has praised—Jane Austen, Willa Cather, Anton Chekhov, and Katherine Anne Porter. By exploring place in her fiction, she brings reality within her grasp, and ours.

"Human life is fiction's only theme," she writes near the end of her essay, and four variations on that theme are conspicuous in her work. Foremost among these is the relatedness of all human life, regardless of differences in place and time. Welty's implicit affirmation of such relatedness in her first novel, *The Robber Bridegroom*, justifies for some critics the mixture there of German fairy tale, Hellenic myth, and American frontier legend—a mixture many have found disturbing. In *The Golden Apples*, Welty's collection of seven related stories, the universal aspects of her theme are kept in better proportion. Most of its principal characters are committed, knowingly or unknowingly, to some quest analogous to the quest of Yeats's Aengus for "the silver apples of the moon, /

The golden apples of the sun.'' What they have glimpsed, however, is not some distant Hesperides, but the continuum underlying all apppearance whereby in varying ways all human beings reenact some part of the eternal human drama. One important recurring figure is King MacLain, an itinerant tea and spice salesman who has fathered legitimately a set of twins in the little town of Morgana, but like the Greek Zeus, continues to father others (at least spiritually) who inherit his restless quest for meaning. Loch Morrison, a Perseus figure, is among these. Capable of seeing through appearances, he does so magnificently one June afternoon when his rational inhibitors have been dulled by an attack of malaria and he sees a near-miraculous transformation of events in the vacant MacLain house next door. Another heir is Virgie Rainey, small-town musician and siren, who flees Morgana but dutifully returns to care for her dying mother. After the funeral she drives to a distant cemetery where the MacLains are buried, and there, hearing the sound of an October rain, she experiences an epiphany that links her to all of Morgana and the universe beyond it. A similar epiphany occurs in *Losing Battles* when Jack Renfro, after returning from prison to resume life with his bride Gloria, hesitates like Paris in Greek legend, uncertain whether to hold her as a gift from Juno (his mother), from Athena (their recently deceased schoolteacher and mentor), or from Aphrodite. He realizes he can take her only from the latter when he, with us, sees the revelation of goddess in his ninety-year-old great-grandmother dancing in the moonlight on an uncleared picnic table. Other revelations of cosmic relatedness occur in the short stories: in Mrs. Larkin's frightening but strangely satisfying penetration of the curtain of green, in William Wallace's unplanned escape from time and care in ''The Wide Net,'' in young Dewey's initiation into the mysteries in ''Ladies in Spring,'' and in the transformation effected in the American girl of ''The Bride of the Innisfallen'' by the appearance of a bride in white at the rail of the channel boat that has just brought her across the choppy Irish Sea. Such intimations of a redeeming coherence in the chaos of appearances that surround us permeate Welty's work; and though sometimes startling, they seldom require more credence than a skeptical reader is likely to give.

A more obvious example of relatedness in Welty's work is the institution of family, her second major theme. Central to *Delta Wedding* and *Losing Battles*, it is conspicuous but secondary in *The Golden Apples*; it hovers at the periphery of both *The Ponder Heart* and *The Optimist's Daughter*. Family relationships as she depicts them are like those that characterize any living organism—continually in metamorphosis as members change status, reproduce, grow old, and die. But also they sometimes see, with varying responses, the introduction of alien members who are capable of producing radical change. Throughout Welty's work, however, change is the prerequisite for survival. For examaple, the persistence of the Fairchild family in *Delta Wedding* and of Granny Vaughn's clan in *Losing Battles* is the consequence of both groups' ability to accede gracefully to the unrelenting pressure to grow and change. In the first of these, the group survives because the wisdom of its senior members makes it possible for young

Dabney Fairchild to surmount a general family reluctance to take in an outsider from the Mississippi hill country. In the later novel, the young people themselves discover the love—their wisdom—that enables them to save their marriage in spite of the more worldly wisdom, clannishness, and hidden family guilts and fears that seem destined to separate them. By saving their marriage, the young people ultimately insure their families' continued life. The moribund Ponder family, reduced to one spinster and an elderly impotent man who is mentally retarded, maintains a kind of twilight life because of the persisting love of its two frail survivors. By contrast, the families in *The Golden Apples*, the MacLains, the Raineys, and the Morrisons, are all unaware of their decay and die before our eyes, leaving only memory and fossil: and the dissolved family of Judge McKelva in *The Optimist's Daughter* leaves only memory, as the Judge's widowed daughter survives, a lonely, reluctant wanderer.

Wanderers are everywhere in Welty's work, and her treatment of them constitues a third theme, that of alienation, or isolation, as Warren has termed it. We see alienation in an angry spinster who retires to her P.O. to escape from an intolerable family; in mad Clytie, who pursues the reflection in a rain barrel to her death; in Zeus-like King MacLain, Miss Eckhart, Loch Morrison, and Virgie Rainey in *The Golden Apples*; in the lonely young women in "The Bride of the Innisfallen" and "No Place for You, My Love"; in Miss Julia Mortimer of *Losing Battles*, whom we never see but who remains a pillar of unrelenting individualism even in death; and, as has been noted, in Laura McKelva of *The Optimist's Daughter*. These isolated characters and others like them may seem to stand in sharp contrast to such characters as Ellen Fairchild and Edna Earle Ponder, but they differ only as the poles of a polar magnet; they are complementary aspects of the principle of process in human relations, whether familial or societal. Both relatedness and isolation have their functions and their special insights. They are opposed precisely as the tragic and the comic are opposed, distinct but inseparable in any comprehensive perception of human life.

The union of these two themes should and does mandate the emergence of a final theme, that of the dream. At least this is true in the work of any author whose portrayals can claim comprehensiveness; and so it is of Welty's work. There the dream takes a variety of forms: the fantasy of Ruby Fisher in "A Piece of News," the epiphany of Mrs. Larkin in "A Curtain of Green," the dreams of universal coherence that come to William Wallace Jamieson in "The Wide Net" and to Virgie Rainey in *The Golden Apples*, the whole of *The Robber Bridegroom* and such stories as "Ladies in Spring" and "Powerhouse," the waking dream of a vanished family life that comes to Laura McKelva during the storm on her last night in the old home at Mount Salus. In such dreams as these, the vividness of Welty's world becomes momentarily apparent. One might say, tangible as well, except that her world is always one and always tangible. The dream in her characters is merely an extension of human sensibility in its perennial effort to perceive a relationship with the world about it; and she never presumes to explain either the dreamer or the dream, the world or our perception of it. Writing of "No Place for You, My Love" and the disembodied shriek that occurs near the end, she calls the whole piece "a circumstantial, realistic story in which the reality *was* a mystery." That characterization could and should be applied to most of her writing.

SURVEY OF CRITICISM

The first significant criticism of Eudora Welty's work was Katherine Anne Porter's introductory essay to *A Curtain of Green* in 1941. Few young writers have been so fortunate. Porter, herself an established author at that time, praised Welty's eye and ear, her directness, her wit, her lack of sentimentality, and above all her "admirable objectivity." The short story, she noted, "is a special and difficult medium," and indirectly she advised the new author to avoid feeling compelled "to do the conventional thing" and attempt a novel. As Porter also noted, however, Welty had already begun writing novels, and her first, *The Robber Bridegroom*, appeared in 1942. Wartime readers were only mildly interested in Welty's works, and critics did not agree. Alfred Kazin, writing in the *Herald-Tribune*, was warm in his praise, whereas John Peale Bishop, writing in the *New Republic*, was critical of her attempt to fuse European fairy tale with tall tales from the American frontier. Lionel Trilling in the *Nation* had misgivings about her playful tone and what he considered her obscurantism. Negative criticism persisted with the appearance of her second collection of stories, *The Wide Net*. Diana Trilling, writing for the *Nation*, found merit in the title story and in "Livvie" but declared the other pieces pretentious. Jean Stafford registered similar disapproval in the *Partisan Review*. Partly in response to Diana Trilling's strictures, Robert Penn Warren wrote a full-length essay for the *Kenyon Review*: he acknowledged Welty's relative immaturity as a writer but noted prophetically that *The Wide Net* gave evidence of an emerging new style, and he discussed the theme of separateness that continues to appear in much of Welty's most distinguished work, notably *The Golden Apples* and *The Optimist's Daughter*. Other sympathetic early critics were Sinclair Lewis and Theodore Spencer.

The appearance of *Delta Wedding* in 1946 seemed at first to justify Katherine Anne Porter's previous warning: critics repeatedly disliked the novel's slow pace and what many viewed as a weak plot. Diana Trilling, again writing in the *Nation*, expressed an opinion that was to remain alive until well into the 1960s: Welty's works had accepted the South passively rather than subjecting it to the scrutiny it deserved. By contrast, John Crowe Ransom, in the *Kenyon Review*, praised highly her portrayal of a doomed way of life and compared her accomplishment to that of Virginia Woolf. The charge that she had taken too little notice of disturbances in her native South was not put to rest until she published the uncannily accurate portrayal of a racist killer, "Where Is The Voice Coming From?," in the *New Yorker* for 6 July 1963, and her essay "Must the Novelist Crusade?" in the *Atlantic Monthly* two years later. In 1949 *The Golden Apples*, a collection of linked stories that resembled a novel, was more warmly received.

While critics such as Ray B. West felt that it represented a continuation of the decline that had begun with *The Robber Bridegroom*, far more—among them Louis D. Rubin, Jr., Granville Hicks, Harry Morris, and Herschel Brickell— praised it as a virtuoso performance; and Welty's stories began to appear in the better anthologies. *The Ponder Heart*, which first appeared in the *New Yorker* in 1953, was a popular success both in hard covers and in the 1956 stage version. And although *The Bride of the Innisfallen* was not widely popular, it greatly enhanced Welty's standing as a writer. By the time Allen Tate in "A Southern Mode of the Imagination" (1968) singled her out, with Stark Young, for comparison with Faulkner ("quite as gifted, though somewhat lower in magnitude and power"), both her respectability and her stature were assured.

In 1962 Ruth M. Vande Kieft published the first book-length study of Welty's career and work. Her book, a Twayne volume, was designed to serve as an introduction, but it gave extended treatments of *Delta Wedding, The Golden Apples*, and *The Bride of the Innisfallen*, and also of several major aspects of Welty's work, among them the metaphysical dimension of her early stories, her use of comic modes, her use of the dream as a device, and her impressionism. Most of Vande Kieft's judgments have been sustained by subsequent criticism, and students continue to find her book valuable. In 1963 Louis D. Rubin, Jr., devoted a chapter of his *The Faraway Country* to Welty's handling of the Mississippi scene. Rubin noted there that, unlike Faulkner, Welty had presented a seemingly tranquil and orderly image of Southern small-town life, and thus she had been dealt with far too often as a mere regionalist. A careful reading of her major works, Rubin showed, revealed their universality. Welty's stature was further enhanced in the early 1960s by a third study, Alfred Appel's *A Season of Dreams: The Fiction of Eudora Welty* (1965). Appel dealt with the entire body of Welty's fiction up to that point and treated at length such matters as the theme of isolation (previously noted by Warren), the Negro, Welty's fascination with the Natchez Trace, and the unification of *The Golden Apples* by recurring theme and symbol. Borrowed from Welty's early story "First Love," Appel's title suggests that he gave special attention to the frequency with which Welty's characters move into what appears to be a dream world, thereby releasing their fears and enriching their lives with enhanced perceptions.

Two other book-length studies should be mentioned. The first is Michael Kreyling's *Eudora Welty's Achievement of Order* (1980). Kreyling takes into account earlier versions of several of the works, including *The Optimist's Daughter, The Golden Apples*, and an unpublished "Delta Cousins," which seems to be the germ from which *Delta Wedding* grew. The special value of Kreyling's book lies in its examination of the evolution of Welty's work, although it also contains a useful defense of *The Robber Bridegroom* and some memorable observations about *Losing Battles*. A more recent book by Albert J. Devlin, *Eudora Welty's Chronicle* (1983), attempts to reconstruct a Mississippi chronicle out of her first four books and thus to define the structure of her historical imagination. The attempt is justifiable, but the aspect Devlin examines is central only to incidental pieces of her work. Another general introduction has appeared: Elizabeth Evans's *Eudora Welty* (1981) in the Ungar Modern Literature Series, which supplements three previous introductions, Vande Kieft's already mentioned, and the ones by J. A. Bryant, Jr. (Minnesota Pamphlet Series, 1977) and Neil Isaacs (Steck-Vaughan Southern Writers Series, 1969). Journal articles and notes have appeared in astronomical numbers recently, but two collections, both sponsored by the University Press of Mississippi, are noteworthy: *Eudora Welty: A Form of Thanks*, edited by Ann J. Abadie and Louis Dollarhide (1979) and Peggy Whitman Prenshaw's *Eudora Welty: Critical Essays* (1979), which in addition to essays by several authors already mentioned contains valuable pieces by such critics as C. E. Eisinger, J. E. Hardy, Warren French, Daniele Patavy-Souques, and R. B. Heilman.

BIBLIOGRAPHY

Works by Eudora Welty

A Curtain of Green and Other Stories. New York: Doubleday, Doran, 1941.
The Robber Bridegroom. New York: Doubleday, Doran, 1942.
The Wide Net and Other Stories. New York: Harcourt, Brace, 1943.
Delta Wedding. New York: Harcourt, Brace, 1946.
The Golden Apples. New York: Harcourt, Brace, 1949.
The Ponder Heart. New York: Harcourt, Brace, 1949.
Selected Stories. New York: Modern Library, 1954.
The Bride of the Innisfallen. New York: Harcourt, Brace, 1955.
The Shoe Bird. New York: Harcourt, Brace and World, 1964.
Losing Battles. New York: Random House, 1970.
One Time, One Place: Mississippi in the Depression: A Snapshot Album. New York: Random House, 1971.
The Optimist's Daughter. New York: Random House, 1972.
The Eye of the Story: Selected Essays and Reviews. New York: Random House, 1978.
The Collected Stories of Eudora Welty. New York: Harcourt Brace Jovanovich, 1980.
Conversations with Eudora Welty, ed. Peggy Whitman Prenshaw. Jackson: University Press of Mississippi, 1984.
One Writer's Beginnings. Cambridge: Harvard, 1984.

Studies of Eudora Welty

Abadie, Ann J. and Louis Dollarhide, ed. *Eudora Welty: A Form of Thanks*. Jackson: University Press of Mississippi, 1979.
Appel, Alfred, Jr. *A Season of Dreams: The Fiction of Eudora Welty*. Baton Rouge: Louisiana State University Press, 1965.
Bryant, J. A., Jr. "Eudora Welty." *Seven American Women Writers of the Twentieth Century: An Introduction*. Ed. Maureen Howard. Minneapolis: University of Minnesota Press, 1977.

Devlin, Albert J. *Eudora Welty's Chronicle*. Jackson: University Press of Mississippi, 1983.

Evans, Elizabeth. *Eudora Welty*. New York: Ungar, 1981.

Isaacs, Neil D. *Eudora Welty*. Austin, Texas: Steck-Vaughn, 1969.

Kreyling, Michael. *Eudora Welty's Achievement of Order*. Baton Rouge: Louisiana State University Press, 1980.

Prenshaw, Peggy Whitman, ed. *Eudora Welty: Critical Essays*. Jackson: University Press of Mississippi, 1979.

Rubin, Louis D., Jr. *The Faraway Country: Writers of the Modern South*. Seattle: University of Washington Press, 1963.

Thompson, Victor H. *Eudora Welty: A Reference Guide*. Boston: G. K. Hall, 1976.

Vande Kieft, Ruth M. *Eudora Welty*. New York: Twayne, 1962.

NANCY M. TISCHLER

Tennessee (Thomas Lanier) Williams (1911–1983)

Few Southerners have been more publicly reviled and more richly rewarded than Tennessee Williams. He was perceived by many as an exploiter of the myth of Southern decadence, by conservative moralists as a force for sexual anarchy, and by many literary critics as a panderer to popular taste. He was nonetheless internationally acclaimed as the South's—and the country's—best playwright. He won two Rockefeller Fellowships, four New York Drama Critics Circle Awards, two Pulitzer Prizes, the Gold Medal for Drama from the American Academy of Arts and Letters and the National Institute of Arts and Letters, the Medal of Honor for Literature from the National Arts Club, and two honorary doctorates. For all of his Bohemian life-style and nonconformist literary technique, by the end of his long and fruitful career, he had become one of America's most celebrated authors.

BIOGRAPHY

Tennessee Williams was an intensely subjective artist who romanticized his own experiences. Names and events in his life took on the mythic quality of private symbols, frequently echoing through his works. He was inclined to see himself as a character whom he romanticized, and he enjoyed anecdotes that exaggerated experience for aesthetic ends.

Williams was born on 29 March 1911, on Palm Sunday (the actual year was one he later varied according to his own convenience). He was named Thomas Lanier Williams III, for his paternal grandfather; the poet Sidney Lanier was one of his father's ancestors—as were Indian fighters of Tennessee. He later used this slender thread to justify the nickname he adopted. He also claimed that St. Francis Xavier's brother Valentine was one of his relatives. He often used the name for himself and for his poetic characters, adopting it formally when he finally converted to Catholicism.

His father was Cornelius Coffin Williams, a man who later served as the model for Stanley Kowalski and Big Daddy—a hard-drinking, loud-talking, poker-playing man's man. His mother, Edwina Dakin Williams, was a prim, high-strung, puritanical Southern lady. He often pictured himself as an outrageous blend of these two American creatures, the Cavalier and the Puritan.

His earliest youth was spent in an Episcopal manse in Clarksdale, Mississippi, where his German grandmother (Grand) and his charming liberal grandfather (the Reverend Edwin Dakin) doted on him. These two people were to form the emotional undergirding for much of his life. The grandfather, who at the end of his life lived with Williams, served as the model for the dying poet in *Night of the Iguana*.

His happy life at the Rectory was broken at age six by an attack of diphtheria, which led the boy into a life of imagination and isolation. His hovering mother discouraged further rough play. And his consequent solitude led him into an intensified love of his sister Rose, his only playmate.

In 1918 this cloistered existence was shattered by Cornelius Williams's promotion from traveling salesman to corporate executive of the International Shoe Company of St. Louis. The move into an urban apartment hastened the emotional disintegration of Rose, who retreated increasingly into her own private world. This tragedy is central to *The Glass Menagerie* and various short stories chronicling her retreat from reality.

The loud presence of the father, the arrival of a new child, Dakin, and the general sense of alienation drove Williams into an intensified private life of books and writing. His adolescent creations—short stories and poems—won him a series of small awards. The alienation of these days made him intensely aware of his Southern speech and manner.

His adolescence was highlighted by a tour of Europe with a group escorted by his grandfather. While in Europe, he became morbidly sensitive about his mortality and had a mystical experience in Cologne Cathedral. Throughout his life, he was concerned with the evanescence of human life and with the need for supernatural intervention. Although he never portrayed a pastor sympathetically and had little enthusiasm for organized religion, he made frequent references to the supernatural in his serious works, and he eventually converted to Roman Catholicism.

College education was a checkered experience for Williams. The quest for a degree led him to the University of Missouri, Washington University in St. Louis, and finally the University of Iowa, from which he graduated in 1938. During this period, he experimented sexually with women and finally with men. He wrote his first plays, joined a theatrical group in St. Louis, and changed his name from Tom to Tennessee.

By the time he left Iowa, he was a published poet, short-story writer, and dramatist, convinced of his homosexuality, determined to escape the International

Shoe Company and to see the world. He went to New Orleans, where he came to know those outcasts who became central to his work. He traveled west and south during those vagabond years, but he never completely cut himself off from his family, although he never again lived with his mother or called St. Louis home.

When he was twenty-six, he subtracted two years from his age, claiming that those years he worked at the shoe factory could not be considered living, and was thereby conveniently eligible for a contest for young playwrights. In 1940 he won a small cash prize for four one-act plays on the Depression, *American Blues*. The award also led him to a long and profitable relationship with an agent, Audrey Wood, who helped him to a Rockefeller grant, several opportunities to publish stories and short plays, a chance at Broadway, and a movie contract.

The most crucial of these was the chance to see *Battle of Angels* produced by the Theatre Guild in Boston in autumn 1940. It failed and Williams was devastated. He continued to revise the play for the rest of his life, unable to accept it as a failure. He insisted that the audience's and the critics' violent reactions to the play taught him that he could not mix sex and religion, leading him next to a "safe" play about mothers—*The Glass Menagerie* (1945). His life became an emotional roller coaster: plays were like children for him. Their very flaws encourged him to love them even harder, to seek to reform them, to defend them in spite of their deficiencies, and to try again and again to find audiences who would love them as he did.

In spite of some lukewarm receptions (of *You Touched Me!* in 1945 and *Summer and Smoke* in 1948), most of his early plays met with wide critical acclaim. At times, several of his plays were on Broadway at once. *A Streetcar Named Desire* (1947) was an even greater success than *The Glass Menagerie*. Later plays continued to increase his wealth and his reputation—notably *Cat on a Hot Tin Roof* (1955) and *Night of the Iguana* (1961). Other plays were treated more coolly by the critics: *Camino Real* (1953) opened to mixed reviews as did *The Rose Tattoo* (1951). Critics laughed at his first effort at longer fiction, *The Roman Spring of Mrs. Stone* (1951), although it was later successful as a film.

His own life became a succession of searches for family and for home. He finally settled into a prolonged liaison with Frank Merlo and bought a home in Key West. His sister, who had been institutionalized and lobotomized, was settled in a comfortable sanatorium, and his grandfather lived the final years of his long life with Williams.

Then some bad reviews and public attacks (such as those directed against *Baby Doll*) led him into a steadily darker mood. In the 1960s, his world seemed to collapse with the decline and death of Merlo. This was followed by a series of deaths of friends and associates, and then by a sense of loneliness and guilt and sorrow, which drove Williams into increasing reliance on drugs. *Slapstick Tragedy* (1966), which reflects this confusion, ran only four days. *The Kingdom of Earth* (1968) was his last respectable Broadway failure. In his *Memoirs* (1975), Williams refers to the 1960s as his "stoned age."

With the help of his brother Dakin, who pointed him to Roman Catholicism but also committed him to a mental institution in St. Louis for three months, he was revived. But he was furious at his mother and brother for this invasion of his life, held his agent equally responsible, cut his brother off from any substantial share in his will, his agent from his life, and renounced the church he had so recently joined.

His final works were more coherent but diminished from his great creative period. A series of small failures marked his last years. Strange references to brutality, death threats, and disappearances occasionally surfaced in the press. He became, however, an increasingly public figure—appearing in his own plays, doing readings, and leading seminars at universities.

He died on 25 February 1983, strangled on a bottle cap in a hotel room in New York City. He was buried, against his expressed desires, in St. Louis, next to his mother. He left the bulk of his vast estate to his sister Rose and to the University of the South, in a fund for young creative writers.

MAJOR THEMES

From the beginning of his long and illustrious career, Tennessee Williams wrote about the extreme situations of human life. Although one of his adolescent plays was about a fatal dinner party in ancient Egypt and another was about coal workers who found strength in union, Williams preferred to write about modern life as it is lived by solitary misfits. He was neither a historian nor a sociologist. He was a poet who celebrated the lyric antitheses of human existence—the tragic and comic moments, love and loss, ecstasy and death, communion and isolation, joy and pain. His early works tended to be more violent and more derivative than his mature efforts. They were often short stories and one-act plays that caught a mood or a relationship.

The beginning of his testing and maturing came with his first recognized full-length play, *Battle of Angels*. Williams found his subject and his voice in this story of the American South. He characterized the materialism of the middle class, their sterile orthodoxy and rigid conformity. Following the Freudian path suggested by D. H. Lawrence, he underscored the terrible frustration and the sexual envy leading to outbursts of brutality. Blacks, foreigners, and nonconformists became lightning rods in such an overcharged world. The play also introduces the mythic Williams hero—the vagabond poet. This secular saint of unfettered sexuality becomes the human sacrifice in the classic Williams apocalypse. Such heroes, however flawed, are inclined to acquire heroic stature as they are incinerated with blow torches, shredded by bloodhounds, castrated by Klansmen, or eaten by adolescents.

Although *Battle of Angels* was not a success, Williams continued to love and revise it, renaming it *Something Wild in the Country* and *Orpheus Descending*, and turning it into a film called *The Fugitive Kind*. Williams's penchant for revision makes neat categorization of periods impossible. *Battle of Angels* is the tragic side of a later comic show that he coauthored. *You Touched Me!* was based on a D. H. Lawrence short story. It, too, was a failure. Again the characters were stereotypes, the ideas too obvious, the plot too clumsy, the imagery too Freudian.

Only in *The Glass Menagerie* did he find the style that was to mark his mature work. A simple autobiographical work that blended tragic insights with comic expression, the play is unpretentious, gently lyrical, and rich in characterization. It is the simple story of a failed dinner party. The people are recognizable and powerfully conceived. Their gestures, voices, silences, clothing, imagery, petulance, laughter, manners, and concerns all blend in a fully theatrical experience. The framing device of the narrator allows the author to indulge in poetry and memory, giving a grandeur to people who would otherwise be simply sad and confused.

More powerful, complex, immediate, and raw in its emotional impact is *A Streetcar Named Desire*, his second mature masterpiece. The characters are again perceived in their totality, their tragedy is again realistic, the conflicts are again totally believable. Williams found that the counterpoint of speech patterns between characters with conflicting backgrounds and needs highlighted their differences and their tragic absurdity. He found by language and gesture the means to demonstrate isolation and the terrible need to communicate.

In *Cat on a Hot Tin Roof* he continued to explore this theme, again celebrating a forceful woman whose will to power makes her too aggressive for Southern taste. He also portrayed a latent homosexual, in this case a wounded ball player, who contrasts with Big Daddy, a materialistic masculine figure. The rich characterization of the loving, domineering father in this play was a triumphant breakthrough for the writer who had hated his own father for so many years.

Other plays of this mature phase shared virtues with these. Although too mannered and precise, *Summer and Smoke* has a sensitively conceived character in its heroine. And the human dichotomy between spirit and flesh was to remain thematic throughout Williams's work. *The Rose Tattoo* was one of several efforts at comedy and the celebration of the flesh. His more sensual and happy figures are usually Mediterranean folks, often Sicilian in recognition of his delightfully sensual memories of life with Frank Merlo, or Mexican in a tribute to his early carefree life in Central America. The heavy use of rose imagery echoes through his work, a recognition of the centrality of human sexuality and love. Tragedy for Williams often results from the harnessing of Pan. He loves to see the goatman running wild.

The later plays began to show signs of a more baroque style. The hero or heroine became more contorted psychologically, the background more grotesque, the action more confused, and the conclusion more violent.

The Night of the Iguana combined the fecundity of the Central American rain forest with the anguish of the trapped iguana. The characters also struggled for freedom and sought to communicate with one another in spite of being in solitary confinement. Williams's grandfather is reflected in this play—less as the defrocked minister who leads tours through God's world than as the aged poet who spends his last breath completing a sonnet.

Sweet Bird of Youth is a tribute to Williams's beloved giants of the theatre. Over the years he saw many of these aging artists triumph over personal tragedy through their determination and their ultimate dedication to their art. As he grew older, he became increasingly committed to the combined power of art and hard work, regardless of personal circumstances.

The sense of nastiness and the focus on mutilation that hover over these plays become more explicit in *Suddenly Last Summer*, the fictionalized account of his sister's lobotomization, which is curiously counterposed with his ambivalent account of his own homosexuality and exploitation of sexual partners. This play and its companion piece, "Something Unspoken," formed *Garden District*, Williams's final big production. Its failure marked the end of his significant contributions to New York theatre.

Coincidental with his personal descent into drugs came an embracing of "experimental theatre." Most of these plays, which were impressionistic, expressionistic, symbolic, and usually brief, were commercial failures. He adopted Oriental dramatic forms, brought mysticism to his stage, tried static drama, and allowed large birds to become onstage characters. Some of these short works have a quality of apocalyptic laughter signaled by the title *Slapstick Tragedy*. Some have moments of self-revelation, as in *Small Craft Warnings* and *In a Bar in Tokyo*. Others have interesting characters or scenes, as in *The Milk Train Doesn't Stop Here Anymore* and *The Seven Descents of Myrtle*. The play of this final group that Williams himself cherished most was *Out Cry*, his intense two-character play.

He attributed this succession of failures to bad casting and bad directing. Some critics insist that the experimental plays never had appropriately sensitive productions. Others believe that the playwright's talent rested in a controlled ambivalence: rather than indulging his lyricism, he wrote better when restraining and parodying it; rather than confessing and lamenting his sexual sins, he was more effective in complex disguises. He was a repetitive playwright whose variations on a handful of themes were impressively complex. Surface simplicity hid remarkable profundity; the real world barely disguised the fantastic world beneath and beyond it.

Williams's range of writing is impressive: poetry, short stories, novels, memoirs, and plays; comedy and tragedy and mixtures; realistic, naturalistic, surrealistic, symbolic; psychological dramas, and slapstick tragedy. He was a writer who could speak to the educated and the uneducated alike of the absurd and the painful world in which helpless human creatures sought moments of comfort and compassion in the face of impending doom. And he could do it with enormous artistry.

SURVEY OF CRITICISM

The best criticism of Tennessee Williams has been written by Tennessee Williams. A sensitive analyst of his own work, though a poor judge of it, he regularly wrote thoughtful essays for newspapers in anticipation of his plays' openings. Most of these appeared in the *New York Times* and have been collected in *Where I Live: Selected Essays* (1978). Like most writers, he has included among his public statements both private insights into and extravagant defenses of his flawed favorites.

Interviews along the way have further enriched the materials close to the primary source. Exhaustive listings of these, most of which appear in popular magazines, are available in bibliographies. The Williams Collection at the Humanities Research Center at the University of Texas at Austin and the Tennessee Williams Fine Arts Center at the Florida Keys Community College have a vast array of his unpublished materials, much of it early drafts of the finished products. The bulk of his papers was donated to Harvard University. Bibliographies that will provide a more detailed listing of primary documents are currently in preparation.

Firsthand knowledge of the author has become available in a series of publications. Members of his own family have been among the most outspoken commentators. His mother wrote about her son from the perspective of a Southern lady in a biography entitled *Remember Me to Tom* (1963). More recently, his brother Dakin, with the help of Shepherd Mead, wrote *Tennessee Williams: An Intimate Biography* (1983). Letters have also surfaced—of particular note being the controversial exchange of letters with Donald Windham (1977), who coauthored the early dramatic adaptation of the D. H. Lawrence short story "You Touched Me." The best source of insights into Williams's life is his own *Memoirs* (1975), an *apologia pro vita sua*. A good source for current and interesting information is the *Tennessee Williams Newsletter*, which includes conversations, letters, and personal memories of Williams.

Because each of Williams's major plays and numerous of his later minor ones became an important theatrical event, the most celebrated theatrical critics— Brooks Atkinson, John Gassner, Henry Hewes—wrote timely pieces about specific works and about the author. It was the defense of *The Glass Menagerie* by Claudia Cassidy that kept the play alive in Chicago and prepared the way for the triumphant entry into New York. These critics and many others have consistently included references to Williams in their writings about the American theatre in the twentieth century and are therefore a rich repository of commentary.

In addition, Williams is regularly anthologized in textbooks and critical studies as a representative of certain trends in modern experience—existential or bohemian or decadent or mythic or violent. The best extended work on the philosophic thrust in Williams's work is Esther Merle Jackson's *The Broken World of Tennessee Williams* (1965).

The book-length assessments, which usually focus on his early work and the public information about his life, began to appear in 1961, when Benjamin Nelson and Nancy M. Tischler both wrote critical studies of Williams. Later studies of the same nature included Signi Falk's book for the Twayne Series (1978) and Gerald Weales's study in the Minnesota Series (1965). At the same time, Williams became a popular topic for scholarly articles. Collections of the more celebrated of these articles have been appearing recently. Twentieth Century Interpretations (1977) has a collection of Williams essays edited by Stephen Stanton, and a much larger collection has also appeared under the title *Tennessee Williams: A Tribute* (1977), edited by Jac Tharpe. This latter collection was followed by a smaller, more select edition under the title of *Thirteen Essays* (1980), also edited by Jac Tharpe. Other collections are still at press, clearly suggesting the vitality of Williams scholarship.

One of the more interesting recent developments has been the proliferation of books and articles dealing with Williams's films. Maurice Yocawar's study (1977) is especially sensitive, and others have followed, bringing new information. The growing interest in film criticism should produce a number of good books in this area. At this point, books on Williams are appearing too fast to chronicle. The enthusiasm for pictorial biographies has resulted in a delightful book by Richard F. Leavitt called *The World of Tennessee Williams* (1978). Rumors abound about potential works, including an authorized biography. Bibliographies have already been published in *The Bulletin of Bibliography* (1973), and others are now at press. It is an exciting time for Williams scholars and a fertile one.

BIBLIOGRAPHY

Works by Tennessee Williams

The Roman Spring of Mrs. Stone: A Novel. New York: New Directions, 1950.
Baby Doll: A Screenplay. New York: New Directions, 1956.
The Knightly Quest: A Novella and Four Short Stories. New York: New Directions, 1966.
Twenty-Seven Wagons Full of Cotton and Other Plays. New York: New Directions, 1966.
Hard Candy: A Book of Stories. New York: New Directions, 1967.
One Arm and Other Stories. New York: New Directions, 1967.
American Blues: Five Short Plays. New York: Dramatists Play Service, 1968.
Dragon Country: A Book of Plays. New York: New Directions, 1970.
The Theatre of Tennessee Williams. New York: New Directions, 1971–76.
    Volume 1: *Battle of Angels* (1940), *The Glass Menagerie* (1945), and *A Streetcar Named Desire* (1947).
    Volume 2: *The Eccentricities of a Nightingale* (1948), *Summer and Smoke* (1948), *The Rose Tattoo* (1951), and *Camino Real* (1953).
    Volume 3: *Cat on a Hot Tin Roof* (1955), *Orpheus Descending* (1957), and *Suddenly Last Summer* (1958).

Volume 4: *Sweet Bird of Youth* (1959), *Period of Adjustment* (1960), and *The Night of the Iguana* (1961).

Volume 5: *The Milk Train Doesn't Stop Here Anymore* (1964), *Kingdom of Earth* (*The Seven Descents of Myrtle*, 1968), *Small Craft Warnings* (1972), and *The Two-Character Play* (*Out Cry*, 1975).

Memoirs. New York: Doubleday, 1975.

Moise and the World of Reason: A Novel. New York: Simon and Schuster, 1975.

Tennessee Williams's Letters to Donald Windham: 1940–65. Ed. Donald Windham. New York: Holt, Rinehart and Winston, 1977.

Where I Live: Selected Essays. Ed. Christine R. Day and Bob Woods. New York: New Directions, 1978.

Studies of Tennessee Williams

Donahue, Francis. *The Dramatic World of Tennessee Williams*. New York: Ungar, 1964.

Falk, Signi. *Tennessee Williams*. 2d ed. Boston: Twayne, 1978.

Hirsch, Foster. *A Portrait of the Artist: The Plays of Tennessee Williams*. London: Kennikat Press, 1979.

Jackson, Esther Merle. *The Broken World of Tennessee Williams*. Madison: University of Wisconsin Press, 1965.

Leavitt, Richard F., ed. *The World of Tennessee Williams*. London: W. H. Arlen, 1978.

Maxwell, Gilbert. *Tennessee Willliams and His Friends*. New York: World, 1965.

Nelson, Benjamin. *Tennessee Williams: The Man and His Work*. New York: Obolensky, 1961.

Phillips, Gene D. *The Films of Tennessee Williams*. Philadelphia: Art Alliance Press, 1980.

Stanton, Stephen, ed. *Tennessee Williams: A Collection of Critical Essays*. Englewood Cliffs, N.J.: Prentice-Hall, 1977.

Tharpe, Jac, ed. *Tennessee Williams: A Tribute*. Jackson: University Press of Mississippi, 1977.

———. *Tennessee Williams: Thirteen Essays*. Jackson: University Press of Mississippi, 1980.

Tischler, Nancy M. *Tennessee Williams*. Austin, Texas: Steck-Vaughn, 1969.

———. *Tennessee Williams: Rebellious Puritan*. New York: Citadel Press, 1965.

Weales, Gerald. *Tennessee Williams*. Minneapolis: University of Minnesota Press, 1965.

Williams, Edwina Dakin. *Remember Me to Tom*. New York: Putnam's, 1963.

Williams, Dakin and Shepherd Mead. *Tennessee Williams: An Intimate Biography*. New York: Arbor House, 1983.

Yocawar, Maurice. *Tennessee Williams and Film*. New York: Frederick Ungar, 1977.

——————— RICHARD S. KENNEDY ———————

Thomas Wolfe
(1900–1938)

Thomas Wolfe was the first Southern novelist to transcend his region and become generally regarded as an "American" writer. His self-consciousness about his American identity, combined with his rhythmic, heightened prose, has brought about his recognition as the representative of the tradition of Melville and Whitman in the twentieth century.

BIOGRAPHY

Thomas Wolfe, the youngest in a family of seven children, was born 3 October 1900 in Asheville, a small city in western North Carolina near the Great Smoky Mountains. His mother, Julia Elizabeth Westall, was a native of that region; his father, William Oliver Wolfe, was a stonecutter from York Springs, Pennsylvania, who had wandered into the South after the Civil War and established a tombstone shop in Asheville. Wolfe's parents, brothers, and sisters, all appear as members of the Gant family in his autobiographical novel *Look Homeward, Angel*. When Thomas was six years old, his mother established a boardinghouse in Asheville, "The Old Kentucky Home," and took him there to live with her. He grew up a lonely child feeling neglected by his mother and disturbed by the fact that the family was now divided between two household centers.

Julia Wolfe's prosperity, however, made it possible for young Wolfe to become a day student at the North State Fitting School, Asheville's newly established preparatory school, where he was trained in Latin, Greek, and German. Here he experienced a new life in his study with a gifted teacher, Mrs. Margaret Roberts, the headmaster's wife, whom he called "the Mother of my Spirit," for she introduced him to the masterpieces of English literature and awakened his love of poetry.

After graduation at age sixteen, he enrolled at the University of North Carolina at Chapel Hill, the first of the Wolfe children to benefit from higher education. During his college years, 1916–20, he concentrated in classics and English literature. In his Latin studies he became familiar with Cicero, Livy, Horace, Catullus, Tacitus, Plautus, and Terence, but he was more attracted by his Greek studies in Homer, Xenophon, Plato, Aeschylus, and Euripides. He was especially fortunate to study under the Renaissance scholar Edwin Greenlaw, who developed his taste for Spenser, Marlowe, Jonson, Milton, and Elizabethan drama. He participated fully in a variety of campus activities: he became a debater, editor of the college newspaper and of the campus humor magazine, and a playwright in the newly formed Carolina Playmakers under Frederick Koch. His one-act plays ''The Return of Buck Gavin'' and ''The Third Night'' were staged at the University in 1919.

His interest in the drama led him to begin graduate study at Harvard in 1920, where he enrolled in Professor George Pierce Baker's English 47, a workshop for practice in play writing. During the next three years he developed a mature talent for literary expression and determined to become a professional writer. At the same time, he earned a master's degree in English, with seminars in Renaissance literature and the Romantic poets. Although he gained confidence in his ability as a writer, he felt very much an outsider at Harvard and during these years began a pattern of solitary existence to which he adhered for the rest of his life, a situation that he later described poignantly in his essay ''God's Lonely Man'' in *The Hills Beyond*.

His hopes for success in the theater were founded on the fact that two of his plays were chosen by Baker for production by the 47 Workshop Players. The first was staged in 1921, ''The Mountains,'' a one-act play about a young doctor who becomes drawn into a family feud against his will. The next year, Wolfe completed a full-length version of *The Mountains* and then went on to write *Welcome to Our City*, a play in ten scenes about a real-estate scheme that provoked a race riot in a small Southern city. When it was produced in spring 1923, many in the Cambridge audience judged that it was the best work ever done by a member of the Workshop. Professor Baker recommended it to the Theatre Guild for a New York production, and Wolfe had visions of a flourishing career in the theater.

A problem arose, however, that was to be a recurring one throughout his life: *Welcome to Our City* was too long. When one of the Guild directors, Lawrence Langer, guaranteed Wolfe a Broadway production if he would cut the playing time by a half hour, Wolfe was unable to do so. His creative talent seemed to be for proliferation, and he lacked the critical perspective for revision. Wolfe's lengthy play was also refused by the Provincetown Playhouse and the Neighborhood Playhouse. Meanwhile, he had moved to New York to accept an instructorship in English at New York University, where during the next six years he taught freshman composition and introduction to literature.

At the end of his first teaching year, he traveled to Europe and toured England, France, Switzerland, and Italy for nine months, writing travel sketches and working to complete a play that he had begun at Harvard, *Mannerhouse*, a historical piece about the decline of a plantation family during the Civil War and Reconstruction period. On the return voyage in 1926, he met and fell in love with Aline Bernstein, a New York theatrical designer and one of the board of directors of the Neighborhood Playhouse. Although Mrs. Bernstein was already married and nineteen years senior to Wolfe, this encounter began the most important relationship of Wolfe's life. Their love affair extended over the next five years.

Discouraged that producers, including Mrs. Bernstein's own theatrical group, turned down *Mannerhouse*, he decided to try prose fiction, a much more suitable form than the drama for his desired fullness of expression. With the encouragement and financial backing of Mrs. Bernstein, Wolfe left teaching for a year and devoted his full energies to writing an autobiographical novel. After eighteen months of compelling himself to write daily, in Europe and in New York, Wolfe completed an intensely introspective, lyrical book about the childhood and youth of a young Southerner, Eugene Gant, and his search for identity. His book, entitled "O Lost," ran over 1,100 typewriten pages: again he had an outsize work that publishers found too long.

Leaving the manuscript in Mrs. Bernstein's hands, Wolfe left New York and wandered aimlessly from one European city to another, trying to write a novel that would be more acceptable to publishers. Eventually, "O Lost" found its way to Maxwell Perkins, a sympathetic editor at Charles Scribner's Sons, who perceived the extraordinary talent displayed in Wolfe's novel and convinced him that it needed to be reduced in size so that it could be published in one volume. When Wolfe was unable to cut the work himself, Perkins went through it with him, cutting out over one-fifth of the material. The novel, retitled *Look Homeward, Angel*, was published in 1929, and Wolfe became recognized as one of the most promising novelists in the country.

Awarded a Guggenheim Fellowship in 1930, he traveled once more to Europe, working on a novel based on his love affair with Mrs. Bernstein yet reflecting the intensity of a young Southerner's response to the urban life of the North. As his pages filled, he seemed unable to find a satisfactory structure, and his narrative plans kept shifting. After three years' work, he had a mountain of manuscript with several disjunctive narrative strands and scattered lyric paeans to the American scene. From time to time he published excerpts from his material as novellas or short stories in magazines: among the most important were "A Portrait of Bascom Hawke," which tied for first place in the Scribner short novel contest in 1932; "The Web of Earth," a monologue based on his mother's reminiscences of her early married years; "Death, the Proud Brother," a young man's account of four deaths he had witnessed in New York; and "No Door," four episodes showing the restless life of the artist.

But the second novel was only an accumulation of fragments. Late in 1933 Wolfe turned in desperation to Perkins for help in organizing what he had written. When Perkins saw that all of Wolfe's work consisted of autobiographical fictional episodes, he urged him to revive the persona of Eugene Gant and pick up his story at the time he went North to Harvard. This simple suggestion solved Wolfe's narrative problem, and thereafter he and Perkins worked together recasting the episodes, as Wolfe wrote necessary material to fill in the gaps. At length, Wolfe completed *Of Time and the River* and also had in hand four additional books, either in outline or partially written, two of which would reach back to Eugene Gant's ancestors and the others carry him forward into the 1930s.

Of Time and the River (1935) was a remarkable performance. Although it dealt with Eugene Gant's struggles to become a playwright, his bewilderment in New York City as a college instructor, and his wanderings in Europe as he tried to release his creative powers, Wolfe had widened his scope from a personal self-consciousness to include a national consciousness as well. This book plus the appearance of a volume of short stories and sketches, *From Death to Morning* (1935), established him as a distinctive figure in American literature.

But his next publication, *The Story of a Novel* (1936), in which he gave an account of his difficulties in writing his book and of Perkins's help in getting it into shape, caused him trouble. A mean-spirited attack by critic Bernard De Voto charged that Wolfe was only able to offer autobiographical outpourings disguised as fiction and that he was helpless and incompetent without editorial assistance. Wolfe's paranoiac personality overreacted to these accusations. As a result, he set aside his six-volume scheme in order to write another novel about the late-nineteenth-century era in the Appalachian region and about a young boy in the early twentieth century observing the transition from the earlier ways.

As months went by, his new book began to include autobiographical sequences, and Wolfe also began taking material written earlier for the projected Eugene Gant volumes and adapting it to his new protagonist. Further, he quarreled with Perkins in order to break away from his seeming dependence on an editor and chose a new publisher. This meant that he abandoned his six-volume American saga and turned his energies to writing about a new alter ego, George Webber, for an ever-expanding novel that he eventually called *The Web and the Rock*. Its principal theme was to be that life does not turn out to be what we expect, a theme broad enough to include an enormous variety of his autobiographical episodes. Eventually, the book came to include everything he had accumulated over the past six years that could possibly fit into his narrative. When the first draft of this work was completed in May 1938, Wolfe left for the Northwest on a vacation trip, to which he added a sweep through eleven National Parks in the Rocky Mountain region. Upon his return to Seattle, he fell ill with pneumonia, a situation which led to the reopening of an old tubercular lesion in his lung. The tubercles were carried through his bloodstream to his brain, and Wolfe died after brain surgery at the Johns Hopkins Hospital in Baltimore, 15 September 1938, just short of his thirty-eighth birthday.

The manuscript of *The Web and the Rock*, over a million words long, was left in the hands of Edward Aswell, his editor at Harper & Brothers. During the next three years, Aswell fashioned three volumes from Wolfe's unfinished manuscript, chiefly by cutting out extraneous material that Wolfe had written for previous projects. *The Web and the Rock* (1939) presented Webber's early years in a small Southern town, his college experiences at the state university, and his love affair with a beautiful stage designer in New York during the time of his writing an autobiographical novel. *You Can't Go Home Again* (1940) showed a more mature Webber developing a social conscience in the midst of the Great Depression and in his visit to Nazi Germany. *The Hills Beyond* (1941) told the story of Webber's maternal ancestors, the Joyners, in the Appalachian region and of the arrival of his father, John Webber, in their town of Libya Hill. Ten other excerpts from the manuscript were included in this volume as additional stories or sketches.

MAJOR THEMES

Because Wolfe's novels have an episodic quality, his first book, *Look Homeward, Angel*, which has a satisfying completeness, is generally regarded as his best achievement. The novel tells the story of Eugene Gant's growing up and his attempt to break free from his possessive mother and from the restrictions of provincial life in the South. But Eugene's development is seen within a naturalistic world of chance that shapes his destiny. "We are the sum of all the moments of our lives," the narrator tells us, describing the evolving process of human life amidst determining forces: "Each moment is the fruit of forty thousand years." But Wolfe's attitude is one of wonder at this "dark miracle of chance which makes new magic in a dusty world." This sense of awe fades, however, when an individual life is seen as isolated, unable to communicate with anyone, lost and searching for meaning.

To express this search, Wolfe employs a Platonic view of human life. Eugene has been brought from a bright world of spirit into this puzzling world of chance where he has lost his bearings and his sense of belonging. In a proem to the novel, the narrator expresses this view in a series of metaphors: "Remembering speechlessly we seek the great forgotten language, the lost lane-end into heaven, a stone, a leaf, an unfound door." The door, stone, and leaf are symbols of a concealed entrance to the world of spirit and imagination.

Thus the book presents a conflict between two kinds of reality. Eugene exists within the mundane life of his hometown, surrounded by the ongoing naturalistic world, but at the same time he yearns for something more, an ideal world of beauty and imagination, a world of spirit. This conflict is resolved at the end of the book in a scene in which Eugene talks to the ghost of his brother Ben. He is afforded a vision of the moments of the past in his own life and eventually a godlike vision of the far past—early civilizations and even prehistoric existence evolving over eons of time. When he tells Ben of his seeking for some ultimate answers to the secrets of life, he asks, in frustration, "Where is the world?" Ben replies, "Nowhere." "*You* are your world." Eugene then understands that he must accept the naturalistic world of chance in which he will continue to live. But he realizes that the search for a world of spirit can be an inward search: "In the city of myself, upon the continent of my soul, I shall find the forgotten language, the lost world, a door where I may enter. . . . ''

In *Of Time and the River*, Eugene's quest continues as he strives to become a writer and to express what truths of life he has found in his experiences. But the new emphasis in this novel is American self-consciousness. The book is filled with incantations to the American earth, reactions to the ugliness of urban squalor, exultations over triumphs of modern technology, and yearnings of an American in Europe for his homeland.

In *The Story of a Novel* Wolfe speaks directly and personally of his struggles to reach into his psyche for the shapes of memory and of his being overwhelmed by the multiplicity of American life. He believes that the American artist, compared to those of other nations, has more difficulty expressing his experience because of "the billion forms of America" and "the savage violence and dense complexity of all its swarming life."

The Web and the Rock and *You Can't Go Home Again* restate Wolfe's themes, but his humor and satire offer some counterpoint to George Webber's intense responses to the vigorous life of his hometown. Also scenes of violence emerge in *The Web and the Rock*, including the account of a sadistic butcher and his family; the lynching of a Negro who had gone berserk and shot several townspeople; Webber's vituperative quarrels with his mistress, Esther Jack; and Webber's fight with a gang of Germans at the Oktoberfest in Munich. Wolfe's pondering over the problem of evil and the human propensity for violence gives a new thematic darkening to his work. In *You Can't Go Home Again*, his pondering develops into social criticism of the waste and heedlessness of the wealthy in New York and a compassion for the downtrodden and exploited lower classes. George Webber's experiences both in New York and Nazi Germany lead to a new awareness of the need for human brotherhood; a generally mature and responsible view of life has now replaced the romantic self-consciousness of the earlier novels.

SURVEY OF CRITICISM

Critics and reviewers, with the notable exception of Bernard De Voto, welcomed Wolfe's novels as they were published, although many pointed to his shortcomings: the episodic quality of his narrative, his tendency toward overstatement, and the excessive length of his novels. As time went on, however, his four novels, taken as a whole, came to be seen as a loosely shaped American epic in prose. Both Maxwell Geismar's edition *The Portable Thomas Wolfe* (1946) and Herbert Muller's *Thomas Wolfe* (1947), the first full-length critical study, helped to establish this view of the Gant-Webber cycle.

Louis D. Rubin, Jr., in *Thomas Wolfe: The Weather of His Youth* (1955), explored in detail Wolfe's debt to Wordsworth and the Romantic poets. Floyd Watkins in *Thomas Wolfe's Characters: Portraits from Life* (1957) examined

Wolfe's use of autobiographical material with perceptive comparisons of fictional characters and their real-life counterparts.

Richard S. Kennedy in *The Window of Memory: The Literary Career of Thomas Wolfe* (1962) was the first critic to make use of the voluminous Wolfe papers at the Harvard Library. His study deals with the mind and art of Thomas Wolfe and traces the development of each of his works as revealed by Wolfe's diaries, notes, and manuscripts. Paschal Reeves in *Thomas Wolfe's Albatross: Race and Nationality in America* (1968) examines Wolfe's attitudes toward minority groups as revealed in his fiction. He demonstrates that Wolfe's racial and ethnic prejudices, common to small Southern communities, gradually wore away as his career developed. An important Wolfe symposium published as *Thomas Wolfe and the Glass of Time*, edited by Paschal Reeves (1971), explores such topics as the question of genre, the use of symbol, the handling of point of view, and the expression of social criticism in Wolfe's work.

Among more recent publications, three critical studies stand out above all others. Malcolm Cowley in "Thomas Wolfe: Homo Scribens" in *A Second Flowering: Works and Days of the Lost Generation* (1973) offers an illuminating treatment of Wolfe's creative process. C. Hugh Holman's *The Loneliness at the Core: Studies in Thomas Wolfe* (1975) is a series of critical meditations on how to account for the value of Wolfe's work without being blind to his limitations. He considers such questions as Wolfe's use of autobiography, the problem of point of view, his developing mastery of the novella form, his contribution to the Southern Renascence, and his place in the epic tradition. Monique Decaux in *La Création romanesque chez Thomas Wolfe* (1977) presents the best psychological study of Wolfe and his work that has yet been published.

A recent critical controversy should be mentioned. John Halberstadt in "The Making of Thomas Wolfe's Posthumous Novels" and in letters to magazines has attacked Wolfe's reputation by the assertion that Edward Aswell and not Thomas Wolfe was the real author of the three posthumous works published from the manuscript Wolfe left behind. Richard S. Kennedy in "The 'Wolfegate' Affair" refuted this charge.

Neither of the full-scale biographies of Wolfe is critically valuable: Elizabeth Nowell's *Thomas Wolfe* (1960) and Andrew Turnbull's *Thomas Wolfe* (1968). There are, however, three publications of Wolfe's own writings that have great biographical value and that are so richly annotated that every Wolfe commentator should be aware of them: *The Letters of Thomas Wolfe*, edited by Elizabeth Nowell (1956); *The Notebooks of Thomas Wolfe*, edited by Richard S. Kennedy and Paschal Reeves (1970); and *My Other Loneliness: The Selected Letters of Thomas Wolfe and Aline Bernstein*, edited by Suzanne Stutman (1983).

Articles on Wolfe and his work appear regularly, especially since 1975 when the first of six annual Wolfe Fests was held at St. Mary's College, Raleigh, North Carolina. These occasions have been superseded by the annual meetings of the Thomas Wolfe Society (founded in 1979) in cities associated with Thomas Wolfe. The semiannual *Thomas Wolfe Review* has now become the best source of biographical and critical articles on Wolfe. This kind of organized and institutionalized activity has brought about a resurgence of interest in his work and solidified his position as an important American writer.

BIBLIOGRAPHY

Works by Thomas Wolfe

Look Homeward, Angel. New York: Charles Scribner's Sons, 1929.
From Death to Morning. New York: Charles Scribner's Sons, 1935.
Of Time and the River. New York: Charles Scribner's Sons, 1935.
The Story of a Novel. New York: Charles Scribner's Sons, 1936.
The Web and the Rock. New York: Harper & Brothers, 1939.
You Can't Go Home Again. New York: Harper & Brothers, 1940.
The Hills Beyond. New York: Harper & Brothers, 1941.
"The Return of Buck Gavin" and "The Third Night," in *Carolina Folk Plays*, 1st, 2d, and 3d Series, ed. Frederick Koch. New York: Henry Holt, 1942.
Mannerhouse: A Play in a Prologue and Three Acts. New York: Harper & Brothers, 1948.
A Western Journal: A Daily Log of the Great Parks Trip. Pittsburgh: University of Pittsburgh Press, 1951.
The Letters of Thomas Wolfe. Ed. Elizabeth Nowell. New York: Charles Scribner's Sons, 1956.
Thomas Wolfe's Purdue Speech: Writing and Living. Ed. William Braswell and Leslie A. Field. West Lafayette, Ind.: Purdue University Press, 1964.
Thomas Wolfe's Letters to his Mother. Ed. C. Hugh Holman and Sue Fields Ross. Chapel Hill: University of North Carolina Press, 1968.
The Notebooks of Thomas Wolfe. Ed. Richard S. Kennedy and Paschal Reeves. Chapel Hill: University of North Carolina Press, 1970.
The Mountains. Ed. Pat M. Ryan. Chapel Hill: University of North Carolina Press, 1970.
Welcome to Our City, a Play in Ten Scenes. Ed. Richard S. Kennedy. Baton Rouge: Louisiana State University Press, 1983.
My Other Loneliness: The Selected Letters of Thomas Wolfe and Aline Bernstein. Ed. Suzanne Stutman. Chapel Hill: University of North Carolina Press, 1983.
Beyond Love and Loyalty: The Letters of Thomas Wolfe and Elizabeth Nowell. Ed. Richard S. Kennedy. Chapel Hill: University of North Carolina Press, 1983.
The Autobiography of an American Novelist. Ed. Leslie A. Field (reprints *The Story of a Novel* and *Writing and Living*). Cambridge, Mass.: Harvard University Press, 1983.
Thomas Wolfe Interviewed, ed. Aldo P. Magi and Richard Walser. Baton Rouge: Louisiana State University Press, 1985.
Holding on for Heaven: The Cablegrams and Postcards of Thomas Wolfe and Aline Bernstein. Ed. Suzanne Stutman. Akron, Ohio: Thomas Wolfe Society.

Studies of Thomas Wolfe

Collections of Essays

Beebe, Maurice and Leslie A. Field, eds. "Thomas Wolfe Special Number." *Modern Fiction Studies* 11 (August 1965): 315–28.

Field, Leslie A., ed. *Thomas Wolfe: Three Decades of Criticism*. West Lafayette, Ind.: Purdue University Press, 1968.

Kennedy, Richard S. *Thomas Wolfe: A Harvard Perspective*. Athens, Ohio: Croissant, 1983.

Phillipson, John S. *Critical Essays on Thomas Wolfe*. Boston: G. K. Hall, 1985.

Rubin, Louis D., Jr. *Thomas Wolfe: A Collection of Essays*. Englewood Cliffs, N.J.: Prentice-Hall, 1973.

Walser, Richard. *The Enigma of Thomas Wolfe*. Cambridge, Mass.: Harvard University Press, 1953.

Individual Studies

Aswell, Edward C. "Thomas Wolfe Did Not Kill Maxwell Perkins." *Saturday Review of Literature* 34, October 6, 1951, pp. 16–17, 44–46.

Blackwelder, James Ray. "Literary Allusions in *Look Homeward, Angel*: The Narrator's Perspective." *Thomas Wolfe Review*, 8 (Fall 1984): 14–25.

Cargill, Oscar. *Thomas Wolfe at Washington Square*. Ed. Thomas Clark Pollock and Oscar Cargill. New York: New York University Press, 1954.

Cowley, Malcolm. *A Second Flowering: Works and Days of the Lost Generation*. New York: Viking Press, 1973.

Decaux, Monique. *La Création romanesque chez Thomas Wolfe*. Etudes Anglaises 71. Paris: Didier, 1977.

De Voto, Bernard. "Genius Is Not Enough." *Saturday Review of Literature* 13 (25 April 1936): 3–4, 14–15.

Evans, Elizabeth. *Thomas Wolfe*. New York: Frederick Ungar, 1985.

Field, Leslie A. "A 'True Text' Experience: Thomas Wolfe and Posthumous Publication." *Thomas Wolfe Review* 6 (Fall 1982): 27–34.

Flora, Joseph M. "Thomas Wolfe at New York University: His Friendship with Vardis Fisher." *Thomas Wolfe of North Carolina*. Ed. H. G. Jones. Chapel Hill: North Carolina Society, 1982.

Gould, Elaine Westall. *Look Behind You, Thomas Wolfe: Ghosts of a Common Tribal Heritage*. Hicksville, N.Y.: Exposition Press, 1976.

Gurko, Leo. *Thomas Wolfe: Beyond the Romantic Ego*. New York: Crowell, 1975.

Hagan, John. "Structure, Theme, and Metaphor in Wolfe's *Look Homeward, Angel*." *American Literature* 53 (May 1981): 266–85.

———. "The Whole Passionate Enigma of Life: Thomas Wolfe on Nature and the Youthful Quest." *Thomas Wolfe Review* 7 (Spring 1983): 32–42.

Halberstadt, John. "The Making of Thomas Wolfe's Posthumous Novels." *Yale Review* 70 (October 1980): 79–94.

Holman, C. Hugh. *The Loneliness at the Core: Studies in Thomas Wolfe*. Baton Rouge: Louisiana State University Press, 1975.

Kennedy, Richard S. *The Window of Memory: The Literary Career of Thomas Wolfe*. Chapel Hill: University of North Carolina Press, 1962.

———. "Thomas Wolfe at New York University." *Thomas Wolfe Review* 5 (Fall 1981): 1–10.

———. "The 'Wolfegate Affair'." *Harvard Magazine* (September 1981): 48–53, 62.

———. "Wolfe's *Look Homeward, Angel* in The Literary Marketplace." *Thomas Wolfe Review* 6 (Fall 1982): 23–27.

Klein, Carole. "In Suffering, A Celebration: Aline Bernstein and Thomas Wolfe." *Thomas Wolfe Newsletter* 3 (Spring 1979): 2–7.

Kussy, Bella. "The Vitalist Trend and Thomas Wolfe." *Sewanee Review* 50 (July 1942): 306–24.

Lanzinger, Klaus. *Die Epik im Amerikanischen Roman*. Studien zur Sprache und Literatur Amerikas, 1. Frankfurt am Main: Diesterweg, 1965.

Ledwig-Rowohlt, H. M. "Thomas Wolfe in Berlin." *American Scholar* 22 (Spring 1953): 185–201.

McElderry, Bruce R., Jr. *Thomas Wolfe*. New York: Twayne, 1964.

Muller, Herbert J. *Thomas Wolfe*. New York: New Directions, 1947.

Nowell, Elizabeth. *Thomas Wolfe: A Biography*. Garden City, N.Y.: Doubleday, 1960.

Perkins, Maxwell. "Thomas Wolfe." *Harvard Library Bulletin* 1 (Autumn 1947): 269–77.

Phillipson, John S. *Thomas Wolfe: A Reference Guide*. Boston: G. K. Hall, 1977.

———. "Thomas Wolfe: A Reference Guide Updated." *Resources for the Study of American Literature* 11 (Spring 1981): 37–80.

———. "Thomas Wolfe's 'Chicamauga': The Fact and the Fiction." *Thomas Wolfe Review* 6 (Fall 1982): 9–22.

Raynolds, Robert. *Thomas Wolfe: Memoir of a Friendship*. Austin: University of Texas Press, 1965.

Reeves, Paschal. *Thomas Wolfe's Albatross: Race and Nationality in America*. Athens: University of Georgia Press, 1968.

———, ed. *Thomas Wolfe and the Glass of Time*. Athens: University of Georgia Press, 1971.

———, ed. *Thomas Wolfe: The Critical Reception*. New York: David Lewis, 1974.

Rothman, Nathan. "Thomas Wolfe and James Joyce: A Study in Literary Influence." *A Southern Vanguard*. Ed. Allen Tate. Englewood Cliffs, N.J.: Prentice-Hall, 1947.

Rubin, Louis D., Jr. *Thomas Wolfe: The Weather of His Youth*. Baton Rouge: Louisiana State University Press, 1955.

———. "In Search of the Country of Art: Thomas Wolfe's *Of Time and the River*." *A Gallery of Southerners*. Baton Rouge: Louisiana State University Press, 1982.

Skipp, Francis E. "The Editing of *Look Homeward, Angel*." *Papers of the Bibliographical Society of America* 57 (1963): 1–13.

Trotti, John Boone. "Thomas Wolfe: The Presbyterian Connection." *Journal of Presbyterian History* 59 (Winter 1981): 517–48.

Turnbull, Andrew. *Thomas Wolfe*. New York: Charles Scribner's Sons, 1968.

Walser, Richard. *Thomas Wolfe, Undergraduate*. Durham, N.C.: Duke University Press, 1977.

———. "Major Thomas Casey Westall." *Thomas Wolfe Review* 8 (Fall 1984): 1–10.

———. *Thomas Wolfe's Pennsylvania*. Athens, Ohio: Croissant, 1978.

———. *The Wolfe Family in Raleigh*. Raleigh, N.C.: Wolfe's Head Press, 1976.

Watkins, Floyd. *Thomas Wolfe's Characters: Portraits from Life*. Norman: University of Oklahoma Press, 1957.

———. "Thomas Wolfe and Asheville Again and Again and Again . . ." *Southern Literary Journal* 10 (Fall 1977): 31–55.

Wheaton, Mabel Wolfe and Legette Blythe. *Thomas Wolfe and His Family*. Garden City, N.Y.: Doubleday, 1961.

——————— THADIOUS M. DAVIS ———————

Richard Wright
(1908–1960)

One of the most distinctive voices from the modern South belongs to Richard Wright. His works of fiction are unrelenting expressions of elemental humanity struggling for self-definition and self-actualization. A realist in his assessment of the pain and tragedy inherent in the lives of human beings trapped within a limiting environment, Wright was an American naturalist, but one who believed in the ultimate strength of individuals to transcend and transform the socioeconomic factors circumscribing their existences. While this belief evolved into his literary experimentation with existentialism, it also initiated his political interest in Communism during his later years. Because his powerful depictions of human beings emerged during his residency in Northern urban areas and because his last thirteen years were spent as an expatriate in France, Wright's career has not generally been associated with the South. The charged social consciousness characteristic of his fiction has resulted more frequently with his being defined as a protest writer; yet at the base of his conceptions of humanity and environment is an intrinsically Southern consciousness, shaped by what he termed "the shocks of Southern living" for black people and imprinted with the reality of racial oppression. His vocation, engendered out of this Southern sensibility and fueled by a concomitant need for an unfragmented life, allowed him to use words, as he said, "to march, to fight, to create a sense of hunger for life that gnaws in us all, to keep alive in our hearts a sense of the inexpressibly human." Throughout his career, Wright sought to express his vision of human identity and to extricate his characters, and society by extension, from oppressive racism.

BIOGRAPHY

Born 4 September 1908 on a Delta cotton plantation 25 miles east of Natchez, Mississippi, Richard Nathaniel Wright bore the given names of his grandfathers,

Richard Wilson and Nathaniel Wright. His first name presaged the closeness throughout his childhood and youth to his maternal grandfather's family, rather than to his paternal relatives. His parents, Ella and Nathan Wright, had settled as sharecroppers in the town of Roxie shortly after their marriage in 1907. Ella Wilson, daughter of a large Natchez family of modest means, had been a country schoolteacher at the time of her marriage to Nathan Wright, an illiterate tenant farmer. The marriage had taken place over the objections of Richard and Margaret Bolden Wilson, who had greater hopes for their daughter.

In 1911, when deteriorating conditions on the farm and a second baby, year-old Leon Alan, strained their resources, Nathan and Ella Wright moved to the Wilson home in Natchez. There they depended upon the help of Margaret Wilson, a midwife and doctor's assistant. For a time, Nathan Wright became an itinerant day laborer before he found a job at a sawmill; however, he rarely had steady employment and none that allowed him to support his family adequately.

The Wrights relocated in Memphis a short time later, so that Nathan would have greater opportunities to provide for his wife and sons. He found work as a night porter at a drugstore, but within two years the lure of the Memphis nightlife and the strain of supporting a family on low wages caused him to desert Ella and his boys. Before his departure in 1913, Nathan Wright had already abandoned most of his financial obligations and parental responsibilities to his wife, who was working as a cook.

Ella Wright struggled to care for her sons; nonetheless, her long hours away from home meant that she had to entrust Alan's supervision to young Richard, and that both boys spent much of their time in the Memphis streets. In 1915 after she became ill, Ella placed Richard and Alan in an orphanage. A year later, she had recovered enough to work off her debt to the orphanage and to leave Memphis for Elaine, Arkansas, where she had been invited to live with her younger sister, Maggie. The move to Arkansas enabled Ella to stop over for the summer in Jackson, Mississippi, where her parents then lived in a large seven-room house, providing her sons with a clean, spacious environment in contrast to their Memphis surroundings.

Initially, the family's settling in Elaine augured well for a stable future for Richard, whose early years had been marked by movement and change. His Aunt Maggie's husband, Silas Hoskins, was a prosperous landowner and saloon keeper. But Wright's early experiences proved to be paradigmatic; the happy stay in Elaine was short-lived, because a white mob killed his uncle and caused his mother and his aunt to flee Arkansas with the two boys. After a brief interlude in Jackson, the Wrights and Maggie Hoskins set out for West Helena, Arkansas, where Ella worked as a cook or domestic until she suffered a series of paralytic strokes and had to be returned to Jackson. During their mother's illness and convalescence, Alan went to live with Maggie in Detroit, and Richard was sent to an uncle in Greenwood, Mississippi, before he was allowed to return to his grandmother's house in Jackson.

From 1919 to 1925 Richard Wright lived under the strict guardianship of his grandmother, Margaret Wilson, an austere Seventh Day Adventist, who restored order to the remaining years of his childhod. Prior to his return to Jackson, Wright's education had been sporadic, even though his mother had first enrolled him at age seven in Memphis's Howard Institute and later had placed him in schools in Elaine and West Helena. During one of his earlier stays in Jackson, he had discovered the world of books from one of his grandmother's boarders, so that by the time he settled into regular attendance at school, he already loved to read. In 1920 he entered an Adventist school taught by his aunt, Addie Wilson, but the experience was traumatic, and the following fall he enrolled in the public Jim Hill School. He went from the fifth to the sixth grade in a few months, and quickly became a good student despite being behind his age group.

Although his school years were not without problems, particularly those stemming from Margaret Wilson's religious discipline and her holding books suspect, these years provided a positive turning point toward dual ambitions: writing and migrating north. Wright began to write stories, and he found jobs to earn money for school books and supplies. He also formed friendships with other youths that he would draw upon in his later writings. As an eighth grader, he wrote his first longer story, "The Voodoo of Hell's Half-Acre," which was published in three installments in the 1924 *Southern Register*, a black weekly newspaper. Selected valedictorian of his ninth-grade class, he wrote and delivered the 1925 graduation address on the theme "The Attributes of Life." Wright's completion of the ninth grade at the Smith-Robinson School marked the end of his formal schooling.

After a series of jobs, including delivery boy for a clothing store and bellhop for a hotel, he left his family and Mississippi for Memphis, where he hoped to earn enough money to move himself and his mother north to Chicago. He worked initially as a dishwasher at the same drugstore where his father had been a porter and later as a delivery boy for an optical company. Saving most of what he earned, he bought secondhand copies of *American Mercury*, *Harper's*, and *Atlantic Monthly*. He borrowed books from the public library with the assistance of a white coworker, as blacks were not allowed to check out books. During this period, Wright prepared to become a writer by reading; he used as his bibliography the authors and works cited by H. L. Mencken in his *Book of Prefaces*. A voracious reader, he discovered Flaubert, Gogol, Nietzsche, and Zola, as well as Edgar Lee Masters, Theodore Dreiser, Sherwood Anderson, and Sinclair Lewis, whose *Main Street* was the first serious novel Wright read. The American writers especially appealed to him because, as he remarked, they "seemed to feel that America could be shaped nearer the hearts of those who lived it."

When Wright boarded an Illinois Central train in 1927, he was migrating to Chicago alone, although he had already managed to get his mother and brother to Memphis. He recalled later that at first Chicago "depressed and dismayed me, mocked all my fantasies"; nevertheless, his ten years in the city were most productive in terms of his apprenticeship as a writer. While holding a sequence of jobs, as dishwasher, insurance salesman, porter, and postal clerk, he also wrote, all the while saving money to send for his mother, who along with his brother arrived in 1928.

Wright's earliest works were poetry and stories encouraged by University of Chicago students whom he met in the John Reed Club. He joined the Communist Party in 1933, a time when the Party's expressed support was for oppressed peoples regardless of their race. The intellectual climate of the radical left inspired Wright to look for publishers; his poems "Rest for the Weary" and "A Red Love Note" appeared in *Left Front*, which named him coeditor in 1934, and one of his more effective poems, "I Have Seen Black Hands," was accepted by *New Masses*, which also published his first essay, "Joe Louis Uncovers Dynamite," in 1935. His poems, articles, and reviews soon began to appear regularly in *New Masses*, *International Literature*, and *Partisan Review*, where in 1935 his best-known poem, the antilynching "Between the World and Me," was published. At the same time, he also became affiliated with the Chicago Federal Negro Theater and the Federal Writers' Project, through which he cemented friendships with a number of other Southern émigrés and writers, including old friends from Jackson and poet Margaret Walker.

Nonetheless, Chicago during the Depression continued the pattern of poverty and hunger that had been a part of life in the South. Wright, the sole wage earner for a family then expanded to include his grandmother Wilson, was frequently out of work. The Public Welfare Bureau assisted with food and temporary jobs as street cleaner and ditchdigger. Reading offered support to persist with his writing. Proust's *Remembrance of Things Past* not only "awed" but also "crushed [him] with hopelessness," for, as he later related, "I wanted to write of the people in my environment with an equal thoroughness, and the burning example before my eyes made me feel that I never could." Yet he completed "Big Boy Leaves Home," a long story published in *The New Caravan* anthology; "Down by the Riverside," "Long Black Song," "Fire and Cloud," all short stories; "Almos' A Man," a story excerpted from an unpublished early novel, "Tarbaby's Sunrise" (alternately titled "Tarbaby's Dawn"); and "Cesspool," a novel published after his death as *Lawd Today*. With the exception of "Big Boy," his short stories were not accepted by magazine editors, and both of his novels were rejected by New York publishers.

Wright decided in 1937 to move to New York. He became Harlem editor of the *Daily Worker*, a Communist publication, and he worked on the post-Harlem Renaissance magazine, the *New Challenge*, with writer Dorothy West. Publishing success in New York City did not come easily. His manuscripts were repeatedly turned down. His break came in December 1937 when he won a $500 first prize in a contest sponsored by *Story* magazine for members of the Federal Writers' Project. With the prize for "Fire and Cloud" and the publicity resulting from its February 1938 publication in *Story*, he was able to obtain a contract from Harper & Brothers for his first book, *Uncle Tom's Children: Four Novellas* (1938), all set in the agrarian South and written during his Chicago period. From that point to 1947, when he left New York for permanent residence in France, Wright achieved the major publications that were to earn him an international reputation. He also established his career-long relationship with the literary agent Paul Reynolds.

Harper accepted and published *Native Son* (1940), Wright's novel treating the life of a black youth in Chicago. The firm pushed the work, which was selected by the Book-of-the-Month Club and sold 200,000 copies in three weeks. The success of *Native Son* insured Wright's position as a significant writer of the 1940s and as the best-known black writer to emerge from that period. Because the novel was a best-seller, Harper published in October 1940 *Uncle Tom's Children: Five Long Stories*, an expanded version that added "The Ethics of Living Jim Crow," an autobiographical essay, and "Bright and Morning Star," a story first appearing in a 1938 issue of *New Masses*. In 1941 a stage adaptation of *Native Son*, written by Wright and playwright Paul Green, capitalized on the popularity of the novel; produced by John Houseman and directed by Orson Welles, the play augmented Wright's reputation so that by the end of 1941 when his first book of nonfiction, *Twelve Million Black Voices: A Folk History of the Negro in the United States* (with Edwin Rosskam), was published by Viking Press, he was the most acclaimed black writer in America.

Married in 1939 to Dhimah Rose Meadman, Wright traveled with her to Mexico in 1940. There, with the aid of a Guggenheim Fellowship, he worked on a novel in progress, "Little Sister," which treated black women and domestic workers and was later entitled "Black Hope." The extended stay in Mexico emphasized differences between Wright and his bride, differences that eventually led to their estrangement and divorce after they returned to New York. Wright traveled back to New York by way of Mississippi, where he saw his relatives and his father after a 25-year separation, but neither man could bridge the gulf that existed between them. Nevertheless, Wright seemed to be settling the ghosts of his past, for before his trip to Mexico, he had visited his mother and brother in Chicago and purchased a house for them.

In 1941 Wright married Ellen Poplar, daughter of Polish immigrants and a Communist Party worker with whom he would have two daughters, Julia (born in 1941) and Rachel (born in 1949). After his marriage he settled into a productive period of writing; he completed an existential fable, "The Man Who Lived Underground" (1942), which, probably because it departed from the naturalism of *Native Son*, failed to find a publisher until 1944, and he completed as well a number of the short stories that were to be published after his death in *Eight Men* (1961). He was also at work on his fictionalized autobiography, *Black Boy: A Record of Childhood and Youth* (1945), another Book-of-the-Month Club best-seller and the last of his major books written in the United States. The Wrights moved to France in 1947 after first making an extended visit in 1946 as guests of the French government.

Wright's early years in Paris were eventful. He met the African and West Indian writers, Léopold Senghor, Alioune Diop, and Aimé Césaire, who started

the Negritude movement and with whom he founded the influential journal
Présence Africaine. He sponsored the Gary Davis movement for peace and world
citizenship and began the French-American Fellowship. In 1950 he starred as
Bigger Thomas in a film version of *Native Son*, shot on location in Buenos Aires
and Chicago by French director Pierre Chenal. During this period he officially
resigned from the Communist Party, after having been estranged from it since
1944 when his essay "I Tried to Be a Communist" appeared in the *Atlantic
Monthly*.

The Outsider (1953), his first novel published after *Native Son*, was intended,
as he explained, "to replace the set of Marxist assumptions which has in the
past more or less guided the direction of my writings." Similar to "The Man
Who Lived Underground" in its metaphysical and existential philosophy, *The
Outsider* evidenced not only the influence of Dostoevsky apparent in the novella,
but also that of Jean-Paul Sartre, whom Wright had come to know in Paris.

A succession of nonfiction books followed *The Outsider* as Wright began to
travel in Africa, Asia, and Europe and to record his responses to social and
political conditions. After a visit to the Gold Coast, now Ghana, he wrote *Black
Power: A Report of Reactions in a Land of Pathos* (1954). His 1955 trip to
Indonesia to attend the Bandoeng Conference resulted in *Bandoeng,
1.500.000.000 hommes* (1955), published in English as *The Color Curtain: A
Report on the Bandung Conference* (1956). Another travel narrative, *Pagan
Spain* (1957), stemmed from excursions in Spain during 1954 and 1955. A series
of lectures delivered in Germany and Scandinavia in 1956 became the collection
of essays, *White Man, Listen!* (1956). None of these books sold well in the
States; undeterred, Wright remained an outspoken political observer.

Although Wright became a prolific essayist, he did not abandon fiction. *Savage
Holiday* (1954), his only novel with a white protagonist, was ignored in the
United States, but considered seriously in France, where it appeared as *Le Dieu
de Mascarade*. In 1958 Doubleday published *The Long Dream*, Wright's last
novel and last book published before his death; *The Long Dream* and its sequel
"Island of Hallucinations," which occupied Wright during his last years, returned to the American South for its black protagonist, Fishbelly, whose odyssey,
like Wright's own, began in Mississippi in the first novel and continued in Europe
in the second.

His final two years were marked by frustration and tension. Critics in the
United States attacked not only *The Long Dream* but also Wright himself for
his long exile in France. The black expatriate community in Paris, which considered him its dean, fell into inner turmoil from suspicions of plots by American
secret agents to discredit some of the writers, Wright in particular, for alleged
anti-American sentiments. Paul Reynolds, his long-term literary agent who had
trouble placing *The Long Dream*, had no success with "Island of Hallucinations." Wright, experiencing financial pressures from the poor sales of his recent
books, faced an uncertain future. His mother's death in January 1959 added to
his sorrow. British officials refused him permission to live in London, where

Julia was to attend Cambridge, but they granted his wife and both daughters visas. Alone in France, Wright suffered from amoebic dysentery, contracted in Africa. In his illness, he turned to writing haiku, and from a group of 4,000 poems, selected 800 for a haiku manuscript. The therapy of poetry, however, was not enough to offset the effects of his physical condition, of his malignment by the press, or of his disappointment when critics panned a New York stage version of *The Long Dream*. World Publishers's acceptance of *Eight Men* (1961) offered little consolation. His novel in progress, "A Father's Law," the study of intergenerational conflict, remained incomplete.

On 26 November 1960 the fifty-two–year–old Wright, recovering from the flu, entered a clinic for a thorough examination and treatment of his recurrent intestinal problem. He died at the clinic of a heart attack on 28 November 1960. Characteristic of the treatment he had received during his last years, the press took two days to announce his "untimely death." Wright's body was cremated, and in a symbolic statement of the meaning of his life, his ashes and those of *Black Boy* were placed in Paris's Columbarium.

MAJOR THEMES

The dominant thematic ideas and motifs in Wright's fiction emanate from his biography, particularly from his formative years in the American South with its life-threatening components of prejudice, bigotry, and brutality. That South, Wright believed, "could recognize but part of a man, could accept but a fragment of his personality, and the rest—the best and the deepest things of heart and mind—were tossed away in blind ignorance and hate." The damaging impact of the Southern world on the personality and humanity of blacks that he observed as a youth became analogous in his fiction to any powerful and destructive physical or psychological environment, whether the urban North, political institutions, or social configurations.

Acutely conscious of such environments, Wright was equally aware of the dynamics of the self-determining personality. In his own life and writings he demonstrated the potential for self-actualization and self-realization despite social or material obstacles. The actual South and the South that became his metaphor for racial oppression were, as he said, so repressive that blacks existed "emotionally on the sheer, thin margin of . . . culture," and that for him, as well as for the majority of his fictional characters, "nothing short of life itself hung upon each of my actions and decisions, and I had grown used to change, to movement, to making adjustments." Poverty, hunger, racism, and oppression may all function as negative factors constricting one's destiny and limiting one's options, but Wright insisted that the individual has the capacity for self-determination and, as in his own case, for creativity. His personal response to adverse environmental conditions was flight from his native region and a search for a place more hospitable to individual development and creativity. He wrote of this flight and search as "taking a part of the South to transplant in alien soil, to see if it could grow differently . . . and perhaps . . . bloom.'' His major themes often encompass a search for identity in temporal or spatial terms and an examination of experience in a linear or sequential progression. The meaning of identity or experience is accentuated by the reality of the human imperative to live fully yet also attenuated by environmental determinism. Wright's conviction, under-lining all of his work, is ''that the humble, fragile dignity of man, buttressed by a tough-souled pragmatism . . . can sufficiently sustain and nourish human life, can endow it with ample and durable meaning.''

Although there is great diversity in the subject of Wright's works from *Uncle Tom's Children* to *The Long Dream* and *Eight Men*, there is a cluster of sustained themes: alienation, flight, becoming, rebellion, oppression, freedom, and self-actualization, all within the emotional nexus of fear, dread, pain, anger or rage, and, in a few instances such as *The Outsider*, despair. He uses black life and thought to signify the human condition, but his messages are not celebratory. He observes, for example, in an essay on his masterpiece *Native Son*, ''How Bigger Was Born,'' ''What made Bigger's social consciousness most complex was the fact that he was hovering unwanted between powerful America and his own stunted place in life—and I took upon myself the task of trying to make the reader feel this No Man's Land. The most that I could say of Bigger was that he felt the *need* for a whole life and *acted* out of that need. . . . '' The statement might well be extended to most of his protagonists, who like Bigger Thomas are trapped by external circumstances but respond, often violently, to an internal need for wholeness even when they are unable to articulate their need or to translate it into a viable existence. Bigger ultimately recognizes, ''what I killed for, I am.'' He asserts his own identity and the meaning of his life and actions, as well as his acceptance of responsibility for both as a way of defining who he is. Although he faces death, and will be executed for committing murder, Bigger comes fully into life in the last part of the novel, ''Fate.'' In effect, he is on the brink of death when he recognizes what his life means.

In ''Fear,'' the first part of *Native Son*, a cornered rat that Bigger kills becomes an emblem for Bigger's existence in an urban ghetto controlled by and isolated from whites. A combination of realistic and naturalistic techniques reveals how he has been reduced to an animal state and his destiny truncated by powers beyond his control. His conclusion in ''Fate'' is that ''a guy gets tired of being told what he can and can't do. . . . you get so you can't hope for nothing. . . . You ain't a man no more.'' He attributes his condition to whites: ''They like God. . . . They don't even let you feel what you want to feel. . . . They kill you before you die.'' His violent acts, the killing of two women, seem inevitable given the overwhelming environmental and societal forces. In the midsection of the novel, ''Flight,'' Bigger experiences freedom from external forces and feels control over his actions, so that by the end of *Native Son*, he defines himself in existential terms through actions: '' . . . I killed. For a little while I was free. I was doing something. It was wrong, but I was feeling all right. . . . I been scared and mad all my life and after I killed that first woman, I wasn't scared no more for a little while."

"Flight" with its emphasis on an awful freedom outside of social constraints and responsibility reiterates one of the prominent themes in Wright's fiction, that of flight and escape from a painful social and experiential reality. In the earliest published fiction, the stories of *Uncle Tom's Children*, the agrarian South is the backdrop for the theme; however, in subsequent works, *Native Son*, "The Man Who Lived Underground," and *The Outsider* in particular, the urban North provides the spatial reality to which characters respond. Flight is psychological as well as literal in Wright's novels and also in his archetypal autobiographical work *Black Boy* and his most fully realized stories, "Big Boy Leaves Home," "The Man Who Lived Underground," and "Almos' A Man." Big Boy is last seen heading north for a chance to live and escape a lynch mob ("Big Boy Leaves Home"); Dave leaves the South to find "somewhere, somewhere where he could be a man" ("Almos' A Man"); Richard extends himself in what he calls "full flight" that is actually a spiritual quest for "some redeeming meaning" (*Black Boy*). Flight, whether voluntary or forced, becomes constructive movement forward in time and condition, even though the end result may be what "The Man Who Went to Chicago" discovers: that blacks were still "locked in the dark underworld of American life"; or the result may be physical annihilation as it is for Fred Daniels ("The Man Who Lived Underground"): shot in a sewer and dehumanized to "a whirling object rushing alone in the darkness, veering, tossing, lost in the heart of the earth."

In depicting hostile environments that simultaneously imprint personality and threaten to eradicate it, Wright develops the theme of becoming in tangent with that of flight. The process of becoming may, in fact, be Wright's major theme. Boys, youths, and men experience initiation into a society, though rites of passage are complicated by racism. Not only do they become "men," but they also become fully human or at least able to recognize what it means to be fully human in a world frequently inhumane. Their movement through states of contact with social forces is at once fearful and painful, but it has the resultant possibility of psychological growth and development. Their search is both for new values that will assert human dignity and for a new identity that will validate those values. The paradigm is clearly evident in *Black Boy*, and to a lesser extent in its continuation *American Hunger*, where movement toward artistic creativity is connected to cumulative levels of personal awareness about familial and cultural configurations and their effect upon the developing personality. As Richard, the protagonist, emerges from early childhood into young manhood, he overcomes fear, cruelty, and despair and establishes a mature faith in living in dignity to his maximum potential. The paradigm is not only evident in *Black Boy* and Wright's works of the 1940s, but it is also visible in *The Long Dream*. Rex "Fishbelly" Tucker is, like Richard, a Southern youth whose racial, sexual, social, and economic initiations occur between his fifth and eighteenth years, which coincide with the period during and after World War II. Dominated by his father Tyree, an undertaker, and by his fear of the dark, Fishbelly has a difficult transition to young manhood, one dominated by dreams and nightmares animated by the powerful parental and racial controls over his life. Wright intended to follow Fishbelly's protracted becoming a man over the course of his mature expatriate years in "Island of Hallucinations," which would, as *American Hunger* does for *Black Boy*, continue the quest for a spiritual and spatial condition amenable to full self-realization.

Older characters in Wright's canon realize themselves in a similar way, despite the fact that their becoming is often compressed into a shorter period of time. Silas of "The Long Black Song," Mann in "Down By the Riverside," and Taylor in "Fire and Cloud" are three such characters from *Uncle Tom's Children*, who, though well into their adult years, become men in an instant of recognizing their own humanity and strength. In his use of the theme of becoming, Wright is masterful in registering what he labeled "the most sensitive and volatile period" in an individual's life, the period during which the individual learns, acknowledges, and acts upon an inviolate humanity.

Underscoring becoming as a thematic imperative in Wright's fiction is a recurrent concern with freedom and rebellion. Whereas a Taylor may state that *"Freedom belongs t the strong!"* and he, Sue ("Bright and Morning Star"), and the other protagonists in *Uncle Tom's Children* may rebel and face violence for their efforts, Cross Damon in *The Outsider* is the Wright character most closely associated with freedom and rebellion. Like Bigger, Cross accidentally becomes a social rebel, but unlike Bigger, who is inarticulate throughout most of *Native Son*, Cross is an intellectual able to formulate the words and concepts necessary for conveying his situation. The four books of the novel, "Dread," "Dream," "Descent," and "Despair," function as signs of Wright's theme and Cross's experience. When presumed dead in a train wreck, Cross walks away from his old life and its attendant problems; he has the freedom to shape for himself a new identity. His situation is a literal portrayal of one subtext in a number of Wright's other works such as *Native Son*, "The Man Who Lived Underground," "Man of All Work," and *Black Boy*; Wright presented that subtext in *White Man, Listen!* as "man stripped of the past and free for the future." Cross dramatizes the individual's responsibility for creating self, but he is an alienated modern man whose journey into identity is a descent into existentialism. He is similar to Camus's Meursault in his indifference to violence and to murder. Cross, however, renounces all authority or power over his existence; for example, he breaks with the Communist Party and political organizations when he realizes that their objective is control of the individual. At the end of a life as a social and moral outsider, Cross confesses, "it was . . . horrible"; "Because in my heart . . . I felt . . . I'm innocent. . . . That's what made the horror. . . ."

Despite his intellectualism, Cross's life apparently is as filled with what Wright called "useless and reasonless suffering" as the lives of Jake Johnson, the physically repulsive and morally empty protagonist of *Lawd Today*, and of

Erskine Fowler, the sexually repressed white killer in *Savage Holiday*. Jake demonstrates in a 24-hour day many of the negative aspects of black manhood; he is a liar, a cheat, a wife-beater who nonetheless feels persecuted. Presented in a naturalistic mode without authorial comment on the apparent determinism, Jake's life, like Bigger's, is comparable to an animal's. The section of the novel depicting his eight hours at work is entitled "Squirrel Cage," while his eight hours after work is "Rat's Alley," and throughout *Lawd Today*, he is presented much like a caged animal moving in a circular fashion without the possibility of change. The white Fowler, on the other hand, experiences freedom in an early retirement from his job with an insurance company; but without work to shape his existence, he becomes a rootless, guilt- and anxiety-ridden man who accidentally kills a child and brutally murders the child's mother. Freudian and Oedipal analogies abound in the novel. Neither Fowler nor Jake comes to understand his life, yet Wright suggests in juxtaposing the seemingly commonplace surface of their lives to their teeming interior realities the complexity of ordinary existence and the tragedy inherent in the indifferent modern world. In his fictional themes, Wright builds philosophically and dramatically "a bridge of words" that makes known a body of experience and meaning that is, he states, "bred in a harsh school of life," but "seek[s] to speak the language of the human heart."

SURVEY OF CRITICISM

In 1938 with the publication of *Uncle Tom's Children*, Wright broke onto the American literary scene as a writer who was not to be ignored, though one not always favored by critics. Reviews of his first collection of stories in leading newspapers and journals, such as the New York *Evening Post*, the *New York Times Book Review*, the *Nation*, *New Masses*, and *Saturday Review of Literature*, were quick to applaud the absence of stereotypes, the proletarian politics, and primarily the narrative style. From the beginning of his major publications, then, both black and white critics recognized the searing truth and aesthetic power of Wright's voice and vision. Sterling Brown, Granville Hicks, and Malcolm Cowley all recognized Wright's talent and predicted that more could be expected of him in the future. Critics on the left welcomed a new strong voice to their ranks, though a few like Alan Comer in the *Daily Worker* criticized his sparse use of social contexts; however, Zora Neale Hurston attacked both the Party politics and what she perceived as hatred in the stories.

When *Native Son* appeared in 1940, Wright's reputation soared. He was compared to Dreiser, Dostoevsky, and Steinbeck; his analysis of social and psychological factors received enthusiastic endorsement. Widely reviewed in nearly all of the important journals of the time, *Native Son* shocked and moved critics who, though not unanimous in their praise of the novel's narrative voice and its antihero Bigger Thomas, recognized that Wright had the unique ability to transform the debilitating racial landscape in American life into an uncompromising art. In fact, the reception of *Native Son* was phenomenal; no black writer before Wright had been the subject of as much extensive and favorable critical commentary.

Although *Black Boy* in 1945 continued both the critical attention accorded Wright and his own attempt to make the obscured experience of blacks in America visible, that work marked the end of nearly wholesale endorsement of his work. The autobiographical book reiterated Wright's discipline and his craftsmanship, and by extension it made clear that the modern black writer was a serious artist; these two achievements helped to pave the way for a new generation of black novelists, in particular Ralph Ellison, Chester Himes, William Gardner Smith, Willard Motley, and James Baldwin.

Nonetheless, at the time of his death in 1960, Wright had received little critical attention in the United States, and what existed was mainly adverse reactions to his work after *Black Boy*. His long absence from the country had alienated many of his American readers and critics, despite his being a fixture in French literary circles. The posthumous publication of his collection of stories, *Eight Men*, and of his first novel, *Lawd Today*, did not measurably affect his diminished literary reputation. By the end of the 1960s, however, the literary climate had appreciably improved for Afro-American writers with the onset of political and cultural activism. As blacks began to reassess their own traditions and to resurrect literary forebears, they rediscovered Wright and his importance. By the early 1970s, one aftermath of the civil rights movement and the new black renaissance was a considerable interest in Wright as a major writer, as a proponent of racial identity and opponent of racial oppression. From that point on, he has been the subject of numerable critical studies, revaluations, and biographies.

Constance Webb's *Richard Wright: A Biography* (1968) and John A. Williams's *The Most Native of Sons: A Biography of Richard Wright* (1970) helped to reinitiate the interest in Wright's life that had marked some of the early reviews of his works. Although both biographies have been superseded by French critic Michel Fabre's *The Unfinished Quest of Richard Wright* (1973), which provided access to more primary sources and biographical details, they still retain usefulness in the perspectives that they present on Wright as friend and fellow writer.

Similarly, Edward Margolies's *Native Sons: A Critical Study of Twentieth-Century Negro American Authors* (1968), with its long chapter "Richard Wright: *Native Son* and Three Kinds of Revolution" and his *Art of Richard Wright* (1969) were among the first book-length treatments of the Wright canon. Since Margolies's books, numerous full studies of Wright's art have added to a rich and diverse body of criticism. Keneth Kinnamon's *The Emergence of Richard Wright: A Study in Literature and Society* (1972), for example, is an extended analysis of Wright's works up to *Native Son* in the contexts of culture and society; Addison Gayle's *Richard Wright: Ordeal of a Native Son* (1980) treats Wright's career and analyzes the impact of his treatment during his Paris years on his writings and creativity.

More recently, collections of criticism have made available the significant articles and reviews that have added to the assessment of Wright's achievements and reputation. Among these, John M. Reilly's *Richard Wright: The Critical Reception* (1978) collects the major periodical reviews of Wright's works, and is especially useful in obtaining a historical overview of Wright studies, because it contains important reviews of his nonfiction work as well as of his less popular fiction. Yoshinobu Hakutani's *Critical Essays on Richard Wright* (1982) is an edition of many of the more significant and ground-breaking early essays on Wright, both general essays on his life, career, and writings and specific essays on individual works of poetry, fiction, and nonfiction. He makes accessible several classic essays in Wright studies: Blyden Jackson's "Richard Wright: Black Boy from America's Black Belt and Urban Ghettos," James Baldwin's "Many Thousands Gone," Irving Howe's "Black Boys and Native Sons," and Ralph Ellison's "Richard Wright's Blues," all of which make evident the singular place that Wright has in modern American literature. Hakutani's collection also brings together previously unpublished and contemporary studies of Wright, and in so doing illustrates the healthy state of Wright scholarship.

Because Wright's work has retained meaning in a changed social and political environment and continues to bear the most rigorous critical analysis, it is apparent that one of the most remarkable canons in American literature will not be lost to future generations of students and scholars. His place has been secured both by his writings and by the vitality of critical interest in them.

BIBLIOGRAPHY

Works by Richard Wright

Uncle Tom's Children: Four Novellas. New York: Harper, 1938.

Native Son. New York: Harper, 1940.

Uncle Tom's Children: Five Long Stories. New York: Harper, 1940.

Native Son, the Biography of a Young American: A Play in Ten Scenes, with Paul Green. New York: Harper, 1941.

Twelve Million Black Voices: A Folk History of the Negro in the United States. New York: Viking Press, 1941.

Black Boy: A Record of Childhood and Youth. New York: Harper, 1945.

The Outsider. New York: Harper, 1953.

Black Power: A Record of Reactions in a Land of Pathos. New York: Harper, 1954.

Savage Holiday. New York: Avon, 1954.

The Color Curtain: A Report on the Bandung Conference. Cleveland and New York: World, 1956.

Pagan Spain. New York: Harper, 1956.

White Man, Listen! New York: Doubleday, 1957.

The Long Dream. New York: Doubleday, 1958.
Eight Men. Cleveland and New York: World, 1961.
Lawd Today. New York: Walker, 1963.

Studies of Richard Wright

Agosta, Lucien L. "Millennial Embrace: The Artistry of Conclusion in Richard Wright's
  'Fire and Cloud.' " *Studies in Short Fiction* 18 (Spring 1981): 121–29.
Bakish, David. *Richard Wright*. New York: Frederick Ungar, 1973.
Bone, Robert. *Richard Wright*. Minneapolis: University of Minnesota Press, 1969.
Brignano, Russell C. *Richard Wright: An Introduction to the Man and His Works*.
  Pittsburgh: University of Pittsburgh Press, 1970.
Bryant, Earle V. "Sexual Initiation and Survival in Richard Wright's *The Long Dream*."
  Southern Quarterly 21 (Spring 1983): 57–66.
Bryant, Jerry H. "The Violence of *Native Son*." *Southern Review* 17 (April 1981): 303–
  19.
Davis, Charles T. and Michel Fabre. *Richard Wright: A Primary Bibliography*. Boston:
  G. K. Hall, 1982.
Fabre, Michel. *The Unfinished Quest of Richard Wright*. New York: William Morrow,
  1973.
Gayle, Addison. *Richard Wright: Ordeal of a Native Son*. Garden City, N.Y.: Anchor
  Press, 1980.
Hakutani, Yoshinobu, ed. *Critical Essays on Richard Wright*. Boston: G. K. Hall, 1982.
Jackson, Blyden. "Richard Wright in a Moment of Truth." *Southern Literary Journal*
  3 (Spring 1971): 3–17.
Kinnamon, Keneth. *The Emergence of Richard Wright: A Study in Literature and Society*.
  Urbana: University of Illinois Press, 1972.
Lee, A. Robert. "Richard Wright's Inside Narratives." *American Fiction: New Readings*.
  Ed. Richard Gray. Totowa, N.J.: Barnes and Noble, 1983, pp. 200–21.
List, Robert N. *Dedalus in Harlem: The Joyce-Ellison Connection*. Washington, D.C.:
  University Press of America, 1982.
McCall, Dan. *The Example of Richard Wright*. New York: Harcourt Brace Jovanovich,
  1969.
McCluskey, John, Jr. "Two Steppin': Richard Wright's Encounter with Blue-Jazz."
  American Literature 55 (October 1983): 332–44.
Margolies, Edward. *The Art of Richard Wright*. Carbondale: Southern Illinois University
  Press, 1969.
———. "Richard Wright: *Native Son* and Three Kinds of Revolution." *Native Sons: A
  Critical Study of Twentieth-Century Negro American Authors*. Philadelphia: J. B.
  Lippincott, 1968, pp. 65–86.
Mebane, Mary E. "Black Folk of the American South: Two Portraits." *The American
  South: Portrait of a Culture*. Ed. Louis D. Rubin, Jr. Baton Rouge: Louisiana
  State University Press, 1980, pp. 86–100.
Moore, Jack B. "The View from the Broom Closet of the Regency Hyatt: Richard Wright
  as a Southern Writer." *Literature at the Barricades: The American Writer in the
  1930's*. Ed. Ralph Bogardus and Fred Hobson. University: University of Alabama
  Press, 1982, pp. 126–43.

Pudaloff, Ross. "Celebrity as Identity: Richard Wright, *Native Son*, and Mass Culture." *Studies in American Fiction* 11 (Spring 1983): 3–18.

Ray, David and Robert Farnsworth, ed. *Richard Wright: Impressions and Perspectives.* Ann Arbor: University of Michigan Press, 1973.

Reilly, John M., ed. *Richard Wright: The Critical Reception.* New York: Burt Franklin, 1978.

Rubin, Steven J. "Richard Wright and Albert Camus: The Literature of Revolt." *International Fiction Review* 8 (Spring 1981): 12–16.

Stepto, Robert B. "Literacy and Ascent: Richard Wright's *Black Boy.*" *From Behind the Veil: A Study of Afro-American Narrative.* Urbana: University of Illinois Press, 1979, pp. 128–62.

Stern, Frederick C. *"Native Son* as Play: A Reconsideration Based on a Revival." *MELUS* 8 (Spring 1981): 55–61.

Tate, Claudia C. "Christian Existentialism in Richard Wright's *The Outsider.*" *CLA Journal* 25 (June 1982): 371–95.

Webb, Constance. *Richard Wright: A Biography.* New York: Putnam, 1968.

Williams, John A. *The Most Native of Sons: A Biography of Richard Wright.* Garden City, N.Y.: Doubleday, 1970.

JOHN PILKINGTON

Stark Young
(1881–1963)

Although Stark Young shares with William Faulkner, Tennessee Williams, and Eudora Welty, his juniors by at least a generation, a major place among Mississipppi's most gifted writers, he is not so well-known to the contemporary public, probably because his major contribution lies in drama criticism, much of it technical and theoretical. With one exception, his novels, important as they are in the history of the Southern literary Renascence, are no longer widely read. His plays and poetry have suffered the same fate, while few are even aware of his contributions to translation and painting. Like James Russell Lowell, Young was a multitalented individual; and though he reached excellence in several fields, he attained the highest achievement in only one. Yet Young's contribution to the fine arts in the third and fourth decades of the twentieth century has been historically impressive. He was, in fact, a complex and rare phenomenon in American cultural history.

BIOGRAPHY

The roots of Stark Young's attitudes and values lie firmly embedded in Como and Oxford, Mississippi. Born in Como, 11 October 1881, Young absorbed the traditions and mores of this small Southern town, established soon after the Treaty of Pontotoc in 1836 ended Indian control over the territory. At that time his ancestors were already on their way westward from Georgia, where they had stopped for almost a generation on their way from Scotland via Virginia. In the seventeenth century, Young's ancestor, James McGregor, a younger son of the McGregor clan in Scotland, changed his name to McGehee and emigrated to Virginia. About the time of the American Revolution, Micajah McGehee, one of James's descendants, moved to Georgia. Three of Micajah's fourteen children, Edward, John, and Hugh, took their families to Mississippi, where Edward became a wealthy planter in the Woodville area and John and Hugh established plantations in Panola County.

In 1848 Hugh McGehee's daughter, Caroline Charlotte (1821–61), married Stephen Gilbert Starks (1816–59), a Methodist preacher, and moved with him to Holly Springs, Mississippi. At their death, Stark Young's mother, Mary Clark Starks (1858–90) and her three siblings were left orphans to be reared by their aunt and uncle in Como. In 1880 Mary Clark married Alfred Alexander Young (1847–1925), a Civil War veteran and physician. At her death, Stark Young and his sister Julia McGehee Young (1884–1962) were left in care of their aunts and uncles. Most of their childhood was spent in Como, where the McGehees permanently imbued Young with Southern attitudes and values.

Young's father's ancestors, like the McGehees, came from the British Isles. Michael Cadet Young, a younger son whose father fell at Blenheim in 1704, emigrated to the Isle of Wight County in Virginia. His fourth son, Thomas Young (1732–1828), moved south to North Carolina and, marrying twice, fathered a large family. Two of his sons, William and Henry, followed the westward trail into Tennessee. One of these Youngs became the father of William Henry Young (1813–88), Stark Young's grandfather. His son, Alfred Alexander Young, grew up in Marshall County, Mississippi. Stark Young recalled both his grandparents and was fond of remarking that his grandmother died from talking too much.

In 1863 Alfred Alexander Young enlisted in the Third Regiment, Mississippi Cavalry and participated in skirmishes near Memphis and Holly Springs. After his regiment was taken into the Confederate army, he fought in battles near Vicksburg, Jackson, and Atlanta. At the end of the war he surrendered with his unit. After the University of Mississippi reopened in 1865, Young entered as a freshman but departed in his sophomore year. He turned to farming but left it to become a physician's apprentice. In 1870 he was graduated from the University of Pennsylvania Medical School. He married and settled in Como. As a child, Stark Young often accompanied his father on visits to patients living in the country, and during the long rides on horseback or in a carriage, the boy absorbed much of the father's philosophy. He never ceased to admire his father for his understanding of people, his compassion for the sick and the poor, and the Southern principles for which he stood.

Young's adoration of his mother seems highly unusual. Always he remembered the joy he felt in her presence, and he once remarked that of all the wounds of his youth, her death, when he was only eight, was the most serious. As a man almost seventy, he could still visualize her beautiful skin, the shape of her face, and her dark hair. He remembered her dying kiss, the drive to the cemetery with his father to direct the gravediggers, and the funeral itself. As a young man he wrote poetry about her. Two of the best poems in *The Blind Man at the Window* (1906), "The Mother" and "Written at My Mother's Grave," reflect his deep feeling for her.

Virtually everyone who commented on Young as a child remarked upon his sensitivity, shyness, and intelligence. His two aunts, who with the McGehees took care of Young and his sister after their mother's death, his teachers, and the McGehee relatives recognized his unique qualities. In school he was almost a prodigy. Though not a "sissy," he cared little for athletics or scientific toys; instead he liked to imagine stories, to act out plays of his own writing, and to draw pictures. He enjoyed the company of his family, especially the conversation of the adults. One of the paradoxes of Young's life was that although he longed for family life his sexual preferences as an adult kept him from ever having any real family of his own. In some ways, his attachment to the huge McGehee family compensated for this lack. They gave him a sense of identity and provided him with a feeling of continuity, a theme that would appear frequently in his creative writing.

In 1895 Dr. Young remarried and moved with his family to Oxford. Soon afterwards, Stark Young entered the University of Mississippi as a special student. Majoring in Greek and Latin, he graduated in 1901 and in the same year enrolled in Columbia University as a graduate student in English. At Columbia Young took Brander Matthews's courses in drama and became an ardent theatergoer. Receiving the M.A. in 1902, he retired to the mountains of North Carolina to read in their original languages the Greek and Latin classics, Dante's *Divina Commedia*, and the English poets, especially Spenser, Keats, and Tennyson. After a brief period of teaching at a military school in Water Valley, Mississippi, Young joined the faculty of the University of Mississippi. In 1906 his volume of poems *The Blind Man at the Window* and his verse play *Guenevere* were published. In 1907 he resigned to become a member of the English faculty at the University of Texas.

For the next eight years Young taught at the University of Texas and spent most of his summers in Italy. While at the university he organized the Curtain Club, founded the *Texas Review*, and published *Addio, Madretto and Other Plays* (1912). As director of the Curtain Club's play performances, Young gained experience in all phases of drama production, and his success placed him in the vanguard of university dramatic companies and the little theater movement then in its inception. In 1915 he accepted a position on the Amherst College faculty. At Mississippi, Texas, and Amherst, Young was a popular teacher. His teaching emphasized the importance of semantics, correct pronunciation, prose rhythms, and poetic interpretation. By 1917 his articles on the theatre and academic subjects began to appear in the *New Republic* and subsequently in the *Nation*, the *North American Review*, the *Yale Review*, the *Dial*, *Bookman*, and *Theatre Arts Magazine*. In 1921 he resigned from Amherst and began a new career as a free-lance writer in New York.

Within a year, Herbert Croly, founder and editor of the *New Republic*, invited Young to become drama critic and a member of the editorial board of the magazine. Young continued to hold this position until his retirement, with the interruption of a single year when he served as drama critic for the *New York Times*. He also became an editor of *Theatre Arts Magazine*. Meanwhile, Young continued to publish in various periodicals. Two of his plays, *At the Shrine* (1919) and *The Queen of Sheba* (1922), appeared in *Theatre Arts Magazine*.

During the next few years, Young's literary and theatrical activities were prodigious. Revising and elaborating his weekly essays in the *New Republic* and monthly articles in *Theatre Arts* on play production and other matters relating to the performing arts, Young published in rapid succession a number of books on art in the theatre: *The Flower in Drama* (1923), *Glamour* (1925), *Theatre Practice* (1926), and *The Theatre* (1927). Together with *Immortal Shadows* (1948), they represent Young's drama criticism at its best. During these years Young also published three plays, *The Colonnade* (1924), *Rose Windows* (1925), and *Sweet Times and the Blue Policeman* (1925), as well as two translations, Molière's *George Dandin* (1924) and Machiavelli's *La Mandragola* (1927). In addition, he directed the Theatre Guild's production of Lenormand's *The Failures* (1923) and Eugene O'Neill's *Welded* (1924) and published *Encaustics* (1926), a volume of essays taken from his nondramatic essays in the *New Republic*.

By the mid–1920s Stark Young had established himself as the leading drama critic in this country. Although he continued to write his weekly essays in the *New Republic*, he used his off-season time to write fictional sketches and stories in Austin, where his sister now lived, and in Italy, which Young found ideally suited for creative activity. Beginning with *The Three Fountains* (1924), he began to express his admiration for Southern values that he had absorbed from the McGehees and his father in Mississippi. *Heaven Trees* (1926), his first published novel, explored the values of a Southern family in an Eden-like plantation setting. *The Torches Flare* (1928) compared the relative positions of the arts in the South and in the North. *River House* (1929), a retelling of the plot of *The Colonnade*, restated the theme of the artist's plight in the South in terms of the businessman. In that same year, Young agreed to write a position paper for *I'll Take My Stand* by Twelve Southerners. His contribution to this Agrarian manifesto was "Not in Memoriam but in Defense," the final essay in the volume. The volumes of fiction and the essay consistently defended Young's Southern philosophy of living. To a lesser degree, similar premises lie behind his volume of stories, *The Street of the Islands* (1930). The *New Republic* treatment of the Scottsboro case and his friendships with Maxwell Perkins, Ellen Glasgow, Allen Tate, Julia Mood Peterkin, Donald Davidson, and others probably encouraged Young to write a final treatment of the Southern theme in *So Red the Rose* (1934). This historical novel, set in Mississippi during the Civil War, soon became a best-seller and has remained popular both as a novel and as a motion picture. With it, Young had said what he wished to say about the South.

With the exception of *Feliciana* (1935), stories and sketches set mainly in Mississippi and Italy, Young published no more volumes of fiction. Instead, he turned to editing and translation. He edited a *Southern Treasury of Life and Literature* (1937) for Scribner's. In 1938 he translated Anton Chekhov's *The Sea Gull* (published in 1939) for the immensely successful production starring Alfred Lunt and Lynn Fontanne. For them he wrote *Belle Isle* (later published in 1942 as *Artemise*), a romantic musical play set near the mouth of the Mississippi River and based upon Lyle Saxon's life of the pirate Jean Lafitte. Although the Lunts at first were enthusiastic over the play, they subsequently did not produce it. Disappointed over his play and the death of his nephew, Young finished his translations of Chekhov's plays—*The Three Sisters* (1941), *The Cherry Orchard* (1947), and *Uncle Vanya* (1956)—and turned to painting as an outlet for his creative energies.

In 1947 Young resigned from the *New Republic* and virtually retired from the theatre. With his friend, William McKnight Bowman, with whom Young had lived since the early 1920s, he traveled to Italy and Greece on several occasions. He enjoyed two one-man shows of his paintings during the 1940s. In 1951 he published his final book, *The Pavilion*, his autobiography to his twenty-first year, dedicated to Allen Tate, his friend of many years. In 1959 he suffered a stroke from which he only partially recovered. On 20 December 1962 his beloved sister Julia died in Austin; two weeks later, 6 January 1963, Stark Young died in New York. On 18 February 1963 a memorial service attended by more than five hundred persons was held at the Morosco Theatre in New York. Such representatives of the art world as Zachary Scott, John Hall Wheelock, Allen Tate, Louis Kronenberger, Harold Clurman, Martha Graham, Mildred Dunnock, Franchot Tone, Kim Stanley, and John Gielgud paid tribute to Young's personal charm and artistic contributions.

MAJOR THEMES

Although Stark Young contributed to American cultural history in a number of different fields, including poetry, play writing, criticism, fiction, translation, and painting, his major work lies in drama criticism and in fiction. In the former, his primary theme was a concept of the art of theatre; in the latter, he identified his philosophy with Southern values. Few writers have been so well equipped as Young to express the problems of the artist in the South; almost no other critic has been so knowledgeable of the drama and the arts that contribute to successful play production and no modern critic has equaled Young in that indefinable sense of what is "right" in the theatre.

The appearance of Stark Young in New York as a drama critic coincided with new developments in the theatre both abroad and in this country. In Europe such men as Adolphe Appia, Max Eastman, Gordon Craig, and Constantin Stanislavsky and in this country the leaders of the Provincetown Players and the little theatre groups worked a renaissance in play production. The decade of the 1920s included some of the best work of such actors and actresses as Eleonora Duse, Giovanni Grasso, Charlie Chaplin, Jacob Ben-Ami, the Lunts, and the Barrymores, such playwrights as Eugene O'Neill, such scenic designers as Robert Edmond Jones, and such producers as Kenneth Macgowan. Consequently, between 1920 and 1940 the American theatre flourished as it had never before or since. This abundance of talent provided Young with superb material for his criticism.

Young's drama criticism originates in his concept of art. He defined art as that something the artist adds to nature, declaring, "Nature was never art." In other words, art translates reality into its own terms and adds to it. This addition becomes art. Hence in Young's view the artist who paints a picture of an apple that is so close to nature that one cannot tell the difference between the painted apple and the actual apple has not created art. In like manner, the actor onstage must not "be" what he stands for. He is not Hamlet but a person acting Hamlet. Only when he adds a dimension to the role, brings himself to the role, does he achieve the art of acting. Were the goal of the actor to "be" the character, a dog onstage would be perfect, since a dog is always a dog. This premise accounts for much of Young's objection to realism in the theatre. The greatest and most enduring art, Young thought, exhibits a central idea that must be translated into the component elements of the particular medium through which the idea is expressed. The function of the critic is to discover this central idea and then evaluate the degree of success that the production achieves in the staging of the play. The apparent simplicity of Young's statement disguises the demands it makes upon the critic.

Young insisted that the art of the theatre is an art distinct from all others. It is not merely a combination of setting, acting, music, direction, lighting, and costume, because when these components are translated into terms of the theatre they do not remain the same. As an example of his meaning, Young cited Robert Edmond Jones's settings for *The Birthday of the Infanta*. The buildings in the set are like no actual buildings in Spain, but they have the qualities that are Spanish. Jones has restated Spanish architecture in theatre terms. "This is the object of all art, to create reality in abstraction and in abstraction reality; to complete, in sum, our living for us." Young argued that the director and producer must insure that each component be translated into theatre art and that the components be harmonized or subordinated to the overall rendering of the dramatist's words. In these terms, theatre becomes an art in itself, albeit perhaps the most complicated of all arts. Young was prepared to explicate and judge the contribution of each component in his discussion of a given performance, a task that only a critic with Young's qualifications could successfully accomplish.

Young recognized that in the production of any play, the actor contributes most to its success or failure. In *Glamour* and elsewhere, he praised Eleonora Duse as the supreme example of the actor as artist. "More than any other [actor] Duse," wrote Young, "brought to the art of acting the largest and most poignant idea, the profoundest sensitivity, the deepest and most exquisite response to experience. Of all the people in the theatre she had most in common with great poetry, great joy and sorrow and beauty, great living." What Duse had in great abundance was character, an inner purity, and an understanding of suffering, and at the same time she was thoroughly Italian.

In *Theatre Practice*, Young continued the discussion of art and the critic begun in *The Flower in Drama* and *Glamour*, reprinting with little change some of the essays he had published in the earlier volumes but adding chapters on "Character Acting" and "Wearing Costumes." Character acting, thought Young, must take second rank to the greatest protagonist roles. Often actors who lack "the magnetism, the control, the direct instinct or whatever it is that would carry their direct selves over the footlights" can achieve success in character roles. For an actor to wear his costume successfully, he must understand the central idea or point of his costume and translate it into his own body. Like other aspects of theatre art, "clothes are translated into something which they were not before, and have added to them something that was not there before."

Young's fourth volume of theatre essays, *The Theater*, was also a reworking of work published earlier in various periodicals. In it he restated the principles upon which he based his drama criticism. He again emphasized the various arts that intervene between the playwright's words and the performance seen by the audience. He noted that a piece of literature may be dramatic without being a good play. "A play," said Young, "is a piece of literature about a section of life written in such a way that it will go over the footlights, in such a way that what it has to say it can say in the theater." Among those elements that intervene between the script and the production, Young included "the sound of the actor's voice," "the time values that he creates" while speaking the lines, "the stage spaces and the positions of the persons on it with regard to each other, the lights, the scene itself," and the audience. In effecting this translation the director can transform the play into his own image or he can give wide latitude to the various components (acting, costume, scene design, etc.). Probably the best directing is a compromise between the two extremes.

The four books on the theatre that Young published in the 1920s continue to have value because they are not, like most of the material in *Immortal Shadows*, his final volume on the theatre, related primarily to specific performances. As Young recognized, a given performance is necessarily ephemeral, since it cannot be exactly revived. The principles enunciated by Young, however, have lasting importance and can be applied to fiction and the other arts.

Stark Young's four novels and the essay for *I'll Take My Stand*, as Donald Davidson noted, possess an "organic unity, whose focus is chiefly upon the South. They apply," as Davidson also suggested, "the artistic principles and moral philosophy" that lie at the core of Young's drama criticism and permeate his autobiographical *The Pavilion*. Thus there is a continuity and consistency between the criticism and the fiction. The two major themes that emerge from the fiction are the relationship of traditional Southern values to the good life and the contrast between the North and the South. A minor but still important theme is the plight of the artist in the South.

In *Heaven Trees* Young dealt with the decade of the 1850s. Heaven Trees is an idyllic plantation in Mississippi. The characters are those of Young's own McGehee and Starks families. Taken together they express the virtues and the weaknesses of the Southern way of life. "Their virtues," wrote Young, "seem always of the heart, wise resolutions of the problem of living. . . . They seem figures of goodness and enduring life.'' In Dr. Clay, Young illustrates the weakness of the South. Clay has a fine intelligence, a splendid education, and a feeling toward the land and his family that Young felt lay at the core of the Southern tradition; yet Clay's life has little purpose to it, and he succumbs to the temptations of easy living and, at times, alcohol. Yet life in the South is seen as preferable to that of the North; the conversion of the Northern governess to Southern gracious living makes this point.

In *The Torches Flare* Young makes the North-South contrast even more vivid. Of the central characters, one is a poet who leaves New York, comes to Mississippi, succumbs to the charm of Southern life, and decides to remain there on a college faculty. Lacking the stimulus of New York, his poetry deteriorates. The other leading character, a young woman, goes to New York from Mississippi, succeeds as an actress, returns to Mississippi, but resists the charm of its living and leaves for New York to resume her artistic career. The agrarian South has shady trees, green grass, quiet, peace, traditions, and roots. Urban New York has its museums, art galleries, symphonies, and theatres; but it is also dirty, noisy, and anonymous. Its citizens are in a hurry to go nowhere, and often their lives are a tangled mess of relationships, lost souls in a harsh world.

In *River House* Young continues the contrast but places greater emphasis upon the weaknesses of the modern South. The plot is similar to that of *The Colonnade* with one significant change. In *River House* the young protagonist is not an artist, as in the play, but a businessman. After working in a St. Louis bank, he returns to manage the family plantation, but he soon discovers that members of the older generation of the family have not been able to adapt to the new and changing South. Instead, they look too much to the past, and their traditional Southern values have been eroded. Beyond the house, the town is full of the kind of persons William Faulkner would later call the Snopeses. Significantly, Young's hero concludes that the best part of the South, its principles of right conduct and its humanity, can return with him to St. Louis and that, although he may leave the South, part of it will always remain with him wherever he is.

Stark Young readily agreed to take part in *I'll Take My Stand* because he found that many of the positions taken by Davidson, Ransom, and Tate coincided with his own. They followed logically from the themes he had presented in his novels. Young began his essay, ''Not in Memoriam, but in Defense,'' with the clear statement that ''we can never go back'' and that no ''intelligent person in the South desires a literal restoration of the old Southern life. . . . But out of any epoch in civilization there may arise things worthwhile.'' He identified these qualities: ''This way of life meant mutuality of interests among more people, an innate code of obligations, and a certain openness of life. It meant self-control . . . ; you controlled yourself in order to make the society you lived in a more decent, affable, and civilized and yourself more amenable and attractive.'' For Young these were the criteria of good living.

The culmination of Young's Southern theme, however, was not the essay in the Agrarian manifesto but *So Red the Rose*. This novel, more than any other Civil War fiction, voiced the Agrarian protest against modern industrialism and extolled the humanistic values of classical civilization; and in it Young, to a greater degree than any other Civil War novelist, made the public event and the private human circumstances coincide. Once more he embodied the virtues of the agrarian way of life in the McGehee family: personal integrity, standards of conduct outside the individual, sympathy for others, love of land, and respect for the order of nature.

Young viewed the Civil War and the defeat of the South as the culmination of the Industrial Revolution. Sherman, the modern man divided between a ruthless amorality of war and his personal feelings toward his child and former friends, becomes the living symbol of the Enemy. He is the harbinger of Samuel Mack, the symbol of unbridled commercial competition, who will "replace" the planter class and the agrarian social values. The defeat of the South and the emergence of the Samuel Macks foretell a dismal future for the South, but in the surviving members of the McGehee family, the traditional Southern values are not entirely extinguished. If Young deplored the pecuniary values of the industrial order that arose after the Civil War, he also reaffirmed his faith in the continuity of the agrarian ideals.

SURVEY OF CRITICISM

Although no full-length biography of Stark Young has been published, the eleven essays providing biographical background for the various groupings of his letters in the two-volume *Stark Young: A Life in the Arts: Letters, 1900–1962*, edited by John Pilkington, together with the letters themselves, in a measure supply helpful material. The publication of the correspondence occasioned a number of thoughtful commentaries about Young and his contribution. Notable among them are those by Harold Clurman, *Nation*, 20 March 1974, 344–46; Howard Mumford Jones, *New Republic*, 21 February 1976, 27–28; James H. Justus, *Mississippi Quarterly* 30 (Fall 1970): 649–57; Kimball King, *Southern Humanities Review* 13 (Summer 1979): 272–73; Thomas F. Marshall, *American Literature* 48 (November 1976): 404–05; Floyd Stovall, *Southern Literary Journal* 9 (Fall 1976): 91–103; Arlin Turner, *South Central Bulletin* 36 (Spring 1976): 32–33; and Gerald Weales, *Southern Review* 12 (Summer 1976): 317–30. These critics varied widely in their estimate of Young's personality, but generally they conceded his brilliance as a drama critic and his significant contribution to the Southern literary Renascence in fiction. Harold Clurman wrote that Young's "observation of acting and directing was more particular and probing in its sensibility than that of any previous American critic and to this day he has not been surpassed" and concluded that "he maintained lofty standards. He stood for something" in the theatre. Howard Mumford Jones, observing that in English literature only Coleridge and Hazlitt are remembered for drama criticism, added that "Young was quite as good as Hazlitt." Floyd Stovall remarked that Young has "much to say to this generation of Americans that would do them good to hear and meditate." On the other side, Gerald Weales referred to Young as a "literary hustler" and asserted "the hypocrisy of so much of his aristocratic pose."

The only book-length study of Young's work is John Pilkington's *Stark Young* (1985). Eric Bentley has written several excellent articles on Young's theatre criticism. In an essay in the *Kenyon Review*, reprinted in his *In Search of Theatre*, Bentley chides Young for his preference for the "Mediterranean" over the "Teutonic," in, for example, his awareness of Ibsen's shortcomings but blindness to those of D'Annuzio, his excusing in Pirandello what he condemns in Shaw, and his animus against "problem plays" and "drama of ideas." Yet Bentley finds Young an expert in all aspects of theatre and calls him "a director in the aisle seat." On Broadway Young was "the opposite of a bull in a china shop." On 11 October 1981 Bentley lectured at the Stark Young Centennial at the University of Mississippi, an address subsequently published in *Theater* [Yale] 14 (Winter 1982): 47–53. Here Bentley perceptively analyzed Young's premises for drama criticism and defended him from those who found him "precious, over-elegant, dandified."

Among the doctoral dissertations that have shed light upon various aspects of Young's work are George Frank Burns, "The Influence of Southern Agrarianism in the Novels of Stark Young" (Vanderbilt, 1973); Frank Wilson Childrey, Jr., "Stark Young: Playwright" (Mississippi, 1976); Malcolm Burton Drexler, "Stark Young's Ideas on Theatre Practice" (Illinois, 1964); Robert M. Lumianski, "Stark Young and His Dramatic Criticism" (Michigan State, 1955); Virginia Rock, "The Making and Meaning of *I'll Take My Stand*" (Minnesota, 1961); Jo Beth Boyd Taylor, "The New York Drama Critics Circle: Its Activities, Procedures, and Achievements" (East Texas State, 1968); and Bedford Thurman, "Stark Young: A Bibliography of His Writings with a Selected Index to His Criticism of the Arts" (Cornell, 1954).

In addition to the dissertations mentioned above that deal primarily with Young's fiction are other studies relating to his novels and place in the Southern literary Renascence. Henry Steele Commager, in "Traditionalism in American Literature," emphasizes the traditional moral values in Young's work and compares him favorably to Ellen Glasgow and others. Donald Davidson's accounts of *I'll Take My Stand* in *Southern Writers in the Modern World* (Athens, 1968) and "*I'll Take My Stand*: A History" discuss Young's contribution to the Agrarian manifesto; Davidson's "Theme and Method in *So Red the Rose*" in *Still Rebels, Still Yankees and Other Essays* (Baton Rouge, 1972), and the introduction to his edition of *So Red the Rose* (New York, 1953), pp. v-xxxviii contain extravagant praise of Young's work. Louis D. Rubin, Jr., in *The Wary Fugitives: Four Poets and the South* (Baton Rouge, 1978), deals with Young's relationship to the agrarians.

BIBLIOGRAPHY

The selected bibliography below does not include a number of Young's books of short fiction, sketches, and essays; excluded also are his poetry, plays, and articles in periodicals and newspapers. For this material, see Bedford Thurman's "Stark Young: A Bibliography of His Writings with a Selective Index to His Criticism of the Arts" (Ph.D. diss., Cornell University, 1954).

Works by Stark Young

The Flower in Drama. New York: Charles Scribner's Sons, 1923.
Glamour: Essays on the Art of the Theatre. New York: Charles Scribner's Sons, 1925.
Heaven Trees. New York: Charles Scribner's Sons, 1926.
Theatre Practice. New York: Charles Scribner's Sons, 1926.
The Theater. New York: George H. Doran, 1927.
The Torches Flare. New York: Charles Scribner's Sons, 1928.
River House. New York: Charles Scribner's Sons, 1929.
So Red the Rose. New York: Charles Scribner's Sons, 1934.
Immortal Shadows: A Book of Dramatic Criticism. New York: Charles Scribner's Sons, 1948.
The Pavilion. New York: Charles Scribner's Sons, 1951.
So Red the Rose, introduction by Donald Davidson. New York: Charles Scribner's Sons, 1953.
The Flower in Drama & Glamour. Rev. ed. New York: Charles Scribner's Sons, 1955.
Trans. *Best Plays of Chekhov: The Sea Gull; Uncle Vanya; The Three Sisters; The Cherry Orchard*, by Anton Chekhov. New York: Modern Library, 1957.
The Theater. New York: Hill & Wang, 1958.
Stark Young: A Life in the Arts: Letters, 1900–1962, ed. John Pilkington. 2 vols. Baton Rouge: Louisiana State University Press, 1975.

Studies of Stark Young

Arthos, John. "In Honor of Stark Young." *Shenandoah* 5 (Summer 1950): 14–27.
Bentley, Eric. "An American Theatre Critic! (or the China in the Bull Shop)." *Kenyon Review* 12 (Winter 1950): 18–47.
———. *In Search of Theatre*. New York: Atheneum, 1975.
———. "Stark Young." *Theater* [Yale] 14 (Winter 1983): 47–53.
Commager, Henry Steele. "Traditionalism in American Literature." *Nineteenth Century* 146 (November 1949): 311–36.
Davidson, Donald. "Counterattack, 1930–1940; The South against Leviathan." *Southern Writers in the Modern World*. Athens: University of Georgia Press, 1968, pp. 31–62.
———. "*I'll Take My Stand*: A History." *American Review* 5 (May 1935): 301–21.
———. "Theme and Method in *So Red the Rose*." *Still Rebels, Still Yankees and Other Essays*. Baton Rouge: Louisiana State University Press, 1972, pp. 84–101.
Isaacs, Edith J. R. "The Theatre of Stark Young." *Theatre Arts* 26 (April 1942): 256–65.

Pilkington, John. *Stark Young*. Jackson: Mississippi Library Commission, 1976.

———. *Stark Young*. Boston: Twayne, 1985.

Rubin, Louis D., Jr. *The Wary Fugitives: Four Poets and the South*. Baton Rouge: Louisiana State University Press, 1978.

Swoope, Charles. "Images in a Vast World: An Appreciation of Stark Young." *Yale/ Theatre* 4 (Spring 1973): 37–41.

Thurman, Bedford. "Stark Young: A Bibliography of His Writings with a Selective Index to His Criticism of the Arts." Ph.D. diss., Cornell University, 1954.

Index

Contributors

JACOB H. ADLER is Professor of English at Purdue University. He is the author of *The Reach of Art: A Study in the Prosody of Pope* (1964) and *Lillian Hellman* (1969).

LAURENCE G. AVERY is Professor of English, University of North Carolina at Chapel Hill. His fields of special interest are modern drama, textual criticism, and computers in the humanities. He has edited *Playwright in America: Letters of Maxwell Anderson, 1912–1958* (1977) and now is at work on an edition of Paul Green's letters.

ROBERT BAIN, Professor of English at the University of North Carolina at Chapel Hill, is the author of *H. L. Davis* and coeditor of *Colonial and Federalist American Writing* and *Southern Writers: A Biographical Dictionary*. He was a contributor to *A Bibliographical Guide to the Study to Southern Literature* and to *Southern Writers* and *The History of Southern Literature*.

LYNN Z. BLOOM is Professor of English at Virginia Commonwealth University. Her most recent books include *Fact and Artifact: Writing Nonfiction* (1985), *Strategic Writing* (1983), and *American Autobiography, 1945–1980: A Bibliography*, with M. Briscoe and B. Tobias (1982). She has received funding from the National Endowment for the Humanities for the latter book, as well as for her current research in progress on *Songs of Ourselves: A History of American Autobiography*.

M. E. BRADFORD is Professor of English at the University of Dallas. He has published over 100 essays on Southern literature and other works dealing with the general culture of the region, its history and politics. He is the author of *A Better Guide Than Reason: Studies in the American Revolution*; *A Worthy Company: Brief Lives of the Framers of the United States Constitution*; and *Remembering Who We Are: Opinions of a Southern Conservative*.

ASHLEY BROWN is Professor of English at the University of South Carolina in Columbia. With Robert S. Haller he edited *The Achievement of Wallace Stevens* (1962). With Frances Neel Cheney, he edited *The Poetry Reviews of Allen Tate, 1924–1944* (1983). With John Kimmey, he edited *The World of Tragedy* (1981).

JAMES A. BRYANT, JR., has written extensively on Shakespeare and other Elizabethan dramatists and on figures of the Southern Renascence. He has taught at Syracuse University, at the University of Nantes (as a Fulbright lecturer), and at various places in the South, among them Vanderbilt, Sewanee, Duke, and the University of North Carolina at Greensboro. Currently he teaches at the University of Kentucky.

RICHARD J. CALHOUN is Alumni Professor of English at Clemson University. With Robert W. Hill, he wrote *James Dickey* (1983). He edited *James Dickey: The Expansive Imagination: A Collection of Critical Essays* (1973). With John Caldwell Guilds, he compiled *A Tricentennial Anthology of South Carolina Literature, 1670–1970* (1971). With Ernest Lander, Jr., he edited *Two Decades of Change: The South Since the Supreme Court Desegregation Decision* (1975).

VIRGINIA SPENCER CARR is head of the English Department at Georgia State University in Atlanta. Her biography of Carson McCullers, *The Lonely Hunter* (1975), won the Francis Butler Simkins Prize of the Southern Historical Association and Longwood College (Virginia) for "distinguished writing in Southern history." Her biography of John Dos Passos, *Dos Passos: A Life* (1984), was nominated for a Pulitzer Prize. She was a Fulbright professor of American literature at the University of Wroclaw (Poland) in 1980–81, conducted an American literature symposium at Age University (Izmir, Turkey), directed Emory University's Summer Creative Writing Institute in 1977, was writer-in-residence at Lynchburg College in 1985, and has just completed a third writing fellowship at Yaddo Artists Colony for work on a novel.

EUGENE CURRENT-GARCIA is Hargis Professor Emeritus of American Literature at Auburn University, where he taught nineteenth-century American and Southern Literature on both undergraduate and graduate levels from 1947 until his retirement in 1978. He helped to found the *Southern Humanities Review* in 1967 and served as editor and coeditor until 1979. Since the 1940s, his articles and reviews have appeared in such journals as *American Literature*, *American*

Quarterly, Studies in Short Fiction, the *Southern Review*, and *Mississippi Quarterly* among others; and his book publications include *What Is The Short Story?*, *O. Henry, Realism and Romanticism in Fiction, Short Stories of the Western World, American Short Stories* (now in its fourth edition), and *The American Short Story Before 1850*. He gave the dedication address at the O. Henry Festival in Greensboro, North Carolina, in 1985.

THOMAS E. DASHER is Associate Professor of English and Head of the Department of English at Valdosta State College in Valdosta, Georgia. The author of *William Faulkner's Characters: An Index to the Published and Unpublished Fiction*, he has written articles on William Goyen and David Madden. He has also been active in developing Writing Across the Curriculum programs.

THADIOUS M. DAVIS teaches at the University of North Carolina, Chapel Hill. Currently at work on a comparative study of William Faulkner and Richard Wright, she has written on major and minor authors of the American South.

JOSEPH M. FLORA is Professor of English and chairman of the Department at the University of North Carolina at Chapel Hill. He edited James Branch Cabell's *The Cream of the Jest* (1975) and is editor of *The English Short Story, 1880–1945* (1985) and coeditor of *Southern Writers: A Biographical Dictionary* (1978). He is the author of *Vardis Fisher* (1965), *William Ernest Henley* (1970), *Frederick Manfred* (1974), and *Hemingway's Nick Adams* (1982).

RUEL E. FOSTER is Benedum Professor of American Literature at West Virginia University, where he was Departmental Chair, 1967–75. Author of *Jesse Stuart* (1968), he coauthored *William Faulkner: A Critical Appraisal* and *Elizabeth Madox Roberts: American Novelist* (1956).

MELVIN J. FRIEDMAN is Professor of Comparative Literature and English at the University of Wisconsin–Milwaukee. He has written extensively about William Styron and Flannery O'Connor. His most recent title is *Critical Essays on Flannery O'Connor* (1985), coedited with Beverly L. Clark. He serves on the editorial boards of *Contemporary Literature, Studies in American Fiction, Studies in the Novel, Journal of Beckett Studies*, and other journals.

HELEN S. GARSON is Professor of English and Professor of American Studies at George Mason University, in Fairfax, Virginia. She teaches and writes about twentieth-century fiction, British and American. Included among her writings on Southern literature is the book *Truman Capote* (1980).

OWEN GILMAN completed his doctorate at the University of North Carolina at Chapel Hill. He is a member of the English Department at Saint Joseph's University in Philadelphia. His articles on American war fiction (including Vietnam) have been published in *Modern Fiction Studies*, the *South Atlantic Quarterly*, and the *Journal of American Culture*.

JOAN GIVNER, who teaches at the University of Regina in Saskatchewan, Canada, is the author of the highly acclaimed biography of Katherine Anne Porter (1982) as well as a writer of short fiction. She is also the editor of *Wascana Review*.

J. LEE GREENE teaches at the University of North Carolina at Chapel Hill. He is the author of *Time's Unfading Garden: Anne Spencer's Life and Poetry* (1977) and articles on Henry Fielding, Ernest Gaines, Alex Haley, Langston Hughes, Anne Spencer, John A. Williams, and others. He has been Managing Editor of the *Southern Literary Journal*. In 1977 he won an Amoco Award for excellence in the teaching of undergraduates.

WILLIAM HARMON, Professor of English at the University of North Carolina at Chapel Hill, is author of five books of poetry, a study of Ezra Pound's work, and *The Oxford Book of American Light Verse*; he prepared the fifth edition of the Thrall-Hibbard-Holman *Handbook to Literature*. His work has appeared in *PMLA*, *Poetry*, *American Anthropologist*, *Antioch Review*, *Kenyon Review*, *Partisan Review*, and other journals. He is an unindicted coconspirator in *l'affaire Uneeda Review*, now merged with the *Lonestar Cavalier Gazette* and the *Everlasting Cooglerite*.

CHARLES B. HARRIS is Professor and Chairperson of the English Department at Illinois State University. He is the author of *Passionate Virtuosity: The Fiction of John Barth* (1983) and *Contemporary American Novelists of the Absurd* (1971) as well as of numerous articles on contemporary American fiction. Professor Harris has served as President of the Executive Committee of the Association of Departments of English.

JOHN J. HINDLE, since receiving his doctorate from Vanderbilt University, has edited two books (with T. D. Young): *The Republic of Letters in America: The Correspondence of Allen Tate and John Peale Bishop*, and *Selected Essays of John Crowe Ransom*. He has also published articles on the fiction of Allen Tate and the literary life of the 1920s and 1930s in America. His primary area of interest is twentieth-century American literature.

RONALD WESLEY HOAG teaches at East Carolina University in Greenville, North Carolina. His work on Southern writers, including Erskine Caldwell, has appeared in *Modern Fiction Studies*, *South Atlantic Review*, *Mississippi Quarterly*, *Paris Review*, *Georgia Review*, *Southern Review*, and elsewhere. He is now preparing a book on the themes of sublimity and wildness in the writings of Henry D. Thoreau.

FRED HOBSON is Professor of English at Louisiana State University. He is the author of *Serpent in Eden: H. L. Mencken and the South* (1974) and *Tell About the South: The Southern Rage to Explain* (winner of the 1983 Jules F. Landry Award), editor of *South-Watching: Selected Essays of Gerald W. Johnson* (winner of the 1983 Lillian Smith Award) and coeditor of *Literature at the Barricades: The American Writer in the 1930s* (1982). He has contributed to a number of journals and quarterlies, including the *Sewanee Review*, the *Southern Literary Journal*, the *Virginia Quarterly Review*, and the *Kenyon Review*.

DAVID MARION HOLMAN received his M.A. and Ph.D. from the University of Michigan. He has taught at the University of North Carolina, Texas A & M University, and the University of Mississippi. He is the author of several articles on American and Southern literature.

ELVIN HOLT, who received his Ph.D. from the University of Kentucky, teaches English at Southwest Texas State University. He wrote his dissertation on Zora Neale Hurston and is doing research in nineteenth- and twentieth-century Afro-American literature.

MARK JOHNSON teaches at Central Missouri State University. He has written on Walker Percy, Robert Duncan, Alan Ginsberg, and others. He is presently completing a book on Duncan.

JAMES H. JUSTUS, currently the president of the Society for the Study of Southern Literature, is Professor of English at Indiana University. He is author of *The Achievement of Robert Penn Warren* (1981) and two chapters in *The History of Southern Literature* (1985).

RICHARD S. KENNEDY is Professor of English at Temple University, where he regularly offers graduate seminars in Fiction of the Modern American South and in Modern American Fiction. He is the author of *The Window of Memory: The Literary Career of Thomas Wolfe* (1962) and *Dreams in the Mirror: A Biography of E. E. Cummings* (1980) and the editor of *The Notebooks of Thomas Wolfe* (1969); *Beyond Love and Loyalty: The Letters of Thomas Wolfe and Elizabeth Nowell* (1983); *Thomas Wolfe: A Harvard Perspective* (1983); *Thomas Wolfe's Welcome to Our City* (1983); and *Etcetera: The Unpublished Poems of E. E. Cummings* (1983). He has contributed numerous articles on Wolfe, Cummings, Melville, Dickens, Joyce Cary, and T. S. Eliot to periodicals and collections of essays.

GEORGE S. LENSING, who received his Ph.D. from Louisiana State University, is Professor of English at the University of North Carolina at Chapel Hill. He has written articles on William Faulkner, Flannery O'Connor, and James Dickey. With Ronald Moran, he is coauthor of *Four Poets and the Emotive*

Imagination (1976). He is the author of *Wallace Stevens' Hard Prize Fully Made* (1986). In 1984 he won the Nicholas Salgo Distinguished Teaching Award at UNC.

MARK T. LUCAS teaches at Centre College in Danville, Kentucky. Currently working on an interdisciplinary study of the "Louse" in Southern life and literature, he has a book—*Andrew Lytle and the South*—due soon from L.S.U. Press.

JULIAN MASON is a Professor of English at the University of North Carolina at Charlotte. His publications include over 50 book or journal articles, including entries for the *Dictionary of Literary Biography*, *American Writers Before 1800*, *Southern Writers: A Biographical Dictionary*, and *A Bibliobiographical Guide to the Study of Southern Literature*. Among his special interests are Southern writers and black writers. He edited *The Poems of Phillis Wheatley*.

JOSEPH R. MILLICHAP is Professor and Head of the English Department at Western Kentucky University. His major scholarly interest is the Southern Renascence, and he has published articles on Faulkner, Wolfe, O'Connor, McCullers, and Horton Foote. His Twayne's United States Authors Series volume on Hamilton Basso was published in 1979.

ROBERT L. PHILLIPS is Professor of English at Mississippi State University. He has served as Secretary/Treasurer for the Society for the Study of Southern Literature and was Managing Editor for the SSSL's *The History of Southern Literature* (1985) and is Book Review Editor for the *Mississippi Quarterly*.

JOHN PILKINGTON, Distinguished Professor Emeritus at the University of Mississippi, received his education at Centre College, Johns Hopkins University, and Harvard University. He is author of *Francis Marion Crawford* (1964), *The Heart of Yoknapatawpha* (1981), *Henry Blake Fuller* (1970), and *Stark Young* (1985). He edited *Stark Young: A Life in the Arts: Letters, 1900–1962* (1975).

WILLIAM PRATT, Professor of English at Miami University in Oxford, Ohio, has edited anthologies of *The Imagist Poem* (1963) and *The Fugitive Poets* (1965), and with his wife, Anne, has translated René Taupin's *The Influence of French Symbolism on Modern American Poetry* (1985). His essays, reviews, poems, and translations have appeared in many journals, including the *Sewanee Review*, *South Atlantic Quarterly*, and *Mississippi Quarterly*. A native of Shawnee, Oklahoma, his B.A. is from the University of Oklahoma and his M.A. and Ph.D. from Vanderbilt University; he has been a Rotary Fellow at the University of Glasgow, Scotland, 1951–52, and a Fulbright Professor at University College, Dublin, Ireland, 1975–76.

PEGGY WHITMAN PRENSHAW is Dean of the Honors College of the University of Southern Mississippi and editor of the *Southern Quarterly*. She has published widely on a variety of topics and has edited several volumes of scholarship, including *Eudora Welty: Thirteen Essays* (1983), *Conversations with Eudora Welty* (1984), and *Women Writers of the Contemporary South* (1984). She is General Editor of the Literary Conversations series (University Press of Mississippi).

DARDEN ASBURY PYRON, who received his Ph.D. from the University of Virginia, is an Associate Professor of History at Florida International University. He has edited *Recasting: "Gone with the Wind" in American Culture* (1982). He is currently working on an intellectual-cultural biography of Margaret Mitchell.

JOHN M. REILLY is Professor of English at the State University of New York at Albany. He edited *Richard Wright: The Critical Reception* (1978) and *Twentieth-Century Interpretations of "Invisible Man"* (1970). His *Twentieth Century Crime and Mystery Writers* won the Edgar Allan Poe Award in 1981.

PAUL SCHLUETER received his Ph.D. from Southern Illinois University. He has taught at several colleges and universities in the United States and West Germany, though in recent years he has devoted most of his time and effort to writing and editing; among his publications are essays and bibliographies on Orwell, Mary McCarthy, Richard Aldington, Edgar Lee Masters, Terry Southern, Keith Waterhouse, G. S. Fraser, Susan Sontag, Kathleen Raine, and others, as well as books on Lessing, Shirley Ann Grau, the modern English novel, modern American literature, and British women writers.

RICHARD R. SCHRAMM is on the staff of the National Humanities Center. He has taught American literature at the University of North Carolina at Chapel Hill and written on Southern literature for a variety of journals.

DOROTHY SCURA is chairman of the English Department at Virginia Commonwealth University. She edited *Henry James 1960–1974: A Reference Guide*. Her articles on Ellen Glasgow, Doris Betts, and other Southern women writers have appeared in the *Mississippi Quarterly*, the *Southern Humanities Review*, the *Southern Quarterly*, and other journals.

FRANK W. SHELTON is Professor of English at Limestone College in Gaffney, S.C. He has numerous publications on modern fiction and modern drama. In addition to Ernest Gaines and Harry Crews, he has written about Cormac McCarthy, Anne Tyler, and Alice Walker.

WILLIAM H. SLAVICK, native of Shelby County, Tennessee, studied at the

University of Notre Dame, where he took his degrees, and the University of Munich. He is author of *DuBose Heyward*, editor of *I Touched White Clover*, and he has written about Faulkner, Roberts, Welty, and Ellison. Professor of English at the University of Southern Maine, he was in 1977 a Senior Fulbright Lecturer at the University of Kassel in West Germany. In 1978 he directed the Downeast Southern Renascence and in 1981 the Roberts Centenary at St. Catharine College in Kentucky.

MARTHA STEPHENS teaches at the University of Cincinnati. She is the author of *The Question of Flannery O'Connor* (1973).

NANCY M. TISCHLER teaches at Pennsylvania State University. She is author of *Tennessee Williams: Rebellious Puritan* (1961), *Tennessee Williams* (1969), *Black Masks: Negro Characters in Modern Southern Fiction* (1969), and *Dorothy L. Sayers, A Pilgrim Soul* (1980).

LINDA WAGNER-MARTIN is Professor of English and Editor of the *Centennial Review* at Michigan State University. She has written about many American modernist writers—Hemingway, Glasgow, Faulkner, Williams, Eliot, Levertov, Oates, Dos Passos, and others. She is currently writing a biography of Sylvia Plath.

ROBERT L. WHITE received his Ph.D. in American Studies from the University of Minnesota and now teaches at York University in Ontario, Canada. He is the author of *John Peale Bishop* (1966).

THOMAS DANIEL YOUNG, Gertrude Conaway Vanderbilt Professor of English at Vanderbilt University, has written or edited 22 books, including *Gentleman in a Dustcoat*, the prize-winning biography of John Crowe Ransom. At present he is working on a book of essays on twentieth-century American fiction and *Conversations with Malcolm Cowley*. He was a Senior Editor of *The History of Southern Literature*.

ANNE R. ZAHLAN teaches at Eastern Illinois University. In addition to her work on the Southern novel, she is interested in twentieth-century British fiction, notably the fiction of expatriate experience. She has spoken and written on George Orwell, Joyce Cary, and Lawrence Durrell.